STRUCTURED COBOL

Fundamentals, second edition

Michael Murach
Mike Murach and Associates

John Padgett
University of Southern Colorado

SRA®

SCIENCE RESEARCH ASSOCIATES, INC.
Chicago, Henley-on-Thames; Sydney, Toronto
A Subsidiary of IBM

Structured COBOL: Fundamentals, second edition

Acquisition Editor	Pamela Cooper
Project Editor	Geof Garvey
Copy Editor	Arlan Bushman
Text and Cover Design	Harry Voigt
Production Director	Steve Leonardo
Composition and Illustrations	Interface Studio

Acknowledgments

Cover photograph: Copyright ©1985, L. R. Lewandowski. All rights reserved. Reproduced by permission of the photographer.

Figures 1-1 and 1-5, pages 4 and 9: Courtesy of International Business Machines, Inc.

Figure 1-2, page 5: Courtesy of TeleVideo Systems, Inc.

Figure 1-4, page 8: Sperry Corporation.

Some of the material appearing on pages 253 through 265, including Figures 7-15 through 7-19 and Figure 7-22, are reprinted from *How to Design and Develop COBOL Programs,* by Paul Noll and Mike Murach, pp. 264 and 283-293. Copyright ©1985 by Mike Murach & Associates. Reprinted by permission.

Some of the material on walkthroughs, pages 309 through 312, including Figures 8-23 and 8-24, is reprinted or adapted from *The COBOL Programmer's Handbook,* by Paul Noll and Mike Murach, pp. 61-65. Copyright ©1985 by Mike Murach & Associates. Reprinted by permission.

Library of Congress Cataloging in Publication Data

Murach, Mike.
Structured COBOL.

Includes index.
Contents: [1] Fundamentals.
1. COBOL (Computer program language) 2. Structured programming. I. Padgett, John, 1936- II. Title.
QA76.73.C25M863 1986 005.13'3 85-26284
ISBN 0-574-21980-3 (v. 1)

Printed in the United States of America.

10 9 8 7 6 5 4 3 2 1

Contents

Part Four: Special Applications of COBOL

Preface for Instructors

The first of a two-volume set, this book is intended for a one-semester (or quarter) course in COBOL. It contains sufficient material for the instructor to be somewhat selective in what is to be taught after the basics of COBOL have been covered. The text presents a subset of the COBOL language that generally conforms to the 1974 standards of the American National Standards Institute. ANSI COBOL is rich in commands that may be used, but only those appropriate to the beginning COBOL programmer and to development of a professional approach to program design, organization, and style are presented. Even though COBOL is a standard language, it is not implemented identically on all computers. The COBOL statements presented here can be executed on the vast majority of computers used today, and where implementation differences occur, the changes should be very modest.

Dozens of COBOL books are available for college and industrial courses. Yet the training of COBOL programmers tends to vary widely in several programmer quality measures. Many students who have completed COBOL courses have not learned how to design and organize a totally efficient program, how to write a readable program, or how to design an efficient and thorough test plan—nor do they understand the meaning of functional modules or the logic of programs because they did not get enough practice writing programs.

In general, there are two basic approaches to teaching the COBOL language. The first teaches the COBOL elements separately until a great deal of detail has been covered. At that point, a few of these elements are combined into a complete program. A book of this sort is easy to identify, since each chapter covers a COBOL division: Identification, Environment, Data, and Procedure. In such an approach, the first complete program commonly is not presented until well into the book. The authors feel that this approach retards the students' learning by asking them to learn too many unrelated facts before they are able to see their relationship in a complete program. Secondly, this approach retards learning since it will take several weeks for the students to have learned enough parts to attempt to write their first COBOL program.

The second approach to the teaching of COBOL is used in this book. This approach encourages the writing of as many programs as possible during the academic session. Writing many programs is of no real benefit unless the programs are of sufficient variety and increasing complexity. That is what this book does: it provides the means for students to write several significant and varied programs. It provides an instructional schedule in which it is not unreasonable to expect the student to complete a significant program every week or two.

This text was designed by the authors to provide students with the training that will enable them to be confident in their abilities while seeking programming positions. In order to accomplish that goal, the book has the following attributes:

- States new terms and objectives at the beginning of each new topic
- Features a strong emphasis on the development of structured programming
- Covers topics a student must know in order to write and test novice-level programs that are significantly challenging without being overpowering
- Provides problems and problem solutions at the end of most topics in order for the student to test his or her new knowledge immediately by seeing the correct answer, which helps with understanding and writing the problem programs
- Provides material based on an analysis of the tasks performed by a typical COBOL programmer trainee in industry
- Places major emphasis on the techniques of structured design and program organization that are used widely in industry
- Models the latest techniques and style in COBOL program development
- Expands the instructor's supplement to include a full set of overhead masters, input record descriptions, problem solutions, terminology quizzes, and suggestions for scheduling the course and assignments

Since there are many COBOL books on the market, the person or committee selecting a COBOL text makes a particularly responsible choice. The selection of a text will directly affect the skills the student takes to the programmer's marketplace to obtain a job and a career. The following points state the educational philosophy that guided the writing of this text and that the authors feel make it an outstanding choice.

- Enables students to *begin writing programs* while they are studying chapter 3. This in turn allows the instructor to make use of lab sessions early in the semester or term. It is possible to make programming assignments in the second or third week.
- Provides a *solid logical foundation* by presenting a thorough discussion of control-break logic and table handling, which, it is felt, will provide the best preparation for the advanced problems of file handling and update. The rich problem set provides the student with ample opportunity to practice the appropriate programming skills.
- Teaches *structured design techniques* used in companies whose data-processing departments do the most extensive COBOL programming in the world, enabling students to learn structured coding as they learn structured design.
- Offers great *relevance to the industry* based on careful selection of content. Although there is continued debate on what the best structured programming techniques are, all of the techniques shown in this book are widely used in industry.

- Promotes emphasis on the "style" in which programs are written. *Structured style* enhances readability and clarity of the program code, thus minimizing development and maintenance time.
- Specifies the differences and the interrelatedness of structured design, structured organization, and structured style. These three aspects of structured programming are *carefully modeled throughout the book*.
- Presents the *core content* of COBOL programming in the first six chapters of the book, allowing the student to see important relationships among elements of the COBOL language from the start. The first two chapters are for the beginning programming student and may be bypassed if the scholastic program provides introductory programming classes. In the next four chapters the student masters a subset of COBOL plus the principles of structured design, coding, and testing. Thereafter, the student learns rapidly by observing and practicing how new COBOL elements relate to the complete COBOL program.

The Development of Structured COBOL: Fundamentals

The variety of experiences brought to the development of this book is felt to be one of its major strengths. A major portion of the contents of the first edition of this text was taken from two earlier books: (1) *Standard COBOL*, Mike Murach, Science Research Associates, 1975, and (2) *Structured Programming, for the COBOL Programmer*, Paul Noll, Mike Murach & Associates, 1977. Mike Murach was responsible for the organization of the book, the coordination of the team, and some of the writing. Paul Noll, a software specialist and independent consultant in industry, was the technical advisor. Judy Taylor did most of the rewriting and new writing that was required. Doug Lowe did some of the writing and wrote all of the programs used in the book. These programs were based on programming standards supplied by Paul Noll.

The second edition involved the co-author, John Padgett, who is currently an Assistant Professor of Computer Science Technology and has been a professional programmer, systems analyst, and management information specialist. Mr. Padgett has used the first edition of the book for several years in his classroom and is intimately familiar with the structured programming philosophy presented by Mike Murach and his associates. Molly Jagger, a student at the University of Southern Colorado, has modernized several of the program examples, and has written program solutions to the programming assignments; the solutions are available in the Instructor's Guide. The addition of Mr. Padgett and Ms. Jagger to this team adds a strong academic viewpoint to the wealth of experience that has gone into the book's development. That experience now spans the range from professional programmers, trainers, and theoreticians to classroom teachers and students.

The first edition of the book was widely used by many colleges and has been used for industry inhouse programmer training. A major reason for the book's success lies with the standards for structured programming developed by Paul Noll, which are widely accepted by the professional programming community. The COBOL he presented was not only accurate but also represented practices in use in the best COBOL shops in the country.

The second edition has remained faithful to Paul Noll's programming standards and any program changes were made to modernize the program and to enhance the standard. A significant improvement on the first edition is the strengthening of the considerations of program organization and style of writing. Most textbooks on the market lack a definitive treatment of these important topics.

Changes from Previous Edition

Problem Set

The format of the expected output has been made more exacting because it is felt that

1. Novice students generally do not know enough about output formatting, and thus should be exposed to good output formats until that topic can be covered in an advanced course.
2. By providing specific output formats, the text enables the instructor to enforce exact adherence to the output specifications. Expecting the student to produce the output exactly as specified is felt to be a desirable goal, since it promotes the attention to detail necessary for good programming.

Terminology and Objectives

Terms and objectives have been moved to the beginning of each topic with the purpose of priming the student to watch for the terms and the objectives to be covered.

Card vs. Terminal Technology

Almost all references to card input and processing have been removed. The only discussion of cards is from a historical viewpoint. Where appropriate, card-punch topics have been replaced with discussions of terminal use.

Interactive Operating Systems

Although not a major discussion, the interactive operating environment is given an introductory treatment, especially as it may apply to the student environment.

Discussion Expansion

In several places the discussions have been expanded to provide improved understanding of the concepts being presented. All chapters have had some revision.

Fundamental vs. Advanced Topics

The advanced subjects, especially file processing and update, have been removed, expanded, and presented in the Advanced volume. The remaining subjects have been strengthened in order to provide a stronger foundation for the novice.

Chapter Length

In some cases, chapter subjects have been separated into two chapters to make chapters of more equal length. For example, the problem-solving discussion (from chapter 1, first edition) has been placed in a separate chapter (chapter 2, second edition) along with an introductory discussion of interactive program development. Also, discussion of the basic subset (chapter 2, first edition) has now been separated into an introduction to the basic subset (chapter 3, second edition), and completion of the basic subset (chapter 4, second edition).

Subject Arrangement

In a few instances, experience has shown that a rearrangement of topics would be beneficial. An example is the presentation of the diagnostic messages from chapter 4 (first edition). This topic is now presented in two places: an early discussion of likely errors (chapter 3, second edition), and a more extensive coverage (chapter 5, second edition) that discusses both syntax errors and execution errors.

COPY Statement

This facility remains in the text and is enhanced by providing the instructor with three versions of the input data descriptions for most problem programs. The intent is that the instructor may choose to assign one version for the students to use on a problem. Students will thus learn some programming efficiency while being exposed to good structured style for data names.

Subroutines

In the same vein as the COPY statement, the subroutine discussion will be left in the novice text and the instructor will be provided with a heading routine that may be implemented with each report program if so desired.

Issue Discussions

In many chapters, and as appropriate to the subject, an issue will be raised and discussed as a final topic in the chapter. Discussions will be brief and may be skipped if desired. Particularly, they will concentrate on those issues that may be of interest (such as the 198x standard), which may provide either an optional method of approaching the chapter subject or simply useful information that is not critical to the subject.

New Subjects

The new topics are of a supplementary or helplful nature. They include execution errors to avoid, a list of structured style guidelines, a list of acceptable abbreviations, top-down coding and testing, and structured walkthroughs.

Acknowledgments

The main portion of credit for this book must go to Paul Noll, Judy Taylor, and Doug Lowe, who made the first edition a great success and who laid down such a solid foundation that the second edition was a pleasure to write.

The authors must accept full responsibility for any shortcomings or failures in the second edition, because it represents their thoughts and decisions. However, the success of any book is truly a team effort and the authors are thankful that they have had so much dedicated, quality help. Our thanks and sincerest expressions of appreciation go to these wonderful people:

Pam Cooper, acquisition editor, was the ramrod for the second edition. Without her drive, hand-holding, and gentle nagging the second edition might not yet be.

C. T. Cadenhead, professor and reviewer, was a tremendous help in discovering those small errors that always sneak in, and had many helpful suggestions that have strengthened the text.

Alan Bush, professor and reviewer, located his share of small errors and provided helpful suggestions.

Geoffrey Garvey, development editor, produced a great-looking, readable book. His advice and patience have helped make the corrections and editing a pleasure and an education.

Molly Jagger, student, not only wrote programs, but was also one of the best technical editors of the revised material.

Mary Padgett, English teacher and long-suffering wife, provided moral support in addition to doing the first copy-editing of the text, which made the whole editing cycle easier for all.

Mike Murach
John J. Padgett
1986

Introduction for Students

COBOL, which stands for *CO*mmon *B*usiness *O*riented *L*anguage, is the most widely used programming language for business applications. It can be used on most business computers, so COBOL programmers can use their skills on many different makes of computers. At present, there are well over 100,000 COBOL programmers working in industry. And each year, thousands of new COBOL programmers are trained. If there is one programming language the business student should become familiar with, it is COBOL.

When you finish this course you will have the fundamental skills necessary for programming any computer system that uses COBOL. From a practical point of view, however, each computer system is likely to have some non-standard peculiarities. So you will usually have to learn these variations as you move from one computer system to another.

Before you begin to use this book, there are several things you ought to know about it:

1. This book is designed so the chapters don't have to be read in sequence. In brief, after you complete the first six chapters, you can skip to any of the other parts of the book. And you can skip to any chapter in part IV without reading the chapters that precede it in that part. So don't worry if your instructor assigns chapters in an unusual way; the book is designed to be used that way.

If you are studying this book on your own, you are encouraged to read it in the standard book sequence, from chapter 1 to chapter 11. But don't feel that you should rigidly adhere to this sequence. Whenever your interest in a subject is aroused, read the appropriate chapter. There is no greater assurance that learning will take place than to study a subject in search of an answer.

2. At the beginning of each topic are lists consisting of the new terms encountered. The intent is not that you be able to define these words but that you feel you understand them. After you read a topic, glance at the list and note any word whose meaning is unclear to you. Then reread the related material. Once the terms are fixed in your mind, continue on.

3. Following the terminology lists for each topic or chapter are one or more behavioral objectives. They describe the activities (behavior) that you should be able to perform upon completion of a topic or chapter. The theory is that you will be a more effective learner if you know in advance what you are expected to do and what you will be tested on. This contrasts with the traditional course in which the student is forced to guess what he will be tested on.

In general, behavioral objectives can be classified as (1) *knowledge objectives* and (2) *application objectives*. A knowledge objective requires you to list, identify, describe, or explain aspects of a subject. For example, the first objective in chapter 1 is to be able to list the components of a typical computer system. Once you are told or have read what these components are, you should have no trouble fulfilling this objective. Although other knowledge objectives will be more involved and more difficult than this one, given the objective and a source of knowledge, you should be able to perform the activity described.

Since COBOL programming is concerned entirely with problem solving, the primary objectives of this book are application objectives—those that require you to apply knowledge to problems. In general, knowledge objectives are given only when they are a prerequisite for applying some aspect of COBOL. If only one objective were given for this entire book, it would be something like this: Given a business programming problem, solve it in COBOL.

4. Following the behavioral objectives are one or more problems for each application objective. These are intended to get you involved. There is much truth in the maxim: I hear and I forget; I see and I remember; I *do* and I understand. If there is one message coming from research in education, it is that meaningful learning depends on what the learner does—not on what is seen, heard, or read.

Because the intent of this book is to teach COBOL programming, the problems, for the most part, ask you to apply COBOL to significant programming tasks. There are no fill-in answers, no multiple-choice questions, and no true/false statements because these types of activity have nothing to do with writing COBOL programs. As much as possible, the problems are intended to stimulate the kind of thinking that would be necessary if you were actually performing the job of a programmer. Because the problems often require you to apply COBOL to situations that go beyond the applications presented in the topics themselves, it is hoped that at times you will experience the joy of discovery and receive the reward of deeper understanding.

Solutions are presented immediately after the problems. This lets you confirm that you are right when you are right, but it also lets you learn from being wrong. By checking the solution when you finish a problem, you can discover when you are wrong and correct false notions before they become habits.

Should you actually work each problem in detail before checking the solution? This may be the surest way of learning, but it isn't necessarily the most efficient or the most practical way. As long as you determine what the problem is and conceive the essential elements of a solution before you check the given solution, learning should take place.

One important message: *Don't skip the problems*. Reading, like listing, can be a very passive activity. Have you ever, for example, read an entire chapter of a book then realized you didn't understand any of it? The problems for each topic or chapter will provide you with check points to reinforce the reading you've done, to teach you application, to keep the learning process active, and to help you achieve deeper understanding.

5. This book assumes no prior knowledge of data processing and programming. However, you may already be familiar with some of the material. For example, if you have had a good introductory course in data processing or have programmed in another language, chapters 1, 2, and 10 will probably be review for you. To help you determine whether or not you should study a topic or chapter, you can check the terminology, objectives, problems, and solutions that apply.

With this as background, you should be ready to start reading this book. Here's hoping that you find it stimulating.

Mike Murach
Fresno, California

John Padgett
Pueblo, Colorado

Part One

Required Background

Before you can start learning about COBOL, you need to understand some basic concepts. As a result, this part presents the minimum background you'll need before you can learn how to program in COBOL. If you have already written programs in another language or if you have had a course in computing or data processing, you probably are familiar with most of the material in this part. If so, you can use this material as a review.

Chapter 1 An Introduction to Computers

Before you can learn to write COBOL programs, you must be familiar with a certain amount of background information. This chapter is designed to provide that background, and covers three topics:

1. An introduction to hardware—reviews the components and size ranges of typical computer systems,

2. An introduction to software—reviews the traditional categories of software and introduces some more modern software concepts,

3. An introduction to the stored program—presents briefly the components of a principal type of program instruction and its effect on memory.

You may be familiar with some or all of this material from a previous course or job experience. To determine whether or not to skip a topic, you should study the terminology list, the behavioral objectives, and the problems for each topic. Behavioral objectives are those changes in behavior that an activity such as studying this text is supposed to effect in individuals. If the terminology, objectives, and problems all appear trivial to you, then you should move on to the next topic. Of course, the instructor may choose to review or to test your knowledge of the subject, such as by administering a terminology quiz.

A computer is a system of hardware and software that accepts input data, processes and manipulates that data, and then provides output information. Note the transformation of data to information. This is a very important concept in planning computer programs; the object is to have the program produce output that is usable by the person requesting the program. This would appear to be self-evident, but it is still surprising, after many years of experience with computers, how much "data" is run through the computer without being converted into truly useful "information." In this chapter a short discussion is presented concerning the relationship between hardware (machinery) and software (programs) and how they work together to change data into information.

Topic 1 **Introduction to Hardware**

Orientation

The first impression that we normally have of a computer system is that of the *hardware*, that is, the actual machinery that may be sitting in a computer center. As microcomputers become more common, our first impressions and experiences derive from proximity and use of the small, but powerful "micros." From whatever source our first experiences with computers come, the *computer* is a system of components (thereby the term *computer system*) that must work together to produce the basic input-process-output (*IPO*) function of computers. For example, a computer can read sales data from an input file, process this data, and provide output in the form of a printed sales report. A computer can accept that input data from many sources: terminals, magnetic tapes and disks, special devices to read checks with *magnetic ink* markings, and punched cards which are, however, rapidly disappearing from the computer scene. Similarly, the output may be sent to any of several devices: printers, terminals, tape and disk drives, and, less often, cards. Because a computer's processing depends on the sequence of instructions (the *program*) that it is given before doing a job, a computer can process data in an almost endless variety of ways.

In general, a computer consists of one or more input devices, one or more output devices, and a *central processing unit (CPU)*. A small system consists of a CPU and only a few *input/output (I/O) devices*, while a large system may consist of one or more CPUs and dozens of I/O devices. Theoretically, at least, the components of a computer system are chosen to fulfill the needs of the user; the system should be large enough to do all the jobs required by the user but not so large that processing capacity goes to waste.

Terminology

The terminology you will be expected to understand and use when this topic is completed consists of the following:

card punch	disk pack	printer
card reader	distributed processing	procedures
central processing unit	executing a program	program
computer	forms control	software
computer system	hardware	spindle
console	input/output device	tape drive
console typewriter	job stream	terminal
continuous form	loading a program	
disk drive	magnetic ink character reader	

Objectives

Remember that behavioral objectives are those changes that are expected as a result of some activity. For this topic you will be expected to demonstrate the following behaviors:

1. *List the components of a typical computer system.*
2. *Understand and correctly use the topic terminology.*

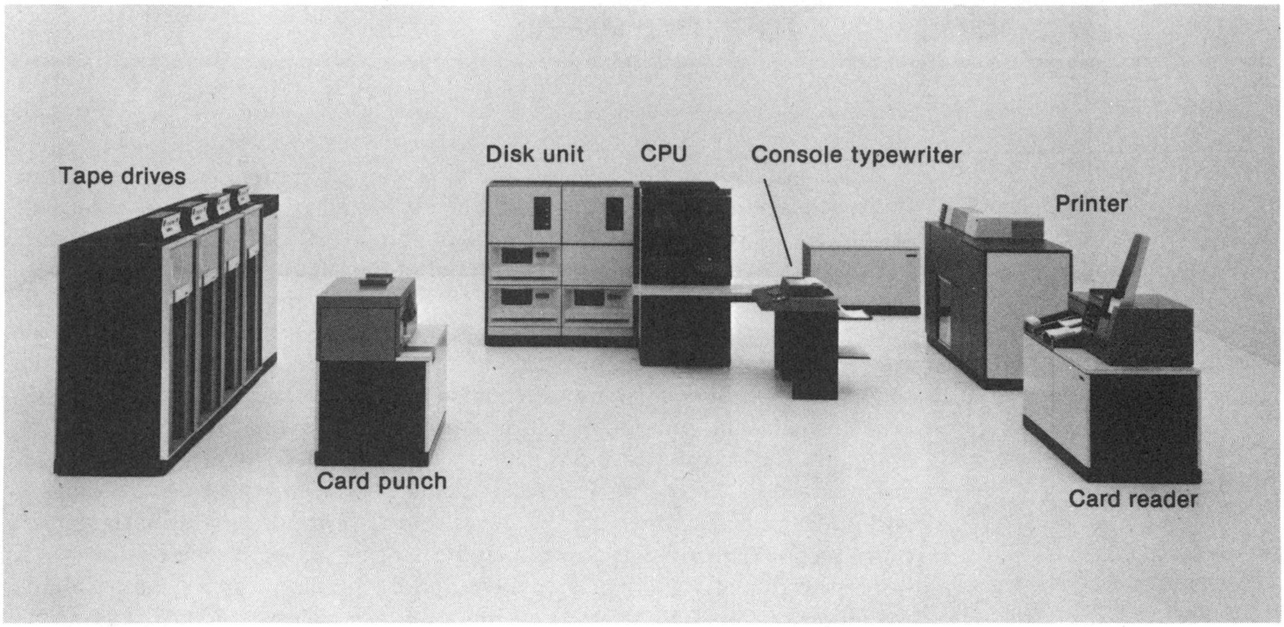
Tape drives
Disk unit
CPU
Console typewriter
Printer
Card punch
Card reader

Figure 1-1
A typical computer system

3. Identify the components of your local computer system and the I/O devices that you will use in writing your COBOL programs.
4. Explain the differences and similarities between your local computer system and the typical system described in the text's other systems.

Typical Computer Systems

Figure 1-1 illustrates an older computer system that one might still see in a moderate-sized installation. It consists of a CPU, a card reader/punch, a printer, two tape drives, two disk drives, a console typewriter, and several terminal stations—which are seldom visible in the computer center, since they are usually distributed out to the various users' offices.

The *card reader* of a computer system usually has one input hopper and one or more output stackers, depending on the model of the device. As the cards are read, one at a time, they pass from the input hopper to one of the stackers. Although some card readers can read over 2000 cards per minute, a card reader in a small system is more likely to read from 200 to 600 cards per minute.

A *card punch*, which looks very much like a card reader, also has one input hopper and one or more output stackers. Although both the punch and the reader may be separate physical units, they are often combined into one unit called a *reader/punch*. In most cases, however, even when combined into one unit, they continue to operate separately. As a rule, card punches operate somewhat slower than card readers—typically, in the range of 100 to 300 cards per minute.

Again, it should be noted that many systems are still leased or purchased with card reader/punches, but these pieces of equipment are quickly being replaced by other more efficient devices, such as terminals or tape and disk.

In fact, the use of cards is disappearing so rapidly that, having acknowledged their infrequent use, we will seldom discuss that topic in this text.

The input device that the student is more likely to encounter is the *terminal*. The terminal is a combined input-output device on which the operator may enter data into the computer system via the attached keyboard and receive information from the system via characters displayed on the cathode ray tube (CRT). The CRT is similar to the television screen in that characters or images are shown on the screen by electronic excitation of a phosphor coating on the inside of the screen. Like television screens, the CRT may be in color or black and white (or, quite often, light green on dark green). Terminals can be very simple or very complex. The simple terminals (often called "dumb" terminals) are connected directly to the computer, which does all of the computing. More complex terminals may have memory and the facility to run programs in the terminal itself. These are able to do a certain amount of computing in the terminal and are known as "smart" terminals. The student will likely use the simpler, less expensive terminals, one of which is shown in Figure 1-2. The terminal shown is one of the products of the TeleVideo Systems, Inc., and is one that has a detached keyboard for easier adjustment to the operator's individual position preference. Many popular terminals have the keyboard and the CRT combined into a single unit.

Printer speeds commonly range from 60–120 lines per minute for the slow, inexpensive character printers to 300–2000 lines per minute for the more typical line printers, and up to several hundred complete pages per minute for the fast, expensive page printers. Character printers produce information that is printed one character at a time. The dot-matrix printer is a typical character printer. Line printers supply information that is printed one whole line at a time. Chain or drum printers are typical examples of this technology although new techniques such as xerography and ink-jet are now being introduced. Page printers print a page at a time and normally use a laser to produce print at high speeds.

Figure 1-2
A typical terminal

To operate at such high speeds, most printers print on continuous, rather than cut, forms. *Continuous forms* are attached to each other in a continuous band of paper, as illustrated in Figure 1-3. They are fed through the printer by a mechanism that fits into the tiny holes on both sides of the forms. After the forms are printed, the sides can be removed and the forms themselves separated, usually at perforations. Because a printer can be adjusted to forms of many widths and lengths, it can be used to print very small forms such as mailing labels as well as 16-inch wide management reports.

A printer also has the capability of skipping to appropriate lines before printing. For example, in preparing the monthly statement illustrated in Figure 1-3, the printer skips to the top of the form before printing the customer's name and address, to the body of the form before printing detailed information about the amounts billed and payments received, and to the total line of the form before printing the balance owed. This capability is commonly called *forms control*. By using forms control, a computer system can meet the printing requirements of almost all business forms.

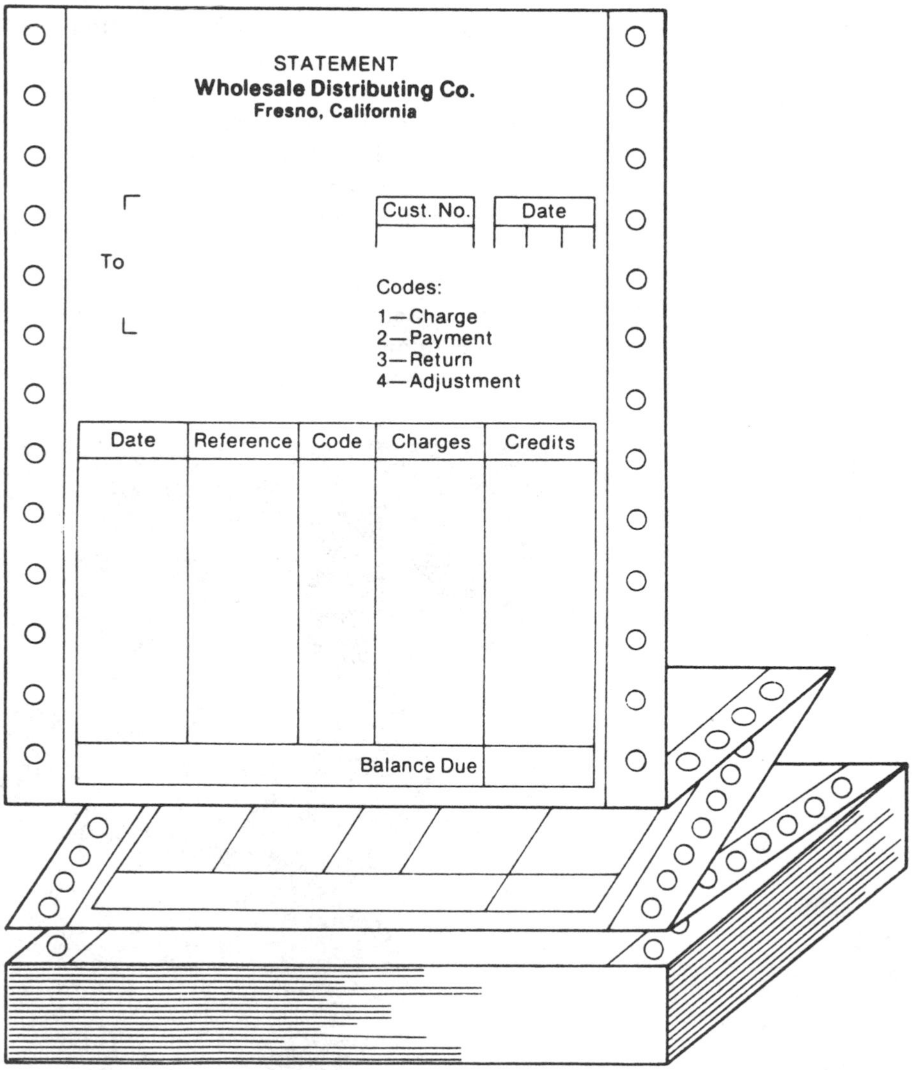
STATEMENT
Wholesale Distributing Co.
Fresno, California
Cust. No.
Date
To
Codes:
1—Charge
2—Payment
3—Return
4—Adjustment
Date
Reference
Code
Charges
Credits
Balance Due

Figure 1-3
A continuous-form statement

A *tape drive* is an I/O device that can read data from or write data on a magnetic tape. The magnetic tape is a long strip of plastic tape that is wound on a reel; it is the big brother of the tape used for home tape recorders. When the reel of tape is mounted on the tape drive, data can be read from it and written on it at speeds much faster than those of card or printing operations. A typical tape drive can transfer data at rates of 60,000 to 320,000 characters per second and more. As disk systems become faster and less expensive, tape drives are becoming less of a factor in computer systems. Many newer systems will not utilize tapes at all.

A disk unit can read data from or write data on disk packs mounted on *disk drives*, or *spindles*, within the unit. The facility shown in Figure 1-1 consists of three separate disk drives. The *disk packs* consist of several platters (disks), somewhat similar to phonograph records, that are stacked on a central spindle. The unique characteristic of the disk is that any one of the records stored on the device can be accessed without reading the other records. For example, 64,000 records might be stored on a disk pack for the device shown in Figure 1-1, yet any one of these records can be accessed and read in an average of about 88/1000 of a second. Contrast this with magnetic type, in which the first 4999 records on a tape must be read before the 5000th record can be read. Disk drives and disk operations will also be covered in detail in chapter 10.

The CPU is the large rectangular unit in Figure 1-1 with the panel of lights, dials, and operational keys on the front. The panel itself is called the *console* of the CPU. The CPU controls the operations of the entire computer system by executing the instructions given it in the form of a program. The CPU contains control circuitry so it can execute a variety of instructions. It also contains storage so it can store the programs while they are executed. As records are read from input devices, they too are stored in the storage of the CPU. The rectangular unit in the upper right of Figure 1-1 contains storage and control circuitry that may be considered a part of the CPU.

The *console typewriter* is usually located near the console of the computer. This typewriter can be used for slow-speed output (it is much slower than a printer), and it can receive input through the keyboard, one character at a time. In normal operation, the console typewriter is used to print a listing of all programs that are run on the system. This listing gives the starting and ending times for each job. If there is an operational problem, a message will be printed on the typewriter, and the computer operator may be called upon to enter a coded response through the keyboard of the console typewriter.

Most modern systems have a video display device in place of the console typewriter, so console output is displayed on a CRT instead of being typed out. In this case, a keyboard beneath the display screen is used to enter console input data.

Although the components shown in Figure 1-1 are physically separate, they are connected by electric cable placed under a raised floor. During operation of the computer the components work together. For instance, when records are read from a tape, the data is transferred to the storage of the CPU where it is processed. When data is printed on the printer or recorded on a disk, the data is transferred from the storage of the CPU to the output device. All of these operations—input, processing, and output—are controlled by program instructions stored in the CPU.

Smaller and larger computer systems

The computer in Figure 1-1 was considered to be a medium-sized computer when it was new in the mid-1970's. But by today's standards it is more likely to be considered to be a small system in power and capacity, if not in physical size. Many of today's systems are physically smaller, but have larger capacity and power. Many modern microcomputers have as much memory capacity and speed as the computer in Figure 1-1 did. Of course, many are considerably larger in capacity, power, and physical size.

The computer in Figure 1-4 is a modern small business system. It has a printer, two disk drives, a small tape system, and a terminal and card reader for input devices. Many modern systems no longer use cards, and all of the input is via one or more terminals attached to the computer.

The computer in Figure 1-5 is a large modern computer system. As you can see, there are several input terminals for monitoring the operation of the system, and most of the storage devices are disks. In modern systems tape is being used as a storage medium less often than before. The system consists of many components. The function of many components is not obvious from the appearance of the cabinets containing them, as the functions of tape drives and printers are.

The system of Figure 1-4 by no means represents the smallest systems that are in use today. Microcomputer systems are available that take up no more room than an office desk and, in fact, often sit on top of the desk. However, only a few of these micro systems can be programmed in COBOL. By the same token, the system in Figure 1-5 does not represent the largest systems available today. In recent years the term "supercomputer" has come into common use to designate the largest systems. A supercomputer is extremely fast, can handle massive amounts of data quickly, and can do complex calculations that were nearly impossible before.

Figure 1-4
A small computer system

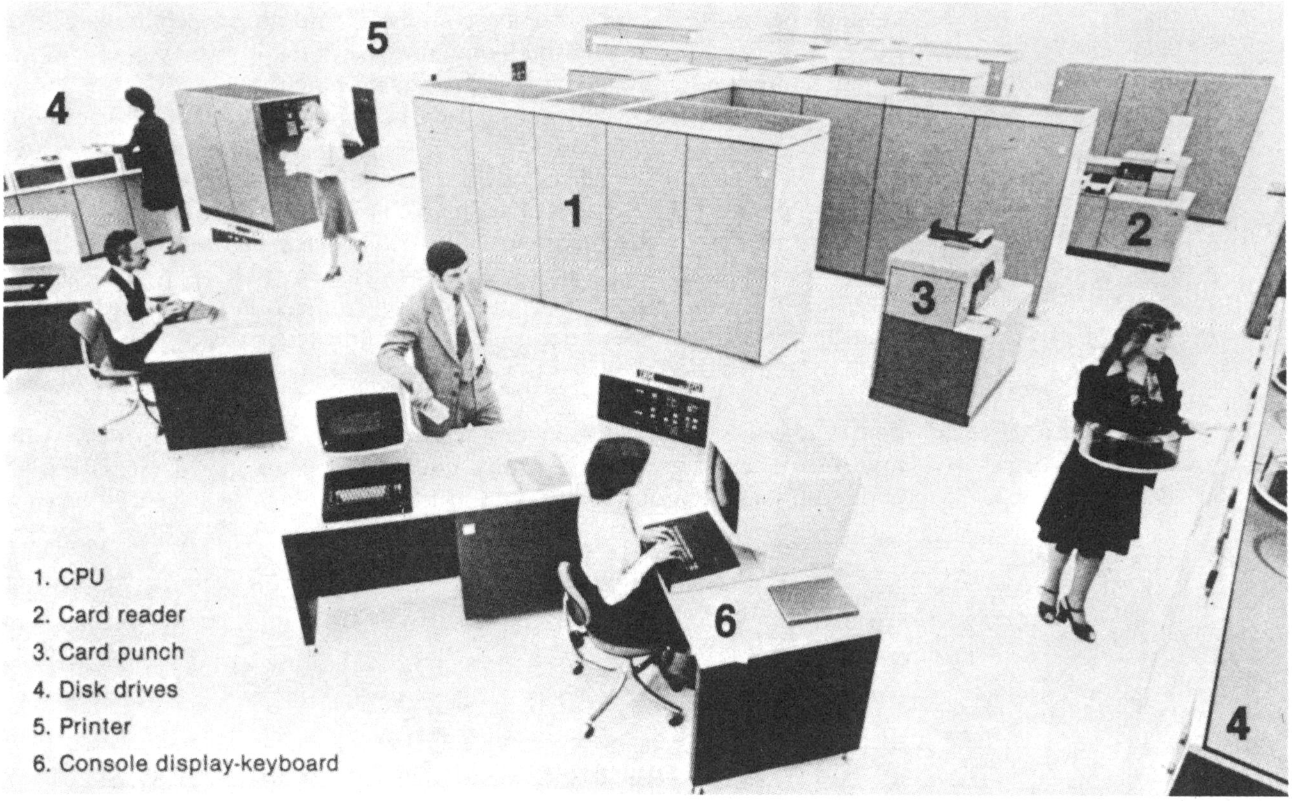
5
4
1
2
3
6
4
1. CPU
2. Card reader
3. Card punch
4. Disk drives
5. Printer
6. Console display-keyboard

Figure 1-5
A large computer system

Distributed processing

When discussing modern computer systems, the topic of distributed systems must be addressed. Thc examples in this book and accompanying discussions may have given the impression that "the computer" is a set of equipment housed in one central location usually called the computer center. Indeed in the past that had been the situation. Usually, there was single computer with various pieces of peripheral equipment that served an entire organization. If any offices in the organization had direct access to the computer, it was generally through the use of on-line terminals. This was a satisfactory situation in the days when computer professionals had to convince other departments of the benefits to be derived from using the computer. However, when those departments began to recognize the benefits, the demand for computing began to mushroom. Now the data processing staff typically has very heavy demands on its services.

One of the problems often arising from the high demand for computer processing is that individual offices or units in an organization feel that they do not receive the service they require. This dissatisfaction may arise from not getting fast enough response from the computer itself. It may be due to too long a wait before a new program can be written and begin working. It may be that a group feels that the information it receives from the central data processing system is not exactly what is needed even though the information output meets the needs of the main office. These problems plus the increased reliability of telecommunications equipment, the decrease in computer costs, the advent of microcomputers, and the availability of appropriate software have provided impetus for a different distribution and organization of equipment and data processing functions.

This realignment typically goes under the name of *distributed processing* and has become a very involved study itself. Normally, the term *distributed processing* creates the image of distributed equipment. However, distributed processing often also includes changing and/or adding centralized staff functions and even the staff who go with those functions. Figure 1-6 is a schematic depicting a typical distributed system. Since this is a physical distribution, a meaningful photograph cannot be utilized. It should be noticed that the photographs used in this chapter could all be parts of a distributed system. Note in the schematic that the various nodes are physically removed from the central system. The nodes may be terminals, intelligent terminals, input and/or output devices, or complete computer systems. Those distributed nodes may be in offices in the same building or located in separate cities, depending on the requirements and office locations of the organization.

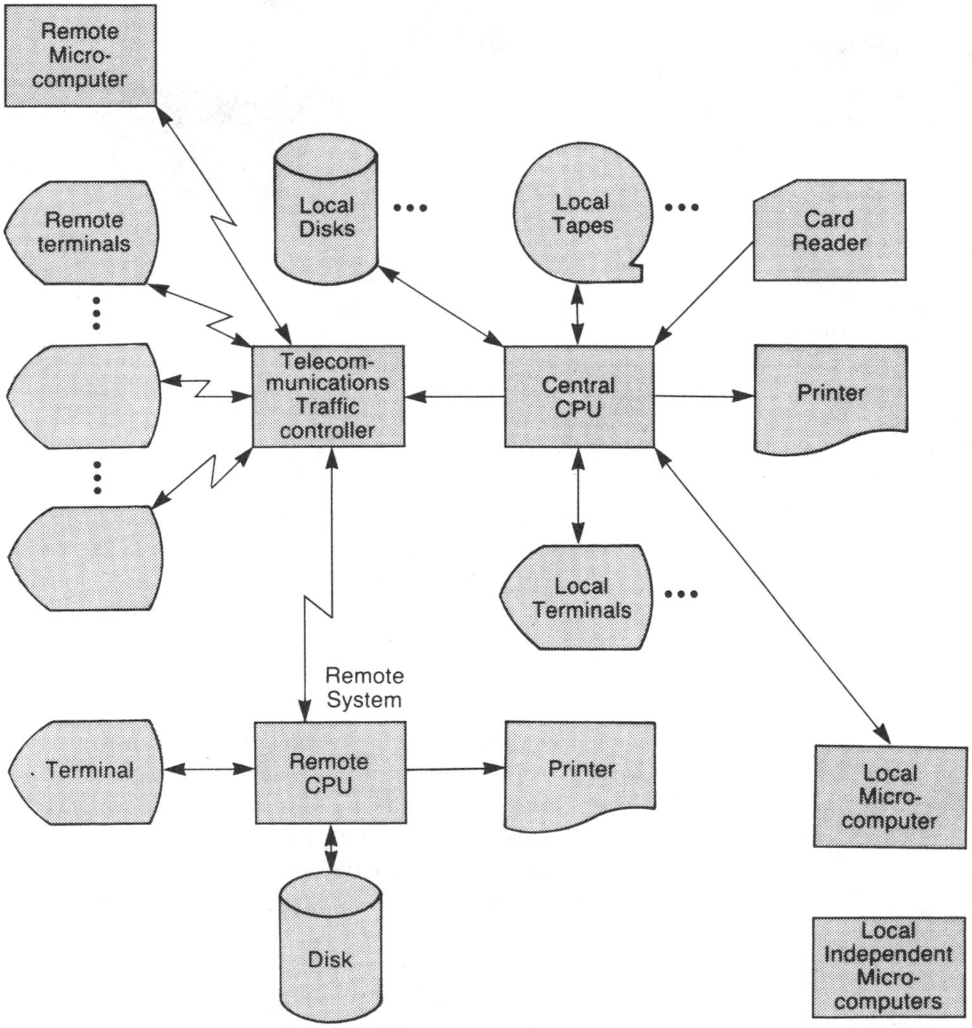
Remote Micro-computer
Remote terminals
Local Disks
Local Tapes
Card Reader
Telecom-munications Traffic controller
Central CPU
Printer
Local Terminals
Remote System
Terminal
Remote CPU
Printer
Local Micro-computer
Disk
Local Independent Micro-computers

Figure 1-6
Schematic of a typical distributed system

Identifying a computer system

To identify a specific computer system, it is common to give the manufacturer's name and the model number of the CPU. For example, one computer is referred to as a Sperry 1100/90, where Sperry is the manufacturer and 1100/90 is the model number. In this case the model number represents a typical situation where the manufacturer has several CPUs in a series; the model number represents both the series and the particular CPU model in that series. Thus, the 1100 is the series and the 90 is the CPU model; Sperry also offers 1100/91 and 1100/92 models. Another computer is referred to as the Burroughs A–15, where Burroughs is the manufacturer and A–15 is the model number. Some other commonly used computers are identified as IBM–4341, DEC VAX/11–780, and Datapoint ARC. The computer in Figure 1-1 is an IBM 370-135; the computer in Figure 1-4 is Sperry Corporation's System 80; and Figure 1-5 shows an IBM 3083/1 computer.

To more specifically identify a computer, the major I/O capabilities are sometimes described. For example, you might hear a programmer describe his or her computer as a Prime 850 with two 300MB (megabyte) disks, two 60KB (kilobyte) tapes, and 48 on-line terminals. Or you might hear a systems designer describe a system as a NCR 9400 with one meg (megabyte) of memory, a 40MB Winchester disk, three CRTs, and a 125 lpm (lines per minute) printer.

Loading and Executing a Program

Before a computer can be used to process data, it must be given a detailed sequence of instructions called a *program*. In other words, the equipment (or *hardware*) must be combined with programs (or *software*). A separate program is required for each job that a computer does; thus, a typical computer installation has hundreds of different programs. Because of the time required to write programs, the amount of money spent for programming in a typical installation is usually far more than the amount spent for computer rental. This is one of the principal reasons the subject of "structured" programming has become so important in recent years. This style of programming is viewed as significantly reducing the time to develop and maintain software.

A program goes through several steps to get to the stage where it can actually direct a computer's actions. When the programmer writes a program in COBOL, he or she is writing in a language that is easy for humans (the programmer, for one) to understand. However, the computer needs a program to be in a different form than humans do. The program must be translated into the language of the computer—machine language. The program that the programmer writes is called the source program, and after it is translated into machine language it is called an object program. The statements of source programs are what will be discussed throughout this text, and the source program is the one to which the techniques and style of structured programming will be applied. The object program is the one that can be run or executed on a computer.

Before an object program can be executed by a computer system, it must be *loaded* into the CPU. From the operator's or user's point of view, this is generally quite simple. The operator may cause a job to be run by keying in its name on the console typewriter or terminal. On the other hand, a user in another office or building may select a program for execution by selecting it from a "menu" of predefined functions available to that particular user. In this latter case, the operator will have started the job earlier so that it will be available to the user on demand. This describes an "on-line" situation where the user may run the program at any time by indicating the selection via key entry on a local terminal.

A request to *execute a program* is normally only a single part of a *job stream*, which is a collection of commands and assignments that indicate to the computer's operating system which programs are to be loaded, which input and output files are required by the program, and which devices will be required for those files. These job steams or *procedures* are normally set up by the systems development department and assigned "job" names or codes before the job is made available for use. The operator causes the job to begin by entering that job's name.

Before a computer system can execute a program, however, the files required by the program must be available to the system. If, for example, a special form is needed, the operator changes the continuous form in the printer and pushes the printer's start button. And if tapes or disk packs are required by the program, the operator must mount the required tapes on appropriate tape drives and the required disk packs on appropriate disk drives. After they are mounted, the operator must push the start buttons on these devices. When all files are available to the system and the I/O devices are ready for operation, the computer system executes the program. If the I/O devices aren't ready when a computer system starts to execute a program, the system will print messages to the operator indicating what files must be mounted on what devices.

To illustrate these operational procedures, suppose that a small system is to prepare payroll checks from two input tapes—one containing weekly payroll data and one containing year-to-date totals. To load and execute the program, the operator will put the *job-control cards* for this program in the card reader and push its start button. As soon as this is done, the cards will be read and the job information will be stored until the computer system is ready for the program. When it is ready, the program will be loaded into the CPU of the system. Before the program can be executed, however, the operator must prepare the I/O devices required by the program. This means mounting the required tapes on the appropriate tape drives and pushing the start buttons on these devices. It also means adjusting the continuous-form payroll checks in the printer of the system and pushing its start button. When all I/O devices are ready for operation, the computer system executes the check-writing program, thus reading the input tapes and printing the payroll checks.

Discussion

It should be clear by now that computer systems vary tremendously as to the components that make them up, their capabilities, and their prices. A small system may rent for $1000 per month or less, a system like the one in Figure 1-1 will rent in the range between $10,000 and $25,000 per month, and a large system may cost well over $100,000 per month. Purchase prices for computer systems vary accordingly. Generally, they are about 45 times as much as the monthly rental price. In most cases, the computer user has the option of either renting or buying a computer system.

Two striking features of even the simplest computer system are the speed and accuracy with which it can process data. The speed can be broken down into I/O speed and CPU speed. In the check-writing program just described, for example, suppose there are 2400 records of 100 characters each on each of the input tapes and that 3 lines are to be printed on each payroll check (a total of 7200 lines for the 2400 employees). At a printing speed of 600 lines per minute, it would take 12 minutes to print 2400 checks. As for reading the input tapes, a typical tape drive would read the 2400 records in less than a minute.

Current CPU speeds, on the other hand, are commonly measured in nanoseconds (billionths of a second). The average speed per program instruction is 4–6 million instructions per second, or about 200 nanoseconds per instruction. At that rate, and assuming 400 instructions per employee, the check-writing program could internally process about 12,500 employees per second. This means that the 2400 employees could be processed in less than ¼ of a second. Thus, one gets a comparison of the relative speeds of the devices: compare the time to print (very slow), with the time to input the data from tape (moderate speed), with the CPU time (extremely fast). This also demonstrates why one CPU can seemingly handle several users at the same time.

As for a computer's accuracy, electronic checking circuitry is built into all I/O devices as well as the CPU to make sure that all errors are caught. A tape drive, for example, doesn't simply read a record. If it did, a faulty reading mechanism might cause inaccurate data to be read into the CPU. Instead, most tape drives have two read heads that read the data twice. Then the data that is read by the first head is compared with the data read by the second head. If the two readings are not the same, an error is recognized and the tape is backed up and the read is attempted again. Similarly, electronic checking circuitry is built into the CPU, printer, disk drives, and all other I/O devices attached to a system. As a result, computer errors that go undetected by a modern computer system are extremely rare. Upon investigation, errors that are blamed on the computer can be traced to errors in system design, programming, or operating procedure.

In addition, modern computer systems have circuitry and software that records and analyzes machine faults so that machine problems may often be identified over the telephone. This often enables maintenance and repair to be done by the local staff without calling out a computer repair specialist, thus saving considerable time and money.

Topic 2 **An Introduction to Software**

Orientation

In the discussion of computer hardware it should have become obvious that a vital component of the computer system is the programs that contain individual commands which cause the hardware to produce the various desired outputs. In the earlier days of computing, the cost of hardware was much more than that of software. Early computer manufacturers often sold the hardware and seemingly "threw in" the available software as part of the package. The sale of the two items with no price distinction for each was called bundling.

Recently, the cost ratio of hardware to software has reversed to the point where one expects that in the near future bundling will be the situation where the hardware is thrown in with the software. The reason for this is that the technology of producing hardware has changed so much that hardware costs have been cut drastically. However, no similar productivity increase has taken place in software production. In fact, the cost per man-hour for programmers has risen. Other reasons for the so-called unbundling of the sale of software from hardware are (1) the results of an antitrust suit against a manufacturer, and (2) the fact that the variety of software available has increased to the point where it is not really practical to give the software away.

This section will discuss the principal categories of software. Since the cost of software has become so significant, it nearly deserves more study when contemplating the acquisition of a computer system than does the hardware. To put together a good system requires thorough knowledge of the role of each software type and careful consideration as to which software best fits the needs of the organization.

Terminology

applications software	operating systems
business applications	program generator
compiler	PROM
data base	redundancy
firmware	scientific applications
information retrieval language	spreadsheet
interpreter	systems software
office automation	word processor

Objectives

1. *Understand and accurately use the terminology.*
2. *Explain the function of the different software types.*
3. *Identify the software category in which COBOL may be placed.*

Typical Software

Systems software

To make the computer easier to use, manufacturers and independent software developers have, over the years, developed a wide range of software that may be put in the category of *systems software*. A satisfactory definition of systems software for the computer novice appears to be "a collection of programs that make the computer easier to use and that enable the user to concentrate on the purpose for which the computer was acquired." Those purposes would be to produce payroll, to keep track of inventory, to calculate stresses on bridge structures, to produce student grade reports, etc. Systems software (except for the category of operating systems) is somewhat comparable to the automobile accessories of power steering, power brakes, power windows, and cruise control which are not really necessary to drive an automobile, but certainly make it more comfortable and easier to use. In the same way systems software is not absolutely necessary, but, in terms of efficiency, is many times more desirable and useful than the auto accessories. The principal systems software categories that are accepted today are operating systems, compilers and interpreters, and data base software.

The previous remarks about the necessity of system software do not really apply to the basic operating system, which is a necessary component of the computer. In the analogy of the automobile, the operating system is more comparable to the ignition system—without which the auto will not start. That is the task of the operating system, to get things started and to smooth the transition from one operation to the other.

Operating systems

The *operating system* software on any particular computer system will vary in size and complexity depending on the size and complexity of the computer system itself. Thus, a home microcomputer's operating system will be relatively simple, but still complex enough that the typical home users will have neither the skill nor the desire to produce their own. The typical home computer's operating system will accomplish the following functions: perform various utility functions, such as initializing a new disk and transfering files and data from one media to another; record which devices are assigned to which computer connection ports or slots; record or change computer configurations; keep track of where files are located on disks and ensure that the data is stored efficiently on disks; catch and inform the user of errors in usage; and, occasionally, keep track of dates and times of machine use.

A larger, professionally used computer will accomplish all of the functions of the microcomputer and many more. In the typical modern computer system, the operating system must also handle traffic into and out of the central processor from several terminals. This means that the operating software must allocate time fairly among the several terminal users so that each user appears to have total control of the computer. In that environment the software must poll each terminal line: to see whether it is requesting access to the computer; to service the requested access by fetching needed disk files, performing calculations, emitting information to printer files, disk files, or to the terminal; and to observe how much time this is taking in order to prevent any one program or user from tying up the computer. If any access takes too much time, the operating system sets that application aside for a time, polls the rest of the lines, and services them in turn. When the polling cycle returns to the user who was set aside, it then allows that application to run for its allotted time or until the function is complete. A larger to super-sized computer system will normally include these functions and many more.

Thus, we are able to get a small impression of the range, complexity, and variety of the topic of operating systems. Remember that the purpose of all operating systems is to make the computer easier to operate.

Compilers and interpreters

The function of *compilers* and *interpreters* arises from the fact that the computer is an electro-mechanical device. As such, its various operations are controlled by the status of its electronic and mechanical parts. Programs are simply a set of commands to the computer to do certain simple functions. When these simple functions are combined in various ways, they become standard commands, and logical combinations of commands become programs. However, the computer understands only the flow of electrons through various "gates" which have only two states—open or closed. Thus comes the need to understand the binary numbering system which is the mathematical representation of a two-state gate. Just as the gate is either open or closed, the binary system has only two digits, zero and one. The binary zero is equated with the gate state of closed or off, and the binary one is equated with the state of open or on.

Early computers required programming to be done in a binary form.

However, this was quickly noted to be very slow and limiting and the effort since that time has been to develop "languages" that are easily understood and quickly used by humans. While the computing industry has developed many languages which are easy to use and understand such as assembler, FORTRAN, BASIC, PL/1, COBOL, RPG, Pascal, and Ada, the computer itself still requires its commands to be in the form of many gates or electronic switches that are either open or closed, on or off. This, then, is the function of compilers or interpreters: to convert or translate the commands given in the languages that humans can easily use to the language of the computer, namely the electronic switch or gate. The function of that set of software called assemblers, compilers, and interpreters is simply that of translating from one language to another.

Data base

As software, in general, develops and grows, the dividing lines between categories begin to become rather fuzzy. There will be many who will argue that *data base* software is not systems software, but rather fits in a different category. Data base is included here as it fits the definition of making the computer system easier to use and greatly enhances the storage, manipulation, and retrieval of data.

Data base software is a collection of complex programs that enable the programmer to store and retrieve data in a more efficient manner than previous record and file techniques allowed. Where the collected data of an organization was (and often still is) stored and processed in separate functional files, such as payroll, inventory, sales, accounts receivable, addresses, etc., data base allows the organization's data to be stored conceptually in one large file. This has the advantage of allowing a programmer to access any piece of data which is required for an application as opposed to having to access two or more files to collect related data for one application. It also enables the reduction of *redundancy* of data—the situation where the same data is stored on several files (e.g., a person's name may appear on the payroll file, the accounts receivable file, and the address file, thus creating redundant data). Data base software allows the user to process certain data more quickly and flexibly.

Applications software

Applications software is that category of software which accomplishes various tasks more efficiently than could be done by hand. Examples of applications functions are: producing payroll checks and sales reports; keeping track of inventory and automatically requesting more stock when it gets too low; and calculating trajectories of space satellites and keeping them on track.

Business applications

The category of *business applications* software includes programs which accomplish the various functions that the efficient running of a business implies. They address the areas of payroll and personnel, inventory, sales, marketing, and manufacture control.

This category implies that certain languages are more appropriate to program those required business applications than others. The typical business languages are COBOL (remember the source of the name COBOL), RPG, and, less often, BASIC, PL/1, and FORTRAN. Which language is used depends quite often on the programmer's or the computer manager's preferance for or familiarity with a language. However, this choice should be made on the basis of the appropriateness of the language to the application. (E.g., COBOL is more appropriate to accounting applications than FORTRAN, whereas

FORTRAN may be considered more appropriate to a marketing survey analysis.) The typical business language tends to only emphasize the basic arithmetic functions, but to be very powerful and flexible in formatting output.

Scientific applications

The category of *scientific applications* software includes functions that are heavily calculation-oriented. Many scientific languages, such as FORTRAN, have very powerful numerical features but tend to be weak in the formatting of good-looking, well-balanced reports. One notable feature of scientific applications versus business applications is that of the potential need of scientific applications to do calculations on very large or very small numbers (numbers as high as $10 \times 10^{+99}$ or as small as $10 + 10^{-99}$) whereas business applications typically encounter numbers in a smaller range.

The typical example of scientific applications is the calculating needed to orbit a satellite or to direct the flights of the space capsules that NASA has sent out and then recovered after flights to other planets. Other examples are the calculating of stresses in the engineering design of structures and the geological calculations required in seismic explorations of the earth.

Recent software advances

Although the following programs probably could be included in the categories already cited, they deserve separate mention because of their relative newness. One of the most popular current uses of the computer is as a glorified typewriter. This is particularly prevalent among microcomputer users as the computers themselves have come within the price range of the average person and very satisfactory *word processors* are available for less than $100. Secretaries, business people, teachers, and students are all finding the word-processing capabilities of microcomputers to be very valuable productivity aids. Other software in this category are simple data bases for recording such data as mailing addresses, electronic *spreadsheets*, and electronic mail.

A productivity aid which is having an increasing impact on the computer arena is the *program generator*. There are, in fact, several software packages available which will generate COBOL programs. As will be seen in studying this book, the readability of programs has become very important. Software exists which will format programs with standard indentations and other readability attributes, thus making the program easier to read while freeing the programmer from the concerns of careful formatting.

Information retrieval languages are simple to learn and use and require the computer staff only to set up standard data names for stored data. These languages may be quickly learned and programmed by office secretaries. Computer staff are freed from the routine production of simple reports, allowing them to concentrate on the more complex programming demands of the organization while providing the user with quicker report generation.

Firmware

Firmware is a recently coined name which identifies things related to computing that are seemingly neither hardware nor software and actually appear to be a combination of both. This feature is due to the advent of the microchip and is sometimes called *PROM* for programmable read only memory. It represents the permanent storage of software on a silicon chip which is plugged into the computer by various means, joining hardware and software into a single entity. Boards which may be plugged into the main board on a microcomputer or modules which may be plugged into an external port are examples of firmware.

Discussion

The preceding material represents a surface view of the wide and expanding world of software. As this is written, more and better software is being produced and made available to an expanding universe of users. With productivity aids software can be produced inexpensively and made available to more users. While it appears that the microcomputer and its software are taking over the world, the real effect is that the world of computing is changing very rapidly. Supercomputers are more in demand than ever while many households now have microcomputers; in fact, the home computer appears to be the modern "toy."

Topic 3 An Introduction to the Stored Program

Orientation

When a program is loaded into a computer, it is placed in the storage of the CPU, or as commonly stated, in memory. This is why a computer program is often referred to as a stored program. In a *multiprogramming* environment several programs may be in the memory of the CPU at the same time. Some programs will be relatively small and some will be very large. The program size is measured by how much memory it takes to store the program. The program's size will depend on the number of tasks that a program is to accomplish and the complexity of those tasks. This topic is intended to present basic concepts regarding the stored program and to insure that a common body of important and basic terms are understood.

Terminology

address	field
ASCII	input area
binary component	K
bit	kilo multiprogramming
byte	output area
conditional branch	storage position
EBCDIC	unconditional branch

Objectives

1. *Understand and accurately use the terminology presented.*
2. *Describe one way in which a field in storage can be identified by a computer's instructions.*
3. *List the four basic types of instructions that can be executed by a typical computer system, and describe the execution of typical instructions within each group. For instance, describe the execution of the move instruction within the data-movement group of instructions.*
4. *Explain what an input or output area in storage is.*

Computer Storage

Small computers have a relatively limited amount of storage. Microcomputers, for instance, typically have storage amounts in the range of 16,384 to 262,144 *storage positions*, whereas some of the larger computers may have several million storage positions. Because the word *kilo* refers to 1000, *K* is often used to refer to 1000 storage positions: a 16K computer has approximately 16,000 storage positions. (I say approximately because 1K is actually 1024 storage positions, so 16K is 16,384 storage positions. In normal conversation, however, the excess storage positions are dropped.)

Associated with each of the storage positions of a computer is a number that identifies it, called the *address* of the storage position. A 16K computer, for instance, has addresses ranging from 0000 to 16,383. You can therefore talk about the contents of the storage position with address 180 or the contents of storage position 14,482.

On many computer systems, each storage position is referred to as a *byte* of storage. Within these bytes of storage, data can be stored in two or more different forms. To keep this explanation simple, however, let's consider only the form in which one character is stored in each storage byte. To illustrate this form, suppose the following boxes represent the twenty bytes from 480 to 499:

Contents:	G	E	O	R	G	E	3	4	3	9	9	8	2		*	1	1	2	1	4
Addresses:	480					485					490					495				

You can then say that byte 480 contains the letter G, byte 487 contains the number 4, byte 494 contains an asterisk, and byte 493 contains a blank. Or you can say that there is a 2 at address 497 and the number 343 is stored in bytes 486 through 488. This is simply the way data-processing people talk about storage and its contents.

Several bytes in a row that contain one item of data, such as an item number or unit price, are commonly referred to as a *field*. For instance, in the above example, bytes 486–490 (which is read as 486 through 490) might represent a balance-on-hand field, while positions 495–499 represent an item-number field. To address a field, a typical instruction specifies the address of the leftmost storage position as well as the number of storage positions in the field. Thus, address 486 with a length of five would address the field in bytes 486–490, while address 1024 with a length of twenty would address the field in bytes 1024–1043.

Of course, a storage position, or byte, isn't really a small box with a character of data in it. Instead, each storage position consists of a number of electronic components called *binary components*, or *bits*, because they can be switched to either of two conditions, commonly referred to as "on" and "off."

In older computers memory was composed of tiny doughnut-shaped cores strung together on wires. Memory was then called core memory or core storage, and this is the reason that you may hear older data processors use those terms. Recent computers use the silicon chip which has microscopic transistor-like circuits or gates imbedded between silicon layers, each of which correspond to a binary component or bit. When these gates are closed, the binary component is said to be on, and when open it is said to be off.

In order to represent data, the several bits that make up a byte of memory are turned on or off in selected combinations. The number of bits in a set which makes up a byte or storage position of memory varies from computer to computer and is the reason one hears them spoken of as 8-bit, 16-bit, 32-bit, or 64-bit computers. Each combination of bits represents a digit or digits, a letter, or a special character. By decoding the combinations of on and off bits at each position, it can be determined which character is stored there. The principles of data representation in storage are: a fixed number of binary components make up one storage position; and one or more storage positions represent a field in storage. There are two prevalent code structures used, known as *ASCII* (American Standard Code for Information Interchange) and *EBCDIC* (Extended Binary Coded Decimal Interchange Code). A few samples of each are shown in Figure 1-7.

Instructions

While a program is being executed, both the instructions of the program and the data being processed are contained in storage. The instructions, in coded form, indicate the operations that are to be performed and give the addresses of the storage bytes that hold the data to be operated upon. The number of storage bytes required to store an instruction varies from computer to computer and from instruction to instruction.

Although a program may consist of thousands of instructions, there are basically only four types that a computer can execute, plus some miscellaneous ones. As a result, a program with 6000 instructions consists of the same types of instructions being executed over and over again. These basic types are (1) input and output, (2) data-movement, (3) arithmetic, and (4) logical (or program-control) instructions.

Input/output instructions

An input/output instruction specifies the type of input or output operation to be performed and the storage bytes to be used in performing the operation. For example, an input instruction, such as a disk-reading instruction, might specify that a disk record is to be read and its data stored in the 200 storage bytes beginning with address 5501. In this case, storage bytes 5501–5700 are called the disk input area, or more typically just the *input area*, of storage. When the read instruction is executed, the data that is read from the disk replaces the data that the input area originally contained. The data from the record position 1 is stored in storage byte 5501, the data from record position 2 is stored in byte 5502, and so on, until the data from record position 200 is stored in byte 5700.

Similarly, an output instruction, such as a write instruction for a printer, specifies the storage bytes from which the output line is to be printed (called the printer output area, or just *output area*, of storage). If a write instruction specifies that a line should be printed from locations 6601 through 6700, the content of storage byte 6601 is printed in print position 1 on the printer, the content of byte 6602 is printed in print position 2, and so on. Since a typical printer may have up to 132 print positions between the left and right margins, the printer output area may require up to 132 storage positions.

Other I/O instructions enable a computer to make use of the other I/O capabilities of the system. For example, a write instruction for a video display terminal will cause a line of text to be written from the output area and to appear on the terminal screen. Similarly, instructions for tape units will cause tape records to be read into input areas or to be written from output blank =

0	0	1	0	0	0	0	0
0	0	●	0	0	0	0	0
128	64	32	16	8	4	2	1

0 =

0	0	1	1	0	0	0	0
0	0	●	●	0	0	0	0
128	64	32	16	8	4	2	1

1 =

0	0	1	1	0	0	0	1
0	0	●	●	0	0	0	●
128	64	32	16	8	4	2	1

2 =

0	0	1	1	0	0	1	0
0	0	●	●	0	0	●	0
128	64	32	16	8	4	2	1

3 =

0	0	1	1	0	0	1	1
0	0	●	●	0	0	●	●
128	64	32	16	8	4	2	1

4 =

0	0	1	1	0	1	0	0
0	0	●	●	0	●	0	0
128	64	32	16	8	4	2	1

5 =

0	0	1	1	0	1	0	1
0	0	●	●	0	●	0	●
128	64	32	16	8	4	2	1

6 =

0	0	1	1	0	1	1	0
0	0	●	●	0	●	●	0
128	64	32	16	8	4	2	1

7 =

0	0	1	1	0	1	1	1
0	0	●	●	0	●	●	●
128	64	32	16	8	4	2	1

8 =

0	0	1	1	1	0	0	0
0	0	●	●	●	0	0	0
128	64	32	16	8	4	2	1

9 =

0	0	1	1	1	0	0	1
0	0	●	●	●	0	0	●
128	64	32	16	8	4	2	1

A =

0	1	0	0	0	0	0	1
0	●	0	0	0	0	0	●
128	64	32	16	8	4	2	1

B =

0	1	0	0	0	0	1	0
0	●	0	0	0	0	●	0
128	64	32	16	8	4	2	1

C =

0	1	0	0	0	0	1	1
0	●	0	0	0	0	●	●
128	64	32	16	8	4	2	1

D =

0	1	0	0	0	1	0	0
0	●	0	0	0	●	0	0
128	64	32	16	8	4	2	1

E =

0	1	0	0	0	1	0	1
0	●	0	0	0	●	0	●
128	64	32	16	8	4	2	1

F =

0	1	0	0	0	1	1	0
0	●	0	0	0	●	●	0
128	64	32	16	8	4	2	1

G =

0	1	0	0	0	1	1	1
0	●	0	0	0	●	●	●
128	64	32	16	8	4	2	1

H =

0	1	0	0	1	0	0	0
0	●	0	0	●	0	0	0
128	64	32	16	8	4	2	1

I =

0	1	0	0	1	0	0	1
0	●	0	0	●	0	0	●
128	64	32	16	8	4	2	1

J =

0	1	0	0	1	0	1	0
0	●	0	0	●	0	●	0
128	64	32	16	8	4	2	1

K =

0	1	0	0	1	0	1	1
0	●	0	0	●	0	●	●
128	64	32	16	8	4	2	1

L =

0	1	0	0	1	1	0	0
0	●	0	0	●	●	0	0
128	64	32	16	8	4	2	1

M =

0	1	0	0	1	1	0	1
0	●	0	0	●	●	0	●
128	64	32	16	8	4	2	1

N =

0	1	0	0	1	1	1	0
0	●	0	0	●	●	●	0
128	64	32	16	8	4	2	1

O =

0	1	0	0	1	1	1	1
0	●	0	0	●	●	●	●
128	64	32	16	8	4	2	1

P =

0	1	0	1	0	0	0	0
0	●	0	●	0	0	0	0
128	64	32	16	8	4	2	1

Q =

0	1	0	1	0	0	0	1
0	●	0	●	0	0	0	●
128	64	32	16	8	4	2	1

R =

0	1	0	1	0	0	1	0
0	●	0	●	0	0	●	0
128	64	32	16	8	4	2	1

S =

0	1	0	1	0	0	1	1
0	●	0	●	0	0	●	●
128	64	32	16	8	4	2	1

T =

0	1	0	1	0	1	0	0
0	●	0	●	0	●	0	0
128	64	32	16	8	4	2	1

U =

0	1	0	1	0	1	0	1
0	●	0	●	0	●	0	●
128	64	32	16	8	4	2	1

V =

0	1	0	1	0	1	1	0
0	●	0	●	0	●	●	0
128	64	32	16	8	4	2	1

W =

0	1	0	1	0	1	1	1
0	●	0	●	0	●	●	●
128	64	32	16	8	4	2	1

X =

0	1	0	1	1	0	0	0
0	●	0	●	●	0	0	0
128	64	32	16	8	4	2	1

Y =

0	1	0	1	1	0	0	1
0	●	0	●	●	0	0	●
128	64	32	16	8	4	2	1

Z =

0	1	0	1	1	0	1	0
0	●	0	●	●	0	●	0
128	64	32	16	8	4	2	1

Figure 1-7a
ASCII Code

Character	zone 8	zone 4	zone 2	zone 1	digit 8	digit 4	digit 2	digit 1
blank =	0	1	0	0	0	0	0	0
A =	1	1	0	0	0	0	0	1
B =	1	1	0	0	0	0	1	0
C =	1	1	0	0	0	0	1	1
D =	1	1	0	0	0	1	0	0
E =	1	1	0	0	0	1	0	1
F =	1	1	0	0	0	1	1	0
G =	1	1	0	0	0	1	1	1
H =	1	1	0	0	1	0	0	0
I =	1	1	0	0	1	0	0	1
J =	1	1	0	1	0	0	0	1
K =	1	1	0	1	0	0	1	0
L =	1	1	0	1	0	0	1	1
M =	1	1	0	1	0	1	0	0
N =	1	1	0	1	0	1	0	1
O =	1	1	0	1	0	1	1	0
P =	1	1	0	1	0	1	1	1
Q =	1	1	0	1	1	0	0	0
R =	1	1	0	1	1	0	0	1
S =	1	1	1	0	0	0	1	0
T =	1	1	1	0	0	0	1	1
U =	1	1	1	0	0	1	0	0
V =	1	1	1	0	0	1	0	1
W =	1	1	1	0	0	1	1	0
X =	1	1	1	0	0	1	1	1
Y =	1	1	1	0	1	0	0	0
Z =	1	1	1	0	1	0	0	1
0 =	1	1	1	1	0	0	0	0
1 =	1	1	1	1	0	0	0	1
2 =	1	1	1	1	0	0	1	0
3 =	1	1	1	1	0	0	1	1
4 =	1	1	1	1	0	1	0	0
5 =	1	1	1	1	0	1	0	1
6 =	1	1	1	1	0	1	1	0
7 =	1	1	1	1	0	1	1	1
8 =	1	1	1	1	1	0	0	0
9 =	1	1	1	1	1	0	0	1

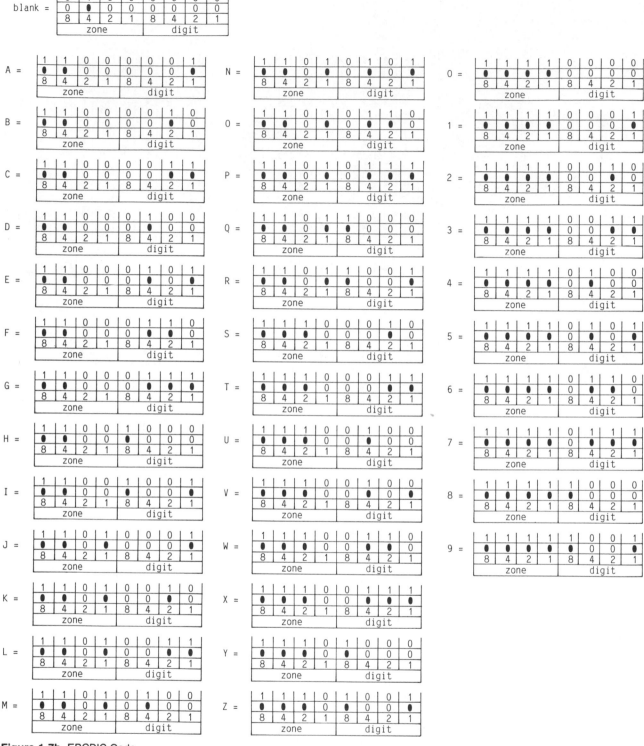

Figure 1-7b EBCDIC Code

areas, and instructions for disk devices will cause disk records to be read into input areas or to be written from output areas.

Data-movement instructions

Data-movement instructions allow a computer to move data from one field in storage to another. The basic data-movement instruction, commonly called the move instruction, causes the data from one field to be copied unchanged to another field. If, for example, a move instruction specifies that the contents of storage bytes 541–545 should be moved to bytes 701–705, the execution of the instruction can be shown as follows:

Before:	0 0 7 0 0	0 0 2 2 5
	541	701
After:	0 0 7 0 0	0 0 7 0 0
	541	701

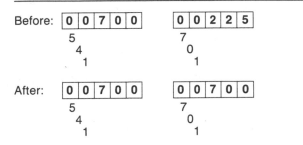

The effect is that the data in the first field is duplicated in the second field.

Another basic data-movement instruction is the edit instruction. The main purpose of this instruction is to move data into a printer output area in a form that will be easier to read when printed. For instance, $3.25 is more understandable than 00325. Computers internally do not require editing since they operate electronically. However, humans who use the output of computers require the use of the eye when they read computer output and so the presentation of output in an easily readable form is a very important study. Most computer languages have made some provision in the instruction set for enabling output fields, particularly the numeric fields, to be edited for human use.

In its simplest form the edit instruction may operate like a move instruction except the insignificant zeros (zeros to the left of a number such as the italicized zeros in *00*140) are suppressed (changed to blanks). This removal of left zeros and replacement with blanks is known as high-order zero suppression. If, for example, the contents of bytes 536–540 are moved with zero suppression to bytes 671–675, the execution takes place as follows:

Before:	0 0 3 0 0	9 9 9 9 9
	536	671
After:	0 0 3 0 0	_ _ 3 0 0
	536	671

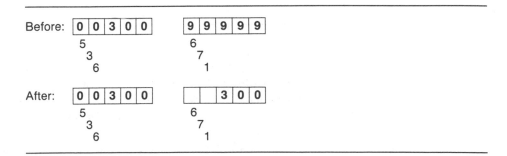

Depending on the codes stored in the receiving field, the edit instruction may also cause decimal points and commas to be inserted into a field, dollar and credit signs to be placed before and after the number, etc. The following example shows how a decimal number in storage is changed to an edited form in preparation for output for human use. Note that the "before" contents at address 925 are left from some prior computer activity and are to be considered "garbage" for this operation. The before contents will be replaced with edited numeric data as a result of the move statement.

	Field	Address	Field	Address
Before:	0 1 2 3 7 5 9 8	783	A 1 4 ; 6 - 9 8 L X	925
After:	0 1 2 3 7 5 9 8	783	1 2 , 3 7 5 . 9 8	925

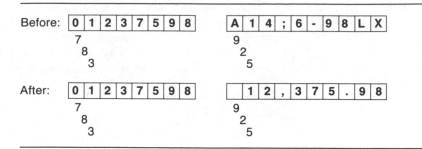

Other data-movement instructions are used to convert data from one form to another. Since two or more forms of data are likely to be used when your COBOL programs are compiled, a significant portion of a program may be made up of data-conversion instructions.

Arithmetic instructions

In general, there are two different ways in which arithmetic instructions operate within a computer. In one way, the instruction specifies the arithmetic operation and the two fields to be operated upon. The result of the arithmetic operation replaces the second field specified, while the first field remains unchanged. This type of instruction is illustrated below.

Typical arithmetic instructions are the add, subtract, multiply, and divide instructions. To illustrate the add, suppose the contents of storage positions 546–550 are to be added to the contents of storage positions 701–705. Then, the execution takes place as follows:

	Field	Address	Field	Address
Before:	0 0 0 7 5	546	0 0 1 5 0	701
After:	0 0 0 7 5	546	0 0 2 2 5	701

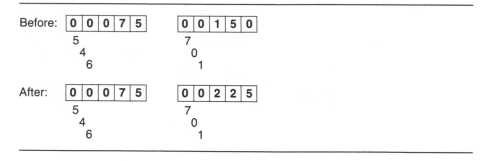

Usually, another form of data storage is used for data involved in arithmetic operations, but conceptually this is what happens. When the subtract, multiply, or divide instructions are executed in this two-field form, the operation takes place in basically the same way.

Because the result of a multiplication or addition may be larger than either field operated upon (for instance, 555 plus 500 equals 1055), one of the fields is usually moved to a larger field before the calculation takes place. Similarly, because the result of a division has a remainder, the number that is divided must be placed in a larger field, part of which becomes the quotient and part of which becomes the remainder.

As will be seen later, some arithmetic instructions do not disturb the contents of either field involved in the calculation, but rather specify a separate result field where the result of the calculation is placed. The instance of subtracting the contents of bytes 252–255 from the contents of bytes 284–287 and placing the result in bytes 488–491 would appear something like the following:

Before:	0 3 8 6	0 5 9 7	9 8 7 6
	252	284	488
After:	0 3 8 6	0 5 9 7	0 2 1 1
	252	284	488

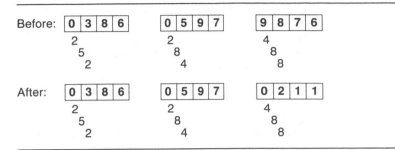

Program control

The basic logical instruction and the basis of logic in the computer is the branch instruction. When a program is initially loaded into storage, the load module specifies in which storage bytes the instructions are to stored and at which storage byte the computer is to begin executing the program. When the computer finishes executing one instruction, it continues with the next instruction in storage. After executing the instruction in bytes 1000–10005, for example, the computer executes the instruction starting with address 1006. The only exception to this sequence results from use of the branch instruction. When the branch instruction is executed, it can cause the computer to break the sequence and jump to the instruction beginning at the address specified in the branch instruction.

For instance, one type of branch instruction tells the computer to branch whenever it is executed. This is called an *unconditional branch*. Suppose then that an unconditional branch instruction, which is stored in bytes 4032–4035, specifies a branch to address 801. When the branch instruction is executed, the computer will continue with the instruction starting at address 801.

Conditional branch instructions cause branching only when specified conditions are met. For example, one type of conditional branch instruction specifies a branch if the result of an arithmetic instruction is negative. Suppose this instruction occupies storage positions 2044–2047 and specifies that the computer should branch to address 1000 if the result of the preceding arithmetic instruction is negative. If the result is zero or positive, the computer continues with the instruction starting at address 2048, the next instruction in storage. If the result is negative, however, the computer continues by executing the instruction starting at address 1000.

Other branch instructions specify that a branch should take place when the result of an arithmetic calculation is zero, when the result of an arithmetic calculation is larger than the result field, or when an I/O device isn't working. Perhaps the most used branch instruction, however, specifies a branch based on the results of a comparison between two fields in storage. This branch instruction is used in conjunction with the second type of logical instruction, the compare instruction.

The compare instruction specifies that two fields are to be compared. When it is executed, the computer determines the relationship between the two fields: Are they equal? Is the first field greater in value than the second? Is the first field less than the second? The branch instruction then specifies a branch based on any of these three conditions. If, for example, the compare instruction compares two fields representing ages, the branch instruction can specify that a branch should take place if the first age is less than the second.

A compare instruction can operate on alphanumeric as well as numeric fields. For example, if two fields containing alphabetic names are compared, the branch instruction can specify that a branch take place when the second name is higher in alphabetic sequence than the first name. Or, if a one-position alphanumeric character is compared with a storage position containing the character M, the branch instruction can specify that a branch take place when the characters are equal.

Discussion

Understanding the nature of the stored program is important because any computer language source program (that which is easy for humans to read and use) is related to its object program (the binary form of the program that the computer must have to run the program). For instance, the COBOL READ and WRITE statements are compiled into input and output instructions. When executed, the instructions resulting from a READ statement cause data to be read from an input device into an input area in storage; the instructions resulting from a WRITE statement cause data to be written on an output device from an output area in storage.

Similarly, a COBOL arithmetic statement such as

```
ADD TR-ON-HAND TO TR-ON-ORDER
```

will cause one or more arithmetic instructions to be compiled into the object program. A COBOL MOVE statement such as

```
MOVE TR-ITEM-NUMBER TO PR-ITEM-NUMBER
```

will cause one or more data-movement instructions to be compiled. And a COBOL IF statement such as

```
IF  QUANTITY-AVAILABLE IS LESS THAN BF-REORDER-POINT
    PERFORM 240-CALC-REORDER-QUANTITY
ELSE
    PERFORM 260-PRODUCE-SHIP-LIST
```

will cause a compare instruction and two or more branch instructions to be compiled. By understanding the general nature of a computer's instructions, you will be better able to understand what happens when COBOL statements are compiled and executed. This understanding will become very important when you get to the stage where sometimes rather obscure logical errors must be found and corrected.

Topic 4 **Issue: The Future of Programmers**

As changes in the world of programmers take place, several things can be observed. First, programmers are much better trained than they were when the profession first became a recognized job. Several years ago a strong interest, and just a little training, which could be self-training, was about all that was required to qualify for a programmer job. Of course, as time passed many college and even high school programs have attempted to provide this training, and have tried to provide students with more than just the minimal skills. Schools are generally doing a good job of educating students to become skilled practitioners of programming and data processing.

Many schools have also accepted the challenge of educating students to become leaders in advancing the practice of computing. Those leaders will continue to find more efficient ways to produce computer outputs which computer users desire. Efficiency is measured in terms of cost and time, and the past ten years have witnessed tremendous increases in the speed of computers, in the quantity of data that can be stored in the system, and in the services performed by operating software. These increases have been accompanied by some significant decreases: decreases in the size and cost of equipment; decreases in the cost of software relative to the tasks performed; and decreases in the level of expertise required to operate the computer systems.

These changes have brought significant changes to the programmer's job. Less and less are programmers expected to provide software for each computer task desired by users. More and more easy-to-use software is available and expertly used by computer neophites. You only have to go to a local computer store (which did not exist a few years ago) and consider the sophistication and ease of use of relatively inexpensive software such as word processors and spreadsheets to understand that computing is open to a world of people who are not "computer trained." Be assured that if the home computer world is experiencing a revolution in the level of expertise required to do sophisticated computing, then, surely, the professional data processing world is also undergoing significant changes. Those same word processors and spreadsheets are being adopted by the business world. Information retrieval languages are enabling users to access the central computer and create their own reports without having to wait in a long line while the computer center programmers work their way through mammoth backlogs of user requests.

Recent theories and implementations of structured programming concepts have enabled significant advances in the speed and accuracy of developing software. This is one of the reasons that most recent programming texts carry the word "structure" somewhere in the title—true structured methods really do increase programming efficiency during the complete life cycle of any program. Literature and seminars available now are going beyond the discussion of structured techniques and beginning to discuss the "4GL" or fourth generation languages. The fourth generation language is one that will be immensely easier to program quickly and accurately. A 4GL will be utilized by less well trained staff and will be able to accomplish more sophisticated tasks than current high-level languages can do.

The preceding discussion raises questions about the future of the programmer. It is, in fact true, that certain experts who study the situation predict that programmers will not be needed in the future since software and hardware have been experiencing sophisticated advances. We have certainly seen that small businesses can buy prewritten accounting packages and have no need for programmers. However, observe that these are the same businesses that a few years ago could not afford computers and thus did not employ programmers. One of the reasons the software mentioned has appeared is that there was a significant demand for it. One point that must be made is that it took programmers to provide that software. The reason that productivity aids appeared was because of demand for more programs. Thus, the outlook for programmers appears to be very good in the foreseeable future, but the quality of a programmer's skill and the level of sophistication is also increasing.

The opinion of the authors is that, first, the job market is currently very good for experienced programmers. Second, entry-level programmers must be more skilled and sophisticated when they enter the profession than were the authors or your instructors. Third, the job environment and tasks of the programmer are changing. Less and less will programmers be expected to churn out simple reports or "one more payroll system." More and more will programmers be setting up data bases and training users how to use those data bases and information retrieval languages. Fourth, programmers will be used less by local data processing centers, but will find more jobs with software developers who sell their products to the computing world at large. Finally, due to the advances in telecommunications, programmers will find more work at home rather than working in a computer center with several colleagues and will be more self-employed "contract programmers" than permanent employees of a business or organization.

The final comment to students is "continue your computer studies, the future is there, and it is bright, but it will change in ways that neither the authors nor your instructors can accurately predict."

Chapter 2 A Student's Procedure for Program Development

Before introducing the various commands of COBOL and the rules and guidelines for their use, an outline for problem solving is presented. If the steps outlined here are followed carefully, the program development process will be much smoother. The first topic will concentrate on the problem-solving steps, while the second will discuss the accessing of the computer through an on-line terminal as the most likely programming environment.

Topic 1 The Problem-Solving Process

Orientation

To write a program, a programmer goes through four general phases: (1) the problem to be solved must be defined; (2) if the problem can be best solved with a program, then that program solution is designed; (3) the chosen solution is implemented, which for a program involves coding and testing; and (4) the programmer carefully documents the program. These four phases are explained in discussion of this topic.

Terminology

bug	functional decomposition	source list
carriage-control tape	literal	source program
clean compilation	logic error	structure chart
compile time error	module	structure diagram
compiler output	object program	structured design
debug	print chart	structured programming
desk checking	program documentation	syntax error
diagnostic	pseudocode	test data
diagnostic list	record layout form	test run
diagnostic message	run time error	variable
documentation		
execution time error		

Objectives

1. *Understand and accurately use the terminology presented.*
2. *Given the record layout form for a programming problem, identify the input record positions of any input data item.*
3. *Given the print chart for a programming problem, identify the print positions where the output data is to be placed, and identify the editing which is to take place on numeric items.*
4. *Given the print chart, identify which items are literal data and which are variable data.*
5. *In general terms, describe how a source program is compiled into an object program and what the outputs of the typical compiler are.*
6. *List the four phases and significant subtasks that a programmer goes through when developing a program.*

Problem Definition

Defining the problem is simply making sure that you know what the program you are going to write is supposed to do. You must understand what the input is going to be, what the output of the program must be, and what calculations or other procedures must be followed in deriving the output from the input. Two documents that are often used for defining input and output are the record layout form and the print chart.

Define desired results

In this text most output will be for the printer, and so the print chart will be utilized. Advanced projects will begin to describe output for other devices such as tape or disk, and in these cases the record layout form will be used. Many programming and systems design texts describe the input record first, then the processing required, and finally show what form the output is supposed to take. This is normal since computing discussions often refer to the input-processing-output path by which useful information is produced from computers. However, this text will present the output (the print chart) first since the final outcome must be understood before one can make determinations about what inputs are required and about what processes must be performed on those inputs to produce the desired output.

Print chart

A *print chart*, such as the one in Figure 2–1, shows the layout of a report that will probably be printed, but which could also be displayed on a terminal. Since printing is still common, the layout form will continue to be referred to as a print chart. The chart indicates that the first or top heading line INVESTMENT REPORT is to be printed or displayed in positions 20–36. Since this heading will remain the same throughout the report, it is referred to as constant or *literal* data. This line is normally called the report title as it identifies the purpose of the report. The next two lines are also literal headings which do not change. They are called column headings as their purpose is to identify the contents of the columns of data below them. Literals are easily identified as their actual contents are spelled out on the chart, such as DESCRIPTION in heading–line–3, positions 16–26.

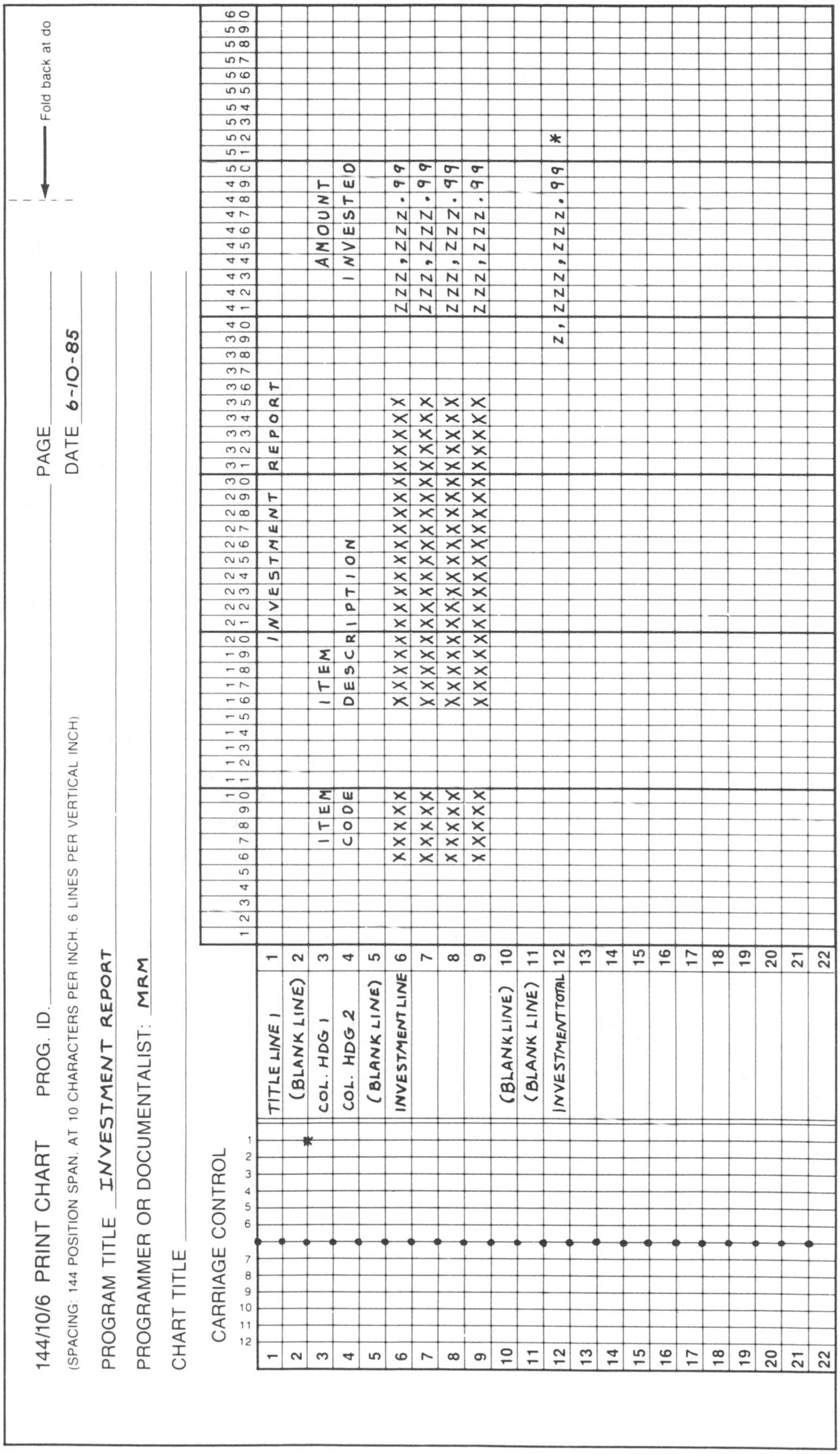

144/10/6 PRINT CHART
PROG. ID.
PAGE
(SPACING: 144 POSITION SPAN, AT 10 CHARACTERS PER INCH, 6 LINES PER VERTICAL INCH)
DATE 6-10-85
PROGRAM TITLE INVESTMENT REPORT
PROGRAMMER OR DOCUMENTALIST: MRM
CHART TITLE
CARRIAGE CONTROL
Fold back at do
TITLE LINE 1
(BLANK LINE)
COL. HDG 1
COL. HDG 2
(BLANK LINE)
INVESTMENT LINE
(BLANK LINE)
(BLANK LINE)
INVESTMENT TOTAL
INVESTMENT REPORT
ITEM
ITEM
AMOUNT
CODE
DESCRIPTION
INVESTED
XXXXX
XXXXXXXXXXXXXXXXXXXXXXXX
ZZZ,ZZZ.99
Z,ZZZ,ZZZ.99 *

Figure 2-1
A print chart

Another category of output is on chart lines 6 through 9 and line 12. These entries indicate the presence of *variable* data, that is, data which will change from one report line to the next and from one report to the next. The chart demonstrates that the item codes will be printed in positions 6–10, the descriptions in 16–35, and the amounts invested in 41–50. The X's indicate that alphanumeric characters will be used for the codes and descriptions, whereas the ZZZ,ZZZ.99 indicates that numeric edited fields will be output under the amount invested columns. The meaning of those symbols will be treated in detail in chapter 3.

Finally, at the end of the report, the total of the amount invested is to be printed after leaving two blank lines to separate the total from the body of the report. This total is indicated by an asterisk (a literal) in position 52. Although Figure 2–1 indicates only 60 print positions from left to right, a complete chart normally has 132 or more positions, which is the number of print positions commonly available on larger printers.

A print chart may also have an area that can be used to show what punches should be made in the *carriage-control tape* for the job. A carriage-control tape is a paper tape that is placed in the carriage-control mechanism in the printer. This tape, which can be punched in 12 different positions, moves in conjunction with the continuous form that is being printed, so the tape can control the skipping of the form. In an invoicing job, for example, a 1-punch may correspond to the first address line of the invoice, a 2-punch to the first line in the body of the form, and a 3-punch to the total line of the form. Then, if the printer is instructed to skip to a 1-punch, the continuous form is skipped to the first address line of the invoice. If it is instructed to skip to a 2-punch, the continuous form skips to the first body line of the invoice, and so on.

In general, you will only use punches 2 through 12 when printing special forms like invoices or payroll checks. When printing standard forms, you can always assume that a carriage-control tape is present in the printer with a 1-punch to represent the first printing line on the form. This is standard operating procedure. Since the programs in this book do not require the use of special forms, the print charts used from now on will not have a carriage-control area. You may find that your printer does not utilize the carriage-control tape, but has some internal coding technique to accomplish the same end. Whether your printer uses the tape or not, the concept is the same, namely, to enable large jumps from one line on the form to other special lines, and to handle forms that are nonstandard length (other than 11 inches long).

Define input available

Record layout format

Record layout forms have many different formats. The one you will see throughout this book is illustrated in Figure 2–2. This format may be used for any kind of input record device—tape, disk, or terminal. The example in Figure 2–2 gives the format for an inventory record that might be input from any of those devices. By studying the field-name and position entries, you can see that the item-code field is in record positions 1–5, the unit-cost field is in positions 26–30, and so on. (The characteristic and usage entries will be explained in chapter 3.)

Define processing required—produce output from input

In addition to the record layout form and print chart, a programmer may be given other written program specifications before writing a program. For example, formulas to be used for calculating output results or a narrative summary of the processing to take place may be supplied.

To further define the problem, a programmer usually questions the person who assigns the program to him, since certain aspects of the problem are likely to be indefinite. For instance, suppose you are asked to write a program that prepares a report like the one in Figure 2–1 from a file with the record format given in Figure 2–2. What additional information would you need from the person who assigned the problem to you? Here are some ideas:

1. How is the amount invested calculated? Is it the on-hand balance multiplied by unit cost, or is it on-hand balance multiplied by unit price?

2. Should the input records be sorted to be sure they're in numerical sequence by item number?

3. Is one line supposed to be printed for each record in the input file or would it be better to print a line for only certain items—say those items with an inventory investment over $10,000?

The point is that you must know exactly what the program is supposed to do before you can write it. Often, an error in testing a program stems from not completely understanding what the program is supposed to do.

File name INVENTORY-FILE Record name INVENTORY-RECORD Date JUNE 10, 1985
Application Inventory Control Designer DAL
Comments

Field Name	Item Code	Item Description	Unit Cost	Unit Price	Reorder Point	On Hand	On Order	Unused	
Characteristics	X(5)	X(20)	999V99	999V99	9(5)	9(5)	9(5)	X(30)	
Usage									
Position	1-5	6-25	26-30	31-35	36-40	41-45	46-50	51-80	

Figure 2–2
A record layout form

Solution Design

General solution—structure chart

Design is a critical stage in the process of program development because it affects the stages that follow. With good design, a program can be coded and tested with maximum efficiency. With poor design, coding is likely to be inefficient and testing is often a nightmare.

In recent years, programming has moved toward a new method of program design called *structured design*. The idea here is to solve a problem by first breaking it down into its functional parts, or *modules*. The program can then be thought of as a series of small, manageable problems rather than as one large, complicated problem.

As the programmer divides a structured program into its functional modules, he or she creates some sort of *structure chart*, or *structure diagram*. The purpose of this chart is to show the program modules and their relationships to each other.

To illustrate, suppose a program is to be written that prepares an investment report like the one charted in Figure 2–1 from a file with the format given in Figure 2–2. The structure chart in Figure 2–3 divides this program into seven modules at four levels. At the top level, level 0, there is one module that represents the entire program. At level 1, the top-level module is divided into two modules, one to produce the report lines and one to print the total line after all the report lines have been printed. Level 2 breaks the produce-report-lines module, module 100, into three more modules: module 110 reads the input records, module 120 does the necessary calculations for figuring the investment amount, and module 130 prints the lines on the output report. Finally, level 3 consists of a module that will print heading lines on each page of the report.

If a program is large, the programmer further subdivides it into as many levels as are necessary. When the structure chart is complete, each of the modules should be small enough that it can be easily coded and tested. The large, complex program thus becomes a collection of small, manageable modules. And both coding and testing are simplified.

Once the structure chart is created, it is the overall guide to program development. However, each of the modules must be documented before coding. Module documentation will be explained in detail in chapter 4.

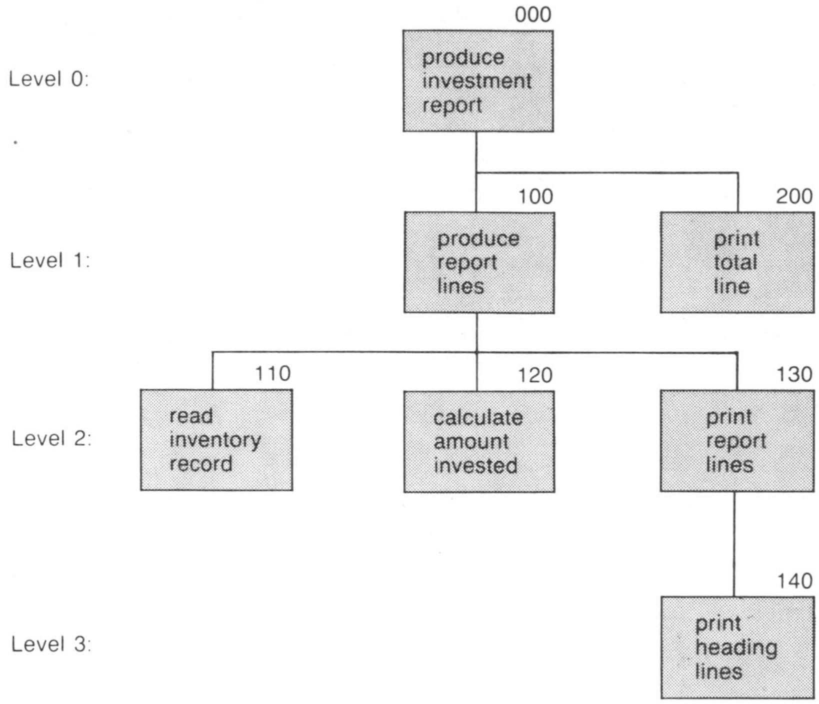
Level 0:
Level 1:
Level 2:
Level 3:
000
produce investment report
100
produce report lines
200
print total line
110
read inventory record
120
calculate amount invested
130
print report lines
140
print heading lines

Figure 2–3
A structure chart for investment report program

Functional decomposition

One thing to notice about the structure chart is that the problem has been broken down into a hierarchy of segments. These segments or modules have been decided on by studying the problem and determining how many distinct functions are involved. The other important determination that is made is which lower-level modules are controlled by which upper-level modules.

This process of developing the hierarchy of functions or the structure chart is called *functional decomposition*. The word *decomposition* refers to the process of "taking the problem apart." The word *functional* refers to the way in which the problem is taken apart, namely by the tasks that must be done.

The process is similar to the process of designing a building where the various functional components must be identified, such as the foundation, walls, roof, electrical, plumbing, etc. The other part of the general design is to determine the interactions of the functions or components (e.g., the walls must be built, but cannot be finished before the electrical wiring is installed).

Specific solution—pseudocode

After the general solution has been determined by developing a structure chart, the specific solution must be developed. The advantage of the functional decomposition approach is that the programmer may plan the program a module at a time rather than all at once. This is comparable to developing separate blueprints for the structural, electrical, and plumbing.

Another aid to easing the programmer's task is the relatively new use of *pseudocode*. This process develops the specifics of each module, but without worrying about following the rules of the programming language exactly. A definition of pseudo is "deceptive similarity." In this instance the similarity is not intended to deceive, but rather to approximate so that the transition to actual program code is easy. The use of pseudocode is also a way to shorten the specific planning process since common or repetitious statements may be generalized. Chapter 6 will present a more thorough discussion of pseudocode.

Synthesis and revision of solutions

An extremely important aspect of any problem-solving process is that of synthesis and revision. Synthesis means having several solutions at hand and using the best of each to derive a solution superior to any prior solution. The same may be accomplished by programmers by developing two or three structure charts independently, comparing them, and attempting to develop a superior approach.

Any solution is improved by the programmer's willingness to go back as far as the structure chart phase and redesign if necessary. Quite often, as one gets into the details, an unanticipated problem arises, or a better approach occurs to the programmer. At that point it is normally advisable to revise the solution. Unfortunately, the novice programmer is often unwilling to go through this synthesis-revision process. The tendency is to make the existing solution work, no matter how poor or difficult it will be. What the novice fails to recognize is that good planning out front makes for quicker implementation and that includes the necessity to revise the plan, even back to the structure chart phase.

Solution Implementation

Code in language of choice

Coding a program in COBOL involves writing the code that eventually is translated into a machine-language program—that is, a program that can be run by the computer. The major purpose of this book, of course, is to teach you how to code in COBOL.

Many languages have special coding forms for use when coding in that language. The purpose of the form is to aid the programmer in observing the boundaries within which the program commands are to be placed and any positions reserved for special use. These forms are a very handy medium for recording the initial program code, but with the increased use of the terminal they appear to be falling into disuse. The COBOL coding form will be discussed in the next chapter.

Test program

An old concept, but a still valid one, is that of *desk checking*. Desk checking simply means that the programmer sits at his or her desk and checks the work done. It cannot be stressed enough at this point that the student needs to develop good desk checking habits. Many student programmers fail because they do not pay enough attention to doing the careful checking implied here. Students have been observed to spend untold hours at the terminal, but still are not able to get a program to run properly. This failure often arises from poor practice of all of the planning and design concepts presented here, but particularly from not checking their work before they try to run it.

When the use of coding forms and key punches was prevalent, desk checking meant coding the program on the forms and then going over the code very carefully before punching the program in cards. Modern usage implies that the programmer studies the program carefully before executing it. Whether the program code is on paper to be studied or on a computer terminal makes no difference in the concept. Once the program is written it needs to be checked for the careless mistakes or omissions that always occur. Desk checking also applies to the test phase. In that phase the output is carefully checked to see if it is accurate.

The bottom line is that the programmer needs to take time to look over the program or its output and try to discover errors, whether they are syntax or logic errors.

Correct syntax errors

After planning the program carefully, the individual commands are typically keyed into the computer and placed in a library for further use. At this point the program commands are readable by humans and are called the *source program*. When the programmer is satisfied that the source code is correct, the program is then presented to a *compiler*. The compiler is in fact a program itself and treats the source program as data, processes it, and produces output from it. Compilers typically produce three outputs (see Figure 2–4):

1. A copy of the source program called the *source list*.

2. A list of coding errors, if any, that can be identified by the compiler. These are called *syntax* or *compile time errors* because they violate the syntax rules of the language and are discovered at compile time. This list of errors (*diagnostics*) is usually appended to the source list and is often called a *diagnostic listing* and is said to contain *diagnostic messages*. Each message on the diagnostic list calls attention to a possible syntax error in the source program. If there are no syntax errors, a message to this effect is usually printed.

3. If there are no disastrous syntax errors, the compile process will then produce a version of the program in machine language. This is in the binary code that the machine will understand and is called the *object program*. Of course, if there are significant syntax errors, there is no point in attempting to produce an object program, and the compile process will be terminated.

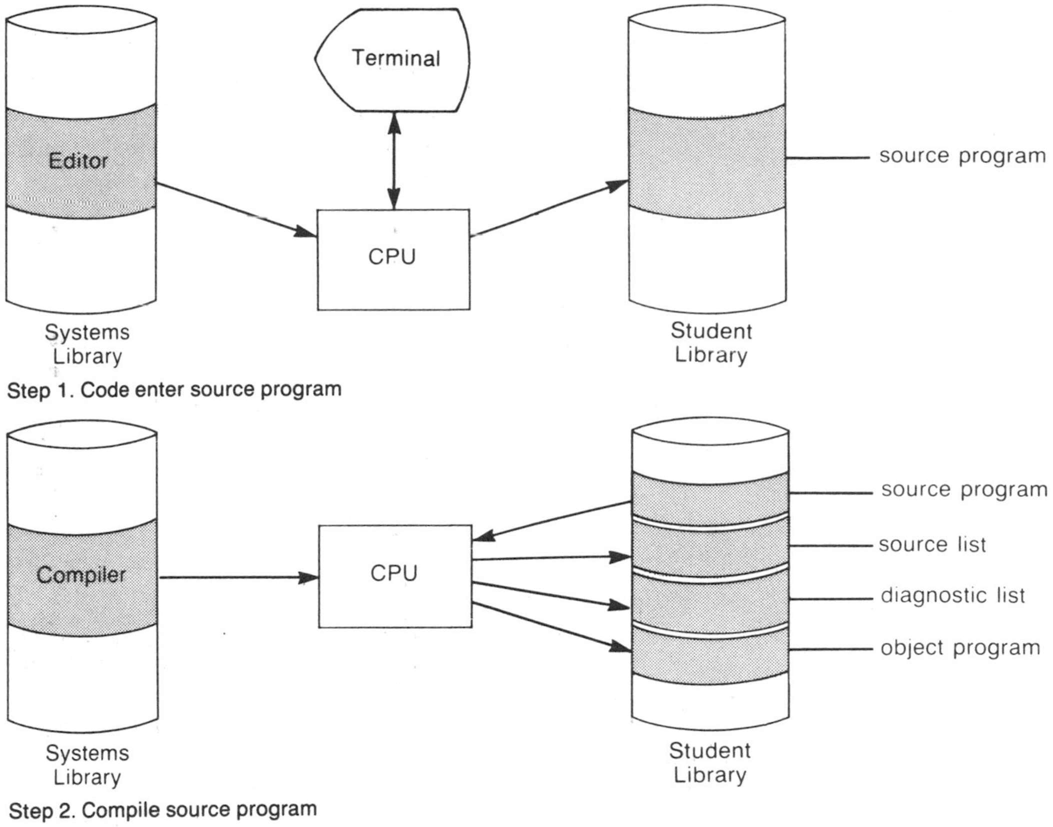
Terminal
Editor
CPU
source program
Systems
Library
Student
Library
Step 1. Code enter source program
Compiler
CPU
source program
source list
diagnostic list
object program
Systems
Library
Student
Library
Step 2. Compile source program

Figure 2–4
Code and compile

If there are diagnostics, the programmer makes the necessary corrections to the source program and the program is recompiled. This process is repeated until there are no more diagnostics or until the only remaining diagnostics are those that do not indicate true syntax errors. This last compilation then is referred to as a *clean compilation*. At this stage, the object program is ready to be tested.

Correct logic errors

To test a program, the programmer tries to run the object program using some *test data*. This test data is intended to simulate all of the conditions that may occur when the program is actually used. When the program is executed, the programmer compares the actual output from the *test run* with the output expected. If they agree, it can be assumed that the program does what it is intended to do.

More likely, however, the actual output and the intended output will not agree because of inappropriate commands in the program. The cause of this mismatch between the expected and the actual output is typically referred to as a *logic error*. These are not syntax errors because the command is correct as far as the compiler is concerned, but are called logic errors because they do not logically accomplish what the program was supposed to accomplish. Note that the detection of a logic error quite often requires careful examination of the program's output. This careful examination involves manually performing all of the calculations that the program was supposed to have made to determine if the output is correct. A common failure of beginning students is to assume that since the computer produced some output it is correct.

Having identified mistakes in the output, the programmer must then *debug* the program by locating the inappropriate commands that are the source of the logical errors (*bugs*). The programmer then makes the necessary changes to the source program, recompiles the program, and makes another test run. This iterative process continues until the program executes as intended.

Another type of error situation that can occur at this time is the *execution* or *run time error*. These are mistakes in providing the correct name of the file to be accessed, in specifying attributes for files which are in conflict with the actual attributes, etc. These errors and the reasons for them happening will be discussed in the chapter on program testing.

In this text the majority of the output is intended to be displayed as a report. Depending on the computer being used, the report may be printed on continuous form paper or may be displayed on the student's terminal screen. Typically, the student may view the test output on the terminal and delay obtaining hard-copy (paper) output until the program and output are error free.

In regard to test data in the typical student environment, the test data may be stored on a general disk library to which all students in the class have access, but which they may read only (not write or change). Other possibilities are providing a means for the students to store the test data in their own libraries, or providing them with a floppy disk that contains the test data. In this text the set of test data provided will contain enough data to test all appropriate situations in each program.

In actual practice, a series of test runs is made using different sets of test data. The test data for the first test run is usually low in volume—perhaps a dozen input records or less—and should be designed to test only the main processing functions of the program. After the program is debugged using this data, it should be tested using data that tries all conditions that may possibly occur during the execution of the program. This set of test data is usually much greater in volume than the first one. After the program executes correctly with this data, a test run may be made using actual, or "live," test data. Then, an entire group of programs may be tested together to be sure that the output from one program is valid input to the next. Only after a program has proved itself under conditions that are as close to real as possible is the program considered ready for use.

Documentation

In data-processing terminology, *documentation* refers to the collection of records that specifies what is being done and what is going to be done within a data-processing system. For each program in an installation, there is a collection of records referred to as *program documentation*. One of the jobs of a programmer is to provide this documentation.

Why is program documentation necessary? Data-processing requirements change. For example, tax laws change: the percent used to calculate social security tax has increased periodically over the last several years as has the maximum amount of social security tax that must be paid in any one year. Company policies also change: discounts may vary from year to year, production departments may switch to new forecasting techniques, and accounting practices may change. For each change, all affected programs must be modified.

Change is so common, in fact, that large companies have special maintenance programmers whose entire job is to modify existing programs. This frees other programmers to work on new programs without interruption. Without adequate documentation, however, maintenance programmers could not make changes within a reasonable period of time. Even when a programmer modifies his or her own programs, documentations is valuable. Three months after writing a program, you may barely remember it.

Some of the more important documents likely to be required by a company's documentation standards are the following:

1. Specifications that give the detailed requirements of the program
2. Layouts of all input and output records on special layout forms
3. A structure chart
4. Specifications for the processing to be done by each of the modules in the structure chart
5. The source listing created during the last compilation
6. Listings of the input data used for testing and listings of the output results of the test runs

Most of these documents, of course, are prepared and used as the program is developed. Nevertheless, a programmer normally spends some time refining and finishing documentation when a program is completed.

Discussion

Traditionally, the major emphasis of a programming course has been on the coding phase of program development. In other words, the typical programming course dealt primarily with the programming language to be taught. In recent years, however, it has become clear that design has more effect on programmer productivity than any other phase of program development. As a result, this course emphasizes design as well as coding. And it also emphasizes testing and debugging, another critical stage in the process of program development.

Although you have been introduced to structured design in this topic, it is only one of several techniques that are associates with *structured programming*. These techniques involve design, documentation, coding, and testing. Since this book teaches structured programming as well as COBOL, most of these techniques are explained in this book. As a result, though you probably have only a hazy notion of what structured programming is all about right now, you will be able to design, document, code, and test structured COBOL programs by the time you finish this book.

Problems

Note: If you have not previously been introduced to record layout forms or print charts, you should do the problems that follow. Otherwise, you will probably want to skip them since they are quite elementary. As you work your way through this book, you will be presented with progressively more complex examples and problems involving the analysis of layout forms and print charts.

1. (Objective 2)
   a. In the layout shown below, which positions contain the hourly-rate field?

Field Name	Employee No.	Employee Name	Hourly Rate	Hours Worked	Unused
Characteristics	X(5)	X(20)	99V99	99V9	X(48)
Usage					
Position	1-5	6-25	26-29	30-32	33-80

b. What data is entered in positions 6–25?

2. (Objective 3)
   a. Based on the print chart in Figure 2–5, in what print positions should the first heading line, OVERTIME REPORT, be printed?
   b. In what print positions is the final total of overtime hours supposed to be printed?
   c. In what print positions is the message, END OF JOB, supposed to be printed?
   d. What character is supposed to print in print position 40 of each detail line?
   e. Should the headings be printed on all pages or only on the first page of the report?

Solutions

1. a. Positions 26–29
   b. Employee name
2. a. Positions 15–29
   b. Positions 35–41
   c. Positions 1–10
   d. A decimal point
   e. You can't tell from a print chart, but it is common to print the headings on all pages of a report.

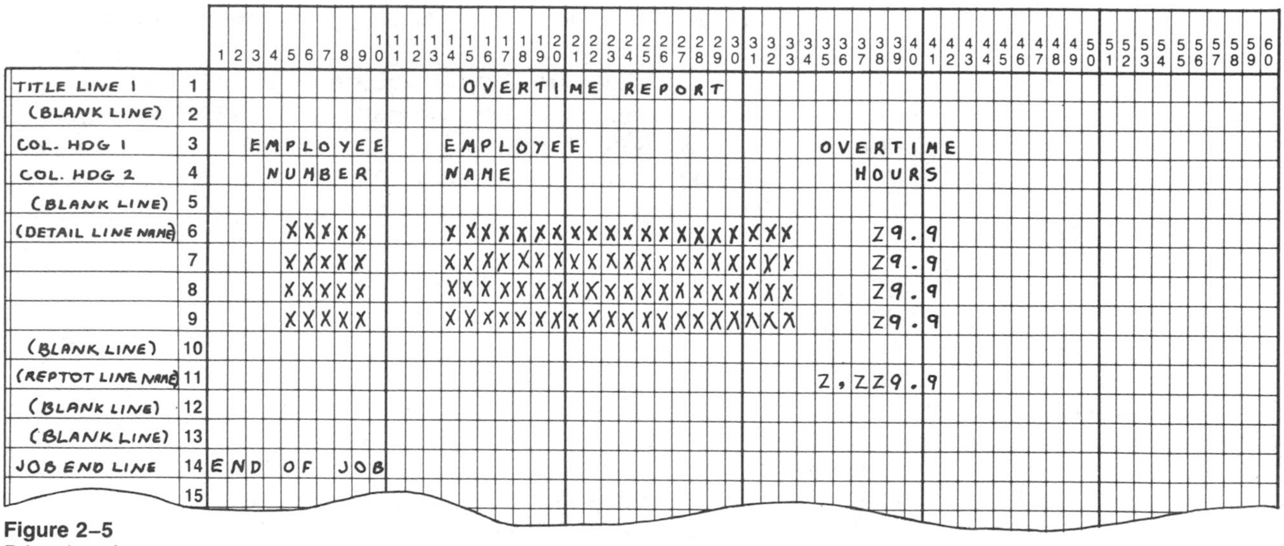
TITLE LINE 1
(BLANK LINE)
COL. HDG 1
COL. HDG 2
(BLANK LINE)
(DETAIL LINE NAME)
(BLANK LINE)
(REPTOT LINE NAME)
(BLANK LINE)
(BLANK LINE)
JOB END LINE
OVERTIME REPORT
EMPLOYEE
NUMBER
EMPLOYEE
NAME
OVERTIME
HOURS
XXXXX
Z9.9
Z,ZZ9.9
END OF JOB

Figure 2–5
Print chart for overtime report

Topic 2 **Interactive Program Development**

Orientation

In the section on software in chapter 1, some concepts about operating systems were introduced. Now, however, you need to extend that knowledge of operating systems to understand how such software is related to the development and running of your programs. Further, it is necessary to provide a short introduction to the terminal—probably the most common input device.

The environment in which programs will be developed and run will vary greatly, depending on the actual combinations of hardware and software being used to practice the skills taught here. This means that you may be learning on a home computer which has the proper compiler. More likely, you will be using a terminal with an on-line operating system to interact with a central computer. Possibly, you may be using your home computer as a terminal to access the central computer over telephone lines by utilizing telecommunications software and a modem. You may even be punching cards and having them read into the computer through a card reader. Since the possibilities for computer access vary so widely, only the most common will be discussed. You must rely on previous experience, your instructor, lab assistants, handouts, manuals, or whatever means have been set up to aid your learning to utilize the local computer system.

Terminology

alpha lock	edit key	monitor
alphanumeric keys	function key	numeric key pad
baud rate	global search and replace	procedure language
break key	JCL	release/return key
character delete	job-control language	supervisor
character insert	key action modifiers	tabulation
control key	library	text editor
control unit		video display
cursor		

Objectives

1. *Understand and accurately use the terms presented.*
2. *Explain the relationship between your computer's operating system and your application programs.*
3. *Learn how you are to store source programs, how to make changes to your source programs, and how to accomplish the compile and execute process.*
4. *Learn to use your input device.*
5. *Be able to identify the principal use of the various keys.*
6. *By studying the text example, be able to locate the various keys on the terminal available to you.*
7. *By discussions with instructors, lab assistants, and/or by reading, become familiar with the terminals to be used.*

Interactive Operating Systems

You will recall that an operating system is a collection of programs designed to improve the efficiency of a computer installation. It does so in two ways. First, an operating system decreases the amount of time a computer is idle by seemingly running several programs or jobs at one time. This facility is normally called multiprogramming. The internal speed of the CPU is so much greater than the ability of the I/O devices to transfer data into or out of the CPU, or our ability to key data quickly, that it only seems that the CPU is doing several things at one time. In reality the CPU does only one operation at a time, such as adding two numbers or issuing a write command. Input or output commands are normally just that, commands only. The actual reading or writing of records is accomplished by separate computer entities called *control units* which do the actual I/O task and then notify the CPU that the task is complete. While the I/O unit was completing its task, the CPU was executing many other commands, perhaps from another program. In this manner the modern computer and operating system vastly increase the time utilization of the CPU.

Secondly, an operating system increases programming efficiency by providing various processing and service programs that eliminate or reduce the programming efforts required of a computer user. Since these services vary widely in function and complexity, the discussion of them will be kept to the most likely ones.

A significant improvement in computer usage has been the advent of the *library*. Instead of programmers running around with large decks of punched cards, they are now able to store the program instructions in a library of some type on a disk drive. A typical educational environment will have several libraries stored on disks. There may be libraries for the professional staff and administrative programs and files of the institution. Separate libraries may be provided for the faculty's purposes, such as program examples and test data for student programs. Libraries are also likely to be provided for the programs and files that students are developing and using.

At the start of a day's computer operations, a supervisor program (or just *supervisor* or *monitor*) is loaded into the storage of the CPU, and control of the computer is transferred to this program. This supervisor, which is one of the programs of the operating system, is responsible for loading all of the other programs to be executed from the appropriate libraries. Note that in modern computer centers the computer may well be turned on when installed and then seldom if ever turned off. If any changes are made to the operating system, they are made and the system simply rebooted.

Most on-line operating systems have a special set of commands that users can combine to cause a coordinated group of actions to occur. These actions will be those required to enable a job to be completed, and the set of commands go by such names as *job-control language* (*JCL*) or *procedure language*. For instance, the student environment may have a standard procedure set up which, when requested by the student programmer, will accomplish the following actions:

1. Ask which compiler to use (COBOL, FORTRAN, Pascal...).
2. Ask which student program to compile.

3. Delete about-to-be-duplicated files on the student library that are left from previous compiles of this program.

4. Find, load into the CPU memory, and execute the program that compiles the student program.

5. Determine if the compile was error-free enough to continue on to the next step in the procedure.

6. End the compile process if significant syntax errors are identified in the program, and go to the step asking whether the student desires a list (see step 10).

7. Access if error-free the program that converts the source code to the object code.

8. Determine which files, if any, are to be used as input to the program when executed, and make those files available.

9. Cause the object program to be executed using the specified input files, making the file contain the output available, and placing the output there.

10. Ask when the program execution is complete if printed output is desired and ask to which printer the output is to be sent if more than one student center is available.

11. Locate the program output on the student's library and move it into the queue of files to be printed on the requested printer.

Each computer center will have many of these job-control streams or procedures set up to accomplish the various actions that must take place in each individual application to accomplish the needs of the user of the computer system.

Using the Terminal

Many older texts contain detailed discussions regarding the use of key punch machines, as these were the means to write programs in machine-readable form. Currently, one finds that key punches for student use have been replaced by terminals, microcomputers, or microcomputers acting as terminals. The use of terminals is the most prevalent form of student program input, and so the terminal is the device to be discussed here.

Since there are many more varieties of terminals commonly in use now than there were key punches in the past, the detailed discussion of terminals is just not as practical. A second legitimate reason for minimizing the discussion of terminal use is that an increasing number of students have had some form of computer terminal experience and need only to determine how the currently available unit differs from others with which they have experience. As this is being written, students in grade school are accomplishing tasks using a computer keyboard; thus new generations of students will have little need for extended explanations on terminal use.

The majority of terminals have some basic attributes in common. Any terminal, whether it is directly connected to the computer or operates in a telecommunications mode, is said to operate at a specified *baud rate*. The baud rate is simply the number of bits of data that can be transmitted in one second. Typical baud rates are 300 and 1200 over phone lines, meaning that 300 or 1200 bits of data are transmitted each second. Again, the bit of data is one on/off switch status from computer memory. Rates of 9600 baud are common in systems that have terminals wired directly into the computer.

All terminals that are used for student work have two main components. One is the *video display* tube, where the data being worked with may be viewed. The second component is the keyboard, which has a layout similar to a typewriter and where data may be entered into the system by striking the various keys. Various keys also cause commands to be given to the operating system, while others allow manipulation of the screen *cursor*. Figure 2–6 displays the keyboard layout on a typical terminal. Notice that the keys on this particular terminal are arranged into the following functional groups:

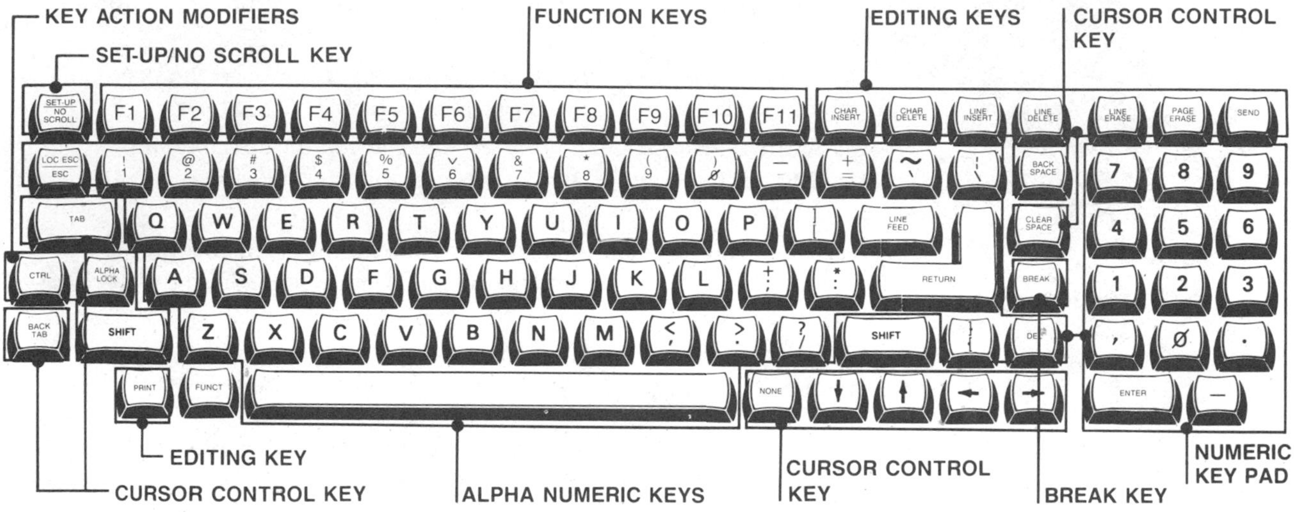
KEY ACTION MODIFIERS
SET-UP/NO SCROLL KEY
FUNCTION KEYS
EDITING KEYS
CURSOR CONTROL KEY
EDITING KEY
CURSOR CONTROL KEY
ALPHA NUMERIC KEYS
CURSOR CONTROL KEY
BREAK KEY
NUMERIC KEY PAD

Figure 2–6
Keyboard layout

1. Alphanumeric keys—the typical typewriter key layout.

2. Function keys—available for assignment of special functions, tailored to the individual needs of the user.

3. Edit keys—cause special text edit functions to occur and typically are to delete/insert characters or lines.

4. Cursor control—cause the cursor to be moved (left, right, up, down, tab (*tabulation*), back tab, back space) on the screen.

5. Numeric keypad—for use when the majority of input is numbers.

6. Key action modifiers—modifies the normal action of keys:
shift—alpha keys generate upper case and other secondary characters;
alpha-lock—locks alphabetic keys into upper case but leaves other keys in original function;
control—generates control codes when used in conjunction with another key.

7. Release/return key—equivalent to the return key on a typewriter. Sends a signal to the system (or the editor) that an entry is complete and the controlling program should act on the entry.

8. Break key—breaks control away from current program and gives it to the appropriate operating function.

The probability is that your local terminals are not the same as shown in the text. The functions will generally be the same for any terminal, even though some may have more and some will have fewer functions and keys. For example, many less expensive terminals will not have a numeric key pad.

Another aspect to be aware of is that the use of some of the terminal's keys depends on the operating system used on the computer, and more especially on the *text editor* available. A text editor is a program with which the programmer will become very familiar, as it is the means for making changes to programs (or any other text) which are entered into the computer system. Text editors allow the user to add, insert, or delete characters, lines, or whole blocks of text. They are the medium through which the program is normally entered into the system to begin with.

Some text editors allow the user to locate a place in the text by searching for a word or a string of text. Many allow a *global search and replace* function which enables the user to replace every occurence of a text string with a new string. A reasonably sophisticated editor will allow the use of the cursor keys, for instance, while an unsophisticated editor may allow only the use of the back space and special editor commands to move around and to change the text. In the simple editor the cursor keys will send unrecognizable codes which become invalid parts of the text and have to be edited out later. The solution to this problem is to lock these keys so that they may not be used. A better solution is to have a sophisticated editor which is more efficient in the long run.

The availability and use of terminals has changed the way in which student and professional programmers work. The use of libraries has been mentioned previously. The modern programmer encodes a program via a terminal, stores the program on the programmer's personal library, and then repeats the compile-test-change cycle until the output produced by the program agrees with the expected output. To make those changes, the programmer recalls the program from the library, makes modifications using the text editor, and restors the modified program to the library where it is found when the compiler accesses it.

Discussion

An introduction to the important facets of interactive program development has been given here. Since operating systems, job-control languages, text editors, and terminals all differ, it is not practical to present more than an overview of those subjects. To become functionally knowledgeable about the system on which you will work, you must study the elements of that particular system. The discussions presented here should help you recognize and understand the separate elements. The first few programs to be written are simple enough that you will probably wish to design, code, and test the complete program all at once. In chapter 5 a top-down technique will be discussed as an efficient method for developing longer programs in the online computer environment where terminals, editors, and libraries are in common use.

Part Two

COBOL: The Core Content

This section presents the critical material of your COBOL training. Chapter 3 presents the basic subset of the COBOL language, and chapter 4 completes the core set of COBOL commands. If you master these chapters, you will be able to design and code complete COBOL programs in a professional style. Furthermore, it will be relatively easy for you to add to this *core content* by learning how to use other COBOL facilities. Please recognize that this part is the critical section of the text. If you, the student, secure a solid grasp of the concepts presented here, the remainder of the course will be like building a house on a solid and level foundation—much easier, more permanent, and with minimal future problems.

The concepts of structured programming include the style in which programs are written. A detailed discussion of that style is delayed until Part III when you will have a better background in COBOL. However, the examples in this part have all been written in a good structured style so that you have a model to learn from, and you are encouraged to observe the organization of the programs, the vertical and horizontal spacings, and the programmer-supplied names used.

Chapter 3 An Introduction to Structured COBOL

This chapter introduces you to the COBOL language that is approved by the American National Standard Institute (ANSI). It does so by presenting programming problems and the COBOL solutions for these problems, and by discussing those solutions in detail so that you can see how the various COBOL commands may be used to provide a computer solution to a problem. Since the solutions use COBOL code that represents the basic capabilities of the language, the code presented can be called a *subset* of the complete ANSI COBOL language.

Effective COBOL programming requires some knowledge of how a computer executes a stored program. That topic was covered in chapter 1, which discussed the stored program and its relationship to the COBOL program in topic 3. If you feel unsure about your understanding of this subject, go back to chapter 1 and review.

The purpose of this chapter is to enable you to quickly learn enough of the COBOL language to code and debug a simple program. Although the program will be simple, the principal language elements of input/output, arithmetic, logic, and data movement will all be given elementary coverage. Topic 1 in this chapter presents the first subset of the COBOL language. Then topic 2 will show some typical syntax errors and diagnostic messages that can occur. A more thorough lesson on program development and debugging will follow in part III.

Topic 1 The Basic Subset of COBOL

Orientation

COBOL, which stands for COmmon Business Orientated Language, is the most widely used language for business applications. It is also one of the oldest programming languages, first introduced in 1959, and has been popular since the mid-1960s. COBOL was designed to be adaptable to equipment of all manufacturers, and, although not available for all computers, is available on the full range of computers from microcomputer to supercomputer.

In an attempt to standardize COBOL, the American National Standards Institute approved a standard COBOL language in 1968. These standards were designed so a standard COBOL compiler could be implemented for computers of varying sizes. This could be done by implementing only a portion (a subset) of the complete language. Thus, subset compilers have been developed for microcomputer systems, while full standard compilers have been developed for large systems. As you might guess, a subset of standard COBOL can be compiled on a full compiler, but full COBOL cannot be compiled on a subset compiler.

Because of the criticism of the 1968 standards and changing requirements in the computer industry, the 1968 standards were revised in 1974. These new standards deleted some of the capabilities of the old standards, modified others, and added a number of capabilities. The new specifications can be referred to as 1974 ANS COBOL in contrast to 1968 ANS COBOL. COBOL is continually being reviewed by user committees, and another revised standard, currently called 198X, is under consideration. The "X" in the 198X indicates that the year of release of the revised standard is unknown. The revised standard attempts to incorporate more of the theoretical constructs of structured programming along with the general updating and changing that occurs in revising a standard.

One reason that a new standard has not been released is that the 1974 standard was a solid, effective revision and has worked very well. Another reason appears to be that the 198X version is thought to be excessively drastic by some COBOL users, particularly in that the new version may render too many old programs out of compliance. The real problem is that old programs could not be compiled on the new compilers, thus necessitating major modification or rewrite of those programs, which is extremely expensive in terms of both time and money. Thus, the new standard has been meeting with a significant amount of resistance by users who are concerned about its compatibility with old programs.

In spite of the attempts at standardization, however, ANS COBOL variations exist from one manufacturer to another. In general, these variations are caused by *extensions* to the standard specifications. These extensions are designed to provide some capability that isn't provided for by the ANS specifications. The 1968 and 1974 standards, in fact, allow such extensions. No matter how many extensions a manufacturer incorporates into his compiler, he can still refer to it as "standard" as long as the rest of the language conforms to the standards.

Because it takes time and money to develop new compilers, computer manufacturers do *not* release new compilers as soon as new standards are released. For example, IBM didn't release an ANS 74 compiler for the System/360–370 until 1977. Furthermore, because it takes a computer user time and money to convert his existing programs from one compiler to another and to retrain his programmers, new compilers are *not* readily accepted when they are released.

Because COBOL will continue to change in the years ahead, we have made every effort in this book to present a subset of the COBOL language that will be in use years from now. As a result, all of the language presented in this book is ANSI standard—no extensions are given. From a practical point of view, however, you will usually want to use some of the extensions that are available on your compiler. If so, you will have to use the reference manuals that are available for your system.

Because of its wide availability and because of its standardization, COBOL has remained popular over the years and tens of thousands of programmers have been trained in it. This topic will present a simple computer problem and its COBOL solution. Then it will discuss the various language elements and how they are used and organized to provide that computer solution.

Terminology

A margin	file name	procedure name
alphanumeric item	imperative statement	program name
B margin	literal	record name
condition	nested IF statements	reserved word
data name	numeric edited item	switch
exception report	numeric item	system name
extension	paragraph name	

Objectives

1. ***Code an acceptable Configuration Section for the compiler that you will be using during this course.***
2. ***Given the description of an input or output file, code acceptable SELECT statements (Environment Division) and data descriptions (Data Division) for it using system names that are compatible with your system.***
3. ***Given the program listing in Figure 3–4 and sample input data, answer questions about the execution of the object program.***

A sample ANS COBOL program—the reorder list

Figure 3–1 gives the characteristics of a reorder-listing program that is to be written in COBOL. The input consists of a file of inventory records with each record containing the data for one inventory item. The output of the program is a listing of those items in inventory that need to be reordered. The illustration indicates the characteristics and placement of each input field in the inventory record and also indicates the print positions for each item to be printed on the output listing. As you can see from the processing specifications, a line is printed whenever an item's available stock (quantity-on-hand plus quantity-on-order) is less than the reorder point. This outputting of information only when a special situation is recognized is a perfect example of providing information and is called *exception reporting*. To simplify your introduction to COBOL, no headings or totals are to be printed on this report.

The structure chart

Figure 3–2 shows a structure chart for this program. The chart is so named because it pictures the main structures of the program. It is also often called a hierarchy chart since the hierarchical relation of one module to another is depicted. The top-level module represents the entire program, thus its functional description is "produce reorder listing." This is probably the easiest module to name as you only have to ask yourself "what is the purpose of the program?" or "what is this program supposed to do?"

Input record layout:

Field Name	Item No.	Item Description	Unit Cost	Unit Price	Reorder Point	On Hand	On Order	Unused
Characteristics	9(5)	X(20)	999V99	999V99	9(5)	9(5)	9(5)	X(30)
Usage								
Position	1-5	6-25	26-30	31-35	36-40	41-45	46-50	51-80

Print chart:

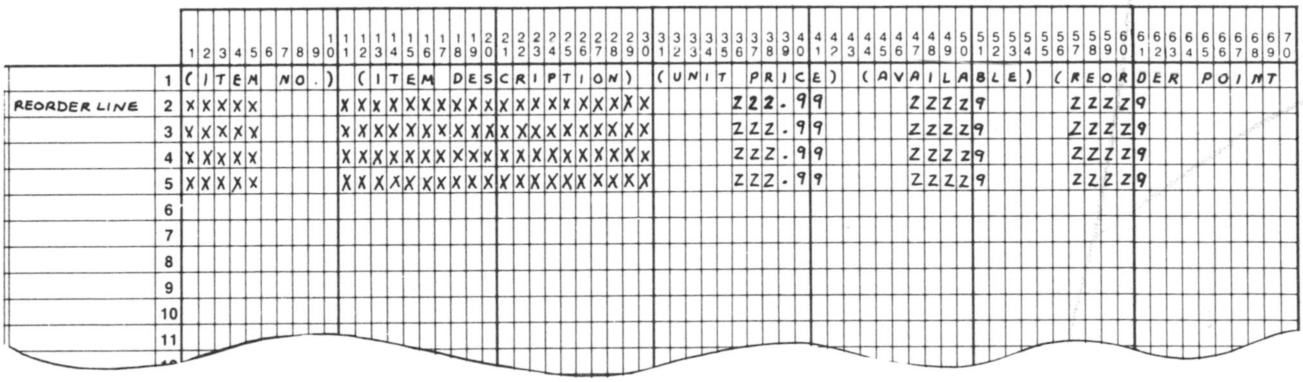
(ITEM NO.)
(ITEM DESCRIPTION)
(UNIT PRICE)
(AVAILABLE)
(REORDER POINT)
REORDER LINE
XXXXX
XXXXXXXXXXXXXXXXXXXX
ZZZ.99
ZZZZ9
ZZZZ9

Narrative:

1. Add on-hand to on-order to derive available.
2. Print a line on the reorder listing only when available is less than the reorder point.

Figure 3–1
The reorder-listing problem

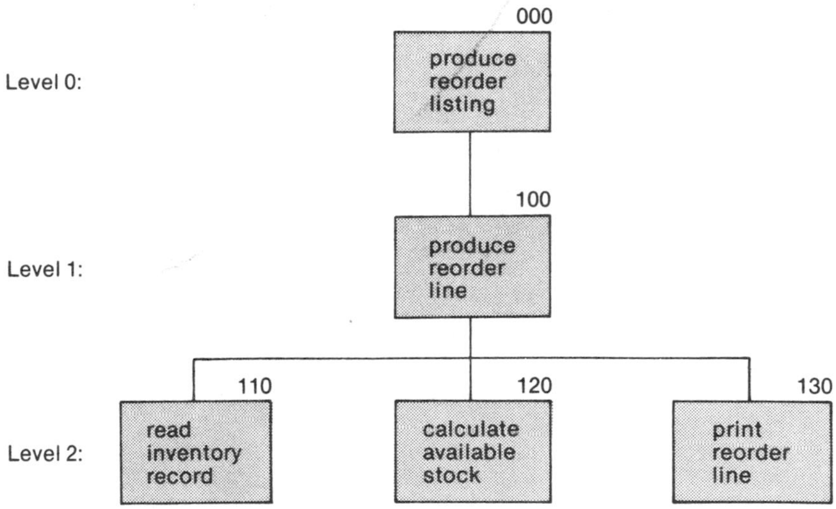
Level 0:
000
produce reorder listing
Level 1:
100
produce reorder line
Level 2:
110
read inventory record
120
calculate available stock
130
print reorder line

Figure 3–2
A structure chart for the reorder-listing problem

Since this is a simple program, the main module has only one module beneath it, a module whose function is to control producing one line of the reorder listing. This module in turn is broken down into three modules or subfunctions:

1. read inventory record—causes one inventory record to be read into memory.

2. calculate available stock—does the arithmetic to determine how much stock is available for this one item.

3. print reorder line—prints a line when the available stock is less than the reorder point.

Later in this chapter you will be shown how the COBOL program relates to this structure chart. Then, in chapter 6, you will learn how to create structure charts of your own.

The COBOL coding form

A special COBOL coding form is available for the programmer to use when writing down the commands that are to be entered into the computer. The form is used because COBOL has a few rules governing placement of certain commands on the coding line. However, with the increasing use of libraries and terminals in the interactive mode, and with the use of pseudocode (covered in chapter 6) as a planning device, the use of coding forms appears to be falling into disuse. Nevertheless, the coding form will be discussed here as it is still used, and many instructors find it to be a valuable aid on tests.

The form in Figure 3–3 is the first page of the reorder listing program. The heading of the COBOL coding form gives information such as program name, data, and programmer. If you study the form, you will see that 80 columns are indicated from left to right. That fact may not be so obvious here, but notice the upper right-hand part of the form where columns 73–80 are indicated. This particular form only lists those columns one time on each page, and the person keying the program is trained that every line is to have the indicated entry in columns 73 through 80. Those last eight columns of the coding line are used for identification purposes. Typically, they identify the program. For example, in this program REORDLST might be entered in columns 73–80 of each line in the source program. Although these columns may contain identifying information, they are considered to be comments by the compiler. Their contents are printed on the printer, but are not checked for syntax errors as the rest of the line would be.

The first three columns are used for the page number of the coding form; the next three columns are used for the line number of the coding line. Thus, 001020 in the first six columns of a source line represents the line numbers 020 on page 001, and 005010 represents the line numbered 010 on page 005. Although lines can be numbered consecutively (001, 002, 003), it is more common to number by tens (010, 020, 030). Then, if a line of coding has to be added to a program, it can be done by using a number of appropriate numerical value. For example, line number 165 would fall between 160 and 170.

Once again, interactive programming is lessening the need to utilize either the numbering scheme or the identification columns of the coding forms. Many programmers no longer put the line numbers or the program identifiers in their programs. However, the positions reserved for the line numbers must still be taken into account when entering the program into the computer. Columns 73–80 may not be used for program commands, so be careful.

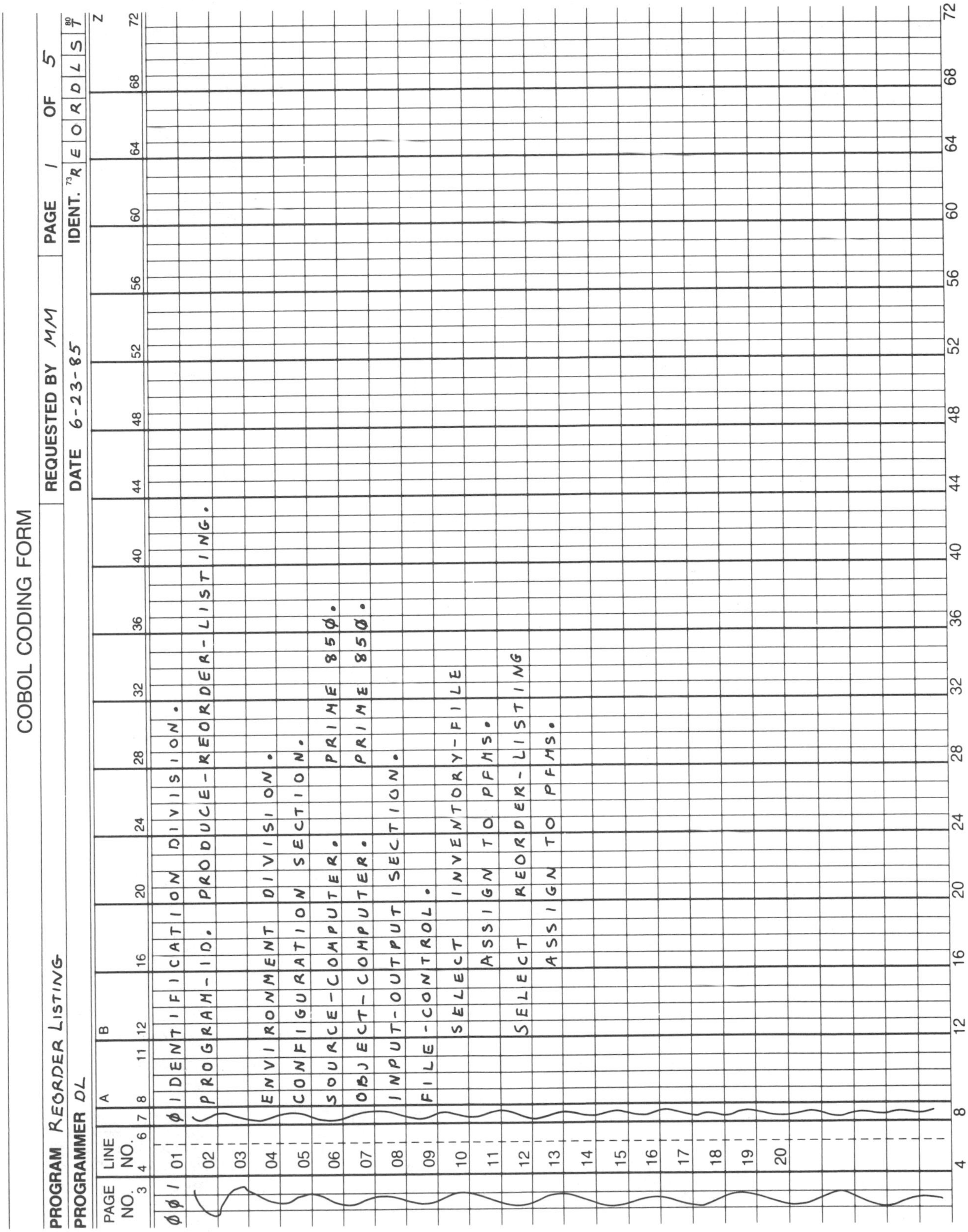
COBOL CODING FORM

PROGRAM REORDER LISTING	REQUESTED BY MM	PAGE 1	OF 5
PROGRAMMER DL	DATE 6-23-85	IDENT. REORDLST	

```
001 01 IDENTIFICATION DIVISION.
    02 PROGRAM-ID.  PRODUCE-REORDER-LISTING.
    03
    04 ENVIRONMENT DIVISION.
    05 CONFIGURATION SECTION.
    06 SOURCE-COMPUTER.  PRIME 85Ø.
    07 OBJECT-COMPUTER.  PRIME 85Ø.
    08 INPUT-OUTPUT SECTION.
    09 FILE-CONTROL.
    10     SELECT INVENTORY-FILE
    11         ASSIGN TO PFMS.
    12     SELECT REORDER-LISTING
    13         ASSIGN TO PFMS.
    14
    15
    16
    17
    18
    19
    20
```

Figure 3–3
The COBOL coding form

Column 7 of the coding form is used to indicate that certain types of coding lines are to be ignored by the compiler. This will be explained in Chapter 4, so ignore this column for now.

The actual program is coded in columns 8–72. Within these columns, only column 8, called the *A margin*, and column 12, called the *B margin*, require special mention. In general, each line of COBOL coding starts in one of these two margins, depending on the function of the coding. In Figure 3–3 the first eight lines of the coding start in the A margin, and the coding on lines 100 and 110 begins at the B margin. Although many compilers give the leeway of starting A-margin coding lines anywhere between column 8 and column 11, you should always start them in column 8. Likewise, you should start all B-margin sentences in column 12, even though your compiler may allow them to begin anywhere between column 12 and column 72.

The heading of the COBOL coding form gives information such as name, date, and programmer. In addition, some forms give instructions to help clarify the difference between certain handwritten symbols which are likely to be confused. In Figure 3–3 the programmer is indicating that a Ø represents the digit zero while 0 represents the letter O. Similarly, the letter Z is written with a bar through it (Ƶ) to distinguish it from the digit 2, and digit 1 is written as a vertical line to distinguish it from the letter I, which is written with top and bottom cross members. Such indications are only done if the person keying the program is different from the one writing it. If the programmer keys his or her own program, then there is no need for such clarification.

Since columns 1–6 and 73–80 of a source program can be disregarded without affecting the program, a COBOL program may be illustrated as in Figure 3–4. The far left margin of the listing is therefore the A margin and the B margin starts four spaces to its right. In the remainder of this book, this is how most programs will be illustrated.

The COBOL divisions

Take a minute to look at the program in Figure 3–4. It is the complete program for printing the reorder listing from the inventory records. It is written for a Prime computer, but, as you will see, only four lines of coding would have to be changed in order to compile the program on any computer system that has a COBOL compiler.

If you scan the program, you can see that it is made up of four divisions: the Identification, Environment, Data, and Procedure Divisions. Although the Identification and Environment Divisions are first, the Data and Procedure Divisions are the essence of the program.

The Identification Division

The Identification Division is used to identify the program. It does not cause any object code to be compiled and requires only two coding lines. In Figure 3–4, the programmer has written

```
IDENTIFICATION DIVISION.
PROGRAM-ID.  PRODUCE-REORDER-LISTING.
```

Except for PRODUCE–REORDER–LISTING, which is the *program name* made up by the programmer, these two coding lines will be the same for all COBOL programs.

```
IDENTIFICATION DIVISION.
PROGRAM-ID.    PRODUCE-REORDER-LISTING.
ENVIRONMENT DIVISION.
CONFIGURATION SECTION.
SOURCE-COMPUTER.    PRIME 850.
OBJECT-COMPUTER.    PRIME 850.
INPUT-OUTPUT SECTION.
FILE-CONTROL.
    SELECT INVENTORY-STATUS-FILE
        ASSIGN TO PFMS.
    SELECT REORDER-LISTING
        ASSIGN TO PFMS.
DATA DIVISION.
FILE SECTION.
FD  INVENTORY-STATUS-FILE
    LABEL RECORDS ARE STANDARD
    RECORD CONTAINS 80 CHARACTERS.
01  INVENTORY-STATUS-RECORD.
    02  IS-ITEM-NO          PICTURE IS 9(5).
    02  IS-ITEM-DESC        PICTURE IS X(20).
    02  FILLER              PICTURE IS X(5).
    02  IS-UNIT-PRICE       PICTURE IS 999V99.
    02  IS-REORDER-POINT    PICTURE IS 9(5).
    02  IS-QTY-ON-HAND      PICTURE IS 9(5).
    02  IS-QTY-ON-ORDER     PICTURE IS 9(5).
    02  FILLER              PICTURE IS X(30).
FD  REORDER-LISTING
    LABEL RECORDS ARE STANDARD
    RECORD CONTAINS 132 CHARACTERS.
01  REORDER-LINE.
    02  RL-ITEM-NO          PICTURE IS X(5).
    02  FILLER              PICTURE IS X(5).
    02  RL-ITEM-DESC        PICTURE IS X(20).
    02  FILLER              PICTURE IS X(5).
    02  RL-UNIT-PRICE       PICTURE IS ZZZ.99.
    02  FILLER              PICTURE IS X(5).
    02  RL-AVAILABLE-STOCK  PICTURE IS Z(5).
    02  FILLER              PICTURE IS X(5).
    02  RL-REORDER-POINT    PICTURE IS Z(5).
    02  FILLER              PICTURE IS X(71).
WORKING-STORAGE SECTION.
01  SWITCHES.
    02  INVENTORY-EOF-SW    PICTURE IS X.
01  WORK-FIELDS.
    02  AVAILABLE-STOCK     PICTURE IS 9(5).
PROCEDURE DIVISION.
000-PRODUCE-REORDER-LISTING.
    OPEN INPUT  INVENTORY-STATUS-FILE
         OUTPUT REORDER-LISTING.
    MOVE 'N'                      TO INVENTORY-EOF-SW.
    PERFORM 100-PRODUCE-REORDER-LINE
        UNTIL INVENTORY-EOF-SW EQUAL 'Y'.
    CLOSE INVENTORY-STATUS-FILE
          REORDER-LISTING.
    STOP RUN.
100-PRODUCE-REORDER-LINE.
    PERFORM 110-READ-INVENTORY-RECORD.
    IF INVENTORY-EOF-SW  EQUAL 'N'
        PERFORM 120-CALCULATE-AVAILABLE-STOCK
        IF AVAILABLE-STOCK LESS THAN IS-REORDER-POINT
            PERFORM 130-PRINT-REORDER-LINE.
110-READ-INVENTORY-RECORD.
    READ INVENTORY-STATUS-FILE
        AT END
            MOVE 'Y'              TO INVENTORY-EOF-SW.
```

Figure 3–4
The reorder-listing program in COBOL (part 1 of 2)

```
120-CALCULATE-AVAILABLE-STOCK.
    ADD IS-QTY-ON-HAND IS-QTY-ON-ORDER
        GIVING AVAILABLE-STOCK.
130-PRINT-REORDER-LINE.
    MOVE SPACES                TO REORDER-LINE.
    MOVE IS-ITEM-NO            TO RL-ITEM-NO.
    MOVE IS-ITEM-DESC          TO RL-ITEM-DESC.
    MOVE IS-UNIT-PRICE         TO RL-UNIT-PRICE.
    MOVE AVAILABLE-STOCK       TO RL-AVAILABLE-STOCK.
    MOVE IS-REORDER-POINT      TO RL-REORDER-POINT.
    WRITE REORDER LINE.
```

Figure 3–4
The reorder-listing program in COBOL (part 2 of 2)

The rules for forming a program name in ANS COBOL are as follows:

1. The name must be 30 characters or fewer and consist of letters, numbers, and hyphens (–) only.

2. The name cannot begin or end with a hyphen or contain blanks.

Thus, X123, ORDLST, and ORDER–LISTING are valid program names, but LIST–, X$YZ, and ORDER LIST are not. Although X123 is a valid name, program names are usually chosen so they indicate the nature of the program. For example, PRODUCE–REORDER–LISTING indicates that the program will produce a listing of inventory items to be reordered. It is also the name given to the top module in the structure chart in Figure 3–2.

Although the standard COBOL specifications allow program names of up to 30 characters in length consisting of letters, numbers, and hyphens, most operating systems have more restrictions than these. Some will only allow a maximum of eight characters and numbers starting with a letter and some only allow seven characters. A few operating systems will allow the program to have the full 30 characters, but will only utilize the first seven or eight and will ignore the rest. You should determine what the rules for program-name formation are for the system you will be using to write the practice programs. Since the seven or eight character limit is so common, the rest of the program examples in this text will be limited to eight. Note that many computer centers have rules for naming programs which often are a combination that indicates which system the program is a part of and a number of other designations identifying the individual program. Since the reorder listing program accesses the inventory file, it might be named INV0005, with INV indicating that it belongs to the inventory system of programs and the 0005 indicating that it is number five in that system.

The Environment Division

The Environment Division of a COBOL program specifies the hardware components that are to be used for the compilation and for the execution of the object program. As a result, this division shows the greatest variance from one computer manufacturer to another. When converting a program from one type of computer to another, this division must always be changed.

The Environment Division for the reorder-listing program in Figure 3–4 is as follows:

```
ENVIRONMENT DIVISION.
CONFIGURATION SECTION.
SOURCE-COMPUTER.    PRIME 850.
OBJECT-COMPUTER.    PRIME 850.
INPUT-OUTPUT SECTION.
FILE-CONTROL.
    SELECT INVENTORY-STATUS-FILE
        ASSIGN TO PFMS.
    SELECT REORDER-LISTING
        ASSIGN TO PFMS.
```

This format will be the same for all programs that have simple input and output. As a result, though it may look confusing, this division is quite routine.

The Configuration Section In the Configuration Section, SOURCE–COMPUTER specifies the computer that will be used for the compilation. In most cases, this will be the same as the computer used for executing the object program, known as the OBJECT–COMPUTER. In the example, the computer used is the Prime 850.

If you were writing a program for an IBM computer, this section may read:

```
CONFIGURATION SECTION.
 SOURCE-COMPUTER.    IBM-4381.
 OBJECT-COMPUTER.    IBM-4381.
```

Since you will generally be writing all of your programs for the same computer, you need only find out how to code these statements once—they will be exactly the same for each program.

A final note about the configuration section. It is important to document the source and object computers when programs are subject to being compiled on one machine and run on another. Some would say that it is important to document the source and object computers all of the time. However, this section is optional on some compilers and may be left out completely. Whether it is required documentation is ultimately up to the computer center management.

The Input–Output Section In the Input–Output Section, the programmer codes SELECT statements. The purpose of the SELECT statement is to give symbolic *file names* to the specific I/O devices that will be used by the program. The format for the SELECT statement is as follows:

```
SELECT file-name ASSIGN TO system-name
```

Here, the capitalized words are always the same (they are part of the COBOL language), while the lowercase words represent names that are assigned by the programmer.

When a programmer makes up a file name, it must conform to these rules:

1. It must be 30 characters or less and consist entirely of letters, numbers, and hyphens.
2. It must not end or begin with a hyphen and cannot contain blanks.
3. It must contain at least one letter.

In Figure 3–4, INVENTORY–STATUS–FILE is the file name for the set of input records, and REORDER–LISTING is the file name for the output report. (Although you might not commonly think of a printed listing as a file, it is considered one in COBOL, and each line on the listing is treated as a record in the file.)

The *system name* given in the SELECT statement pertains to the I/O device that is going to be used for a file. Since this name must meet the specifications of the computer manufacturer, system names must be changed as you move from one type of computer to another. Before writing a COBOL program, then, you have to find out the system names for the I/O devices that your program will use.

In this book the complete programs use system names that are valid for the Prime 850. As you can see in Figure 3–4, these names are fairly simple: PFMS is the name for PRIME FILE MANAGEMENT SYSTEM. In the Prime interactive system, all input and output files may be stored on disk files. When printing is desired, a separate function is invoked to do so. Other systems may use input names such as READER or TERMINAL and output names such as PRINTER or LOCAL–PRINTER. On some systems the names may be quite complex. For example, on an IBM system such as the 4381 the SELECT statements for the files in Figure 3–4 might read as:

```
SELECT BAL-FWD-FILE     ASSIGN TO UT-S-INVFLE.
SELECT REORDER-LISTING ASSIGN TO UT-S-ORDLST.
```

Here, each system consists of three different parts separated by hyphens. It's obvious, then, that system names vary quite a bit from manufacturer to manufacturer.

As you will notice in Figure 3–4, the SELECT clause is on one line and the ASSIGN clause is on the next and indented 4 spaces. Although not required by any compiler, a structured style guideline directs programmers to put no more than one clause on a line, to place succeeding clauses in a statement on the next line, and then to indent 4 spaces. The program examples in this text will follow those style guidelines so that you may observe models of the recommended style. Discussion of the style will continue throughout the book, but detailed presentation will begin in the chapter on structured programming.

The Data Division

The Data Division can consist of two sections. The first section, called the File Section, gives the characteristics of the input and output files and records. The Working–Storage Section describes the other fields of storage required by the program.

The File Section ***The input file*** The file and record descriptions for the inventory input are as follows:

```
FD  INVENTORY-STATUS-FILE
    LABEL RECORDS ARE STANDARD
    RECORD CONTAINS 80 CHARACTERS.
01  INVENTORY-STATUS-RECORD.
    02  IS-ITEM-NO            PICTURE IS 9(5).
    02  IS-ITEM-DESC          PICTURE IS X(20).
    02  FILLER                PICTURE IS X(5).
    02  IS-UNIT-PRICE         PICTURE IS 999V99.
    02  IS-REORDER-POINT      PICTURE IS 9(5).
    02  IS-QTY-ON-HAND        PICTURE IS 9(5).
    02  IS-QTY-ON-ORDER       PICTURE IS 9(5).
    02  FILLER                PICTURE IS X(30).
```

FD stands for file description and is followed by the file name that was originally created in the SELECT statement of the Environment Division. The next two lines give information about the file.

The LABEL RECORDS clause is required in every FD statement. For most files, the label records are either STANDARD or OMITTED—that is, either the file has beginning and ending labels in a standard format or it doesn't have beginning and ending labels at all. Labels are magnetically encoded wordings at particular places on a magnetic file (such as the header and trailer labels on a tape file) that identify the individual file and differentiate it from all other files. Such labels are especially important on devices such as tape or disk since the contents may not be determined by merely looking at the piece of tape or disk. Some devices, such as card reader/punches, terminals, and printers, do not, of course, have labels. Since these devices don't have labels, it may seem logical to code their LABEL RECORDS clauses like this:

```
LABEL RECORDS ARE OMITTED
```

In fact, some compilers require this.

Most compilers, however, allow you to code STANDARD labels, rather than OMITTED, even though some files don't have labels. If this is done, the programmer can direct the file to a tape or direct-access device if perhaps a printer isn't available when the program is run. In this book, then, STANDARD labels are specified for all files. Be sure to check whether this is acceptable to your compiler before you code your FD statements for card and printer files. As noted before, some systems can be programmed to automatically store output for printing on disk files where it may be called up and viewed on a terminal. The output file may be used this way until hard copy is desired, at which time the file may be "spooled" to the printer.

RECORD CONTAINS 80 CHARACTERS means just what it says—there are a total of 80 characters defined in the record, whether named and used or not. The 80 characters are the length of a card record and a complete line on most terminals. However, any tape or disk record may be shorter or longer, and so you will have to adjust this coding to the actual lengths of the records used. As you will see in a moment, this clause provides a check on the actual length of the record.

The line starting with 01 begins the description of the record. The 01 level number indicates that the name following is the name for an entire record. In other words, INVENTORY-STATUS-RECORD is the *record name*. The rules for forming a record name are the same as those for forming a file name—up to 30 letters, numbers, or hyphens and containing at least one letter.

The 02 level numbers indicate that the lines describe fields within the 01 record. Following the 02 numbers are *data names*, which are made up using the rules for file or record names, or the word FILLER, which is used for those fields or card columns that are not used by the program. For example, the first two 02 lines give the data names IS-ITEM-NO and IS-ITEM-DESC to the item-number and item-description fields of the input records. The third 02 line, which is FILLER, indicates that the third field in the input record will not be used by the program. If you refer to Figure 3-1, you can see that the third field is the unit-cost field, which is not required on the output record.

Although the programmer could have used names like S241 and B11 for item number and item description, he made up names that reflect their use. In this program, IS in a name refers to the input file—INVENTORY-STATUS—and the remainder of the name refers to the field. Thus, IS-ITEM-DESC indicates the item-description field in the inventory-status file. This is a common naming technique.

One point to remember when creating names such as file names, record names, or data names is that you must avoid duplicating COBOL *reserved words*. For example, the words SELECT, LABEL, RECORDS, ARE, and STANDARD are reserved words—words that are a part of the COBOL language. As a result, you cannot use any of these words for a name that you make up. If LABEL is used as a file name, for instance, the COBOL compiler will diagnose an error. Since you will use a prefix like IS for most of the names you create (as in IS–ITEM–NO), you normally have little chance of duplicating a reserved word. You can find a complete list of the reserved words for your compiler in the compiler's reference manual.

The PICTURE IS clauses that follow the data names give the characteristics of the fields and correspond to the characteristics entries in the record layout form. The number or letter outside the parentheses tells what kind of data the field contains; the number inside parentheses tells how long the field is. For example, 9(5) means the field is numeric and consists of five columns. And X(20) means that the field is alphanumeric and consists of twenty columns. (An alphanumeric field can contain letters, numbers, or special characters.)

Do you understand so far? The data names give each of the fields in the record a symbolic name that can be used later in the Procedure Division. The PICTURE IS clauses, which may start one or more spaces after the data names, indicate the nature of the data and the size of the field.

Now, look a little further. The PICTURE for the field named IS–UNIT–PRICE is 999V99. This means that the field is five columns long (there are five 9s) and contains numeric data with a decimal point two places from the right. In other words, a 9 indicates one numeric column and the V indicates the position of the assumed decimal point. When the COBOL compiler works with decimal numbers, it cannot handle having the decimal point as an actual part of the number field, because numeric fields must contain only numeric digits. However, the place where the decimal is supposed to be must be indicated. So the symbol V is used to stand for an implied decimal point, that is, the symbol implies that the number has three whole number digits and two decimal places.

When the source program is compiled, the computer adds up the number of columns indicated in the PICTURE clauses for a record and compares the sum to the character count in the RECORD CONTAINS clause. If they don't match, a diagnostic message is printed. For the INVENTORY–STATUS–RECORD, the sum of the PICTUREs is 80. Since this is the count in the RECORD CONTAINS clause, no error is indicated. Figure 3–5 illustrates the names assigned to the input area and the fields within it.

The printer file The next file description is for the report that is to be printed on the printer. Its coding lines are as follows:

```
FD  REORDER-LISTING
    LABEL RECORDS ARE STANDARD
    RECORD CONTAINS 132 CHARACTERS.
```

Except for the file name, REORDER–LISTING, the three lines of coding are like those for the input file. They say that the file either has standard labels or none at all and that the file contains fixed-length records that are 132 characters long. Most printers have a print line that is 132 characters long, but you may have to adjust the RECORD CONTAINS clause for the printer you will be using.

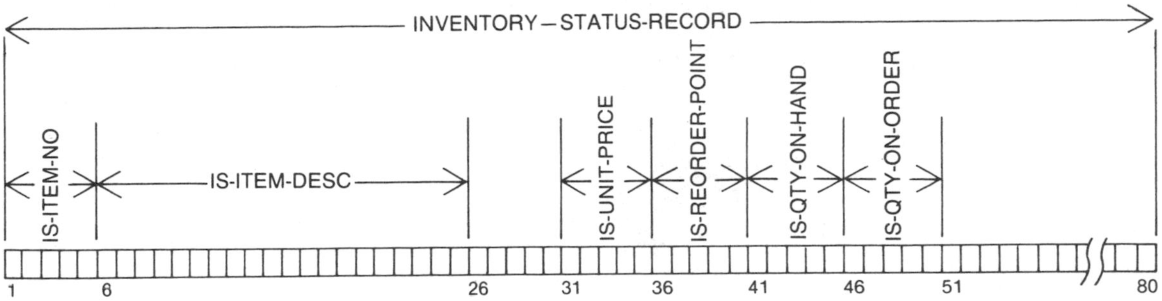
INVENTORY—STATUS-RECORD
IS-ITEM-NO
IS-ITEM-DESC
IS-UNIT-PRICE
IS-REORDER-POINT
IS-QTY-ON-HAND
IS-QTY-ON-ORDER
1
6
26
31
36
41
46
51
80

Figure 3–5
The input area

The record description that follows the FD statement is this:

```
01  REORDER-LINE.
    02  RL-ITEM-NO          PICTURE IS X(5).
    02  FILLER              PICTURE IS X(5).
    02  RL-ITEM-DESC        PICTURE IS X(20).
    02  FILLER              PICTURE IS X(5).
    02  RL-UNIT-PRICE       PICTURE IS ZZZ.99.
    02  FILLER              PICTURE IS X(5).
    02  RL-AVAILABLE-STOCK  PICTURE IS Z(5).
    02  FILLER              PICTURE IS X(5).
    02  RL-REORDER-POINT    PICTURE IS Z(5).
    02  FILLER              PICTURE IS X(71).
```

Here, the 01 line assigns the name REORDER–LINE to the output record. Thus, REORDER–LINE is the record name.

As you can see, the 02 levels and the PICTURE clauses define the fields of the printed line just as they did the fields of the input records. The only new symbols used are the Z as in Z(5) and the decimal point as in ZZZ.99. Z(5) means that a five-digit numeric field is to be printed and the high-order zeros should be suppressed. ZZZ.99 means that a five-digit numeric field is to be printed with two decimal places and a decimal point. The high-order zeros to the left of the decimal point are to be zero-suppressed. Thus, the number 00718 will print as 7.18; the number 00003 will print as .03. The data names in these descriptions begin with RL, which refers to the record name, REORDER–LINE.

The total number of characters in the PICTURE clauses for the printer area equals 132, which is the number of print positions on the printer. It is also the count given in the RECORD CONTAINS clause. As a result, no error is indicated. Figure 3–6 illustrates the names assigned to the output area and the fields within it. Notice that the FILLER lines in the printer description determine the spacing of the output report.

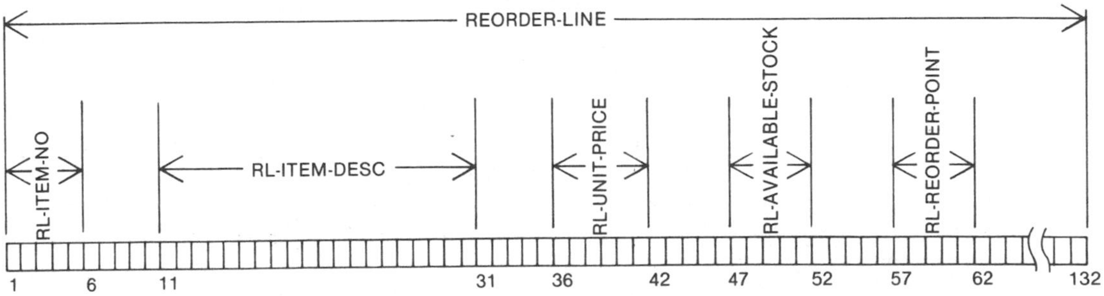
REORDER-LINE
RL-ITEM-NO
RL-ITEM-DESC
RL-UNIT-PRICE
RL-AVAILABLE-STOCK
RL-REORDER-POINT
1
6
11
31
36
42
47
52
57
62
132

Figure 3–6
The printer output area

The Working–Storage Section The Working–Storage Section of the Data Division defines all other data fields that are to be used by the program. For this program, the Working–Storage Section is as follows:

```
WORKING-STORAGE SECTION.
01  SWITCHES.
    02  INVENTORY-EOF-SW        PICTURE IS X.
01  WORK-FIELDS.
    02  AVAILABLE-STOCK         PICTURE IS 9(5).
```

Here, the 01 levels, SWITCHES and WORK–FIELDS, aren't record names for input or output areas. Instead, they are used to logically group the fields the program will need during the processing of the INVENTORY–STATUS–RECORDs.

We define a *switch* as a field that can have one of two possible values; these values indicate the switch is either "off" or "on." In this book, a value of N is used to mean "off"; a value of Y is used to mean "on." Whenever you move one of these values to a switch field, you are "setting the switch."

The one switch in this program, INVENTORY–EOF–SW, indicates when all the records in the input file have been read. (Since EOF is a commonly used abbreviation for end-of-file, you are likely to see it often.) Like all switches, INVENTORY–EOF–SW is described as a one-position alphanumeric field. It will have a value of either Y or N moved to it during the course of this program, depending on whether any input records remain to be read. Switches are quite common in structured programs, so you will learn more about how and when to use them as you go through this book.

WORK–FIELDS hold the results of calculations that must be made to produce the output data from the input data. In this program, a five-position numeric field named AVAILABLE–STOCK will hold the result when the available stock for each inventory status record is calculated. This result will then be used to decide whether a line should be printed on the reorder listing.

Incidentally, when coding a PICTURE clause, 9(5) and 99999 are equivalent. Similarly, 9(3) V9(2) and 999V99 are equivalent as are Z(3).9(2) and ZZZ.99. In general, the programmer chooses the form that is easier for him or her to code or to understand. As a rule of thumb, use parentheses when four or more characters in a row are required.

The Procedure Division

As you will see in chapter 6, a programmer begins to document the modules of a program after designing its structure chart. At that time, the programmer creates many of the file, record, and data names used to code the Environment and Data Divisions. In addition, the programmer creates names for the groups of instructions that make up the Procedure Division. These names are called *procedure*, or *paragraph names*. Since they always start at the A margin, they are easy to identify. In figure 3–4, for example, 000– PRODUCE–REORDER–LISTING, 100–PRODUCE–REORDER–LINE, 110– READ–INVENTORY–RECORD, and so forth are the procedure names used. These names are formed using the same rules as for file names with one exception: **they don't have to contain any letters.**

In general, there should be one paragraph name for each module in the structure chart for a program. As a result, there are five paragraph names in the Procedure Division of Figure 3–4, one for each of the five module blocks in Figure 3–2. As you can see, a paragraph name is created by taking the block number and the module description from the structure chart and separating

Procedure Division Formats

I/O statements:

```
OPEN INPUT file-name.

OPEN OUTPUT file-name.

READ file-name RECORD
    AT END
        imperative-statement.

WRITE record-name.

CLOSE file-name.
```

Data-movement statements:

```
MOVE SPACE TO data-name.

MOVE literal TO data-name.

MOVE data-name-1 TO data-name-2.
```

Arithmetic statements:

```
ADD data-name-1 TO data-name-2.

ADD data-name-1 data-name-2
    GIVING data-name-3.

SUBTRACT data-name-1 FROM data-name-2.

SUBTRACT data-name-1 FROM data-name-2
    GIVING data-name-3.

MULTIPLY data-name-1 BY data-name-2.

MULTIPLY data-name-1 BY data-name-2
    GIVING data-name-3.

DIVIDE data-name-1 INTO data-name-2.

DIVIDE data-name-1 INTO data-name-2
    GIVING data-name-3.
```

Sequence-control statements:

```
IF condition
    statement-1
[ELSE
    statement-2].

PERFORM procedure-name.

PERFORM procedure-name
    UNTIL condition.
```

Miscellaneous statements:

```
STOP RUN.
```

Figure 3–7
Simplified statement formats showing recommended indentation

the number and words by hyphens. The paragraphs are in sequence by module number, so it is easy to locate a paragraph in a large program when you know its paragraph name.

The lines of coding that start in the B margin of the Procedure Division are COBOL statements that specify operations that are to take place on the fields, records, and files previously defined. These symbolic statements follow consistent formats, some of which are given in Figure 3–7. To use any of these statements, the programmer substitutes the names of the files, records, or fields that are to be operated on for the lowercase words in the statement formats. The capitalized words in each statement are written just as they appear in the statement format. To execute a procedure named 110–READ–INVENTORY–RECORD, for example, the programmer codes

```
PERFORM 110-READ-INVENTORY-RECORD.
```

The problem for the beginning programmer, then, is to learn the format and function of each of the available COBOL statements.

In the remainder of this topic, the operation of each of the paragraphs in the reorder-listing program will be explained. Although this may be somewhat confusing at first, you should understand the operation of this program by the time you complete this topic.

Module 000: Produce Reorder Listing The top-level module in the structure chart in Figure 3–2 represents the entire program. Its primary function is to determine which of the level-1 modules should be executed, when they should be executed, and how many times these modules should be executed. Since there is only one level-1 module for this program, module 000 determines how many times module 100 should be executed. In addition, it gets the input and output files ready for processing at the start of the program, and it deactivates the files at the end of the program. The COBOL code for this module is duplicated in Figure 3–8.

```
000-PRODUCE-REORDER-LISTING.
    OPEN INPUT  INVENTORY-STATUS-FILE
         OUTPUT REORDER-LISTING.
    MOVE 'N'                      TO INVENTORY-EOF-SW.
    PERFORM 100-PRODUCE-REORDER-LINE
        UNTIL INVENTORY-EOF-SW EQUAL 'Y'.
    CLOSE INVENTORY-STATUS-FILE
          REORDER-LISTING.
    STOP RUN.
```

Figure 3–8
Module 000:
Produce Reorder Listing

The OPEN statement An OPEN statement is required for each file that is to be read or written by a program. Therefore, the OPEN statements usually are found in the top-level module. If you look at the formats for the OPEN statement in Figure 3–7, you can see how the OPEN statements in Figure 3–8 relate to the formats. The programmer simply substitutes into the OPEN statements the file names defined in the Environment Division. The word INPUT is used for an input file, the word OUTPUT for an output file.

The OPEN statements are required. On devices that do not have labels, such as terminals and printers, they do not actually cause any processing to be done other than ensuring that the device is ready to operate. For files on devices such as tape and disk files, the OPEN statement does several checks on the file labels. The principal check done is to examine the labeled name of the file and ensure that it matches with the file label expected. If the file label and the expected label do not match, the operating system emits an error for the operator's action.

The MOVE statement The MOVE statement that follows the OPEN statements is this:

```
MOVE "N" TO INVENTORY-EOF-SW
```

It sets the field named INVENTORY-EOF-SW to a value of N, for "no," meaning that the end of the file has *not* been reached. As you will see later, this switch is set to a value of Y, for "yes," when all of the input records have been read. In this program, then, when INVENTORY-EOF-SW is equal to N, it means there are still some more records to be processed. When it is equal to Y, it means there are no more records to be processed.

The PERFORM UNTIL statement The PERFORM UNTIL statement in module 000 is this:

```
PERFORM 100-PRODUCE-REORDER-LINE
    UNTIL INVENTORY-EOF-SW IS EQUAL TO "Y".
```

It will cause the paragraph named 100-PRODUCE-REORDER-LINE to be executed until INVENTORY-EOF-SW has a value of Y. In other words, module 100 will be executed until there are no more input records to be processed. The program will then continue with the next statements in sequence, the CLOSE statements.

If you compare this PERFORM UNTIL statement with the format in Figure 3-7, you'll see that the *condition* in the statement is this:

```
INVENTORY-EOF-SW IS EQUAL TO "Y".
```

Each time the statement is executed, the program tests the value of INVENTORY-EOF-SW to see whether the condition has been met *before* performing 100-PRODUCE-REORDER-LINE. Thus, module 100 will not be performed the first time INVENTORY-EOF-SW is found to be equal to Y.

Conditions are formed by using the general format shown in Figure 3-9. In other words, two values can be compared to see whether value-A is greater than value-B, value-A is equal to value-B, or value-A is less than value-B. The values can be values stored in fields or values specified in the statement itself (*literals*). In the condition in Figure 3-8, the first value is the value stored in the field named INVENTORY-EOF-SW, the second value is the literal value Y.

Condition format:

```
{literal-1    }  {IS [NOT] GREATER THAN}  {literal-2    }
{data-name-1  }  {IS [NOT] EQUAL TO    }  {data-name-2  }
                 {IS [NOT] LESS THAN   }
```

Examples:

```
1.  RECORD-EOF-SW IS NOT EQUAL TO "Y"
2.  ITEM-CODE-1 IS GREATER THAN ITEM-CODE-2
3.  TR-CODE IS LESS THAN 5
4.  "N" IS NOT GREATER THAN EMP-NAME
```

Figure 3-9
Basic condition tests

Chapter 4 will explain in detail how to create literals. For now, accept the fact that a non-numeric literal is expressed by enclosing the literal value in quotation marks. Thus, the literal in the condition is "Y"; the literal value is Y.

NOT is an optional word in a condition. It is used to state the negative of a condition. Thus, the PERFORM UNTIL statement could be written like this with the same results:

```
PERFORM 100-PRODUCE-REORDER-LINE
    UNTIL INVENTORY-EOF-SW IS NOT EQUAL TO "N".
```

Module 100 would still be executed until INVENTORY–EOF–SW equals Y.

The CLOSE statement. Just as files must be opened at the start of a program, they must be closed at the end. As a result, module 000 uses these CLOSE statements:

```
CLOSE INVENTORY-STATUS-FILE.
CLOSE REORDER-LISTING.
```

After CLOSE statements are executed, the files are no longer available for processing. You should realize, however, that the real significance of the CLOSE statement, like the OPEN, pertains to tape and direct-access files.

The STOP statement. STOP RUN means that the program has finished and the computer system should go on to the next program. It causes a branch to the supervisor so the next program can be loaded into storage and executed.

Module 100: Produce Reorder Line Module 100 is the level-1 module in Figure 3–2. Its coding is shown in Figure 3–10. Its primary function is to see that all the level-2 modules that it controls are executed in the proper sequence. Each time module 100 is given control by module 000, it is executed one time; then control passes back to the PERFORM UNTIL statement in module 000. Remember that the PERFORM UNTIL statement will cause module 100 to be executed again and again until INVENTORY–EOF–SW is equal to Y. Thus, it will be executed once for each inventory-status record.

```
100-PRODUCE-REORDER-LINE.
    PERFORM 110-READ-INVENTORY-RECORD.
    IF INVENTORY-EOF-SW IS NOT EQUAL TO "Y"
        PERFORM 120-CALCULATE-AVAILABLE-STOCK
        IF AVAILABLE-STOCK IS LESS THAN IS-REORDER-POINT
            PERFORM 130-PRINT-REORDER-LINE.
```

Figure 3–10
Module 100: Produce Reorder Line

The PERFORM statement The PERFORM statement causes one paragraph to be executed. The program then continues with the first statement following the PERFORM statement. As a result, the first statement in module 100 causes the paragraph named 110–READ–INVENTORY–RECORD to be executed. After this, the IF statement that follows the PERFORM statement is executed.

The IF statement The IF statement is the logical statement (in structured programming terms, the selection statement) of the COBOL program. It usually compares two values and continues based on the results of the comparison. Some examples follow:

```
1.  IF   VALID-TRAN-SWITCH IS EQUAL TO "Y"
         PERFORM 240-PRINT-SALES-LINE
    ELSE
         PERFORM 250-PRINT-ERROR-MESSAGE.
2.  IF   SR-PERIOD-SALES IS LESS THAN SALES-QUOTA
         MOVE "C" TO COMMISSION-CODE
         PERFORM 320-CALCULATE-REGULAR-COMMISSION
    ELSE
         MOVE "A" TO COMMISSION-CODE
         PERFORM 320-CALCULATE-REGULAR-COMMISSION
         PERFORM 330-CALCULATE-BONUS-COMMISSION.
```

In these examples, the programmer has used indentation to show that the IF–ELSE structure provides for two conditions—true and false. If the condition in the IF statement is true, all statements before the ELSE are executed; if the condition is false, all the statements after the ELSE are executed. Notice that only one period is used in the IF–ELSE structure, after the last statement of the ELSE clause. The condition formats you can use are summarized in Figure 3–9.

If you look at the IF-statement format in Figure 3–7, you'll see that the ELSE clause is enclosed in brackets. This means that the clause is optional. As a result, IF statements like these can be coded:

```
1.  IF ER-HOURS-WORKED IS GREATER THAN OVERTIME-HOURS
         PERFORM 320-CALCULATE-OVERTIME-PAY.
2.  IF TRAN-EOF-SWITCH IS NOT EQUAL TO "Y"
         PERFORM 120-ACCUMULATE-CUST-TOTAL.
```

Here, if the condition is true, the statements following the condition are executed. If the condition is false, processing continues with the statement following the IF statement.

Nested IF statements When an IF statement contains one or more other IF statements, they are referred to as *nested IF statements.* In Figure 3–10, nested IF statements are used in module 100 as follows:

```
IF INVENTORY-EOF-SW IS NOT EQUAL TO "Y"
    PERFORM 120-CALCULATE-AVAILABLE-STOCK
    IF AVAILABLE-STOCK IS LESS THAN IS-REORDER-POINT
        PERFORM 130-PRINT-REORDER-LINE.
```

Once again, indentation is used to show the relationships between the parts of the IF statements.

Figure 3–11 shows how these nested IF statements operate when executed. In brief, if INVENTORY–EOF–SW isn't equal to Y (meaning there are still cards to be processed), the available stock is calculated. Then, if the available stock is less than the reorder point, a reorder line is printed. If, however, the condition in either IF statement is *not* true, processing should continue with the next statement after the IF. As a result, ELSE clauses aren't required.

Because COBOL allows many levels of nesting, nesting can become very confusing if it isn't handled correctly. To better understand it, look at Figure 3–12. It shows the logic of IF statements nested within both the IF and ELSE portions of a primary IF statement.

One key point to remember when nesting is that the compiler will pair each ELSE with the first IF that precedes it that doesn't already have an ELSE, regardless of how you have paired IFs and ELSEs through indentation. So to eliminate errors when coding nested IF statements, you should be sure that each IF statement has a corresponding ELSE if it requires one. You should

Statement:

```
IF INVENTORY-EOF-SW NOT EQUAL TO "Y"
    PERFORM 120-CALCULATE-AVAILABLE-STOCK
    IF AVAILABLE-STOCK IS LESS THAN IS REORDER-POINT
        PERFORM 130-PRINT-REORDER-LINE.
```

Logic flow:

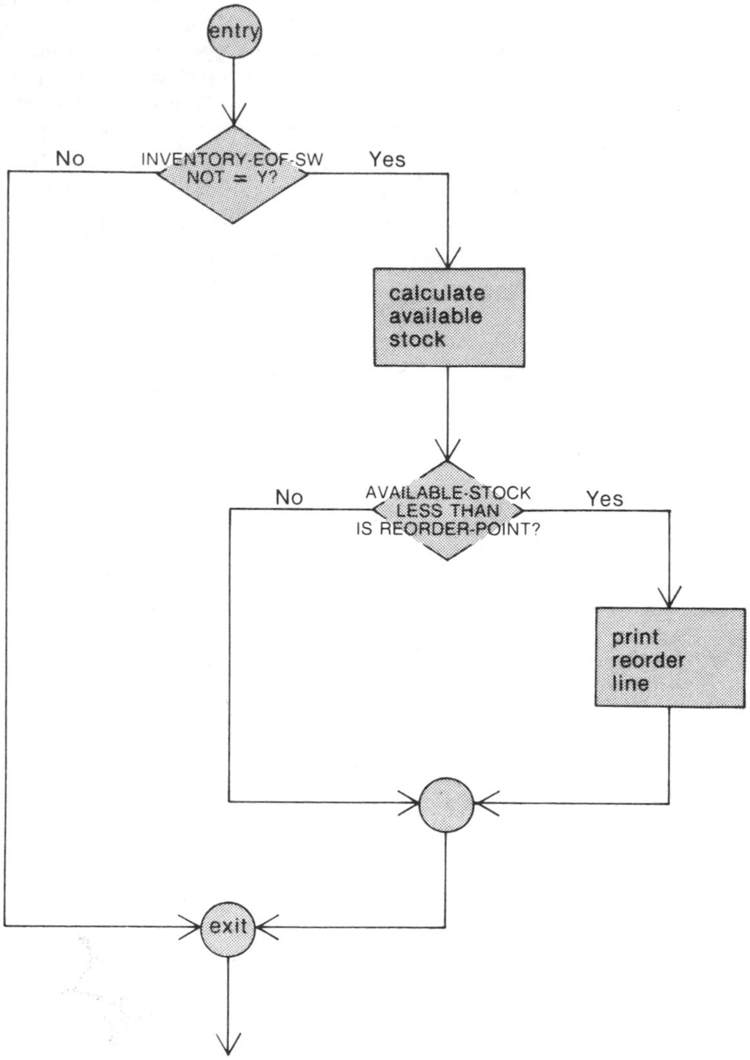
entry
No
INVENTORY-EOF-SW NOT = Y?
Yes
calculate available stock
No
AVAILABLE-STOCK LESS THAN IS REORDER-POINT?
Yes
print reorder line
exit

Figure 3–11
Operation of the nested IF statements in module 100

also use indentation to make sure you have properly paired your IFs and ELSEs, as well as to show the logical structure of the nesting. If you do both of these things, several levels of nesting can be used with limited confusion.

Warning: Be aware that nesting is terminated by the first period, regardless of indentation. Forgetting this has caused COBOL programmers untold hours of debugging toil. You should also keep in mind the fact that a missing period will include unintended lines in the range of the IF. The lines so included will be those that follow until a period is encountered. In fact, a misplaced period is one of the more difficult errors to detect for the beginning programmer.

Coding:

```
IF condition-1
    IF condition-2
        statement-group-A
    ELSE
        statement-group-B
ELSE
    IF condition-3
        statement-group-C
    ELSE
        statement-group-D
```

Logic flow:

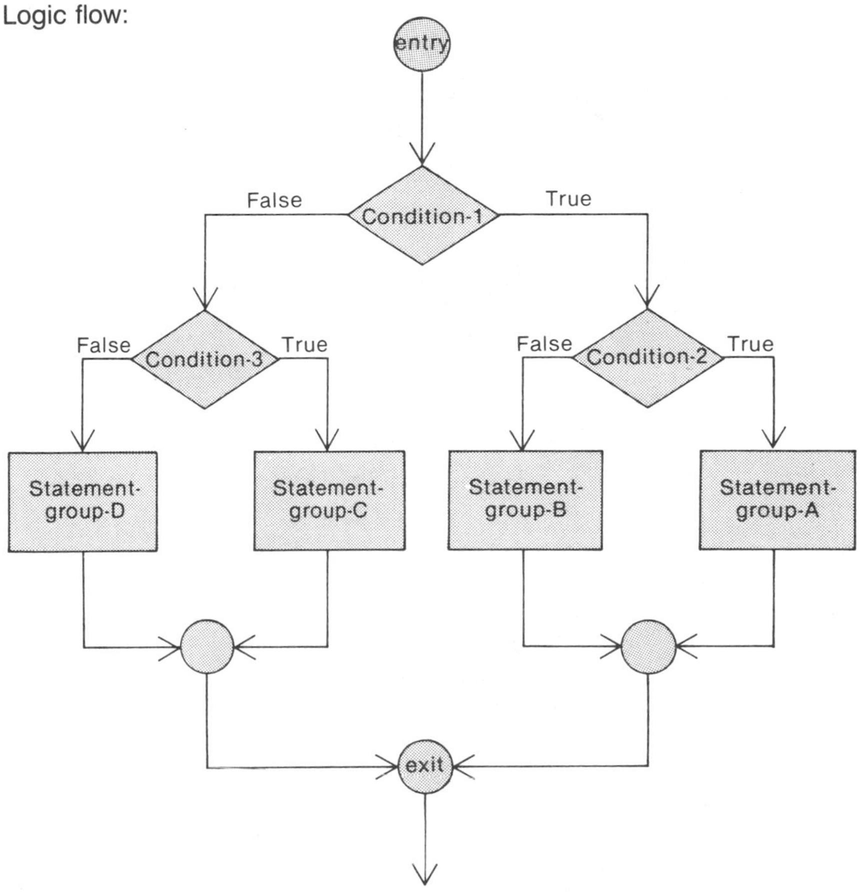
entry
False
Condition-1
True
False
Condition-3
True
False
Condition-2
True
Statement-group-D
Statement-group-C
Statement-group-B
Statement-group-A
exit

Figure 3–12
Nested IF statements—coding and logic

Module 110: Read Inventory Record ***The READ statement*** This module consists of only one statement, the READ statement:

```
READ INVENTORY-STATUS-FILE
    AT END
        MOVE 'Y'              TO INVENTORY-EOF-SW.
```

It causes one inventory record to be read. When there are no more records to be processed (AT END), the program moves a value of Y into the field named INVENTORY–EOF–SW.

How does the READ statement know when there are no more records to be processed? This varies somewhat by computer system. So you'll want to find out how *your* system is told that there are no more records to be read. For now, however, simply be aware that the AT END clause is executed when an attempt is made to read another record and no more records are available.

If you check the format for the READ statement in Figure 3–7, you will see that AT END must be followed by an *imperative statement*. That means that conditional statements like the IF statement are not allowed. In most cases, the AT END clause is used to move a value into an end-of-file switch. This value is then tested by a PERFORM UNTIL statement in a higher-level module to determine whether or not processing should continue.

Module 120: Calculate Available Stock ***Arithmetic statements*** This module consists of only one statement, an ADD statement:

```
ADD IS-QTY-ON-HAND IS-QTY-ON-ORDER
    GIVING AVAILABLE-STOCK.
```

It adds the contents of IS–QTY–ON–HAND to the contents of IS–QTY–ON–ORDER and stores the result in AVAILABLE–STOCK.

In general, there are two formats for each type of arithmetic statement (see Figure 3–7). In the first format, the result of the arithmetic operation replaces the contents of the second field named (data-name-2), while the contents of the first field named are unchanged. For instance,

```
ADD IS-QTY-ON-HAND TO IS-QTY-ON-ORDER
```

would execute this way:

Field name:	IS-QTY-ON-HAND	IS-QTY-ON-ORDER
Contents before:	00050	00070
Contents after:	00050	00120

The second format, which uses GIVING and a third data name, is the one used in module 120. By using GIVING, the statement has the effect of a move and an add instruction, so neither data-name-1 nor data-name-2 is changed. For example, the ADD statement in module 120 would execute this way:

Field name:	IS-QTY-ON-HAND	IS-QTY-ON-ORDER	AVAILABLE-STOCK
Before:	00070	00050	?
After:	00070	00050	00120

Although all four arithmetic statements have the same basic formats, it should be noted that the remainder in a DIVIDE statement is lost when the statement is executed. Thus,

```
DIVIDE TR-MONTHS INTO WS-TOTAL
```

executes in this way:

Field name:	TR-MONTHS	WS-TOTAL
Before:	10	23
After:	10	02

and

```
DIVIDE TR-MONTHS INTO WS-TOTAL GIVING AVERAGE
```

executes in this way:

Field name:	TR-MONTHS	WS-TOTAL	WS-AVERAGE
Before:	10	23	?
After:	10	23	02

When using arithmetic statements, you should make sure that all result fields are large enough to store the results. Also, all fields except the GIVING field in the second format must be numeric. For now, that means that they must have PICTUREs that consist of 9s and Vs only, while a GIVING field may consist of either Zs, 9s, and a decimal point or of 9s and Vs.

Module 130: Print Reorder Line Module 130 is the last paragraph in the program in Figure 3–4. It consists of these statements:

```
MOVE SPACES                  TO REORDER-LINE.
MOVE IS-ITEM-NO              TO RL-ITEM-NO.
MOVE IS-ITEM-DESC            TO RL-ITEM-DESC.
MOVE IS-UNIT-PRICE           TO RL-UNIT-PRICE.
MOVE AVAILABLE-STOCK         TO RL-AVAILABLE-STOCK.
MOVE IS-REORDER-POINT        TO RL-REORDER-POINT
WRITE REORDER-LINE.
```

It moves the requires data to the printer output area and prints one reorder line. Remember that this module is only executed when the available stock is less than the reorder point.

The MOVE statements The first statement

```
MOVE SPACE TO REORDER-LINE
```

simply does what it says: it puts spaces, or blanks, in all 132 positions of the printer output area. (SPACE is a COBOL reserved word that represents one or more spaces.) As a result, it clears the area of any data remaining from a previous program or from a previous line of printing. A statement such as this is often used prior to statements that move data to an output area.

After the output record is cleared (set to spaces), a series of MOVE statements moves the data to the output record. These statements indicate the power of the MOVE statement in COBOL. If zero suppression or the insertion of a decimal point is necessary when a field is moved, the MOVE statement does it. For example, when IS-UNIT-PRICE is moved to RL-UNIT-PRICE, a decimal point is inserted and the leading zeros before the decimal point are suppressed, as in this example:

Field:	IS-UNIT-PRICE	RL-UNIT-PRICE
PICTURE:	999V99	ZZZ.99
Before:	00449	?????
After:	00449	4.49

Data item table:

Item name	PICTURE contains	PICTURE examples
Alphabetic	As	A(20) AA
Alphanumeric	Xs	X(20) XXX
Numeric	S, V, and 9s	9(5) S999V99
Numeric edited	Decimal point, Zs, 9s, and other editing characters	Z(5) ZZZ.99

MOVE table:

Sending Item	Receiving Item			
	Alphabetic	Alphanumeric	Numeric	Numeric edited
Alphabetic	OK	OK	Illegal	Illegal
Alphanumeric	OK	OK	Questionable	Questionable
Numeric	Illegal	Whole numbers OK; others questionable	OK	OK
Numeric edited	Illegal	OK	Illegal	Illegal

Figure 3–13
Data items and the MOVE statement

If 00005 were moved instead of 00449, RL–UNIT–PRICE would print as .05. As you can see, the result of a COBOL MOVE depends on the PICTUREs given for each of the fields involved in the statement.

To classify data items, most reference manuals use the terminology in Figure 3–13. Alphabetic items, which have not yet been mentioned, have PICTUREs that consist of As. Since they contain letters and spaces only, they have limited use and *alphanumeric items* will always work just as well. As a result, alphabetic items aren't used in this book.

Numeric items consist primarily of 9s, but they may also have one V (decimal point) and one S (a sign as explained later). *Numeric edited items* can consist of 9s, Zs, decimal points, and any of several other editing characters that will also be covered later.

The bottom table in Figure 3–13 uses this terminology to indicate which types of moves are legal, which are illegal, and which, though legal, should never be done. As you can see, it is always an error to move an alphabetic field to a numeric or numeric edited field. In contrast, it is always okay to move a numeric field to a numeric edited field. In this type of move, the number of digits (9s) in the sending field should be the same as the number of digits (9s or Zs) in the receiving field.

The moves marked "Questionable" in the chart are allowed by most compilers; however, in almost all cases they should be avoided. For example, if an alphanumeric field were moved to a numeric field, it would be treated as though it contained an integer, which might not be the case at all. As a result, the value in the receiving field would be unpredictable. In general, then, treat the moves marked "Questionable" as though they were illegal, and avoid them entirely.

The WRITE statement The WRITE statement causes one line to be printed and the form to be moved up one line. In other words, after all fields are moved to the printer output area, the WRITE statement prints the output line. Note that the format for the WRITE statement (see Figure 3–7) requires the record name. In contrast, the format for the READ statement requires the file name. You can remember this requirement by the saying "read a file—write a record."

Discussion

The key to understanding the reorder-listing program just described is in following the flow of control from one module to another. To recap, first remember that the top module (module 000) is executed only once. However, control passes from module 000's PERFORM UNTIL statement to module 100 once for each record in the input file until at last there are no more records in the input file and Y is moved to INVENTORY–EOF–SW. Then, the program moves from the PERFORM UNTIL statement to the CLOSE statements that follow it.

Each time module 100 is executed, it causes module 110 to be executed. And as long as module 110 reads another data record, module 100 also causes module 120 to be executed. Finally, for each data record, if the available stock is less than the reorder point, module 100 causes module 130 to be executed and a reorder line is printed.

Because the program illustrated in this topic is written in ANS COBOL, it could be compiled on any computer that has an ANS compiler. To do so, only the shaded words in the Environment Division that follows would have to be changed:

```
ENVIRONMENT DIVISION.
CONFIGURATION SECTION.
SOURCE-COMPUTER.    PRIME 850.
OBJECT-COMPUTER.    PRIME 850.
INPUT-OUTPUT SECTION.
FILE-CONTROL.
    SELECT INVENTORY-STATUS-FILE
        ASSIGN TO PFMS.
    SELECT REORDER-LISTING
        ASSIGN TO PFMS.
```

That is, the computer names in the Configuration Section would have to be changed along with the system names in the Input–Output Section.

As you can see from this program, coding the Identification, Environment, and Data Divisions is a rather trivial job. The difficulties are encountered in the Procedure Division. If you don't yet understand how the reorder-listing program works, you should after you do the problems for this topic.

Problems

1. (Objective 1) Code the Configuration Section for the compiler you will be using in this course.

2. (Objective 2) Write a SELECT statement and file, record, and field descriptions for an input file consisting of invoice records in this format:

Record positions	Field	Form
1	Record code	Alphanumeric
2–4	Salesperson number	Numeric
5–9	Customer number	Numeric
15–19	Invoice number	Numeric
20–25	Invoice date	Numeric
26–47	Customer name	Alphanumeric
48–54	Invoice amount	Numeric (two decimal places)

3. (Objective 2) Write a SELECT statement and file, record, and field descriptions for a printer file that prints an invoice register with this line format:

Print positions	Field	Form
1–5	Invoice Number	Numeric
10–14	Customer number	Numeric
19–40	Customer name	Alphanumeric
45–51	Invoice amount	Numeric (decimal point must print)

   Suppress the left zeros in all numeric fields and coordinate your descriptions with the input data descriptions of problem 2.

4. (Objective 3) The data in the table in Figure 3–14 represents six input records for the reorder-listing program shown in Figure 3–4. Assuming that positions 51–80 of all the input records are blank, answer the following questions:

Field name:	Item no.	Item description	Unit cost	Unit price	Reorder point	Quantity On hand	Quantity On order
Record positions	1-5	6-25	26-30	31-35	36-40	41-45	46-50
Record 1:	00101	GENERATOR	04000	04900	00100	00070	00050
	00103	HEATER SOLENOID	00330	00440	00050	00034	00000
	03244	GEAR HOUSING	06500	07900	00010	00012	00000
	03981	PLUMB LINE	00210	00240	00015	00035	00000
	04638	STARTER SWITCH	00900	00980	00030	00016	00000
Record 6:	A record that indicates the end of the file						

Figure 3–14
Input data for the reorder-listing program

   a. Give the verbs for the first four statements that will be executed by this program.

   b. Other than module 000, list in sequence the modules that will be executed for record 1.

c. What does the field named INVENTORY–EOF–SW contain after the first input record has been processed? What does AVAILABLE–STOCK contain?

d. What is the next statement to be executed after the ADD statement for record 1?

e. Other than module 000, list in sequence the modules that will be executed for record 2.

f. After module 110 has been executed for record 2, what do IS–UNIT–PRICE, IS–QTY–ON–ORDER, and AVAILABLE–STOCK contain?

g. After module 120 has been executed for record 2, what does AVAILABLE–STOCK contain?

h. After module 130 is executed for record 2, what do RL–ITEM–NO, RL–ITEM–DESC, RL–UNIT–PRICE, and RL–AVAILABLE–STOCK contain?

i. When the WRITE statement is executed for record 2, what is printed in the first 51 print positions of the printer?

j. What is the next statement to be executed after the WRITE statement for record 2?

k. Assume that the program is back at the PERFORM UNTIL statement prior to processing record 3. List in sequence the modules that will be executed up to the time that the program ends. Do not include module 000.

l. What will be printed in the first 51 print positions for record 3?

m. What will be printed in the first 51 print positions for record 4?

n. What will be printed in the first 51 print positions for record 5?

o. What happens when the READ statement is executed for record 6? What are the next two statements to be executed after this?

p. What happens when the PERFORM UNTIL statement is executed after record 6 has been processed?

q. What happens when the STOP RUN statement is executed?

Solutions

1. Code the Configuration Section for your compiler right here so you can refer to it whenever you need it:

2. Your SELECT statement should have this form:

```
SELECT INVOICE-FILE ASSIGN TO system-name.
```

And the system name should conform to the requirements of your compiler.

These are acceptable file and data descriptions:

```
FD   INVOICE-FILE
     LABEL RECORDS ARE STANDARD
     RECORD CONTAINS 80 CHARACTERS.
01   INVOICE-RECORD
     02  IR-CODE            PICTURE IS X.
     02  IR-SLSPERS-NO      PICTURE IS 9(3).
     02  IR-CUST-NO         PICTURE IS 9(5).
     02  FILLER             PICTURE IS X(5).
     02  IR-INV-NO          PICTURE IS 9(5).
     02  IR-INV-DATE        PICTURE IS 9(6).
     02  IR-CUST-NAME       PICTURE IS X(22).
     02  IR-INV-AMOUNT      PICTURE IS 9(5)V99.
     02  FILLER             PICTURE IS X(26).
```

3. Your SELECT statement should have this form:

```
SELECT INVOICE-REGISTER ASSIGN TO system-name
```

And the system name should conform to the requirements of your compiler.

These are acceptable file and data descriptions:

```
FD   INVOICE-REGISTER
     LABEL RECORDS ARE STANDARD
     RECORD CONTAINS 132 CHARACTERS.
01   INV-REG-LINE.
     02  IR-INV-NO           PICTURE IS Z(5).
     02  FILLER              PICTURE IS X(4).
     02  IR-CUST-NO          PICTURE IS Z(5).
     02  FILLER              PICTURE IS X(4).
     02  IR-CUST-NAME        PICTURE IS X(22).
     02  FILLER              PICTURE IS X(4).
     02  IR-INV-AMOUNT       PICTURE IS Z(5).99.
     02  FILLER              PICTURE IS X(80).
```

Note: Your compiler may require that you specify OMITTED rather than STANDARD for printer files.

4. a. OPEN, OPEN, MOVE, PERFORM UNTIL
   b. 100, 110, 120
   c. N, 00120
   d. The second IF statement in module 100 (part of the nested IFs)
   e. 100, 110, 120, 130
   f. 00440, 00000, and 00120
   g. 00034
   h. ØØ103, HEATERbSOLENOIDbbbbb,bb4.40, and bbb34 (where b equals one blank)
   i. ØØ103bbbbbHEATERbSOLENOIDbbbbbbbbbbbb4.40bbbbbbbb34 (where b equals one blank)
   j. PERFORM UNTIL
   k. 100, 110, 120, 100, 110, 120, 100, 110, 120, 130, 100, 110
   l. Nothing
   m. Nothing

n. Ø4638bbbbbSTARTERbSWITCHbbbbbbbbbbbbb9.80bbbbbbbb16 (where b equals one blank)

o. The AT END clause is executed, so Y is moved into INVENTORY–EOF–SW. Then, the IF statement in module 100 is executed followed by the PERFORM UNTIL statement in module 000.

p. Control falls through to the first statement following the PERFORM UNTIL statement.

q. The program ends and a branch to the supervisor takes place.

Topic 2 **Introduction to Program Errors**

Orientation

This topic will introduce you to the typical mistakes that novice programmers usually make. The kind of error that will be discussed is the type that the compiler can catch, and is called *syntax error* because a language rule was violated. Syntax errors will be given a more extensive treatment in the chapter on debugging. This topic will first present desk checking as a method to minimize program errors; then the reorder-listing program with a few syntax errors and the necessary corrections will follow; and finally, typical syntax errors to check for will be listed.

Terminology

compiler output	diagnostic listing	source listing
desk checking	diagnostic messsage	syntax error

Objectives

1. *Understand and use the terminology of this topic.*

2. *Understand and begin to practice the desk checking technique on the first programming assignment.*

3. *Write and compile a first COBOL program, and correct the syntax errors.*

4. *Identify which of the typical syntax errors were made in the beginning program.*

5. *Find and correct all errors in the first program and produce accurate output.*

Desk Checking

A programmer should *desk check* his or her program before entering it into the computer. This saves computer time and programmer time because desk checking almost always catches an error or two and thus saves a compilation or a test run. Although the saving of one run may seem unimportant, you will probably find it to be a significant factor if you are competing with many other students for computer time, especially toward the end of the course. Thus, it is strongly recommended that you make it a standard practice to desk check your program carefully.

Before you enter your program into the computer, you should go over your coding forms several times, *checking them for a different type of error each time through*. Here are some guidelines on what to look for:

1. Check for completeness and the spelling of reserved words. Are all required division, section, and paragraph names present, and are they spelled correctly? A misspelled division name (such as ENVIROMNENT DIVISION), a missing section name (such as FILE SECTION), or a missing hyphen in a paragraph name (such as 150–WRITE REPORT–LINE) can lead to dozens of diagnostics in a long program. Likewise, misspelling a reserved word like STANDARD in the LABEL RECORDS clause will cause problems.

2. Check each statement for punctuation and spacing. Is the end of each statement or series of statements marked by a period? Are there spaces between data names, literals, and reserved words? Is every non-numeric literal enclosed in quotation marks?

3. Check all file, record, data, and procedure names used in the statements of the Procedure Division to be sure they are defined elsewhere in the program. You can often catch a misspelled name this way.

4. Sketch record layouts as described by the PICTUREs of your program and compare them to the layouts given in the problem definition. Be sure the I/O work areas are the proper size for the actual records.

5. The initial data in your working-storage fields, print line areas, and so on, may be important. If so, you must define them with an initial value or else code instructions to set or reset the values in these areas. Check to make sure that these values are properly established.

6. Check position 7 of each statement to make sure it is blank or contains an asterisk. If any other character is punched in this column, it can lead to diagnostics.

When you have checked for errors in this manner, your program is ready for entry into the computer. Unfortunately, the process of entry provides another opportunity for errors to get into the source code. Most of these errors will happen because of inaccurate keying, even if you have someone else enter the program for you. For instance, if another person does your program entry, you may discover that your twos (2) looked like Z's, or it was not obvious which character was a zero and which was a capital O. Thus, you should also write carefully.

Compiler Output

When a program is compiled, a number of different types of output can be printed as part of the *compiler output*. The two most common types are illustrated in Figure 3–15 (parts 1–2). They are (1) the source listing and (2) the diagnostic listing. Figure 3–15 illustrates the output from our Prime compiler, but the output from any COBOL compiler will be basically the same.

The *source listing* is shown in parts 1–2 of Figure 3–15. This is primarily a listing of the source program. On the far left of the listing is a column of statement numbers generated by the compiler. There is one number for each program line. This is typical of most compilers, but some may follow different

```
IDENTIFICATION DIVISION.
PROGRAM-ID.    PRODUCE-REORDER-LISTING.
ENVIRONMENT DIVISION.
CONFIGURATION SECTION.
SOURCE-COMPUTER.    PRIME 850.
OBJECT-COMPUTER.    PRIME 850.
INPUT-OUTPUT SECTION.
FILE-CONTROL.
    SELECT INVENTORY-STATUS-FILE
        ASSIGN TO PFMS.
    SELECT REORDER-LISTING
        ASSIGN TO PFMS.
DATA DIVISION.
FILE SECTION.
FD  INVENTORY-STATUS-FILE
    LABEL RECORDS ARE STANDARD
    RECORD CONTAINS 80 CHARACTERS.
01  INVENTORY-STATUS-RECORD.
    05  IS-ITEM-NO          PIC 9(5).
    05  IS-ITEM-DESC        PIC X(20).
    05  FILLER              PIC X(5).
    05  IS-UNIT-PRICE       PIC 999V99.
    05  IS-REORDER-POINT    PIC 9(5).
    05  IS-QTY-ON-HAND      PIC 9(5).
    05  IS-QTY-ON-ORDER     PIC 9(5).
    05  FILLER              PIC X(30).
FD  REORDER-LISTING
    LABEL RECORDS ARE STANDARD
    RECORD CONTAINS 132 CHARACTERS.
01  REORDER-LINE.
    05  RL-ITEM-NUMBER      PIC X(5).
    05  FILLER              PIC X(5).
    05  RL-ITEM-DESC        PIC X(20).
    05  FILLER              PIC X(5).
    05  RL-UNIT-PRICE       PIC ZZZ.99.
    05  FILLER              PIC X(5).
    05  RL-AVAILABLE-STOCK  PIC Z(5).
    05  FILLER              PIC X(5).
    05  RL-REORDER-POINT    PIC Z(5)
    05  FILLER              PIC X(71).
WORKING-STORAGE SECTION.
01  SWITCHES.
    05  INVENTORY-EOF-SW    PIC X.
01  WORK-FIELDS.
    05  AVAILABLE-STOCK     PIC 9(5).
PROCEDURE DIVISION.
000-PRODUCE-REORDER-LISTING.
    OPEN INPUT  INVENTORY-STATUS-FILE
         OUTPUT REORDER-LISTING.
    MOVE 'N'                        TO INVENTORY-EOF-SW.
    PERFORM 100-PRODUCE-REORDER-LINE
        UNTIL INVENTORY-EOF-SW EQUAL 'Y'.
    CLOSE INVENTORY-STATUS-FILE.
          REORDER-LISTING.
    STOP RUN.
100-PRODUCE-REORDER-LINE.
    PERFORM 110-READ-INVENTORY-RECORD.
    IF INVENTORY-EOF-SW  EQUAL 'N'
        PERFORM 120-CALCULATE-AVAILABLE-STOCK
        IF AVAILABLE-STOCK LESS THAN IS-REORDER-POINT
            PERFORM 130-PRINT-REORDER-LINE.
110-READ-INVENTORY-RECORD.
    READ-INVENTORY-STATUS-FILE
        AT END
            MOVE 'Y'                TO INVENTORY-EOF-SW.
120-CALCULATE-AVAILABLE-STOCK.
```

Figure 3–15
Source listing (part 1 of 2)

```
(0067)           ADD IS-QTY-ON-HAND IS-QTY-ON-ORDER
(0068)               GIVING AVAILABLE-STOCK.
(0069)       130-PRINT-REORDER-LINE
(0070)           MOVE SPACES                TO REORDER-LINE.
(0071)           MOVE IS-ITEM-NO            TO RL-ITEM-NO.
(0072)           MOVE IS-ITEM-DESC          TO RL-ITEM-DESC.
(0073)           MOVE IS-UNIT-PRICE         TO RL-UNIT-PRICE.
(0074)           MOVE AVAILABLE-STOCK       TO RL-AVAILABLE-STOCK.
(0075)           MOVE IS-REORDER-POINT      TO RL-REORDER-POINT.
(0076)           WRITE REORDER-LINE.

 0040  /W/ PERIOD ASSUMED ABOVE.
 0054  UNRECOGNIZABLE ELEMENT IS IGNORED. [REORDER-LISTING   ]
 0063  UNRECOGNIZABLE ELEMENT IS IGNORED. [READ-INVENTORY-STATUS-FILE  ]
 0064  UNRECOGNIZABLE ELEMENT IS IGNORED. [AT  ]
 0064  UNRECOGNIZABLE ELEMENT IS IGNORED. [END   ]
 0070  PERIOD ASSUMED AFTER PROCEDURE-NAME DEFINITION.
 0071  UNRECOGNIZABLE ELEMENT IS IGNORED. [RL-ITEM-NO  ]
 0000  /W/ INCONSISTENT READ USAGE. [INVENTORY-STATUS-FILE   ]
 0001  /W/ FILE NEVER CLOSED. [REORDER-LISTING   ]

 P R O G R A M    S T A T I S T I C S

 Executable Code Size: 225 Words.
 Constant Pool Size: 22 Words.
 Total Pure Procedure Size: 247 Words.

 Working-Storage Size: 8 Bytes.
 Total Linkframe Size: 388 Words.

 Stack Size: 16 Words.

 Trace Mode: Off.

 No Arguments Expected.

 76 Source Lines.

 6 Errors, 3 Warnings, Prime V-Mode COBOL, Rev 19.1 <PRODUC>
```

Figure 3–15
Source Listing (part 2 of 2)

rules, such as generating a line number only for those lines that contain COBOL verbs. In Figure 3–15 each source statement of the program can be referred to by a statement number from 1 through 76.

Most compilers check the sequence of the line numbers that are coded into the source program. If any numbers are out of sequence a designator such as an S is printed next to the line number to indicate to the programmer that an out of sequence condition exists. With the move away from coding forms and the use of on-line libraries to hold source code, there is a corresponding move away from the use of line numbers in the source program. The need for line numbers was clearer when source code was punched into cards—which could easily get out of order. The line numbers helped maintain the order. The programs in this book will not use coded line numbers since they were done in an interactive environment using libraries to hold the source code.

The last part of the compiler output is the *diagnostic listing.* The compiler used provides two items of information: (1) the source code line number to which the error can be connected, and (2) the *diagnostic message* itself. Some compilers will also give message numbers that can be used to reference the manufacturer's COBOL reference manual for more detailed explanations of the error if required. The majority of COBOL compilers provide self-explanatory diagnostics, and if you study the messages carefully, you should seldom need to refer to the manual.

Many compilers also print the level of severity of the diagnostic. A W category of severity indicator is a warning that something of minor consequence has been detected and may cause the program trouble, but the detected error will not cause the compilation to be cancelled. A D type severity indicator means that a disastrous error has occurred and will cause the compile to be cancelled after all of the program has been examined for errors. Different compilers have varying methods of indicating whether the error is minor or disastrous to the continuation of the compile process, but you will quickly adapt to your compiler.

Correcting Diagnostics

To correct diagnostics, you should normally take them in sequence and correct each statement as needed. If you come to a message you can't figure out, skip over it since one of the later diagnostics may indicate its cause. After going through all the diagnostics, if there are still a few you can't figure out, you might try recompiling the program with all other errors corrected. Sometimes, this will solve your problem because the problem diagnostics are caused by errors you have already corrected. However, it is recommended that you do not jump to this stage too quickly. Most of the time you will be able to determine whether the current error was caused by a prior one if you give the diagnostics careful and thoughtful study.

Figure 3–15 is the reorder-listing program as it may have been compiled on an early trial. It contains syntax errors, and the compiler has listed the diagnostic messages that tell about those errors. The following discussion will introduce you to correcting compile time errors.

To correct the syntax errors in Figure 3–15, look at the first diagnostic listed on the diagnostic messages page (part 3). The first diagnostic is the one with the number 0040 in the left column. The /W/ is a severity designator indicating a warning. The message is that a period has been left out in the preceding line and that the compiler will assume the presence of one for this compile. You should fix these minor errors unless there is some overriding reason not to do so. To fix this error, look at the line preceding line 40 in part 1 (line 39). That is what the number in the left column of the diagnostic page does—it tells the line number where the error was recognized. Line 39 reads:

```
05  RL-REORDER-POINT      PICTURE IS Z(5)
```

Notice that there is no period after the PICTURE clause—that was the cause of the diagnostic. So to fix the problem, simply place a period after the PICTURE clause:

```
05  RL-REORDER-POINT      PICTURE IS Z(5).
```

Now work on the next diagnostic. It points to line 54, says that an element is unrecognizable, will be ignored, and in the brackets gives a data-name which is the unrecognized element. Look at line 54. It is the file name REORDER–LISTING by itself. Given its position in the program, you might expect that it needs a CLOSE statement to precede it, and you would be right. There are two solutions here: (1) change line 54 to read:

```
CLOSE REORDER-LISTING.
```

or (2) remove the period terminating line 53 which will cause the CLOSE statement on line 53 to control (CLOSE) succeeding file names, such as the one on line 54. This is a facility of many COBOL commands that has not been discussed yet. This facility of one verb to have several objects is called statements in a series, and is discussed thoroughly in chapter 4.

The third diagnostic refers to line 63 and is another unrecognizable element. The offending element is shown to be READ–INVENTORY–STATUS–FILE. The problem here is the hyphen between the verb, READ, and the file name, INVENTORY–STATUS–FILE. The solution is to remove the hyphen so that the statement reads: READ INVENTORY–STATUS–FILE. The misplacement of hyphens is a typical mistake of the novice programmer. Another common error is to leave out required hyphens in required places such as paragraph names.

The fourth and fifth errors both point to elements on line 64 which are parts of a valid READ command. However, due to the hyphen problem, the compiler could not recognize a valid READ and so the AT and the END seemed to be out of place to the compiler. These two diagnostics are examples of diagnostics that will automatically disappear when a prior error is fixed. Some compilers are less sophisticated than others and, after an error is identified, will list all succeeding words in a sentence as being unrecognizable. If you have this type of compiler, you will soon learn when to ignore those succeeding errors.

The sixth diagnostic points to line 70 and indicates another omitted period, but one that should follow a paragraph name. When you examine line 70 you will see that it is not a paragraph name, but you should also observe that line 69, just above, is a paragraph name and has no period following it. The solution is to enter a period after the paragraph name in line 69. This diagnostic is an example of the type where the error is not discovered until the compiler begins to examine succeeding statements. When that happens, most compilers emit a diagnostic message that references a line other than the one on which the error actually occurred. When you have this type of diagnostic, you must get in the habit of looking at the parts of the program that are close to the line referenced.

Diagnostic seven points to line 71 and references RL–ITEM–NO as the unrecognized element. When you examine line 71 there will appear to be nothing wrong with it. In fact there is nothing wrong with the line as it stands. However, when a data name is involved, you need to look back to the data division where the data element was defined to determine if the spellings match. Line 31 in the output record description has the element named RL–ITEM–NUMBER. Now you have a choice, correct the data division statement or the procedure division statement. Look back at line 19 in the input. It uses the abbreviation NO for number, as does the procedure division statement. As you gain experience, you will suspect that the intention was to use NO rather than spell out NUMBER, because one of our style guidelines will be to achieve consistency with data names. Such consistency will be accomplished by making the input and the output data names exactly the same except for the prefixes. In this situation line 31 in the data divison should be changed to read RL–ITEM–NO. Be careful with always changing the data division name, however. In longer programs you may find that the data name is used several times in the procedure division and that to change the data name will result in errors for all of the other statements in the procedure division which referenced that data element.

The eighth diagnostic references line zero, and is a warning. It is saying that the file named INVENTORY–STATUS–FILE has inconsistent read usage. Think back to the third diagnostic. Now you should be able to see that the program as written had no valid read for that file, hence the diagnostic. This is another that will disappear when the third error is fixed.

The final diagnostic is another warning. It is related to the second error and will disappear when that error is fixed.

The rest of the information on the page is a set of program statistics provided by the individual compiler. The statistics will vary with compilers and operating systems, but most will provide similar information. The information presented on the last two lines is fairly common and, as you can see, tells the number of source lines in the program and the number of errors and warning messages. Of course, the most important information for the programmer is the diagnostic messages themselves.

Syntax Errors to Avoid

Here are some syntax errors that novice programmers are prone to make. Study the list and use it in conjunction with the process suggested in the discussion on desk checking.

Nonunique data names: Two different fields have been assigned the same data name, such as using ITEM–NUMBER for both the input field and the output field.

COBOL reserved word as a data name: Since COBOL has about 300 reserved words, it is easy to use one of them for a data name. Data names such as CODE, COUNT, DATE, ERROR, and OUTPUT are examples of such words. To avoid the problem the easiest technique is to use two words connected by a hyphen for any data name. To decide which two words to use, pick one that defines the use of the field, such as COUNT, and one that answers the question "of what?" as in "count of what?" Thus, data names that use reserved words but cause no problems would be RECORD–COUNT, BIRTH–DATE, and ERROR–MESSAGE.

Spelling problems: Be careful how you spell the COBOL reserved words. The compiler can only deal with what was actually presented, not with what you intended. Also watch out for consistent spelling of programmer-supplied data names. It is easy to name a field ACCOUNTS–PAYABLE in the data division, and then refer to it as ACCOUNT–PAYABLE in the procedure division.

Omitting or inserting hyphens: Remember that DATA DIVISION does not use a hyphen, but FILE–CONTROL does. The data name IR–ITEM–NUMBER will not be recognized when referred to as IR–ITEM NUMBER in a procedure statement. Also note that the command READ PAYROLL–FILE becomes an error when coded as READ–PAYROLL–FILE.

Code entered in the wrong columns: Remember to observe margins A and B on the coding line. Margin A begins in position 8, and margin B begins in position 12. This is easy to overlook when using a terminal and not using line numbers. Also remember that any code beyond position 72 will be treated as comments, and even though the code appears on the list, the compiler will not consider it to be part of the program.

Invalid numeric picture: If a data name is used in a arithmetic command it must be defined as a numeric field, and the picture clause may only use the symbols 9, S (for sign), and V.

Receiving field too small: The field that is the object of a MOVE statement or the GIVING in an arithmetic command must be large enough to contain what is being sent to it. A sending field of length X(5) must have a receiving field of at least the same size. A common error is not counting the periods and commas in a numeric edited picture, so that a field of 9(5) is incorrectly moved to a field with picture Z,ZZZ. The error is that there must be a Z for each 9, or a picture of ZZ,ZZZ. Most compilers generate warning diagnostics, but since they are warnings they are easy to overlook and then the output gets truncated.

Record contains and FD conflict: The RECORD CONTAINS should always be used as it provides an automatic check on the correct record description count. If the record size computed by the compiler does not agree with that stated in the RECORD CONTAINS clause, a diagnostic will be generated. The diagnostic can also result from other errors, namely those that cause an entry to be ignored and thus throw the count off. In some compilers this diagnostic is often the last one to disappear before obtaining a clean compile.

Omitted periods: Every COBOL sentence must end with a period. When they are omitted in the data division, the compiler may simply warn that a period is missing in an expected place and will put one in for that compile. The compiler may do the same at certain places in compiling the procedure division. However, the primary cause of logical grief for programmers is the omitted period in procedural statements, especially when IF statements are involved. The only remedy is careful program design and careful checking.

Discussion

You have been given a short introduction to error detection that concentrates on the syntax error. The syntax error, of course, will be the very first error you will have to deal with unless you are unlucky enough to write a program that runs the first time. No, that is not a misprint. One of the intriguing aspects of programming is that those who make a reasonable number of errors and are able to figure out how to fix them in a reasonable amount of time seem to be those who learn the most about the language. So don't be afraid of making errors, but try to look on them as a valuable part of the learning process.

Chapter 5 will cover program testing in more depth, and will present testing techniques which will ease the testing process. However, it is believed that this presentation at this point is helpful as you are now ready to begin coding and testing your first program.

Problem

Rather than provide a book problem at this point, it is suggested that you begin to code the first assignment and spend some time discussing the various syntax errors which you will have generated.

Chapter 4 Completing the COBOL Core

In chapter 3 you were introduced to the basic structure for the COBOL programming language. In this chapter you will build on that base by learning some additional COBOL elements. The first topic presents many elements that are necessary to broaden your COBOL knowledge. The second topic presents an introduction to two advanced COBOL facilities. The first is the use of condition names, which is a very useful facet of COBOL. The second is the COPY facility, and it may be bypassed if you are not going to use the several predefined input record descriptions that are provided by your instructor. The COPY discussion presents enough information to be able to copy the predefined data descriptions. The third topic presents some techniques that provide alternatives to the programming style presented in the text.

This also seems an appropriate time for a little pep talk. Writing programs in any language is a skill that requires a considerable time investment to develop. For the novice, COBOL probably requires more careful thought and continuous effort than most. Thus, you are encouraged to recognize the time investment and positive attitude that are required, and to remember that the key ingredient to building any skill is practice. When an assignment is made, start on it immediately and persevere, and you will be surprised at what you will have learned by the end of the course.

Topic 1 Completing the Basic Subset

Orientation

Chapter 3 presented a program with a simple output format. There were no headings and no spacing complications. This, of course, is not the normal output format, but was used as a starting point. Now you are ready for a more challenging output. The first part of this topic will present the enhanced statements needed to write a program with headings and variable spacings. After that, new data division and procedure division elements will be discussed. The topic will end with an explanation of how to read general COBOL language formats and with a presentation of a refined version of the reorder list program.

Terminology

alphanumeric literal	forms overflow	numeric literal
comment	group item	numeric-edited item
comment line	implementor name	stroke
editing	mnemonic name	
elementary item	non-numeric literal	

Objectives

1. ***Given a programming problem and a structure chart for its solution, code a program solution in COBOL. The proper program solution will require several of the functions described in this chapter.***

Enhancement Facilities in COBOL

Comment lines

Under the ANS 74 standards, a programmer may use *comments* in a program to explain or give extra information about a certain segment of code. A *comment* line has an asterisk in column 7 and a comment or note written by the programmer in the remaining columns. During compilation, the contents of comments are printed, but otherwise the lines are ignored. Thus, they can be placed in a program without affecting the resulting object code.

Because a structured COBOL program is relatively easy to follow by virtue of its structure alone, it rarely requires any comments at all. In general, then, you should only use comments when they actually contribute to the clarity of the program. Don't use them to document or restate something that is made clear by the code itself.

Blank comment lines

In contrast to comment lines with notes entered in them, blank comments should be used regularly to help make your program listings easier to follow. A blank comment also has an asterisk in column 7, but nothing is entered in the rest of the line. Using blank comment lines before the logical breaks in your programs will space your program listings and make them more readable. In general, you should use blank comment cards before division names, section names, paragraph names, FD items and 01-level items, as shown in Figure 4-1. As you go through this book you will see many examples showing the use of blank comment lines.

If your compiler doesn't provide for comment lines with an asterisk in column 7, you can use completely blank lines, with nothing written in them, to space your output listings. The only drawback here is that the COBOL compiler has to search a blank line column-by-column to make sure that it

```
 IDENTIFICATION DIVISION.
      .
      .
*
 ENVIRONMENT DIVISION.
      .
      .
*
 DATA DIVISION.
*
 FILE SECTION.
*
 FD   .
      .
*
 01   .
      .
      .
*
 PROCEDURE DIVISION.
*
 000-PRODUCE-REORDER-LISTING.
      .
      .
```

Figure 4–1
Using blank comment lines to space the source listing

doesn't contain any source code. In contrast, once the compiler encounters an asterisk in column 7, it knows it can ignore the rest of the lines. So for efficiency's sake, only use blank lines if your system doesn't allow you to use blank comment lines.

Spacing the printed output form

In many applications, the vertical spacing of a printed form must be varied. For example, when printing an invoice, the customer name and address are printed, several lines are skipped to the body of the form where one or more body lines are printed, several more lines are skipped, and the total line is printed, and then the form is skipped to the heading of the next invoice. In COBOL, this skipping is generally done by using the following formats of the WRITE statement:

```
1.  WRITE record-name
         AFTER ADVANCING integer LINES.
2.  WRITE record-name
         AFTER ADVANCING data-name LINES.
3.  WRITE record-name
         AFTER ADVANCING mnemonic-name.
```

In the first format, the integer must be a positive number. (An integer is simply a whole number.) When the statement is executed, the form in the printer moves up as many lines as indicated before the output record is printed. Depending on the compiler used, there may be limits on how large the interger may be. Be sure to check what the maximum-sized integer allowed by your computer is. Some computers allow only 1, 2, or 3 to be used, and some allow it to be as large as 100.

In the second format, the WRITE statement uses the name of a data element described in the Working-Storage of the Data Division. Spacing of the form depends on the value of the field at the time the WRITE statement is executed.

For example,

```
WRTTE PAYROLL-RECORD
    AFTER ADVANCING SPACE-CONTROL LINES
```

causes triple spacing if SPACE–CONTROL contains a 3 at the time of execution. The field must always contain a positive integer, with its maximum value limited by the compiler being used.

The third form of the AFTER ADVANCING clause provides for skipping to various places that are preassigned in the carriage control facility of the printer. Some printers use punches in a carriage-control tape. There are normally about a dozen positions available for assignment in the carriage-control facility. These positions are typically called channels and are numbered C01 through C12. The most common predefined position is at the top of the page and can vary depending on the length of the paper being used. This top-of-page position is usually given the number C01. The position at the bottom of the page is often indicated by C12. Other positions will vary depending on the individual application, but most will be used in conjunction with a special form that is used for the application (refer to Figure 1-2 for an example).

When it is used, *mnemonic names* are assigned to specific carriage-control positions in the Configuration Section of the Environment Division. For example, as mentioned, a channel 1 (CO1) is typically used to locate the top of the next page when standard forms are used. The following Special–Names assignment may be used on several computer systems to give the mnemonic name PAGE–TOP to the channel 1 position:

```
ENVIRONMENT DIVISION.
CONFIGURATION SECTION.
SPECIAL-NAMES.
    C01 IS PAGE-TOP.
```

As you can see, a paragraph named SPECIAL–NAMES is required. PAGE–TOP conforms to the rules for forming mnemonic names, which are the same as those for data names.

The Special–Names assignment is an implementor-dependent function, and different computer systems will often use different wordings to accomplish that assignment. These wordings are called *implementor names* because they are created by the implementor of the compiler being used. The following shows other computer system's versions of the PAGE–TOP assignment:

```
SPECIAL-NAMES.
    1 IS PAGE-TOP.

SPECIAL-NAMES.
    NEXT-PAGE IS PAGE-TOP.
```

When the third format of the WRITE statement is executed, the printer skips to the portion of the printed page that is represented by the mnemonic name. Thus, on all three of the systems just described

```
WRITE PAYROLL-RECORD
    AFTER ADVANCING PAGE-TOP
```

will cause the form to be skipped to the top of the next page before printing.

If you are using an ANS 74 compiler, you may also skip to the top of a page without using a mnemonic name assigned in the SPECIAL–NAMES paragraph. In place of the mnemonic name, you use the reserved word PAGE.

Thus, the following will cause a skip to the top of the next page:

```
WRITE PAYROLL-RECORD
    AFTER ADVANCING PAGE
```

When using the ADVANCING option of the WRITE statement, you should take note that some compilers (especially ANS 1968) require that if AFTER ADVANCING appears in one WRITE statement for a file, it must be used in *all* of the WRITE statements for that file.

Another point to pay attention to is that some compilers (IBM for example) take the first position of the print line for carriage control when the ADVANCING option is used. You should check what your compiler does for carriage control, but if your program has data printing in position 1 of the line and it does not appear when the line is printed, then you probably have such a compiler. The solution to this problem is simply to provide one FILLER byte at the first position of the printer line description. You will see this modeled in the programs in this text.

In general, you will use only formats 2 and 3 of the WRITE AFTER statement to control spacing. Furthermore, you will use format 3 primarily for skipping to the top of a new page. Although some systems allow you to use other carriage-control channels to skip to other lines on a page, you would only use these when you're working with special forms. And even then, the channels wouldn't be required. You could simply keep a count of how many lines it takes to reach a desired line on a form, and then skip that many lines using format 1 or 2 of the WRITE AFTER statement.

Incidentally, the word BEFORE can be used in place of the word AFTER in any of the three formats just described. Then, the printing of the line takes place before the indicated spacing or skipping. In general, however, only one of the words should be used in any one program since mixing them can easily lead to programming errors in which one line is printed over a previously printed line. As a result, it is recommended that you use the AFTER forms in all the programs you write.

Field description in the Data Division

In chapter 3, you were introduced to some basic ways of describing fields in the Data Division of the program. As you will see in this section, there are a number of other clauses that can further define data fields. Before getting to them, though, let's examine how additional level numbers can be used to define fields within fields.

Level numbers

In chapter 3, 01 and 02 level numbers were used in the Data Division to describe the fields within a record. Additional level numbers are used to describe fields within fields—such as month, day, and year fields within the larger data field. To illustrate, consider the accounts receivable record and its associated data descriptions in Figure 4–2. Here, AR–CUST–ID refers to the first 20 record positions, while AR–CUST–NO refers to positions 1–5 and AR–CUST–NAME refers to positions 6–20. Similarly, AR–BAL–FWD refers to positions 58–70, AR–BF–DATE to positions 58–63, and AR–BF–YEAR to positions 62 and 63.

The description of fields within fields creates the need for two more terms to describe the relationship of fields. A field which is not further broken down or subdivided is called an *elementary item* because it is the base or elementary description, and has an attached PICTURE clause. A field which is subdivided, or has subdescriptions, is called a *group item* because it is the

Field Name	Customer ID		Customer Address				Balance Forward		
	Cust No.	Customer Name	Street	City	State	ZIP Code	Mo.	Day	Year
Characteristics	X(5)	X(15)	X(15)	X(15)	X(2)	X(5)	9(2)	X(2)	X(2)
Usage									
Position	1-5	6-20	21-35	36-50	51-52	53-57	58-59	60-61	62-63

Field Name	Balance Fwd Contd. Amount	Unused	
Characteristics	9(5)V99	X(10)	
Usage			
Position	64-70	71-80	

```
01  AR-RECORD.
    05  AR-CUST-ID.
        10  AR-CUST-NO              PICTURE IS 9(5).
        10  AR-CUST-NAME            PICTURE IS X(15).
    05  AR-CUST-ADDRESS.
        10  AR-CUST-STREET          PICTURE IS X(15).
        10  AR-CUST-CITY            PICTURE IS X(15).
        10  AR-CUST-STATE           PICTURE IS X(2).
        10  AR-CUST-ZIP             PICTURE IS 9(5).
    05  AR-BAL-FWD.
        10  AR-BF-DATE.
            15  AR-BF-MONTH         PICTURE IS 9(2).
            15  AR-BF-DAY           PICTURE IS 9(2).
            15  AR-BF-YEAR          PICTURE IS 9(2).
        10  AR-BF-AMOUNT            PICTURE IS 9(5)V99.
    05  FILLER                      PICTURE IS X(10).
```

Figure 4–2
Level numbers

name for a group of descriptions. Group items do not have PICTURE clauses attached to them since the subdescription PICTURE clauses will define the length of the field named by the group item name. Note that the subdescriptions may be all numeric items, all alphanumeric items, or may contain a mix of numeric and alphanumeric pictures. Whatever the mix happens to be, the group item is always considered to be an alphanumeric item and treated as such when used in any COBOL statements such as a MOVE.

Note also that the level numbers used are 01, 05, 10, and 15, not 01, 02, 03, and 04. Although 01, 02, 03, and 04 could be used, leaving a gap between the level numbers makes it easier to further divide a record later. Thus, leaving gaps is a common programming practice.

Depending on your compiler, you can use level numbers from 01 to 10 or from 01 to 49 to describe items. As long as one level number is greater than a preceding level number, it is considered to be part of the larger field. By using a group item such as AR–CUST–ADDRESS as well as elementary items such as AR–CUST–STREET and AR–CUST–ZIP, you can operate on the entire field or any of its parts when writing statements in the Procedure Division.

Signed numbers

So far the issue of positive and negative numbers has not been addressed. The PICTURE clause rules for numeric fields discussed up to now are fine for positive numbers, but COBOL requires that an additional character be added to the PICTURE clause if there is a possibility that the number contained in the field may be negative and that the program is to recognize that fact. In COBOL the character S should be used in the PICTURE clause of any input or working-storage field to indicate the presence of an operational sign. The following are examples:

```
05   SALES-AMOUNT       PICTURE IS S9(4)V99.
05   NET-PAY            PICTURE IS S999V9.
```

The S does not require an extra record position in an input field, and it does not require an extra storage position. Also, it must be the leftmost character of the PICTURE clause. When the PICTURE clause for a numeric field includes the sign indicator, any data which is stored in the field as the result of a MOVE statement or an arithmetic statement will have the appropriate positive or negative sign stored with it. Whenever the sign indicator S is not included as part of the PICTURE clause for a numeric field, then the absolute value of the result of any arithmetic operation will be placed in the field regardless of the sign that the calculation generated. For example, if S is not specified for a field and the field becomes negative as the result of a calculation, the minus sign will be removed. Thus, −200 would be converted to an unsigned 200, which is treated as +200. If removing the sign isn't the intention of the programmer, errors are sure to occur.

In general, you should use an S on all numeric fields in working-storage unless you deliberately intend to remove plus or minus signs that may occur during the execution of the program. This will lead to more efficient object code because additional code is generated by the compiler to ensure that the data in the field is stored as an absolute value (no sign), and such coding is generally unnecessary. As for numeric input fields, you should use S for fields that may carry a sign.

VALUE clauses

Many programs require fields that have a certain starting or constant value. In COBOL, these initial values are given in the Data Division by using VALUE clauses. For example, the following description in the Working-Storage Section of a program gives the field named INTEREST–RATE a value of .005:

```
05   INTEREST-RATE  PICTURE IS V999 VALUE IS .005.
```

A numeric value used in the VALUE clause can have as many digits as are allowed by the compiler as long as the value doesn't exceed the PICTURE size for a field. A value can have a leading plus or minus sign as in +.005 or −32, and it can have a decimal point.

In the example above, .005 is called a *numeric literal*. In general, the numeric literal used in the VALUE clause should be consistent with the PICTURE for the field. That is, it should have the same number of decimal positions; and if the field is signed, the literal should have a sign too. If the VALUE and the PICTURE for the field aren't consistent, diagnostics will occur.

A VALUE clause can also be used to give a non-numeric value to a field in storage. In this case, a *non-numeric* or *alphanumeric literal* is used as in the following:

```
05   IR-TITLE      PICTURE IS X(16)
                   VALUE IS "INVENTORY REPORT".
```

The non-numeric literal is "INVENTORY REPORT" and all characters between the quotation marks (") are stored in the field named IR–TITLE. In other words, IR–TITLE is given an initial value of INVENTORY REPORT.

Because the quotation mark is used to mark the beginning and end of a non-numeric literal, it cannot be used within the literal itself. The word

QUOTE can be used in those instances when a quotation-mark literal value is needed. With the exception of the quotation mark, all other characters can be used in the normal way within a non-numeric literal.

In strict ANS COBOL, the double quotation mark (''), rather than the single quotation mark ('), is used for non-numeric literals. However, the single quotation mark is a common substitute. So check your compiler and find out which you should use.

A VALUE clause can also contain the COBOL words SPACE or ZERO. Thus,

```
05   AMOUNT    PICTURE IS 9(4)  VALUE IS ZERO.
05   BLANKS    PICTURE IS X(10) VALUE IS SPACE.
```

gives a starting value of zero to AMOUNT and a value of spaces to BLANKS.

VALUE clauses are often used for fields whose values might have to be changed from time to time. For example, in a report-printing program, you usually have to determine when you've come to the end of one page of printed output and need to skip to the top of the next page (this is called *forms overflow*). To do this, you can create a working-storage field with an appropriate name—like LINES–ON–PAGE—and assign it a value equal to the maximum number of lines per page. You can then use an IF statement to compare LINES–ON–PAGE with a field that counts the lines as they are printed, as in this example:

```
IF LINE-COUNT IS GREATER THAN LINES-ON-PAGE
```

If the condition is true, your program can skip to a new page. If the number of lines per page ever needs to be adjusted, you can quickly and easily change the value of LINES–ON–PAGE without having to recode any Procedure Division statements.

Another common use of VALUE clauses is to store data that is to be printed as the heading of a report. For example, the COBOL code in the Working–Storage Section of Figure 4–3 would print this heading before processing data:

```
                 INVESTMENT REPORT
      ITEM       UNIT   QUANTITY        DOLLAR
     NUMBER      COST   ON HAND         VALUE
```

USAGE clauses

USAGE clauses are not absolutely necessary in a COBOL program. However, they can significantly affect the efficiency of the object program that is compiled. The USAGE clause allows the programmer to specify the form in which a field of data should be stored. Although it usually isn't necessary for a COBOL programmer to know how data is actually stored, you should know that most computers can store data in more than one form. Normally, data is stored in one way when it is not involved in arithmetic operations and in another way when it is. COBOL refers to these forms as DISPLAY and COMPUTATIONAL.

The DISPLAY form of storage means that there is one character of data in each storage position. This is how storage was described in Chapter 3. In the COMPUTATIONAL form, which applies to numeric fields only, more than one digit of a number is usually stored in a single storage position.

```
       .
       .
 ENVIRONMENT DIVISION.
*
 CONFIGURATION SECTION.
       .
       .
 SPECIAL-NAMES.
     C01 IS PAGE-TOP.
       .
       .
 DATA DIVISION.
 FILE SECTION.
       .
       .
 FD  INVESTMENT-LISTING
     LABEL RECORDS ARE STANDARD
     RECORD CONTAINS 133 CHARACTERS.
*
 01  PRINT-AREA.
     05  FILLER                 PIC X(133).
*
 WORKING-STORAGE SECTION.
       .
       .
 01  REPORT-NAME-LINE.
     05  FILLER                 PIC X(12)      VALUE SPACE.
     05  FILLER                 PIC X(11)      VALUE 'INVESTMENT'.
     05  FILLER                 PIC X(110)     VALUE 'REPORT'.
*
 01  COL-HD-LINE-1.
     05  FILLER                 PIC X(12)      VALUE '  ITEM '.
     05  FILLER                 PIC X(7)       VALUE 'UNIT'.
     05  FILLER                 PIC X(15)      VALUE 'QUANTITY'.
     05  FILLER                 PIC X(98)      VALUE 'DOLLAR'.
*
 01  COL-HD-LINE-2.
     05  FILLER                 PIC X(12)      VALUE ' NUMBER'.
     05  FILLER                 PIC X(22)      VALUE 'COST   ON HAND'.
     05  FILLER                 PIC X(98)      VALUE 'VALUE'.
       .
       .
 PROCEDURE DIVISION
       .
       .
 140-PRINT-HEADING-LINES.
     MOVE REPORT-NAME-LINE       TO PRINT-AREA.
     PERFORM 160-WRITE-PAGE-TOP-LINE.
     MOVE COL-HD-LINE-1          TO PRINT-AREA.
     MOVE 2                      TO SPACE-CONTROL.
     PERFORM 150-WRITE-REPORT-LINE.
     MOVE COL-HD-LINE-2          TO PRINT-AREA.
     PERFORM 150-WRITE-REPORT-LINE.
     MOVE 2                      TO SPACE-CONTROL.
*
 150-WRITE-REPORT-LINE.
     WRITE PRINT-AREA
         AFTER ADVANCING SPACE-CONTROL.
     ADD SPACE-CONTROL           TO LINE-COUNT
     MOVE 1                      TO SPACE-CONTROL.
*
 160-WRITE-PAGE-TOP-LINE.
     WRITE PRINT-AREA
         AFTER ADVANCING PAGE.
     MOVE 1                      TO LINE-COUNT.
```

Figure 4–3
Printing report headings—
Environment and Data Divisions

The two standard forms of the USAGE clause are as follows:

```
USAGE IS DISPLAY
USAGE IS COMPUTATIONAL
```

The USAGE clause is one of the clauses that can come after a data name, as in these examples:

```
1.  05    FIELD-A  USAGE IS COMPUTATIONAL
                   PICTURE IS S9(3)V99.
2.  05    FIELD-B  PICTURE IS S9(4)  VALUE IS +1244
                   USAGE IS COMPUTATIONAL.
3.  05    FIELD-C  PICTURE IS 9(5)   USAGE IS DISPLAY.
```

Notice that the sequence of PICTURE, VALUE, and USAGE clauses is not significant. However, to keep your programs clear and readable, you should align similar clauses whenever possible.

When the data from a field of one usage is moved to a field of another usage, it is converted to the form of the receiving field. As a result, the data in a field can be converted from one form to another by using the MOVE statement. However, other statements can lead to data conversion, too, and this can result in an inefficient object program. For example, all arithmetic takes place in the computational form of storage, whether it is specified in a USAGE clause or not. So when arithmetic operations are performed on DISPLAY fields, the data in the fields must be converted to the computational form before the arithmetic can take place. Then, after the fields have been operated upon, they must be converted back to their original usage (DISPLAY) before the program can continue. Assigning the fields the proper usage (in this case, COMPUTATIONAL) in the Data Division would save all this data conversion and lead to a more efficient object program.

When should you use each of the USAGE forms? In the Working-Storage Section, you should use COMPUTATIONAL for all numeric fields that are going to be involved in arithmetic operations or numeric comparisons (IF statements). You should use DISPLAY for all other fields in working storage. And you *must* use DISPLAY for all fields coming from or going to devices external to the system—such as card, terminal, or printer—whether they are operated on arithmetically or not. However, if you omit the USAGE clause entirely, USAGE IS DISPLAY will be assumed by the compiler. So most programmers don't bother to code the DISPLAY form of the USAGE clause. As a result, USAGE IS DISPLAY is never used in the programs in this book. Since there are no USAGE clauses in the program in Figure 3–4, all of the fields have DISPLAY usage.

COMPUTATIONAL is a binary mode of storage. Another mode of storage, called COMPUTATIONAL-3 (which is more appropriate for decimal numbers), is often available. Even though the current ANS standard does not call for COMPUTATIONAL-3 usage, many compilers utilize it and the ANSI will include it in the new 198X standard. The programs in this text will specify COMPUTATIONAL-3 usage for storage of numeric fields (except for subscripts, which are discussed in a later chapter).

Group	Sending field		Receiving field	
	PICTURE	Data	PICTURE	Edited result
1 Basic editing	S999V99	12345	ZZZ.99	123.45
	S999V99	00123	ZZZ.99	1.23
	S999V99	-00123	ZZZ.99	1.23
2 Comma insertion	S9(4)V99	142090	Z,ZZZ.99	1,420.90
	S9(4)V99	001242	Z,ZZZ.99	12.42
	S9(4)V99	000009	Z,ZZZ.99	.09
3 Credit symbol	S9(6)	001234	ZZZ,ZZZCR	1,234
	S9(6)	-001234	ZZZ,ZZZCR	1,234CR
	S9(4)V99	-001234	Z,ZZZ.99CR	12.34CR
4 Fixed dollar sign	S9(6)	001234	$ZZZ,ZZZ	$ 1,234
	S9(4)V99	123456	$ZZZZ.99	$1234.56
	S9(4)V99	000012	$ZZZZ.99	$ .12
5 Floating dollar sign	S9(4)V99	142090	$$,$$$.99	$1,420.90
	S9(4)V99	001242	$$,$$$.99	$12.42
	S9(4)V99	000009	$$,$$$.99	$.09
	S99V99	1234	$$$.99CR	$12.34
	S99V99	-0012	$$$.99CR	$.12CR
6 Asterisk check protection	S9(4)V99	142090	$*,***.99	$1,420.90
	S9(4)V99	001242	$*,***.99	$***12.42
	S9(4)V99	000009	$*,***.99	$*****.09
	S9(4)V99	123456	**,***.99	*1,234.56
7 Floating plus sign	S9(4)V99	142090	++,+++.99	+1,420.90
	S9(4)V99	-142090	++,+++.99	-1,420.90
	S9(4)V99	001242	++,+++.99	+12.42
	S9(4)V99	-001242	++,+++.99	-12.42
	S9(4)V99	000009	++,+++.99	+.09
	S9(4)V99	-000009	++,+++.99	-.09
8 Floating minus sign	S9(4)V99	001242	--,---.99	12.42
	S9(4)V99	-001242	--,---.99	-12.42
	S99V99	1234	---.99	12.34
	S99V99	-1234	---.99	-12.34
9 Insertion character 0	S9(4)	1234	ZZZ,Z00	123,400
	S9(4)	-1234	++,+++.00	-1,234.00
	S9(4)	-0012	ZZZ,Z00CR	1,200CR
	S9(4)	0012	$$,$$$.00	$12.00
10 Insertion character B	S9(4)	-1234	ZZZZBCR	1234 CR
	S9(6)	040339	99B99B99	04 03 39
	S9(6)	001234	ZZZB999	1 234
11 Stroke (ANS 74)	S9(6)	040339	ZZ/99/99	4/03/39
	S9(4)	0775	99/99	07/75

Figure 4–4
Editing numeric fields

The PICTURE clause and editing

When numeric data is moved to a numeric edited item, the data is normally coverted to a more readable form. In group 1 of Figure 4–4, for example, the numbers 12345 and 00123 are converted to 123.45 and 1.23 by using PICTURE clauses consisting of Zs, 9s, and decimal points. This conversion of a numeric item to a more readable form is often referred to as *editing*.

To further refine numeric data, editing characters such as the comma and the CR symbol are used. For example, commas are normally used when printing a field that has four or more digits to the left of the decimal point. This usage is shown in group 2 of Figure 4–4. Since the numbers 001242 and 000009 do not have four or more significant digits to the left of the decimal point, the comma is suppressed along with the insignificant zeros. Otherwise, the comma prints as desired. If a field can have a value in the millions or billions, additional commas may be used as in this example: ZZ,ZZZ,ZZZ,ZZZ.99.

In the examples so far, a negative field moved to a numeric edited item would be stripped of its sign and printed as if it were positive. As shown in group 3, the credit symbol (CR) is used to indicate that a field is negative. When coding the picture of the receiving field, CR is placed to the right of the digits that are to be printed. CR is then printed to the right of the field if the number being edited is negative; if the number is positive, nothing is printed.

Group 4 illustrates the use of a fixed dollar sign. Here, one dollar sign is used as the leftmost character of an editing PICTURE. When data is moved to this numeric edited field, editing takes place as usual with the dollar sign remaining unchanged in the leftmost position of the field.

Group 5 represents the use of the floating dollar sign. Here, the dollar signs replace the Zs that would otherwise be used and one additional dollar sign is placed to the left of the field. Since there are four digit positions (9s) to the left of the decimal point in the first three examples, five dollar signs and one comma are used. When numeric data is moved to a field described with a floating dollar sign, the dollar sign prints just to the left of the first printed digit.

The asterisk (*), illustrated in group 6, is often used when printing checks to make sure that no one changes the amount printed. A fixed dollar sign is normally used at the far left of the field, but it may be omitted. At least one asterisk is used for each digit position to the left of the decimal point. When data with insignificant zeros is moved to a field like this, asterisks replace the zeros, and, if necessary, the commas.

A floating plus (+) or minus (–) sign may be used in place of the CR symbol to indicate whether a field is positive or negative. Groups 7 and 8 give some examples. In either case, the number of signs used in the numeric edited item is one more than the number of digit positions to the left of the decimal point in the sending item. Since there are four digit positions to the left of the decimal point in all of the examples in group 7 and in the first two examples in group 8, five plus or minus signs appear in the PICTURE for each corresponding receiving field. When the plus sign is used (group 7), it prints to the left of the result if the value is positive; a minus sign prints if the value is negative. When the minus sign is used (group 8), nothing prints if the value is positive; the minus sign prints if the value is negative.

Occasionally, a value in storage—such as 12—may represent a larger number—such as 1200 or 12,000. Then, zeros could be added to the field when it is printed. For this purpose, the insertion character 0 (zero) may be used as in group 9. When the value 1234 is moved to a field with a PICTURE of ZZZ,Z00, for example, the result is 123,400. In other words, the 0 is inserted into the result. The zero character may be used in combination with any of the other editing characters and may be placed anywhere in a field.

To insert a blank into a field, the insertion character B may be used as in group 10. Wherever the B appears in the PICTURE, a blank is inserted when the field is printed. Bs may also be used in combination with any of the other editing characters.

Group 11 illustrates the use of the *stroke* (slash) as an insertion character. This edit character is only available on 1974 compilers. It is used for editing date fields.

Although there are other ways in which numeric fields may be edited, those just illustrated satisfy the requirements of most business programs. When coding these PICTUREs, always try to have the same number of decimal places in the sending and the receiving fields—that is, align decimal points.

Otherwise, inefficient object code is likely to result. By the same token, you should try to have as many Zs and 9s in the receiving field as there are 9s in the sending field. When using floating characters, there should be one more $, +, or – than would be used if coding Zs. Incidentally, the USAGE of the sending field doesn't affect the editing that is performed when a numeric item is moved to a numeric edited field.

When you want to edit an alphanumeric field, as opposed to a numeric field, the editing that can be done is limited. In this case, the only valid editing characters are the insertion characters 0 (zero), B (blank), and / (stroke). Editing takes place just as in groups 9, 10, and 11 in Figure 4–4; however, the picture of the sending field is described with Xs and the picture of the receiving field is described with Xs and the insertion characters, as in these examples:

Sending field		*Receiving field*	
PICTURE	Data	PICTURE	Data
X(3)	123	XXX000	123000
X(3)	MRM	XBXBX	M R M
X(6)	123456	XX/XX/XX	12/34/56

Here again, insertion of the stroke (slash) is only available on 1974 compilers.

The BLANK WHEN ZERO clause

If a value of zero is move to a field with this PICTURE:

```
$$,$$$.99BCR
```

$.00 will be printed. Since this printing is usually unnecessary, the BLANK WHEN ZERO clause is often used as follows:

```
05  CR-AMOUNT-OWED    PICTURE IS $$,$$$.99BCR
                      BLANK WHEN ZERO.
```

Here, CR-AMOUNT-OWED is converted to blanks when a value of zero is moved to it.

Procedure Division elements

This section presents some additional statements and coding refinements that will make it easier for you to code certain functions in the Procedure Division.

Literals in the Procedure Division

As you have seen, both numeric and non-numeric literals can be used in VALUE clauses in the Data Division. They can also be used, as shown in the reorder-listing program, in statements in the Procedure Division. The following are some examples:

```
1.  PERFORM 100-PRODUCE-REORDER-LINE
        UNTIL INVENTORY-EOF-SW IS EQUAL TO "Y".
2.  ADD 1.57 TO RESULT-FIELD.
3.  IF SL-ACCOUNT IS GREATER THAN 10000
        PERFORM 150-PRINT-REPORT-LINE.
4.  IF TR-TRAN-CODE IS EQUAL TO "R"
        PERFORM 240-PROCESS-RETURN-RECORD.
```

A literal cannot, however, be used as the receiving field in an arithmetic instruction. For example,

```
ADD RESULT-FIELD TO 1.57
```

would cause a diagnostic.

Statements with items in a series

In many COBOL statements, a series of items can be coded in one statement, as in these examples:

```
1.  OPEN INPUT  BAL-FWD-FILE
         OUTPUT REORDER-LISTING.
```

(Both input and output files are opened in one statement.)

```
2.  ADD HOSPITAL-DEDUCT
        RETIREMENT-DEDUCT
        WITHHOLDING-TAXES
        GIVING EMPL-PAYROLL-DEDUCTS.
```

(Three fields are added together and the result is placed in the fourth field.)

```
3.  MOVE ZERO-QTY        TO BRANCH-TOTAL
                            DIVISION-TOTAL
                            CUSTOMER-TOTAL.
```

(The contents of one field are moved to three fields.)

```
4.  CLOSE BAL-FWD-FILE
          REORDER-LISTING
          NEW-BAL-FILE.
```

(Three files are closed in one statement.)

By using a string of three periods, the format for a statement indicates that a series of data names can be used. For example, the expanded formats of the OPEN and CLOSE statements are:

```
OPEN INPUT file-name ... OUTPUT file-name ...
CLOSE file-name ...
```

ROUNDED and ON SIZE ERROR options for arithmetic statements

For all arithmetic statements, there are two optional clauses that may be used. The first is the ROUNDED clause, which is used as follows:

```
MULTIPLY EMP-HOURS-WORKED BY EMP-HOURLY-RATE
    GIVING NET-PAY ROUNDED.
```

To illustrate how this statement works, suppose EMP–HOURS–WORKED is 40.5, EMP–HOURLY–RATE is 2.25, and NET–PAY is a field with two decimal places. Although the result of the multiplication is 91.125, the statement would round the result to 91.13:

Field name	*PICTURE*	*Value before execution*	*Value after execution*
EMP–HOURS–WORKED	99V9	40.5	40.5
EMP–HOURLY–RATE	99V99	2.25	2.25
NET–PAY	999V99	?????	91.13

Without the ROUNDED option, the third decimal place in the answer would be dropped, and 91.12 would be placed in the NET–PAY field.

You should consider using the ROUNDED option whenever the result of a calculation will have more decimal places than is specified in the PICTURE of the receiving field. However, because of efficiency considerations, you should avoid using it unless you really need a rounded result.

The second arithmetic option is the ON SIZE ERROR option, which is used as follows:

```
MULTIPLY EMP-HOURS-WORKED BY EMP-HOURLY-RATE
    GIVING NET-PAY
    ON SIZE ERROR
        PERFORM 330-PRINT-ERROR-MESSAGE.
```

This means that the program should perform the procedure named 330–PRINT–ERROR–MESSAGE if the result of the calculation has more digits than is specified in the PICTURE of the receiving field. For example, if NET–PAY has a PICTURE of 999V99 and the result of the multiplication is 2125.90, a size error has occurred, and the program will perform the error-message procedure. Without the ON SIZE ERROR clause, the computer would continue to execute the program, but you couldn't be sure of the value in the result field; it would depend on the compiler.

In general, you should avoid using ON SIZE ERROR whenever possible. As you might guess, it affects the efficiency of the object program because a test for size overflow must be made each time a calculation is performed. As a more efficient alternative, I recommend that you check your input fields for valid values before you use them in an arithmetic statement. Then you can be sure the values are small enough that size overflow won't occur.

The REMAINDER clause

High-level ANS COBOL provides for the remainder in a DIVIDE statement to be saved by using the REMAINDER clause. For instance, consider this example:

```
DIVIDE MINUTES-PER-HOUR INTO TIME-IN-MINUTES
    GIVING TIME-IN-HOURS
    REMAINDER MINUTES-REMAINING.
```

When this statement is executed, TIME–IN–HOURS will receive the quotient and MINUTES–REMAINING will receive the remainder.

If the ROUNDED and ON SIZE ERROR clauses are needed, they are used as in this example:

```
DIVIDE MINUTES-PER-HOUR INTO TIME-IN-MINUTES
    GIVING TIME-IN-HOURS ROUNDED
    REMAINDER MINUTES-REMAINING
    ON SIZE ERROR
       PERFORM 330-PRINT-DIVIDE-ERROR.
```

The rounding is done after the remainder has been stored in MINUTES–REMAINING, so MINUTES–REMAINING will still contain the remainder after the statement has been executed. For example, suppose MINUTES–PER–HOUR contains the value 60 and TIME–IN–MINUTES contains the value 156. Then the results of the two DIVIDE statements above will differ as follows:

	Unrounded result	Rounded result
MINUTES–PER–HOUR	60	60
TIME–IN–MINUTES	156	156
TIME–IN–HOURS	2	3
MINUTES–REMAINING	36	36

The DISPLAY statement

The DISPLAY statement can be used for infrequent output within a program. For example, if an END OF JOB message is to be written at the end of a program, the DISPLAY statement, rather than the WRITE statement, can be used.

The format of the DISPLAY statement is as follows:

```
DISPLAY {data-name}
        {literal  }   ...
```

Therefore, the following are examples of valid DISPLAY statements:

```
DISPLAY OUTPUT-DATA.
DISPLAY "END OF JOB".
DISPLAY "RECORD NUMBER " INV-ITEM-NUMBER " IS IN ERROR.".
```

In example 1, the contents of the field named OUTPUT–DATA would be written. In example 2, END OF JOB (a literal) would be written. In example 3—which uses a series of a literal, a data name, and another literal—if the field named INV–ITEM–NUMBER contains 7904, this line would be displayed:

```
RECORD NUMBER 7904 IS IN ERROR.
```

When a numeric field is displayed, it is first converted to DISPLAY usage. If the field has a sign, the rightmost digit of the number will be written as a letter or the equivalent of a digit plus a hexadecimal C or D in the zone position of the EBCDIC code. In other words, the data isn't edited before being displayed. Thus, +184 is written as 18D, where D is the combination of the digit 4 and the zone for the hexidecimal C. A –184 is written as 18M, where M is the combination of the digit 4 and the zone for a hexidecimal D. Of course, if Ss aren't used in the PICTUREs of the fields that are displayed, the fields will not carry signs.

Because the data written by a DISPLAY statement is never considered to be part of a file, the output device doesn't have to be specified in a SELECT statement and an FD description isn't required. However, a DISPLAY statement is executed much more slowly than a WRITE statement. As a result, you should never use the DISPLAY statement for writing more than a few lines within a program.

In general, then, the DISPLAY statement is used to write messages about the operation of a program during its execution. On some systems, these messages will be written on the console typewriter or will appear on the console screen; on others, they will be printed by one of the system's printers; and on others, you can specify which output device you want to use through your job-control language.

When the DISPLAY messages are printed, they are often interspersed with the printer output resulting from the WRITE statement. However, on some larger systems, the messages are printed separately from the normal printer output. In any case, it should always be easy to identify the program that issued the message, and the message should always be understandable. The message form we recommend is this:

$$\texttt{program-name} \quad \left\{\begin{matrix} \texttt{I} \\ \texttt{A} \end{matrix}\right\} \quad \texttt{message-number} \quad \texttt{message}$$

Here, the braces show that you must code either an I or an A as part of the message. An I means the message is only for Information, while an A is used when some outside Action is required to correct the condition causing the message. The message number refers to the numbers given in the instructions for running the program in which a complete description of the message can be found. You will see this format used in programs at the end of this topic.

Punctuation and spacing in your coding

Thus far, the only punctuation marks used in the COBOL examples in this book have been the period, quotation marks, and parentheses. For low-level ANS COBOL, this is all that is allowed. High-level COBOL, however, allows the use of the comma and semicolon in much the same way that they would be used in English. As a result, you might see statements such as these in COBOL programs:

```
ADD FIELD-A, FIELD-B, FIELD-C, GIVING FIELD-D.

READ BALCRD RECORD;
    AT END MOVE "Y" TO CARD-EOF-SWITCH.
```

When the compiler encounters a comma or semicolon, it simply ignores it.

The intent of the comma and semicolon, of course, is to improve the readability of a program. Unfortunately, they do more harm than good. In actual practice, they lead to keying errors and unwanted diagnostics. As a result, it is recommended that the comma and semicolon be avoided, and none of the programs in this book use them.

As for spacing, the only requirement is that COBOL reserved words, names supplied by the programmer, and literals be separated by one or more spaces. As a result, statements can be written on more than one line, as they have been throughout this chapter:

```
1.  MULTIPLY EMP-HOURS BY EMP-HOURLY-RATE
        GIVING GROSS-PAY ROUNDED
        ON SIZE ERROR
            PERFORM 330-PRINT-ERROR-MESSAGE.

2:  05  INTEREST-RATE  PICTURE IS S9V99
                       VALUE IS +4.50
                       USAGE IS COMPUTATIONAL-3.
```

Statements can also be written one after the other as shown here:

```
290-PRINT-REPORT-HEADING.  MOVE-HEADER-LINE TO OUTPUT-LINE.
    WRITE OUTPUT-LINE AFTER ADVANCING TO-PAGE-TOP.  MOVE
    COLUMN-HEADING TO OUTPUT-LINE.  MOVE 2 TO SPACE-CONTROL.
    WRITE OUTPUT-LINE AFTER ADVANCING SPACE-CONTROL LINES.
```

Coding in this way makes it immensely more difficult to read and understand the source code, and thus is not recommended programming practice. In a later chapter when structured style guidelines are presented, you will be told that the recommended practice is to only code one clause per line. Thus, when following that guideline, the above example would read as follows:

```
290-PRINT-REPORT-HEADING.
    MOVE-HEADER-LINE           TO OUTPUT-LINE.
    WRITE OUTPUT-LINE
        AFTER ADVANCING TO-PAGE-TOP.
    MOVE COLUMN-HEADING        TO OUTPUT-LINE.
    MOVE 2                     TO SPACE-CONTROL.
    WRITE OUTPUT-LINE
        AFTER ADVANCING SPACE-CONTROL LINES.
```

The real key to readability in a COBOL program is the proper use of indentation. For instance, the IF statement should be coded with indentation as in Figure 3–11 and 3–12 to show the relationships between the true and false clauses. Similarly, conditional clauses like AT END and ON SIZE ERROR should be indented four spaces from the start of the statements that contain them. In chapter 6, you will be given some specific rules for the use of indentation in the Data and Procedure Divisions. In the meantime, you will use indentation to good advantage if you use the programs shown in this chapter as guides.

COBOL reference formats

So far, this book has used somewhat simplified formats when presenting a new COBOL element. Not all of the variations of a statement or clause have been given, and, as much as possible, the common technical notation has been avoided. In contrast, a COBOL technical manual normally expresses COBOL formats as shown in the samples in Figure 4–5. Here, the following notation is used:

1. All words printed entirely in capital letters (such as DATA DIVISION) are COBOL reserved words.

2. Words that are printed in lowercase letters (such as file-name) represent names or words supplied by the programmer.

3. Braces ({ }) enclosing a stack of items indicate that the programmer must use one of the items. In the PICTURE clause, for example, the programmer can use either PICTURE or the shortened form, PIC.

4. Brackets ([]) are used to indicate that the enclosed item may be used or omitted, depending on the requirements of the program. For example, the ROUNDED clause in the ADD statement is optional.

5. The ellipsis (...) indicates that an element may appear once or any number of times in succession. Thus, a series of fields may be added together in the ADD statement.

6. Underlined reserved words are required unless the element itself is optional, but reserved words that are not underlined are optional. Thus, the LABEL RECORDS clause can be written

```
LABEL RECORDS STANDARD
```

Since this notation is common to all COBOL manuals, it is used in the COBOL chapters that follow.

```
DATA DIVISION.

FILE SECTION.

FD      file-name
        LABEL RECORDS ARE {OMITTED }
                          {STANDARD}

        RECORD CONTAINS integer CHARACTERS.

01-49   {data-name}
        {FILLER   }

        {PICTURE}    IS character-string
        {PIC    }

         BLANK WHEN ZERO

WORKING-STORAGE SECTION.

01-49   {data-name}
        {FILLER   }

        {PICTURE}
        {PIC    }    IS character-string

                   {DISPLAY      }
         USAGE IS  {COMPUTATIONAL}
                   {COMP         }

         VALUE IS literal

         BLANK WHEN ZERO

PROCEDURE DIVISION.
        ADD  {data-name-1}  {data-name-2}   ...
             {literal-1  }  {literal-2  }

             TO data-name-m [ROUNDED]  [data-name-n  [ROUNDED]] ...

             [ON SIZE ERROR imperative-statement]

        CLOSE file-name-1 [file-name-2] ...

        READ file-name RECORD AT END imperative-statement

        WRITE record-name  [{BEFORE}  ADVANCING  {integer LINES  }]
                           [{AFTER }             {data-name LINES}]
                           [                     {mnemonic-name  }]
```

Figure 4–5
Some sample COBOL formats

By studying the formats in Figure 4–5, you can see that a large amount of coding can be eliminated by using shortened forms of words. For example, a COMPUTATIONAL field can be described as follows:

```
05 DATA-FIELD PIC S999V99 VALUE +3.40 COMP.
```

It also reduces coding to eliminate all optional words. However, it is good practice to use the optional words if they add to the sense of a Procedure Division statement because the program is then easier to read. As a result, a WRITE statement is usually written as

```
WRITE record-name
    AFTER ADVANCING SPACE-CONTROL LINES
```

rather than

```
WRITE record-name AFTER SPACE-CONTROL
```

Both are acceptable COBOL, however. In the Data Division, it is common to omit all optional words in PICTURE, VALUE, and USAGE clauses and to use the shortened forms of the words PICTURE (PIC) and COMPUTATIONAL (COMP).

The Refined Reorder-Listing Program

Because it was the first program presented, the reorder-listing program in chapter 3 was much simplified. In actual practice, a program like this would print headings at the top of each page of the report and, at the end of the report, would probably print a count of the number of records processed. This count would be used to verify that all inventory records were processed—that is, no records were missing from the input file. These printing lines are shown on the print chart in Figure 4–6. In addition, a normal end-of-job message should be displayed when the program ends. This message, too, is shown on the print chart.

Notice that a record name has been given to each type of output line on the print chart in Figure 4–6. For instance, the name REPORT–NAME–HDG has been given to the first heading line of the report and the name REORDER–LINE to the body or detail lines of the report. Later on those names will probably be used in the module documentation and COBOL code. This practice is recommended because it relates one form of documentation to another. From now on you will see record names given on all print charts. Incidentally, the last line on the print chart in Figure 4–6 was not given a name as it will be written by a DISPLAY statement.

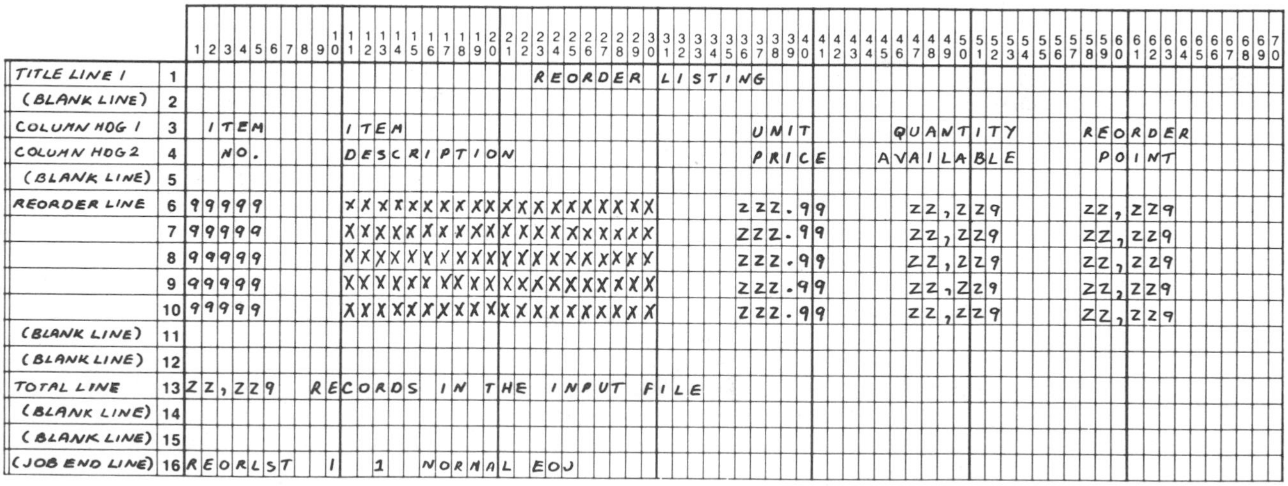
TITLE LINE 1
REORDER LISTING
(BLANK LINE)
COLUMN HDG 1
ITEM
ITEM
UNIT
QUANTITY
REORDER
COLUMN HDG 2
NO.
DESCRIPTION
PRICE
AVAILABLE
POINT
(BLANK LINE)
REORDER LINE
99999
XXXXXXXXXXXXXXXXXXXX
ZZZ.99
ZZ,ZZ9
ZZ,ZZ9
(BLANK LINE)
(BLANK LINE)
TOTAL LINE
ZZ,ZZ9
RECORDS IN THE INPUT FILE
(BLANK LINE)
(BLANK LINE)
(JOB END LINE)
REORLST
I
1
NORMAL EOJ

Figure 4–6
The refined reorder-listing print chart

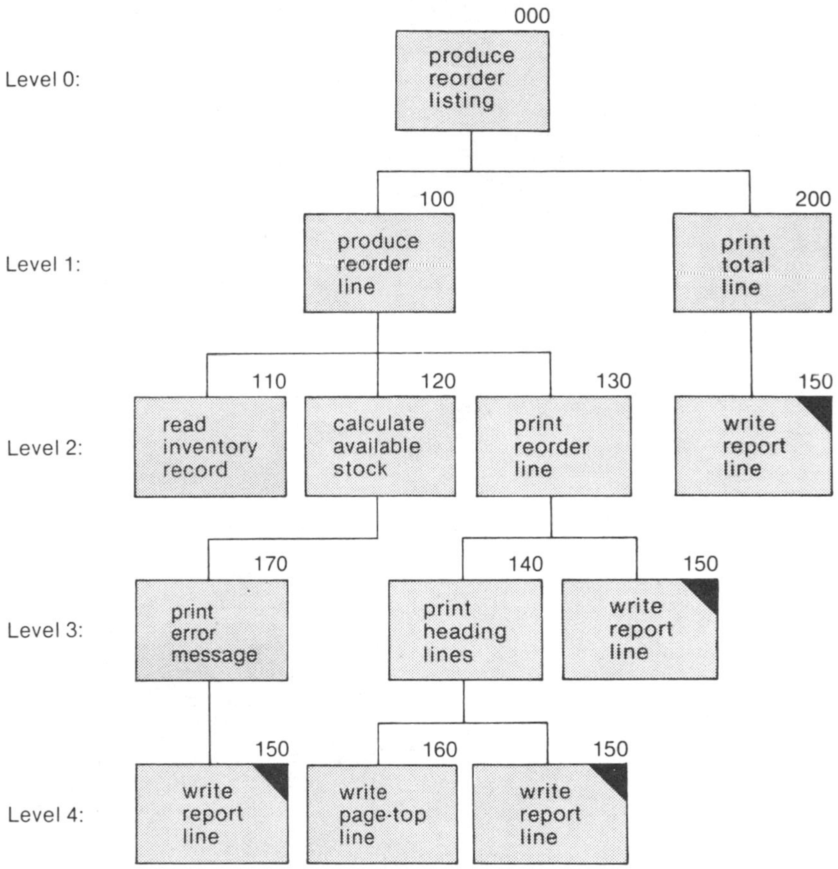
Level 0:
Level 1:
Level 2:
Level 3:
Level 4:
000
produce reorder listing
100
produce reorder line
200
print total line
110
read inventory record
120
calculate available stock
130
print reorder line
150
write report line
170
print error message
140
print heading lines
150
write report line
150
write report line
160
write page-top line
150
write report line

Figure 4–7
Structure chart for the refined reorder-listing program

The structure chart

A structure chart for the refined reorder-listing program is given in Figure 4–7. Here, modules 000, 100, 110, and 120 are the same as in the simplified reorder-listing program. However, since a total line is needed, module 200 is used at level 1 to print the total line after all inventory records have been processed. Similarly, since heading lines are required on this report, module 140 has been added subordinate to module 130. It will be performed by module 130 whenever the heading lines should be printed.

Module 150 is used in three different places in the structure chart. Its function is to write a line on the report whether it be a heading, reorder, or total line. The use of this module makes it possible for only one WRITE statement to be used for writing all but the first line on each page. Since each WRITE statement generates several dozen bytes of object code, using one WRITE statement rather than several can reduce the size of the object program. In this book, a maximum of two WRITE statements will be used for each print file: one for skipping to the top of a page and printing the first heading line (module 160 in Figure 4–7); and one for printing all other report lines (module 150).

To show that module 150 is used in more than one place in the program, the right corner is shaded. You will now see how this module and this structure chart are related to the COBOL coding.

```
 IDENTIFICATION DIVISION.
*
 PROGRAM-ID.    REOLST.
*
 ENVIRONMENT DIVISION.
 CONFIGURATION SECTION.
 SOURCE-COMPUTER.    PRIME 850.
 OBJECT-COMPUTER.    PRIME 850.
 INPUT-OUTPUT SECTION.
*
 FILE-CONTROL.
     SELECT INVENTORY-STATUS-FILE
         ASSIGN TO PFMS.
     SELECT REORDER-LISTING
         ASSIGN TO PFMS.
*
 DATA DIVISION.
 FILE SECTION.
*
 FD  INVENTORY-STATUS-FILE
     LABEL RECORDS ARE STANDARD
     RECORD CONTAINS 80 CHARACTERS.
*
 01  INVENTORY-STATUS-RECORD.
     05  IS-ITEM-NO           PIC 9(5).
     05  IS-ITEM-DESC         PIC X(20).
     05  FILLER               PIC X(5).
     05  IS-UNIT-PRICE        PIC 9(3)V99.
     05  IS-REORDER-POINT     PIC 9(5).
     05  IS-QTY-ON-HAND       PIC 9(5).
     05  IS-QTY-ON-ORDER      PIC 9(5).
     05  FILLER               PIC X(30).
*
 FD  REORDER-LISTING
     LABEL RECORDS ARE STANDARD
     RECORD CONTAINS 133 CHARACTERS.
*
 01  PRINT-AREA.
     05  FILLER               PIC X(133).
*
 WORKING-STORAGE SECTION.
*
 01  SWITCHES.
     05  INVENTORY-EOF-SW     PIC X       VALUE 'N'.
*
 01  WORK-FIELDS.
     05  AVAILABLE-STOCK      PIC S9(5)                 COMP-3.
*
 01  PRINT-CONTROL-FIELDS                               COMP-3.
     05  LINE-COUNT           PIC S99     VALUE +99.
     05  LINES-ON-PAGE        PIC S99     VALUE +57.
     05  SPACE-CONTROL        PIC S9.
*
 01  COUNT-FIELDS                                       COMP-3.
     05  RECORD-COUNT         PIC S9(5)   VALUE ZERO.
*
 01  HEADING-LINE-1.
     05  FILLER               PIC X(24)   VALUE SPACE.
     05  FILLER               PIC X(8)    VALUE 'REORDER'.
     05  FILLER               PIC X(123)  VALUE 'LISTING'.
*
 01  HEADING-LINE-2.
     05  FILLER               PIC X(11)      VALUE ' ITEM'.
     05  FILLER               PIC X(27)      VALUE 'ITEM'.
     05  FILLER               PIC X(8)       VALUE 'UNIT'.
     05  FILLER               PIC X(12)      VALUE 'QUANTITY'.
```

Figure 4–8
The refined-reorder listing program (part 1 of 3)

```
       05  FILLER              PIC X(75)    VALUE 'REORDER'.
*
 01  HEADING-LINE-3.
       05  FILLER              PIC X(14)    VALUE ' NO.'.
       05  FILLER              PIC X(22)    VALUE 'DESCRIPTION'.
       05  FILLER              PIC X(9)     VALUE 'PRICE'.
       05  FILLER              PIC X(12)    VALUE 'AVAILABLE'.
       05  FILLER              PIC X(76)    VALUE 'POINT'.
*
 01  REORDER-LINE.
       05  FILLER              PIC X        VALUE SPACE.
       05  RL-ITEM-NO          PIC X(5).
       05  FILLER              PIC X(5)     VALUE SPACE.
       05  RL-ITEM-DESC        PIC X(20).
       05  FILLER              PIC X(5)     VALUE SPACE.
       05  RL-UNIT-PRICE       PIC ZZZ.99.
       05  FILLER              PIC X(5)     VALUE SPACE.
       05  RL-AVAILABLE-STOCK  PIC Z(5).
       05  FILLER              PIC X(5)     VALUE SPACE.
       05  RL-REORDER-POINT    PIC Z(5).
       05  FILLER              PIC X(71)    VALUE SPACE.
*
 01  TOTAL-LINE.
       05  TL-RECORD-COUNT     PIC ZZ,ZZZ.
       05  FILLER              PIC X(13)    VALUE '  RECORDS IN'.
       05  FILLER              PIC X(4)     VALUE 'THE'.
       05  FILLER              PIC X(110)   VALUE 'INPUT FILE'.
*
 01  ERROR-DESCRIPTION-LINE.
       05  FILLER              PIC X(16)    VALUE ' REORDER  A  2'.
       05  FILLER              PIC X(12)    VALUE 'CALCULATION'.
       05  FILLER              PIC X(15)    VALUE 'ERROR FOR ITEM'.
       05  FILLER              PIC XXX      VALUE 'NO'.
       05  EL-ITEM-NO          PIC X(5).
       05  FILLER              PIC X(9)     VALUE '--RECORD'.
       05  FILLER              PIC X(73)    VALUE 'IGNORED'.
*
 PROCEDURE DIVISION.
*
 000-PRODUCE-REORDER-LISTING.
       OPEN INPUT  INVENTORY-STATUS-FILE
            OUTPUT REORDER-LISTING.
       PERFORM 100-PRODUCE-REORDER-LINE
            UNTIL INVENTORY-EOF-SW EQUAL 'Y'.
       PERFORM 200-PRINT-TOTAL-LINE.
       CLOSE INVENTORY-STATUS-FILE
             REORDER-LISTING.
       DISPLAY 'REORDER  I  1  NORMAL EOJ'.
       STOP RUN.
*
 100-PRODUCE-REORDER-LINE.
       PERFORM 110-READ-INVENTORY-RECORD.
       IF INVENTORY-EOF-SW  EQUAL 'N'
           PERFORM 120-CALCULATE-AVAILABLE-STOCK
           IF AVAILABLE-STOCK LESS THAN IS-REORDER-POINT
               PERFORM 130-PRINT-REORDER-LINE.
*
 110-READ-INVENTORY-RECORD.
       READ INVENTORY-STATUS-FILE
           AT END
               MOVE 'Y'              TO INVENTORY-EOF-SW.
       IF INVENTORY-EOF-SW IS NOT EQUAL TO 'Y'
           ADD 1 TO RECORD-COUNT.
*
 120-CALCULATE-AVAILABLE-STOCK.
```

Figure 4-8
The refined reorder-listing program (part 2 of 3)

```
           ADD IS-QTY-ON-HAND IS-QTY-ON-ORDER
               GIVING AVAILABLE-STOCK
               ON SIZE ERROR
                   PERFORM 170-PRINT-ERROR-MESSAGE
                   MOVE 99999          TO AVAILABLE-STOCK.
      *
       130-PRINT-REORDER-LINE.
           IF LINE-COUNT GREATER THAN LINES-ON-PAGE
               PERFORM 140-PRINT-HEADING-LINES.
           MOVE IS-ITEM-NO             TO RL-ITEM-NO.
           MOVE IS-ITEM-DESC           TO RL-ITEM-DESC.
           MOVE IS-UNIT-PRICE          TO RL-UNIT-PRICE.
           MOVE AVAILABLE-STOCK        TO RL-AVAILABLE-STOCK.
           MOVE IS-REORDER-POINT       TO RL-REORDER-POINT.
           MOVE REORDER-LINE           TO PRINT-AREA.
           PERFORM 150-WRITE-REPORT-LINE.
      *
       140-PRINT-HEADING-LINES.
           MOVE HEADING-LINE-1         TO PRINT-AREA.
           PERFORM 160-WRITE-PAGE-TOP-LINE.
           MOVE HEADING-LINE-2         TO PRINT-AREA.
           MOVE 2                      TO SPACE-CONTROL.
           PERFORM 150-WRITE-REPORT-LINE.
           MOVE HEADING-LINE-3         TO PRINT-AREA.
           PERFORM 150-WRITE-REPORT-LINE.
           MOVE 2                      TO SPACE-CONTROL.
      *
       150-WRITE-REPORT-LINE.
           WRITE PRINT-AREA
               AFTER ADVANCING SPACE-CONTROL.
           ADD SPACE-CONTROL           TO LINE-COUNT
           MOVE 1                      TO SPACE-CONTROL.
      *
       160-WRITE-PAGE-TOP-LINE.
           WRITE PRINT-AREA
               AFTER ADVANCING PAGE.
           MOVE 1                      TO LINE-COUNT
      *
       170-PRINT-ERROR-MESSAGE.
           MOVE IS-ITEM-NO             TO EL-ITEM-NO.
           MOVE ERROR-DESCRIPTION-LINE TO PRINT-AREA.
           PERFORM 150-WRITE-REPORT-LINE.
      *
       200-PRINT-TOTAL-LINE.
           MOVE RECORD-COUNT           TO TL-RECORD-COUNT
           MOVE TOTAL-LINE             TO PRINT-AREA.
           MOVE 3                      TO SPACE-CONTROL.
           PERFORM 150-WRITE-REPORT-LINE.
```

Figure 4–8
The refined reorder-listing program (part 3 of 3)

The program listing

Figure 4–8 is a program listing of the refined reorder-listing program. The program is presented here because it illustrates many of the elements presented in this topic. The following comments summarize some of the main points:

1. Blank comment lines are used to vertically space the listing for improved readability. The vertical spacing helps identify where major program segments begin.

2. In the PROGRAM-ID statement, the program name is only seven characters long. As mentioned in chapter 3, seven or eight characters is the maximum allowed on several operating systems. Although the Prime computer being used allows 30 characters as a maximum, all of the program names that follow will be limited to eight characters since that is more common.

3. Because forms overflow is required by this program, the PAGE option is used with the AFTER ADVANCING in the 160 module. An optional technique that may be necessary on some computers would be to assign a name, such as PAGE–TOP, to channel 1 in the SPECIAL–NAMES paragraph of the Configuration Section. However, if your compiler allows the PAGE option, it is the simplest technique to use.

4. In the Input–Output Section, Prime system names are used in the SELECT statements. To run this program on a different computer, the system names would have to be changed.

5. No fields are defined within the output area for the printer (PRINT–AREA). Instead, all print lines are defined in working storage. As a result, PRINT–AREA is an elementary item and it requires a PICTURE clause.

6. In the Working–Storage Section, the fields that are needed to control the processing done by the program are grouped under four different 01-levels: SWITCHES for the fields that determine the logical flow of the program; WORK–FIELDS for the fields that will contain the results of calculations done by the program; PRINT–CONTROL–FIELDS for the fields that control the printing of the output report; and COUNT–FIELDS for the fields that contain a running tally of certain records in the program. These fields are then followed by the descriptions of the printer output areas. Note that there is a different output area for each line that will be printed on the report.

7. INVENTORY–EOF–SW is set to an initial value of N in working storage rather than in module 000.

8. AVAILABLE–STOCK and RECORD–COUNT are both defined in working storage as signed (S) COMP–3 fields. COMP–3 is the most efficient usage for these fields since they are involved in arithmetic operations in the program.

9. The PRINT–CONTROL–FIELDS in working storage are assigned COMP–3 usage at the 01 (or group) level. Whenever a USAGE clause is given at the group level, it applies to all the elementary items within the group. So LINE–COUNT, LINES–ON–PAGE, and SPACE–CONTROL are all COMP–3 fields.

10. LINES–ON–PAGE, the field that specifies how many lines can be printed on a page of the output report, is given a starting literal value of +57. Later on, if the programmer wants to adjust the number of lines per page, he can simply change the value of this field. Note that the literal has a plus sign, since the PICTURE for the field is signed.

11. Because all print lines are constructed in working storage and all FILLER areas are given a starting value of SPACE, the print area doesn't have to be cleared to spaces before constructing each output line. In other words,

```
MOVE SPACE TO PRINT-AREA
```

isn't needed before moving the working-storage areas to the print area. In your programs from now on all output records should be constructed in working storage.

12. In module 000, one OPEN statement is used to open both files. Also, the DISPLAY statement is used to display an end-of-job (EOJ) message when the program reaches its normal conclusion. Notice that this message is in the form recommended for operational messages (see the writeup on the DISPLAY statement earlier in this topic).

13. Module 100, the module that drives the subordinate modules, is unchanged.

14. In module 110, an ADD statement adds one to RECORD–COUNT for each input record. Note that RECORD–COUNT was given a starting value of zero in working storage, so it will represent the total number of data records read when the program ends.

15. In module 120, the ON SIZE ERROR is used when calculating AVAILABLE–STOCK. If a size error occurs, module 170 is performed which prints a message in the recommended form. After 170 is performed a value of 99999 is moved to AVAILABLE–STOCK. Since AVAILABLE–STOCK then contains a value larger than any value that would be stored in REORDER–POINT, no reorder line will be printed for a record with a size error.

16. Module 130 gives the logic for printing heading and reorder lines. If LINE–COUNT is greater than LINES–ON–PAGE, the heading lines are printed. Then, whether heading lines have been printed or not, a reorder line is formatted and printed and a spacing value of 1 is moved into SPACE–CONTROL. Since LINE–COUNT is given a starting value of +99 and LINES–ON–PAGE has a value of +57, heading lines will be printed before the first reorder line. LINE–COUNT is given a value of +99 so that if LINES–ON–PAGE is ever increased, the logic for printing the heading lines on the first page will still work without changing the initial value of LINE–COUNT.

Note that the first action taken in module 130–PRINT–REORDER–LINE is to test for possible forms overflow. Although this may seem backward, it is the logic that works best, and you should get in the habit of planning all detail print modules like this—to test for forms overflow before doing anything else. In fact, the general hierarchical logic flow of a program can be stated as "test first for the last condition that will happen." If you note the 000 module, you will see that the first test is for the EOJ switch being 'Y' which won't happen until the last record has been read.

17. Module 140 prints the first heading line by performing module 160, which contains one of the two WRITE statements used for the printer file. The second and third heading lines are printed by performing module 150, which contains the second WRITE statement. After each heading line is printed, a spacing value is moved to SPACE–CONTROL.

18. Module 150 contains the primary WRITE statement of the program. It is called by modules 130, 140, and 200. If the program wasn't coded in this fashion, three more WRITE statements would be required. This module also keeps track of the number of lines that have been printed on a page by adding the SPACE–CONTROL value to LINE–COUNT after printing each line.

19. Module 160 prints the first line on each page of the report. It does this by executing a WRITE statement that causes a skip to PAGE–TOP (a channel–1 position in the carriage-control) before printing. After the line is printed, the module resets LINE–COUNT to zero.

20. Module 200 moves the output data to the printer output area and performs module 150. Once again, module 150 causes the output line to be printed.

21. As mentioned in item 15, module 170 moves the on-size-error error message to the output line and prints it. Sometimes this might be done via a DISPLAY statement. However, preferred practice is to create an 01-level working-storage element that documents the contents of the message and to output it via the standard module 150, which writes all lines except the top of the page.

Discussion

If you understand the refined reorder-listing program, you should now be able to begin writing programs of your own. However, you will probably have difficulty in creating proper structure charts. After all, this book has given only superficial treatment to structured design thus far. In chapter 6 structured design and documentation will be covered in detail.

Input record layout:

Field Name	Item No.	Item Description	Unit Cost	Unit Price	Reorder Point	On Hand	On Order	Unused
Characteristics	9(5)	X(20)	999V99	999V99	9(5)	9(5)	9(5)	X(30)
Usage								
Position	1-5	6-25	26-30	31-35	36-40	41-45	46-50	51-80

Print chart:

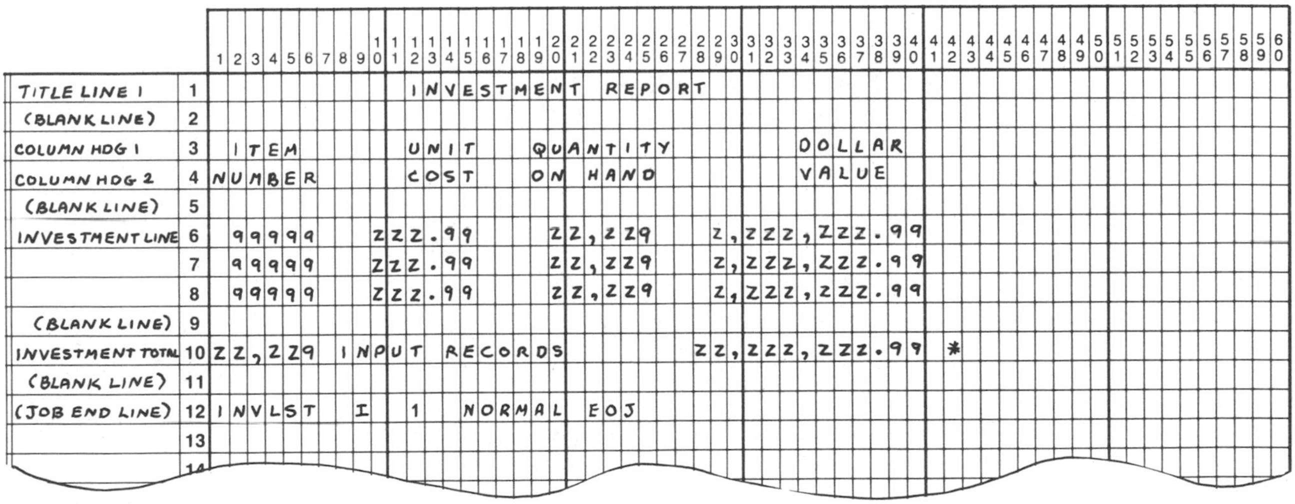
TITLE LINE 1
INVESTMENT REPORT
(BLANK LINE)
COLUMN HDG 1
ITEM
UNIT
QUANTITY
DOLLAR
COLUMN HDG 2
NUMBER
COST
ON HAND
VALUE
(BLANK LINE)
INVESTMENT LINE
99999
ZZZ.99
ZZ,ZZ9
Z,ZZZ,ZZZ.99
(BLANK LINE)
INVESTMENT TOTAL
ZZ,ZZ9
INPUT RECORDS
ZZ,ZZZ,ZZZ.99
*
(BLANK LINE)
(JOB END LINE)
INVLST
I
1
NORMAL
EOJ

Narrative:

1. Amount invested = on-hand × unit-cost.
2. Forms overflow should be provided for and headings should be printed on each overflow page.
3. Do not suppress lead zeros on the item-number field; on other numeric fields, use zero suppression.

Figure 4–9
The investment-listing problem

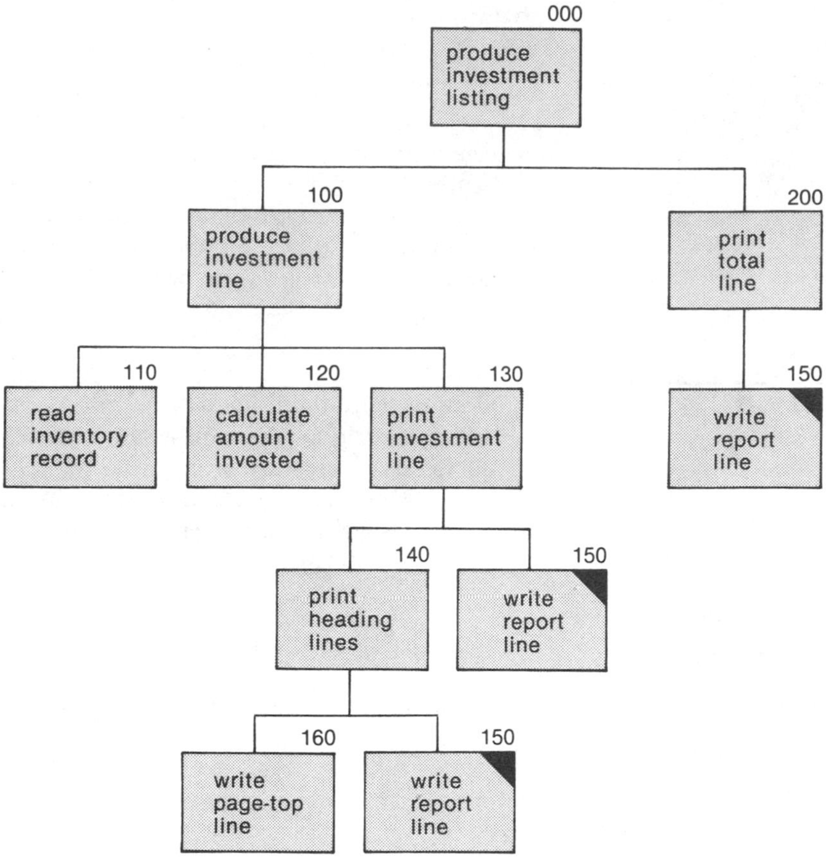
000
produce investment listing
100
produce investment line
200
print total line
110
read inventory record
120
calculate amount invested
130
print investment line
150
write report line
140
print heading lines
150
write report line
160
write page-top line
150
write report line

Figure 4–10
Structure chart for the investment-listing program

Problems

1. Figure 4–9 defines a problem that consists of printing an investment report from a file of inventory records like those used for the reorder-listing program. At the end of the report, a total line consisting of a count of the number of input records and a total of the amounts invested are to be printed. Using the structure chart in Figure 4–10 for this program, code a COBOL solution. You don't have to provide for size errors in the calculations.

2. Figure 4–11 is a listing of a solution for problem 1 above. Suppose there is a request for an extra total line that gives the average amount invested in inventory for each item, using this format:

```
AVERAGE INVESTMENT PER ITEM IS ZZ,ZZ9.99
```

   Code the changes that would have to be made to the original program to cause the new total line to print on the line immediately after the original total line.

```
IDENTIFICATION DIVISION
*
PROGRAM-ID.    INVSLST.
*
ENVIRONMENT DIVISION.
CONFIGURATION SECTION.
SOURCE-COMPUTER.    PRIME 850.
OBJECT-COMPUTER.    PRIME 850.
INPUT-OUTPUT SECTION.
*
FILE-CONTROL.
    SELECT INVENTORY-FILE
        ASSIGN TO PFMS.
    SELECT INVESTMENT-LISTING
        ASSIGN TO PFMS.
*
DATA DIVISION.
*
FILE SECTION.
*
FD  INVENTORY-FILE
    LABEL RECORDS ARE STANDARD
    RECORD CONTAINS 80 CHARACTERS.
*
01  INVENTORY-RECORD.
    05  IR-ITEM-NO          PIC 9(5).
    05  FILLER              PIC X(20).
    05  IR-UNIT-COST        PIC 999V99.
    05  FILLER              PIC X(10).
    05  IR-ON-HAND          PIC 9(5).
    05  FILLER              PIC X(35).
*
FD  INVESTMENT-LISTING
    LABEL RECORDS ARE STANDARD
    RECORD CONTAINS 133 CHARACTERS.
*
01  PRINT-AREA.
    05  FILLER              PIC X(133).
*
WORKING-STORAGE SECTION.
*
01  SWITCHES.
    05  INVENTORY-EOF-SW    PIC X          VALUE 'N'.
        88  LAST-INVENTORY-REC             VALUE 'Y'.
        88  MORE-INVENTORY-RECS            VALUE 'N'.
*
01  WORK-FIELDS                                         COMP-3.
    05  ITEM-INVESTMENT     PIC S9(7)99.
*
01  PRINT-CONTROL-FIELDS                                COMP-3.
    05  LINE-COUNT          PIC S99        VALUE +99.
    05  LINES-ON-PAGE       PIC S99        VALUE +57.
    05  SPACE-CONTROL       PIC S9.
*
01  COUNT-FIELDS                                        COMP-3.
    05  RECORD-COUNT        PIC S9(5)      VALUE ZERO.
*
01  TOTAL-FIELDS                                        COMP-3.
    05  TOTAL-INVESTMENT    PIC S9(7)V99   VALUE ZERO.
*
01  REPORT-NAME-LINE.
    05  FILLER              PIC X(12)      VALUE SPACE.
    05  FILLER              PIC X(11)      VALUE 'INVESTMENT'.
    05  FILLER              PIC X(110)     VALUE 'REPORT'.
*
01  COL-HD-LINE-1.
    05  FILLER              PIC X(12)      VALUE '  ITEM '.
    05  FILLER              PIC X(7)       VALUE 'UNIT'.
```

Figure 4–11
The investment-listing program
(part 1 of 3)

```
    05  FILLER                  PIC X(15)      VALUE 'QUANTITY'.
    05  FILLER                  PIC X(98)      VALUE 'DOLLAR'.
*
01  COL-HD-LINE-2.
    05  FILLER                  PIC X(12)      VALUE ' NUMBER'.
    05  FILLER                  PIC X(22)      VALUE 'COST   ON HAND'.
    05  FILLER                  PIC X(98)      VALUE 'VALUE'.
*
01  INVESTMENT-LINE.
    05  FILLER                  PIC XX         VALUE SPACE.
    05  IL-ITEM-NO              PIC 9(5).
    05  FILLER                  PIC XXX        VALUE SPACE.
    05  IL-UNIT-COST            PIC ZZZ.99.
    05  FILLER                  PIC X(4)       VALUE SPACE.
    05  IL-ON-HAND              PIC ZZ,ZZZ.
    05  FILLER                  PIC XXX        VALUE SPACE.
    05  IL-ITEM-INVESTMENT      PIC Z,ZZZ,ZZZ.99.
    05  FILLER                  PIC X(92)      VALUE SPACE.
*
01  TOTAL-LINE.
    05  FILLER                  PIC X          VALUE SPACE.
    05  TL-RECORD-COUNT         PIC ZZZ,ZZZ.
    05  FILLER                  PIC X(7)       VALUE ' INPUT'.
    05  FILLER                  PIC X(14)     VALUE 'RECORDS'.
    05  TL-TOTAL-INVESTMENT     PIC ZZ,ZZZ,ZZZ.99.
    05  FILLER                  PIC X(92)      VALUE ' *'.
*
PROCEDURE DIVISION.
*
000-PRODUCE-INVESTMENT-LISTING.
    OPEN INPUT  INVENTORY-FILE
         OUTPUT INVESTMENT-LISTING.
    PERFORM 100-PRODUCE-INVESTMENT-LINE
        UNTIL LAST-INVENTORY-REC.
    PERFORM 200-PRINT-TOTAL-LINE.
    CLOSE INVENTORY-FILE
          INVESTMENT-LISTING.
    DISPLAY 'INVSLST  I  1  NORMAL EOJ'.
    STOP RUN.
*
100-PRODUCE-INVESTMENT-LINE.
    PERFORM 110-READ-INVENTORY-RECORD.
    IF MORE-INVENTORY-RECS
        PERFORM 120-CALCULATE-AMOUNT-INVESTED
        PERFORM 130-PRINT-INVESTMENT-LINE.
*
110-READ-INVENTORY-RECORD.
    READ INVENTORY-FILE
        AT END
            MOVE 'Y'              TO INVENTORY-EOF-SW.
*
120-CALCULATE-AMOUNT-INVESTED.
    MULTIPLY IR-UNIT-COST BY IR-ON-HAND
        GIVING ITEM-INVESTMENT.
    ADD ITEM-INVESTMENT           TO TOTAL-INVESTMENT.
*
130-PRINT-INVESTMENT-LINE.
    IF LINE-COUNT GREATER THAN LINES-ON-PAGE
        PERFORM 140-PRINT-HEADING-LINES.
    MOVE IR-ITEM-NO               TO IL-ITEM-NO.
    MOVE IR-UNIT-COST             TO IL-UNIT-COST.
    MOVE IR-ON-HAND               TO IL-ON-HAND.
    MOVE ITEM-INVESTMENT          TO IL-ITEM-INVESTMENT.
    MOVE INVESTMENT-LINE          TO PRINT-AREA.
    PERFORM 150-WRITE-REPORT-LINE.
    ADD 1                         TO RECORD-COUNT.
*
```

Figure 4–11
The investment-listing program (part 2 of 3)

```
 140-PRINT-HEADING-LINES.
     MOVE REPORT-NAME-LINE       TO PRINT-AREA.
     PERFORM 160-WRITE-PAGE-TOP-LINE.
     MOVE COL-HD-LINE-1          TO PRINT-AREA.
     MOVE 2                      TO SPACE-CONTROL.
     PERFORM 150-WRITE-REPORT-LINE.
     MOVE COL-HD-LINE-2          TO PRINT-AREA.
     PERFORM 150-WRITE-REPORT-LINE.
     MOVE 2                      TO SPACE-CONTROL.
*
 150-WRITE-REPORT-LINE.
     WRITE PRINT-AREA
         AFTER ADVANCING SPACE-CONTROL.
     ADD SPACE-CONTROL           TO LINE-COUNT.
     MOVE 1                      TO SPACE-CONTROL.
*
 160-WRITE-PAGE-TOP-LINE.
     WRITE PRINT-AREA
         AFTER ADVANCING PAGE.
     MOVE 1                      TO LINE-COUNT.
*
 200-PRINT-TOTAL-LINE.
     MOVE RECORD-COUNT           TO TL-RECORD-COUNT.
     MOVE TOTAL-INVESTMENT       TO TL-TOTAL-INVESTMENT.
     MOVE TOTAL-LINE             TO PRINT-AREA.
     MOVE 2                      TO SPACE-CONTROL.
     PERFORM 150-WRITE-REPORT-LINE.
```

Figure 4–11
The investment-listing program (part 3 of 3)

Solutions

1. Figure 4–11 is an acceptable solution for a Prime computer system. On another system, the SOURCE– and OBJECT–COMPUTER lines would be different; the implementor name for channel 1 (CO1) in the SPECIAL–NAMES paragraph might be required; and the system names in the SELECT statements would be different. If you weren't able to code a solution by yourself, be sure to study this one until you're confident you understand how it works.

2. The coding form in Figure 4–12 gives an example of acceptable changes. Note that the DIVIDE statement puts the result in a numeric edited field, TL2–AVG–INVESTMENT. This illustrates that the data name used in a GIVING clause can be either numeric or numeric edited. Note also that the result is rounded.

COBOL CODING FORM

PROGRAM | REQUESTED BY | PAGE OF
PROGRAMMER | DATE | IDENT.

```
           (Insert after Total-line-1)
      *
       Ø1  TOTAL-LINE-2
           Ø5  FILLER              PIC X(Ø9)   VALUE ' AVERAGE '.
           Ø5  FILLER              PIC X(14)   VALUE 'INVESTMENT PER'.
           Ø5  FILLER              PIC X(Ø9)   VALUE ' ITEM IS'.
           Ø5  TL2-AVG-INVESTMENT  PIC ZZ,ZZZ.99.
           Ø5  FILLER              PIC X(92)   VALUE SPACE.



           Insert at end of Module 200
           DIVIDE RECORD-COUNT INTO TOTAL-INVESTMENT
               GIVING TL2-AVG-INVESTMENT ROUNDED.
           MOVE TOTAL-LINE-2            TO PRINT-AREA.
           PERFORM 15Ø-WRITE-REPORT-LINE
```

Figure 4–12
Modifications to the investment-listing program

Topic 2 Two Advanced COBOL Facilities

Orientation

The COBOL facilities presented here are quite often presented at a later time. Condition names and the COPY statement are being presented here because they are very helpful concepts, and the student should learn them as early as possible. The use of condition names is a great aid in making a program more readable. The COPY statement is a definite efficiency factor in professional programming as it takes some of the coding burden off the programmer and helps enforce standard data names. The latter facet, standard data names for input records, will be the principal emphasis of use in this text.

Terminology

condition	source library
condition name	source-statement library
library name	

Objectives

1. *Understand and use correctly the terms presented here.*
2. *Immediately begin to use the condition name concept for the end-of-file switches in all program assignments.*
3. *Be able to identify appropriate situations for condition name use and use the concept effectively.*
4. *Determine how to invoke the COPY facility on your operating system. (Note that due to computer center restrictions or crowded facilities, the use of the COPY facility may not be possible).*
5. *If possible, use the COPY statement to include standard input record descriptions in your problem programs where assigned. (Note that the standard input records supplied with this text have three versions.)*
6. *Given a programming problem and a description of available entries in the source-statement library, code a COBOL solution using the COPY statement.*

Condition names

A *condition name* is a facility of COBOL that, if used thoughtfully, can help make programs much more understandable. Although this discussion is often left for more advanced parts of the text, such as the chapter on the professional subset, condition names are so useful that they are being presented here so that you will develop the habit of using them. Do not worry about the concept being too advanced. Condition names are really simple once you have a clear understanding of what a condition is.

First, review the general form of the IF statement that was presented in chapter 3:

```
 IF  condition
     imperative-statement-1
[ELSE
     imperative-statement-2].
```

Notice the word *condition*. The IF statement has several parts, of which the "IF" is the COBOL command and the "condition" is the statement of the test to be made. For instance, recall the first IF that was used (see Figure 3–4):

```
IF  INVENTORY-EOF-SW IS NOT EQUAL TO 'Y'
    PERFORM 120-CALCULATE-AVAILABLE-STOCK
    IF  AVAILABLE-STOCK IS LESS THAN IS-REORDER-POINT
        PERFORM 130-PRINT-REORDER-LINE.
```

Here a nested IF was shown, but the parts to study now are the two conditions:

```
    1.   INVENTORY-EOF-SW IS NOT EQUAL TO 'Y'
and 2.   AVAILABLE-STOCK IS LESS THAN IS-REORDER-POINT
```

When anyone reads those statements, it is reasonably clear what conditions will actually be tested. However, there are several common conditions that will lend very little understanding to the program. For example, consider the following:

```
1.   IF  SR-STUDENT-CLASS IS EQUAL TO 4
2.   IF  CR-COMMISSION-LEVEL-FLAG IS EQUAL TO 3
3.   IF  TR-TRANS-CODE IS EQUAL TO 2
```

In each of the above you are probably left with a question as to what situation the program is trying to identify. In other words, is test 1 trying to identify a senior? Is test 2 attempting to find a salesperson with a high or low commission rate or is it a product which carries a high or low rate? What is the transaction that test 3 is seeking? Of course, SR–STUDENT–CLASS could be defined as a longer alphanumeric field and have the actual class names, such as "sophomore" or "senior" stored in it. The practice in computing, however, is to store codes—single digits that represent a specific status for the record entity. Thus, a code of 1 would probably represent a freshmen, 2 a sophomore, 3 a junior, etc. As you can see, anytime a field has several different but specific codes, any IF tests made may not be clear as to which state the program is trying to identify.

COBOL has a facility called the condition name which is identified in the program code by an 88-level number in the Data Division. The purpose of the 88 level is to give names to the condition part of IF commands when the use of codes are involved and, thus, to make the meaning of the test more obvious. Figure 4–13 shows several examples of how a condition name may be assigned to each code by using the 88 level.

There are several things to notice about the use of condition names:

1. Condition names may be used in either the File Section or the Working–Storage Section of the Data Division.

2. The 88 level must follow an elementary item with a PICTURE clause. The condition name clause may not contain a PICTURE, but must have a VALUE. The associated field may be either a numeric or an alphanumeric item.

3. If the PICTURE clause is for a numeric item the value assigned to the condition name must be a number without quotes—that is, a numeric literal.

4. If the PICTURE clause is for a non-numeric or alphanumeric item, the value assigned to the condition name may be any valid symbol (alphabetic, numeric, or special characters), but must be bracketed by quotes—that is, a non-numeric literal.

5. One condition name may include several different codes as in the SPECIAL–COMMISSION condition name of Figure 4–13. Those several codes may be listed individually or as a group if they comprise a segment of the collating sequence. For example:

```
1. 88  INDIVIDUAL-CODES          VALUE 1 5 10.
2. 88  GROUP-CODES               VALUE 'J' THRU 'N'.
3. 88  VALID-GRADES              VALUE 'A'THRU 'D'
                                       'F' 'IN' 'NC'.
```

As you can see, example 1 listed 3 individual numeric values for the condition name. This means that the test IF INDIVIDUAL–CODES would be true anytime the related field contained a value of 1, 5, or 10. Example 2 assigned a series of codes to the name GROUP–CODES,

```
DATA DIVISION.
FILE SECTION.
    .
    .
    05  SR-STUDENT-CLASS              PIC 9.
        88  FRESHMAN                            VALUE 1.
        88  SOPHOMORE                           VALUE 2.
        88  JUNIOR                              VALUE 3.
        88  SENIOR                              VALUE 4.
        88  GRADUATE                            VALUE 5.

    .
    .
    05  TR-TRANS-CODE                 PIC X.
        88  ISSUE                               VALUE '1'.
        88  RECEIPT                             VALUE '2'.
        88  RETURNS                             VALUE '3'.
    .
    .
WORKING-STORAGE SECTION.
*
01  SWITCHES.
    05  SALES-EOF-SW                  PIC XXX   VALUE 'NO'.
        88  LAST-SALES-RECORD                   VALUE 'YES'.
        88  MORE-SALES-RECORDS                  VALUE 'NO'.
    .
    .
    05  INVENTORY-EOF-SW              PIC X   VALUE 'N'.
        88  END-INVENTORY-FILE                VALUE 'Y'.
        88  NOT-END-INVENTORY-FILE            VALUE 'N'.
    .
    .
01  FLAGS.
    05  COMMISSION-LEVEL-FALG         PIC X.
        88  TRAINEE-COMMISSION                VALUE '1'.
        88  STANDARD-COMMISSION               VALUE '2'.
        88  BONUS-COMMISSION                  VALUE '3'.
        88  SPECIAL-COMMISSION                VALUE '4' 'D' THRU 'F'.
```

Figure 4–13
Defining condition names in the Data Division

and the condition name applies to the beginning and ending values and all values in the collating sequence that are in between. This means that the test IF GROUP–CODES is true whenever the associated field contains one of the letters J, K, L, M, or N. Finally, example 3 combines individual and series codes to define what a valid grade would be, and the test IF VALID–GRADES is true whenever the grade field contains A, B, C, D, F, IN, or NC.

To understand how these condition names are used in the Procedure Division, study Figure 4–14 which presents two skeleton examples of the uses of condition names.

1. In the first example about the sales file (part 1), notice that the condition names may also be used with the UNTIL clause of a PERFORM statement. Thus, a condition name may name any condition, not just those that are part of IF statements.

2. The word NOT can be used with any condition name to form a negative condition. For example, the following could be a logical statement in part 2:

```
IF NOT ISSUE
    ADD TR-QUANTITY - TO WS-QTY-AVAILABLE.
```

Example 1

```
 PROCEDURE DIVISION.
*
 000-PRODUCE-SALES-SUMMARY.
     .
     .
     PERFORM 100-PREPARE-SALES-LINE
         UNTIL LAST-SALES-RECORD.
    .
    .
 100-PREPARE-SALES-LINE.
     PERFORM 110-READ-SALES-RECORD.
     IF  MORE-SALES-RECORDS
         PERFORM 120-DETERMINE-SALES-COMMISSION
         PERFORM 130-PRINT-SALES-LINE.
     .
     .
 110-READ-SALES-RECORD.
     READ SALES-FILE
         AT END
              MOVE 'YES'              TO SALES-EOF-SW.
     .
     .
 120-DETERMINE-SALES-COMMISSION.
     IF  STANDARD-COMMISSION
         MOVE STANDARD-COMM-PCT      TO COMMISSION-PCT
     ELSE
     IF  BONUS-COMMISSION
         MOVE BONUS-COMM-PCT         TO COMMISSION-PCT
     ELSE
     IF  TRAINEE-COMMISSION
         MOVE TRAINEE-COMM-PCT       TO COMMISSION-PCT
     ELSE
         MOVE SPECIAL-COMM-PCT       TO COMMISSION-PCT.
     .
     .
```

Example 2

```
 000-PRODUCE-INVENTORY-STATUS.
     .
     .
     PERFORM 100-PRODUCE-STATUS-LINE
         UNTIL END-INVENTORY-FILE.
     .
     .
 100-PRODUCE-STATUS-LINE.
     PERFORM 110-READ-INVENTORY-RECORD.
     IF  NOT-END-INVENTORY-FILE
         PERFORM 120-DETERMINE-INVENTORY-STATUS
         PERFORM 130-PRINT-STATUS-LINE.
     .
     .
 110-READ-INVENTORY-RECORD.
     READ INVENTORY-FILE
         AT END
             MOVE 'Y'                 TO INVENTORY-EOF-SW.
     .
     .
 120-DETERMINE-INVENTORY-STATUS.
     IF  ISSUE
         PERFORM 150-PROCESS-INV-ISSUE
     ELSE
         IF  RECEIPT
             PERFORM 160-PROCESS-INV-RECEIPT
         ELSE
             IF  RETURNS
                 PERFORM 170-PROCESS-INV-RETURNS
             ELSE
                 PERFORM 180-PRINT-CODE-ERROR.
```

Figure 4–14
Using condition names in the Procedure Division

3. In both parts 1 and 2, note how two condition names are used for the end-of-file test. Use of the two names avoids the necessity of making a NOT condition test, which some people find confusing. In module 000 the condition takes a positive approach (LAST–SALES–RECORD) as does the condition in module 100 (MORE–SALES–RECORDS). If the two conditions were not defined, then one of the conditions would have to be the negation of the other. For instance, the test in module 100 may then read: IF NOT LAST–SALES–RECORD.

4. These comments do not add much to your knowledge of condition names, but will bring up some points of style and general programming responsibilities. In part 1 the IF statements are vertically aligned. This is valid form for a situation where there are several tests on the same field and there are too many to indent each one.

The last test, for SPECIAL–COMMISSION, is not made. It is assumed that after the program has been tested for the other three conditions and found them all to be false that the only remaining possibility is the SPECIAL–COMMISSION condition. Thus, why make the test? This coding assumes that there are no invalid codes on the record, as should be the case on a permanent file. To ensure that no invalid codes are on a permanent file is the responsibility of the systems designer and the programmer who writes any routines that update the file.

5. In part 2 the concepts exemplified by the code are the same as part 1—it is just a different example. The only significant conceptual difference is found in module 120 where all three conditions are tested, and if none are true, then an error is printed. This implies that the record is not from a permanent file and may have coding errors.

The following are general comments about the use of condition statements:

1. This text defines two types of code fields. The first is switches, which are those fields that act like a switch, meaning that they only have two states—on or off, yes or no. The end-of-file fields are switch-type fields. The other is type called flags. This simply means that the field may have several codes, and certainly more than two, otherwise it would be a switch. Note that names may be given to any code that may be stored in the field. This is obvious for flags, but many times programmers forget that both the "on" and the "off" states of a switch may be assigned a condition name. When you observe the SALES–EOF–SW of Figure 4–13, you will see that both states have been assigned a name.

2. It is desirable to keep the names consistent, and to do so the condition names should be related to the data names whenever practical. For a switch, the condition name should make clear what state is being tested. The data name should be an explanatory name for the switch and have a suffix of –SWITCH or –SW.

For a flag, the condition names may or may not be closely related to the flag name. For flags like the COMMISSION–LEVEL–FLAG in Figure 4–13, it is sensible to repeat the word COMMISSION in the condition names (e.g., BONUS–COMMISSION) as this helps explain that the condition has to do with commissions. Just the words TRAINEE, STANDARD, etc., do not make this clear and, in fact, may cause confusion. However, in the inventory example the words ISSUE, RECEIPT, and RETURNS seem to be adequate indicators as to what happened to an item in inventory.

Note that it does take some careful thought to effectively use condition names. The use of them should always improve the clarity of the program.

3. You will discover how valuable condition names are when you have to change a program because the codes in it have been changed. Without condition names, every statement in the Procedure Division that refers to the codes would have to be found and changed. With condition names, only the 88-level clauses in the Data Division need to be changed.

Because condition names are valuable in programs that have code fields or various types of switches or flags, you should use them often. As a result, you will see them used continuously in the programs in the rest of this book. You are encouraged to use them in all of your programs since they will all have at least the end-of-file switch.

Introduction to the COPY Facility

A large part of most COBOL programs is taken up with routine descriptions of files, records, and data fields. Since a file is normally processed by several programs, a lot of effort would be wasted if each programmer had to code the same descriptions. Also, there would probably be minor differences in the way each programmer defined the files and records. Unfortunately, these minor differences could cause major problems. To avoid this, COBOL descriptions may be written once, stored in a *source-statement library* (or just *source library*) on a direct-access device, and retrieved as needed by other programs using the same descriptions.

In the same way, processing modules that are used by more than one program can be stored in the source library. For example, a routine that calculates federal withholding tax might be stored in the source library, available to any programmer who needed it. Again, the advantages of using the library are the savings in programmer time and the standardization and compatibility of programs written by different programmers.

To illustrate the use of the source-statement library, suppose the field descriptions in the top part of Figure 4–15 are stored in the library under the *library name* TRANREC. To get these descriptions into a program, the programmer has to code a COPY statement in the Data Division that specifies this library name:

```
COPY TRANREC.
```

When the source program is compiled, the statements from the source-statement library are inserted (copied) into the program and printed on the source listing, as shown in Figure 4–15.

Some computers designate copied statements by placing the character C to the left of each statement that was copied, as is demonstrated in Figure 4–15. The Prime system used for programs in the book designates copied statements by placing square brackets around the line numbers of the copied statements (e.g., [0001]) and restarting the numbering of each copied group with 0001 so that the line numbering of the copied part is independent of the line numbers of the rest of the source program. The original source statement lines are surrounded by parentheses and are numbered continuously

```
TRANREC entry in the source-statement library:

         01   TRANSACTION-RECORD.
              05  TR-CODE                      PIC X(01).
              05  TR-ITEM-NUMBER               PIC 9(05).
              05  TR-QUANTITY                  PIC 9(05).
              05  TR-REF-NUMBER                PIC X(05).
              05  TR-REF-DATE.
                  10  TR-REF-YEAR              PIC X(02).
                  10  TR-REF-MO                PIC X(02).
                  10  IR-REF-DAY               PIC X(02).
              05  FILLER                       PIC X(58).

COBOL statement in the Data Division:

              COPY TRANREC.

Statements in the source listing:

              COPY TRANREC.
C        01   TRANSACTION-RECORD.
C             05  TR-CODE                      PIC X(01).
C             05  TR-ITEM-NUMBER               PIC 9(05).
C             05  TR-QUANTITY                  PIC 9(05).
C             05  TR-REF-NUMBER                PIC X(05).
C             05  TR-REF-DATE.
C                 10  TR-REF-YEAR              PIC X(02).
C                 10  TR-REF-MO                PIC X(02).
C                 10  TR-REF-DAY               PIC X(02).
C             05  FILLER                       PIC X(58).
```

Figure 4–15
Using the COPY statement

beginning with (0001). Your system may treat copied statements in the source list differently than either of these examples.

The COPY statement

The actual simple format of the COPY statement is:

```
                   ┌ ┌ OF ┐                ┐
COPY text-name     │ ┤    ├  library-name  │
                   └ └ IN ┘                ┘
```

Modern interactive operating systems typically have been organized with several libraries so that the student programmers may have their own individual libraries which are separate from faculty libraries, from computer center libraries, from special-project libraries, etc. If the Data Division entry that you wish to copy is in your own library, then all that needs to be specified is the text-name, which in this case is really a file name of a file of COBOL statements on a library. If the Data Division entry is on a library that is separate from the students' libraries, then the OF or IN options followed by the library name where the statements are stored will be needed, as in the following:

```
COPY INVREC IN  STUDENT_DATA.
```

Again, exactly how you utilize the COPY command depends upon your compiler, your operating system, and how and where the source statements to be copied are stored.

The COPY statement can be used wherever a programmer-defined word (name), a reserved word, a literal, a PICTURE character string, or a comment entry can be used. It can also be used wherever a separator like a space or a period can be used. In other words, a COPY statement can generally be used in any logical place within a program.

Library names

The library name for a group of source statements is created when the statements are stored in the library. It must be unique and must follow the rules for forming library names. Since these rules vary from system to system, you'll have to check the reference manual for your system to find out what's permissible.

Guidelines for use

You have been given some general ideas on when and how to use the COPY statement. Note that the simplest use of the COPY has been presented, but it is also the most typical. What follows is some perspective on how this facility should be used by COBOL programmers in the professional environment in industry.

File and record descriptions

Storing file and record descriptions is the most important job of the source library. (By record description, is meant all code that describes the fields within the record, whether this code is in the File Section or the Working–Storage Section of the Data Division.) Besides saving programmer time by eliminating repetitious coding, this function of the library ensures that all programs within an installation will use the same names for the records and fields within a file. This, in turn, reduces confusion, program bugs, and interface problems between programs written by different programmers. At the least, then, the source library should contain all file and record descriptions.

Tables

A second specific function of the source library is to store commonly used tables that aren't subject to a lot of change. For example, suppose a table contains the names of the 50 states as well as their two-letter abbreviations. This table is quite stable and could be used constantly by programmers who wanted to convert a state code to the expanded state name or vice versa. If it were stored in the source library, each programmer could enter it into the Working–Storage Section of his or her program simply by using a COPY statement. Again, there's an obvious savings in programmer time—a programmer wouldn't have to code all 50 entries each time the table was needed.

Procedure Division paragraphs

Commonly used Procedure Division routines should also be stored in the source library. They may consist of one or more paragraphs; however, the paragraphs shouldn't be numbered. You'll give the number and name from your VTOC to the top-level module in the library routine when you copy the routine into your program. For example, in this code

```
 100-STORE-ITEM-TABLE.
*
     COPY LOADITAB.
```

100–STORE–ITEM–TABLE would be the name taken from your VTOC for the program. If the procedure stored under the library name LOADITAB consisted of more than one paragraph, the second and subsequent paragraphs would have the paragraph names given to them when they were stored.

The REPLACING clause

This part of the COPY statement was not presented. One of the advantages of the COPY facility is the coordination of data names among all the programs that use the same fields. And this is in keeping with structured programming, which aims to perform standard tasks in a standard way, thereby eliminating the chance for confusion and errors. The REPLACING clause of the COPY statement works against these goals. It encourages variations from program to program. This is particularly true under the 1974 standards where a programmer can change entire lines of code. So, as a general rule, avoid the REPLACING clause. Strive for consistency instead.

Program development

As a programmer, you should make use of the source library early in the development of a structured program. In fact, right after you have complete specifications for a program, you should get listings of all the library code—both data descriptions and processing modules—that might be applicable to the program. As you create the VTOC for the program, you may decide not to use some or all of the processing modules. But it's important to get copies of them before you start the VTOC because in some cases they will affect your design. As for the data descriptions, they may be used in your module documentation, depending on your installation's standards. And, of course, you will use them in the COBOL code itself.

Discussion

If you have understood this portion, you will realize how valuable the COPY statement is, especially for the professional programmer. If you consider that a large part of the coding in a COBOL program is in the Data Division, the COPY statement used in that division alone can reduce programming time considerably. In fact, if a company doesn't make use of the source-statement library, COBOL can be an expensive language to use in terms of programming costs. So you'll find that the source library and COPY statement are widely used in professional COBOL shops.

Problems

1. Assume that you are to write a program using a file that contains Accounts Receivable data.

   a. Code just the FD and file name for this file.

Code the following program parts using condition names.

   b. Code the Working–Storage data definitions for the switch that is used for the end-of-file test on the Accounts Receivable file.

   c. Code a PERFORM statement to execute module 100 to prepare and print each line of an aging report using the data in the Accounts Receivable file. The PERFORM should call for the execution of module 100 until the end of the Accounts Receivable file is reached.

d. Code the IF statement in the module 100 that performs the module 120 to calculate how long the charge has been on the file without being paid, and performs the module 130 to print the aging line.

2. Assume that you are working with a personnel file that includes codes for job level. Code the data description for that field along with the condition names for the required job categories. The categories and codes are salaried = 1, hourly = 2, civil-service = 3, craft-apprentice = 11, craft-journeyman = 12, craft-master = 13.

3. Suppose a source listing of a COBOL program contains the following file and record descriptions:

```
       *
        FD  TRANSACTION-FILE COPY TRANFILE.
C           LABEL RECORDS ARE STANDARD
C           RECORD CONTAINS 80 CHARACTERS.
C      *
C       01  TRAN-RECORD.
C      *
C               05  TR-CUST-NO   PIC 9(6).
C               05  TR-REF-NO    PIC X(6).
C               05  TR-REF-DATE  PIC X(6).
C               05  TR-CODE      PIC X.
C               05  TR-ITEM-NO   PIC 9(6).
C               05  TR-QUANTITY  PIC 9(5).
C               05  FILLER       PIC X(50).
```

a. Write a valid READ statement for this file.

b. Write a statement that compares the customer number in the record above to a field named OLD–CUSTOMER–NO. If the transaction customer number is larger, execute a paragraph named 120–PRINT–CUSTOMER–LINE.

4. Suppose you are writing a billing program in which some of the customers will get a discount on the merchandise they purchased. To calculate the amount of the discount, you are going to copy a routine from the source-statement library. The library name is DISCALC, and your module name is going to be 250–CALCULATE–DISCOUNT–AMOUNT. Write the COPY statement required for this program.

Solutions

1. a. The following is an acceptable file name:

```
FD  ACCOUNTS-RECEIVABLE
```

b. Here's a good switch definition:

```
01  SWITCHES.
    05  ACCT-RECEIVABLE-EOF-SW       PIC X      VALUE 'N'.
        88  END-ACCT-RECV-FILE                  VALUE 'Y'.
        88  MORE-ACCT-RECV-RECS                 VALUE 'N'.
```

Note that both states of the switch have been given names.

c. This will be your typical PERFORM statement that uses the UNTIL clause:

```
PERFORM 100-PRODUCE-AGING-LINE
    UNTIL END-ACCT-RECV-FILE.
```

d. This is a good IF statement using condition names:

```
IF  MORE-ACCT-RECV-RECS
    PERFORM 120-CALCULATE-AGED-DURATION
    PERFORM 130-PRINT-AGING-LINE.
```

Note that the two 88-level names were defined so that there was no need to use the NOT (or negation) with either condition name or data value.

2. An acceptable solution for the job categories is:

```
05  JOB-CATEGORY            PIC X(02).

    88  EMPL-SALARIED                   VALUE '1'.
    88  EMPL-HOURLY                     VALUE '2'.
    88  EMPL-CIVIL-SVC                  VALUE '3'.
    88  CRAFT-APPRENTICE                VALUE '11'.
    88  CRAFT-JOURNEYMAN                VALUE '12'.
    88  CRAFT-MASTER                    VALUE '13'.
    88  VALID-JOB-CATEGORY              VALUE '1' THRU '3'
                                              '11' THRU '13'.
```

Notice that an extra condition name has been coded to be used whenever a test needs to be made to determine whether the code is a valid one. If the VALID-JOB-CATEGORY name were not used, several IF statements or a compound IF would be needed to replace the following test:

```
IF  VALID-JOB-CATEGORY ...
```

This is another example of careful consideration of the problem and thoughtful coding, marking you as a professional-level programmer.

3. a. The following is an acceptable READ statement:

```
READ TRANSACTION-FILE
    AT END
        MOVE "Y" TO TRAN-EOF-SW.
```

Notice that you use the name assigned to the file in the program, not the library name. The library name simply identifies which entry is to be copied.

b. Here's an acceptable IF statement:

```
IF TR-CUST-NO GREATER OLD-CUSTOMER-NO
    PERFORM 120-PRINT-CUSTOMER-LINE.
```

As you can see, the fields in the library entry are used just as though the programmer had coded them in his program himself.

4. Here's an acceptable COPY statement:

```
 250-CALCULATE-DISCOUNT-AMOUNT.
*
     COPY DISCALC.
```

Topic 3 Issue: Coding Practices

PERFORM READ Option

There are two acceptable techniques for accessing the read module in a structured COBOL program. The technique presented so far uses only one PERFORM statement to access the read module. This technique has the advantage of that single PERFORM. However, it does cause a slight logic problem in that it necessitates testing of the last record switch before accessing following routines, such as calculation and print modules. Also, it often requires the use of a first record switch which must be constantly tested, even when no longer really useful. The second technique requires a "priming" read call. That is, a PERFORM of the read module early in the main control module gets the first record and eliminates the logic test for last record in the principal module. Note that use of the priming read necessitates the movement of the read PERFORM from the first line in the principal logic module to the last line. Study Figure 4–16 carefully, and observe how the code used here differs from the previous examples.

As you can see, this technique has several advantages, but it does have module 110 being accessed from more than one point. Of course, this is not an error nor a violation of structured guidelines, but is a factor that should be minimized and not indulged in frivolously. The examples in this text will continue with the single PERFORM of the read module, but you might try this option on one or two of your problem programs. There will be more discussion of this concept in the chapter on control breaks.

A single I/O command per file

It is worth mentioning one more time that this text promotes the practice of allowing only one READ command or one WRITE command per file. To implement this requires a separate module for the READ command and a separate module for the WRITE command. Then, whenever an I/O command is required, the appropriate module is accessed via a PERFORM statement. The only exception to this is the use of an additional WRITE command in a separate module to advance to the top of the page for printed output. You have already been shown how to implement this practice in the previous discussions and examples. There will seem to be other exceptions when you study disk I/O, but the rule will still be enforceable when you begin to discriminate between the types of READ and WRITE commands. Learn the practice now; it will simplify the whole development process when the more complex problems come along.

Naming files and fields

A constant and key concept in this text is the goal of providing clarity and readability in every program. A basic place to start occurs when you, the programmer, select names for files, records, and fields. The following is a list of guides that will aid your selection of meaningful names.

1. Never use words that tie the element to a physical device. This is a practice that some fall into when naming files and records. For example, never name a file as TAPE–FILE. Your documentation is lost when a system revision puts the file on a disk instead. Then you have to

```
 PROCEDURE DIVISION.
 000-PRODUCE-REORDER-LISTING.
     OPEN INPUT  INVENTORY-STATUS-FILE
          OUTPUT REORDER-LISTING.
     PERFORM 110-READ-INVENTORY-RECORD.                 (added command)
     PERFORM 100-PRODUCE-REORDER-LINE
         UNTIL LAST-INVENTORY-RECORD.
     PERFORM 200-PRINT-INVENTORY-TOTALS.
     CLOSE INVENTORY-STATUS-FILE
           REORDER-LISTING.
     STOP RUN.
*
 100-PRODUCE-REORDER-LINE.
     PERFORM 120-CALCULATE-AVAILABLE-STOCK
     IF AVAILABLE-STOCK-LESS THAN IS-REORDER-POINT
         PERFORM 130-PRINT-REORDER-LINE.
     PERFORM 110-READ-INVENTORY-RECORD.             (command moved, EOF
                                                     test eliminated)
*
 110-READ-INVENTORY-RECORD.
     READ INVENTORY-STATUS-FILE
         AT END
             MOVE 'Y'              TO INVENTORY-EOF-SW.
*
 120-CALCULATE-AVAILABLE-STOCK.
     (logic and statements in this module
      not affected by the subject under discussion)
*
 130-PRINT-REORDER-LINE.
     (no effect on this module)
*
 200-PRINT-INVENTORY-TOTALS.
     (no effect on this module)
```

Figure 4–16
Optional treatment of PERFORM READ logic

change all references to the file name if you want to maintain accurate documentation in the program.

2. Do not use words that identify the file or record as an input or an output entity. Examples are INPUT–MASTER–FILE or INVENTORY–OUTPUT–FILE. The I/O commands that are used on the file should make its I/O direction obvious. In addition there are more useful names to use.

3. Do specify names for fields that clarify their function. Function means the type of data the file, record, or field contains. Thus, names such as INVENTORY–FILE, PAYROLL–RECORD, ACCOUNTS–RECEIVABLE–RECORD, AR–CHANGE–DATE, etc., are names that make clear the function of the particular entity being named.

4. As mentioned before, when naming data entities specify a name that answers the question "what?" This implies that most data names should be a two-word name. For instance, DATE as a data name seems clear as it is obvious that the data concerns a date. But it can certainly be improved because it does not answer the question "what?" In other words, what DATE is it? Is the field about a birth date, a charge date, a payment date, or what? Even if the name has a prefix, such as EMPL as in EMPL–DATE, you now know the date has something to do with employees, but it is still not specific enough and doesn't answer the "what?" question. Now if the name is changed to EMPLOYMENT–DATE, it becomes clear that this is probably the date that the employee was hired.

Part Three

Program Development Techniques and Report Control Logic

You now have learned the basic set of COBOL statements and commands. If you were given problem statements for an uncomplicated program, you could probably write an adequate program. However, there are more sophisticated methods of programming, and there are some more powerful COBOL commands to learn. So this part will complete your introduction to the basic subset of COBOL facilities. Part IV and the Advanced book will present a professional subset of the language.

Chapter 5 extends your knowledge of how to identify and remove program errors and introduces control-break logic. Chapter 6 covers structured programming: background, structure charts, bridging the gap between structure chart and coding with pseudocode, and structured style guidelines. Chapter 7 completes the chapter 5 discussion about report control breaks, presents a concept of testing, and, finally, gives a list of recommended abbreviations and verb conventions.

When you have completed Part III you will have cleared three major learning hurdles: basic COBOL statements, structured programming style, and control breaks. Then you will be ready to move to the next learning level.

Chapter 5 Compiling and Testing COBOL Programs and An Introduction to Report Logic

You have now had some experience debugging your first programs. As you would expect, the program assignments will become more complex and difficult, and for a time you can be expected to make more complex errors. This chapter presents material which will extend your ability to determine quickly the cause of your program errors and to correct them. Chapter 3 introduced you to syntax errors. The first topic in this chapter demonstrates a program with more syntax errors than the one in chapter 3. Topic 2 dicusses some techiques to help find logic errors. Topic 3 lists several errors that do not show up until the program actually executes and so are called execution time errors, as most execution time errors represent some failing in understanding the problem program or how to provide the correct computer solution. Topic 4 introduces the subject of Report Control Logic, which is the beginning of your training in more complex programming logic.

Topic 1 More Syntax Errors

Orientation

This topic presents the revised reorder-listing program with a more typical list of syntax errors. The situation presented is just as the program might have been after its first compile. You may have had to deal with the same number of diagnostics already, but probably not with the same variety. The examples in this text try to show a variety of errors rather than the single error type made several times in one program.

Terminology

There is no new terminology presented here. You might review the terms presented in chapter 3 to ensure that you understand them.

Objectives

1. *Understand the diagnostic messages presented in the example.*

2. *Understand the programming errors that caused the diagnostics and what must be done to correct the errors.*

3. *Be able to correct the syntax errors in your own programs.*

4. *Begin to take a more careful approach to writing your programs so as to minimize syntax errors.*

Revised reorder listing—first compile

Before the discussion of the example begins, a goal is recommended for you as a programmer: namely, that you have your program syntax error-free by the third compile. Sometimes, especially at the beginning of the course, this will be difficult to accomplish, but having the goal will cause you to be more careful in writing the program and entering it into the computer. As you struggle to meet this goal, you will find that your skill at developing and coding programs will increase faster than if you did not have such a goal.

Figure 5–1 is the compiler output of the revised reorder-listing program. It represents the typical first compile of a program and the attendant diagnostic messages generated by common syntax errors that a novice programmer might make. First, study the program and the diagnostics and attempt to figure out the error causes yourself. Do this before reading further in the text.

```
 IDENTIFICATION DIVISION.
*
 PROGRAM ID.    REOLST.
 ENVIRONMENT DIVISION.
*
 CONFIGURATION SECTION.
*
 SOURCE-COMPUTER.    PRIME 850.
 OBJECT-COMPUTER.    PRIME 850.
*
 INPUT-OUTPUT SECTION.
*
 FILE-CONTROL.
     SELECT INVENTORY-STATUS-FILE
         ASSIGN TO PFMS.
     SELECT REORDER-LISTING
         ASSIGN TO PFMS.
*
 DATA DIVISION.
*
 FILE SECTION.
*
 FD  INVENTORY-STATUS-FILE
     LABEL RECORDS ARE STANDARD
     RECORD CONTAINS 80 CHARACTERS.
*
 01  INVENTORY-STATUS-RECORD.
     05  IS-ITEM-NO           PIC 9(5).
     05  IS-ITEM-DESC         PIC X(20).
     05  FILLER               PIC X(5).
     05  IS-UNIT-PRICE        PIC 9(3)V99.
     05  IS-REORDER-POINT     PIC 9(5).
     05  IS-QTY-ON-HAND       PIC 9(5).
     05  IS-QTY-ON-ORDER      PIC 9(5).
```

Figure 5–1
More syntax errors (part 1 of 4)

```
               05  FILLER              PIC X(25).
          *
           FD  REORDER-LISTING
                   LABEL RECORDS ARE STANDARD
                   RECORD CONTAINS 133 CHARACTERS.
          *
           01  PRINT-AREA.
               05  FILLER              PIC X(133).
          *
           WORKING-STORAGE SECTION.
          *
           01  SWITCHES.
               05  INVENTORY-EOF-SW    PIC X         VALUE 'N'.
          *
           01  WORK-FIELDS.
               05  AVAILABLE-STOCK     PIC S9(5)                 COMP-3.
          *
           01  PRINT-CONTROL-FIELDS                              COMP-3.
               05  LINE-COUNT          PIC S99       VALUE +99.
               05  LINES-ON-PAGE       PIC S99       VALUE +57.
               05  SPACE-CONTROL       PIC S9.
          *
           01  COUNT-FIELDS                                      COMP-3.
               05  RECORD-COUNT        PIC S9(5)     VALUE ZERO.
          *
           01  HEADING-LINE-1.
               05  FILLER              PIC X(24)     VALUE SPACE.
               05  FILLER              PIC X(8)      VALUE 'REORDER'.
               05  FILLER              PIC X(101)    VALUE 'LISTING'.
          *
           01  HEADING-LINE-2.
               05  FILLER              PIC X(4)      VALUE ' ITEM'.
               05  FILLER              PIC X(12)     VALUE SPACE.
               05  FILLER              PIC X(20)     VALUE 'ITEM'.
               05  FILLER              PIC X(19)     VALUE 'UNIT'.
               05  FILLER              PIC X(77)     VALUE 'REORDER.
          *
          01   HEADING-LINE-2.
** SYNTAX ERROR **  "QLIT"
               05  FILLER              PIC X(14)     VALUE ' NO.'.
** SYNTAX ERROR **  "QLIT"  LENGTH? PUNCT?
               05  FILLER              PIC X(22)     VALUE '     DESCRIPTION
** SYNTAX ERROR **  "QLIT"
               05  FILLER              PIC X(9)      VALUE 'PRICE'.
               05  FILLER              PIC X(12)     VALUE 'AVAILABLE'.
               05  FILLER              PIC X(76)     VALUE 'POINT'.
          *
           01  REORDER-LINE.
               05  FILLER              PIC X         VALUE SPACE.
               05  RL-ITEM-NO          PIC X(3).
               05  FILLER              PIC X(5)      VALUE SPACE.
               05  RL-ITEM-DESC        PIC X(20).
               05  FILLER              PIC X(5)      VALUE SPACE.
               05  RL-UNIT-PRICE       PIC ZZZ.99.
               05  FILLER              PIC X(5)      VALUE SPACE.
               05  RL-AVAILABLE-STOCK  PIC Z(5).
               05  FILLER              PIC X(5).     VALUE SPACE.
               05  RL-REORDER-POINT    PIC  (5).
** SYNTAX ERROR **  PIC = X
               05  FILLER              PIC X(71)     VALUE SPACE.
          *
           TOTAL-LINE.
               05  TL-RECORD-COUNT     PIC ZZ,ZZZ.
               05  FILLER              PIC X(13)     VALUE '  RECORDS IN'.
               05  FILLER              PIC X(4)      VALUE 'THE'.
```

Figure 5–1
More syntax errors (part 2 of 4)

```
               05  FILLER              PIC X(110)    VALUE 'INPUT FILE'.
          *
           01  ERROR-DESCRIPTION-LINE.
               05  FILLER              PIC X(16)     VALUE ' REORDER  A  2'.
               05  FILLER              PIC X(12)     VALUE 'CALCULATION'.
               05  FILLER              PIC X(15)     VALUE 'ERROR FOR ITEM'.
               05  FILLER              PIC XXX       VALUE 'NO'.
               05  EL-ITEM-NO          PIC X(5).
               05  FILLER              PIC X(9)      VALUE '--RECORD'.
               05  FILLER              PIC X(73).    VALUE 'IGNORED'.
          *
           PROCEDURE DIVISION.
          *
           000-PRODUCE-REORDER-LISTING.
               OPEN INPUT  INVENTORY-STATUS-FILE
                    OUTPUT REORDER-LISTING.
               PERFORM 100-PRODUCE-REORDER-LINE
                   UNTIL INVENTORY-EOF-SW EQUAL'Y'.
** SYNTAX ERROR **  PUNCT?
               PERFORM 200-PRINT-TOTAL-LINE.
               CLOSE INVENTORY-STATUS-FILE
                     REORDER-LISTING.
               DISPLAY 'REORDER  I  1  NORMAL EOJ'.
               STOP RUN.
          *
           100-PRODUCE-REORDER-LINE.
               PERFORM 110-READ-INVENTORY-RECORD.
               IF INVENTORY-EOF-SW  EQUAL 'N'
                   PERFORM 120-CALCULATE-AVAILABLE-STOCK
                   IF AVAILABLE-STOCK LESS THAN IS-REORDER-POINT
                       PERFORM 130-WRITE-REORDER-LINE.
          *
           110-READ-INVENTORY-RECORD.
               READ INVENTORY-STATUS-FILE
                   AT END
                       MOVE 'Y'             TO INVENTORY-EOF-SW.
          *
               120-CALCULATE-AVAILABLE-STOCK.
               ADD IS-QTY-ON-HAND IS-QTY-ON-ORDER
                   GIVING AVAILABLE-STOCK
                   ON SIZE ERROR
                       PERFORM 210-PRINT-ERROR-MESSAGE
                       MOVE 99999           TO AVAILABLE-STOCK.
          *
           130-PRINT-REORDER-LINE.
               IF LINE-COUNT GREATER THAN LINES-ON-PAGE
                   PERFORM 140-PRINT-HEADING-LINES.
               MOVE IS-ITEM-NO              TO RL-ITEM-NO.
               MOVE IS-ITEM-DESC            TO RL-ITEM-DESC.
               MOVE IS-UNIT-PRICE           TO RL-UNIT-PRICE.
               MOVE AVAILABLE-STOCK         TO RL-AVAILABLE-STOCK.
               MOVE IR-REORDER-POINT        TO RL-REORDER-POINT.
               MOVE REORDER-LINE            TO PRINT-AREA.
               PERFORM 150-WRITE-REPORT-LINE.
               ADD 1                        TO RECORD-COUNT.
          *
           140-PRINT-HEADING-LINES.
               MOVE HEADING-LINE-1          TO PRINT-AREA.
               PERFORM-160-WRITE-PAGE-TOP-LINE.
** SYNTAX ERROR **  LENGTH?
               MOVE HEADING-LINE-2          TO PRINT-AREA.
               MOVE 2                   TO SPACE-CONTROL.
               PERFORM 150-WRITE-REPORT-LINE.
               MOVE HEADING-LINE-3          TO PRINT-AREA.
               PERFROM 150-WRITE-REPORT-LINE.
```

Figure 5–1
More syntax errors (part 3 of 4)

```
(0159)          MOVE 2                           TO SPACE-CONTROL.
(0160)      *
(0161)       150-WRITE-REPORT-LINE.
(0162)          WRITE PRINT-AREA
(0163)              AFTER ADVANCING SPACE-CONTROL.
(0164)          ADD SPACE-CONTROL                TO LINE-COUNT.
(0165)          MOVE 1                           TO SPACE-CONTROL.
(0166)      *
(0167)       160-WRITE-PAGE-TOP-LINE.
(0168)          WRITE PRINT-AREA
(0169)              AFTER ADVANCING PAGE.
(0170)          MOVE 1                           TO LINE-COUNT.
(0171)      *
(0172)       200-PRINT-TOTAL-LINE.
(0173)          MOVE RECORD-COUNT                TO TL-RECORD-COUNT.
(0174)          MOVE TOTAL-LINE                  TO PRINT-AREA.
(0175)          MOVE 3                           TO SPACE-CONTROL.
(0176)          PERFORM 150 WRITE-REPORT-LINE.
(0177)      *
(0178)       210-PRINT-ERROR-MESSAGE.
(0179)          MOVE IS-ITEM-NO                  TO EL-ITEM-NO.
(0180)          MOVE ERROR-DESCRIPTION-LINE TO PRINT-AREA.
(0181)          PERFORM 150-WRITE-REPORT-LINE.

0003  AREA-A VIOLATION; RESUMES AT  NEXT PARAGRAPH/SECTION/DIVISION/VERB.  [PR  ]
0037  RECORD MIN/MAX DISAGREES WITH RECORD CONTAINS; LATTER SIZES  PREVAIL.
0066  /W/ LITERAL TRUNCATED TO ITEM SIZE.
0073  UNRECOGNIZABLE ELEMENT IS IGNORED. [NO  ]
0074  UNRECOGNIZABLE ELEMENT IS IGNORED. [DESCRIPTION   ]
0075  UNRECOGNIZABLE ELEMENT IS IGNORED. [FILLER  ]
0075  UNRECOGNIZABLE ELEMENT IS IGNORED. [X    ]
0075  /W/ PERIOD ASSUMED ABOVE.
0074  GROUP ITEM; PIC/VALUE/JUST/BLANK/SIGN/SYNC IGNORED.
0075  NAME OMITTED; ENTRY BYPASSED.  [)   ]
0075  INVALID VALUE IGNORED. [05  ]
0076  LEVEL 01 ASSUMED.
0078  LEVEL 01 ASSUMED.
0092  UNRECOGNIZABLE ELEMENT IS IGNORED. [TOTAL-LINE  ]
0105  SOURCE BYPASSED UNTIL NEXT FD/SECTION. [VALUE   ]
0105  SOURCE BYPASSED UNTIL NEXT FD/SECTION. [IGNORED   ]
0123  /D/ UNRESOLVED PROCEDURE-NAME; STATEMENT DELETED.  [120-CALCULATE-AVAI  ]
0125  /D/ UNRESOLVED PROCEDURE-NAME; STATEMENT DELETED.   [130-WRITE-REORDER-  ]
0130  UNRECOGNIZABLE ELEMENT IS IGNORED. [MOVE  ]
0130  UNRECOGNIZABLE ELEMENT IS IGNORED. [Y   ]
0130  UNRECOGNIZABLE ELEMENT IS IGNORED. [TO  ]
0130  UNRECOGNIZABLE ELEMENT IS IGNORED. [INVENTORY-EOF-SW   ]
0132  UNRECOGNIZABLE ELEMENT IS IGNORED. [120-CALCULATE-AVAILABLE-STOCK     ]
0146  STATEMENT DELETED DUE TO ERRONEOUS SYNTAX. [IR-REORDER-POINT  ]
0146  UNRECOGNIZABLE ELEMENT IS IGNORED. [TO  ]
0146  UNRECOGNIZABLE ELEMENT IS IGNORED. [RL-REORDER-POINT  ]
0150  AREA-A VIOLATION; RESUMES AT  NEXT PARAGRAPH/SECTION/DIVISION/VERB.   [*   ]
0151  PERIOD ASSUMED AFTER PROCEDURE-NAME DEFINITION.
0153  UNRECOGNIZABLE ELEMENT IS IGNORED. [PERFORM-160-WRITE-PAGE-TOP-LIN  ]
0157  STATEMENT DELETED DUE TO ERRONEOUS SYNTAX. [HEADING-LINE-3  ]
0157  UNRECOGNIZABLE ELEMENT IS IGNORED. [TO  ]
0157  UNRECOGNIZABLE ELEMENT IS IGNORED. [PRINT-AREA  ]
0158  UNRECOGNIZABLE ELEMENT IS IGNORED. [PERFROM  ]
0158  UNRECOGNIZABLE ELEMENT IS IGNORED. [150-WRITE-REPORT-LINE   ]
0174  STATEMENT DELETED DUE TO ERRONEOUS SYNTAX. [TOTAL-LINE  ]
0174  UNRECOGNIZABLE ELEMENT IS IGNORED. [TO  ]
0174  UNRECOGNIZABLE ELEMENT IS IGNORED. [PRINT-AREA  ]
0176  STATEMENT DELETED DUE TO NON-NUMERIC OPERAND.
0181  /D/ UNRESOLVED PROCEDURE-NAME; STATEMENT DELETED.  [150-WRITE-REPORT-L  ]
0000  /W/ INCONSISTENT READ USAGE. [INVENTORY-STATUS-FILE   ]
```

Figure 5–1
More syntax errors (part 4 of 4)

By now you should be able to read and understand the messages. The format of the explanations will refer to the line number listed in the message and then explain what is required to fix the error.

Line No.	Explanation
0003	COBOL reserved word not recognized due to missing hyphen between PROGRAM and ID. Insert hyphen making the entry read PROGRAM–ID.
0037	A recount of the number of positions defined in the INVENTORY-STATUS-RECORD adds up to 75. Change PIC X (25) to X(30) on the FILLER at line 35.
0066	Picture and literal disagree. Change PIC X(4) to X(5).
0073	through 0078 See line 0070; the subsequent errors may have been generated by the missing quote after the literal 'REORDER'.
0092	The entry in margin A (to be valid) needs a 01 before the name TOTAL–LINE.
0105	There is a period between the PICTURE clause and the VALUE clause. Remove it.
0123	Note that line 0132, the paragraph name for module 120, does not begin in margin A, and the compiler did not recognize it as a paragraph name. Hence the command to PERFORM it was invalid since the name could not be found. Fix line 0132.
0125	Observe the paragraph name on line 0139. That name and the PERFORM command on line 0125 do not match. Change line 0125 to 130–PRINT–REORDER–LINE.
0130	A very subtle error. The character "O" in the MOVE command is really the numeric digit zero ("0"). Correct the MOVE command. Watch out for this one, it will drive you crazy.
0132	Remember line 0123. Move the paragraph name over into margin A.
0146	Check back to the record description (line 0032), and you see that the data names do not match. Change line 0146 to IS–REORDER–POINT.
0150	The asterisk character for indicating a blank line to the compiler was not placed in position 7. Move the asterisk (*) one space to the left.
0151	Correcting line 0150 should clear this message.
0153	Remove the hyphen between the PERFORM and the paragraph name.
0157	Look back to lines 0065 and 0072. Both have the same name. Line 0072 should be named HEADING–LINE–3, not 2. Making that change should also clear several of the syntax error indicators in the source list at that point.
0158	A common keying error. The "O" and "R" are transposed in the command PERFORM, thus creating an invalid command, PERF*RO*M.
0174	Recall error 0092. The name TOTAL–LINE is not recognized due to that error. Fixing line 0092 will clear these diagnostics.
0176	Missing hyphen in paragraph name. Place hyphen between 150 and WRITE–REPORT–LINE.
0181	Similar to line 0130 error, only this time the entry had a character "O" when it should have had a zero. Change 15O to 150.
0000	Recall error 0003. This message should clear when that one is fixed.
** SYNTAX ERROR **	Some compilers do not list this type of error. When listed, generally, they indicate an error in coding the line in which periods, quotes, or a similar indicator is missing. You need to look at the code around the message, especially at the code above it. The syntax problems around line 70 have already been discussed.
0089	Look at the PICTURE. The type designator "X" is missing after the PIC.
0113	Study the UNTIL statement. The phrase EQUAL 'Y' has no space after the EQUAL.
0153	Discussed previously, the error at this line is questioning the length of the programmer-supplied name which appears to be too long to the compiler. Of course, it is, since the line contains a misplaced hyphen.

```
IDENTIFICATION DIVISION.
*
PROGRAM-ID.    REOLST.
ENVIRONMENT DIVISION.
*
CONFIGURATION SECTION.
*
SOURCE-COMPUTER.    PRIME 850.
OBJECT-COMPUTER.    PRIME 850.
*
INPUT-OUTPUT SECTION.
*
FILE-CONTROL.
    SELECT INVENTORY-STATUS-FILE
        ASSIGN TO PFMS.
    SELECT REORDER-LISTING
        ASSIGN TO PFMS.
*
DATA DIVISION.
*
FILE SECTION.
*
FD  INVENTORY-STATUS-FILE
    LABEL RECORDS ARE STANDARD
    RECORD CONTAINS 80 CHARACTERS.
*
01  INVENTORY-STATUS-RECORD.
    05  IS-ITEM-NO          PIC 9(5).
    05  IS-ITEM-DESC        PIC X(20).
    05  FILLER              PIC X(5).
    05  IS-UNIT-PRICE       PIC 9(3)V99.
    05  IS-REORDER-POINT    PIC 9(5).
    05  IS-QTY-ON-HAND      PIC 9(5).
    05  IS-QTY-ON-ORDER     PIC 9(5).
    05  FILLER              PIC X(30).
*
FD  REORDER-LISTING
        LABEL RECORDS ARE STANDARD
        RECORD CONTAINS 133 CHARACTERS.
*
01  PRINT-AREA.
    05  FILLER              PIC X(133).
*
WORKING-STORAGE SECTION.
*
01  SWITCHES.
    05  INVENTORY-EOF-SW    PIC X          VALUE 'N'.
*
01  WORK-FIELDS.
    05  AVAILABLE-STOCK     PIC S9(5)                   COMP-3.
*
01  PRINT-CONTROL-FIELDS                                COMP-3.
    05  LINE-COUNT          PIC S99        VALUE +99.
    05  LINES-ON-PAGE       PIC S99        VALUE +57.
    05  SPACE-CONTROL       PIC S9.
*
01  COUNT-FIELDS                                        COMP-3.
    05  RECORD-COUNT        PIC S9(5)      VALUE ZERO.
*
01  HEADING-LINE-1.
    05  FILLER              PIC X(24)      VALUE SPACE.
    05  FILLER              PIC X(8)       VALUE 'REORDER'.
    05  FILLER              PIC X(101)     VALUE 'LISTING'.
```

Figure 5-2
Syntax errors second pass (part 1 of 4)

```
(0064)          *
(0065)           01  HEADING-LINE-2.
(0066)               05  FILLER             PIC X(5)       VALUE ' ITEM'.
(0067)               05  FILLER             PIC X(12)      VALUE SPACE.
(0068)               05  FILLER             PIC X(20)      VALUE 'ITEM'.
(0069)               05  FILLER             PIC X(19)      VALUE 'UNIT'.
(0070)               05  FILLER             PIC X(77)      VALUE 'REORDER'.
(0071)          *
(0072)           01  HEADING-LINE-3.
(0073)               05  FILLER             PIC X(14)      VALUE ' NO.'.
(0074)               05  FILLER             PIC X(22)      VALUE '     DESCRIPTION
(0075)               05  FILLER             PIC X(9)       VALUE 'PRICE'.
** SYNTAX ERROR **     "QLIT"  PUNCT?
(0076)               05  FILLER             PIC X(12)      VALUE 'AVAILABLE'.
** SYNTAX ERROR **     "QLIT"  PUNCT?
(0077)               05  FILLER             PIC X(76)      VALUE 'POINT'.
** SYNTAX ERROR **     "QLIT"  PUNCT?
(0078)          *
(0079)           01  REORDER-LINE.
** SYNTAX ERROR **     "QLIT"
(0080)               05  FILLER             PIC X          VALUE SPACE.
** SYNTAX ERROR **     "QLIT"  LENGTH?
(0081)               05  RL-ITEM-NO         PIC X(3).
** SYNTAX ERROR **     "QLIT"  LENGTH?
(0082)               05  FILLER             PIC X(5)       VALUE SPACE.
** SYNTAX ERROR **     "QLIT"  LENGTH?
(0083)               05  RL-ITEM-DESC       PIC X(20).
** SYNTAX ERROR **     "QLIT"  LENGTH?
(0084)               05  FILLER             PIC X(5)       VALUE SPACE.
** SYNTAX ERROR **     "QLIT"  LENGTH?
(0085)               05  RL-UNIT-PRICE      PIC ZZZ.99.
** SYNTAX ERROR **     "QLIT"  LENGTH?
(0086)               05  FILLER             PIC X(5)       VALUE SPACE.
** SYNTAX ERROR **     "QLIT"  LENGTH?
(0087)               05  RL-AVAILABLE-STOCK PIC Z(5).
** SYNTAX ERROR **     "QLIT"  LENGTH?
(0088)               05  FILLER             PIC X(5)       VALUE SPACE.
** SYNTAX ERROR **     "QLIT"  LENGTH?
(0089)               05  RL-REORDER-POINT   PIC X(5).
** SYNTAX ERROR **     "QLIT"  LENGTH?
(0090)               05  FILLER             PIC X(71)      VALUE SPACE.
** SYNTAX ERROR **     "QLIT"  LENGTH?
(0091)          *
(0092)           01  TOTAL-LINE.
** SYNTAX ERROR **     "QLIT"  LENGTH?
(0093)               05  TL-RECORD-COUNT    PIC ZZ,ZZZ.
(0094)               05  FILLER             PIC X(13)      VALUE '  RECORDS IN'.
(0095)               05  FILLER             PIC X(4)       VALUE 'THE'.
(0096)               05  FILLER             PIC X(110)     VALUE 'INPUT FILE'.
(0097)          *
(0098)           01  ERROR-DESCRIPTION-LINE.
(0099)               05  FILLER             PIC X(16)      VALUE ' REORDER  A  2'.
(0100)               05  FILLER             PIC X(12)      VALUE 'CALCULATION'.
(0101)               05  FILLER             PIC X(15)      VALUE 'ERROR FOR ITEM'.
(0102)               05  FILLER             PIC XXX        VALUE 'NO'.
(0103)               05  EL-ITEM-NO         PIC X(5).
(0104)               05  FILLER             PIC X(9)       VALUE '--RECORD'.
(0105)               05  FILLER             PIC X(73)      VALUE 'IGNORED'.
(0106)          *
(0107)           PROCEDURE DIVISION.
(0108)          *
(0109)           000-PRODUCE-REORDER-LISTING.
(0110)               OPEN INPUT  INVENTORY-STATUS-FILE
```

Figure 5–2
Syntax errors second pass (part 2 of 4)

```
                 OUTPUT REORDER-LISTING.
           PERFORM 100-PRODUCE-REORDER-LINE
               UNTIL INVENTORY-EOF-SW EQUAL 'Y'.
           PERFORM 200-PRINT-TOTAL-LINE.
           CLOSE INVENTORY-STATUS-FILE
                 REORDER-LISTING.
           DISPLAY 'REORDER  I  1  NORMAL EOJ'.
           STOP RUN.
      *
       100-PRODUCE-REORDER-LINE.
           PERFORM 110-READ-INVENTORY-RECORD.
           IF INVENTORY-EOF-SW  EQUAL 'N'
               PERFORM 120-CALCULATE-AVAILABLE-STOCK
               IF AVAILABLE-STOCK LESS THAN IS-REORDER-POINT
                   PERFORM 130-PRINT-REORDER-LINE.
      *
       110-READ-INVENTORY-RECORD.
           READ INVENTORY-STATUS-FILE
               AT END
                   MOVE 'Y'              TO INVENTORY-EOF-SW.
      *
       120-CALCULATE-AVAILABLE-STOCK.
           ADD IS-QTY-ON-HAND IS-QTY-ON-ORDER
               GIVING AVAILABLE-STOCK
               ON SIZE ERROR
                   PERFORM 210-PRINT-ERROR-MESSAGE
                   MOVE 99999            TO AVAILABLE-STOCK.
      *
       130-PRINT-REORDER-LINE.
           IF LINE-COUNT GREATER THAN LINES-ON-PAGE
               PERFORM 140-PRINT-HEADING-LINES.
           MOVE IS-ITEM-NO               TO RL-ITEM-NO.
           MOVE IS-ITEM-DESC             TO RL-ITEM-DESC.
           MOVE IS-UNIT-PRICE            TO RL-UNIT-PRICE.
           MOVE AVAILABLE-STOCK          TO RL-AVAILABLE-STOCK.
           MOVE IS-REORDER-POINT         TO RL-REORDER-POINT.
           MOVE REORDER-LINE             TO PRINT-AREA.
           PERFORM 150-WRITE-REPORT-LINE.
           ADD 1                         TO RECORD-COUNT.
      *
       140-PRINT-HEADING-LINES.
           MOVE HEADING-LINE-1           TO PRINT-AREA.
           PERFORM 160-WRITE-PAGE-TOP-LINE.
           MOVE HEADING-LINE-2           TO PRINT-AREA.
           MOVE 2                    TO SPACE-CONTROL.
           PERFORM 150-WRITE-REPORT-LINE.
           MOVE HEADING-LINE-3           TO PRINT-AREA.
           PERFORM 150-WRITE-REPORT-LINE.
           MOVE 2                        TO SPACE-CONTROL.
      *
       150-WRITE-REPORT-LINE.
           WRITE PRINT-AREA
               AFTER ADVANCING SPACE-CONTROL.
           ADD SPACE-CONTROL             TO LINE-COUNT.
           MOVE 1                        TO SPACE-CONTROL.
      *
       160-WRITE-PAGE-TOP-LINE.
           WRITE PRINT-AREA
               AFTER ADVANCING PAGE.
           MOVE 1                        TO LINE-COUNT.
      *
       200-PRINT-TOTAL-LINE.
           MOVE RECORD-COUNT             TO TL-RECORD-COUNT.
```

Figure 5–2
Syntax errors second pass (part 3 of 4)

```
 (0174)              MOVE TOTAL-LINE            TO PRINT-AREA.
 (0175)              MOVE 3                     TO SPACE-CONTROL.
 (0176)              PERFORM 150-WRITE-REPORT-LINE.
 (0177)          *
 (0178)           210-PRINT-ERROR-MESSAGE.
 (0179)              MOVE IS-ITEM-NO            TO EL-ITEM-NO.
 (0180)              MOVE ERROR-DESCRIPTION-LINE TO PRINT-AREA.
 (0181)              PERFORM 150-WRITE-REPORT-LINE.
0075  UNRECOGNIZABLE ELEMENT IS IGNORED. [PRICE   ]
0076  UNRECOGNIZABLE ELEMENT IS IGNORED. [AVAILABLE    ]
0077  UNRECOGNIZABLE ELEMENT IS IGNORED. [POINT   ]
0092  /W/ PERIOD ASSUMED ABOVE.
0091  /W/ LITERAL TRUNCATED TO ITEM SIZE.
0142  UNRECOGNIZABLE ELEMENT IS IGNORED. [RL-ITEM-NO  ]
0143  UNRECOGNIZABLE ELEMENT IS IGNORED. [RL-ITEM-DESC  ]
0144  UNRECOGNIZABLE ELEMENT IS IGNORED. [RL-UNIT-PRICE   ]
0145  UNRECOGNIZABLE ELEMENT IS IGNORED. [RL-AVAILABLE-STOCK  [
0146  UNRECOGNIZABLE ELEMENT IS IGNORED. [RL-REORDER-POINT  ]
0147  STATEMENT DELETED DUE TO ERRONEOUS SYNTAX. [REORDER-LINE  ]
0147  UNRECOGNIZABLE ELEMENT IS IGNORED. [TO  ]
0147  UNRECOGNIZABLE ELEMENT IS IGNORED. [PRINT-AREA  ]
 P R O G R A M    S T A T I S T I C S

27 Errors, 2 Warnings, Prime V-Mode COBOL, Rev 19.1 <REOLST>
```

Figure 5–2
Syntax errors second pass (part 4 of 4)

Revised Reorder Listing—Second Compile

One aspect to note about most compilers is that one error can mask one or more other errors. These other errors will not show up until the current error has been fixed. This is what happens when the program is compiled after having all of the above errors fixed. Study Figure 5–2 and see if you can find what the cause of the diagnostics in the second compile are. You will find the cause to be a rather obscure one.

Amazingly, all of the diagnostics listed here are caused by one mistake. This is a good example of how one error can throw a whole section off in some compilers. Recall that you were instructed to look around when a syntax error appeared in the source code. If you look above the first message to line 0074, you will notice that the literal has no ending.quote, nor does the clause have an ending period. If you were trying to debug this one on the terminal, you might not discover the problem, since the quote and period might appear on the terminal. The problem is that the entry went beyond position 72, and the quote and period are in 73 and 74. This compiler did not print anything in positions 73–80, so the mistake was somewhat more noticeable.

The solution is to change the Picture in line 0073 to X(19), which will cause the literal 'NO.' to pad that area with blanks to the right of the NO. Then change line 0074 to read PIC X(17) VALUE 'DESCRIPTION'. That will pull the clause back out of the 73–80 area and get rid of all of these diagnostics.

After this situation was fixed, a clean compile was obtained, and now the programmer was able to begin testing the logic of the problem.

Topic 2 **Execution Time Errors**

Orientation

Getting the syntax errors out of the program is only part of the battle—probably the easy part because you have the diagnostics to indicate where the problems are. Once you obtain a clean compile, you then must test the program to ensure that the output is (1) in the form specified and (2) is accurate. The type of errors that can occur here are called *execution time* or *logic errors*. This topic first discusses how to test for accurate output, and second provides a beginning list of execution errors for which to look.

Terminology

execution error   logic error   left or right justified

Objectives

1. *Understand the difference between syntax and logic or execution time errors.*

2. ***Begin to develop precise techniques for testing the correctness of the output both in terms of format and accuracy of the data.***

3. ***Begin to develop a standard list of problems to look for when testing a program, and through experience begin to associate certain output problems with their likely causes.***

Testing for Correct Output Format

The correctness of the form should be easy to determine. At this point in the text, all of the output is formatted for the printer. The aspects of printed output to check for are:

1. **Horizontal positioning**—Make sure that each heading literal and each data element is printed in the relative position indicated on the print chart given for the output. If the chart indicated that the report name should begin in position 17, then it should be in 17. If it indicated 5 spaces between two literals or variables, then there should be 5 spaces on the output. Sometimes variable fields, such as names or numbers, have varying lengths for different records. In this case one side or the other should be in a fixed position. With alphanumeric fields the left side is usually in a fixed position (called *left justified*) whereas numeric fields have the right digit in a fixed position (*right justified*). Another alignment indicator that is handy, if used on a numeric field, is the decimal point.

2. Vertical positioning—The print chart will usually specify blank lines between certain groups of output. For instance, the following is typical:

Top line	**report heading**	**Gas light**
line 2	blank	
line 3	column heading 1	
line 4	column heading 2	
line 5	blank	
line 6	first detail line	
line 7 to n	other detail lines on page	
line n	blank	
line n+1	total line	
line n+2	blank	
line n+3	blank	
line n+4	EOJ message	

It is expected that your program will have single spacing where it is specified, double spacing where specified, and triple spacing when called for.

3. Correct literal spelling—If the output specs call for a column heading to read ITEM NUMBER, do not output it as ITEM NO.

4. Correct numeric variable edition—Be sure that your edit pictures of numeric fields follow the format indicated on the output specs. If a number is to have the high-order zeroes removed, be sure to do so. If the specs don't call for zero suppression, don't do it. Be careful about following the specified placement and use of commas, floating or fixed dollar signs, and other special characters such as the check protection asterisk.

A useful tool for checking horizontal positioning is a ruler to help you identify the position number on a line. In the past most printers were impact type that had a hammer which hit a preformed character slug against the ribbon and paper, thereby leaving an imprint of the character. When this was the common type of printer, the plastic flowchart templates commonly available also had an edge that was used for character counting. These were inexpensive tools for measuring in which position a character or group of characters appeared on a line. They were effective because most print character slugs were a standard size. However, when dot-matrix printers became common, there was no longer a guarantee of a standard since the size of any character can be varied even on a single printer. You may have to make a template yourself by creating a number line that can be printed out with your program, cut off, and used as a ruler to measure for correct positioning.

Some instructors will insist that you reproduce the output format exactly, and some will be more relaxed in this regard. It is recommended that you be exact with your output, as it will train you in the art of "attention to detail" which is a necessary skill in programming.

Testing for Correct Output Data

Sometimes this is an exercise with a calculator, sometimes you need to play computer, and sometimes you merely need to check that the input data did not get garbled before it got to the output.

Computers are very complex machines and occasionally do some strange things. But a working rule is that computers do not mess up your data, you the programmer did it. If a computer hiccups at the wrong time, the result will be so obvious that there will be little trouble identifying the cause. The output in that case will be extremely garbled or more likely just nonexistent. Computers do not make subtle errors, such as having the number 125.78 appear as 1.25. That is a programmer error. So take a very long time to conclude that "the computer fouled up." Spend time looking at your input and output specifications to see whether you have coded a record incorrectly. A common mistake is to make one of the field specifications in the input record either too long or too short, which will cause garbled data. That would be the likely cause of the 125.78 appearing as 1.25.

Another common mistake of novices is to conclude that the output they generate is correct. You must get out your calculator and add up the numbers to see if the totals printed are really correct. If you have subtotals, are they accurate? Are they really a total of their group? Check more than one group to be sure that you haven't been accumulating running totals rather than group totals. Do the subtotals add up to the major total? Try to imagine ways in which you could have misprogrammed and double check those situations.

Check back to the input and manually calculate the results of the required arithmetic operations. Do your manual calculations match those of the program? If not, why not?

Remember that your program is providing information that someone will use as a basis for making decisions. If you do not provide them with accurate information, you are leading them into some potentially poor decisions. People are learning to put more faith in the accuracy of computers. Help them learn to have faith in the skill and professionalism of programmers.

Common Execution Errors

There are a set of mistakes that novices are prone to make, but even the most experienced professional still makes them occasionally. The difference is in the frequency of occurrence and in the speed with which the mistake is found and corrected. This discussion presents a list of commonly made errors. You should refer to this list when debugging your program, as such a list can help speed the problem-solving process.

1. Failure to initialize a field—Depending on the operating system, a program may give bad data or have an abnormal termination if certain fields are not given a proper initial value:

Counters—normally should be set to zero

Switches—set to appropriate initial state

Totals and subtotals—set to zero

Control fields—capture initial value and new values whenever changes occur

As your programs become more complex, many of the above field types will have to be reset during the program execution. The most common ones are resetting subtotals after they have been printed and the new values for control fields. Be sure to pay special attention to these situations, as they are common sources of mistakes for the novice.

2. Inappropriate MOVE—Though simple in concept, the MOVE can cause problems if you do not pay attention to some of the more subtle rules associated with it. Especially learn the consequences of:

Sending and receiving fields of different length

Group item moved to elementary numeric field

Elementary numeric moved to a group item

3. Signed numbers—Remember that negative numbers can only be recognized by signed numeric PICTURE clauses. If you have the possibility of negative numbers, but forget the S designator, all of the numbers will be positive.

4. Field size too small—If an arithmetic operation generates a number that is too large to be contained in the specified size of the result field, the left most digits of the number will simply be truncated. Unless you have specified the ON SIZE option, you will normally get no warning. Plan your result fields carefully so that they will be able to handle the maximum possible size field for the data that the program will be handling.

5. Inappropriate use of comments—Once programmers become convinced of the value of comments in a program, they often tend to overcomment. Actually, a COBOL program requires very little commentary if the programmer specifies meaningful data names and functional paragraph names (more about this in the chapter on structured programming).

Overcommenting is often troublesome when maintenance is required, as there is a tendency to forget to change the comments which then are no longer consistent with the source code.

Some programmers have caused commands to become comments by placing an asterisk in position 7 when the code should have been eliminated. They mistakenly did this with the notion that doing so maintained a historical perspective, or that the code might be needed again at a future date. This is a bad practice as the resultant code is not as readable and could be very misleading. The guideline here: do not do it.

6. Nested IF problems—you know that whenever there are two or more IF statements in a sentence, this is called a nested IF. Remember that if the ELSE is used, the compiler associates it with the closest previous IF which is not already paired with an ELSE. You must take care that the nested logic the compiler generates is the logic you intended. There are a few techniques that can help:

Limiting the IFs—do not put more than three (maximum four) IF–ELSE combinations in a sentence. If the logic requires more, break them up into more sentences or perform paragraphs with subtests in them.

An ELSE for every IF—some guidelines recommend that each IF in a nested situation have an associated ELSE, even if there is no action required in the ELSE path. As you will see later, there is a way of handling that situation. Note that not all are in favor of this guideline, especially as an absolute.

Consistent indentation—a very valuable visual guide to what is taking place in the nested IF is to adopt an indentation pattern that promotes clarity of code, and to use it carefully in all appropriate situations. You will be provided with such a pattern in the discussion on structured style.

7. Misplaced periods—This in another of those subtle mistakes that can drive you crazy. If you forget the period at the end of an IF sentence, the following command may become a part of the IF logic when you don't want it to be. On the other hand, when there are several commands to be executed as part of an IF condition and one is ended with a period, the following commands will not be under control of the IF when they should have been. There are other situations where a misplaced period can cause inaccurate, but executable logic, so be careful with them.

8. Invalid file access—COBOL will not let you access a file before it has been opened or after it has been closed. You may not normally access the input area in the file section after the AT END switch in the READ command has been turned on. Inappropriate execution of READ or WRITE commands will sometimes cause the first input record to be bypassed, the last detail line to be printed twice, detail lines to contain data from the previous and the current record, etc. You should always check the first and last output records to ensure that such an error has not occurred.

Discussion

There are other common execution errors, but they are the type that happen with advanced processes, such as table handling and disk file access, so discussion of them now is premature. Again, be sure to refer back to this list whenever you are checking for execution time errors. And be on the lookout for others to add to your personal list and to share with your fellow programmers.

Topic 3 Introduction to Testing and Debugging

Orientation

Testing and debugging refer to the process of executing the object program to see if it works as intended, finding errors, correcting them, and trying again. More specifically, the object of testing is to find errors, while the object of debugging is to remove them.

One of the major pitfalls in the process of programming is inadequate testing. In other words, a program is not tried on enough combinations of input data to be sure all of its routines work. Nevertheless, it is considered to be tested and is put into production. Then, when actual data causes inaccurate output to be produced or causes program cancellation, a crisis often occurs. Imagine the scurrying that goes on when a program that prints payroll checks is cancelled prematurely. Or when a payroll check for double the amount owed to an employee is discovered.

Terminology

abend
abnormal termination
acceptance test
data exception
divide exception
operation exception
overflow exception
program check
storage dump
storage printout
systems test
test plan
unit test
utility program

Objective

Given test data, expected output, compiler output, and test run output, debug any program ending in normal termination.

Testing

To guard against inadequate testing, a program is usually tested in three phases: unit test, systems test, and acceptance test. The *unit test* is the programmer test in which the programmer tries to make sure that all modules in the program are adequately tested. The *systems test* is designed to test the relationships between the programs within a system; if, for example, the output from one program in a system is input to another program, the systems test helps determine whether the programs are properly coordinated. Finally, the *acceptance test* is designed to determine whether the instructions to the operations department are clear enough that the program can be run without any help from the program developers.

To prepare for the unit test, you should develop a *test plan*. To do this, you first make a list of all of the conditions that should be tested in each module. Then you decide in what sequence the conditions should be tested. In general, you want to discover the major problems first, so you start by using only valid data to see whether the major modules are entered properly and whether control passes from one major module to another as intended. Then you can test for independent errors, after which you can test for errors that result when one condition has an effect on another condition. Finally, you can test conditions that depend on volume; to test a page overflow routine, for example, you need enough data to force 60 or more print lines.

Once you have a test plan, you create data that will test the conditions specified in your plan. As you create the data, you also determine what output to expect.

After a test run is made, you compare the actual output with the expected output. If the program involves tape or disk input or output, listings of the contents of these files must be made before and after the test run. In a disk update run, for example, the contents of the disk file must be printed before and after testing to determine what changes were made in the file during the test run.

To get a listing of a file's contents, you may have to write your own programs or you may use *utility programs* that are supplied with an operating system. In any event, if the actual output disagrees with the expected output, you must find the cause of the error, change the source code, recompile, and test again.

After you make a test run, you should document it. The documentation for each test run should include the following:

1. The compiler output for the run
2. Listing of each input file used
3. Listings of each output file created during the test run

In addition, you should mark any output errors on the output listing, and, on the source listing, you should mark what changes you made to correct these errors. Since a programmer in a typical data-processing department is frequently coding, testing, and debugging several programs at one time, this documentation can save backtracking and confusion.

Debugging

Debugging is one of the most challenging jobs of a programmer. In a large, complex program, debugging an error can be much like solving a mystery. To determine what happened, you begin with clues and trace backward until you find the culprit: a coding error or input error.

When a program is tested, there are two possible outcomes: (1) it can run to completion (STOP RUN), or (2) it can be abnormally terminated or cancelled. If a program runs to completion, the programmer discovers any errors or bugs by comparing actual output with expected output. If a program is abnormally terminated, the programmer must discover the cause of the termination, correct it, and test again.

Normal termination (end of job)

The reorder-listing program will be used again to illustrate debugging after normal termination of a test run. This time some minor errors which will cause defective output have been introduced into the source code of this program. Of the several test cases that could be designed to fully test the program, the two following test records have been selected for this illustration:

	Case 1	Case 2
Item number	00101	00103
Description	GENERATOR	HEATER SOLENOID
On-hand quantity	00070	00034
On-order quantity	00050	00000
Reorder point	00100	00050

The first item does not require reordering, so it should not appear on the report; the second item should appear on the report.

Figure 5–3 gives the output of the test run. Parts 1-3 show the source listing that resulted from the compilation step, and the printer output that resulted from the execute step begins at the bottom of part 3. As you can see, there are three different errors in the printer output: (1) there is some unexpected data (garbage) in the first heading line; (2) in the second heading line, the whole first column-heading line after the second ITEM is shifted to the left and is not aligned with the headings in the second column-heading line; and (3) the detail line for the second input record did not print.

Can you determine the cause of these errors? Those in the heading lines are fairly easy to debug. Quite simply, statement 66 doesn't give an initial value of SPACE to the last 94 positions of the work area. As a result, data from the previous program prints in the last 94 print positions. As for the misplacement of the first column heading line, statement 71 should have a PICTURE of X(27), not X(7).

```
 IDENTIFICATION DIVISION.
*
 PROGRAM-ID.    REORLST.
 ENVIRONMENT DIVISION.
*
 CONFIGURATION SECTION.
*
 SOURCE-COMPUTER.    PRIME 850.
 OBJECT-COMPUTER.    PRIME 850.
*
 INPUT-OUTPUT SECTION.
*
 FILE-CONTROL.
     SELECT INVENTORY-STATUS-FILE
         ASSIGN TO PFMS.
     SELECT REORDER-LISTING
         ASSIGN TO PFMS.
*
 DATA DIVISION.
*
 FILE SECTION.
*
 FD  INVENTORY-STATUS-FILE
     LABEL RECORDS ARE STANDARD
     RECORD CONTAINS 80 CHARACTERS.
*
 01  INVENTORY-STATUS-RECORD.
     05  IS-ITEM-NO          PIC 9(5).
     05  IS-ITEM-DESC        PIC X(20).
     05  FILLER              PIC X(5).
     05  IS-UNIT-PRICE       PIC 9(3)V99.
     05  IS-REORDER-POINT    PIC 9(5).
     05  IS-QTY-ON-HAND      PIC 9(5).
     05  IS-QTY-ON-ORDER     PIC 9(5).
     05  FILLER              PIC X(30).
*
 FD  REORDER-LISTING
     LABEL RECORDS ARE STANDARD
     RECORD CONTAINS 133 CHARACTERS.
*
 01  PRINT-AREA.
     05  FILLER              PIC X(133).
*
 WORKING-STORAGE SECTION.
*
 01  SWITCHES.
     05  INVENTORY-EOF-SW    PIC X          VALUE 'N'.
         88  LAST-INVENTORY-RECORD          VALUE 'Y'.
         88  MORE-INVENTORY-RECORDS         VALUE 'N'.
*
 01  WORK-FIELDS.
     05  AVAILABLE-STOCK     PIC S9(5)                      COMP-3.
*
 01  PRINT-CONTROL-FIELDS                                   COMP-3.
     05  LINE-COUNT          PIC S99        VALUE +99.
     05  LINES-ON-PAGE       PIC S99        VALUE +57.
     05  SPACE-CONTROL       PIC S9.
*
 01  COUNT-FIELDS                                           COMP-3.
     05  RECORD-COUNT        PIC S9(5)      VALUE ZERO.
*
 01  HEADING-LINE-1.
     05  FILLER              PIC X(24)      VALUE SPACE.
```

Figure 5–3
Execution errors—reorder listing (part 1 of 4)

```
           05  FILLER                PIC X(8)      VALUE 'REORDER'.
           05  FILLER                PIC X(7)      VALUE 'LISTING'.
           05  FILLER                PIC X(94).
      *
       01  HEADING-LINE-2.
           05  FILLER                PIC X(6)      VALUE '  ITEM'.
           05  FILLER                PIC X(5)      VALUE SPACE.
           05  FILLER                PIC X(7)      VALUE 'ITEM'.
           05  FILLER                PIC X(8)      VALUE 'UNIT'.
           05  FILLER                PIC X(12)     VALUE 'QUANTITY'.
           05  FILLER                PIC X(75)     VALUE 'REORDER'.
      *
       01  HEADING-LINE-3.
           05  FILLER                PIC X(11)     VALUE '   NO.'.
           05  FILLER                PIC X(26)     VALUE 'DESCRIPTION'.
           05  FILLER                PIC X(8)      VALUE 'PRICE'.
           05  FILLER                PIC X(14)     VALUE 'AVAILABLE'.
           05  FILLER                PIC X(74)     VALUE 'POINT'.
      *
       01  REORDER-LINE.
           05  FILLER                PIC X         VALUE SPACE.
           05  RL-ITEM-NO            PIC X(5).
           05  FILLER                PIC X(5)      VALUE SPACE.
           05  RL-ITEM-DESC          PIC X(20).
           05  FILLER                PIC X(5)      VALUE SPACE.
           05  RL-UNIT-PRICE         PIC ZZZ.99.
           05  FILLER                PIC X(5)      VALUE SPACE.
           05  RL-AVAILABLE-STOCK    PIC ZZ,ZZ9.
           05  FILLER                PIC X(5)      VALUE SPACE.
           05  RL-REORDER-POINT      PIC ZZ,ZZZ.
           05  FILLER                PIC X(71)     VALUE SPACE.
      *
       01  ERROR-DESCRIPTION-LINE.
           05  FILLER                PIC X(16)     VALUE ' REORDER  A  2'.
           05  FILLER                PIC X(12)     VALUE 'CALCULATION'.
           05  FILLER                PIC X(15)     VALUE 'ERROR FOR ITEM'.
           05  FILLER                PIC XXX       VALUE 'NO'.
           05  EL-ITEM-NO            PIC X(5).
           05  FILLER                PIC X(9)      VALUE '--RECORD'.
           05  FILLER                PIC X(73)     VALUE 'IGNORED'.
      *
       01  TOTAL-LINE.
           05  FILLER                PIC X         VALUE SPACE.
           05  TL-RECORD-COUNT       PIC ZZ,ZZZ.
           05  FILLER                PIC X(13)     VALUE '  RECORDS ON'.
           05  FILLER                PIC X(4)      VALUE 'THE'.
           05  FILLER                PIC X(109)    VALUE 'INPUT FILE'.
      *
       PROCEDURE DIVISION.
      *
       000-PRODUCE-REORDER-LISTING.
           OPEN INPUT  INVENTORY-STATUS-FILE
                OUTPUT REORDER-LISTING.
           PERFORM 100-PRODUCE-REORDER-LINE
               UNTIL LAST-INVENTORY-RECORD
           PERFORM 200-PRINT-TOTAL-LINE.
           CLOSE INVENTORY-STATUS-FILE
                 REORDER-LISTING.
           DISPLAY 'REORLST  I  1  NORMAL EOJ'.
           STOP RUN.
      *
       100-PRODUCE-REORDER-LINE.
           PERFORM 110-READ-INVENTORY-RECORD.
           IF MORE-INVENTORY-RECORDS
```

Figure 5–3
Execution errors—reorder listing (part 2 of 4)

```
                PERFORM 120-CALCULATE-AVAILABLE-STOCK
                IF AVAILABLE-STOCK LESS THAN IS-REORDER-POINT
                    PERFORM 130-PRINT-REORDER-LINE.
      *
       110-READ-INVENTORY-RECORD.
           READ INVENTORY-STATUS-FILE
               AT END
                   MOVE 'Y'             TO INVENTORY-EOF-SW.
      *
       120-CALCULATE-AVAILABLE-STOCK.
           ADD IS-QTY-ON-HAND IS-QTY-ON-ORDER
               GIVING AVAILABLE-STOCK
               ON SIZE ERROR
                   PERFORM 140-PRINT-ERROR-MESSAGE
                   MOVE 99999           TO AVAILABLE-STOCK.
      *
       130-PRINT-REORDER-LINE.
           IF LINE-COUNT GREATER THAN LINES-ON-PAGE
               PERFORM 150-PRINT-HEADING-LINES.
           MOVE IS-ITEM-NO              TO RL-ITEM-NO.
           MOVE IS-ITEM-DESC            TO RL-ITEM-DESC.
           MOVE IS-UNIT-PRICE           TO RL-UNIT-PRICE.
           MOVE AVAILABLE-STOCK         TO RL-AVAILABLE-STOCK.
           MOVE IS-REORDER-POINT        TO RL-REORDER-POINT.
           MOVE REORDER-LINE            TO PRINT-AREA.
           ADD 1                        TO RECORD-COUNT.
      *
       140-PRINT-ERROR-MESSAGE.
           MOVE IS-ITEM-NO              TO EL-ITEM-NO.
           MOVE ERROR-DESCRIPTION-LINE TO PRINT-AREA.
           PERFORM 160-WRITE-REPORT-LINE.
      *
       150-PRINT-HEADING-LINES.
           MOVE HEADING-LINE-1          TO PRINT-AREA.
           PERFORM 170-WRITE-PAGE-TOP-LINE.
           MOVE HEADING-LINE-2          TO PRINT-AREA.
           MOVE 2                       TO SPACE-CONTROL.
           PERFORM 160-WRITE-REPORT-LINE.
           MOVE HEADING-LINE-3          TO PRINT-AREA.
           PERFORM 160-WRITE-REPORT-LINE.
           MOVE 2                       TO SPACE-CONTROL.
      *
       160-WRITE-REPORT-LINE.
           WRITE PRINT-AREA
               AFTER ADVANCING SPACE-CONTROL.
           ADD SPACE-CONTROL            TO LINE-COUNT.
           MOVE 1                       TO SPACE-CONTROL.
      *
       170-WRITE-PAGE-TOP-LINE.
           WRITE PRINT-AREA
               AFTER ADVANCING PAGE.
           MOVE 1                       TO LINE-COUNT.
      *
       200-PRINT-TOTAL-LINE.
           MOVE RECORD-COUNT            TO TL-RECORD-COUNT.
           MOVE TOTAL-LINE              TO PRINT-AREA.
           MOVE 3                       TO SPACE-CONTROL.
           PERFORM 160-WRITE-REPORT-LINE.
P R O G R A M   S T A T I S T I C S


Executable Code Size: 511 Words.
Constant Pool Size: 66 Words.
Total Pure Procedure Size: 577 Words.
```

Figure 5–3
Execution errors—reorder listing (part 3 of 4)

```
Working-Storage Size: 822 Bytes.
Total [inkframe Size: 805 Words.

Stack Size: 40 Words.

Trace Mode: Off.

No Arguments Expected.

185 Source Lines.


No Errors, No Warnings, Prime V-Mode COBOL, Rev 19.2  REORLS


                    REORDER LISTING /BSUP        BSS   $002F           (0067)        pt

ITEM      ITEM   UNIT      QUANTITY      REORDER
 NO.      DESCRIPTION              PRICE    AVAILABLE       POINT

     2 RECORDS ON THE INPUT FILE
```

Figure 5–3
Execution errors—reorder listing (part 4 of 4)

But why didn't the detail line print? There are several possibilities. The second data record could contain incorrect data. Such incorrect data could cause the calculation of quantity available to be greater than the reorder point, which, of course, prevents the line from printing. The statements for calculating available could be in error so available was considered to be larger than reorder point. The IF statement that determines whether available is less than the reorder point could be worded wrong so the PERFORM statement wasn't executed as intended. The paragraph that prints the detail line could be incomplete so that the reorder line never reached the PRINT–AREA or was never actually written. Or perhaps the program ended before the second record was completely processed. By checking out each of these possibilities, you should be able to determine that a PERFORM statement is missing near the end of the paragraph named 130–PRINT–REORDER–LINE. Thus, the program never reached paragraph 150–WRITE–REPORT–LINE, and the reorder line wasn't printed.

Using DISPLAY statements

Since this program is short, debugging is relatively simple. However, if a program is long or the calculations are complex, it may be very difficult to determine why the output is not as expected. In this case, you may want to use debugging statements (such as DISPLAY statements) to provide output messages as the program executes. These statements are inserted in your program during testing, and they are removed after the errors are corrected. The messages given by these statements can show the contents of selected storage fields or they can indicate which modules were executed. They can thus help you find the bugs. After the errors are corrected, the statements are removed from the source program, the program is recompiled, and a final test run is made.

To illustrate the use of DISPLAY statements for debugging, suppose you couldn't figure out why the reorder line wasn't printed during the test run that is documented in Figure 5–3. You might then insert the DISPLAY state

```
Display statements inserted in module 120:

DISPLAY "BF-ON-HAND        = " BF-ON-HAND.                    DEBUG
DISPLAY "BF-ON-ORDER       = " BF-ON-ORDER.                   DEBUG
DISPLAY "AVAILABLE-STOCK   = " AVAILABLE-STOCK.               DEBUG
DISPLAY "BF-REORDER-POINT  = " BF-REORDER-POINT.              DEBUG


DISPLAY statement output:

BF-ON-HAND        = 00070
BF-ON-ORDER       = 00050
AVAILABLE-STOCK   = 0012
BF-REORDER-POINT  = 00100
BF-ON-HAND        = 00034
BF-ON-ORDER       = 00000
AVAILABLE-STOCK   = 0003D
BF-REORDER-POINT  = 00050
REORLST  I  1  NORMAL  EOJ
```

Figure 5–4
Using DISPLAY statements to show the contents of selected fields during the execution of a test run

ments shown in Figure 5–4 at the end of module 120. This time when the program is tested using the two records given earlier, you will have the additional output shown in Figure 5–4. By analyzing this output, you can see that the input data and available-stock calculation are correct, so you must check out other possibilities.

There are a couple of points you should note about the DISPLAY statements in Figure 5–4. First, depending on how your system stores data, the DISPLAY statement output may contain some characters you wouldn't normally expect. For example, if a numeric field carries a sign, the rightmost digit of the field may be displayed as a letter, a special character, or a blank (look at the rightmost position in the values for AVAILABLE–STOCK). Also, notice that DEBUG was coded in columns 73–77 of the source list so the DISPLAY statements will be easy to remove from the program at the end of the test run.

If you still couldn't figure out why the reorder line wasn't printed, you might use DISPLAY statements to show the sequence in which the modules of the program were executed. For instance, you could take out the DISPLAY statements of Figure 5–4 (since you know the data values are correct) and insert the DISPLAY statements of Figure 5–5 into the reorder-listing program. One DISPLAY statement is to be inserted into each paragraph of the program to print the module number of the paragraph. As a result, the output from these statements, as shown in Figure 5–5, clearly indicates that module 160 was executed only twice. By checking the module documentation, you can see that this module should be called twice by module 150 and once by module 130, so the problem is probably within module 130.

On most systems, there are more sophisticated ways to trace the execution of a program and to find out the values of certain fields during a test run. For now, though, the DISPLAY statement will help you get the information you need to debug a program that ran to completion.

Abnormal termination

If a program is *abnormally terminated*, it is referred to as a *program check*. This means the object program tried to do something impossible—such as trying to operate arithmetically on non-numeric data. When a program check

```
DISPLAY statements inserted in modules 100 through 200:

DISPLAY 100.                                                   DEBUG
DISPLAY 110.                                                   DEBUG
DISPLAY 120.                                                   DEBUG
DISPLAY 130.                                                   DEBUG
DISPLAY 140.                                                   DEBUG
DISPLAY 150.                                                   DEBUG
DISPLAY 160.                                                   DEBUG
DISPLAY 200.                                                   DEBUG

DISPLAY statement output:

100
110
120
100
110
120
130
140
160
150
150
100
110
200
REORLST  I  1  NORMAL EOJ
```

Figure 5–5
Using DISPLAY statements to list the modules that are executed during a test run

occurs, an error message is usually displayed on the operator console or printed in the program output. In either case, the program is cancelled.

Debugging a program that terminates abnormally (or *abends*) can be a very difficult process. Many systems provide additional output when a program abends to help you in debugging. For example, on some systems you can get a *storage dump*, or *storage printout*, that lists the contents of a computer's storage at the time the program check occurred. Rather than detail the extra output produced by any one computer system, though, here are some general ideas on what to look for in finding the cause of a program check no matter what system you're using.

In many cases, you will be able to tell which record was last to be processed before the program check occurred. This is your first debugging clue. If, for example, the program prints one line for each input record, you can tell which record was last to be processed by analyzing the printed output up to the time of the program check. Similarly, if a program prints one line for each group of input records, you will be able to narrow the problem down to a group of records by analyzing the output that was printed before the program check occurred. Then, by analyzing the record that was being processed at the time of the program check, you can often find something unusual that is likely to have caused the program check.

A second debugging help is knowing that the vast majority of all program checks result from a relatively limited number of causes. The four most common types of program checks are data exception, divide exception, overflow exception, and operation exception. These are described in more detail below.

Data exception

The most common type of program check is called *data exception*. It occurs when an arithmetic statement tries to operate on non-numeric data. In general, there are two cases in which data exception occurs in COBOL programs.

In the first case, the input data doesn't conform to the input descriptions in the Data Division. If, for example, blanks are read into a storage field with a picture of 9(3), data exception will result when the field is operated upon by an ADD statement. This type of error is caused either by faulty input data or by faulty data descriptions.

In the second case, a field in working storage isn't initialized properly. If, for example, a field is supposed to have a starting value of zero but is given no starting value, data exception may occur when an ADD statement tries to add a number to it.

If you can figure out which record was being processed at the time of the program check, it's usually rather easy to debug a program that was ended because of data exception. If the program check occurs during the processing of the first input record, it's likely that some field in working storage wasn't initialized properly or that a field description in the Data Division is wrong. If the program check occurs during the processing of a later record, it's likely that one of the input fields contains invalid data.

Divide exception

When a program tries to divide a field by zero, a *divide exception* occurs. In this case, you should be able to locate the bug by checking the DIVIDE statements in your program along with the data in the record that was being processed at the time of the program check. As a good programming practice, your program should always check to make sure that the divisor isn't zero before executing a DIVIDE statement; then the divide exception should never occur.

Overflow exception

When the execution of an arithmetic statement leads to a result that is larger than the receiving field can hold and the ON SIZE ERROR clause hasn't been used, an *overflow exception* can occur. Here again, you should be able to find the bug by analyzing the data in the record that was being processed at the time of the program check. If you follow this data through your program, you should reach a set of arithmetic instructions in which the result exceeds the size of the receiving field. This in turn means that either your size specifications in the Data Division are inaccurate or the data exceeds its expected limits. As a good programming practice, your program should check the input data whenever possible to make sure it's a reasonable size; then the overflow exception should never occur.

Operation exception

When the computer tries to execute an invalid machine-language operation code, an *operation exception* occurs. In a COBOL program, this often means a file-handling problem. For example, the following questions may lead you to the cause of an operation exception in COBOL:

1. Did a READ statement attempt to read a file before it was opened?
2. Did a READ or WRITE statement try to operate on a file after it was closed?

3. Did a statement refer to a field in the input area of storage after the AT END clause for the file had been executed?

4. Did a statement attempt to operate on a field in the input area before the first READ statement was executed for the file?

5. Did SPACE–CONTROL have an invalid value at the time a WRITE statement was executed? In other words, was it left blank or did it contain some value other than a positive integer?

6. Was a STOP RUN statement executed before all files were closed?

Although these errors don't cause operation exceptions on all systems, they are common causes on some systems.

This book isn't designed to teach you how to debug all types of program checks, but this introduction to program checks should help you debug most of the abnormal terminations you will run into using the COBOL elements presented in this book. Later on, you may learn more sophisticated methods of debugging abnormal terminations. Even then, however, you should always look for the obvious bug first.

Discussion

As you will see, structured programs that conform to the recommended organization and style will contain fewer bugs to begin with. In addition, these bugs are likely to be simple keying or clerical mistakes rather than complex logical errors. Finally, due to the structured design, the bugs will be relatively easy to find and correct.

Problem

Figure 5–6 gives the output for a test run made on the reorder-listing program using the following test data:

Record Positions	1–5	6–25	26–30	31–35	36–40	41–45	46–50
	00101	GENERATOR	04000	04900	00100	00070	00050
	00103	HEATER SOLENOID	00330	00440	00050	00034	00000
	03244	GEAR HOUSING	06500	07900	00010	00012	00000
	03981	PLUMB LINE	00210	00240	00015	00035	00000
	04638	STARTER SWITCH	00900	00980	00030	00016	00000

The output includes (1) the source listing and (2) the printer output. However, reorder lines have printed for all five input records when they should have only printed for two of the records. In addition, the amounts in the AVAILABLE column aren't correct. How should these errors be corrected?

Solution

IS–QTY–ON–HAND in statement 33 should have a PICTURE of 9(5).

```
       IDENTIFICATION DIVISION.
      *
       PROGRAM-ID.   REORLST.
       ENVIRONMENT DIVISION.
      *
       CONFIGURATION SECTION.
      *
       SOURCE-COMPUTER     PRIME 850.
       OBJECT-COMPUTER.    PRIME 850.
      *
       INPUT-OUTPUT SECTION.
      *
       FILE-CONTROL.
           SELECT INVENTORY-STATUS-FILE
               ASSIGN TO PFMS.
           SELECT REORDER-LISTING
               ASSIGN TO PFMS.
      *
       DATA DIVISION.
      *
       FILE SECTION.
      *
       FD  INVENTORY-STATUS-FILE
           LABEL RECORDS ARE STANDARD
           RECORD CONTAINS 80 CHARACTERS.
      *
       01  INVENTORY-STATUS-RECORD.
           05  IS-ITEM-NO          PIC 9(5).
           05  IS-ITEM-DESC        PIC X(20).
           05  FILLER              PIC X(5).
           05  IS-UNIT-PRICE       PIC 9(3)V99.
           05  IS-REORDER-POINT    PIC 9(5).
           05  IS-QTY-ON-HAND      PIC 999V99.
           05  IS-QTY-ON-ORDER     PIC 9(5).
           05  FILLER              PIC X(30).
      *
       FD  REORDER-LISTING
           LABEL RECORDS ARE STANDARD
           RECORD CONTAINS 133 CHARACTERS.
      *
       01  PRINT-AREA.
           05  FILLER              PIC X(133).
      *
       WORKING-STORAGE SECTION.
      *
       01  SWITCHES.
           05  INVENTORY-EOF-SW    PIC X         VALUE 'N'.
               88  LAST-INVENTORY-RECORD         VALUE 'Y'.
               88  MORE-INVENTORY-RECORDS        VALUE 'N'.
      *
       01  WORK-FIELDS.
           05  AVAILABLE-STOCK     PIC S9(5)                    COMP-3.
      *
       01  PRINT-CONTROL-FIELDS                                 COMP-3.
           05  LINE-COUNT          PIC S99       VALUE +99.
           05  LINES-ON-PAGE       PIC S99       VALUE +57.
           05  SPACE-CONTROL       PIC S9.
      *
       01  COUNT-FIELDS                                         COMP-3.
           05  RECORD-COUNT        PIC S9(5)     VALUE ZERO.
      *
       01  HEADING-LINE-1.
           05  FILLER              PIC X(24)     VALUE SPACE.
           05  FILLER              PIC X(8)      VALUE 'REORDER'.
           05  FILLER              PIC X(101)    VALUE 'LISTING'.
```

Figure 5-6
Execution errors—reorder listing, 2nd type (part 1 of 4)

```
      *
       01  HEADING-LINE-2.
           05  FILLER                  PIC X(6)     VALUE '  ITEM'.
           05  FILLER                  PIC X(5)     VALUE SPACE.
           05  FILLER                  PIC X(27)    VALUE 'ITEM'.
           05  FILLER                  PIC X(8)     VALUE 'UNIT'.
           05  FILLER                  PIC X(12)    VALUE 'QUANTITY'.
           05  FILLER                  PIC X(75)    VALUE 'REORDER'.
      *
       01  HEADING-LINE-3.
           05  FILLER                  PIC X(11)    VALUE '   NO.'.
           05  FILLER                  PIC X(26)    VALUE 'DESCRIPTION'.
           05  FILLER                  PIC X(8)     VALUE 'PRICE'.
           05  FILLER                  PIC X(14)    VALUE 'AVAILABLE'.
           05  FILLER                  PIC X(74)    VALUE 'POINT'.
      *
       01  REORDER-LINE.
           05  FILLER                  PIC X        VALUE SPACE.
           05  RL-ITEM-NO              PIC X(5).
           05  FILLER                  PIC X(5)     VALUE SPACE.
           05  RL-ITEM-DESC            PIC X(20).
           05  FILLER                  PIC X(5)     VALUE SPACE.
           05  RL-UNIT-PRICE           PIC ZZZ.99.
           05  FILLER                  PIC X(5)     VALUE SPACE.
           05  RL-AVAILABLE-STOCK      PIC ZZ,ZZ9.
           05  FILLER                  PIC X(5)     VALUE SPACE.
           05  RL-REORDER-POINT        PIX ZZ,ZZZ.
           05  FILLER                  PIC X(71)    VALUE SPACE.
      *
       01  ERROR-DESCRIPTION-LINE.
           05  FILLER                  PIC X(16)    VALUE ' REORDER  A  2'.
           05  FILLER                  PIC X(12)    VALUE 'CALCULATION'.
           05  FILLER                  PIC X(15)    VALUE 'ERROR FOR ITEM'.
           05  FILLER                  PIC XXX      VALUE 'NO'.
           05  EL-ITEM-NO              PIC X(5).
           05  FILLER                  PIC X(9)     VALUE '--RECORD'.
           05  FILLER                  PIC X(73)    VALUE 'IGNORED'.
      *
       01  TOTAL-LINE.
           05  FILLER                  PIC X        VALUE SPACE.
           05  TL-RECORD-COUNT         PIC ZZ,ZZZ.
           05  FILLER                  PIC X(13)    VALUE '  RECORDS ON'.
           05  FILLER                  PIC X(4)     VALUE 'THE'.
           05  FILLER                  PIC X(109)   VALUE 'INPUT FILE'.
      *
       PROCEDURE DIVISION.
      *
       000-PRODUCE-REORDER-LISTING.
           OPEN INPUT  INVENTORY-STATUS-FILE
                OUTPUT REORDER-LISTING.
           PERFORM 100-PRODUCE-REORDER-LINE
               UNTIL LAST-INVENTORY-RECORD
           PERFORM 200-PRINT-TOTAL-LINE.
           CLOSE INVENTORY-STATUS-FILE
                 REORDER-LISTING.
           DISPLAY 'REORLST  I  1  NORMAL EOJ'.
           STOP RUN.
      *
       100-PRODUCE-REORDER-LINE.
           PERFORM 110-READ-INVENTORY-RECORD.
           IF MORE-INVENTORY-RECORDS
               PERFORM 120-CALCULATE-AVAILABLE-STOCK
               IF AVAILABLE-STOCK LESS THAN IS-REORDER-POINT
                   PERFORM 130-PRINT-REORDER-LINE.
      *
```

Figure 5-6
Execution errors—reorder listing, 2nd type (part 2 of 4)

```
       110-READ-INVENTORY-RECORD.
           READ INVENTORY-STATUS-FILE
               AT END
                   MOVE 'Y'            TO INVENTORY-EOF-SW
      *
       120-CALCULATE-AVAILABLE-STOCK.
           ADD IS-QTY-ON-HAND IS-QTY-ON-ORDER
               GIVING AVAILABLE-STOCK
               ON SIZE ERROR
                   PERFORM 140-PRINT-ERROR-MESSAGE
                   MOVE 99999          TO AVAILABLE-STOCK.
      *
       130-PRINT-REORDER-LINE.
           IF LINE-COUNT GREATER THAN LINES-ON-PAGE
               PERFORM 150-PRINT-HEADING-LINES.
           MOVE IS-ITEM-NO             TO RL-ITEM-NO.
           MOVE IS-ITEM-DESC           TO RL-ITEM-DESC.
           MOVE IS-UNIT-PRICE          TO RL-UNIT-PRICE.
           MOVE AVAILABLE-STOCK        TO RL-AVAILABLE-STOCK.
           MOVE IS-REORDER-POINT       TO RL-REORDER-POINT.
           MOVE REORDER-LINE           TO PRINT-AREA.
           PERFORM 160-WRITE-REPORT-LINE.
           ADD 1                       TO RECORD-COUNT.
      *
       140-PRINT-ERROR-MESSAGE.
           MOVE IS-ITEM-NO             TO EL-ITEM-NO.
           MOVE ERROR-DESCRIPTION-LINE TO PRINT-AREA.
           PERFORM 160-WRITE-REPORT-LINE.
      *
       150-PRINT-HEADING-LINES.
           MOVE HEADING-LINE-1         TO PRINT-AREA.
           PERFORM 170-WRITE-PAGE-TOP-LINE.
           MOVE HEADING-LINE-2         TO PRINT-AREA.
           MOVE 2                      TO SPACE-CONTROL.
           PERFORM 160-WRITE-REPORT-LINE.
           MOVE HEADING-LINE-3         TO PRINT-AREA.
           PERFORM 160-WRITE-REPORT-LINE.
           MOVE 2                      TO SPACE-CONTROL.
      *
       160-WRITE-REPORT-LINE.
           WRITE PRINT-AREA
               AFTER ADVANCING SPACE-CONTROL.
           ADD SPACE-CONTROL           TO LINE-COUNT.
           MOVE 1                      TO SPACE-CONTROL.
      *
       170-WRITE-PAGE-TOP-LINE.
           WRITE PRINT-AREA
               AFTER ADVANCING PAGE.
           MOVE 1                      TO LINE-COUNT.
      *
       200-PRINT-TOTAL-LINE.
           MOVE RECORD-COUNT           TO TL-RECORD-COUNT.
           MOVE TOTAL-LINE             TO PRINT-AREA.
           MOVE 3                      TO SPACE-CONTROL.
           PERFORM 160-WRITE-REPORT-LINE.
P R O G R A M    S T A T I S T I C S

Executable Code Size: 515 Words.
Constant Pool Size: 68 Words.
Total Pure Procedure Size: 583 Words.

Working-Storage Size: 822 Bytes.
Total Linkframe Size: 805 Words.
```

Figure 5-6
Execution errors—reorder listing, 2nd type (part 3 of 4)

```
Stack Size: 40 Words.

Trace Mode: Off.

No Arguments Expected.

185 Source Lines.

No Errors, No Warnings, Prime V-Mode COBOL, Rev 19.2  REORLS

                           REORDER LISTING

 ITEM       ITEM                         UNIT     QUANTITY      REORDER
  NO.       DESCRIPTION                  PRICE    AVAILABLE      POINT

00101       GENERATOR                    49.00        50          100
00103       HEATER SOLENOID               4.40         0           50
03244       GEAR HOUSING                 79.00         0           10
03981       PLUMB LINE                    2.40         0           15
04638       STARTER SWITCH                9.80         0           30

        5    RECORDS ON THE INPUT FILE
```

Figure 5-6
Execution errors—reorder listing, 2nd type (part 4 of 4)

Topic 4 **Introduction to Control Breaks**

Orientation

One of the major goals for this text is to develop your logical programming ability by having you learn some specific programming techniques. One of those techniques is learning how to organize and specify the code for *control breaks*. Control break processing simply means that input data is organized or sorted into groups. The groups are identified by indicators of some sort which are stored in one of the fields in the record. Typical grouping indicators are customer numbers, class codes, department numbers, warehouse numbers, etc. Whenever the group indicator changes, it is said that a control break has occurred. There can be control breaks within control breaks, and when there are n number of them, it is said that you are programming an n-level control break. This topic will introduce you to the single- or one-level control break.

Terminology

column heading	detail report	report total
control break	grand total	subtotal
control field	heading line	summary report
detail line	report heading	total line

Objectives

1. *Understand and use the terms that apply to control break logic.*
2. *Given the problem statement for a single-level control break problem, provide the coding for the programmed solution.*
3. *Learn how print chart specifications indicate the type of control break logic required for the output.*

Report Line Types

Before getting into the topic of control breaks, it is appropriate to define some terms more precisely. In any discussion about reports and reporting, you will recognize that a report is composed of lines. The main problem you will be faced with in writing report logic is when and how to output the various kind of lines that comprise a report. The principal line types are defined below:

Report heading(s). One or more lines of literals (and possibly variables) that define the purpose of the report and probably the name of the company or department for which the report is being made. Generally called a *heading line* it may also contain times, dates, and page numbers.

Column heading(s). One or more lines which clearly denote for the user of the report what data is being listed in the column below. This is also a heading line.

Detail line(s). Normally several lines which represent one line of information for each input record read. These lines are said to contain the "details" of the report.

Total line(s). Lines that contain various accumulations of the quantities listed in the detail lines. There are commonly *subtotals* (totals of one or more data groups) and *grand totals* or *report totals*, which are the accumulations of all of the detail quantities for the whole report. Sometimes page totals are given, which, of course, are merely the totals of all quantities shown on that page.

Figure 5–7 contains the specifications for a new program that will be presented for study. The print chart shows the output format for a one-level customer sales report. The report lists the customer numbers and the calculated amount of the sale for each transaction to each customer. The print chart uses all of these line types—report, heading, detail, and total. These will be commonly used terms in the discussions that follow in this text.

The Single-Level Control Break—Subtotals

The most common programming application of control break logic is the accumulation and printing of subtotals. As mentioned before, data is grouped by a code and, whenever the code changes, different actions are specified if you are doing control break programming. A very typical action at that time is to print the total that was accumulated from the previous group.

System flowchart:

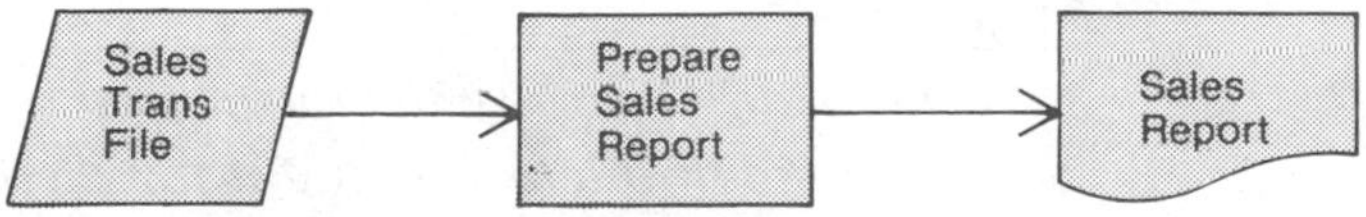
Sales Trans File
Prepare Sales Report
Sales Report

Print chart:

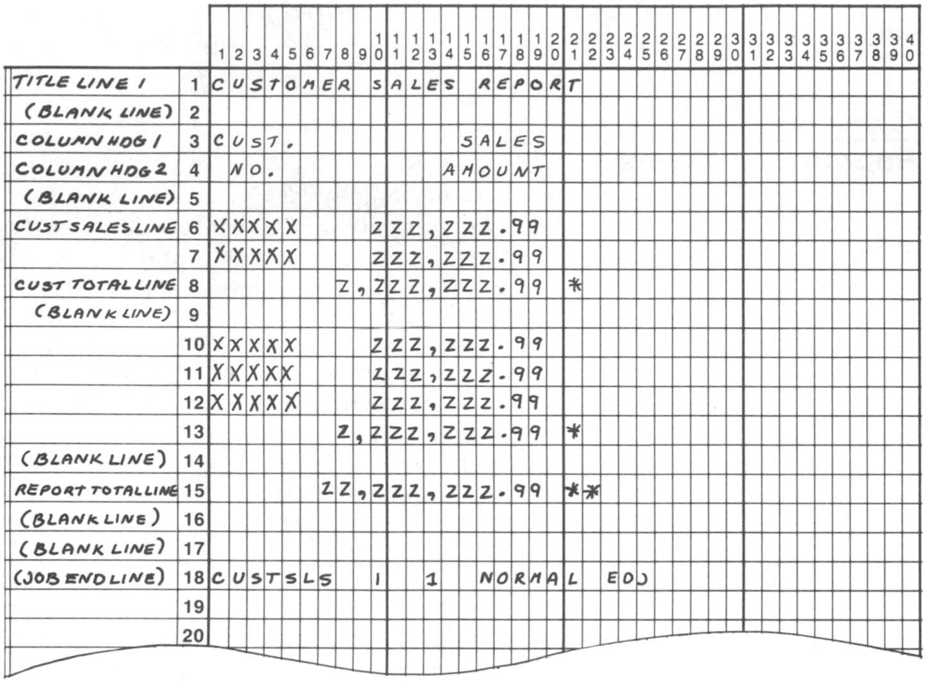
TITLE LINE 1
(BLANK LINE)
COLUMN HDG 1
COLUMN HDG 2
(BLANK LINE)
CUST SALES LINE
CUST TOTAL LINE
(BLANK LINE)
(BLANK LINE)
REPORT TOTAL LINE
(BLANK LINE)
(BLANK LINE)
(JOB END LINE)
CUSTOMER SALES REPORT
CUST. SALES
NO. AMOUNT
XXXXX ZZZ,ZZZ.99
Z,ZZZ,ZZZ.99 *
ZZ,ZZZ,ZZZ.99 **
CUSTSLS 1 1 NORMAL EOJ

Input record layout:

Field Name	Order Number	Order Date	Salesman Number	Customer Number	Quantity	Item Number	Unit Cost	Unit Price	Unused
Characteristics	X(5)	9(6)	X(2)	X(5)	9(3)	X(5)	999V99	999V99	X(44)
Usage									
Position	1-5	6-11	12-13	14-18	19-21	22-26	27-31	32-35	37-80

Figure 5–7
Specifications for a one-level control break sales report.

Observe the output shown in Figure 5–8, and you will note that there are one or more transactions (lines) for each customer. When each input record has an output line printed for it, the report is called a *detail report.* If you use your calculator, you will see that the subtotals (indicated by single asterisks) printed are the total of the amounts in the lines between the last subtotal (or the beginning of the program) and the current one. In Figure 5–8 the first subtotal is the accumulation of all the quantities printed in the sales amount column for customer number 01052, the second subtotal is the accumulation of all quantities printed for customer number 01940, and so on. The last subtotal is the accumulation of all quantities for customer 58111. The final total (indicated by the double asterisks) is the accumulation of all the subtotals.

The output of these subtotals is considered to be "breaks" in the normal logic flow. They occur when a control field changes, thus the derivation of the name "control break." After that break to output the subtotal, the normal

```
CUSTOMER SALES REPORT

CUST.        SALES
 NO.         AMOUNT

01052         376.75
01052         800.00
01052         200.00
            1,376.75 *

01940         505.00
01940         620.00
            1,125.00 *

13498         448.00
13498         576.00
            1,024.00 *

19763         875.00
19763       2,000.00
19763       2,000.00
            4,875.00 *

26888         295.25
              295.25 *

31284       1,500.00
31284         257.39
31284         500.00
            2,257.39 *

33480         320.00
33480         665.20
              985.20 *

49200         500.00
49200         800.00
49200          54.95
            1,354.95 *

58111         540.75
              540.75 *

           13,834.29 **

CUSTSLS  I  1  NORMAL EOJ
```

Figure 5–8
Output from one-level control break CUSTSLS program

logic flow continues. Of course, if no change occurs, there is no break and the normal logic flow goes on. One small logic problem to be cautious about is not to overlook processing the first record in the new group.

To enable this break in the normal logic flow to occur, some new program parts must be introduced. First, study Figure 5–9 which is the structure chart for the program CUSTSLS that produced the output shown in Figure 5–8. This is the program that will be used to demonstrate the additions needed for a control break program. In studying the structure chart, did you observe any significant differences from previous charts? If you look back, you will probably see that there was only one PRINT–something–LINE module under the 100–PRODUCE–something–LINE module. Now you should note that there are two PRINT–something–LINEs which are actually named 130–PRINT–CUSTOMER–LINE and 140–PRINT–CUSTOMER–TOTAL. This,

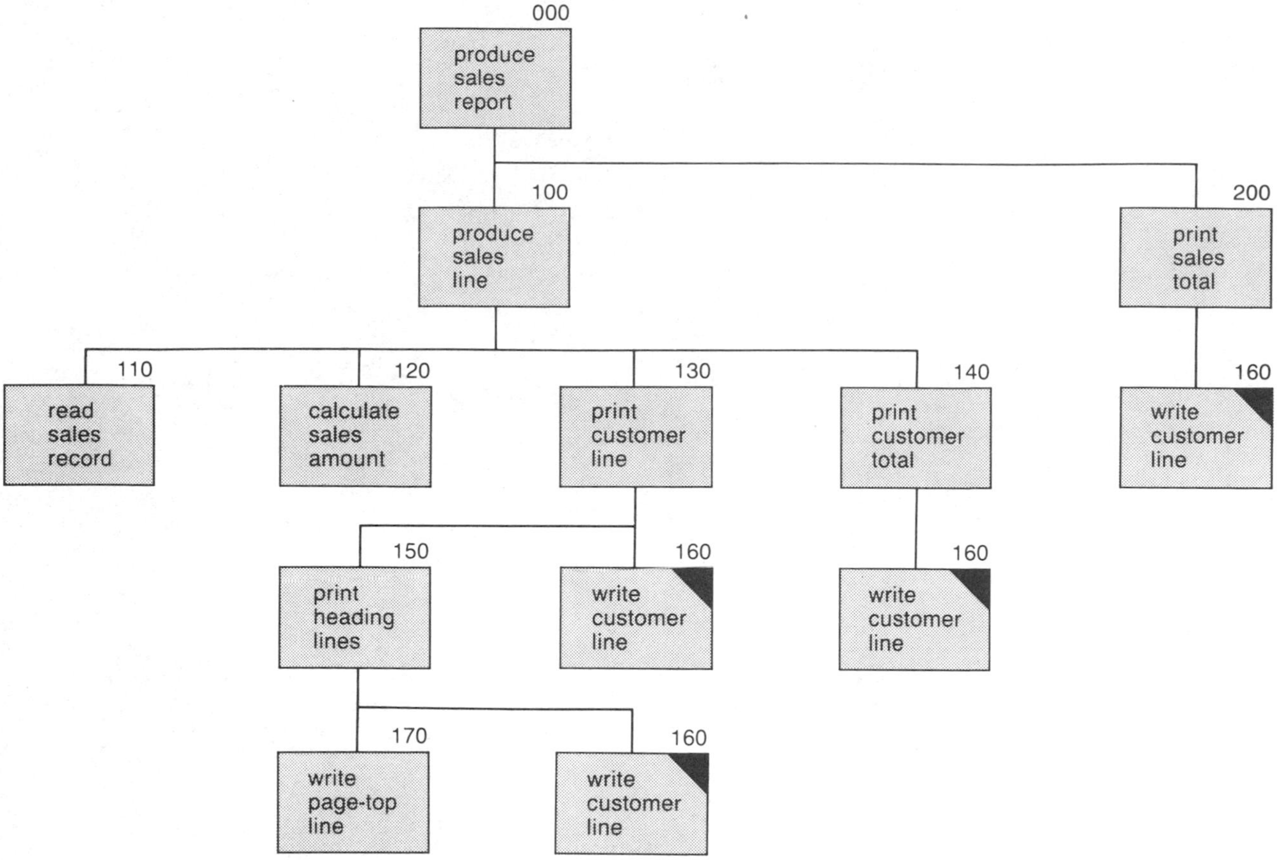
000
produce sales report
100
produce sales line
200
print sales total
110
read sales record
120
calculate sales amount
130
print customer line
140
print customer total
160
write customer line
150
print heading lines
160
write customer line
160
write customer line
170
write page-top line
160
write customer line

Figure 5–9
Structure chart for CUSTSLS one-level control break report

of course, indicates that there is one additional module in this program that was not in the others that you have seen.

An important note can be inserted here. You might have begun to note that modules and their relationship to one another are beginning to fall into a rather standard pattern. This, in fact, is true. There is a rather standard pattern, especially for printed output. Since the text tries to avoid making any overly large conceptual jumps, the program problems build on the concepts learned in previous problems. As programs become more complex, the structure charts just tend to have a few changes and additions to that basic pattern. The sooner you learn this pattern, the quicker and easier it will be for you to solve your problem programs.

Figure 5–10 is the source code list for the CUSTSLS program that produces the output of Figure 5–8. First, observe in Figure 5–10 that a new group, CONTROL–FIELDS, has been added in Working–Storage at the 01 level. The field shown, PRIOR–CUSTOMER–NO, is called a *control field.* This field will contain the group indicator from the current group being printed, so that when the next record is read into memory its indicator may be compared to PRIOR–CUSTOMER–NO to determine if a change has occurred. If the fields are different, then the logic performs the routine to print the subtotal for the previous group and to take care of getting ready for a new group. Other significant Working–Storage additions are:

1. The CUSTOMER–TOTAL field under the 01-level TOTAL–FIELDS. This is the accumulator for the calculated sales amounts from each transaction.

```
 IDENTIFICATION DIVISION.
*
 PROGRAM-ID.    CUSTSLS.
*
 ENVIRONMENT DIVISION.
*
 CONFIGURATION SECTION.
*
 SOURCE-COMPUTER.    PRIME 850.
 OBJECT-COMPUTER.    PRIME 850.
*
 INPUT-OUTPUT SECTION.
*
 FILE-CONTROL.
     SELECT SALES-TRAN-FILE
         ASSIGN TO PFMS.
     SELECT SALES-REPORT.
         ASSIGN TO PFMS.
*
 DATA DIVISION.
*
 FILE SECTION.
*
 FD  SALES-TRAN-FILE
     LABEL RECORDS ARE STANDARD
     RECORD CONTAINS 56 CHARACTERS.
*
 COPY 'SALES-TRAN-RECORD'.
 01  SALES-TRAN-RECORD.
     05  ST-ORDER-NO          PIC X(5).
     05  ST-ORDER-DATE        PIC 9(6).
     05  ST-SALESPERS-NO      PIC XX.
     05  ST-CUSTOMER-NO       PIC X(5).
     05  ST-QUANTITY          PIC 9(3).
     05  ST-ITEM-NUMBER       PIC X(5).
     05  ST-UNIT-COST         PIC 999V99.
     05  ST-UNIT-PRICE        PIC 999V99.
     05  FILLER               PIC X(20).
 COPY 'SALES-TRAN-RECORD'.
*
 FD  SALES-REPORT
     LABEL RECORDS ARE STANDARD
     RECORD CONTAINS 133 CHARACTERS.
*
 01  PRINT-AREA.
     05  FILLER               PIC X(133).
*
 WORKING-STORAGE SECTION.
*
 01  SWITCHES.
     05  SALES-TRAN-EOF-SW    PIC X          VALUE 'N'.
         88  END-SALES-FILE                  VALUE 'Y'.
         88  MORE-SALES-RECORDS              VALUE 'N'.
     05  FIRST-RECORD-SW      PIC X          VALUE 'Y'.
         88  FIRST-SALES-RECORD              VALUE 'Y'.
*
 01  WORK-FIELDS                                          COMP-3.
     05  SALES-AMOUNT         PIC 9(5)V99.
*
 01  CONTROL-FIELDS.
     05  PRIOR-CUSTOMER-NO    PIC X(5).
*
 01  PRINT-CONTROL-FIELDS                                 COMP-3.
     05  LINE-COUNT           PIC S99        VALUE +99.
```

Figure 5–10
Single-level control break program CUSTSLS (part 1 of 3)

```
           05  LINES-ON-PAGE        PIC S99          VALUE +57.
           05  SPACE-CONTROL        PIC S99          VALUE +1.
      *
       01  TOTAL-FIELDS                                      COMP-3.
           05  CUSTOMER-TOTAL       PIC S9(5)V99     VALUE ZERO.
           05  REPORT-TOTAL         PIC S9(7)V99     VALUE ZERO.
      *
       01  REPORT-HEADING-LINE.
           05  FILLER               PIC X(10)        VALUE 'CUSTOMER'.
           05  FILLER               PIC X(123)       VALUE 'SALES REPORT'.
      *
       01  COL-HEADING-1.
           05  FILLER               PIC X(15)        VALUE ' CUST.'.
           05  FILLER               PIC X(118)       VALUE 'SALES'.
      *
       01  COL-HEADING-2.
           05  FILLER               PIC X(14)        VALUE '  NO.'.
           05  FILLER               PIC X(119)       VALUE 'AMOUNT'.
      *
       01  CUSTOMER-LINE.
           05  FILLER               PIC X            VALUE SPACE.
           05  CL-CUSTOMER-NO       PIC X(5).
           05  FILLER               PIC X(4)         VALUE SPACE.
           05  CL-SALES-AMOUNT      PIC ZZZ,ZZZ.99.
           05  FILLER               PIC X(113)       VALUE SPACE.
      *
       01  CUSTOMER-TOTAL-LINE.
           05  FILLER               PIC X(8)         VALUE SPACE.
           05  CT-CUSTOMER-TOTAL    PIC Z,ZZZ,ZZZ.99.
           05  FILLER               PIC X(113)       VALUE ' *'.
      *
       01  REPORT-TOTAL-LINE.
           05  FILLER               PIC X(7)         VALUE SPACE.
           05 RT-REPORT-TOTAL       PIC ZZ,ZZZ,ZZZ.99.
           05  FILLER               PIC X(113)       VALUE ' **'.
      *
       PROCEDURE DIVISION.
      *
       000-PRODUCE-SALES-REPORT.
           OPEN INPUT  SALES-TRAN-FILE
                OUTPUT SALES-REPORT.
           PERFORM 100-PRODUCE-SALES-LINE
               UNTIL END-SALES-FILE.
           PERFORM 200-PRINT-SALES-TOTAL.
           CLOSE SALES-TRAN-FILE
                 SALES-REPORT.
           DISPLAY 'CUSTSLS  I  1  NORMAL EOJ'.
           STOP RUN.
      *
       100-PRODUCE-SALES-LINE.
           PERFORM 110-READ-SALES-RECORD.
           IF ST-CUSTOMER-NO GREATER THAN PRIOR-CUSTOMER-NO
               PERFORM 140-PRINT-CUSTOMER-TOTAL.
           IF MORE-SALES-RECORDS
               PERFORM 120-CALCULATE-SALES-AMOUNT
               PERFORM 130-PRINT-CUSTOMER-LINE.
      *
       110-READ-SALES-RECORD.
```

Figure 5–10
Single-level control break program CUSTSLS (part 2 of 3)

```
               READ SALES-TRAN-FILE
                   AT END
                       MOVE 'Y'               TO SALES-TRAN-EOF-SW
                       MOVE HIGH-VALUE        TO ST-CUSTOMER-NO.
               IF FIRST-SALES-RECORD
                   MOVE ST-CUSTOMER-NO        TO PRIOR-CUSTOMER-NO
                   MOVE 'N'                   TO FIRST-RECORD-SW.
          *
           120-CALCULATE-SALES-AMOUNT.
               MULTIPLY ST-QUANTITY BY ST-UNIT-PRICE
                   GIVING SALES-AMOUNT.
               ADD SALES-AMOUNT               TO CUSTOMER-TOTAL.
          *
           130-PRINT-CUSTOMER-LINE.
               IF LINE-COUNT GREATER THAN LINES-ON-PAGE
                   PERFORM 150-PRINT-HEADING-LINES.
               MOVE ST-CUSTOMER-NO            TO CL-CUSTOMER-NO.
               MOVE SALES-AMOUNT              TO CL-SALES-AMOUNT.
               MOVE CUSTOMER-LINE             TO PRINT-AREA.
               PERFORM 160-WRITE-CUSTOMER-LINE.
          *
           140-PRINT-CUSTOMER-TOTAL.
               MOVE CUSTOMER-TOTAL            TO CT-CUSTOMER-TOTAL.
               MOVE CUSTOMER-TOTAL-LINE       TO PRINT-AREA.
               PERFORM 160-WRITE-CUSTOMER-LINE.
               ADD CUSTOMER-TOTAL             TO REPORT-TOTAL.
               MOVE ZERO                      TO CUSTOMER-TOTAL.
               MOVE ST-CUSTOMER-NO            TO PRIOR-CUSTOMER-NO.
               MOVE 2                         TO SPACE-CONTROL.
          *
           150-PRINT-HEADING-LINES.
               MOVE REPORT-HEADING-LINE       TO PRINT-AREA.
               PERFORM 170-WRITE-PAGE-TOP-LINE.
               MOVE COL-HEADING-1             TO PRINT-AREA.
               MOVE 2                         TO SPACE-CONTROL.
               PERFORM 160-WRITE-CUSTOMER-LINE.
               MOVE COL-HEADING-2             TO PRINT-AREA.
               PERFORM 160-WRITE-CUSTOMER-LINE.
               MOVE 2                         TO SPACE-CONTROL.
          *
           160-WRITE-CUSTOMER-LINE.
               WRITE PRINT-AREA
                   AFTER ADVANCING SPACE-CONTROL.
               ADD SPACE-CONTROL              TO LINE-COUNT.
               MOVE 1                         TO SPACE-CONTROL.
          *
           170-WRITE-PAGE-TOP-LINE.
               WRITE PRINT-AREA
                   AFTER ADVANCING PAGE.
               MOVE 1                         TO LINE-COUNT.
          *
           200-PRINT-SALES-TOTAL.
               MOVE REPORT-TOTAL              TO RT-REPORT-TOTAL.
               MOVE REPORT-TOTAL-LINE         TO PRINT-AREA.
               MOVE 2                         TO SPACE-CONTROL.
               PERFORM 160-WRITE-CUSTOMER-LINE.
```

Figure 5–10
Single-level control break program CUSTSLS (part 3 of 3)

2. 01 CUSTOMER–TOTAL–LINE, which is the description of the line that will contain the customer total amount and which will be printed when the control break occurs.

3. Under the 01 SWITCHES is FIRST–RECORD–SW. This is a switch employed in the READ module to control actions required to capture the first customer number. You will soon see that those actions are required only once in the program execution.

Carefully study Figure 5–10 during the following discussion of the changes and additions in the Procedure Division. You may be surprised to observe that there will be only one new module added and just small changes made to two other modules. The new Procedure Division statements are:

1. The most significant logical change to the program is the addition of the two lines in module 100:

```
IF   ST-CUSTOMER-NO GREATER THAN PRIOR-CUSTOMER-NO
     PERFORM 140-PRINT-CUSTOMER-TOTAL.
```

This is the logical comparison where the program discovers whether the group indicators have changes or not. As you can see the module to print the subtotal, 140–PRINT–CUSTOMER–TOTAL, is executed only when the indicator has changed. If no change occurs, the program moves on to the next sentence where it tests the last record switch.

Note the comparison used is GREATER whereas most people might be inclined to test EQUAL. This is a somewhat minor point, but the reason for the GREATER test is that the way in which the records are grouped is by sorting on the group indicator. Since most sorts of this kind are in ascending order, the lower numbers will be first and the highest numbers last, thus the numbers are always getting larger and the test for greater is appropriate. If the groups are in descending order, then the test would be LESS. In the event that you are not able to predict the order, then an EQUAL test would probably be more appropriate.

2. Two code change shave been made to the 110–READ... module. The first is the addition of the

```
MOVE HIGH-VALUE     TO ST-CUSTOMER-NO.
```

statement to the action controlled by the AT END clause of the READ command. The purpose of this statement is to force the highest possible code in the computer's collating sequence into the input customer number. The reason for doing so is to ensure that the contents of ST–CUSTOMER–NO is greater than the contents of the control field, PRIOR–CUSTOMER–NO, which causes the IF test discussed above to be true which then allows module 140–PRINT–CUSTOMER–TOTAL to be performed. How else would you easily make sure that the total for the last group was printed? Some programmers go to much trouble getting the last subtotal printed when the end of file happens. This is the cleanest method, as it used the existing code in module 100 and only requires the addition of the above MOVE statement.

A note about the HIGH–VALUE. It is a COBOL reserved word which is in the category of figurative constants like ZERO and SPACE. The constant in this case is the highest internal code possible on the individual computer, normally resulting in having all of the bits in the receiving field turned on. COBOL also has a LOW–VALUE figurative constant which would be the appropriate value to move if the file were in descending order. That would normally result in all of the bits of the receiving field being turned off.

3. The second code change to the 110–READ module is the sentence:

```
IF  FIRST-SALES-RECORD
    MOVE ST-CUSTOMER-NO       TO PRIOR-CUSTOMER-NO
    MOVE 'N'                  TO FIRST-SALES-REC-SW.
```

This allows the capture of the group indicator of the first record. This is necessary so that there will be a valid customer number present in the control field when the IF test in module 100 takes place. Of course, when processing the first customer, the numbers will be equal, the test will be false, and no break will occur. But then there was no reason to want to print a total at that point anyhow.

If you think about the situation for a time, you will agree that this is necessary as the program cannot be expected to have the PRIOR–CUSTOMER–NO field initialized to the first customer on the file. If at first you think "why not?" ask yourself what would happen if the first customer quit the company and was subsequently removed from the file. The next customer on file would now become the first one, but the program would still have the removed customer number in the control field.

The move of the 'N' to the switch field merely sets the switch to an "off" state, which prevents the two moves from being done again.

4. The module 140–PRINT–CUSTOMER–TOTAL is the one that takes care of printing the total line and preparing for processing the next group. It has several different subfunctions which should be done in the following order:

a. Move necessary variables to the print line.

b. Move the Working–Storage record to the File Section output record (PRINT–AREA).

c. If other than single space, adjust the SPACE–CONTROL field. This example has no need to do this since the output specifications called for single space between the detail and the total line.

d. Perform the WRITE module (160).

e. Roll the subtotal amount just printed forward to the next level of total. Here you add the subtotal to the report total.

f. Set the subtotal to zero. This gets it ready for the next group. Failure to do this is a common mistake and results in what is called a "cumulative total." This mistake is one reason for the strong recommendation to check your output with a calculator before deciding that the program is accurate.

g. Move the customer number of the new record in memory to the control field. This captures the number of the new group and prevents printing of the subtotal line until the group changes again or the end of the file is reached.

Although the list of tasks for the subtotal print module seems rather long, note that there is often only one command per point discussed.

Another important point to pay attention to in coding this kind of module is that of testing for the page overflow. Observe that module

140 does not make that test. There is an excellent reason for not doing so. When the total for a group is being printed, it should appear on the same page as the details that generated the total. If the print total module tested for overflow, the total line could wind up as the first line on the next page, which is generally thought to be poor report form. If you look at the structure chart of Figure 5–9, you will see that none of the page-top modules are connected to the subtotal module.

Discussion

Study the control break example and discussion carefully. Mastery of the control break logic is one of the major milestones in your pursuit of programming skills of which you can be proud.

Problems

You are to write a program for a food sales report. The report is to have a one-level report control break. The input records will be in franchise number order within district number. The report is to be a detail report. This means that a group total is to be printed whenever the district number changes and a line is to be printed for each input record read. The following gives specific instructions for working the problem:

1. The program specifications for the food sales report problem are given in Figure 5–11.

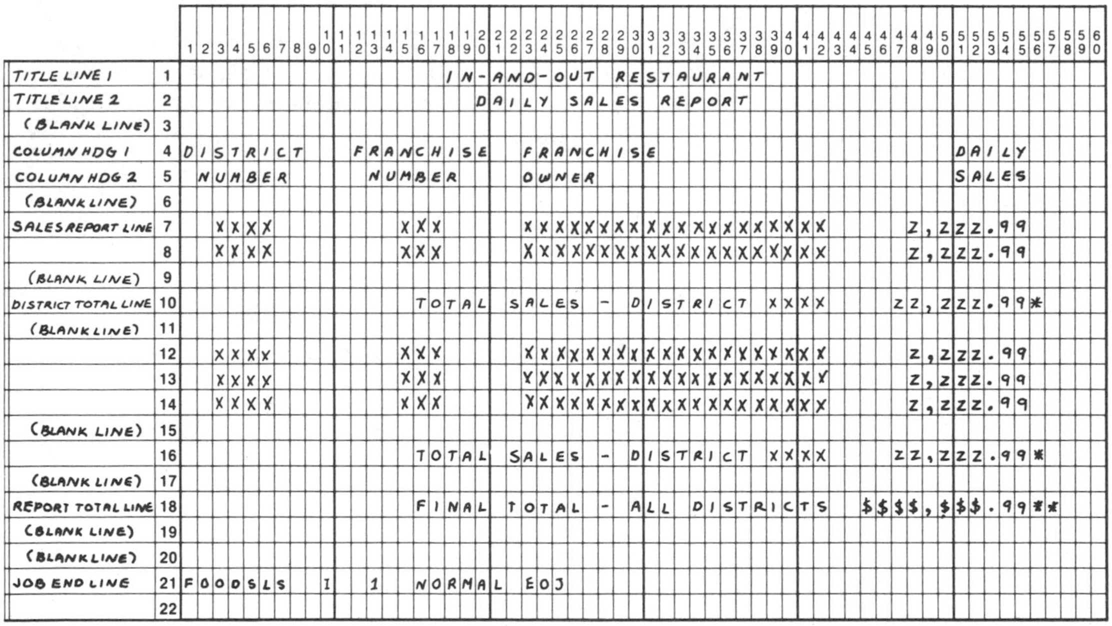
TITLE LINE 1 — IN-AND-OUT RESTAURANT
TITLE LINE 2 — DAILY SALES REPORT
(BLANK LINE)
COLUMN HDG 1 — DISTRICT FRANCHISE FRANCHISE DAILY
COLUMN HDG 2 — NUMBER NUMBER OWNER SALES
(BLANK LINE)
SALES REPORT LINE — XXXX XXX XXXXXXXXXXXXXXXXXXXX Z,ZZZ.99
XXXX XXX XXXXXXXXXXXXXXXXXXXX Z,ZZZ.99
(BLANK LINE)
DISTRICT TOTAL LINE — TOTAL SALES - DISTRICT XXXX ZZ,ZZZ.99*
(BLANK LINE)
XXXX XXX XXXXXXXXXXXXXXXXXXXX Z,ZZZ.99
XXXX XXX XXXXXXXXXXXXXXXXXXXX Z,ZZZ.99
XXXX XXX XXXXXXXXXXXXXXXXXXXX Z,ZZZ.99
(BLANK LINE)
TOTAL SALES - DISTRICT XXXX ZZ,ZZZ.99*
(BLANK LINE)
REPORT TOTAL LINE — FINAL TOTAL - ALL DISTRICTS $$$$,$$$.99**
(BLANK LINE)
(BLANK LINE)
JOB END LINE — FOODSLS I 1 NORMAL EOJ

Field Name	District Number	Franchise Number	Franchise Owner	Daily Sales
Characteristics	X(4)	X(3)	X(20)	9(4)V99
Usage				
Position	1-4	5-7	8-27	28-33

Figure 5–11
Program specifications for Food Sales 1-level report

2. The first two levels of the structure chart for the food sales program are given in Figure 5–12. Complete the structure chart, being careful to use the naming and numbering conventions.

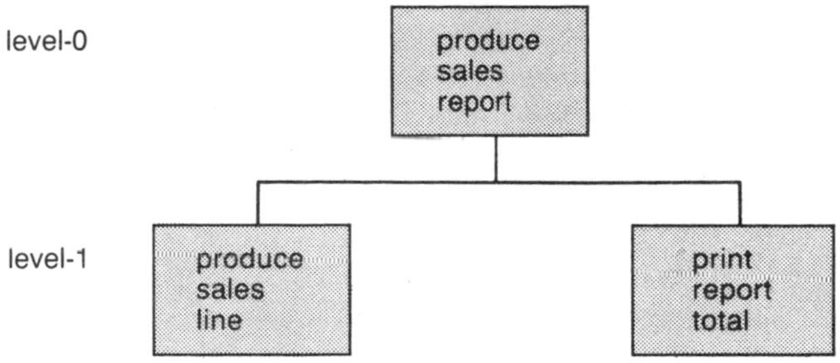
level-0
produce sales report
level-1
produce sales line
print report total

Figure 5–12
First two levels of one-level control break food sales report

3. Partial coding for the first three divisions of the food sales program solution are shown in Figure 5–13. Complete the coding as specified below:
   a. ***point-A—provide the input record description.
   b. ***point-B—provide the specifications for the necessary switches.
   c. ***point-C—provide the specifications for the necessary control fields.
4. Provide the Procedure Division statements necessary to solve the problem.

```
       IDENTIFICATION DIVISION.
      *
       PROGRAM-ID.    FOODSLS.
      *
       ENVIRONMENT DIVISION.
      *
       CONFIGURATION SECTION.
      *
       SOURCE-COMPUTER.    PRIME 850.
       OBJECT-COMPUTER.    PRIME 850.
      *
       INPUT-OUTPUT SECTION.
      *
       FILE-CONTROL.
           SELECT DAILY-FOOD-RECEIPTS
               ASSIGN TO PFMS.
           SELECT DAILY-FOOD-SALES-REPT.
               ASSIGN TO PFMS.
      *
       DATA DIVISION.
      *
       FILE SECTION.
      *
       FD  DAILY-FOOD-RECEIPTS
           LABEL RECORDS ARE STANDARD
           RECORD CONTAINS 33 CHARACTERS.
      *
***point-A
      *
       FD  DAILY-FOOD-SALES-REPT
           LABEL RECORDS ARE STANDARD
           RECORD CONTAINS 133 CHARACTERS.
      *
       01  PRINT-AREA.
           05  FILLER               PIC X(133).
      *
       WORKING-STORAGE SECTION.
```

Figure 5–13
First three divisions for one-level control break food sales report (part 1 of 2)

```
*
***point-B
*
***point-C
*
 01  PRINT-CONTROL-FIELDS                                  COMP-3.
     05  LINE-COUNT          PIC S99        VALUE +99.
     05  LINES-ON-PAGE       PIC S99        VALUE +50.
     05  SPACE-CONTROL       PIC S99        VALUE +1.
*
 01  TOTAL-FIELDS                                          COMP-3.
     05  DISTRICT-TOTAL      PIC 9(5)V99    VALUE ZERO.
     05  REPORT-TOTAL        PIC 9(6)V99    VALUE ZERO.
*
 01  TITLE-LINE-1.
     05  FILLER              PIC X(18)      VALUE SPACE.
     05  FILLER              PIC X(11)      VALUE 'IN-AND-OUT'.
     05  FILLER              PIC X(104)     VALUE 'RESTAURANT'.
*
  01  TITLE-LINE-2.
     05  FILLER              PIC X(20)      VALUE SPACE.
     05  FILLER              PIC X(12)      VALUE 'DAILY SALES'.
     05  FILLER              PIC X(101)     VALUE 'REPORT'.
*
  01  COL-HEADING-1.
     05  FILLER              PIC X(12)      VALUE ' DISTRICT'.
     05  FILLER              PIC X(11)      VALUE 'FRANCHISE'.
     05  FILLER              PIC X(28)      VALUE 'FRANCHISE'.
     05  FILLER              PIC X(82)      VALUE 'DAILY'.
*
 01  COL-HEADING-2.
     05  FILLER              PIC X(13)      VALUE '  NUMBER'.
     05  FILLER              PIC X(10)      VALUE 'NUMBER'.
     05  FILLER              PIC X(28)      VALUE 'OWNER'.
     05  FILLER              PIC X(82)      VALUE 'SALES'.
*
 01  SALES-REPORT-LINE.
     05  FILLER              PIC XXX        VALUE SPACE.
     05  SR-DISTRICT-NO      PIC X(4).
     05  FILLER              PIC X(8)       VALUE SPACE.
     05  SR-FRANCHISE-NO     PIC XXX.
     05  FILLER              PIC X(5)       VALUE SPACE.
     05  SR-FRANCHISE-OWNER  PIC X(20).
     05  FILLER              PIC X(5)       VALUE SPACE.
     05  SR-DAILY-SALES      PIC Z,ZZZ.99.
     05  FILLER              PIC X(76)      VALUE SPACE.
*
 01  DISTRICT-TOTAL-LINE.
     05  FILLER              PIC X(16)      VALUE SPACE.
     05  FILLER              PIC X(14)      VALUE 'TOTAL SALES -'.
     05  FILLER              PIC X(9)       VALUE 'DISTRICT'.
     05  DT-DISTRICT-NO      PIC X(4).
     05  FILLER              PIC X(4)       VALUE SPACE.
     05  DT-DISTRICT-TOTAL   PIC ZZ,ZZZ.99
     05  FILLER              PIC X(76)      VALUE '*'.
*
 01  REPORT-TOTAL-LINE.
     05  FILLER              PIC X(16)      VALUE SPACE.
     05  FILLER              PIC X(14)      VALUE 'FINAL TOTAL -'.
     05  FILLER              PIC X(15)      VALUE 'ALL DISTRICTS'.
     05  RT-REPORT-TOTAL     PIC $$$$,$$$.99.
     05  FILLER              PIC X(77)      VALUE '**'.
```

Figure 5–13
First three divisions for one-level control break food sales report (part 2 of 2)

Solutions

2. Figure 5–14 shows the full VTOC for the food sales program:

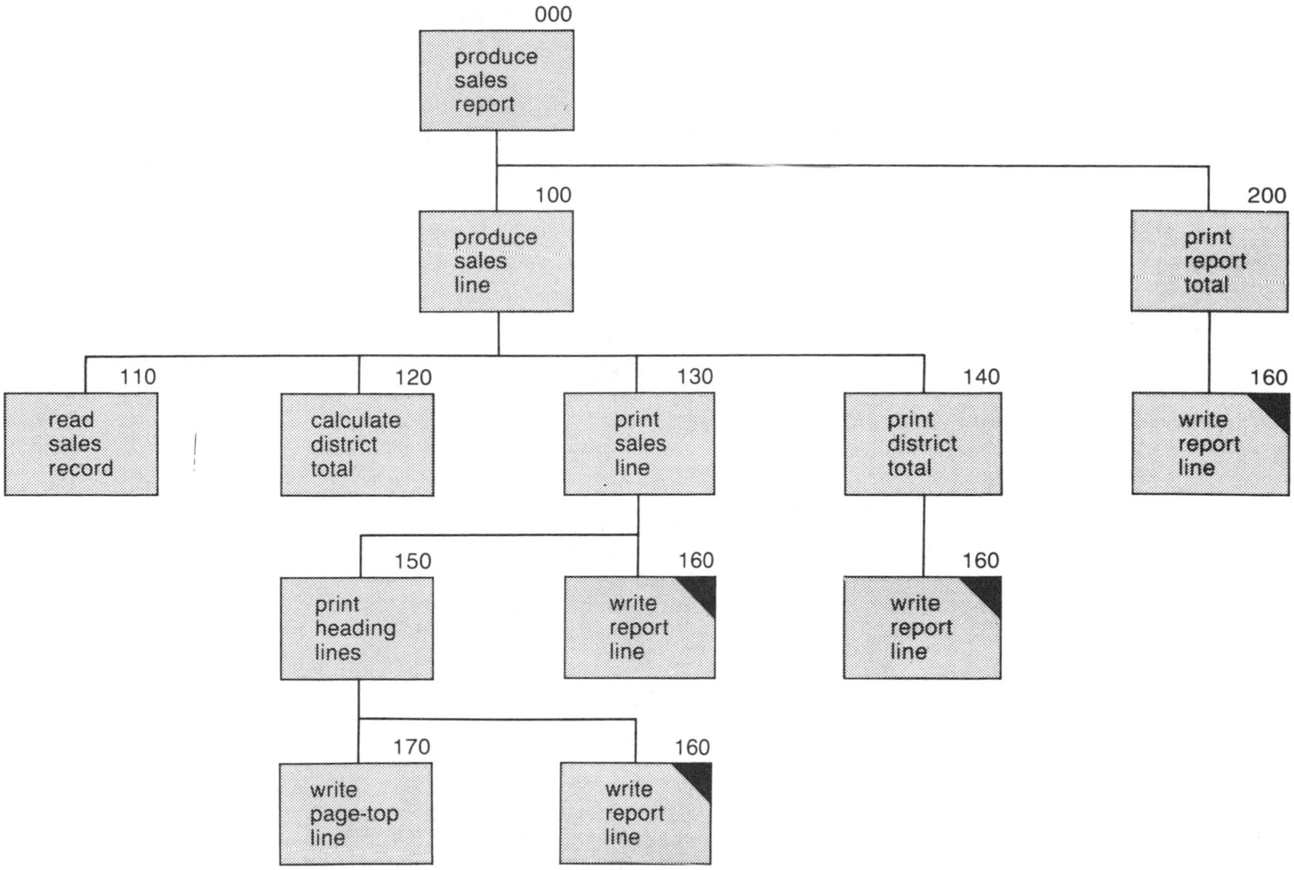
000
produce sales report
100
produce sales line
200
print report total
110
read sales record
120
calculate district total
130
print sales line
140
print district total
160
write report line
150
print heading lines
160
write report line
160
write report line
170
write page-top line
160
write report line

Figure 5–14
Full structure chart for one-level control break food sales report

3. ***point-A, the input record description, can be specified like this:

```
01  DAILY-SALES-RECORD.
    05  DS-DISTRICT-NO       PIC X(4).
    05  DS-FRANCHISE-NO      PIC XXX.
    05  DS-FRANCHISE-OWNER   PIC X(20).
    05  DS-DAILY-SALES       PIC 9(4)V99.
```

***point-B, the switch declarations, should look similar to the following:

```
01  SWITCHES.

05  DAILY-SALES-EOF-SW  PIC X          VALUE 'N'.
    88  LAST-DAILY-SALES-REC           VALUE 'Y'.
    88  MORE-DAILY-SALES-RECS          VALUE 'N'.
05  FIRST-SALES-REC-SW  PIC X          VALUE 'Y'.
    88  FIRST-SALES-RECORD             VALUE 'Y'.
```

***point-C, the following is a proper declaration for the control break field.

```
01  CONTROL-FIELDS.
    05  PRIOR-DISTRICT-NO     PIC X(4).
```

4. Figure 5–16 contains an appropriately coded COBOL solution for the food sales report. Figure 5–15 shows the pseudocode solution to the same problem. Pseudocode is discussed in chapter 6. Compare the statements in the two figures to see the steps in the development of a completed program.

```
000-PRODUCE-SALES-REPORT.
    1. Open files.
    2. Do 100-PRODUCE-SALES-LINE
           until file end recognized.
    3. Do  200-PRINT-REPORT-LINE.
    4. Close files.
    5. Stop.

100-PRODUCE-SALES-LINE.
     1. Do 110-READ-SALES-RECORD.
     2. IF control break occurs
            Do 140-PRINT-DISTRICT-TOTAL.
     3. IF have more records to process
            Do 120-CALC-DISTRICT-TOTAL
            Do 130-PRINT-SALES-LINE.

110-READ-SALES-RECORD.
     1. Read the input file
            AT END
                set end of file switch
                MOVE HIGH-VALUE to the control field.
     2. IF just read first input record
            save the first group control field
            set the first record switch off.

120-CALC-DISTRICT-TOTAL.
    1. calculate the district total.

130-PRINT-SALES-LINE.
    1. IF  page overflow occurs
           Do 150-PRINT-HEADING-LINES.
    2. Format the detail print line in W-S.
    3. Move the detail print line to the output area.
    4. Do 160-WRITE-REPORT-LINE.

140-PRINT-DISTRICT-TOTAL.
    1. Format the subtotal print line.
    2. Move the subtotal print line to the output area.
    3. Do 160-WRITE-REPORT-LINE.
    4. Add the subtotal amount to the final total.
    5. Set the subtotal amount to zero for the next group.
    6. Save the new group control field.

150-PRINT-HEADING-LINES.
    1. Move the first report title line to the output area.
    2. Do 170-WRITE-PAGE-TOP-LINE.
    3. Move the second report title line to the output area.
    4. Do 160-WRITE-REPORT-LINE.
    5. Move the first column heading to the output area.
    6. Set the spacing control field for double space.
    7. Do 160-WRITE-REPORT-LINE.
```

Figure 5–15
Pseudocode solution for one-level food sales report (part 1 of 2)

```
    8.  Move the second column heading to the output area.
    9.  Do 160-WRITE-REPORT-LINE.
    10. Set the spacing control field for double space.

160-WRITE-REPORT-LINE.
    1.  Write out the contents of the output area
            AFTER ADVANCING SPACE-CONTROL.
    2.  ADD SPACE-CONTROL            TO LINE-COUNT.
    3.  MOVE 1                       TO SPACE-CONTROL.
*
170-WRITE-PAGE-TOP-LINE.
    1.  WRITE PRINT-AREA
            AFTER ADVANCING PAGE.
    2.  MOVE 1                       TO LINE-COUNT.
*
200-PRINT-REPORT-TOTAL.
    1.  Format the report total line in W-S.
    2.  Move the report total line to the output area.
    3.  Do 160-WRITE-REPORT-LINE.
```

Figure 5–15
Pseudocode solution for one-level food sales report (part 2 of 2)

```
*
PROCEDURE DIVISION.
*
000-PRODUCE-SALES-REPORT.
    OPEN INPUT  DAILY-FOOD-RECEIPTS
         OUTPUT DAILY-FOOD-SALES-REPT.
    PERFORM 100-PRODUCE-SALES-LINE
        UNTIL LAST-DAILY-SALES-REC.
    PERFORM 200-PRINT-REPORT-TOTAL.
    CLOSE DAILY-FOOD-RECEIPTS
          DAILY-FOOD-SALES-REPT.
    DISPLAY 'FOODSLS  I  1  NORMAL EOJ'.
    STOP RUN.
*
100-PRODUCE-SALES-LINE.
    PERFORM 110-READ-SALES-RECORD.
    IF DS-DISTRICT-NO GREATER THAN PRIOR-DISTRICT-NO
        PERFORM 140-PRINT-DISTRICT-TOTAL.
    IF MORE-DAILY-SALES-RECS
        PERFORM 120-CALC-DISTRICT-TOTAL
        PERFORM 130-PRINT-SALES-LINE.
*
110-READ-SALES-RECORD.
    READ DAILY-FOOD-RECEIPTS
        AT END
            MOVE 'Y'             TO DAILY-SALES-EOF-SW
            MOVE HIGH-VALUE      TO DS-DISTRICT-NO.
    IF FIRST-SALES-RECORD
        MOVE DS-DISTRICT-NO      TO PRIOR-DISTRICT-NO
        MOVE 'N'                 TO FIRST-SALES-REC-SW.
*
120-CALC-DISTRICT-TOTAL.
    ADD DS-DAILY-SALES           TO DISTRICT-TOTAL.
*
130-PRINT-SALES-LINE.
    IF LINE-COUNT GREATER THAN LINES-ON-PAGE
        PERFORM 150-PRINT-HEADING-LINES.
    MOVE DS-DISTRICT-NO          TO SR-DISTRICT-NO.
    MOVE DS-FRANCHISE-NO         TO SR-FRANCHISE-NO.
    MOVE DS-FRANCHISE-OWNER      TO SR-FRANCHISE-OWNER.
    MOVE DS-DAILY-SALES          TO SR-DAILY-SALES.
    MOVE SALES-REPORT-LINE       TO PRINT-AREA.
    PERFORM 160-WRITE-REPORT-LINE.
```

Figure 5–16
COBOL code solution for one-level food sales report (part 1 of 2)

```
*
 140-PRINT-DISTRICT-TOTAL.
     MOVE PRIOR-DISTRICT-NO      TO DT-DISTRICT-NO.
     MOVE DISTRICT-TOTAL         TO DT-DISTRICT-TOTAL.
     MOVE DISTRICT-TOTAL-LINE    TO PRINT-AREA.
     MOVE 2                      TO SPACE-CONTROL.
     PERFORM 160-WRITE-REPORT-LINE.
     ADD DISTRICT-TOTAL          TO REPORT-TOTAL.
     MOVE ZERO                   TO DISTRICT-TOTAL.
     MOVE DS-DISTRICT-NO         TO PRIOR-DISTRICT-NO.
     MOVE 2                      TO SPACE-CONTROL.
*
 150-PRINT-HEADING-LINES.
     MOVE TITLE-LINE-1           TO PRINT-AREA.
     PERFORM 170-WRITE-PAGE-TOP-LINE.
     MOVE TITLE-LINE-2           TO PRINT-AREA.
     PERFORM 160-WRITE-REPORT-LINE.
     MOVE COL-HEADING-1          TO PRINT-AREA.
     MOVE 2                      TO SPACE-CONTROL.
     PERFORM 160-WRITE-REPORT-LINE.
     MOVE COL-HEADING-2          TO PRINT-AREA.
     PERFORM 160-WRITE-REPORT-LINE.
     MOVE 2                      TO SPACE-CONTROL.
*
 160-WRITE-REPORT-LINE.
     WRITE PRINT-AREA
         AFTER ADVANCING SPACE-CONTROL.
     ADD SPACE-CONTROL           TO LINE-COUNT.
     MOVE 1                      TO SPACE-CONTROL.
*
 170-WRITE-PAGE-TOP-LINE.
     WRITE PRINT-AREA
         AFTER ADVANCING PAGE.
     MOVE 1                      TO LINE-COUNT.
*
 200-PRINT-REPORT-TOTAL.
     MOVE REPORT-TOTAL           TO RT-REPORT-TOTAL.
     MOVE REPORT-TOTAL-LINE      TO PRINT-AREA.
     PERFORM 160-WRITE-REPORT-LINE.
```

Figure 5–16
COBOL code solution for one-level food sales report (part 2 of 2)

Chapter 6 The Principles of Structured Programming

This is probably the most important chapter in this text. Although it does not really teach you any COBOL, it does show you how to write programs that are well organized, very readable, and easy to understand and maintain. It presents a developmental process which will enable you to develop structured programs quickly and accurately. The first topic discusses unstructured code and the history of structured programming. The second topic presents a detailed discussion of structure charts and how to develop them. The structure chart is a tool to use at the general level when designing a program. The third topic discusses pseudocode, which is the tool of the specific design level. Topic four lists structured programming style guidelines.

Topic 1 The Background of Structured Programming

Orientation

To appreciate structured programming, you almost have to have written and tested unstructured programs. If you are new to programming, it is impractical to have you write programs the wrong way just so you will understand the mistakes of the past. Sometime in your programming career you will probably have the opportunity to perform maintenance on an unstructured program; then you will begin to understand the significant differences. For the time being, a short program written in the old style will be presented.

Terminology

conditional branch	proper program	structured style
dummy module	selection structure	top-down coding
GO TO	sequence structure	top-down design
iteration structure	structured design	top-down testing
program flowchart	structured programming	unconditional branch
program stub		

Objectives

1. *Explain why structured programming has become such an important topic for professional programmers.*
2. *Explain how the four significant events of structured programming affected the practice of programming.*

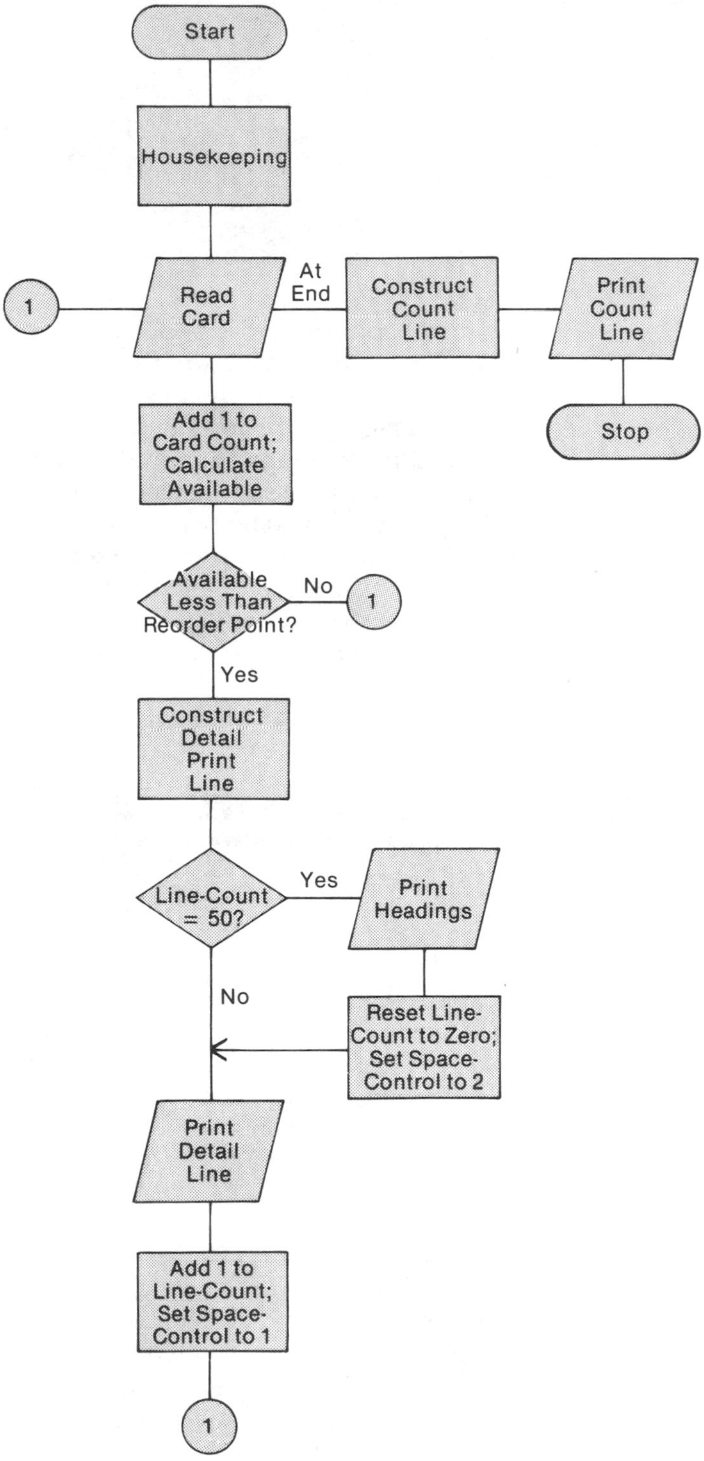
Start
Housekeeping
Read Card
At End
Construct Count Line
Print Count Line
Stop
1
Add 1 to Card Count; Calculate Available
Available Less Than Reorder Point?
No
1
Yes
Construct Detail Print Line
Line-Count = 50?
Yes
Print Headings
Reset Line-Count to Zero; Set Space-Control to 2
No
Print Detail Line
Add 1 to Line-Count; Set Space-Control to 1
1

Figure 6–1
Flowchart for the refined reorder-listing program

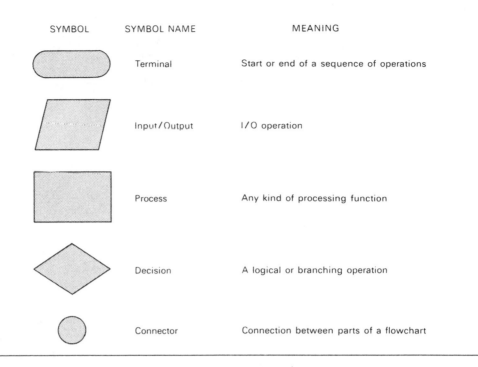

SYMBOL	SYMBOL NAME	MEANING
	Terminal	Start or end of a sequence of operations
	Input/Output	I/O operation
	Process	Any kind of processing function
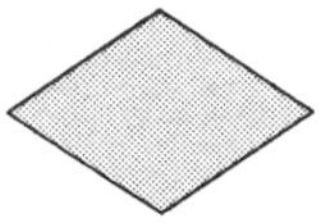	Decision	A logical or branching operation
	Connector	Connection between parts of a flowchart

Figure 6–2
ANSI flowcharting symbols

Unstructured Program Development

Although it's a simple example, suppose the refined reorder-listing program shown in Figure 4–8 were developed in an unstructured fashion. After the programmer had the problem definition clearly in mind, he would probably draw a *program flowchart* for its solution...something like the one in Figure 6–1. A flowchart like this is supposed to show the sequence of instructions to be used for the program and the logic required to derive the output from the input. The meanings of the symbols used in this flowchart are shown in Figure 6–2.

To follow a flowchart like the one in Figure 6–1, you start at the top and read down and to the right unless arrows indicate otherwise. When you come to a connector circle with a number in it, you continue at a connector circle containing the same number. For example, after calculating the available stock, the program reaches a connector circle with a 1 in it if the available stock is *not* less than the reorder point. This means that the flow of the program continues at the connector circle leading into the Read Card symbol. If the available stock is less than the reorder point, the program continues by constructing a detail print line for the output report.

After finishing the program flowchart, the programmer would code the unstructured program using the flowchart as a guide. If you study Figure 6–3 carefully and compare it with program examples that have been used so far, you should be able to understand some of the pitfalls of unstructured code. Figure 6–3 is easy to compare as it is the now familiar reorder-listing program.

```
FD  INPUT-CARD
    LABEL RECORDS ARE OMITTED
    RECORD CONTAINS 80 CHARACTERS.
01  INPUT-RECORD.
    05  ITEM         PIC 9(5).
    05  DESC         PIC X(20).
    05  FILLER       PIC X(5).
    05  PRICE        PIC 9(3)V99.
    05  REORDER-POINT  PIC 9(5).
    05  ON-HAND      PIC 9(5).
    05  ON-ORDER     PIC 9(5).
    05  FILLER       PIC X(30).
FD  PRINT-OUT
    LABEL RECORDS ARE OMITTED
    RECORD CONTAINS 63 CHARACTERS.
01  PRINT-AREA  PIC X(63).
WORKING-STORAGE SECTION.
77  AVAILABLE  PIC S9(5) COMP-3.
01  REORDER-LINE.
    05  FILLER          PIC X  VALUE SPACE.
    05  ITEM-OUT        PIC X(3).
    05  FILLER          PIC X(5)  VALUE SPACE.
    05  DESC-OUT        PIC X(20).
    05  FILLER          PIC X(5)  VALUE SPACE.
    05  PRICE-OUT       PIC ZZZ.99.
    05  FILLER          PIC X(5)  VALUE SPACE.
    05  AVAILABLE-OUT   PIC Z(5).
    05  FILLER          PIC X(5)  VALUE SPACE.
    05  REORDER-POINT-OUT PIC X(5).
77  LINE-COUNT  PIC S99  VALUE +50.
01  HEADING-LINE-1  PIC X(63)
    VALUE '                          REORDER LISTING'.
01  HEADING-LINE-2  PIC X(63)
    VALUE ' ITEM           ITEM                 UNIT
-   '   REORDER'.
01  HEADING-LINE-3  PIC X(63)
    VALUE '  NO.        DESCRIPTION            PRICE      AVAILABL
-   'E   POINT'.
77  COUNTER  PIC S9(5)  VALUE ZERO.
01  TOTAL-LINE.
    05  CARD-COUNT      PIC ZZZ,ZZZ.
    05  FILLER  PIC X(26) VALUE '  CARDS IN THE INPUT DECK'.
PROCEDURE DIVISION.
SET-UP.
    OPEN INPUT INPUT-CARD, OUTPUT PRINT-OUT.
MAINLINE-ROUTINE.
    READ INPUT-CARD AT END GO TO END-OF-JOB.
    ADD 1 TO COUNTER.
    ADD ON-HAND ON-ORDER GIVING AVAILABLE-STOCK
        ON SIZE ERROR DISPLAY 'ERROR IN AVAILABLE CALC FOR ITEM '
        ITEM ' CARD IGNORED.' GO TO MAINLINE-ROUTINE.
    IF AVAILABLE-STOCK LESS THAN REORDER-POINT
        GO TO PRINT-ROUTINE.
    GO TO MAINLINE-ROUTINE.
PRINT-ROUTINE.
    MOVE ITEM TO ITEM-OUT.
    MOVE DESC TO DESC-OUT.
    MOVE PRICE TO PRICE-OUT.
    MOVE AVAILABLE TO AVAILABLE-OUT.
    MOVE REORDER-POINT TO REORDER-POINT-OUT.
    IF LINE-COUNT IS EQUAL TO 50 GO TO HEADING-ROUTINE.
DETAIL-PRINTING.
    MOVE REORDER-LINE TO PRINT-AREA.
    WRITE PRINT-AREA AFTER ADVANCING 1 LINES
    ADD 1 TO LINE-COUNT.
    GO TO MAINLINE-ROUTINE.
```

Figure 6–3
Unstructured reorder listing (part 1 of 2)

```
HEADING-ROUTINE.
    MOVE HEADING-LINE-1 TO PRINT-AREA.
    WRITE PRINT-AREA AFTER ADVANCING PAGE-TOP LINES
    MOVE HEADING-LINE-2 TO PRINT-AREA.
    WRITE PRINT-AREA AFTER ADVANCING 2 LINES
    MOVE HEADING-LINE-3 TO PRINT-AREA.
    WRITE PRINT-AREA AFTER ADVANCING 1 LINES
    MOVE SPACES TO PRINT-AREA.
    WRITE PRINT-AREA AFTER ADVANCING 1 LINES
    MOVE 4 TO LINE-COUNT
    GO TO DETAIL-PRINTING.
END-OF-JOB.
    MOVE COUNIER TO CARD-COUNT.
    MOVE TOTAL-LINE TO PRINT-AREA.
    WRITE PRINT-AREA AFTER ADVANCING 3 LINES.
    MOVE SPACES TO PRINT-AREA.
    WRITE PRINT-AREA AFTER ADVANCING 3 LINES.
    CLOSE INVENTORY-STATUS-FILE, REORDER-LISTING.
    DISPLAY 'REORDER  I  1  NORMAL EOJ'.
    STOP RUN.
```

Figure 6–3
Unstructured reorder listing (part 2 of 2)

The example begins with the File Section of the Data Division since there are few significant differences between structured and unstructured concepts that affect the first two divisions. At this time you do not have names for them, but the following is a list of problems with typical unstructured code that you might be able to recognize in part 1, the Data Division:

1. inconsistent clause alignment
2. more than one clause per line
3. data names that are unclear as to their functional use
4. file and record names that identify data flow directions and I/O devices rather than identifying their functional use and contents
5. no data groupings in working storage
6. no visual group separation (blank lines)
7. not aligning value clauses, and continuing value clauses over more than one line

In part 2, the Procedure Division, one of the more interesting exercises is to draw lines on the page following the code as it moves from one paragraph to another. Go ahead and do this. You will find it to be a revealing activity even for such a short program. The Procedure Division unstructured problem list is:

1. again, inconsistent clause alignment. Note that all previous programs aligned the TOs, and as you will find out, had rules for other alignments.
2. use of the GO TO statement. No other programs used this. It is one of the main attributes of unstructured code. You will seldom have to use the GO TO.
3. again, no visual separation of paragraphs by use of blank lines
4. absolutely no top-down organization. This will be one of the principal issues in structured code.
5. placement of more than one clause on a line
6. use of more than one I/O statement per file

Actually, the program example in Figure 6–3 is not the worst example of unstructured coding that might have been presented. You probably found following the logic of the program to be a little confusing, but imagine how bad it would be if a large, complex program were coded in this manner. If you talk to programmers who have been in the profession for several years, they can probably show you some really great examples of "how not to do it." After you have completed this chapter, refer back to Figure 6–3 and study it again from your new perspective.

The GO TO statement is referred to as a branch instruction since it interrupts the top-to-bottom flow of the source program and directs the program to continue execution at the point (paragraph name) named as the object of the GO TO. A GO TO that is a sentence by itself is called an *unconditional branch*, such as the last sentence in the paragraph called MAINLINE–ROUTINE:

```
GO TO MAINLINE-ROUTINE.
```

In other words, when the program execution arrives at this point, it is continually and unconditionally directed to resume execution back at the top of the paragraph.

When a GO TO is the statement following some sort of conditional test, such as an IF or AT END, then the situation is said to be a *conditional branch*, for instance:

```
READ CARD-FILE
     AT END GO TO END-OF-JOB.
```

In this case program flow always continues at the next sentence following the READ command, except when the AT END condition is recognized. Under that condition the flow is then directed to the paragraph named END–OF–JOB.

Since this program is short, its flowchart and its Procedure Division are relatively easy to follow. But what if the program required several thousand instructions? What if the program had extensive logical requirements? Then, the program might require hundreds of GO TO statements, and its logic would be as difficult to follow as the pieces of pasta in a plate of spaghetti. In fact, unstructured code is often referred to as "spaghetti coding."

To put it bluntly, unstructured methods of program development have shortcomings in the areas of design, coding, and testing. In the design stage, the flowchart is difficult to create and once created is difficult to change. Furthermore, it's easy to leave out important details of the program when creating the flowchart. Most damning of all, however, the flowchart doesn't help simplify large or complex programs. As a result, the flowchart is a poor guide for coding and is usually incomplete as documentation.

In the coding stage, unstructured coding is just that ... unstructured. The programmer is free to determine in what sequence the paragraphs will be coded and in what sequence they will be placed in the program. Using the flowchart in Figure 6–1, for example, the programmer might code the end-of-job routine right after coding the READ statement for the card file. Or the programmer might code the entire mainline routine and then code all other paragraphs required by that routine. During coding the programmer has to create paragraph names and be sure that these paragraphs are included in the program later on. Is it any wonder that important details are frequently overlooked and required paragraphs are missing?

If you compare Figure 6–3 with the structured examples in this book, you can observe that the structured programs are organized so that individual parts are easy to locate. Statements are organized by function, and the numbering system makes it easy to locate a program module.

A serious problem with unstructured design is not with the flowchart concept itself but with its use. Formerly, programmers began to draw a flowchart immediately upon being given a programming assignment. That meant they bypassed the general design stage when the structure chart would be developed and moved immediately into the specific design level. This ultimately made for a confused development and was similar in concept to drawing the foundation, plumbing, and wiring blueprints for a house before deciding whether it is to be a ranch style or colonial, a single or two-story, energy efficient or traditional, etc. No builder would think of beginning construction on a house until those questions had been resolved, but this is essentially what unstructured design attempts to do.

As for testing, it is far too often a nightmare. In this stage, all of the mistakes made in design and coding come back to haunt you. When a bug is detected, you have to locate it. But if the program lacks structure, how do you know where to look? Using traditional techniques, then, a program of several thousand source records might contain hundreds of errors and take months to debug.

The ultimate criticism of unstructured methods, however, can be stated in terms of programmer productivity. In a study done in 1965, the average COBOL programmer was found to produce only ten lines of tested code per day. A study done in 1975 showed no improvement. Since this lack of productivity is a significant problem for the computer industry, it's clear that new methods of program development are needed.

The History of Structured Programming

As it became apparent that programming was not very efficient, various computer scientists began to study the situation and to develop more exacting concepts for the structure of a *proper program*. This discussion will quickly track the four steps in the commercial success of any concept:

1. theoretical conceptualization
2. translation of the concept into practical terms
3. successful demonstration, and
4. commercial adoption

In 1964 two mathematicians, Corrado Bohm and Guiseppe Jacopini, presented a paper at an international meeting that represented the first step in the development of structured programming concepts. The meeting was the International Colloquium on Algebraic Linguistics and Automata Theory in Israel and their paper presented proof that any program logic could be expressed in three structures: sequence, selection, and iteration structures. Bohm and Jacopini's paper was published in Italian, and it was not until 1966 that it was translated to English. Even then it did not cause a significant immediate impact since it was very theoretical and complex.

A letter written by Professor Edsger W. Dijkstra in 1968 did cause a significant stir in practical computer science circles, and may be viewed as the beginning of the second step. The letter, written to *Communications of the ACM*, was entitled "GO TO Statement Considered Harmful." Professor Dijkstra stated that the more GO TOs a program contained, the worse the quality of the program became, and suggested that GO TOs be eliminated from all high-level languages.

The concepts of Bohm and Jacopini, coupled with the challenge of Dijkstra, and pushed by recognition that programmer productivity was falling drastically, provided impetus for improved programming practices. During the period from 1969 to 1971, the IBM Corporation used structured programming concepts along with other improved practices on a project that is viewed as the first large-scale, commercial implementation of "structured programming"—the third step. The significant result of this trial, the New York Times Project, was that the productivity of the programmers using these new techniques was four to six times higher than those using traditional methods. Possibly the most significant statistic was that the program bug rate of those using the new approach dropped drastically to about .0004 errors per line of code.

When the success of the New York Times Project became known, the hard-pressed data processing community began to show interest. By the mid-1970s structured practices began to be adopted by more and more commercial data processing installations. The fourth requirement for a concept's success, commercial acceptance, was in place and structured programming was on its way.

The Theory of Structured Programming

As the various computer scientists began to give rigid definitions for the structure of a *proper program*, their efforts led to a discipline known as *structured programming*. This discipline is intended to improve program clarity, simplify debugging, and increase programmer productivity.

The basic assumption in structured programming is that any program can be written using only three logical structures. These structures are summarized in Figure 6–4. They are called the sequence, selection, and iteration structures.

The *sequence structure* is simply the idea that imperative program statements are executed in sequence. For instance, if the COBOL MOVE, ADD, and SUBTRACT statements are coded in sequence in a program, they are executed one after the other. As a result, a sequence box can consist of one imperative statement or many. And two sequence boxes can be combined into one without changing the basic sequential structure.

The *selection structure* is a choice between two and only two actions based on a condition. If the condition is true, one function is done; if false, the other is done. Either one of the two actions may be null, or not expressly stated; in other words, an action may be specified for only one result of the condition test. Then, when the other result occurs, the program continues by executing the next statement in sequence. This structure is often referred to as the IF–THEN–ELSE structure, and many programming languages have code that closely approximates it.

The *iteration structure*, often called the DO–WHILE structure, provides for doing a function as long as a condition is true. When the condition is no longer true, the program continues with the next structure. A common alternate structure for interation is the fourth one shown in Figure 6–4, the DO–UNTIL structure. Logically related to the DO–WHILE, the DO–UNTIL does a function *until* a condition becomes true.

Although COBOL doesn't directly provide for either the DO–WHILE or DO–UNTIL structure, it does offer the PERFORM–UNTIL structure. This is the third iteration structure shown in Figure 6–4. As you can see, it is closely related to the DO–UNTIL structure. In fact, it differs from the DO–UNTIL only in that the condition is tested *before* the function is done rather than after.

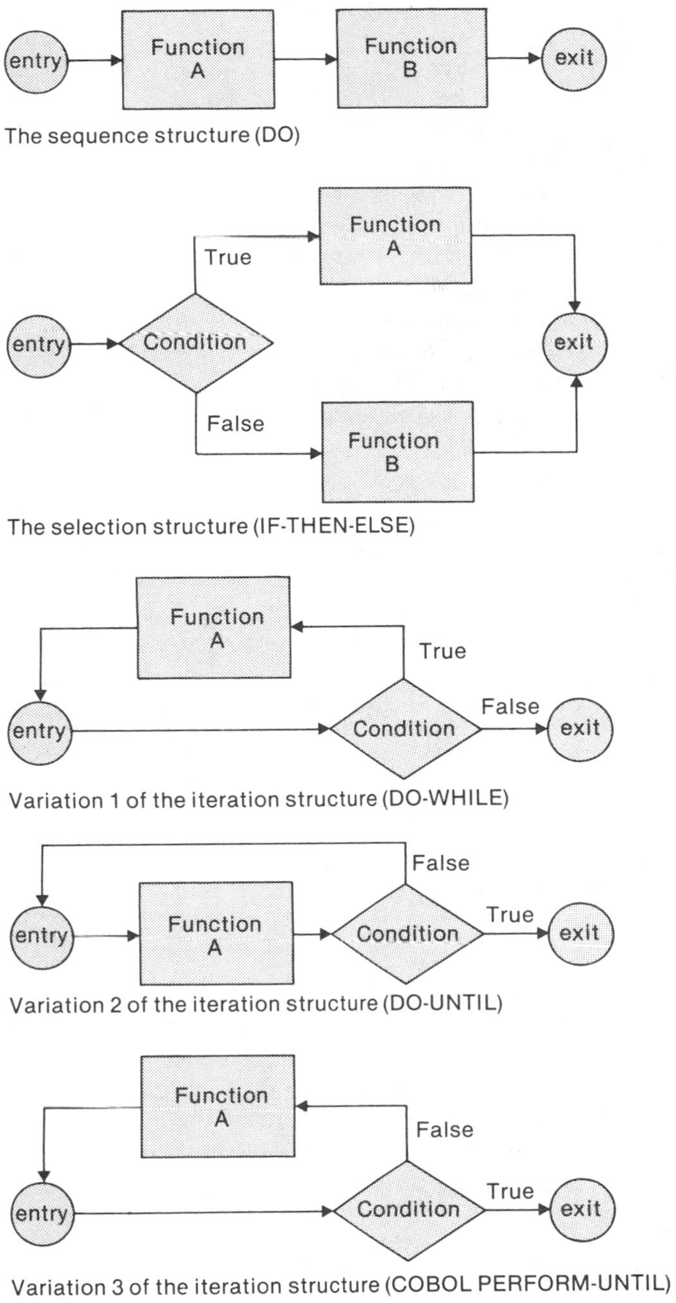
entry
Function A
Function B
exit
The sequence structure (DO)
Function A
True
entry
Condition
exit
False
Function B
The selection structure (IF-THEN-ELSE)
Function A
True
entry
Condition
False
exit
Variation 1 of the iteration structure (DO-WHILE)
False
entry
Function A
Condition
True
exit
Variation 2 of the iteration structure (DO-UNTIL)
Function A
False
entry
Condition
True
exit
Variation 3 of the iteration structure (COBOL PERFORM-UNTIL)

Figure 6–4
The basic structures of structured programming

In actual practice, the PERFORM–UNTIL structure is often referred to as a DO–UNTIL structure since the difference is more academic than real. When reference is made to a DO–UNTIL structure in this book, you can imagine coding it with the COBOL PERFORM–UNTIL statement.

Notice that all of the structures in Figure 6–4 have only one entry and one exit point. As a result, a program made up of these structures will have only one entry and one exit. Thus, the program will be executed in a controlled manner from the first statement to the last. These characteristics make up a proper program.

One of the principles of structured programming is that any of the three basic structures can be substituted for a function box in any of the other structures. The result will still be a proper program. Similarly, two or more of the basic structures in sequence can be treated as a single function box. This means that structures of great complexity can be created with the assurance that they will have only one entry and one exit point and that they will be executed in a controlled manner from start to finish.

Structured programming has contributed to programmer productivity because it has placed necessary restrictions on program structure. The GO TO statement that is so widely used in unstructured programs is illegal in structured programming. As a result, uncontrolled branching is impossible. This in turn reduces the likelihood of program bugs and makes it easier to find errors when there are bugs. In addition, when handled correctly, the structured program is easier to read and understand than the unstructured program.

Structured Design and Documentation

Although it is possible to draw flowcharts for structured programs, new design and documentation techniques have been developed in conjunction with structured programming. The one you were introduced to in chapter 2 is called *top-down design*, or *structured design*.

When structured design is used, the program flowchart is replaced by some sort of structure chart as you have seen in chapter 3. For instance, Figure 6–5 duplicates the structure chart for the refined reorder-listing program. To create a chart like this, the programmer first tries to divide the program into its major functional modules. These modules in turn are divided into their subordinate modules, and so forth. When the programmer is finished, the structure chart shows all modules required by the program as well as the relationships between these modules. Later on, these modules can be coded with one entry and one exit point using only the sequence, selection, and iteration structures. Thus, the complete program is a proper program. In topic 2 of this chapter, you will learn how to create structure charts of your own.

After creating the structure chart, the programmer documents each of the modules in the chart before coding them. It is only at this stage that the programmer considers the detailed specifications required by the program. Although a program flowchart can be used to document each of the modules, new methods of documentation are rapidly replacing the flowchart, even for this purpose. In topic 3, you will learn how to use pseudocode, a design language for structured COBOL programs.

Structured Coding and Testing

When structured design is used, the structure chart is the guide for coding. Unlike the program flowchart, it gives the paragraph names, the sequence numbers for the paragraphs, and an indication of the sequence in which the modules should be coded. When the programmer finishes coding, it is a simple matter to make sure that there is one paragraph in the program for each module in the structure chart.

Beyond this, using structured programming to develop COBOL programs implies that a number of structured coding techniques should be used. These are designed (1) to ensure that the modules are independent with only one entry and one exit point and (2) to make the COBOL program easy to read and understand. These techniques were introduced in chapter 3 and will be expanded throughout this text.

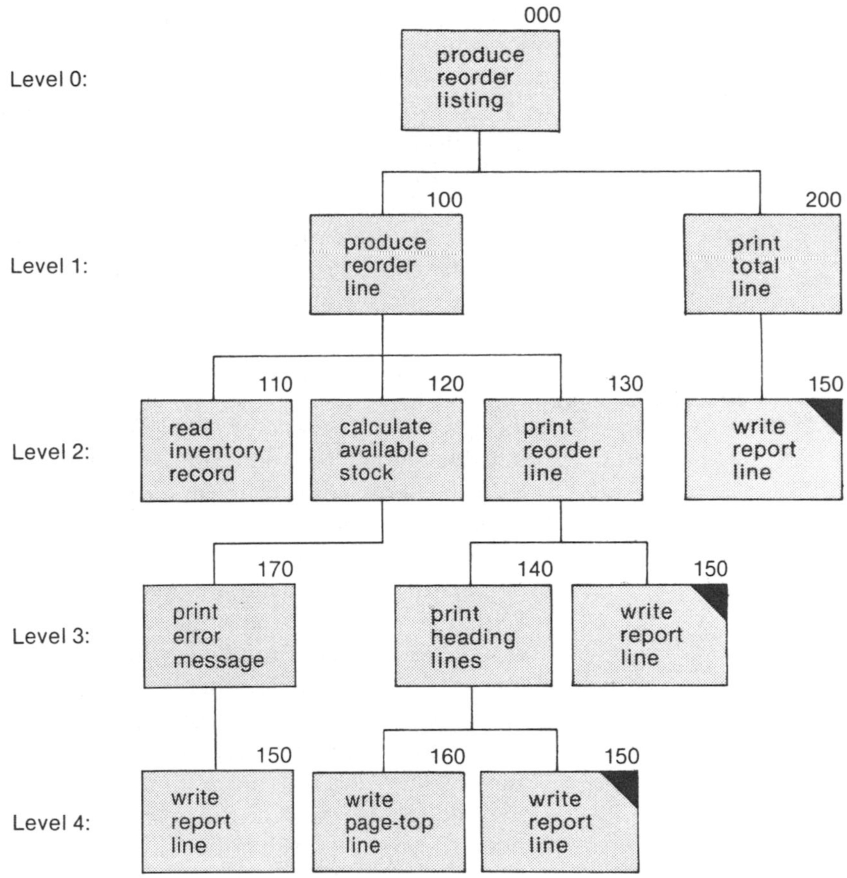
Level 0:
Level 1:
Level 2:
Level 3:
Level 4:
000
produce reorder listing
100
produce reorder line
200
print total line
110
read inventory record
120
calculate available stock
130
print reorder line
150
write report line
170
print error message
140
print heading lines
150
write report line
150
write report line
160
write page-top line
150
write report line

Figure 6–5
Structure chart for the refined reorder-listing program

The benefits of structured programming are perhaps most obvious when it comes to testing. Because the program consists of independent modules and because these modules have only one entry and one exit point, the structured program is almost sure to have fewer bugs than the unstructured program. In addition, these bugs are likely to be simply clerical errors rather than complex logical errors. Finally, due to the structured design, the bugs will be relatively easy to find and correct.

Structured programming also makes *top-down coding and testing* (or simply *top-down testing*) possible. This implies coding and testing the program one level or one module at a time. For instance, the first test run might test only the operation of the level-0 and level-1 modules. Then, depending on the complexity of the program, all of the level-2 modules or only a few of the level-2 modules can be added to the program for the next test run. Eventually, the lowest-level modules will be tested in combination with all the other modules of the program.

The advantage of top-down testing is that testing is controlled. If a bug is detected when using the same test data as in the previous test run, it is clearly the result of the module or modules added since that run. Since these modules are independent, it is relatively easy to find the cause of the bug and correct it. Top-down testing sharply contrasts traditional test methods in which the entire program with its dozens or hundreds of bugs is tested at once.

To use top-down testing, the programmer codes *dummy modules*, or *program stubs*, for those modules that aren't ready to be tested. For instance, modules 100 and 200 would be dummy modules when testing module 000 in Figure 6–5. In this case, the modules would receive control from module 000, print a message saying that they have received control, and pass control back to module 000. Module 100 would also set INVENTORY-EOF-SWITCH to Y as required by the COBOL code so that module 000 could run to completion.

Since top-down testing is more helpful in testing large programs than in testing small ones, a more thorough discussion will be delayed until later in the book. The technique will be expanded and explained in more detail at the point where your program assignments are becoming difficult enough to benefit from a top-down development and testing approach.

Discussion

Although the term *structured programming* originally meant creating programs consisting of only the three proper structures (sequence, selection, and iteration), it has now come to mean far more. Today, it refers to a collection of techniques that includes structured design, module documentation, and top-down coding and testing. In addition, structured programming implies that programs are organized into functional modules, and are written in a *structured style* that is clear and easy to follow. All of these techniques depend on the notion of independent modules with only one entry and one exit point. And all of them are designed to increase programmer productivity.

At present, the techniques of structured programming are by no means standard. Structure charts are done in a variety of ways throughout the computer industry, and module documentation is done in many different ways. There is even debate as to the proper techniques for coding and testing structured programs. Nevertheless, structured programming is here to stay. It is simply a more efficient way to design, document, code, and test programs.

Topic 2 **The Structure Chart—A General Design Tool**

Orientation

Structured design (or top-down design) sharply contrasts traditional methods of program design. Instead of worrying about programming details, the top-down designer tries to focus on the overall structure of the program. After the major modules have been designed, the designer works on the design of the next level down. The designer continues this process until the entire program is divided into functional modules that can be coded with limited difficulty.

When structured design is used, the program designer creates some sort of structure chart like the one in Figure 6–5. Although there are many different forms of structure charts, this book uses a standard form called a *visual table of contents*, or a *VTOC* (pronounced VEE-tock). The VTOC is part of a method of documentation called *HIPO* (Hierarchy plus Input–Process–Output). As a result, you will sometimes hear the VTOC referred to as a *hierarchy chart*. No matter what term you use, you need to know how to create and evaluate structure charts if you're going to be an effective structured COBOL programmer.

Terminology

called module	heirarchy chart	span of control
calling a module	HIPO	structure chart
calling module	module independence	visual table of contents
common		
module	passing a control code	VTOC
control span	proper subordination	

Objectives

1. *List the four steps you should follow when creating a VTOC.*
2. *Explain how you can tell when a module is* functional.
3. *List and describe seven characteristics you should analyze when you review a VTOC.*

Note: If you are new to structured programming, you will probably have difficulty creating your own VTOCs at this time. That's why being able to create your own VTOCs isn't one of the objectives of this topic, though it will be one after topic 4.

Step 1—Create the First Draft of the VTOC

Before this discussion begins, you should be alerted to another advantage of the VTOC or structure chart. The problem specifications for this example use a process involving the loading of a table. That should bother you when you get to thinking about it, as you do not yet know how to load or work with tables.

Many teachers would not give you such an example at this time since you are not prepared to program it. However, using this example points out a very important aspect of the use of structure charts—namely, that you merely need to be able to identify the functions to be placed in the chart and to specify the relationship of one function (module) to another. You do not necessarily need to know exactly how to program a function.

There will be many similar situations you will encounter as a professional programmer, where you are not exactly sure how to do something. However, you will be able to identify the need for that something (a program module) and you should be able to place it in relation to the other modules. Then you can do the research and learning necessary to actually program the module.

To illustrate the procedure for creating VTOCs, take a minute and study the problem specifications in Figure 6–6. This program is supposed to read a file of inventory transaction records and check (or edit) them for validity. If a record is invalid, the program is to print a line on a report so the record can be corrected. Although the narrative in Figure 6–6 is brief, this problem should serve to illustrate how VTOCs are created.

Design by levels

When creating a VTOC, you begin with the top-level, or level-0, module. This module represents the entire program, so it should be given an appropriate functional name. For this program, something like "verify inventory transactions" or "edit inventory transactions" is appropriate.

System flowchart:

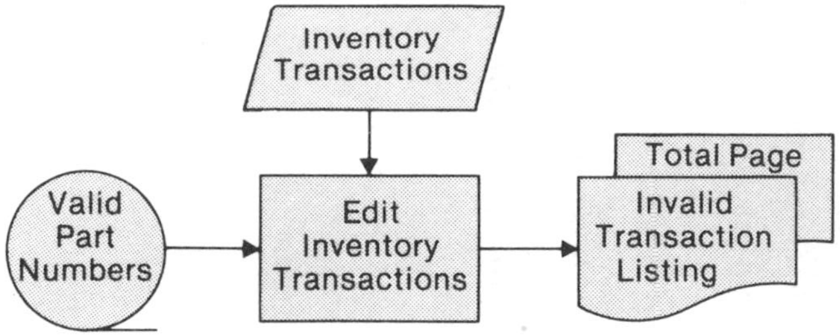
Inventory Transactions
Valid Part Numbers
Edit Inventory Transactions
Total Page
Invalid Transaction Listing

Record layouts:

Valid part number records

Field Name	Part Number	Date of Last Price Change	Unit Cost	Unit Price
Characteristics	X(5)	9(6)	9999V99	9999V99
Usage				
Position	1-5	6-11	12-17	18-23

Sales transactions

Field Name	Update Code	Tran. Type	Customer Order No.	Order Date	Branch Number	Salespers Number	Customer Number	Quantity	Part Number	Unused
Characteristics	C	1	X(10)	9(6)	X(2)	X(3)	X(5)	9(5)	X(5)	X(42)
Usage										
Position	1	2	3-12	13-18	19-20	21-23	24-28	29-33	34-38	39-80

Return transactions

Field Name	Update Code	Tran. Type	Customer Memo No.	Return Date	Unused	Customer Number	Quantity	Part Number	Return Authorization Code	Unused
Characteristics	C	2	X(10)	9(6)	X(5)	X(5)	9(5)	X(5)	X(4)	X(38)
Usage										
Position	1	2	3-12	13-18	19-23	24-28	29-33	34-38	39-42	43-80

Figure 6–6
Specifications for the edit-inventory-transactions program (part 1 of 2)

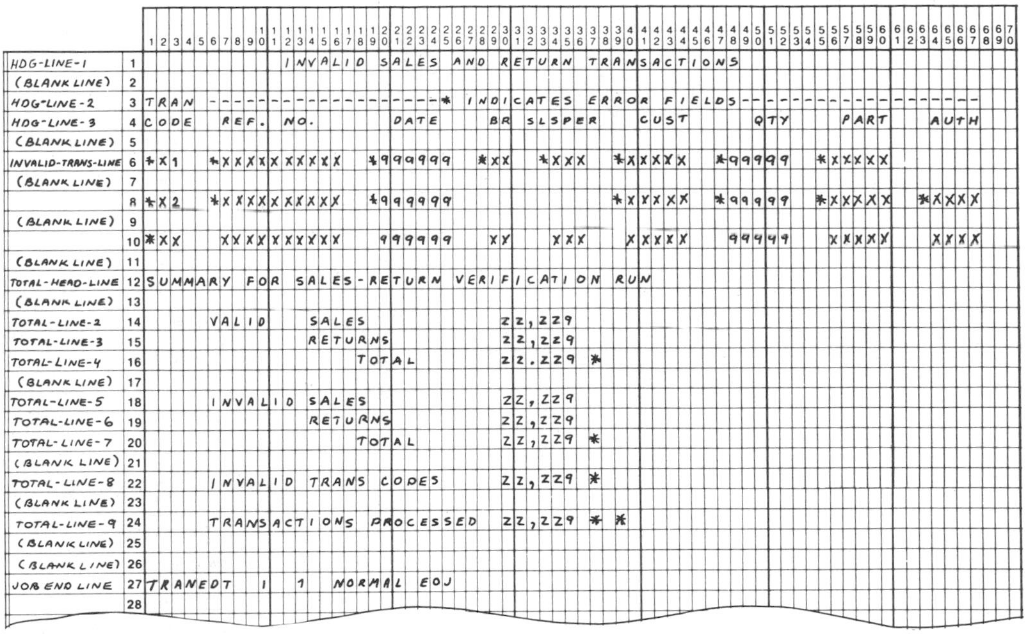
HDG-LINE-1 1 INVALID SALES AND RETURN TRANSACTIONS
(BLANK LINE) 2
HDG-LINE-2 3 TRAN ------------------* INDICATES ERROR FIELDS--------------------
HDG-LINE-3 4 CODE REF. NO. DATE BR SLSPER CUST QTY PART AUTH
(BLANK LINE) 5
INVALID-TRANS-LINE 6 *X1 *XXXXXXXXXX *99999 *XX *XXX *XXXXX *99999 *XXXXX
(BLANK LINE) 7
8 *X2 *XXXXXXXXXX *99999 *XXXXX *99999 *XXXXX *XXXX
(BLANK LINE) 9
10 *XX XXXXXXXXXX 99999 XX XXX XXXXX 99999 XXXXX XXXX
(BLANK LINE) 11
TOTAL-HEAD-LINE 12 SUMMARY FOR SALES-RETURN VERIFICATION RUN
(BLANK LINE) 13
TOTAL-LINE-2 14 VALID SALES ZZ,ZZ9
TOTAL-LINE-3 15 RETURNS ZZ,ZZ9
TOTAL-LINE-4 16 TOTAL ZZ.ZZ9 *
(BLANK LINE) 17
TOTAL-LINE-5 18 INVALID SALES ZZ,ZZ9
TOTAL-LINE-6 19 RETURNS ZZ,ZZ9
TOTAL-LINE-7 20 TOTAL ZZ,ZZ9 *
(BLANK LINE) 21
TOTAL-LINE-8 22 INVALID TRANS CODES ZZ,ZZ9 *
(BLANK LINE) 23
TOTAL-LINE-9 24 TRANSACTIONS PROCESSED ZZ,ZZ9 * *
(BLANK LINE) 25
(BLANK LINE) 26
JOB END LINE 27 TRANEDT 1 1 NORMAL EOJ
28

Narrative:

1. Detailed editing specifications for each type of transaction will be developed later on. For both transaction types, however, the transaction part number must be matched against the valid part numbers in the valid part-number file. To do this, the file of valid part numbers must be read and stored in a part-number table at the start of the program. If no match is found, the transaction part number will be considered invalid.
2. The transaction code should be a 1 (sale) or 2 (return). Anything else is an error.
3. The size and location of the fields in a transaction record will vary depending on whether the transaction is a sale or a return.
4. All invalid transactions are printed on the listing. An asterisk should be used to mark each invalid field.

Figure 6–6
Specifications for the edit-inventory-transactions program
(part 2 of 2)

To name a module, you should use one verb, one or at most two adjectives, and one object. Although this may seem limiting, you will find that it will be all that you need. As you will see, all of the structure charts in this book use this naming technique.

After the top-level module has been named and a block drawn for it at the top of the VTOC, the program designer tries to determine what functions (modules) the top-level module consists of. For instance, a simple report-

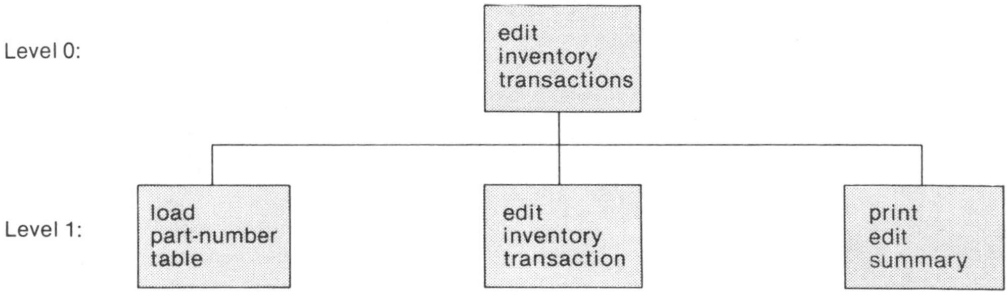
Level 0:
edit inventory transactions
Level 1:
load part-number table
edit inventory transaction
print edit summary

Figure 6–7
The first two levels of the VTOC for the edit-inventory-transactions program

printing program like the reorder-listing program consists of a module that produces the body lines of the report and a module that produces that total lines.

For the edit-inventory-transactions program, the designer has decided on the level-1 modules shown in Figure 6–7. As you can see, the entire program consists of three major modules: (1) a module that loads the part-number table from tape into computer storage at the start of the program, (2) a module that edits one inventory transaction, and (3) a module that prints the total page of the report after all transactions have been edited.

To create the level-1 modules in a VTOC, you should begin by deciding on one primary functional module that will be performed repeatedly during the execution of the program. In Figure 6–7, this is the edit-inventory-transaction module. In other words, the level-0 module represents the processing for all input records; the primary level-1 module represents processing for only one input record (or set of records).

At first, the development of a VTOC seems to be confusing, especially at the first two levels. Study and keep in mind the following summary comments:

1. The module at level-0 is the main control module. To name the module at level-0, state the purpose of the program in the verb-adjective-noun format (edit-inventory-transactions).

2. At level-1 there is always at least one principal function or task to be done, and that will be the name of the principal module (edit-inventory-transaction). The names of the level-0 module and the level-1 principal module are always very similar (note the name goes from plural at level-0 to singular at level-1, and the change from print . . . report at level-0 to print . . . line at level-1 in previous examples).

3. At level-1 there may (or may not) be what could be called a get-ready or a set-up module. This is a function or task that must be accomplished before the principal module's task can begin. In previous examples no get-ready function was needed. In the current example a list of part numbers must be loaded into a table since one of the edit subtasks is to see if the incoming part numbers are valid, and that is done by checking each one against an official list. The task of the load-part-number-table module is to make the official list available to the edit program.

4. At level-1 there may (or may not) be what could be called a follow-up module. This is a function or task that must be done after (and only after) the principal module's task has been completed. A very typical function of the follow-up type of module is to print out some totals or summary information that was accumulated while the principal module was running.

After you have decided upon the primary level-1 module, you should think about functional modules that need to be performed before the primary module. In Figure 6–7, this is the load-part-number-table module, because the part-number table must be loaded before any of the transactions can be checked for validity. Then, you should think of functional modules that need to be performed after the primary module. In Figure 6–7, this is the print-edit-summary module. In other words, after all transaction records have been processed by the primary module, the total page should be printed.

In general, the left-to-right placement of modules in the VTOC indicates the probable sequence of module execution. This is certainly true for the level-1 modules in Figure 6–7. However, this isn't always the case. In some instances, subordinate modules will be executed in a sequence that isn't

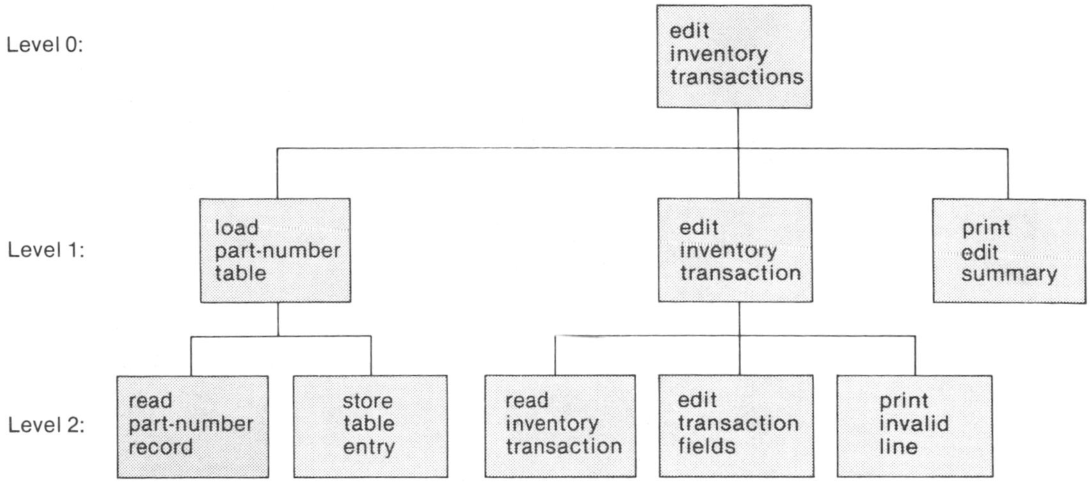
Level 0:
Level 1:
Level 2:
edit inventory transactions
load part-number table
edit inventory transaction
print edit summary
read part-number record
store table entry
read inventory transaction
edit transaction fields
print invalid line

Figure 6–8
The first three levels of the VTOC for the edit-inventory-transactions program

apparent at the time the VTOC is created. You should not be concerned about the sequence of module execution when you make your first draft of the VTOC. First, they can be rearranged when you make the final draft; second, the order may not become clear until the programmer gets to the detailed logic.

After the level-1 modules have been created, the program designer tries to decide whether any of these consist of subordinate functions. If so, subordinate modules should be created. Here, the designer is thinking in terms of clearly defined functions.

For the edit-inventory-transactions program, the designer has decided on the level-2 modules shown in the VTOC in Figure 6–8. Thus, the load-part-number-table module has been broken down into two subordinate modules: one for reading the part-number records and one for storing the records in the part-number table in the COBOL program. If you haven't coded table handling routines in another language, you may have a hard time understanding this part of the program right now. As you'll see later, though, the read and store modules both represent clearly defined functions that are required if the table is to be stored properly.

The edit-inventory-transaction module is also subdivided into subordinate modules: one will read a transaction record, one will edit the individual fields in the record, and one will print a line on the report for each invalid transaction. As you might guess, the read-inventory-transaction and edit-transaction-fields modules will be performed once for each transaction record. However, the print-invalid-line module will only be executed when the transaction record is invalid.

Notice that the three basic submodules for the edit-inventory-transaction module follow the basic computer concept of input-processing-output. Although the output submodule (print-invalid-line) may not be executed in each cycle of the level-1 module, it is still an integral part of that basic concept.

As for the print-edit-summary module, it isn't subdivided any further. The designer feels that it is a clearly defined function that needs no more simplification.

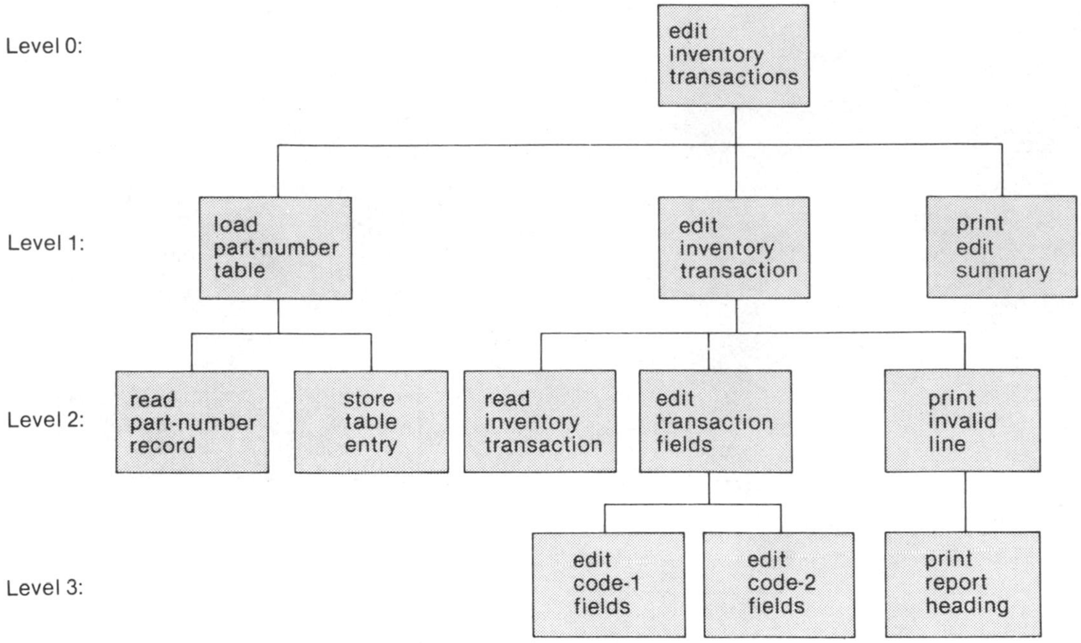
Level 0:
edit inventory transactions
Level 1:
load part-number table
edit inventory transaction
print edit summary
Level 2:
read part-number record
store table entry
read inventory transaction
edit transaction fields
print invalid line
Level 3:
edit code-1 fields
edit code-2 fields
print report heading

Figure 6–9
The first four levels of the VTOC for the edit-inventory-transactions program.

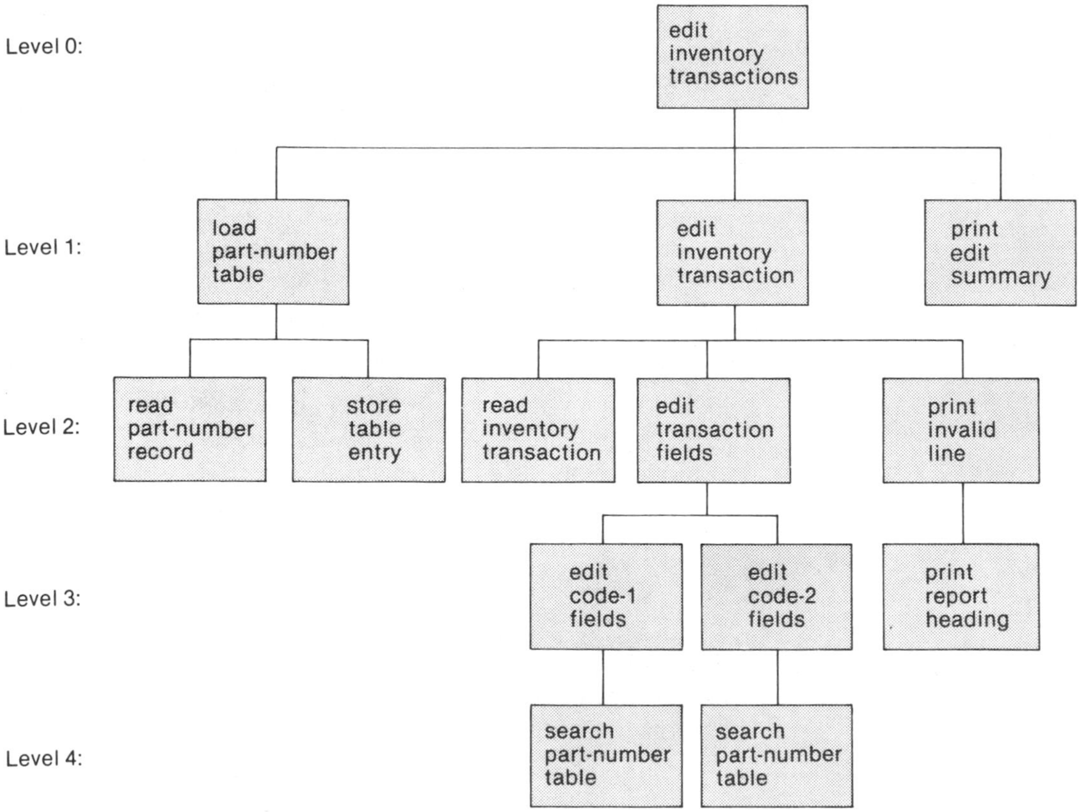
Level 0:
edit inventory transactions
Level 1:
load part-number table
edit inventory transaction
print edit summary
Level 2:
read part-number record
store table entry
read inventory transaction
edit transaction fields
print invalid line
Level 3:
edit code-1 fields
edit code-2 fields
print report heading
Level 4:
search part-number table
search part-number table

Figure 6–10
The first five levels of the VTOC for the edit-inventory-transactions program.

The programmer next decides whether any of the level-2 modules can be subdivided into clearly defined functions. Thus, the edit-inventory-transactions program can be further subdivided as shown in Figure 6–9. Here, the edit-transaction-fields module is broken down into two modules that edit the fields in the transaction records—one module for each of the two types of transactions. Here too, the print-invalid-line module is given a subordinate module that will print a heading on each page of the report. In this case, then, a single subordinate module is broken out of a higher-level module.

When the designer decides on the modules for editing the fields in each of the two record types, he or she realizes that the part-number field must be edited by searching the part-number table for an equal comparison. The programmer also realizes that this module must be subordinate to each of the edit-fields modules. Thus, the programmer adds one more level to the VTOC as shown in Figure 6–10. As you can see, the search-part-number-table module is subordinate to the edit-code-1-fields module as well as to the edit-code-2-fields module.

At this stage, the VTOC in Figure 6–10 is logically complete; all modules have been broken down into their functional components. Note, however, that you do *not* need to concern yourself with the details of the program to create a VTOC like this. For instance, the designer has created the edit modules without even knowing what the editing rules are going to be. All the designer knows is that the rules will probably be different for each type of transaction, so a separate module has been provided for each.

Whether you are given all specifications or not, you should make every effort to avoid the details of a program when you're designing the VTOC. Once you have convinced yourself that the function of any given module can be programmed, forget the details. You shouldn't have to confront them again until you are called on to document or code the module.

You very likely will be tempted to start coding without going to the "trouble" of preparing a VTOC. You may think, "I can always do the VTOC after I finish the program." This is a near-fatal, although common, mistake of beginning programming students. It will invariably cost many extra hours of debugging time that will far exceed the time required to develop an appropriate design. Avoid this trap by thoughtfully making the VTOC first. And remember this little phrase that seems to be so very applicable: "If you do not have time to do it right, when will you have time to do it over?"

Add one read or write module for each file

After the VTOC is logically complete as in Figure 6–10, the designer adds read and write modules that are specific to each physical file required by the program. The idea here is that there should only be one READ statement in the program for each file read by the program. Similarly, there should only be one WRITE statement for each output file.

It isn't always possible, however, to have only one WRITE statement for each output file. For instance, as we saw in chapter 4, COBOL print files usually require one WRITE statement that skips to the top of a page as well as one WRITE statement that spaces one or more lines based on the value in a space-control field. In most cases, though, you should be able to follow the rule of one READ or WRITE statement per file.

To limit the number of READ and WRITE statements for each file, the READ and WRITE statements must be coded in separate read and write modules. These modules can then be performed whenever a record needs to be read or written. By isolating the READ and WRITE statements in this way, you end up with a more efficient program and one that is easy to modify.

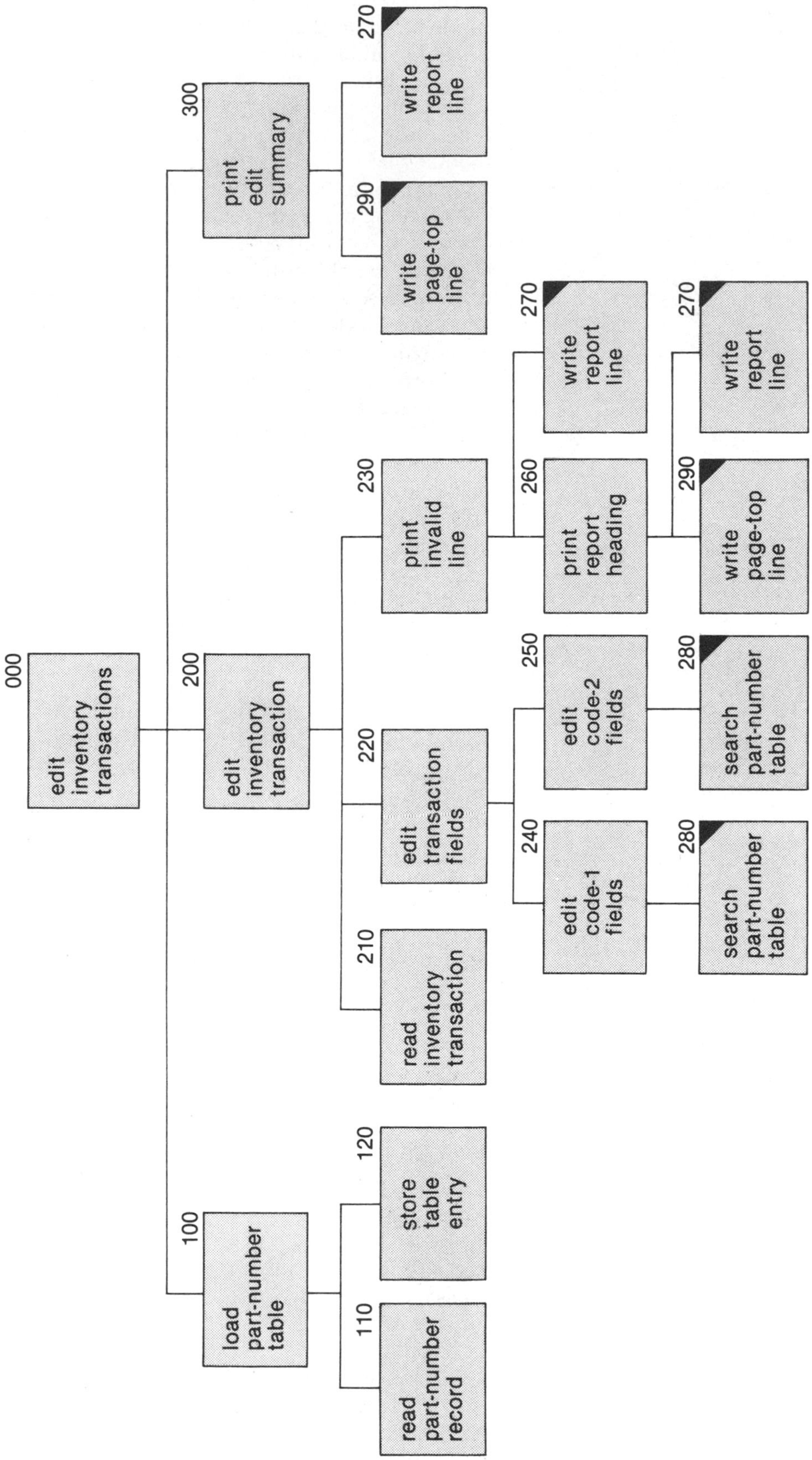
000
edit inventory transactions
100
load part-number table
110
read part-number record
120
store table entry
200
edit inventory transaction
210
read inventory transaction
220
edit transaction fields
240
edit code-1 fields
280
search part-number table
250
edit code-2 fields
280
search part-number table
230
print invalid line
260
print report heading
290
write page-top line
270
write report line
270
write report line
300
print edit summary
290
write page-top line
270
write report line

Figure 6–11
Complete VTOC for the edit-inventory-transactions program

Because there are already two read modules in Figure 6–10, one for each of the input files, the designer doesn't have to add any other specific read modules. However, since the printer file needs both page-top and body lines, specific write modules should be added subordinate to the three print modules. These write modules are shown in the VTOC for the edit-inventory-transactions program in Figure 6–11. One of them will write a line after skipping to the top of the next page (module 290); the other will write a line after spacing one or more lines as determined by a space-control field (module 270). You can see this use of write modules in the refined reorder-listing program in Figure 4–8.

Although the read and write modules will often consist of only one COBOL statement, it is worthwhile to isolate the statements. Later on, if you want to count the number of records read or the number of lines printed, the code can easily be added to these modules. The alternative in a large program is to have several READ or WRITE statements for each file dispersed in many different modules, an inefficient and confusing practice.

Shade common modules

Because the search and write modules in Figure 6–11 are subordinate to more than one module, they are called *common modules*. As a result, the upper righthand corners of these blocks are shaded. This simply shows that the modules are used in more than one place in the VTOC. Thus, module 280 is common to modules 240 and 250; module 270 is common to modules 230, 260, and 300; and module 290 is common to modules 260 and 300.

Use more than one page for large charts

If a structure chart is so large that it is difficult to get it on a single page, it should extend to two or more pages. In a case like this, the first page should contain the top-level module and the level-1 modules, such as those shown in Figure 6–7. Then, subsequent pages will start with one of the level-1 modules: page 2 will contain the first level-1 module and all its subordinates; page 3 will contain the second level-1 module and its subordinates; and so on. If, for example, the edit-inventory-transactions program were larger, page 3 of the structure chart might be as shown in Figure 6–12. This is the level-1 module called "edit inventory transaction" along with all of its subordinate modules.

Step 2—Review and Analyze

Once you have your first version of a VTOC, you should give it a thorough review. Are all modules functional? Are all modules independent? Are all functions required by the program accounted for by the VTOC? Are all common modules shaded?

After you are convinced that your VTOC is complete and proper, you should review it with someone else who is involved with the program—a manager, a systems analyst, a user of the program. Your primary purpose here is to make sure your VTOC has accounted for everything.

Based on your review, you are likely to change your VTOC. Sometimes this means changing or moving only a block or two. Sometimes this means redrawing the entire chart. Later on, as you document the individual modules, you may decide that other changes are also needed. These changes, however, are usually minor.

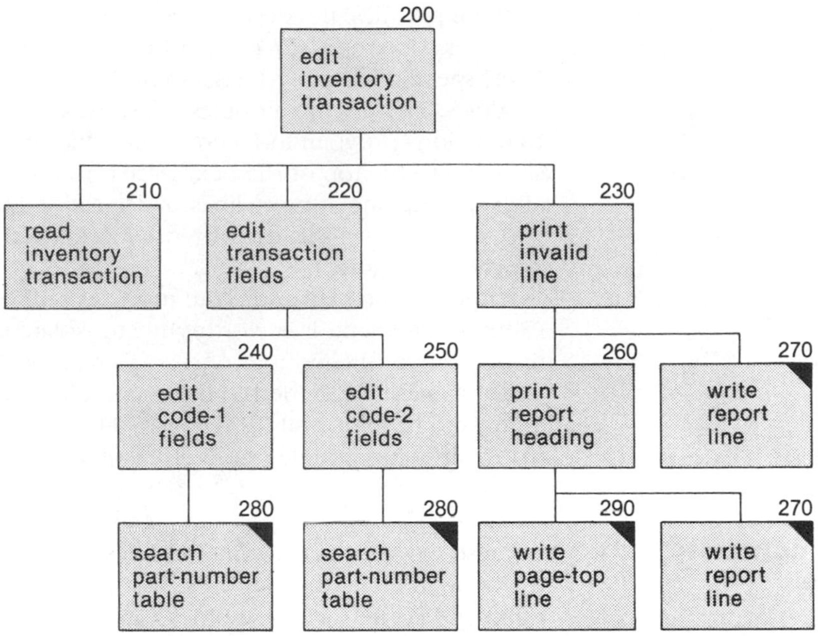
200
edit inventory transaction
210
read inventory transaction
220
edit transaction fields
230
print invalid line
240
edit code-1 fields
250
edit code-2 fields
260
print report heading
270
write report line
280
search part-number table
280
search part-number table
290
write page-top line
270
write report line

Figure 6–12
Page 3 of the VTOC for the edit-inventory-transactions program: the edit-inventory-transaction branch

When you review your VTOC, there are a number of things you should watch for. Above all, you should ask yourself (1) whether all the modules are functional and (2) whether the VTOC is complete. After that, you should consider verb consistency, module independence, proper subordination, span of control, and module size.

Are all the modules functional?

Perhaps you've noticed the emphasis on function as VTOC creation has been described. This emphasis, as you might guess, is one of the important principles of effective top-down design. In brief, *all* modules should represent one and only one program function.

You can be sure your modules are functional if you can describe them in a single imperative sentence such as "print the heading lines," "update the records in the master files," or "search the customer table." This, of course, is what you do when you name the module by using one verb, one or two adjectives, and an object. If you can't describe your modules in this way, they probably aren't functional and your program design is probably faulty.

One type of module that isn't functional is a module that refers to time. Thus "perform end-of-file processing" isn't a functional description. The elements in a module like this are only related by the fact that they are done *after* all records have been processed. Similarly, "perform initialization" modules aren't functional. Their elements are only related because they are done *before* the main processing routines. They too are related by time.

Another type of module description to watch out for is one that refers to a class of data. Traditionally, for example, programs contained "process input data" modules. The elements in these modules were only related insofar as they operated on the same type of data (input data). In other words, these modules were simply a conglomeration of all the functions that had to do with any part of the input data. Thus, the modules weren't functional and were indicative of faulty program design. So watch out for modules built around classes of data—they aren't likely to be functional.

If your module description requires the use of the word *and* or *or*, it is a good indication that the module contains more than one function. Thus, a "read and store table records" module should be divided into two functional modules. And a "print valid or invalid message" module should be two modules.

Sometimes, as shown above, you may find that when you feel it is necessary to use an *and* or an *or* that the problem is (1) a need to be more thoughtful and creative in choosing module names and (2) a strong indication that the module under consideration really requires two subordinate modules. The above example of "read and store table records" has this problem. Look back to Figure 6–11 and note how the load-part-number-table module contains separate read and store subfunctions which address the original need of creating a read and store module.

In any event, strive for functional modules. Test all of them to see whether they can be described in a single imperative sentence. Test all of these sentences to see whether they represent a function rather than a collection of elements related by time or class of data. If your modules are functional, they will be relatively easy to document, code, and test. If they aren't functional, you will run into problems as you develop the program.,

Is the VTOC complete?

When you're sure that each module represents one function, your next question should be this: Does the VTOC provide for all functions that must be done by the program? When a VTOC consists of a hundred or more modules, however, this can be a difficult question to answer.

The way to approach this question is one level at a time, from the top down. In Figure 6–11, for example, you should first ask whether the three level-1 modules do everything implies by their boss, module 000. In other words, does editing the inventory transactions consist only of loading the part-number table (module 100), editing the individual transactions (module 200), and printing the total page (module 300)? Or should there be other level-1 functions (modules)? It appears level 1 is complete as shown.

In terms of major functions addressed, level-1 is complete as shown. To help clarify that implication analysis, consider the production of a cake for dessert at supper. It may be a major subfunction to the preparation of a meal. What are the subfunctions of the cake production process itself? They would appear to be: (1) obtain-cake-recipe, (2) obtain-cake-ingredients, (3) bake-supper-cake, (4) decorate-supper-cake. Notice that there are two get-ready modules here, one principal module, and one follow-up module. If you were inclined to include more modules, perhaps you need to spend more study on the concept of distinction between major functions and subfunctions. On the other hand, the first two modules could have very well been subfunctions under a major get-ready function called prepare-cake-ingredients.

After you have analyzed one level for completeness, you continue with the next level down. For instance, do modules 110 and 120 provide for everyting that module 100 implies? Do modules 210, 220, and 230 provide for everything module 200 implies? And do modules 290 and 270 provide for everything module 300 implies?

Since this analysis seems to give a lot of people trouble, a good aid is to jot down what is meant by a certain module description on a piece of scratch paper. In Figure 6–11, for example, what does load part-number table (module 100) mean to you? It means (1) reading the table records and (2) loading the records into a working-storage area. As a result, level-2 beneath module 100 seems to be complete.

Module Type	Function Required		
	Input	**Process**	**Output**
Get-ready	usually	often	hardly ever
Principal	almost always	almost always	almost always
Follow-up	hardly ever	sometimes	almost always

Figure 6–13
Table of functions required by module types

You can use this scratch-pad idea whenever you have doubts about completeness. It is particularly useful when reviewing a VTOC with another person. As questions arise, you can list the functions that you think a boss module implies. Then, you can discuss the items on the list to determine (1) whether all functions are accounted for and (2) whether all functions contribute to the objective of the boss module. If you decide that all functions are *not* accounted for, you simply add the required modules and continue your analysis.

Recall the discussion about the level-1 modules in relation to the input-process-output functions. Another question you might ask is "does the boss module require all three processes?" Figure 6–13 is a table which may help your thinking about the level-1 modules and their subordinate modules.

When you design modules at level-2 and below, you will find that they are the input, process, and output modules. As such, any subordinate modules are normally those of processing functions.

Are the verbs precise and consistent?

When you do a scratch-pad analysis, you will often discover problems with the verbs used in module descriptions. The major problem seems to be using verbs that are too general. For example, it's tempting to name a module "process sales record" when you're not sure what it's going to require. What you really mean is that the module should do everything that is required—but you don't know what that is—or that the module should do everything that isn't done by other modules at that level. In either case, you will *not* be able to list the functions required by the module. So avoid using a general verb like "process"; whenever possible, find a more precise verb to use in the module description. Only after you have a clear idea of what the module must do will you be able to continue your analysis.

Besides using precise verbs in your module descriptions, you should try to be consistent in their use. In other words, one verb should mean the same thing throughout a VTOC and, if possible, throughout a programming department. For instance, the word *print* is used to mean at the least (1) formatting the output record in storage (if necessary) and (2) writing the record on the printer; the word *write* means physically placing the record on the output device (as in the COBOL WRITE statement). Similarly, use the word *get* to mean (1) reading a record, (2) checking the record for validity, and (3) doing something with the invalid records; use the word *read* to mean physically reading the record from the input device (as in the COBOL READ statement).

Quite frankly, the way that these words are used can be debated. However, the key is that the use of these words is consistent throughout this book. Once you understand what is meant by the verbs used, you will be able to understand the module descriptions in Figure 6–11. Further, you will be able to understand what is implied by any of the VTOC modules in the rest of this text. People who have agreed on the meaning of certain words can communicate quickly and effectively. That is why it is so important for a computer center's programming staff to have a single set of documentation standards and program coding techniques. In a programming class, you should be able to quickly understand what each other's programs are doing; when you see a module named "print-sales-line" you should expect the same actions to take place and those actions to be in the same order.

The important thing, then, is consistency. As you review your VTOCs for completeness, you should keep a close eye on the verbs you use. Whenever you see the same verb used in more than one way, you should change the VTOC so the verbs are consistent.

Are the modules independent?

Structured programming depends on the use of independent modules. This means a module should only be *called* by the module above it in the VTOC. Thus, module 220 in Figure 6–11 (the *called module*) should only be called by module 200 (the *calling module*).

To maintain independence, control codes created in a called module should only be used by the calling module. To say it another way, codes created in the subordinate module should only be *passed* to the calling module. For example, the end-of-file code that must be created by module 210 in Figure 6–11 should only be passed to module 200. If the code is required by the print-invalid-line module, module 230, this latter module isn't properly independent.

Although a code should only be required by the calling module, it is okay to pass a code from one calling module to another. For example, the end-of-file switch created by module 210 is passed to and tested by module 200, which is module 210's calling module. Module 200 in turn passes the code up to the next calling module, module 000, which also tests the code. In other words, it's okay to pass a code up the line, from one calling module to another. But a code created in one module should *not* be required by modules at the same level or at lower levels in the VTOC; if it is, it indicates that the modules aren't independent.

Note here that it was said *control codes* shouldn't be passed erratically from one module to another. Nothing was said about data. On the contrary, it is perfectly all right for data that is created in one module to be used in modules other than the calling module. In Figure 6–11, for example, data read by the read-inventory-transaction module (module 210) is used in modules 220, 230, 240, 250, and 280. And these modules are at the same level as module 210 or at lower levels. Similarly, data created in a computational module is likely to be used in print modules at the same or lower levels.

In some cases, it is difficult or impossible to decide whether a module is independent by looking at a VTOC. If the modules are functional, there is a good chance that they will be properly independent. Nevertheless, the programmer should keep the goal of module independence in mind. This is important when creating the VTOC, and it is important when creating the documentation for the individual modules.

Is proper subordination shown?

When we refer to *proper subordination*, it means that called modules are related to the correct calling module. Since the program designer has many options when creating a VTOC, it is not always easy to achieve proper subordination. To some extent, at least, it is only achieved after a program designer has gained some experience with the techniques of structured design and documentation.

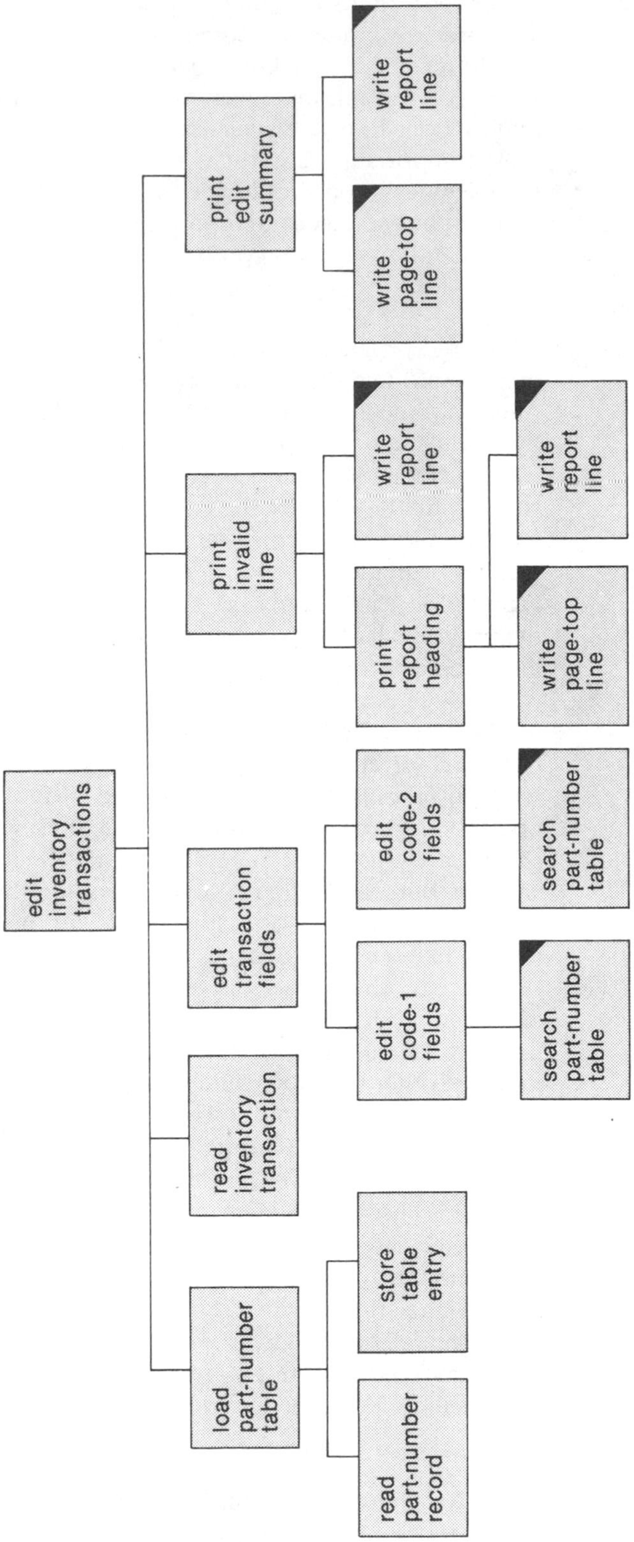
edit inventory transactions
load part-number table
read inventory transaction
edit transaction fields
print invalid line
print edit summary
read part-number record
store table entry
edit code-1 fields
edit code-2 fields
print report heading
write report line
write page-top line
write report line
search part-number table
search part-number table
write page-top line
write report line

Figure 6–14
Improper subordination for the edit-inventory-transactions program

To illustrate, look at the VTOC in Figure 6–14. It is for the edit-inventory-transactions program that is charted in Figure 6–11. Here, the program designer has decided on five level-1 modules. Now the question is: Why is this improper subordination and why do the three level-1 modules in Figure 6–11 represent proper subordination?

The ability to answer this question depends to some extent on experience. In brief, however, you won't be able to code the VTOC in Figure 6–14 in structured code. Specifically, the top-level module in a structured program must repeatedly execute the major level-1 module using a DO–UNTIL structure. This level-1 module in turn must control the major functions of the program. Since the VTOC in Figure 6–14 doesn't provide for this level-1 control module, it doesn't represent proper subordination.

If you study the following coding, which would be in the level-0 module edit-inventory-transactions, you should soon understand why the VTOC of Figure 6–14 does not have proper subordination.

```
    .
    .
    .
PERFORM 100-LOAD-PART-NUMBER-TABLE
    UNTIL LAST-PART-RECORD.
PERFORM 200-READ-INVENTORY-TRANSACTION
    UNTIL LAST-INVENTORY-RECORD.
PERFORM 300-EDIT-TRANSACTION-FIELDS
    UNTIL LAST-INVENTORY-RECORD.
PERFORM 400-PRINT-INVALID-LINE.
PERFORM 500-PRINT-EDIT-SUMMARY.
    .
    .
```

Some study will show that the perform of module 200 would read all of the inventory records without doing any processing at all on them. It would just "flush" them through the computer. You might then argue for removal of the UNTIL clause, with that PERFORM statement looking like this:

```
    .
    .
    .
PERFORM 200-READ-INVENTORY-TRANSACTION.
PERFORM 300-EDIT-INVENTORY-TRANSACTION
    UNTIL LAST-INVENTORY-RECORD.
    .
    .
```

Here you can see that only one inventory transaction would be read, the PERFORM of module 300 would keep processing that first record, and fall into that programmer's bane, the infamous "infinite loop."

Although you may not be able to detect improper subordination at this point, it will show up when you document the modules. As a result, you will be better able to detect improper subordination after you learn how to document the modules in topic 3. For now, though, try to use this guideline: Use level-1 for the one major function of the program, for functions that must be done before the major function, and for functions that must be done after the major function.

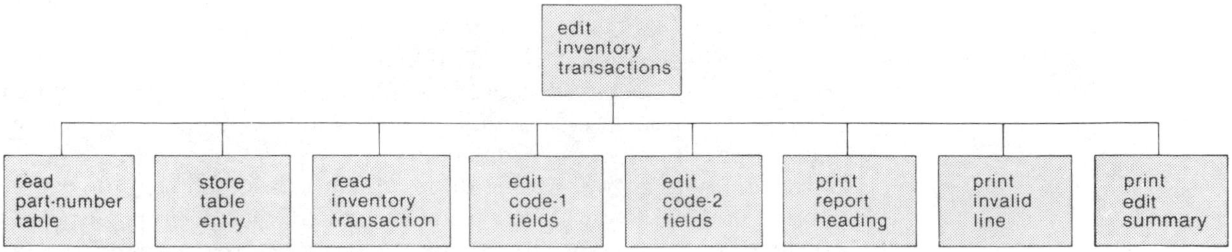
edit
inventory
transactions
read
part-number
table
store
table
entry
read
inventory
transaction
edit
code-1
fields
edit
code-2
fields
print
report
heading
print
invalid
line
print
edit
summary

Figure 6–15
Improper subordination reflected by a broad span of control

Are the control spans reasonable?

If a module has three other modules subordinate to it, its *span of control*, or *control span*, is three. In other words, it controls the operation of three modules. Span of control is useful because it can indicate problems in program design.

As a rule of thumb, the span of control for a module should be no more than nine and no less than two. If, for example, the edit-inventory-transactions program were charted as in Figure 6–15, the span of control for the top-level module would be eight. This large span of control, then, could indicate that the modules were not designed with proper subordination. Also, it could be that a module that calls eight subordinates will require so many levels of nested IF statements that it will be very difficult to follow once it is coded. On the other hand, if the modules are simply executed in sequence (that is, the boss module consists of one simple PERFORM statement after another), the large span of control may not indicate any problem at all.

The other extreme is illustrated in Figure 6–16. Here the VTOC has several modules that have a span of control of one. Although this is usually less of a problem than a too large span of control, it is likely that this VTOC could be improved.

Span of control, then, is simply a measure that can indicate design problems. Although perfectly proper programs may have modules that have a span of control of ten or more, they deserve a second look. Similarly, though some programs may require a structure like that in Figure 6–16, it isn't common and it may indicate design flaws.

Are the modules too large?

Part of the theory of structured design says that each module should be small enough to be manageable. For COBOL programs, this means that a module should be around 50 statements or less (50 statements is about the number that will fit on one page of the source listing). Studies have shown that the larger a module is, the more difficult it is to read and understand. Furthermore, the difficulty does not increase in direct proportion to the size of the module. For example, a 100-statement module is often three or four times as difficult to read and understand as a 50-statement module, rather than being only twice as troublesome.

Needless to say, you can't tell how large a module will be by looking at a VTOC. As a result, you may have to make changes to the VTOC when coding the program. If, for example, you code a module that requires 500 statements, you should attempt to divide it into smaller component parts.

The simplest rule to go by is to develop your VTOC down to the lowest functional level. Although some books on structured design recommend that modules range from 10 to 50 statements, this is unrealistic. If a module requires

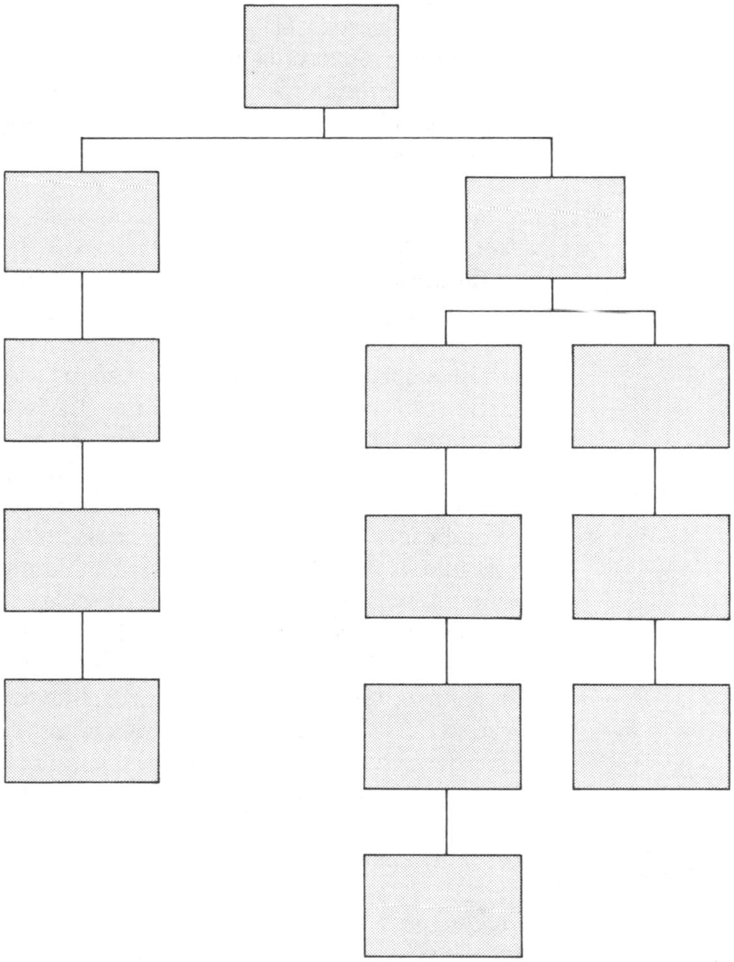

Figure 6–16
Questionable control spans

only one statement but it is a clearly defined function, there is no point in combining it with someother function just to increase the module size. On the other hand, a 100-statement module may be perfectly acceptable, particularly if it consists primarily of imperative statements executed in sequence. In general, though, if you design down to the lowest level, you will find that relatively few modules require more than 50 lines of COBOL code.

Step 3—Number the Modules

After you have your VTOC in final form, it is time to number the modules. These numbers are then used in combination with the module descriptions to form the COBOL paragraph names for the modules. You have already seen this in the example programs.

Although some companies use complicated numbering schemes, the recommended numbering is shown in Figure 6–11. Here, the top-level module is given the number 000. Then, the first level-1 module is given the number 100. After this, all modules subordinate to module 100 are numbered by tens starting with 110. Then, the second level-1 module is given a number that is the next available multiple of 100—in Figure 6–11 this is number 200. After the modules subordinate to module 200 are numbered by tens starting with 210, the third level-1 module is given a number that is the next available multiple of 100. Since the last number used for module 200's subordinate modules in Figure 6–11 is 290, the next level-1 module is assigned number 300.

In programs that consist of several dozen modules, you may find that your level-1 modules will be numbered something like 100, 300, and 500. In other words, there will be more than ten modules subordinate to module 100 and more than ten subordinate to module 300.

In this numbering scheme, the numbers do not *not* indicate at what level the module can be found. This means that changes can be made to the VTOC without changing module numbers. In contrast, when more complex numbering systems are used, a change to the VTOC usually means a change to the module number, which in turn means a change to the module documentation, which in turn means a change in the COBOL source code.

For instance, some numbering systems use a number like 1.2.4 to indicate the fourth block under block number 1.2, which is the second block under block number 1.0. If the chart is changed so block 1.2.4 should be the first block under block 3.1, its number must be changed to 3.1.1. In brief, you can easily become a slave to a numbering system like this.

Numbering by hundreds and tens also allows for great flexibility if additional blocks must be added to the VTOC after the programmer thinks it is complete. For example, if another module must be added subordinate to module 100 in Figure 6–11, it can be numbered 130 without having to change any other module number. Likewise, if a programmer needs two subordinate modules for module 210, they can easily and logically be numbered 211 and 212 without affecting the rest of the VTOC.

Incidentally, in some systems the numbers are placed inside the blocks themselves, in the lower righthand corner. However, by placing them outside the boxes as in Figure 6–11, you have more room for the module description, and the numbers are easier to locate.

Step 4—If Necessary, Shorten Module Names

When you document each of the modules in your VTOC as described in topic 3, you will create the actual COBOL paragraph names for each of the modules. To create the COBOL name, you will use the module number followed by the module description with the number and words separated by hyphens. Thus, module 000 in Figure 6–11 will be coded in the paragraph named

```
000-EDIT-INVENTORY-TRANSACTIONS
```

Unfortunately, however, this name is invalid since it has more than 30 characters.

After you number the modules, then, you should inspect the module names to make sure they're not too long. In general, you will only have to be careful when two of the words in the module description are long, like *inventory* and *transaction*, or when a four-word module description is used. Then, if the paragraph name will be over 30 characters, you should shorten the description by abbreviating one or more words, Make every effort, however, to keep the module name on the VTOC meaningful. In Figure 6–11, the module descriptions for modules 000, 200, and 210 were too long or on the borderline, so they were shortened as shown in Figure 6–17. The words were changed from *transactions* and *transaction* to *trans* and *tran*. Figure 6–17, then, represents the final VTOC for the edit-inventory-transactions program.

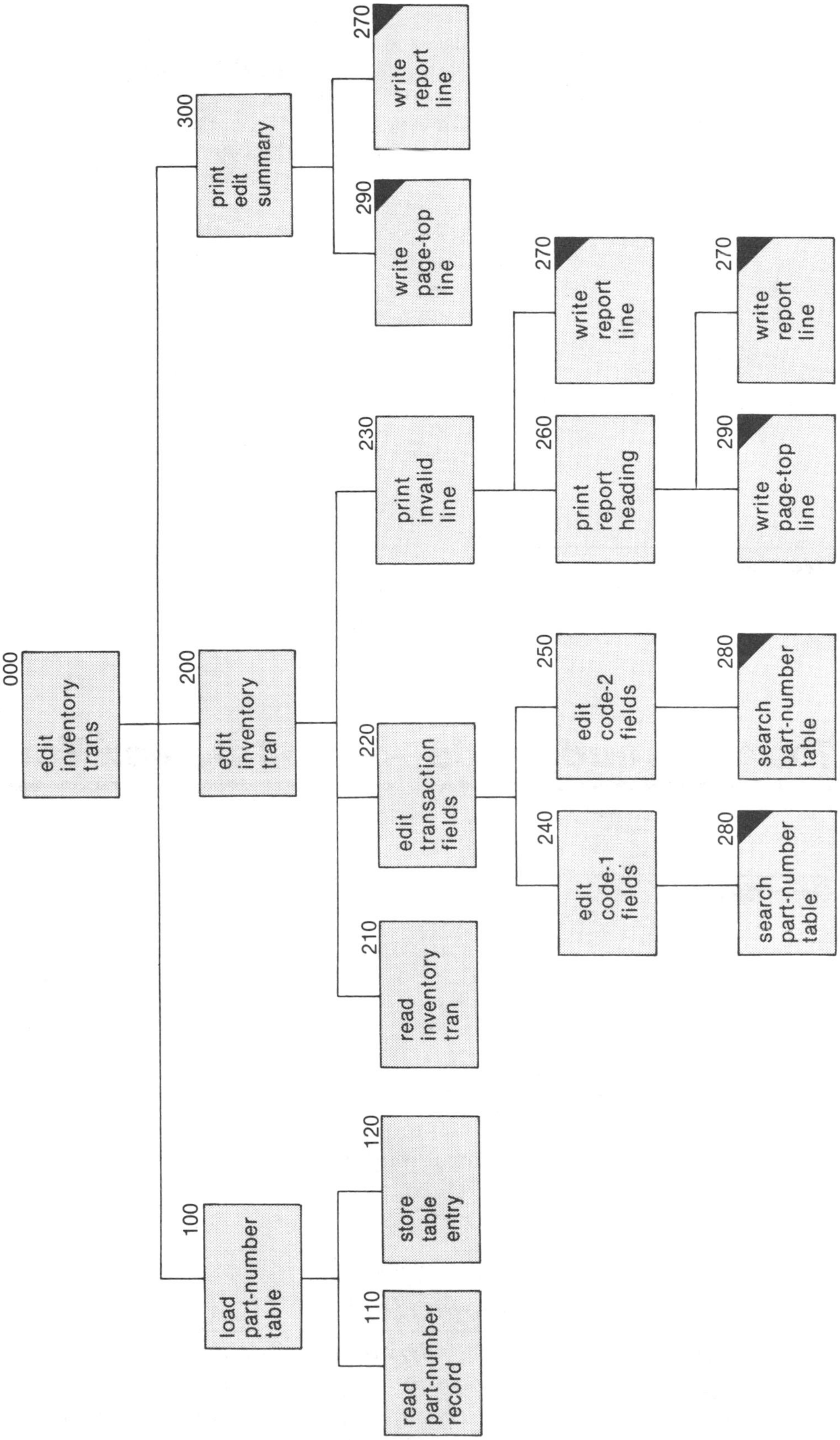
000
edit inventory trans
100
load part-number table
110
read part-number record
120
store table entry
200
edit inventory tran
210
read inventory tran
220
edit transaction fields
230
print invalid line
240
edit code-1 fields
250
edit code-2 fields
260
print report heading
270
write report line
280
search part-number table
290
write page-top line
300
print edit summary

Figure 6–17
Complete VTOC for the edit-inventory-transactions program after the module descriptions have been shortened

Discussion

As mentioned at the start of this topic, there are other forms of structure charts besides the VTOC. Some of these use arrows and other symbols to indicate the data and codes that are passed from one module to another. Other types of charts indicate whether a module is always executed or whether it depends on a condition that varies during processing. It is felt that this type of information is best omitted from the structure chart. Not only does it make the structure chart more difficult to create, it makes it more difficult to change. Furthermore, some of this information is difficult to develop without actually documenting the modules. Finally, it forces the programmer to think in terms of procedure and details—just the type of thinking you should try to avoid during design. This information should be recorded only as part of the module documentation.

In summary, then, the purpose of the structure chart is to show the relationships of the modules required by the program. Once created, it is a guide for program development. The module documentation will follow this guide. The program itself will follow this guide. As for the detailed processing specifications, they are documented by HIPO diagrams or pseudocode as you will see in the next topic.

Problem

At this point, you probably will be working on program assignments. You should use the discussion on structure charts to help design and check the VTOCs for your programs.

Topic 3 **Pseudocode—Detail Design Tool**

Orientation

After the structure chart or VTOC is created, the programmer documents the processing required by the individual modules. As a result, the documentation for a structured program before coding consists of (1) the VTOC and (2) module documentation. Now that you have learned how to create VTOCs, this topic concentrates on module documentation.

Terminology

branch module	IPO diagram	principal control
control module	leaf module	pseudocode
HIPO diagram	main control	work module
IPO	minor control	

Objectives

1. *Understand the function of pseudocode in the development process and use the specialized pseudocode for COBOL.*

2. *Learn the guidelines for documenting program modules and especially learn to create functional modules.*

3. ***Understand the functional difference between the logic/control modules on the higher levels and the work modules on the lower levels.***
4. ***Given the proper definition for a program and the VTOC for its program design, write the pseudocode to document the processing done by any of the modules.***

Pseudocode Tools

Although it is possible to use traditional program flowcharts for module documentation, the trend in industry is to avoid program flowcharts altogether. As mentioned before, flowcharts are difficult to create and maintain, and they don't represent a problem solution in a form that is an efficient guide for coding. Worst of all, they force you to focus on how the processing can be done before you have documented what it is that must be done.

At present, many different forms of module documentation are being used. One of the most common forms is the *HIPO diagram* (also known as an *IPO diagram* or simply an *IPO*). The HIPO diagram is part of the HIPO (Hierarchy plus Input–Process–Output) system of documentation developed and promoted by IBM. Complete HIPO documentation for a program consists of the VTOC and one HIPO or IPO diagram for each module in the VTOC.

Figure 6–18 illustrates the characteristics of a HIPO diagram. It is a HIPO for the top-level module in Figure 6–17. The heading on the form gives the programmer's name, the program name, the date, and the number and name of the module being documented (these are taken from the VTOC). Below the heading, there are three boxes on the HIPO diagram: the left box for describing input, the right box for describing output, and the middle box for describing processing. For this module, there are two input requirements—two working-storage (WS) fields—and no output requirements. As for processing, six steps are documented. To the right of each step that calls another module, the number of the called module is written and boxed. The calling module for the module being documented—in this case, the operating system (OS)—is listed next to the "from" arrow that points into the process box. You can see, then, that a HIPO diagram is complete documentation for a module. It shows all the input, processing, and output requirements for the module and indicates the module's relationships to its called and calling modules.

If you analyze the HIPO diagram in Figure 6–18, you can see that the critical portion of the documentation is that shown in the process box. In contrast, it is usually a trivial task to record the input and output requirements once you have figured out the processing requirements. As a result, many companies and programmers feel that they can get by just by documenting the processing steps using a simple language called *pseudocode*. Because the trend in industry is away from the more formal types of module documentation, like HIPO diagrams, this topic will simply explain how to use pseudocode.

Using Pseudocode

The processing steps in Figure 6–18 are written in the kind of pseudocode used throughout this book. In this form of pseudocode, all the words that relate to the basic structures of structured programming—words like DO,

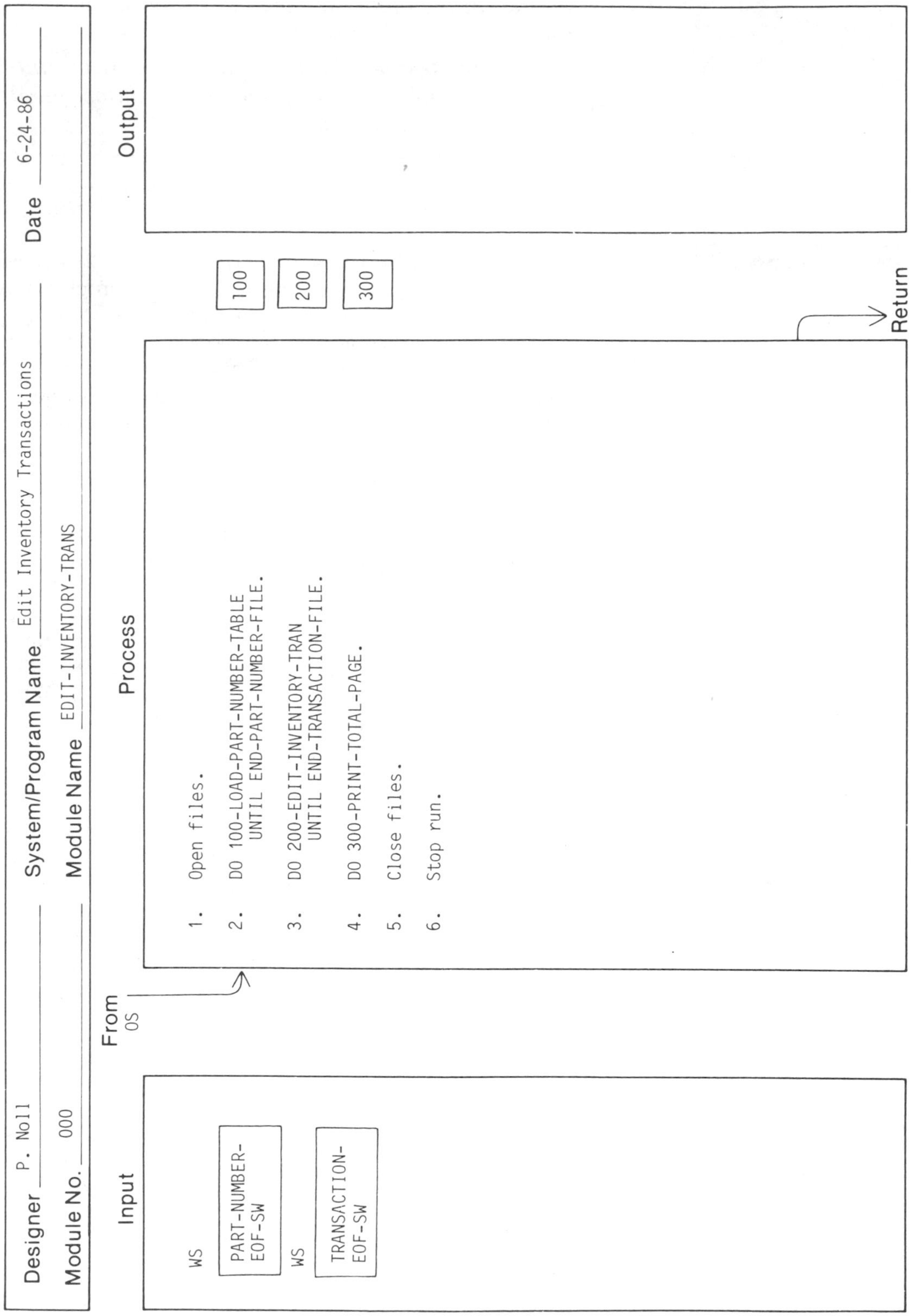
Designer P. Noll
System/Program Name Edit Inventory Transactions
Date 6-24-86
Module No. 000
Module Name EDIT-INVENTORY-TRANS
Input
WS
PART-NUMBER-EOF-SW
WS
TRANSACTION-EOF-SW
From OS
Process
1. Open files.
2. DO 100-LOAD-PART-NUMBER-TABLE UNTIL END-PART-NUMBER-FILE.
3. DO 200-EDIT-INVENTORY-TRAN UNTIL END-TRANSACTION-FILE.
4. DO 300-PRINT-TOTAL-PAGE.
5. Close files.
6. Stop run.
100
200
300
Return
Output

Figure 6–18
HIPO diagram for module 000 of the edit-inventory-transactions program

UNTIL, IF, THEN, and ELSE—are capitalized. These words indicate the logical structure of the module. All COBOL names—like the names of files, records, data items, and modules—are created at this time and are capitalized as well. Aside from the structure and COBOL words, the processing functions are explained in everyday English using lowercase letters.

One suggestion is made here in regard to the creation of names (file, record, data, or module). It is helpful to keep an extra sheet of paper handy as you are documenting the modules. Use that sheet to record any new names that you create. Thus, when you need to refer to that name, you have a record of it in one place and do not have to shuffle back through your pseudocode trying to recall what the name was.

When you begin the pseudocode, you should already have determined what your file names, record names, and field names are in the records. You will either have a copied input record to use, or you should develop the input record from the program problem specifications. Similarly, you should develop the output record description from the problem specifications before you begin with the pseudocode. Then as you discover the need for more names, you can add them to the list.

Given this explanation of pseudocode, can you follow the processing steps in Figure 6–18? First, the files are opened. Second, module 100 is repeatedly executed until the end of the part-number file has been reached. Third, module 200 is repeatedly executed until the end of the transaction file has been reached. Then in the last three steps, module 300 is executed, the files are closed, and the program ends.

You should be aware that the pseudocode in Figure 6–18 is a "customized" form of the language. It's "customized" because it allows you to use COBOL names. In strict pseudocode, there would be no COBOL words, so the processing specifications for module 000 of the edit program would be something like what is shown in Figure 6–19. If you compare this with the processing steps shown in Figure 6–18, you can see that no COBOL words are used, so the pseudocode is not related to any one programming language.

Although some companies go out of their way to avoid the use of COBOL words in their pseudocode, there is little point in this. If a program is definitely going to be written in COBOL, why not use COBOL data names and even COBOL verbs? In fact, in short modules, there is nothing wrong with using COBOL itself to document a module. Be careful, though. One thing you don't want to do is code the program twice, once in the module documentation and again on the coding forms. So in general, resist the urge to code.

```
1. Open files.
2. DO module-100
       UNTIL no more table records.
3. DO module-200
       UNTIL no more transaction records.
4. DO module-300.
5. Close files.
6. Stop run.
```

Figure 6–19
Strict pseudocode for module 000 of the edit-inventory-transactions program

Figure 6–20
Psueodocode for module 200 of the edit-inventory-transaction program

```
1.     DO 210-READ-INVENTORY-TRAN.
2.     IF MORE-INVENTORY-RECS
           DO 220-EDIT-TRANSACTION-FIELDS
           IF INVALID-TRANS
               DO 230-PRINT-INVALID-LINE.
```

As in COBOL, indentation is used to make pseudocode easy to read and understand. For instance, look at Figure 6–20. It gives the pseudocode for module 200 of the edit program. Here, the first step performs the module reading a transaction record (module 210). The second step uses nested IF logic to show when modules 220 and 230 are to be executed. Nested IF structures in pseudocode should always be indented and aligned as shown in this example. Similarly, the UNTIL phrase should be indented from the start of the DO phrase as shown in Figure 6–18. This corresponds closely to the proper use of indentation from COBOL code, as shown throughout this text.

Although capital and lowercase words have been mixed in Figure 6–18 and 6–20, in practice many programmers prefer to use all capitals when using pseudocode. In general, this should cause no confusion. For instance,

```
1.     OPEN FILES.
2.     DO  100-LOAD-PART-NUMBER-TABLE
           UNTIL END-PART-NUMBER-FILE.
3.     DO  200-EDIT-INVENTORY-TRAN
           UNTIL END-TRANSACTION-FILE.
```

is as easy to understand as the pseudocode in Figure 6–18. So feel free to use all capitals if you prefer them to a combination of capital and lowercase letters.

Guidelines for Documenting Modules

When you start to document modules for your own programs, you'll probably find that a number of minor questions are raised. For instance, what level of detail should be shown? Or, in which module should a subfunction be placed if it could logically be placed in two or more different modules? The material that follows will give you some ideas that should help you answer many of the questions that come up.

Always handle switches in a standard way

Switches are quite common in structured programming. For example, Figure 6–18 uses two of them to control the processing in module 000 of the edit program. PART-NUMBER-EOF-SW marks the end of the part-number file, while TRANSACTION-EOF-SW is turned on at the end of the transaction file.

Because they are so common, switches should always be used in a standard way. Here are the standards used in this book:

1. All switch-field names end with the suffix -SW.

2. The purpose of the switch-field should be obvious if you were to drop the -SW. Thus, TRANSACTION-EOF indicates that the switch's purpose is to keep track of the status of the end condition for the transaction file. PART-NUMBER-EOF is used to record the end status for the Part file.

```
1.      DO 280-SEARCH-PART-NUMBER-TABLE.
2.      IF INVALID-PART-NUMBER
            move "N" to VALID-TRAN-SW
            move "*" to mark error field in INVALID-TRANS-LINE.
3.      IF any remaining fields in the INVENTORY-TRANS-REC are invalid
            move "N" to VALID-TRAN-SW
            move "*" to mark error field.
4.      IF INVALID-TRANSACTION
            add 1 to INVALID-SALES-COUNT
        ELSE
            add 1 to VALID-SALES-COUNT.
```

Figure 6–21
Pseudocode for module 240 of the edit-inventory-transaction program

3. All conditions that will be tested in the program should have condition names set up for them. Rather than testing for a negative condition such as IF NOT END–TRANSACTION–FILE, that condition should have a name given to it so that the negative test could be written with a positive statement—IF MORE–TRANSACTION–RECS.

4. A switch is considered to be off if it contains a value of N (for "no") and considered to be on if it contains a value of Y (for "yes").

5. All switches are initialized to their starting values in Working–Storage.

The use of switches was illustrated in COBOL in chapter 3, and the use of condition names was discussed in chapter 4. Those concepts are followed in the programs and the pseudocode throughout the rest of this book.

How much detail should be shown?

One question that comes up when using pseudocode is this: To what level should the logical details be recorded? For instance, look at Figure 6–21. It's the pseudocode for module 240 of the edit program, the module that controls the editing of the transactions that have a 1 in the transaction-type field. The pseudocode uses one search-table step and three IF structures to indicate the editing requirements of the entire module. When actually coding this module, however, many IF statements are likely to be required since there are seven transaction fields to edit. As a result, the pseudocode could be taken to another level of detail as shown in Figure 6–22.

Is this documentation better than that of Figure 6–21? The answer is debatable. Both are acceptable because they clearly indicate the processing requirements for the module. Yet some would argue that version 1 is better because it's simpler, while others would argue that version 2 is better because it's a better guide for COBOL coding. In practice, you, the programmer, must make these decisions. I think you'll find that in most cases you'll use pseudocode that's closer to COBOL in the higher-level modules; in the lower-level modules, you'll find it easier to summarize what processing must be done. However, if you ever feel you need to refine the processing steps to better understand the processing requirements, by all means go to whatever level of detail you feel is required for clarity. Remember, clarity is the goal.

If you have been paying careful attention to the problem statement, you may have questioned why Figure 6–22 did not test some of the fields indicated on the input format for this problem. First, note that the module presented in Figure 6–22 was for the type-1, sales transaction record only, not for the type-2 record. Secondly, one field of the type-1 record, the reference number, was not tested. The answer here is that the field is actually a customer-supplied number, and the company using this program has no practical way of checking that type of field, as they may be assumed to have many customers.

```
1.      DO 280-SEARCH-PART-NUMBER-TABLE.
2.      IF INVALID-PART-NUMBER
            move "N" to VALID-TRAN-SW
            move "*" to mark error field in INVALID-TRANS-LINE.
3.      IF ITR-UPDATE-CODE is invalid
            move "N" to VALID-TRAN-SW
            move "*" to mark error field.
4.      IF ITR-ORDER-DATE is invalid
            move "N" to VALID-TRAN-SW
            move "*" to mark error field.
5.      IF ITR-BRANCH-NO is invalid
            move "N" to VALID-TRAN-SW
            move "*" to mark error field.
6.      IF ITR-SALESMAN-NO is invalid
            move "N" to VALID-TRAN-SW
            move "*" to mark error field.
7.      IF ITR-CUST-NO is invalid
            move "N" to VALID-TRAN-SW
            move "*" to mark error field.
8.      IF ITR-QUANTITY is invalid
            move "N" to VALID-TRAN-SW
            move "*" to mark error field.
9.      IF INVALID-TRANSACTION
            add 1 to INVALID-SALES-COUNT
        ELSE
            add 1 to VALID-SALES-COUNT.
```

Figure 6–22
Expanded pseudocode for module 240 of the edit-inventory-transaction program

Keep the modules independent

As you create your module documentation, remember that the modules of a structured program must be independent. In theory, then, you should be able to document one module without referring to the documentation for other modules. In other words, you shouldn't need to know what is happening in any of the other modules.

In practice, however, you will often need to refer to other modules for the proper names of files, records, and fields. Also, you may want to check another module to see whether you remembered to set a switch or move a field or something like that. But that's all. If you find that you continually need to refer to the processing steps in one module in order to document another module, something's wrong. Either your modules aren't independent or your functions aren't clearly defined.

Move subfunctions down the line

Perhaps the most difficult task when documenting modules is deciding in which module a subfunction should be placed. For instance, you know that a report-printing program like the reorder-listing program must count lines and reset the LINE-COUNT field to zero after page overflow. But subfunctions like these don't really require their own separate modules since they are not major functions and usually consist of just a line or two of code. So how do you decide in which existing module to place them?

Whenever you are in doubt as to the proper placement of a subfunction, try moving the subfunction down the line in the VTOC. In Figure 6–17, for example, you could count the number of valid and invalid transactions in either module 220 or in modules 240 and 250. Using the down-the-line guideline, modules 240 and 250 will be responsible for these subfunctions. Similarly, you should move subfunctions like resetting total fields down the line whenever you're in doubt about where they should go.

Remember, however, that decisions like these are debatable. So the main thing is to strive for consistency. If you develop a pattern for your decisions, like always moving subfunctions down the line, you will minimize clerical errors and simplify debugging. And remember, too, that this applies only to *subfunctions*; a major function should always have its own module, regardless of how few lines of coding it will require. Of course, it should be pointed out that you will be following the standards of the computer installation when you work as a professional. Now, you should consider yourself to be working for a company whose standards are those laid out in this book.

Document only the function named

Another point that should be emphasized is this: Only document the function described by the module name. In other words, never place a subfunction in a module where it doesn't belong just because you can't find a good place for it. It is better to add another module to the VTOC for a subfunction like this, even if it is only a few coding lines long, than to place it where you won't be able to find it later on.

With this in mind, you might object to the down-the-line guideline just recommended. For example, since the program in Figure 6–17 is supposed to count the number of input transactions read, the down-the-line rule will place the counting statement in module 210, the read-inventory-tran module. But doesn't this violate the principle of documenting only the function specified in the module name?

The answer here is to think of it as a convention. Whenever input or output records must be counted, it will be done in the associated read or write module. In other words, counting is included in the notion of reading or writing. In the long run, this convention will simplify module design, documentation, and coding.

One approach for which you should be prepared is that of the use of conventions to guide your actions. Many facets of society have conventions for that purpose, and computing is no different. To demonstrate this with a practical situation, the following conventions apply to the print module for simple reports. The print module would typically include code that would do the following:

1. Test for page overflow and call the page-top print routine if overflow has occurred.

2. Format the output line by moving all data to be printed into the output line.

3. Move the output line from Working–Storage to the File Section print area.

4. Call the write module that physically outputs the print area.

The conventions this book promotes for the module that physically outputs the print area (not the page-top routine) are listed below:

1. Give the WRITE command with the AFTER ADVANCING option to space the printer the required number of spaces and physically print the line.

2. Increment the line counter by adding the object field of the ADVANCING option to the field that is being used to accumulate the number of lines printed. Typically this command would be ADD SPACE–CONTROL TO LINES–PRINTED.

3. Set the field containing the lines to advance to the standard number. Typically this would read MOVE 1 TO SPACE–CONTROL.

These conventions will be expanded after the discussion on multilevel report control has been presented. For now, the conventions discussed should help you decide where to place many common subfunctions. In addition, you may want to develop other conventions either on your own or in conjunction with other members in your programming group. In the absence of conventions, however, don't be misleading: only document the function named in the VTOC.

A Pseudocode Example—the Edit Program

In general, all structured programs are made up of two types of modules. The lower-level modules do most of the actual work required by the program such as reading input records, performing calculations, and formatting output records. So these are called *work modules*. In contrast, the upper-level modules that call two or more subordinate modules do little work. Their primary job is to control the execution of their subordinates. As a result, they are called *control modules*. The control modules may actually be divided into three subtypes: *main*, *principal*, and *minor control*. The following discussion is a definition of the control modules and the work module.

Control and work modules

The control module's primary function is to control the execution sequence of subordinate work modules. The typical command contained in a control module will be start-up or shut-down commands such as OPEN or CLOSE; commands to invoke other modules such as the PERFORM, or the PERFORM–UNTIL; and the condition testing command, IF–ELSE. A control module will typically call two or more work modules. Any so-called work done in a control module will be incidental to its "control" function. These will be upper-level modules. As you see from Figure 6–23, three categories of control modules are defined:

1. Major control—the main program control module at the 0-level that controls the execution of the modules on level-1.

2. Principal control—previously defined as the principal level-1 function, this module controls execution of the input-process-output modules which are part of the vertical mainline program function.

3. Minor control—modules that contain minor control logic such as recognizing page overflow and calling for the page-top routine. These modules may occur at any level except the lowest and often contain more work-type commands than control commands.

Work modules give the so-called work commands. These would be: the MOVE, the input/output READ and WRITE, any calculation command such as the ADD, and often the PERFORM.

Study Figure 6–23 carefully. It is a VTOC model showing the relationship between the various types of modules in a typical report program. The model depicts the get-ready, principal, and follow-up module relationship on level-1. It does not assign module names, but rather labels each block in the VTOC as a control module or a work module.

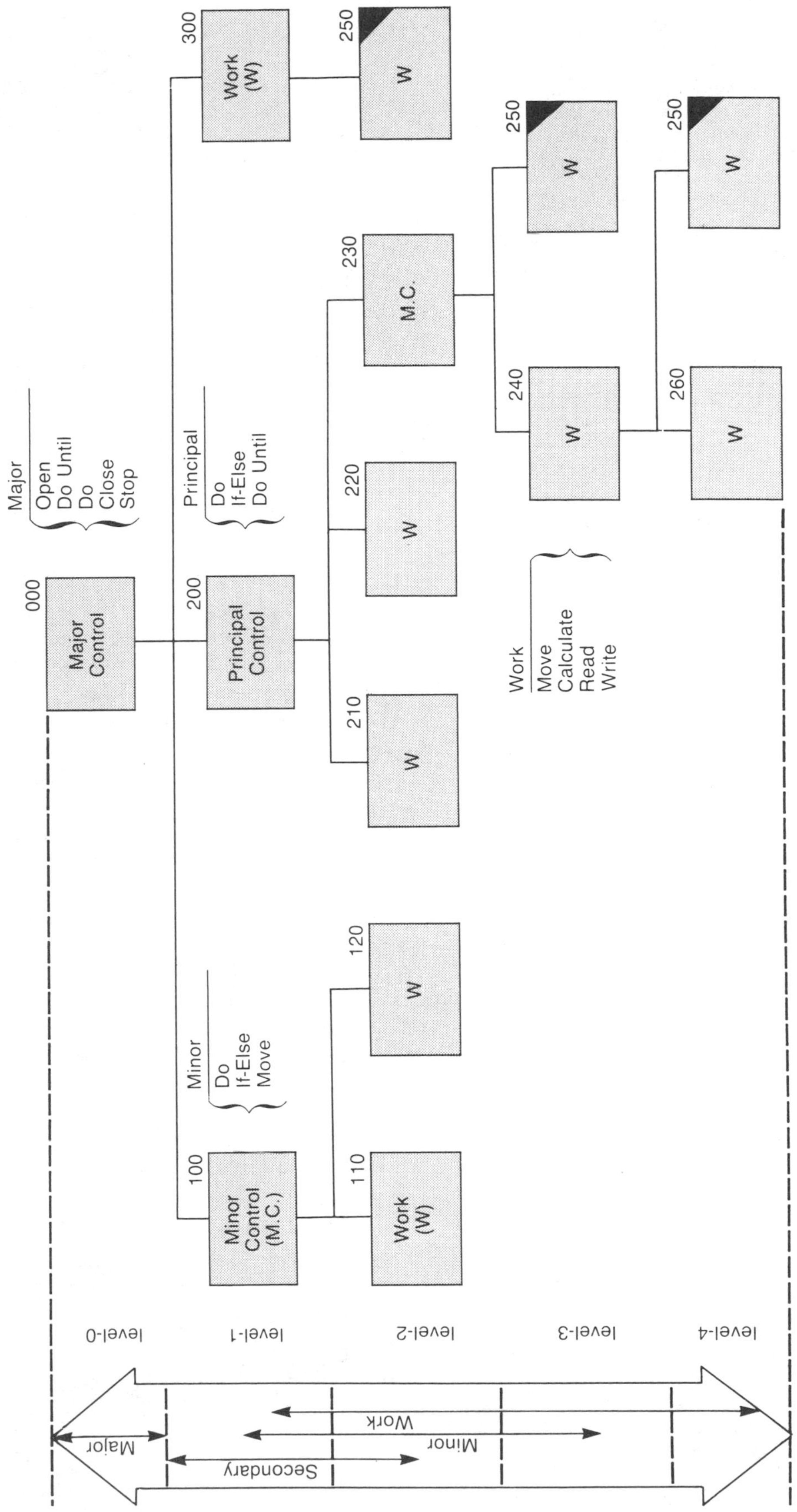
000
Major Control
Major
Open
Do Until
Do
Close
Stop
100
Minor Control (M.C.)
Minor
Do
If-Else
Move
110
Work (W)
120
W
200
Principal Control
Principal
Do
If-Else
Do Until
210
W
220
W
230
M.C.
240
W
250
W
260
W
250
W
300
Work (W)
250
W
Work
Move
Calculate
Read
Write
level-0
level-1
level-2
level-3
level-4
Major
Secondary
Minor
Work

Figure 6–23
Relationship of modules in typical report program with typical commands

```
1.      Read INVENTORY-TRANSACTIONS
            AT END
                move "Y" to TRAN-EOF-SW.
2.      IF MORE-INVENTORY-RECS
            add 1 to TRANS-PROCESSED-COUNT.
```

Figure 6–24
Pseudocode for module 210 of the edit-inventory-transaction program

In the VTOC in Figure 6–17, modules 000, 100, 200, and 220 are the primary control modules. The other modules do most of the work. Module 230, as you will see, is primarily a work module even though it does control the execution of two subordinate I/O modules.

In some books, you will see control modules called *branch modules* because they are always part of a branchlike structure. Similarly, you will see work modules called *leaf modules* since they can be compared to leaves on the branches. Use whichever terminology you prefer, but be aware of the distinction between control and work modules since it is a useful one.

Understanding the edit program

In general, you should be able to understand the operation of a structured program if you have the problem specifications, the VTOC, and the pseudocode for the primary control modules. You shouldn't need to know much about the work modules since each one should represent a single, clearly defined function. To help you understand the operation and documentation of the edit-inventory-transactions program, you will be shown the pseudocode for a few more of the key modules.

As you have seen in the HIPO diagram in Figure 6–18, module 000 of the edit program performs module 100 until all part-number records have been read, performs module 200 until all transaction records have been read, and performs module 300 to print the total page. As you have seen in the pseudocode in Figure 6–20, module 200 performs module 210 to read one transaction, performs module 220 to edit the transaction, and performs module 230 *if the transaction is not valid*. So now let's look at modules 210, 220, and 230.

The pseudocode for module 210 is shown in Figure 6–24. It reads one transaction record and moves the value Y into TRAN–EOF–SW if the end-of file record is read. This switch in turn is tested by module 200 before processing continues and by module 000 after each execution of module 200. If the end-of-file record isn't read, module 210 adds one to TRANS–PROCESSED–COUNT for use by module 300.

The pseudocode for module 220 is shown in Figure 6–25. In step 1, the value Y is moved to VALID–TRAN–SW. This means that module 220, 240, or 250 must change the switch to N if an invalid field is detected. In step 2, the invalid-transaction-line record in working storage is cleared to spaces.

```
1.      Move "Y" to VALID-TRAN-SW.
2.      Move spaces to INVALID-TRANS-LINE.
3.      IF INVENTORY-SALE
            DO 240-EDIT-CODE-1-FIELDS
        ELSE
            IF INVENTORY-RETURN
                DO 250-EDIT-CODE-2-FIELDS
            ELSE
                move "*" to mark error field in INVALID-TRANS-LINE
                move "N" to VALID-TRAN-SW
                add 1 to INVALID-TRAN-CODE-COUNT.
```

Figure 6–25
Pseudocode for module 220 of the edit-inventory-transaction program

```
1.      Move output fields
                  from INVENTORY-TRANS-REC to INVALID-TRANS-LINE.
2.      IF LINE-COUNT is greater than LINES-ON-PAGE
            DO 260-PRINT-REPORT-HEADING.
3.      Move INVALID-TRANS-LINE to PRINT-AREA.
4.      DO 270-WRITE-REPORT-LINE.
```

Figure 6–26
Pseudocode for module 230 of the edit-inventory-transaction program

In step 3, nested IF statements are used to determine whether module 240 or 250 is to be performed or whether the transaction code itself is invalid.

The pseudocode for module 230 is shown in Figure 6–26. This is more of a work module than a control module. In step 1, it prepares the invalid-transaction-line record in working storage. In step 2, it performs module 260 if the output page is full. Then, in steps 3 and 4, the invalid-transaction-line record is moved to the print area and module 270 is performed. This causes the invalid-transaction line to be printed. Although a value could be added to LINE–COUNT in this module to keep track of the number of lines printed, this subfunction was moved down the line to the write-report-line module.

Can you understand the operation of the edit program now that you have seen the documentation for the primary modules? Because the module documentation is spread all over this topic, the processing steps for the major modules have been duplicated in Figure 6–27. This should make the documentation easier to follow.

If you are reviewing the documentation for someone else's program, a pseudocode summary of the control modules like the one in Figure 6–27 is sometimes an aid to understanding. Similarly, if you are having trouble doing a VTOC design because you can't visualize how the control modules will work, a pseudocode summary on scratch paper can be helpful. In any event, studying Figure 6–27 should help you understand the major processing done by the edit program. All modules not shown are simple control modules or straightforward work modules.

Discussion

By now you should recognize the advantage of HIPO diagrams or pseudocode over flowcharts. Without question, these types of structured documentation are easier to create than flowcharts. And they are much better guides to coding a program.

At one time, it seemed that HIPO diagrams might become the standard method of module documentation in industry. However, HIPO documentation has been the target of frequent criticism lately. For one thing, it's cumbersome. If you have a VTOC consisting of 20 modules, you will end up with at least 21 pages of documentation (1 VTOC and 20 IPOs). More important, though, a HIPO diagram is relatively difficult to create and maintain. So more and more companies seems to be using pseudocode alone to document the processing a module does.

A related trend in industry is to drop module documentation altogether once the coding is completed. In this case, a programmer may use something like HIPO diagrams or pseudocode as working tools to code the modules. But after coding, these working tools are thrown away. The VTOC and COBOL source listing then become the primary elements of program documentation—documentation that is always up-to-date. This can increase programming efficiency because the programmer doesn't have to spend time revising module documentation every time a change is made to a program.

```
000-EDIT-INVENTORY-TRANS

    1.   Open files.
    2.   DO 100-LOAD-PART-NUMBER-TABLE
             UNTIL END-PART-NUMBER-FILE.
    3.   DO 200-EDIT-INVENTORY-TRAN
             UNTIL END-INVENTORY-TRANS-FILE.
    4.   DO 300-PRINT-TOTAL-PAGE.
    5.   Close files.
    6.   Stop run.

200-EDIT-INVENTORY-TRAN

    1.   DO 210-READ-INVENTORY-TRAN.
    2.   IF MORE-INVENTORY-RECS
             DO 220-EDIT-TRANSACTION-FIELDS
             IF INVALID-TRANS
                    DO 230-PRINT-INVALID-LINE.

210-READ-INVENTORY-TRAN

    1.   Read INVENTORY-TRANSACTIONS
             AT END
                 move "Y" to TRAN-EOF-SW.
    2.   IF MORE-INVENTORY-RECS
             add 1 to TRANS-PROCESSED-COUNT.

220-EDIT-TRANSACTION-FIELDS

    1.   Move "Y" to VALID-TRAN-SW.
    2.   Move spaces to INVALID-TRANS-LINE.
    3.   IF INVENTORY-SALE
             DO 240-EDIT-CODE-1-FIELDS
         ELSE
             IF INVENTORY-RETURN
                 DO 250-EDIT-CODE-2-FIELDS
             ELSE
                 move "*" to mark error field in INVALID-TRANS-LINE
                 move "N" to VALID-TRAN-SW
                 add 1 to INVALID-TRAN-CODE-COUNT.

230-PRINT-INVALID-LINE

    1.   Move output fields
                    from INVENTORY-TRANS-REC to INVALID-TRANS-LINE.
    2.   IF LINE-COUNT is greater than LINES-ON-PAGE
             DO 260-PRINT-REPORT-HEADING.
    3.   Move INVALID-TRANS-LINE to PRINT-AREA.
    4.   DO 270-WRITE-REPORT-LINE.
```

Figure 6–27
Pseudocode summary of key modules in the edit-inventory-transaction program

In any event, this book will teach you structured design and coding regardless of the method of module documentation that you end up using. In general, the principles you have just learned about using pseudocode will apply to any effective method of module documentation that you may come in contact with. So if you can use pseudocode, you shouldn't have any trouble documenting the processing done by a module.

Problems

Refer to the VTOC in Figure 6–17 and the problem definition in Figure 6–6.

1. Document module 260 using pseudocode.

2. Document module 270 using pseudocode.

3. Document module 290 using pseudocode.

4. Document module 300 using pseudocode.

Solutions

Figure 6–28 gives acceptable pseudocode for modules 260, 270, 290, and 300.

1. This module is just like module 140 in the refined reorder-listing program. It moves the heading lines to PRINT–AREA, moves the proper spacing values to SPACE–CONTROL, and calls subordinate modules to actually write the lines on the report.

2. In this module, the SPACE–CONTROL value is added to LINE–COUNT to keep track of the number of lines that have been printed on a page.

3. Again in this module, COBOL itself is used to describe the processing. Also note that resetting LINE–COUNT to zero has been moved down the line into this module.

```
260-PRINT-REPORT-HEADING

    1. Move HDG-LINE-1 to PRINT-AREA.
    2. DO 290-WRITE-PAGE-TOP-LINE.
    3. Move HDG-LINE-2 to PRINT-AREA.
    4. Move 2 to SPACE-CONTROL.
    5. DO 270-WRITE-REPORT-LINE.
    6. Move HDG-LINE-3 to PRINT-AREA.
    7. DO 270-WRITE-REPORT-LINE.
    8. Move 2 to SPACE-CONTROL.

270-WRITE-REPORT-LINE

    1. WRITE PRINT-AREA
           AFTER ADVANCING SPACE-CONTROL LINES.
    2. ADD SPACE-CONTROL TO LINE-COUNT.
    3. Move 1 to SPACE-CONTROL.

290-WRITE-PAGE-TOP-LINE

    1. WRITE PRINT-AREA
           AFTER ADVANCING PAGE-TOP.
    2. MOVE 1 TO LINE-COUNT.

300-PRINT-TOTAL-PAGE

    1. Add VALID-SALES-COUNT
           VALID-RETURN-COUNT
               giving VALID-COUNT.
    2. Add INVALID-SALES-COUNT
           INVALID-RETURN-COUNT
               giving INVALID-COUNT.
    3. Move TOTAL-LINE-1 to PRINT-AREA.
    4. DO 290-WRITE-PAGE-TOP-LINE.
    5. Prepare total lines 2 through 9 for printing.
    6. When each line is ready for printing
           DO 270-WRITE-REPORT-LINE.
```

Figure 6–28
Pseudocode for modules 260, 270, 290, and 300 of edit-inventory-transactions program

4. Because there are nine different lines to be printed by this module, the processing for the last eight lines has been summarized in steps 5 and 6. Remember, you don't want to code the module twice. If it's straightforward, simplify. Step 5 means that for each output line, the output area must be formatted and a proper character must be moved into the SPACE-CONTROL field. Step 6 means that module 270 should be executed after the preparation of each output line.

Topic 4 COBOL Structured Style Guidelines

Orientation

The previous topics presented the structured programming concepts that concentrated principally on program development and organization. This topic lists guidelines which are designed to promote coding in a visual "style" that is balanced and easy to read. There are more guidelines needed to complete the list for this book. Since they are only understandable after the more advanced topics have been discussed, they will be presented later. The list presented at this time is still an extensive one, and this is an appropriate place in the study of COBOL to begin concentrating on creating programs that conform to a structured style as well as structured organization.

This means that certain parts of the code are vertically aligned so that the eye does not need to search around to determine where a particular piece of the code is located. It means that major segments of the code are visually separated by blank lines. It means that other parts are logically grouped and ordered in a consistent fashion so that all programs of a computer department have similar organization, thus making location of similar code elements easier no matter which program is being studied. It means paying careful attention to the details, not only of the logic, but also to the appearance, which ultimately ensures efficiency in development and maintenance.

Most professional computer programming organizations will have some form of guidelines for program code style. Professional style guidelines may be more or less restrictive than those presented here, but they are all designed for local code standardization, which improves communication among the organization's staff and increases efficiency.

Some will claim that such standards stifle creativity, but the opposite is really true. A standard approach and its attendant efficiency gains enable the programmer to avoid becoming tied up in relatively minor coding bugs and frees him or her to concentrate on more challenging logical problems.

The following guidelines should be adapted in each program that you write and should be used as a checklist for good structured style before turning in any program assignment. Study the guidelines carefully, use them consistently, and think about adding your own special ideas to the list. Remember, the idea is to create a well-organized, readable program in which the intent of the code is clear to the programmer who is studying it.

General Conventions

Make user-defined words meaningful so that they describe their function. Field names should answer the question "of what?"; that is, use name REC–COUNT instead of just COUNT, and HOURS–WORKED instead of HOURS.

Hyphens should be used in user-defined words to make the separate multiple English words and abbreviations more readable.

Commas or semicolons should not be used as punctuation as they add nothing to the meaning of the statement and are often a source of confusion and keystroke error.

Provide visual separation between divisions, sections, all paragraphs, and WORKING–STORAGE 01-level groups by inserting blank lines.

Only one COBOL sentence, statement, clause, or phrase should be written on each coding line. Multiple clauses in a sentence should be placed on separate lines and indented after the first clause.

When indenting, do so in four-space units. Exceptions may be made when vertical alignment of certain entries is desirable. When the four-space indentation pattern consumes too much space on the coding line, other patterns may be used. If four-space indentation is not practical, indent three or two spaces. Never indent only one space. Note: exceptions to the four-space rule should be made infrequently and very judiciously.

Indentification Division Conventions

The program-name should be limited to the maximum number of characters allowed by the operating system being used. (Many computers have a maximum of 8 characters on external names.) Local programming style conventions will, of course, override these guidelines.

Environment Division Conventions

Write the SELECT statements in I/O sequence so that the input files are listed first, followed by the output files.

The SELECT statements should follow the one clause per line rule. That is, the ASSIGN clause should begin on a separate line and should be indented four spaces.

Choose file names which describe the file content and its function in the program, such as ACCOUNTS–RECEIVABLE–FILE (for the input detail file), and ACCOUNTS–RECEIVABLE–LIST (for the printed output).

Never choose file names (such as CARD–FILE, TAPE–FILE, or DISK–FILE) that refer to specific input-output devices since system changes may change the physical device, thus rendering the program documentation inaccurate. Also do not choose names that refer to input or output (such as INPUT–FILE, OUTPUT–FILE, or PRINT–FILE).

Data Division Conventions

Each clause of the FD entry should be placed on a separate line.

The optional RECORD CONTAINS clause of the FD should always be used as it provides automatic record length checking.

The optional DATA RECORDS clause of the FD should be omitted as it adds little to the program documentation.

Each data-item subdivision should be indented four spaces (level number 05 at position 12, level number 10 at position 16, etc.). When the four-space indentation rule consumes too much space on the coding line, two-space indentations can be used.

The gap level-number assignment should be in increments of five after level 01 (01, 05, 10, 15, etc.). This allows easy insertion of new levels if necessary.

All data names of a record should be prefixed with a two-, three-, or four-character abbreviation for that record (with two preferred). Be careful to ensure that the prefix for each record of the program is unique so that the remainder of the data names do not have to be. For example, this pattern allows input and output names to be SR–ITEM–NUMBER and SL–ITEM–NUMBER, respectively.

Always use the abbreviation PIC rather than the word PICTURE so as to conserve space on the coding line and to minimize keystrokes.

When describing records and fields in WORKING STORAGE or in the FILE SECTION:

1. vertically align *all* PICTURE (PIC) by beginning the word PIC in the same column (depending on the length of data-names, good positions are 32, 36, 40, 44, or 48)

2. vertically align all other clauses such as VALUE and COMP–3. (the goal is consistency throughout the data division)

Nonarithmetic integer fields (numeric fields not involved in calculations or subject to numeric editing) should be described as alphanumeric rather than numeric. Because of the need for arithmetic sign handling, numeric PICTURE clauses are usually less efficient, and, on some computer systems, invalid numeric fields may cause data exceptions and undesired abnormal program termination.

The field length in the picture character string should be expressed by a number enclosed in parentheses rather than by the repetition method. To promote precise clause alignment, it is desirable to use a two-digit repetition number (03) versus the single digit form (3). (Note, however, that keystrokes are saved by using X or XX versus X(01) or X(02), with the break-even point being 4 digits.)

The optional word IS should not be used in the VALUE clause. Nor should the optional words USAGE or IS be used when specifying the usage for a data item. Such words do not materially enhance program documentation and consume space on the coding line.

Since DISPLAY usage is the default value for the Usage clause, the DISPLAY statement should be omitted. DISPLAY usage will be provided automatically.

Since the abbreviations COMP and COMP–3 conserve space on the coding line and are equally understandable, they should be used in preference to COMPUTATIONAL and COMPUTATIONAL–3.

Organize WORKING–STORAGE data items into groups of logically related fields, using level numbers 01 through 49. A preferred order for groups of fields is switches, flags, work-fields (to hold intermediate results), control fields (for control breaks), print control fields, counters (other than for print control), total fields, subscripts, index, tables, and finally input/output records (in the order of processing and reporting). (Note: prestructured COBOL allowed a 77-level elementary item called an independent data item. Its use is discouraged since it promotes chaos in Working–Storage.)

Output records should be defined in WORKING–STORAGE. Doing this has several advantages, some of which are:

1. VALUE clauses may be used for the initialization of constant fields within the record.
2. Double-buffering problems are eliminated.
3. Fields of a record that have already been written to an output device may still be referenced.
4. When referring to a storage dump, it is easier to determine which output record was being processed at the time of termination.

The advantages of defining input record in WORKING–STORAGE are not as great as those for output record definition, but it is good practice and has the following advantages:

1. Fields of a record may still be referenced after the next record has been read if the READ INTO is not used.
2. When referring to a storage dump, it is easier to determine which input record was being processed at the time of termination.
3. The READ INTO statement is easy to use when there is only one input record type per file.
4. It allows description of the input record to be in closer physical proximity to the output records.

Longer records in WORKING–STORAGE which contain primarily non-numeric, external, constant values (e.g., headings) should be defined in *logical* groups of 20 characters or less. Do not break a literal in the middle of the word.

Constant fields should be initialized with VALUE clauses in the Data Division. Initializing variable fields with Procedure Division statements does aid program documentation and helps to make modules reentrant. It is often desirable to initialize certain fields in the Data Division and to reinitialize them in the Procedure Division at the appropriate time (e.g., Subtotals).

Procedure Division Conventions

Open and close all files with single OPEN and CLOSE statements followed by a file list with each file name on a separate line and vertically aligned.

The PERFORM–UNTIL statement should be written with the UNTIL condition on a separate line and indented four spaces under the PERFORM.

The READ statement should be written with the AT END phrase on a separate line and indented four spaces. The imperative command(s) which are controlled by the AT END clause should be written on separate lines and indented four spaces under the AT END clause.

The WRITE statement should be written with the AFTER ADVANCING phrase on a separate line and indented four spaces.

Align *all* of the reserved words TO used in MOVE statements in the same position on the coding line throughout the program.

Any MOVE statement which will not fit on one coding line should be written with the reserved word TO and the receiving field(s) on a separate line and indented four spaces.

Any MOVE statement which has multiple receiving fields should be written with each receiving field after the first one on a separate line and aligned vertically under the first receiving field name.

Only a single entry point and a single exit point should be provided for each program module (Note: use of the PERFORM statement ensures this structured programming rule.)

Each program module should be numbered in accordance with a module numbering system, and the program modules should be arranged in order according to that number. The numbering system should be easy to implement and easy to change when program maintenance is required.

Each program module should be named in the form nnn-verb-adjective-noun, where nnn is the number in the above mentioned numbering system (e.g., 110–READ–INVENTORY–FILE or 220–CALCULATE–SALES–TOTAL).

Only one READ and/or one WRITE module should be established for each file. When printing reports, the establishment of two WRITE modules is generally acceptable, if one WRITE module is used to skip to the top of a new page and one WRITE module is used for all other output.

Parentheses within COMPUTE statement arithmetic expressions should be used to control the sequence of arithmetic operations rather than relying on the normal sequence of operations. Parentheses make the expression easier to read and understand and help ensure that the correct computation is made.

Each COMPUTE statement arithmetic expression should be limited to three or a maximum of four factors to prevent overly complicated logic. If more than four factors are required in the calculation, break it up into several COMPUTE statements and calculate the final result with the intermediate results.

Do not use the GO TO statement. (Note: there are situations which require the use of the GO TO. They have not been discussed yet.)

Appropriate indentation should be provided to enhance the clarity of the IF statement. Appropriate indention is, for example:

1. for AND related IFs:

```
IF  condition-1
    statement-a
    IF  condition-2
        statement-b
        IF  condition-3...
```

2. for OR related IFs:

```
IF  condition-1
    statement-a
ELSE
    IF  condition-2
        statement-b
    ELSE
        IF  condition-3
```

Note the placement of the ELSE on a line by itself, and directly beneath its corresponding IF. Subordinate IFs are indented four spaces underneath their controlling ELSEs.

Nested IF statements should be limited to three or four levels to prevent them from becoming overly complex. If necessary to have more levels, break them up by PERFORMing module(s) which do additional testing.

If the COBOL standard PAGE option is available, it should be used in preference to the mnemonic-name option to advance printer forms to the next page.

The WRITE/FROM statement should be avoided because its use limits WRITE module use, particularly on printed reports.

Any arithmetic statement which will not fit on a single coding line should be separated at a logical point and continued with indentation on the following coding line. Logical separation points are at phrases such as the TO or GIVING parts of the commands. Begin the next line with the TO or the GIVING.

Use of the ON SIZE ERROR phrase can be minimized and even eliminated in many programs. Define fields large enough to ensure that SIZE errors do not occur. Data should normally be prevalidated via a prior process or program to prevent SIZE errors.

Chapter 7 Multilevel Control Breaks and Top-Down Development and Testing

Previous chapters have developed the essentials of COBOL and structured programming, including an introduction to control breaks. This chapter takes the control break concept two steps further and discusses two- and three-level control break reporting. The third topic presents additional approaches to development and testing that are appropriate to more complex programs. The final topic adds helpful concepts to structured style by presenting some ideas for building data and module names.

Topic 1 Two–Level Control Breaks

Orientation

Chapter 6 introduced you to the basics of how to design and document structured programs. The last topic in chapter 5 introduced you to reporting with control breaks. Many new ideas have been presented in a rather short time; this topic aids your review of many of the concepts of control break processing. It presents another control break example, which is intended to help synthesize these concepts and to help solidify your understanding of control break logic and program organization.

The example presented here has the advantage of extending your knowledge of control breaks by moving on to the discussion of two-level breaks. Actually, understanding the concept behind the single-level break facilitates understanding two-, three-, or any-level control break logic.

Carefully study the example presented here. It is based on the same input record as the example in chapter 5. The example here shows a typical professional situation where the same input record is used to produce more than one output report for different purposes and/or users. Compare it with the single-level control break program so that you can discover the similarities and the differences. You will be surprised to find many similarities and few differences.

Terminology

control field
multilevel report
summary report
two-level report

Objectives

1. ***Given the specifications for a programming problem, create an acceptable VTOC for it.***
2. ***Given the problem definition for a program and the VTOC for its program design, write pseudocode to document the processing done by any of the modules.***

The Program Specifications

Figure 7–1 gives the specifications for a report-printing program. It is like the reorder-listing program in that it prepares a printed report from a sequential input file. However, it is more complicated than the reorder-listing program because it summarizes the information in one or more sales transaction records and prints a single total line for each customer and for each salesman.

System flowchart:

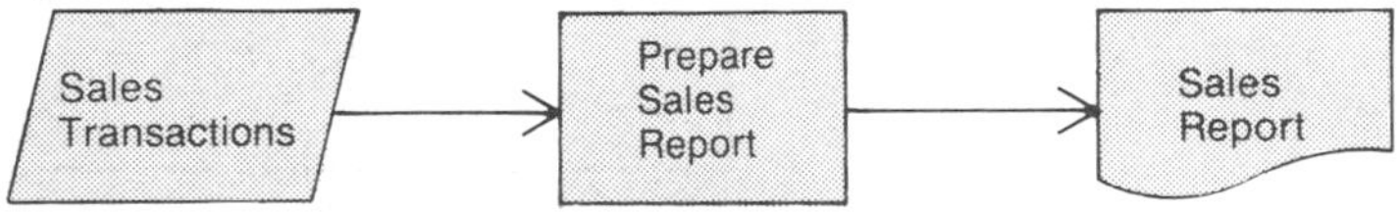
Sales
Transactions
Prepare
Sales
Report
Sales
Report

Print chart:

Field Name	Order Number	Order Date	Salesperson Number	Customer Number	Quantity	Item Number	Unit Cost	Unit Price
Characteristics	X(5)	9(6)	X(2)	X(5)	9(3)	X(5)	999V99	999V99
Usage								
Position	1-5	6-11	12-13	14-18	19-21	22-26	27-31	37-56

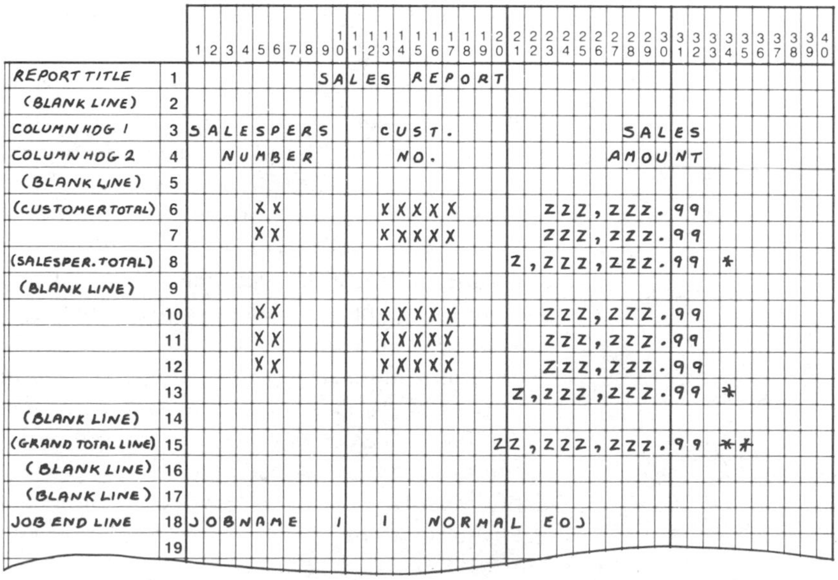
REPORT TITLE
(BLANK LINE)
COLUMN HDG 1
COLUMN HDG 2
(BLANK LINE)
(CUSTOMER TOTAL)
(SALESPER. TOTAL)
(BLANK LINE)
(BLANK LINE)
(GRAND TOTAL LINE)
(BLANK LINE)
(BLANK LINE)
JOB END LINE
SALES REPORT
SALESPERS
CUST.
SALES
NUMBER
NO.
AMOUNT
XX
XXXXX
ZZZ,ZZZ.99
Z,ZZZ,ZZZ.99 *
ZZ,ZZZ,ZZZ.99 **
JOBNAME
NORMAL EOJ

Figure 7–1
Specifications for a two-level report summary program (part 1 of 2)

Sample output:

```
                SALES REPORT

     SALESPERSON  CUST.        SALES
         NO.       NO.         AMOUNT

         31        1052      1,376.75
         31       13498      1,024.00
         31       19763      4,875.00
         31       24291        188.75
                             7,464.50 *

         37        1940      1,125.00
         37       22341        913.00
                             2,038.00 *

         44       26888        295.25
         44       27430        175.43
         44       31284      2,257.39
         44       32290        874.50
         44       32292      1,573.20
         44       33480        985.20
         44       49200      1,354.95
         44       58111        540.75
                             8,056.67 *

            GRAND TOTAL     $17,559.17 * *
```

Narrative:

1. The input records have been sorted in customer-number within salesperson number sequence. There will be one or more records for each customer line printed on the report.
2. The sales amount printed for each customer is the sum of the extensions for each customer; the extension is quantity multiplied by unit price.
3. Totals will be printed for each salesperson. At the end of the report, the grand total of all sales will be printed.

Figure 7–1
Specifications for a two-level report summary program (part 2 of 2)

When a report contains summary lines for various groups of input records, it is called a *summary report*. A sales-by-salesperson report, for example, is a summary report with one summary line for each salesperson. When a summary report contains summary lines for more than one type of group, it is called a multilevel summary report, or just a *multilevel report*. The report in Figure 7–1 is a multilevel report because it gives sales totals at two levels—sales by customer and sales by salesperson. As a result, it can be called a *two-level report*. In a typical business system, multilevel reports of up to three levels—for instance, customer within salesperson within branch—are quite common.

When a summary report is prepared, the input file must be in sequence based on the data in a *control field*. For instance, item number is the control field if a sales-by-item report is to be prepared, so the transaction file must be in item-number sequence before the report-printing program is run. Similarly, a file must be in sequence by a control field within a control field for a two-level summary report. For the program in Figure 7–1, then, the input file must be in sequence by customer number within salesperson number.

To prepare a summary report, the control field from one record must be compared to the control field from the previous record. If the new control field is greater than the old control field, it indicates that a summary line should be printed. For example, in a program that prints a sales-by-item report, a greater-than comparison would indicate the start of the records for a new item. So a summary line for the previous item would be printed. If the control fields are equal, it means that the data from the new record should be applied to the group being processed, so no line should be printed. And if the new control field is less than the old control field, it indicates that the input file is not in sequence (an error condition). Needless to say, when a multilevel report like the one in Figure 7–1 is to be prepared, the problem is complicated because comparisons must be done based on more than one control field.

Beyond the control-field logic, however, the program in Figure 7–1 requires only two fairly simple calculations to produce the summary lines. By multiplying quantity times unit price for each input record and accumulating the total sales amount for each customer, the customer lines can be printed. By accumulating the customer totals for each salesperson, the salesperson total lines can be printed. Keep in mind that only one summary line is printed for each customer or salesperson, regardless of the number of input records for that customer or salesperson.

Look again at Figure 5–7 to see that the input record is the same for these two different outputs. This is a very typical situation since different people in an organization have different information needs. An account clerk will want to see all of the detail transactions that have occurred so that totals, balances, and other amounts can be verified. In other words, someone must have the data at hand to answer a customers' questions about their account balances. On the other hand, the vice president of sales is not concerned about this level of detail, and, in fact, those details are distracting to that person's function. So the example in this topic might be the type of report that the vice president would wish to see, whereas the version presented in chapter 5 was a detailed report and would be more appropriate to an account clerk's function.

The VTOC

Figure 7–2a shows a VTOC for the sales-report program. At level 1, it requires only two modules: the main module that produces the sales lines and a module that prints the grand total line after all records have been processed. Module 100 is subdivided into four modules: one for reading the sales records, one for accumulating the sales amounts for customers, one for printing customer total lines, and one for printing salesperson total lines.

Following are some specific highlights:

1. Module 100 has the largest span of control in this VTOC, so it will probably be the most complex in terms of nested IF statements. It will process one sales record at a time and print customer and salesperson totals whenever necessary.

2. Modules 110 and 120 will be performed once for each input record. Modules 130 and 140 will only be performed when there's a control-field change, signifying that a summary line should be printed.

3. Modules 130 and 140, the two main print modules, will probably contain code to accomplish a number of tasks, including (1) formatting the appropriate output line in working storage, (2) moving the proper forms-control character into a space-control field, (3) adding the total for the line that's printed to totals at a higher level, and (4) resetting the

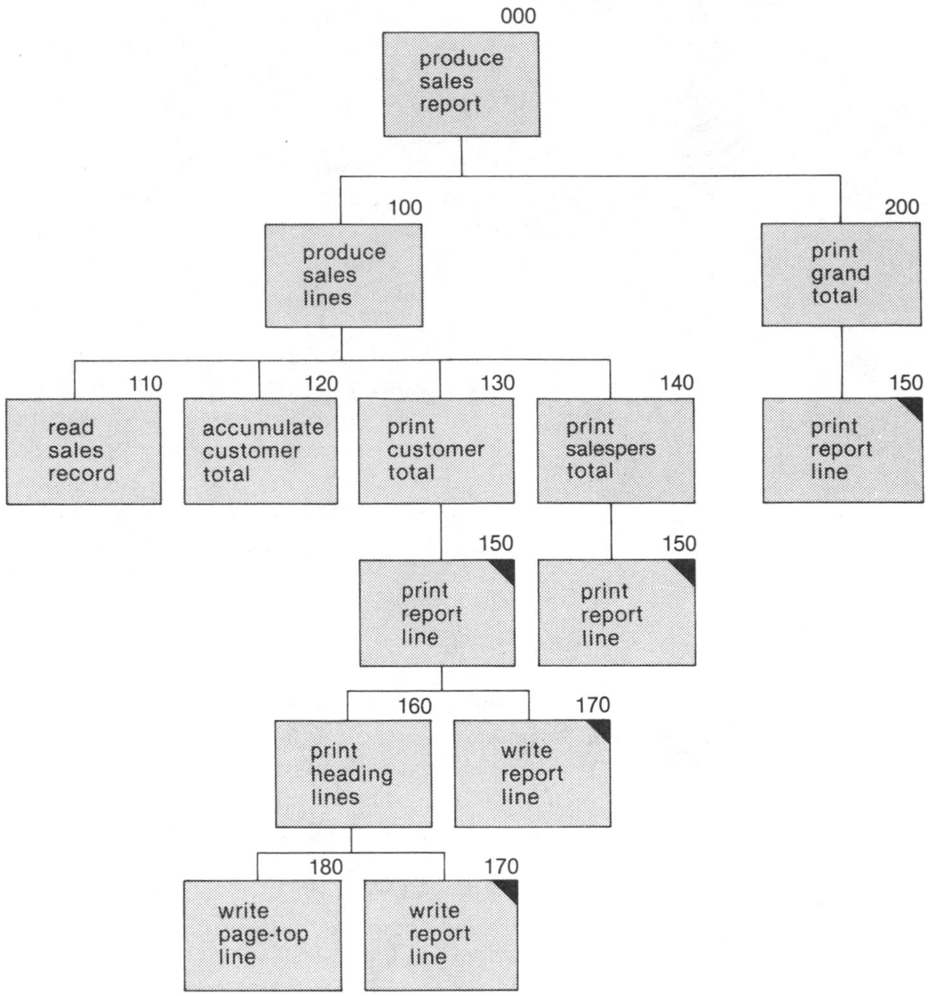
000
produce sales report
100
produce sales lines
200
print grand total
110
read sales record
120
accumulate customer total
130
print customer total
140
print salespers total
150
print report line
150
print report line
150
print report line
160
print heading lines
170
write report line
180
write page-top line
170
write report line

Figure 7–2a
Complete VTOC for the two-level report summary program

total for the line that's printed to zero so the records for the next customer or salesperson can be processed.

4. Modules 150 through 180, which are subordinate to each module that prints a line, represent a general print routine that you may find useful in many programs. Module 150 tests to see whether the output page is full. If it is, module 150 calls module 160, which skips to the top of the next page and prints headings. then module 150 calls module 170, which prints the data for the next report line. The description for module 150, "print report line," is intended to imply that every line on the report will be physically printed by the execution of this module. This module is particularly useful in programs that print many different types of lines.

5. Rather than show modules 160, 170, and 180 every time module 150 is used, module 150's subordinates will be omitted after they've been shown once. This makes the VTOC easier to read and change. Understand, however, that module 150 will always have modules 160 and 170 subordinate to it even when they've not shown. And module 160 will always call modules 180 and 170.

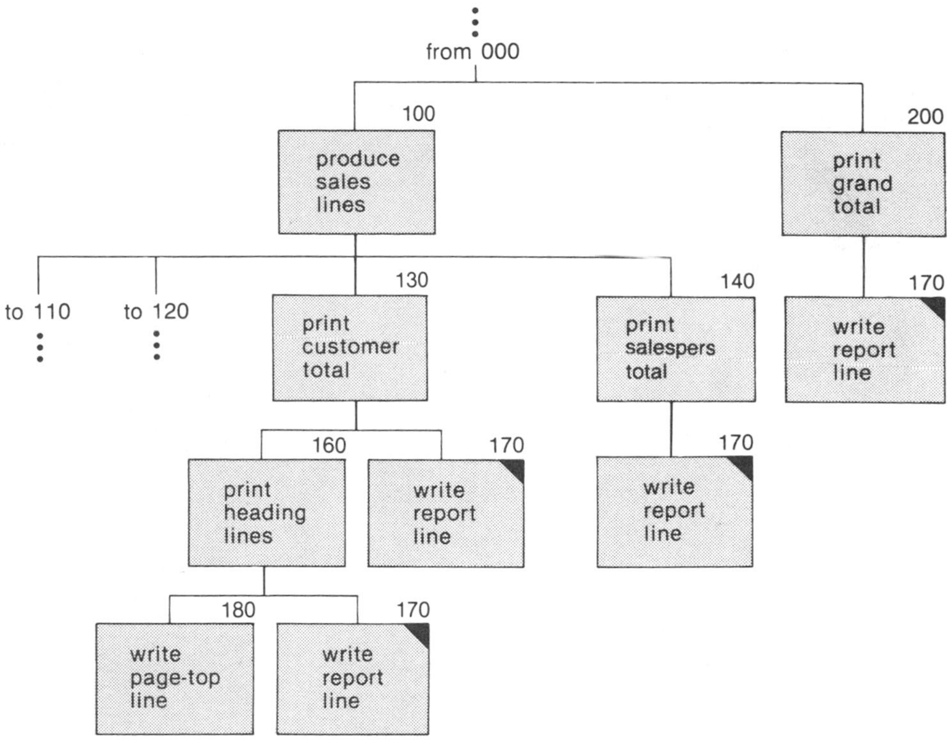
from 000
100
produce sales lines
200
print grand total
to 110
to 120
130
print customer total
140
print salespers total
170
write report line
160
print heading lines
170
write report line
170
write report line
180
write page-top line
170
write report line

Figure 7–2b
Alternative to Figure 7–2a (totals print on same page)

Another solution

A workable VTOC for a program usually won't spring fullblown into your mind; it will be the result of thought, time, and experience. For a beginning programmer, it is frequently easier to refer to a VTOC from a previous, similar program and use it as a "model" to construct the new VTOC. In fact, as you shall shortly see, you can use the examples given in this book as your model VTOCs. Furthermore, you'll usually be able to come up with more than one workable VTOC for any program you design. For example, Figure 7–3 shows the basic structure of another solution to the problem in Figure 7–1. Here, module 130 controls the printing of the detail lines. Again, a general print routine (modules 150 through 180 in Figure 7–2) would be used subordinate to modules 140, 150, and 200.

For a simple two-level report, the extra control level in Figure 7–3 isn't really necessary. After all, the control span of module 100 in Figure 7–2a is only four. However, as you go on to more complicated problems that print totals at three or more levels, you might find the VTOC in Figure 7–3 much easier to work with. To adapt it to more complex problems, you would simply put one module subordinate to module 130 for each different type of body line (not heading or total lines) that is to be printed.

The Module Documentation

To understand the logic needed to code a multilevel-report program, you must study the module documentation. So look now at the pseudocode for the control modules in the sales-report program.

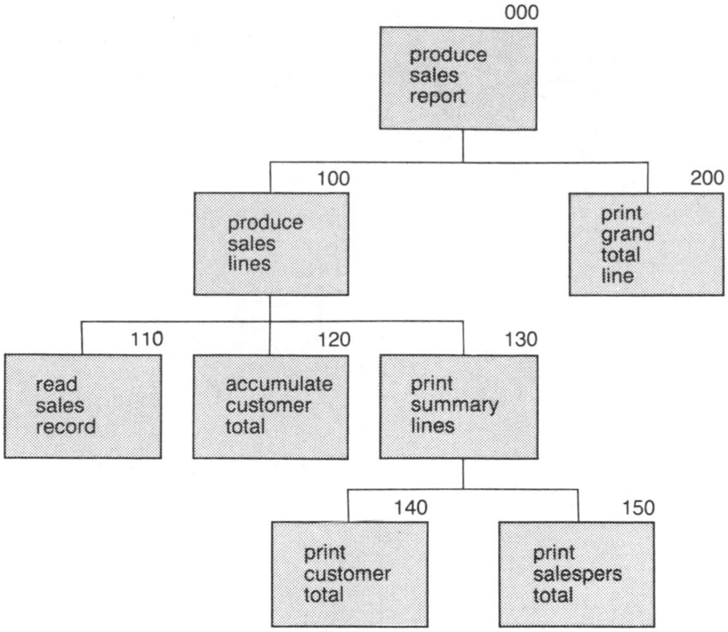
000
produce sales report
100
produce sales lines
200
print grand total line
110
read sales record
120
accumulate customer total
130
print summary lines
140
print customer total
150
print salespers total

Figure 7–3
An acceptable structure for the report summary program

100–PRODUCE–SALES–LINES

The major control module, as you can see from the VTOC in Figure 7–2a, is module 100. Figure 7–4 shows its pseudocode. In step 1, it performs module 110. This module reads one record and, if the end-of-file condition is detected (AT END), moves the value Y into TRAN–EOF–SW and moves the highest value in the computer's collating sequence (HIGH–VALUE) into the salesperson-number field in the transaction record (TR–SALESPERS–NO). Thus, if TR–SALESPERS–NO is compared to any other value after the AT END condition has been detected, the computer will find TR–SALESPERS–NO to be greater than the other value.

Step 2 in module 100 consists of three levels of nested IF statements. The first level tests the value of the FIRST–RECORD–SW. To understand the reason for this, back up a moment.

Remember, the logic in a summary report program is based on comparing the control field of the record just read with the control field of the previous record. But what happens when the record just read is the first record in the file and there is no value for a previous record? To provide for this condition, you need a first-record switch. As you can see from the pseudocode, when the switch is on, the control-field values in the transaction (TR–SALESPERS–NO and TR–CUSTOMER–NO) are moved to two working-storage fields (OLD–SALESPERS–NO and OLD–CUSTOMER–NO). These working-storage fields, or holding fields, always contain the values of the control fields of the previous record. Thus, these are the fields that are compared to the control fields in the transaction just read to determine what further processing should be done.

If the first-record switch is on, it is turned off after the holding fields are set up and step 2 is finished. Otherwise, the program executes the ELSE portion of the first IF statement in step 2. In this case, if TR–SALESPERS–NO is greater than OLD–SALESPERS–NO, the transaction marks both a new salesperson and a new customer. So customer and salesperson total lines are printed for the previous customer and salesperson by modules 130 and 140, and the holding fields in working-storage are adjusted. If TR–CUSTOMER–NO is greater than

```
1. DO 110-READ-SALES-RECORD.

2. IF FIRST-RECORD
     move TR-SALESPERS-NO to OLD SALESPERS-NO
     move TR-CUSTOMER-NO to OLD-CUSTOMER-NO
     move "N" to FIRST-RECORD-SW
   ELSE
     IF TR-SALESPERS-NO is greater than OLD-SALESPERS-NO
       DO 130-PRINT-CUSTOMER-TOTAL
       DO 140-PRINT-SALESPERS-TOTAL
       move TR-CUSTOMER-NO to OLD-CUSTOMER-NO
       move TR-SALESPERS-NO to OLD-SALESPERS-NO
     ELSE
       IF TR-CUSTOMER-NO is greater than OLD-CUSTOMER-NO
         DO 130-PRINT-CUSTOMER-TOTAL
         move TR-CUSTOMER-NO to OLD-CUSTOMER-NO.

3. IF not TRAN-EOF
     DO 120-ACCUMULATE-CUSTOMER-TOTAL.
```

Figure 7–4
Pseudocode for module 100 of the produce-sales-report program

OLD–CUSTOMER–NO, the total line for the previous customer is printed by module 130, and only the customer holding field is adjusted. This ends step 2.

You may have noticed that step 2 doesn't indicate what should be done if the transaction control fields are equal to the holding fields. This is taken care of in step 3 when module 120 is executed. In addition, step 2 doesn't indicate what should be done if the transaction control fields are less than the holding fields, thus indicating that the input records are out of sequence. Although you may have to provide for out-of-sequence records in some of the programs you write, it is assumed that out-of-sequence records are impossible in this program. (In actual practice, the input file for a program like this would probably be a tape or disk file that has been sorted, so you wouldn't have to provide for out-of-sequence records.)

In step 3, the sales total for the record just read is added to the customer total by module 120 if the end-of-file switch is off. This means module 120 is executed for all transaction records including the first record. The IF condition is necessary so module 120 won't be performed after the end-of-file condition has been reached. If it were performed after the end of the file, the program would probably operate a second time on the data in working storage. Thus, the report wouldn't match the expected output.

If you desk check the logic in module 100, you will see that step 2 depends on having HIGH–VALUE in the TR–SALESPERS–NO field after the end of the file has been reached. Otherwise, this module won't print the last customer and salesperson lines.

```
1. Move OLD-SALESPERS-NO
        OLD-CUSTOMER-NO
        CUSTOMER-TOTAL
            to CUSTOMER-TOTAL-LINE.

2. Move CUSTOMER-TOTAL-LINE to NEXT-REPORT-LINE.

3. DO 150-PRINT-REPORT-LINE.

4. Move 1 to SPACE-CONTROL.

5. Add CUSTOMER-TOTAL to SALESPERS-TOTAL.

6. Move zero to CUSTOMER-TOTAL.
```

Figure 7–5a
Pseudocode for module 130 of the produce-sales-report program

```
130-PRINT-CUSTOMER-TOTAL.
    1.  IF LINE-COUNT is greater than LINES-ON-PAGE
            Do 160-PRINT-HEADING-LINES.
    2.  Move OLD-SALESPERS-NO
             OLD-CUSTOMER-NO
             CUSTOMER-TOTAL         to CUSTOMER-TOTAL-LINE.
    3.  Move CUSTOMER-TOTAL-LINE    to PRINT-AREA.
    4.  Move 1                      to SPACE-CONTROL.
    5.  Do 170-WRITE-REPORT-LINE.
    6.  Add CUSTOMER-TOTAL          to SALESPERS-TOTAL.
    7.  Move zero                   to CUSTOMER-TOTAL.

140-PRINT-SALESPERS-TOTAL.
    1.  Move OLD-SALESPERS-NO
             SALESPERS-TOTAL        to CUSTOMER-TOTAL-LINE.
    3.  Move SALESPERS-TOTAL-LINE   to PRINT-AREA.
    4.  Move 2                      to SPACE-CONTROL.
    5.  Do 170-WRITE-REPORT-LINE.
    6.  Add SALESPERS-TOTAL         to REPORT-TOTAL.
    7.  Move zero                   to SALESPERS-TOTAL.
```

Figure 7–5b
Alternative to module 130
(to print totals on the same page)

130–PRINT–CUSTOMER–TOTAL

Once you understand module 100, you should understand the operation of the entire program since the other modules are primarily work modules. For instance, module 130, shown in Figure 7–5a, simply formats the output line (step 1), prints it (steps 2 and 3), and sets the proper space-control value for the next line to be printed (step 4). In addition, this module adds the customer total to the salesman total (step 5) and returns the customer total to zero in preparation for the next customer line (step 6). In other words, this print module is allowed to do everything remotely associated with printing the line; this is the convention suggested previously. If you don't use this convention, you will have difficulty placing the code for steps 5 and 6.

150–PRINT–REPORT–LINE

Module 150 is the control module for the general printing routine, and its pseudocode is shown in Figure 7–6. Quite simply, step 1 prints heading lines (module 160) if the page is full. Then, step 2 moves the next line to be printed into the output area, and step 3 prints it (module 170).

By looking at this module, you can see why module 130 must move each customer line to a holding area in working storage (NEXT–REPORT–LINE) after the line is formatted. If the module moved the line directly to the output area (PRINT–AREA), the line would be destroyed if module 150 caused heading lines to be printed. As you might guess, module 140 must handle the salesperson line the same way.

Pseudocode summary

To help you understand the overall operation of this program, the pseudocode for modules 000, 100, and 110 has been isolated in Figure 7–7a. These three modules contain all of the control code, and they take care of all necessary changes in control fields and switches. As mentioned before, a pseudocode

```
1. IF LINE-COUNT is greater than LINES-ON-PAGE
      DO 160-PRINT-HEADING-LINES.

2. Move NEXT-REPORT-LINE to PRINT-AREA.

3. DO 170-WRITE-REPORT-LINE.
```

Figure 7–6
Pseudocode for module 150 of
the produce-sales-report program

```
000-PRODUCE-SALES-REPORT

    1. Open files.
    2. DO 100-PRODUCE-SALES-LINE
           UNTIL TRAN-EOF.
    3. DO 200-PRINT-GRAND-TOTAL-LINE.
    4. Close files.
    5. Stop run.

100-PRODUCE-SALES-LINE

    1. DO 110-READ-SALES-RECORD.
    2. IF FIRST-RECORD
         move TR-SALESPERS-NO to OLD-SALESPERS-NO
         move TR-CUSTOMER-NO to OLD-CUSTOMER-NO
         move "N" to FIRST-RECORD-SW
       ELSE
         IF TR-SALESPERS-NO is greater than OLD-SALESPERS-NO
           DO 130-PRINT-CUSTOMER-TOTAL
           DO 140-PRINT-SALESPERS-TOTAL
           move TR-CUSTOMER-NO to OLD-CUSTOMER-NO
           move TR-SALESPERS-NO to OLD-SALESPERS-NO
         ELSE
           IF TR-CUSTOMER-NO is greater than OLD-CUSTOMER-NO
             DO 130-PRINT-CUSTOMER-TOTAL
             move TR-CUSTOMER-NO to OLD-CUSTOMER-NO.
    3. IF not TRAN-EOF
         DO 120-ACCUMULATE-CUSTOMER-TOTAL.

110-READ-SALES-RECORD

    1. Read TRANSACTION-FILE
           AT END
               move "Y" to TRAN-EOF-SW
               move HIGH-VALUE to TR-SALESPERS-NO.
```

Figure 7–7a
Pseudocode summary of key modules in the produce-sales-report program

summary of key modules can help you understand someone else's program and can help you check out the flow of control between modules in your own programs.

An issue of concern regarding printed output is whether the designer wants to have subtotals print on the same page as the detail lines when page overflow occurs. If you study Figure 7–2a, 7–4, 7–5a, and 7–6 you will see that if a salesperson total control break happens at the same time that the line-count exceeds the lines-on-page, the salesperson total will be printed on the next page. When that occurs, it means that the totals are separated from the details or other subtotals associated with the totals being printed. Quite often report designers specify that the group totals should always appear on the same page as the details. To demonstrate how to avoid printing subtotals on the next page a few changes will be made to the figures just discussed.

Observe Figure 7–2b, which is a modification of Figure 7–2a. Modules not directly affected have been left out of the figure. Note that the 150–PRINT–REPORT–LINE module has been removed completely from the VTOC and that module 130 calls modules 160–PRINT–HEADING–LINES and 170–WRITE–REPORT–LINE directly rather than going through module 150. Also modules 140 and 200 call module 170, the write module, directly and do not go through module 150.

Figure 7–5b, pseudocode for module 130, has been changed to reflect this approach. You can see that module 130 tests for the page overflow in the same way that the detail print module in previous chapters has done. In fact,

```
000-PRODUCE-SALES-REPORT
    1. Open files
    2. Do 100-PRODUCE-SALES-LINE
           UNTIL TRAN-EOF.
    3. Do 200-PRINT-GRAND-TOTAL-LINE.
    4. Close files.
    5. Stop run.

100-PRODUCE-SALES-LINE
    1. Do 110-READ-SALES-RECORD.
    2. IF TR-SALESPERS-NO is greater than OLD-SALESPERS-NO
           Do 130-PRINT-CUSTOMER-TOTAL
           Do 140-PRINT-SALESPERS-TOTAL
       ELSE
           IF TR-CUSTOMER-NO is greater than OLD-CUSTOMER-NO
               Do 130-PRINT-CUSTOMER-TOTAL.
    3. IF not TRAN-EOF
           Do 120-ACCUMULATE-CUSTOMER-TOTAL.

110-READ-SALES-RECORD.
    1. Read TRANSACTION-FILE
           AT END
               move 'Y'            to TRAN-EOF-SW
               move HIGH-VALUE     to TR-SALESPERS-NO.
    2. IF FIRST-RECORD
           move TR-SALESPERS-NO    to OLD-SALESPERS-NO
           move TR-CUSTOMER-NO     to OLD-CUSTOMER-NO
           move 'N'                to FIRST-RECORD-SW.
```

Figure 7–7b
Revision of Figure 7–7a to demonstrate "pushing subfunction down the line"

the original Figures 7–2a and 7–5a represent a departure from the program organization presented before. Also notice that the Figure 7–5b pseudocode performs 170–WRITE–REPORT–LINE directly rather than going through 150–PRINT–REPORT–LINE.

The pseudocode for module 140–PRINT–SALESPERS–TOTAL has been added to Figure 7–5b to show the complete relationship between the two PRINT modules and to demonstrate that module 140 does not test for page overflow—so that the salesperson total will be printed on the same page as the customer total. Also, Figure 7–2b implies that module 200–PRINT–GRAND–TOTAL will not test for page overflow either, since it now performs only module 170. Thus, when the program ends, the logic will automatically print the salesperson, customer, and grand totals on the same page.

Another issue in programming is a guideline given in Chapter 6: to "push subfunctions down the line," meaning that minor or incidental parts of modules should be taken out of high-level modules and placed in lower-level modules if possible. The 100–PRODUCE–SALES–LINE module logic displayed in Figures 7–4 and 7–7a can be changed under this guideline. The principal logic that must be shown in this module is the comparison between the current control fields and the prior control fields to determine when to take a control break. The part of the module that can be considered to be a subfunction is the one that tests for the first record and saves the control fields. This is a one-time function to capture the control fields out of the first record. It is a subfunction that can be moved to a lower-level module, preferably a work module. Which module should it be moved to, then? Since it is directly connected with reading the input records and since the 110–READ–SALES–RECORD module is considered a work module, put that subfunction in the 110 module. Figure 7–7b is a rewrite of Figure 7–7a to show how implementing that guideline will change modules 100 and 110.

At this point in the discussion of the two-level control break program, it is important to compare Figure 7–2b with the VTOC of Figure 5–9. Physically they look nearly alike. Modules 130 and 140 are important to consider in each figure. In Figure 5–9, 130 is named PRINT–CUSTOMER–LINE, and 140 is named PRINT–CUSTOMER–TOTAL. In Figure 7–2, 130 is named PRINT–CUSTOMER–TOTAL, and 140 is named PRINT–SALESPERS–TOTAL. You should observe that there are only two PRINT . . . modules controlled by module 100. You might ask "Why is that when one VTOC is for a single-level control, and the other is for a two-level control program?"

The answer is that the first (Figure 5–9) is for a *detail* report and the other (Figure 7–2b) is for a *summary* report. Remember that a detail report prints a line for each input record, whereas a summary report prints a line only when a control group changes. Thus, the detail report (Figure 5–9) should have a module named PRINT–something–LINE that indicates the printing of the detail line. The summary report will have no such module, since no detail line is to be printed. Since Figure 7–2b is for a two-level control break summary program, it still has two PRINT modules, but note that these are both named PRINT–something–TOTAL, which indicates that a total line is to be printed. Of course, any total line printing is under the control of a control-field change. Note that if Figure 7–2a were a detail rather than a summary report, it would have three print modules under control of module 100. Module 130 would print the detail line, 140 would print the customer total, and 150 would print the salesperson total.

Discussion

Now that you have seen the VTOC and pseudocode for another typical business program, you should feel more confident of your own ability to design and document structured programs. Maybe it will help you to know that you can adapt the VTOCs and module documentation you've seen in the recent topics to a wide range of report-preparation programs. For example, all single-level report-printing programs will have a basic structure like the one for the reorder-listing program in Figure 6–5. And all multilevel report-printing programs will have a structure similar to that in Figure 7–2a or 7–3. Likewise, the control logic for all summary report-printing programs will be similar to that in the sales-report program. In fact, in some cases the logic may be so similar that you'll be able to transfer the pseudocode for the control modules from one program to another simply by changing procedure and data names.

This, then, is a major advantage of structured programming. Because all programs are made up of independent modules, you don't have to start every new program from scratch. Instead, you can begin by asking yourself how it is like other programs you have written and go on from there.

You should now be able to start to use the important techniques of structured design and documentation. As you get more experience and as you learn more about COBOL coding, you will gain proficiency in structured design and documêntation. By the time you complete this book, you should be able to create VTOCs and pseudocode for a wide range of programming problems.

Problem

At this point in the course you should be heavily involved in doing program assignments and so no problem exercises are being provided at the end of this topic. If you feel that a problem exercise would be useful at this time, skip ahead to the end of the next topic where a two-level control break problem is given.

Topic 2 Three–Level Control Breaks

Orientation

Now that you have studied the one- and two-level control break examples, you should begin to have a better grasp of the concepts of control breaks and how to program them. It is hoped that you are beginning to observe that once you know how to do a one-level break, it is a rather easy step to doing multilevel breaks. This topic discusses the three-level break, and when you have completed it, you should be comfortable with the concept of control breaks.

The approach to three-level breaks taken here will be to present a model—a very general example rather than a specific example. Also, this topic will discuss some of the finer points of control break processing, such as *group printing* and *group indication*.

Terminology

detail report	group printing
group indication	summary report

Objectives

1. ***Understand the terminology and how to implement the concepts those terms represent.***

2. ***Observe and identify the general pattern of control break processing, especially multilevel.***

3. ***Given program specifications, be able to create an appropriate VTOC for a two-level control break program.***

4. ***Given program specifications, be able to document (in pseudocode) the critical modules for a two-level control break program.***

The General Model

The structural patterns—overall design

Figure 7–8 is the VTOC for a three-level control break program. Note that it is also a detail type report as opposed to a summary report. The module names are designed to be general in nature so that this figure may function as a "model" rather than a VTOC for any specific program. The model concept is useful since you can apply it to several situations by merely changing a few of the parts. One of the parts that can be changed to apply to a specific situation is the word "general," which is the adjective used in all the modules except 140, 150, 160, and 190.

Suppose that you were planning a program to produce a three-level control report program for an employee overtime application. The report is entitled "Overtime Report," and the data is taken from the employee payroll file. Subtotals are to be taken when the shift changes, when the department changes, and when the plant changes. The file, of course, must be presorted in order by (1) plant, (2) department, (3) shift, and (4) employee name.

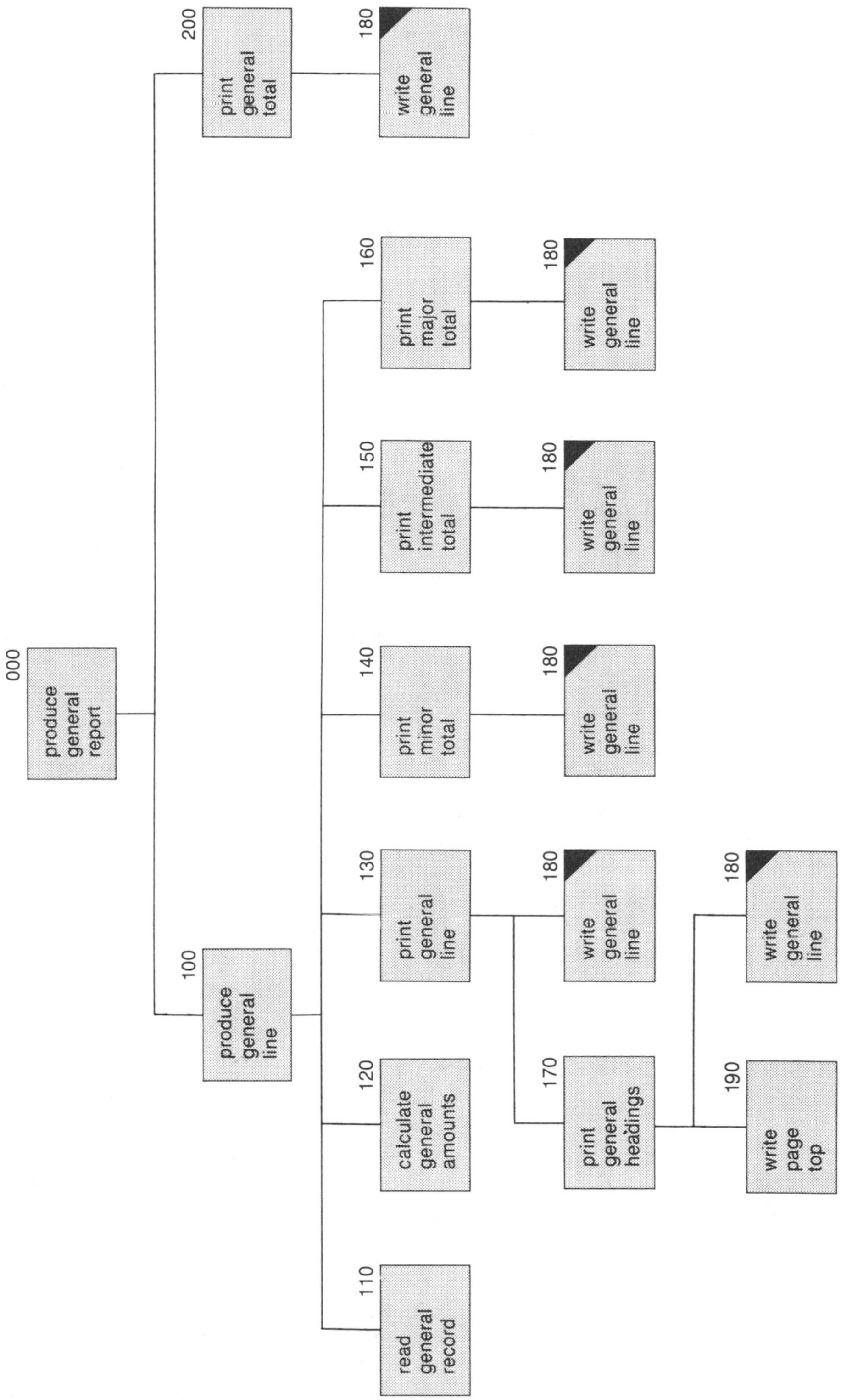
000
produce general report
100
produce general line
200
print general total
110
read general record
120
calculate general amounts
130
print general line
140
print minor total
150
print intermediate total
160
print major total
170
print general headings
180
write general line
180
write general line
180
write general line
180
write general line
180
write general line
180
write general line
190
write page top

Figure 7–8
Structure chart for the general model of a detail, three-level control break report

The employee file used as input contains the standard employee data plus overtime data for those who received overtime. The file has been sorted in the desired order via a prior sorting program. Employees not working overtime will not appear on the report, and will be eliminated by testing in an appropriate place in the program. Note, however, that elimination of those employees is not a problem that you need to be concerned about when developing the VTOC.

Using the above information the general model could be changed in the following manner:

1. Substitute the word "overtime" for the word "general" in all modules except 110.

2. Substitute the word "employee" for the word "general" in module 110 since the employee file is the one being read.

3. Substitute the word "shift" for the word "minor" in module 140 since the break when the shift changes will be the minor control break. That is the meaning of it being third in order when the order of sorting was listed above.

4. Substitute the word "department" for the word "intermediate" in the module 150. The break on department change is the intermediate control since it was second in the sort order.

5. Substitute the word "plant" for the word "major" in module 160. This break is the major control as it was first in the order of sort.

One of the important aspects of any problem-solving situation is that of pattern recognition. The general model presented here is really just a pattern. That pattern can be adapted to the different situations for which it applies. As you will find later, it is obviously not an appropriate pattern for table handling nor for file update. But it is a good pattern for reporting. One of the vital learning hurdles is passed when you learn the importance of patterns, their uses, and adaptations in your daily life. As you can see here, patterns certainly make program design easier.

Another point is that this general model or pattern may be adapted to other than three-level control break reporting with detailed output. Consider the following points:

1. To produce a summary type report rather than a detail report, module 130's concept can be eliminated. Module 130 will still be there, but its function will now be to print the minor total, the function of module 140. Thus, module 100 will now control only three print modules (130 through 150), but those will be printing "totals," not any "line." Of course, the control of the heading print will now be connected to the print minor total module.

2. To produce a report with four levels of control break, merely add another PRINT–level–TOTAL module. When this is done, you will have to change the general names concept since the minor-intermediate-major concept works only for three levels. However, this is really no problem as you will not be using the general words of minor, intermediate, and major anyhow. You would use specific words such as customer, branch, department, etc., to indicate the control fields.

3. To produce a report with only two or one levels of control, you merely eliminate the printing of the higher-level totals. For a two-level control program, eliminate printing of the intermediate total and just print minor and major totals (obviously the intermediate total concept doesn't make any sense when there are only two totals). For a one-level control program, eliminate printing of the two higher-level totals and retain only the minor total, which now becomes just the single total for whatever group is being totaled.

To focus better the preceding discussion, analyze some of the previous examples, and compare them to the general model.

1. Figure 5–9 was the VTOC for a single-level control break report. It was also a detail report and thus had two print modules controlled directly by module 100. Module 100 was to print the customer line (the detail line) and module 140 printed the one subtotal (the customer total).

2. Figure 5–14 was also the VTOC for a detail, single-level control break report. Compare Figure 5–12 with Figure 5–9, and you will see that the VTOC patterns are the same. Just the names of the modules are different to reflect the different specific situations.

3. Figure 7–2b has the same pattern as Figure 5–9 and 5–14. But Figure 7–2a is the VTOC for a two-level control break program. Why do all three of these have the same structural pattern? The reason is that Figure 7–2b is a summary report and has no module to print the customer line (the detail line). The two print modules named print the totals of the customer group and the salesperson group. Study this situation until you are sure that you could explain it to a classmate. Incidentally, the summary report also has another name for it: *group printing*, which means that only a total is printed for the group rather than any of the details.

4. Now study Figure 7–8 again. Has it become obvious why this is the pattern for a detail, three-level control break program? If not, review this topic's discussion and the examples a few more times. It is important that the design structure is clear to you.

The pseudocode—specific design

Figure 7–9 is the pseudocode for the general model. Note that it uses non-specific names just as the structure chart did. You would substitute specific names for the file, record, data, and paragraph names just as was done in the VTOC. In this particular instance, however, you would probably be developing the pseudocode from scratch rather than adapting a previous set of code. There is nothing, though, to keep you from referring to this model when developing the detailed planning for a program. The model can still be used as a pattern and can also be used as a checklist to help ensure that you have documented all of the major and minor functions required by the program.

The following discussion highlights the specific modules one by one and the new concepts of the control break logic.

Mod 000

Standard major control module. Usually it has the same pattern unless there is a get-ready process required.

Mod 100

Sentence 2 is the critical one for multilevel control programs. The three IF tests control the printing of the three subtotals. If there were only two subtotals, there would be only two IF tests for control break.

```
000-PRODUCE-GENERAL-REPORT.
    1.  Open files.
    2.  Do 100-PRODUCE-GENERAL-LINE
            UNTIL LAST-GENERAL-RECORD.
    3.  Do 200-PRINT-GENERAL-TOTALS.
    4.  Close files.
    5.  Stop run.

100-PRODUCE-GENERAL-LINE.
    1.  Do 110-READ-GENERAL-RECORD.
    2.  IF GEN-MAJOR-CONTROL GREATER THAN PRIOR-MAJOR-CONTROL
            Do 140-PRINT-MINOR-TOTAL
            Do 150-PRINT-INTERM-TOTAL
            Do 160-PRINT-MAJOR-TOTAL
        ELSE
            IF GEN-INTERM-CONTROL GREATER THAN PRIOR-INTERM-CONTROL
                Do 140-PRINT-MINOR-TOTAL
                Do 150-PRINT-INTERM-TOTAL
            ELSE
                IF GEN-MINOR-CONTROL GREATER THAN PRIOR-MINOR-CONTROL
                    Do 140-PRINT-MINOR-TOTAL.
    3.  IF MORE-GENERAL-RECORDS
            Do 120-CALCULATE-GENERAL-AMOUNTS
            Do 130-PRINT-GENERAL-LINE.

110-READ-GENERAL-RECORD.
    1.  READ GENERAL-FILE
            AT END
                MOVE end indicator      TO GENERAL-FILE-END-SW
                MOVE HIGH-VALUES        TO GEN-MAJOR-CONTROL.
    2.  IF FIRST-GENERAL-RECORD
            MOVE GEN-MAJOR-CONTROL      TO PRIOR-MAJOR-CONTROL
            MOVE GEN-INTERM-CONTROL     TO PRIOR-INTERM-CONTROL
            MOVE GEN-MINOR-CONTROL      TO PRIOR-MINOR-CONTROL
            MOVE 'N'                    TO FIRST-GENERAL-REC-SW.

120-CALCULATE-GENERAL-AMOUNTS.
    1.  Do calculations as required.
    2.  Accumulate minor total.

130-PRINT-GENERAL-LINE.
    1.  IF LINES-PRINTED GREATER THAN LINES-ON-PAGE
            Do 170-PRINT-GENERAL-HEADINGS.
    2.  Prepare GENERAL-LINE for printing.
           (note - includes: (1) moving input and working storage fields to the
            print line, (2) moving the line to the print buffer, and (3) setting
            the spacing control.)
    3.  Do 180-WRITE-GENERAL-LINE.
    4.  Set control fields to spaces for group indication as required.
            (e.g. MOVE SPACES   TO GL-MAJOR-CONTROL
                                   GL-INTERM-CONTROL
                                   GL-MINOR-CONTROL.)

140-PRINT-MINOR-TOTAL.
    1.  Move appropriate minor data fields to MINOR-TOTAL-LINE fields.
    2.  Set spacing control to appropriate value if different than the
            common space value.
    3.  MOVE MINOR-TOTAL-LINE           TO GENL-PRINT-BUFFER.
    4.  Do 180-WRITE-GENERAL-LINE.
    5.  Add minor total(s)              to interm total(s).
    6.  Set minor total(s)              to zeroes.
    7.  MOVE GF-MINOR-CONTROL           TO PRIOR-MINOR-CONTROL
                                           GL-MINOR-CONTROL.
    8.  Set space control for next detail line.

150-PRINT-INTERM-TOTAL.
    1-7. Use the same general logic as module 140.
```

Figure 7–9
General model for detail, 3-level control (part 1 of 2)

```
160-PRINT-MAJOR-TOTAL.
    1-7. Use the same general logic as module 140.

170-PRINT-GENERAL-HEADINGS.
    1.  MOVE GL-REPORT-HEADING           TO GENL-PRINT-BUFFER.
    2.  Do 190-WRITE-PAGE-TOP.
    3.  Prepare other headings for printing as required.
            (includes: (1) moving identifying fields to heading fields, (2)
             moving the heading lines to the print buffer, (3) and setting
             appropriate spacing control if different than the common
             space value.)
    4.  Do 180-WRITE-GENERAL-LINE after each heading line prepared.
    5.  Move control fields to detail line fields for group indication.
            (e.g. MOVE PRIOR-MAJOR-CONTROL    TO GL-MAJOR-CONTROL.
                  MOVE PRIOR-INTERM-CONTROL   TO GL-INTERM-CONTROL.
                  MOVE PRIOR-MINOR-CONTROL    TO GL-MINOR-CONTROL.)
    6.  Set space control for first detail line on page.

180-WRITE-GENERAL-LINE.
    1.  WRITE GENL-PRINT-BUFFER
            AFTER ADVANCING SPACE-CONTROL.
    2.  ADD SPACE-CONTROL                     TO LINES-PRINTED.
    3.  MOVE the common space value           TO SPACE-CONTROL.

190-WRITE-PAGE-TOP.
    1.  WRITE GENL-PRINT-BUFFER
            AFTER ADVANCING PAGE.
    2.  MOVE 1                                TO LINES-PRINTED.

200-PRINT-GENERAL-TOTALS.
    1.  Move report total field(s) to the GENERAL-TOTAL-LINE fields.
    2.  MOVE GENERAL-TOTAL-LINE               TO GENL-PRINT-BUFFER.
    3.  Set the appropriate spacing control value.
    4.  DO 180-WRITE-GENERAL-LINE.
            (unless the totals are to be placed on a separate page, in which
             case call the page top write module instead of the general
             write module.)
    5.  If there is more than one total line repeat lines 1-4 as required.
    6.  Format the job end message.
    7.  DO 180-WRITE-GENERAL-LINE.
```

Figure 7–9
General model for detail, 3-level control (part 2 of 2)

When any one control break occurs, the program calls all appropriate print total modules. This is important for documentation as it shows in a top-level module exactly which significant modules are being called and under what conditions. Do not call the major module and have it call the intermediate one which calls the minor one. That approach hides the significant logic.

Always use a nested IF for the control logic versus three separate IF sentences. There is no reason to ask a question that already has been answered, plus separate IF sentences can cause trouble in this case. The nested IF is much more straightforward logic for this situation.

The control fields are tested from major to minor, whereas the print modules are called from minor to major. When you think about that for a time, it makes complete sense. Of course, you print the lower-level subtotal first followed by higher-level totals. The control fields should be tested from major to minor because a break at any high level automatically implies breaks at all other levels—thus there would be no need to test lower control fields.

When the last record has been processed, the major control field will be set to HIGH–VALUE, and the end-of-file switch will be set on (see module 110). Those actions of module 110 will cause the major control break to occur and call the print modules for all of the subtotals (sentence 2). The calculation module and detail print module will be bypassed because the end-of-file switch is set on (sentence 3). This is a somewhat subtle bit of logic coordination which greatly simplifies the coding when the end of file is reached.

Mod 110

The key to simplifying control logic is the use of the reserved word HIGH–VALUE moved into the major control field when the end of the input file is reached. As discussed previously, these two actions have important impact.

Sentence 2 captures all of the control fields when the first record has been read and sets off the first record switch. Sometimes programmers also want to take care of group indication here, but as you will see that is only unnecessary duplication of code. The group indication will be discussed and taken care of in the page heading module 170.

Mod 120

Does whatever calculations are required to prepare the data for the detail line, and adds any accumulated detail quantities to the lowest-level subtotal.

Mod 130

The standard detail line printing module with which you have become very familiar. It tests for page overflow and formats and causes the detail line to be printed. Since this is the printing of the detail line, you must remember that the heading lines will have been printed already. Observe that sentence 4 moves spaces to the control fields so that the data will not be repeated when not needed. The new group indications have already been set in the page top module or in the appropriate subtotal printing module.

Mod 140

Formats and prints the first or minor subtotal. If other than normal spacing is required before printing of the subtotal (such as double spacing), that is done just before moving the line to the printing area.

Since this is a module that handles subtotals, it has some additional chores. First, it adds the total amount(s) just printed to the next level of total. Second, it sets the amount(s) just added back to zero to get ready for accumulating the total for the next group. Finally, it moves the control field from the new input record to the corresponding control field in Working–Storage, and also moves it to the detail print line so the new group may be identified for group indication.

Mod 150 and 160

Use the same general logic as module 140 in these two subtotal modules. The only real difference will be the substitution of appropriate data names in the individual commands. Note that for a three-level control program module 150 would add the intermediate total to the major total and save the intermediate control field. Module 160 would add the major total to the final, grand, or report total and save the new major control field.

Mod 170

Is the standard module to print the report headings. The only thing new is in sentence 5, which deals with the movement of control fields to the detail print line. When a report is using group indication, a new page should not start without identifying each of the groups on the first detail line, even if a control break has not occurred. Thus, each time the page overflow is recognized the control fields are moved to the detail line again.

Therefore, it was not necessary to move them to the detail line in the read module at first record time. Since the printing of the heading lines had to take place first, the group indication would be taken care of and placing the code to move those fields in the read module was a duplication.

Mod 180

Is the standard write line for all except the page top. It also accumulates the page count and is a good place to move the common spacing value (typically one) to the space control field. This is an example of the concept of shoving subfunctions down the line and normally will save a few coding lines as this only needs to be written once. Note that it is placed at the *end* of the module so it won't interfere with other space control adjustments and the line counting.

Mod 190

Standard page top routine which merely causes print at the top of the page and initialization of the line counting field. Note that here it is set to one. While this is more accurate than zero, since one line was printed, it is a minor point.

Mod 200

Standard printing of the report or grand total routine. If there is more than one line to be printed, some of the instructions have to be repeated. Sometimes it is required that the final totals be printed on a separate page, in which case the page top routine would also be called.

Discussion

As mentioned previously in this topic, there are two principal concepts to learn here. The first is to understand how a detail, three-level control break report is designed, organized, and coded. The second is to understand the importance of pattern recognition and to develop the ability to apply this in problem solving, whether in a computing situation or in any other life situation. A critical aspect of the pattern recognition concept is to be able to adapt applicable parts of the pattern and to reject the parts which do not apply.

Stop and review programs that have been discussed so far for common patterns. You should not be surprised to find that the pattern has been fairly consistent and has changed gradually as new concepts have been introduced.

Print chart:

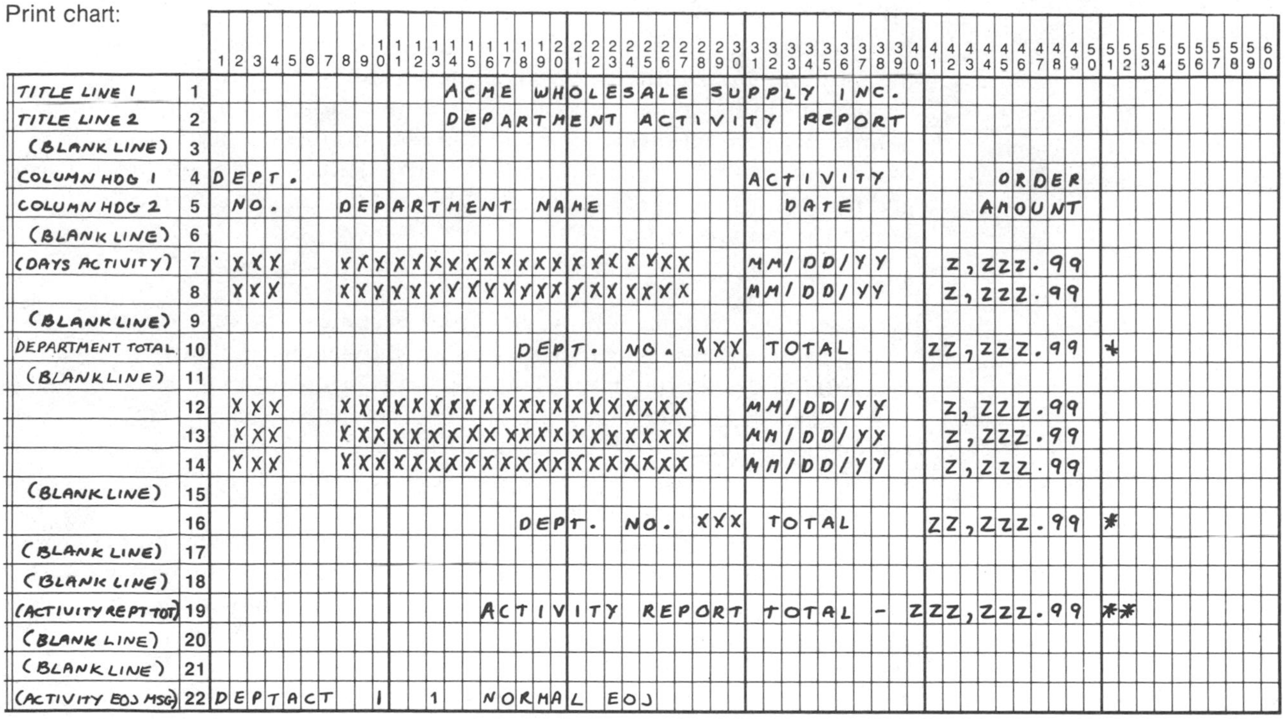

TITLE LINE 1 — ACME WHOLESALE SUPPLY INC.
TITLE LINE 2 — DEPARTMENT ACTIVITY REPORT
(BLANK LINE)
COLUMN HDG 1 — DEPT. ACTIVITY ORDER
COLUMN HDG 2 — NO. DEPARTMENT NAME DATE AMOUNT
(BLANK LINE)
(DAYS ACTIVITY) — XXX XXXXXXXXXXXXXXXXXXXX MM/DD/YY Z,ZZZ.99
XXX XXXXXXXXXXXXXXXXXXXX MM/DD/YY Z,ZZZ.99
(BLANK LINE)
DEPARTMENT TOTAL — DEPT. NO. XXX TOTAL ZZ,ZZZ.99 *
(BLANK LINE)
XXX XXXXXXXXXXXXXXXXXXXX MM/DD/YY Z,ZZZ.99
XXX XXXXXXXXXXXXXXXXXXXX MM/DD/YY Z,ZZZ.99
XXX XXXXXXXXXXXXXXXXXXXX MM/DD/YY Z,ZZZ.99
(BLANK LINE)
DEPT. NO. XXX TOTAL ZZ,ZZZ.99 *
(BLANK LINE)
(BLANK LINE)
(ACTIVITY REPT TOT) — ACTIVITY REPORT TOTAL - ZZZ,ZZZ.99 **
(BLANK LINE)
(BLANK LINE)
(ACTIVITY EOJ MSG) — DEPTACT 1 1 NORMAL EOJ

Instructions:

1. The input records are sorted in activity date order within department number.
2. There will be one or more records for each date. Print only one line for the transactions on each date.
3. Calculate the order amount by multiplying the quantity sold by the wholesale cost.

Record layout:

Field Name	Record Code	Product Number	Dept. No.	Dept. Name	Activity Date	Quantity Sold	Whlse Cost	Retail Price
Characteristics	XX	X-XXX	X(3)	X(20)	YYMMDD	99	99V99	99V99
Usage								
Position	1-2	3-7	8-10	11-30	31-36	37-38	39-42	43-46

Figure 7–10
Specifications for two-level control break problem

Problems

1. Figure 7–10 gives the specifications for a two-level control break program. Create an appropriate VTOC for it.

2. Analyze your VTOC and revise it as required. This is a good opportunity to compare notes with your classmates.

3. After revising your VTOC as necessary, add the switch, print control, control field, total field, detail, and total lines to the program skeleton of the first three divisions shown in Figure 7–11.

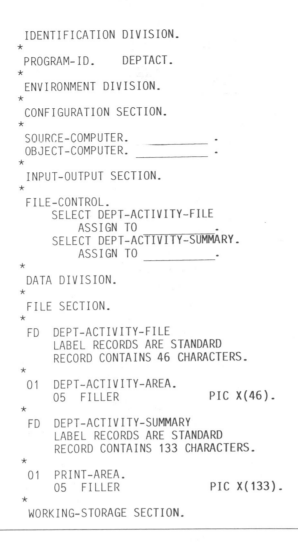

```
 IDENTIFICATION DIVISION.
*
 PROGRAM-ID.    DEPTACT.
*
 ENVIRONMENT DIVISION.
*
 CONFIGURATION SECTION.
*
 SOURCE-COMPUTER.  __________ .
 OBJECT-COMPUTER.  __________ .
*
 INPUT-OUTPUT SECTION.
*
 FILE-CONTROL.
     SELECT DEPT-ACTIVITY-FILE
         ASSIGN TO __________.
     SELECT DEPT-ACTIVITY-SUMMARY.
         ASSIGN TO __________.
*
 DATA DIVISION.
*
 FILE SECTION.
*
 FD  DEPT-ACTIVITY-FILE
     LABEL RECORDS ARE STANDARD
     RECORD CONTAINS 46 CHARACTERS.
*
 01  DEPT-ACTIVITY-AREA.
     05  FILLER             PIC X(46).
*
 FD  DEPT-ACTIVITY-SUMMARY
     LABEL RECORDS ARE STANDARD
     RECORD CONTAINS 133 CHARACTERS.
*
 01  PRINT-AREA.
     05  FILLER             PIC X(133).
*
 WORKING-STORAGE SECTION.
```

Figure 7–11
First three divisions of department activity report

4. When you feel satisfied with the tasks of number 3, develop a specific design for the problem by developing the processing modules in pseudocode.

Solutions

1. & 2. Figure 7–12 shows an acceptable VTOC for the two-level control break problem.

3. Figure 7–13 contains appropriate Data Division elements for the two-level control break problem. Notice that the order in which they are listed is a logical organization based on program function.

4. The pseudocode in Figure 7–14 is a good solution for the problem. You should carefully review this solution and note the differences between your solution and the text solution. Are the differences significant? You are advised to treat even minor differences as significant at this point. A good question to ask yourself is "Why is the text solution better than mine here?"

Principal reason for differences are concepts such as: (1) order of groups, (2) order of code, (3) meaningful data names, (4) functional modules, and (5) conventions.

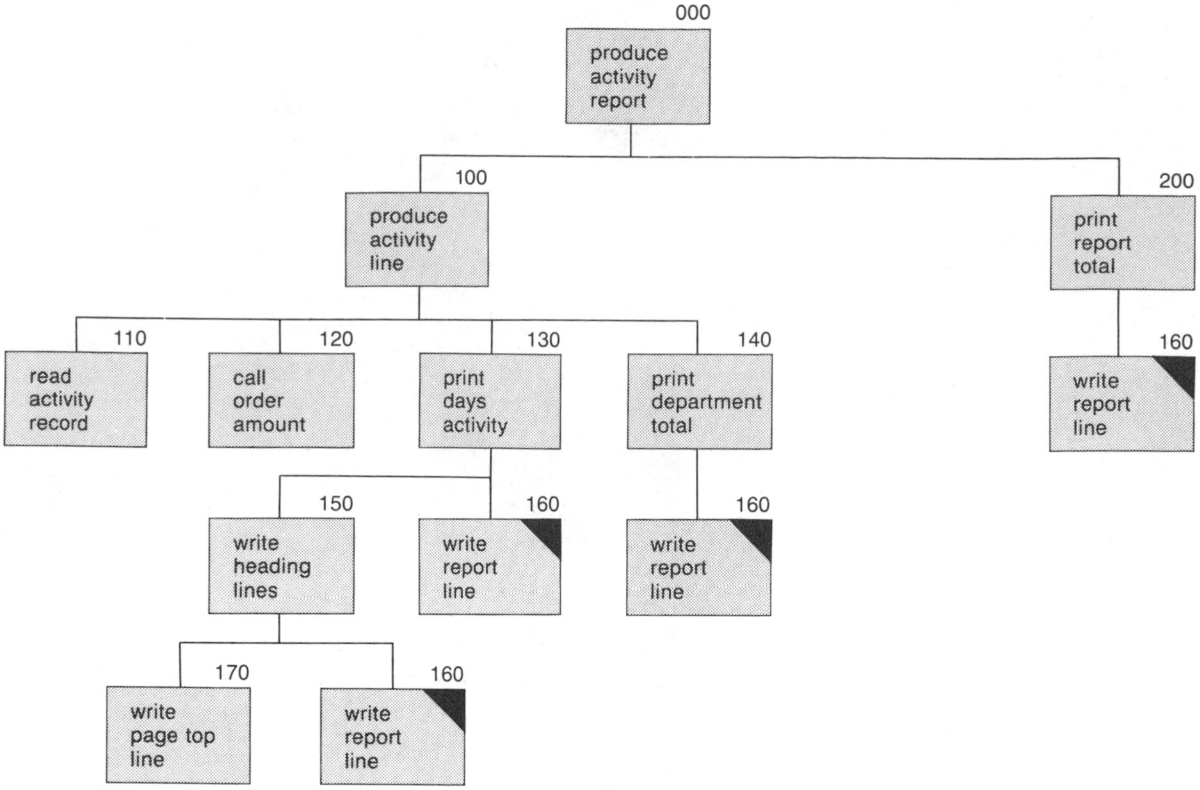
000
produce activity report
100
produce activity line
200
print report total
110
read activity record
120
call order amount
130
print days activity
140
print department total
160
write report line
150
write heading lines
160
write report line
160
write report line
170
write page top line
160
write report line

Figure 7–12
VTOC for Department Activity Report

```
 WORKING-STORAGE SECTION.
*
 01  SWITCHES.
     05  ACTIVITY-EOF-SW     PIC X          VALUE 'N'.
         88  LAST-ACTIVITY-REC              VALUE 'Y'.
         88  MORE-ACTIVITY-RECS             VALUE 'N'.
     05  FIRST-ACT-RECORD-SW PIC X          VALUE 'Y'.
         88  FIRST-ACT-RECORD               VALUE 'Y'.
*
 01  WORK-FIELDS                                         COMP-3.
     05  ORDER-AMOUNT        PIC 9(4)V99.
*
 01  CONTROL-FIELDS.
     05  PRIOR-DEPT-NO       PIC XXX.
     05  PRIOR-DEPT-NAME     PIC X(20).
     05  PRIOR-DATE.
         10  PRIOR-YEAR      PIC XX.
         10  PRIOR-MONTH     PIC XX.
         10  PRIOR-DAY       PIC XX.
*
 01  PRINT-CONTROL-FIELDS                                COMP-3.
     05  LINE-COUNT          PIC S99        VALUE +99.
     05  LINES-ON-PAGE       PIC S99        VALUE +50.
     05  SPACE-CONTROL       PIC S99        VALUE +1.
*
 01  TOTAL-FIELDS                                        COMP-3.
     05  DAYS-TOTAL          PIC S9(4)V99   VALUE ZERO.
     05  DEPT-TOTAL          PIC S9(5)V99   VALUE ZERO.
     05  REPORT-TOTAL        PIC S9(6)V99   VALUE ZERO.
*
```

Figure 7–13
Working-Storage section of the department activity report (part 1 of 2)

```
 01  ACTIVITY-RECORD.
     05  AR-CODE              PIC XX.
     05  AR-PRODUCT-NO        PIC X(5).
     05  AR-DEPT-NO           PIC XXX.
     05  AR-DEPT-NAME         PIC X(20).
     05  AR-DATE.
         10  AR-YEAR          PIC XX.
         10  AR-MONTH         PIC XX.
         10  AR-DAY           PIC XX.
     05  AR-QUANTITY          PIC 99.
     05  AR-WHLSE-COST        PIC 99V99.
     05  AR-RETAIL-PRICE      PIC 99V99.
*
 01  TITLE-LINE-1.
     05  FILLER               PIC X(14)      VALUE SPACE.
     05  FILLER               PIC X(15)      VALUE 'ACME WHOLESALE'.
     05  FILLER               PIC X(104)     VALUE 'SUPPLY INC.'.
*
 01  TITLE-LINE-2.
     05  FILLER               PIC X(14)      VALUE SPACE.
     05  FILLER               PIC X(11)      VALUE 'DEPARTMENT'.
     05  FILLER               PIC X(9)       VALUE 'ACTIVITY'.
     05  FILLER               PIC X(99)      VALUE 'REPORT'.

*
 01  COL-HEADING-1.
     05  FILLER               PIC X(31)      VALUE ' DEPT.'.
     05  FILLER               PIC X(14)      VALUE "ACTIVITY'.
     05  FILLER               PIC X(88)      VALUE 'ORDER'.
*
 01  COL-HEADING-2.
     05  FILLER               PIC X(8)       VALUE '  NO.'.
     05  FILLER               PIC X(11)      VALUE 'DEPARTMENT'.
     05  FILLER               PIC X(14)      VALUE 'NAME'.
     05  FILLER               PIC X(11)      VALUE 'DATE'.
     05  FILLER               PIC X(89)      VALUE 'AMOUNT'.
*
 01  DAYS-ACTIVITY-LINE.
     05  FILLER               PIC XX         VALUE SPACE.
     05  DA-DEPT-NO           PIC XXX.
     05  FILLER               PIC XXX        VALUE SPACE.
     05  DA-DEPT-NAME         PIC X(20).
     05  FILLER               PIC XXX        VALUE SPACE.
     05  DA-MONTH             PIC XX.
     05  FILLER               PIC X          VALUE '/'.
     05  DA-DAY               PIC XX.
     05  FILLER               PIC X          VALUE '/'.
     05  DA-YEAR              PIC XX.
     05  FILLER               PIC XXX        VALUE SPACE.
     05  DA-DAYS-TOTAL        PIC Z,ZZZ.99.
     05  FILLER               PIC X(83)      VALUE SPACE.
*
 01  DEPT-TOTAL-LINE.
     05  FILLER               PIC X(18)      VALUE SPACE.
     05  FILLER               PIC X(10)      VALUE 'DEPT. NO.'.
     05  DT-DEPT-NO           PIC XXX.
     05  FILLER               PIC X(10)      VALUE ' TOTAL'.
     05  DT-DEPT-TOTAL        PIC ZZ,ZZZ.99.
     05  FILLER               PIC X(83)      VALUE ' *'.
*
 01  REPORT-TOTAL-LINE.
     05  FILLER               PIC X(16)      VALUE SPACE.
     05  FILLER               PIC X(9)       VALUE 'ACTIVITY'.
     05  FILLER               PIC X(15)      VALUE 'REPORT TOTAL -'.
     05  RT-REPORT-TOTAL      PIC ZZZ,ZZZ.99.
     05  FILLER               PIC X(83)      VALUE ' **'.
```

Figure 7–13
Working Storage section of the department activity report (part 2 of 2)

```
000-PRODUCE-ACTIVITY-REPORT.
    1. Open files.
    2. DO 100-PRODUCE-ACTIVITY-LINE
           UNTIL LAST-ACTIVITY-REC.
    3. DO 200-PRINT-REPORT-TOTAL.
    4. Display job end message.
    5. Close files.
    6. Stop run.

100-PRODUCE-ACTIVITY-LINE.
    1. DO 110-READ-ACTIVITY-RECORD.
    2. IF AR-DEPT-NO is greater than PRIOR-DEPT-NO
           DO 130-PRINT-DAYS-ACTIVITY
           DO 140-PRINT-DEPARTMENT-TOTAL
       ELSE
           IF AR-DATE is greater than PRIOR-DATE
               DO 130-PRINT-DAYS-ACTIVITY.
    3. IF MORE-ACTIVITY-RECS
          DO 120-CALC-ORDER-AMOUNT.

110-READ-ACTIVITY-RECORD.
    1. Read DEPT-ACTIVITY-REC into ACTIVITY-RECORD
           AT END
               move 'y' to ACTIVITY-EOF-SW
               move HIGH-VALUE to AR-DEPT-NO.
    2. IF FIRST-ACTIVITY-REC
           move AR-DEPT-NO          to PRIOR-DEPT-NO
           move AR-DEPT-NAME        to PRIOR-DEPT-NAME
           move AR-DATE             to PRIOR-DATE
           move 'n'                 to FIRST-ACT-RECORD-SW.

120-CALC-ORDER-AMOUNT.
    1. Multiply AR-WHLSE-COST by AR-QUANTITY
          to determine ORDER-AMOUNT.
    2. Add ORDER-AMOUNT to DAYS-TOTAL.

130-PRINT-DAYS-ACTIVITY.
    1. IF LINE-COUNT is greater than LINES-ON-PAGE
           DO 150-PRINT-HEADING-LINES.
    2. Move DAYS-TOTAL               to DA-DAYS-TOTAL.
    3. Move DAYS-ACTIVITY-LINE       to PRINT-AREA.
    4. DO 160-WRITE-REPORT-LINE.
    5. Add DAYS-TOTAL to DEPT-TOTAL.
    6. Set DAYS-TOTAL to zero.
    7. Save date of current record.
    8. Format date in DAYS-ACTIVITY-LINE.

140-PRINT-DEPARTMENT-TOTAL.
    1. Move DEPT-TOTAL               to DT-DEPT-TOTAL.
    2. Move DEPT-TOTAL-LINE          to PRINT-AREA.
    3. Set SPACE-CONTROL to 2.
    4. DO 160-WRITE-REPORT-LINE.
    5. Add DEPT-TOTAL to REPORT-TOTAL.
    6. Set. DEPT-TOTAL to zero.
    7. Move AR-DEPT-NO               to PRIOR-DEPT-NO
                                        DA-DEPT-NO
                                        DT-DEPT-NO.
    8. Move AR-DEPT-NAME             to DA-DEPT-NAME.
    9. Set SPACE-CONTROL to 2.

150-WRITE-HEADING-LINES.
    1. Format, move to print-area, and output
       the title lines and column headings.
    2. Format DAYS-ACTIVITY-LINE for a new page.
    3. Set SPACE-CONTROL to 2.
```

Figure 7–14
Pseudocode for department activity report (part 1 of 2)

```
160-WRITE-REPORT-LINE.
    1. Write PRINT-AREA
           AFTER ADVANCING SPACE-CONTROL.
    2. Inrcrement the LINE-COUNT.
    3. Set standard spacing.

170-WRITE-PAGE-TOP-LINE.
    1. Write PRINT-AREA
           AFTER ADVANCING PAGE.
    2. Set LINE-COUNT to 1.

200-PRINT-REPORT-TOTAL.
    1. Move REPORT-TOTAL           to RT-REPORT-TOTAL.
    2. Move REPORT-TOTAL-LINE      to PRINT-AREA.
    3. Set SPACE-CONTROL to 3.
    4. DO 160-WRITE-REPORT-LINE.
```

Figure 7–14
Pseudocode for department activity report (part 2 of 2)

Topic 3 Top–Down Coding and Testing

Orientation

Although you have probably coded and tested all of the modules of your structured programs at once, there is a better way to do it. This better way is called *top-down coding and testing*. For professionals it is recommended that the method be used for any program that takes more than a day to develop. As a student, you should use the method for all remaining assignments as it will help you learn top-down testing as well as aid your development efficiency.

In this topic the theory and advantages of top-down coding and testing are introduced. Then, techniques related to the effective use of top-down coding and testing are presented. When you finish this topic, you should know how to use top-down coding and testing and should be motivated to use it for the new programs you develop.

Terminology

dummy module	processing stub	top-down coding and testing
input stub	program stub	top-down testing
output stub		

Objectives

1. *Develop an effective top-down test plan for programming assignments.*
2. *Using the top-down test plan, code program stubs for each phase of the test plan at the appropriate time.*

Program: INV2100 EDIT INVENTORY TRANSACTIONS		Page: 1
Designer: Anne Prince		Date: 01-18-86
Test phase	**Data**	**Data source**
1. Modules 000, 200, and 300	None	Not applicable
2. Add modules 210, 310, 320, 330, 340, and 350	Three part-number records; Two valid transactions: one for each transaction code, and one with the first part number in the table, one with the last part number	Self
3. Add modules 100, 360, 370, 380, 390, 400, and 500	Invalid transactions that will test all possible causes of invalid fields	Self
4. Contingencies	Mixed data from steps 2 and 3; any new records that might cause contingent errors	Self
5. Page overflow and maximum table size	As many part-number records as the program is supposed to provide for; 150 transactions with enough invalid transactions to cause page overflow	Test data generator

Figure 7–15
A test plan for the edit program using top-down testing to test the major modules first

An Introduction to Top-Down Coding and Testing

When you use top-down coding and testing, you don't code the entire program and then test it. Instead, you code and test in phases. You normally start by coding and testing the level-0 module and one or more of the level-1 modules. Then, after correcting any bugs, you add one or more modules to this coding and test again. When this much of the program runs without bugs, you code a few more modules, add them to what you have, and test again. You continue in this way until all of the modules have been coded and you are testing the entire program. Because top-down coding and testing always go together, the phrase *top-down testing* implies top-down coding as well.

To illustrate top-down testing, Figure 7–15 gives a test plan for an edit program similar to the edit program shown in Figure 6–11. Figure 7–15 is somewhat more sophisticated than Figure 6–11 and is a better example for demonstrating the top-down testing method.

Rather than test all 16 modules at once, however, the programmer has decided to code and test only modules 000, 200, and 300 in the first phase of testing. This is illustrated by the structure chart in Figure 7–16. Although the unshaded modules will be called during the test run, they won't be tested until later. After modules 000, 200, and 300 run without error, the programmer continues with the next phase of the test plan.

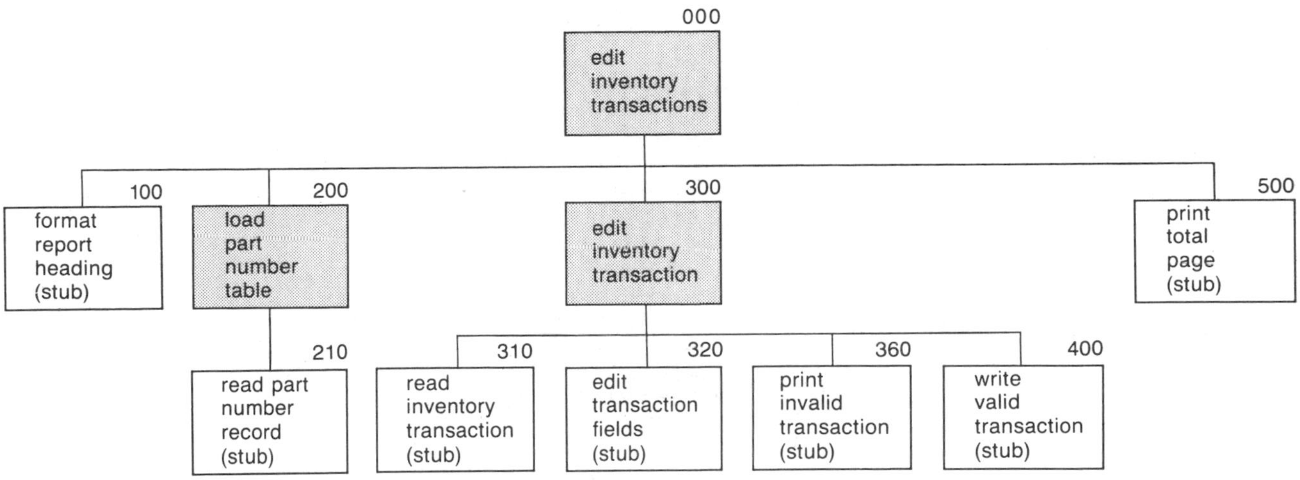
000
edit
inventory
transactions
100
format
report
heading
(stub)
200
load
part
number
table
300
edit
inventory
transaction
500
print
total
page
(stub)
210
read part
number
record
(stub)
310
read
inventory
transaction
(stub)
320
edit
transaction
fields
(stub)
360
print
invalid
transaction
(stub)
400
write
valid
transaction
(stub)

Figure 7–16
The first phase of coding and testing for the edit program using the test plan in Figure 7–15

As you will see later, the programmer has considerable choice as to which modules are coded and tested next. For instance, module 210 could be coded next, or modules 310 and 320, or modules 360, 370, 380, and 390. And whether one, two, or more modules are added at a time depends on the length and complexity of the modules.

In the test plan in Figure 7–15, the programmer has decided to add six modules to the program in the second phase of testing. This is illustrated by the structure chart in Figure 7–17. Then, when all of these modules run without error, the programmer adds the remaining modules of the program.

To use top-down coding and testing, the programmer must code *program stubs*, or *dummy modules*, for all modules called by the modules that are being tested. In Figure 7–16, for example, the unshaded modules are program stubs. The coding for program stubs, as you will see, varies depending on whether the modules supply input, process data, or give output.

You might bc curious about the two structure blocks in Figure 7–17 which are labeled DATEDIT. Those blocks demonstrate how to designate the intended use of a subrouting call in the VTOC. Subroutines will be discussed in a later chapter, but it is instructive to show here how a VTOC deals with them.

Another thing about Figure 7–17 that may bother you is, where are modules 370, 380, and 390 mentioned in the test plan? Those were left off Figure 7–17 since they were just the typical print-heading, write-page-top, and write-line modules, and you should know now where their appropriate placement is. Depending on the programmer's preference, they can be tested at later or earlier points just like the other modules.

The benefits of top-down testing

The primary benefit of top-down testing is improved testing efficiency (or improved productivity). To illustrate this benefit, imagine a program of 2000 lines or more with 1000 statements in the Procedure Division. If you test the entire program at once with all of its bugs, there is a good possibility that the first few days of testing will be very inefficient. If, for example, a couple of minor clerical errors cause some part of the program to execute improperly, it may be difficult to determine just where in the program the bug originates.

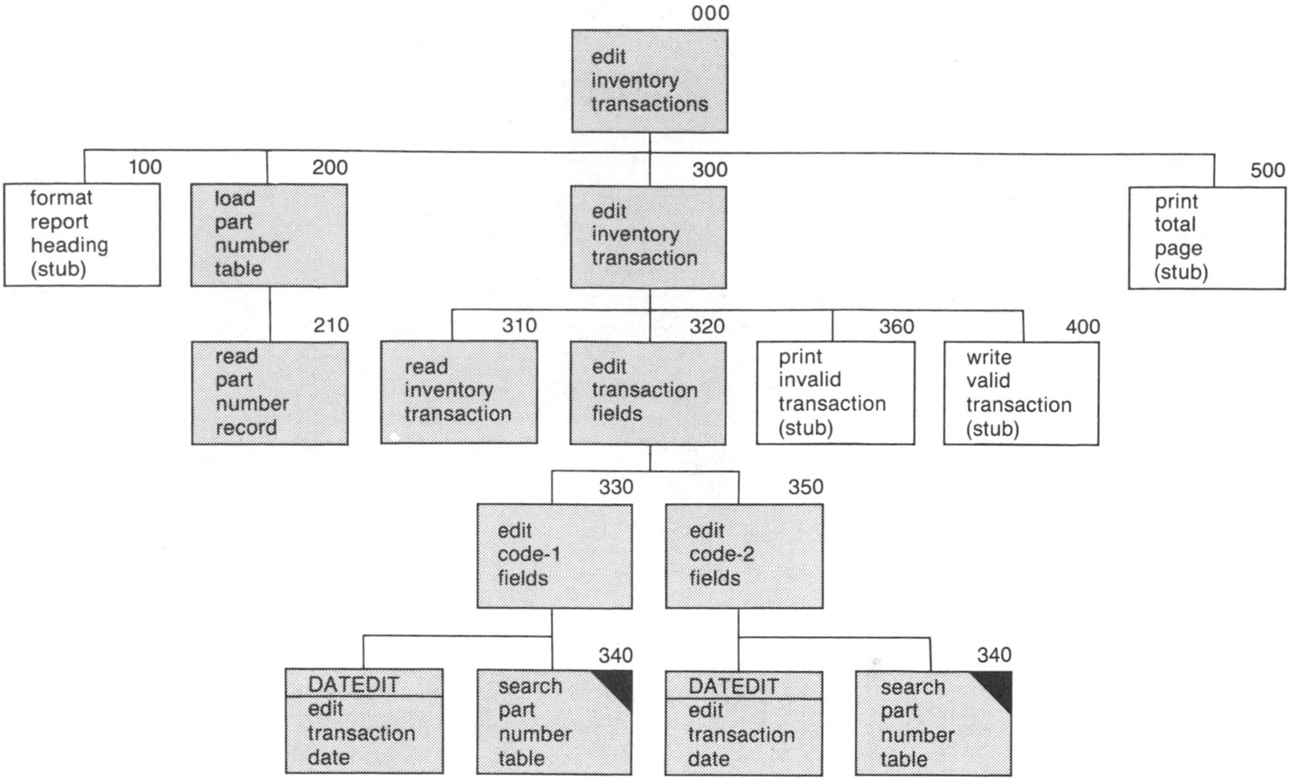
000
edit inventory transactions
100
format report heading (stub)
200
load part number table
300
edit inventory transaction
500
print total page (stub)
210
read part number record
310
read inventory transaction
320
edit transaction fields
360
print invalid transaction (stub)
400
write valid transaction (stub)
330
edit code-1 fields
350
edit code-2 fields
DATEDIT
edit transaction date
340
search part number table
DATEDIT
edit transaction date
340
search part number table

Figure 7–17
The second phase of coding and testing for the edit program using the test plan in Figure 7–15

And this in turn can lead to wasted effort: the addition of debugging statements in the source code, an unnecessary test run or two, and so on.

But if a program like this is tested from the top down, testing proceeds in increments of a few modules, perhaps 150 statements or less, at a time. As a result, it should be easy to locate the source of any bugs that are discovered during testing. They almost have to be in the modules just added or in the interfaces between the old modules and the new modules. Then, by the time all 1000 statements are tested together, all of the major control modules should be error-free, so any additional errors should be relatively trivial. In short, an unwieldy test run is turned into a series of easily managed steps when you use top-down testing.

After improved testing efficiency, the second biggest benefit you get from using top-down testing may be improved programmer morale. To some, variety is the spice of life, so it may get depressing to be involved in a large project in which the coding task alone will take a couple of weeks or more. While you are coding, you have to wonder whether you have made any major omissions or logical errors. And because you're not getting any feedback, your mind tends to get jumbled up as thoughts about one module interfere with thoughts about another.

How much better it is to code a couple hundred lines of COBOL and to test them before going any further. Besides giving a little variety to the project, it clears the mind. Once you know the top levels of the program are okay, you have confidence that you're on the right track. Furthermore, by proceeding in this way, you know that you won't be facing the task of debugging the entire program when you complete the coding.

A third benefit of top-down testing is improved program quality; in particular, improved program reliability. Although there is no formal data to prove this, it is felt that a program is more likely to be reliable if it is tested on a top-down basis. Because a programmer is only concerned with a few modules each test run, it seems more likely that each module will actually be tested, thus making the resulting program more reliable. In contrast, it's easy to forget to test a module or two when you test all of the modules at once.

Later on, some minor benefits of top-down testing will be presented, but these are the important ones. If you use top-down testing, you should improve your productivity along with your program quality and you should enjoy programming more than ever before.

Some Related Ideas

With this as background, you should start using top-down testing right away. To use it well, however, you need to know (1) how to code program stubs, (2) when to use top-down testing, and (3) in what sequence to code and test the modules of a program. What follows, then, are some ideas in these areas.

How to code program stubs

In general, there are three types of program stubs: input stubs, processing stubs, and output stubs. An *input stub* replaces a module that is supposed to supply data to a program. For instance, modules 210 and 310 in Figure 7–16 are input modules, so their replacements are input stubs. A *processing stub* replaces a module that operates upon the data within a program, such as module 320 in Figure 7–16. And an *output stub* replaces a module that produces output in a program, such as module 360, 400, or 500 in Figure 7–16. How you code any of these three types of stubs will depend on the requirements of the program and on your test plan.

To illustrate, the coding for some typical program stubs are shown in Figure 7–18. The coding shown in Figure 7–18 is for the stubs that would be used for the first test phase of the edit program. The VTOC of Figure 7–16 is a visual display of the modules that will be treated as stubs in the plan's first test phase. When the modules are coded later on, the stubs will be deleted and replaced with actual code. Notice that a stub was not coded for module 100. Since it is not needed until a report line is actually printed, its coding may be put off until then.

The minimum amount of code that an input stub should contain is shown in Figure 7–18 for module 210. This stub simply displays the module number and indicates that the last record in the file has been read. A step up from this is the code shown for module 310. This simulates the reading of one input record the first time the module is executed and sets the end-of-file switch the second time the module is executed. Beyond this level, you may want to use a counter to simulate the reading of several records before setting the end-of-file switch. Or you may want to take records one at a time from a table that you created for the stub and pass them back to the calling module. At some point, of course, it becomes more practical to code the actual module and use actual input data than to code an extensive stub that will be thrown away later. So you must have solid reasons for going beyond the levels of detail shown in Figure 7–18.

A processing stub should supply the codes or answers that the calling modules look for, but they don't have to be the right codes or answers. For instance, the code for module 320 in Figure 7–18 moves an N into the valid-transaction switch. It will do this whether the transaction is valid or invalid. Nevertheless, this is all that module 300 needs to continue processing. Similarly, a calculate module may pass a constant value back to the program each time it is executed. For instance, a stub for a gross-pay calculation may return

Input stubs

```
 210-READ-PART-NUMBER-RECORD.
*
     DISPLAY '210-READ-PART-NUMBER-RECORD'.
     MOVE 'Y' TO PART-NUMBER-EOF-SW.

 310-READ-INVENTORY-TRANSACTION.
*
     DISPLAY '310-READ-INVENTORY-TRANSACTION'.
     IF FIRST-RECORD
         MOVE 'C1AAAAAAAAAA0911841122233333444455555
              TO INVENTORY-TRANSACTION-RECORD
         MOVE 'N' TO FIRST-RECORD-SW
     ELSE
         MOVE 'Y' TO TRAN-EOF-SW.
```

Processing stubs

```
 320-EDIT-TRANSACTION-FIELDS.
*
     DISPLAY '320-EDIT-TRANSACTION-FIELDS'.
     MOVE 'N' TO VALID-TRAN-SW.
```

Output stubs

```
 360-PRINT-INVALID-TRANSACTION.
*
     DISPLAY '360-PRINT-INVALID-TRANSACTION'.
     DISPLAY INVENTORY-TRANSACTION-RECORD.

 400-WRITE-VALID-TRANSACTION.
*
     DISPLAY '400-WRITE-VALID-TRANSACTION'.
     DISPLAY INVENTORY-TRANSACTION-RECORD.

 500-PRINT-TOTAL-PAGE.
*
     DISPLAY '500-PRINT-TOTAL-PAGE'.
     DISPLAY VALID-SALES-COUNT.
     DISPLAY VALID-RETURN-COUNT.
     DISPLAY INVALID-SALES-COUNT.
     DISPLAY INVALID-RETURN-COUNT.
     DISPLAY INVALID-TRAN-CODE-COUNT.
     DISPLAY TRANS-PROCESSED-COUNT.
```

Figure 7–18
Program stubs for the first test phase of the edit program

a constant value of $100.00 each time it is entered. Since this will allow the calling module to continue, it is acceptable.

For an output stub, you will generally use a DISPLAY statement to show what the output data is. This is illustrated in the code for modules 360, 400, and 500 in Figure 7–18. For modules 360 and 400, the DISPLAY statement is used to print the contents of the entire transaction record. For module 500, DISPLAY statements are used to print the values of the fields named. Since the DISPLAY statements won't print the data in a neatly edited format, an output stub should only be used for a low-volume test run.

In some cases, due to the test data used, a program stub should never be reached at all. If, for example, only good transaction data is used in phase 2 of the test plan in Figure 7–15, module 360 should never be executed during this test run. In a case like this, the stub should consist of a single statement that displays the module number so the error will be obvious if the module is called.

In Figure 7–18, you can see that each program stub displays the paragraph name before doing any dummy processing. This helps the programmer determine whether all modules were called as intended. Although a DISPLAY statement was recommended for this purpose in each dummy module, you should realize that this isn't essential and creating these statements can be unnecessary work. So, to some extent, this use of DISPLAY statements should depend on your program's complexity and your personal preferences.

When to use top-down testing

The main benefits of top-down testing have been presented. You probably have experienced just enough frustration with development and testing of your student programs to understand these benefits and to be motivated to want to use the method. Just to support the need for learning top-down testing, more reasons follow.

In some cases, you can use top-down testing to help you get around incomplete specifications. As you get the specifications for the edit program, for example, suppose you can't find out what the editing rules are going to be for each field of the transaction records. By using top-down design, this omission in the specifications shouldn't stop you from designing the program and coding all of the modules except the ones with incomplete specifications. In addition, though, by using top-down testing, you can test all of the modules except modules 330 and 350. So you can all but complete the program without knowing the editing rules.

You may also want to use top-down testing to help you get around a module or a group of modules that seem overwhelming to you. Suppose, for example, that you're a trainee and you haven't really mastered the table-handling feature of COBOL. As a result, modules 200 and 210 in the edit program bother you. To clear the air, then, you code a stub for module 200 using code with subscripts that you understand as shown in Figure 7–19. This lets you forget about these modules until you have time to research the table-handling feature of COBOL and code them properly.

When a program is getting more attention than it deserves because the user is concerned about it, you may have another good reason for using top-down testing. In this case, you can stub off all of the modules that the user isn't worried about, and test the ones he or she is worried about. If, for example, the user is worried about the format of a printed report, you can code the print modules early in your development sequence. Then, you can show the user a sample of the output and get reactions to it early in the development of the program. As always, the earlier you discover problems in specification or design, the better off you are.

In the student environment, implement top-down testing by creating the VTOC for a program assignment as soon as the topic which is to be practiced in the assignment is introduced. Even though you may not have a completely accurate VTOC, especially at the lower levels, you should be able to create an accurate VTOC of the first two levels. The pattern recognition idea will

```
 200-LOAD-PART-NUMBER-TABLE.
*
     DISPLAY '200-LOAD-PART-NUMBER-TABLE'.
     MOVE 00001 TO PN-TABLE-ENTRY (1).
     MOVE 55555 TO PN-TABLE-ENTRY (2).
     MOVE 99999 TO PN-TABLE-ENTRY (3).
     MOVE 3 TO PN-ENTRY-COUNT.
     MOVE 'Y' TO PART-NUMBER-EOF-SW.
```

Figure 7–19
A program stub that simulates the functions of modules 200 and 210 in the edit program

enable you to produce most of the VTOC accurately. Then you can code the first two levels and leave the other levels as stubs until you have: (1) tested the coded modules, and (2) understood the rest of the problem and how the new concepts apply to it.

In summary, then, there are many reasons for using top-down testing. So the real question is this: When is a program long enough to justify the use of top-down testing?

As a guideline here, the basic rule is this: If a program takes longer than a day to develop, it's worth using top-down testing when you develop it. That way, you'll produce a measurable amount of tested code each day. And you'll improve your productivity and your program's quality as you code and test the program.

How to decide on the coding sequence when using top-down testing

As you may have realized by now, you can develop the modules in a program in many different sequences when you use top-down coding and testing. If there are no outside influences, your goal should be to use the sequence that will be most efficient in terms of coding and testing. When you develop your test plan, then, you should ask questions like: Where are the major module interfaces in the program? Where, if anywhere, in the structure chart do I have doubts about the design? In what modules do I have doubts about how the coding should be done? Once again, you should attempt to detect the major errors first.

If you have no particular concerns about your program or module designs, you have great flexibility as to your development sequence. After you test the first two or three levels, it becomes a case of mop up. Eventually, you have to code and test all of the modules, so you may as well take them one leg at a time, introducing data that applies to each leg as you go along.

To illustrate another sequence for developing the modules of the edit program, look at the test plan in Figure 7–20. In contrast to the one in the Figure 7–15, the programmer planned this coding sequence with his or her own efficiency in mind. In the first phase, the programmer codes the top-level module and some of the trivial formatting and printing modules. It is known when these modules are tested, that only the summary page should print with zeros in the total areas. But the programmer also knows that most of the time can be spent in this phase developing the code in the first three divisions of the program. So it's all right if the coding in the Procedure Division is trivial.

Then, in the second testing phase, the programmer can concentrate on the coding that will load the part-number file, print invalid transaction records, and write valid transaction records on the output file. Note that the modules that do the actual editing aren't going to be tested, but the one transaction with the invalid transaction code should be listed by the program and the two valid transactions should be written on the output file. This coding should go quite easily, because the programmer coded most of the entries in the first three divisions of the program during the first phase of coding and testing. As a result, there will be no doubt about the names to use in the Procedure Division statements.

Finally, in phase 3, the programmer adds the modules that actually edit the fields in the two types of transaction records. These, of course, are the most difficult modules of the program. But now that most of the trivial modules have already been developed, this coding and testing should proceed quite easily too.

Program: INV2100 EDIT INVENTORY TRANSACTIONS		Page: 1
Designer: Anne Prince		Date: 08-18-86
Test phase	**Data**	**Data source**
1. Modules 000, 100, 380, 390, and 500	None	Not applicable
2. Add modules 200, 210, 300, 310, 320, 360, 370, and 400	Three part-number records; Two valid transactions: one with each transaction code, and one with the first part number in the table and one with the last; one invalid transaction due to an invalid transaction code	Self
3. Add modules 330, 340, and 350	Same data as in phase 2	
4. Invalid transactions	Invalid transactions that will test all possible causes of invalid fields	Self
5. Contingencies	Mixed data from steps 2 and 4; any new records that might cause contingent errors	Self
6. Page overflow and maximum table size	As many part-number records as the program is supposed to provide for; 150 transactions with enough invalid transactions to cause page overflow	Test data generator

Figure 7–20
Another test plan for the edit program using top-down testing with the emphasis on coding efficiency

Is the sequence of testing Figure 7–20 better than the one in Figure 7–15? Not necessarily. It was only presented to show you that there is more than one way to code and test the modules of a program from the top down. In the test plan in Figure 7–15, the programmer decided to test the most difficult modules first and the trivial modules last; in the test plan in Figure 7–20, the programmer took the opposite approach. Both plans are acceptable, so the approach you take will often depend on your own working style.

Incidentally, in case it isn't obvious, you have considerable flexibility when it comes to coding the first three divisions of a program on a top-down basis. Normally, you will code the entries in the Identification Division when you code the modules for the first phase of testing. But you don't have to code the entries in the Environment and Data Divisions until they are needed by the modules in the Procedure Division. For instance, you don't have to code the Data Division entries for the part-number table in the edit program until you code the modules that load the table. Similarly, you don't have to code the SELECT statement, FD statement, or record description for the part-number file until you code an I/O statement for the file.

Since you normally issue OPEN and CLOSE statements for all files in the top-level module of a program though, it is common to code the entries for all files and records in the first phase of testing, even if you don't operate on them in this phase. Otherwise, you have to omit them from your OPEN and CLOSE statements in module 000 until a later phase of testing. But this too is up to the individual programmer.

Discussion

The primary benefits of top-down testing are improved productivity, improved program quality (reliability), and improved programmer morale. As the size of a program increases, these benefits take on more and more significance. A manager, then, might insist that top-down testing be used for all nontrivial programs. A programmer should probably make top-down testing a way of life. It is simply a more enjoyable way to develop programs.

In an informal COBOL survey, though, only 20 percent of the shops said they used top-down testing for all programs. Another 30 percent said they used it "often." And about half of the shops said they didn't use it very much. So for those shops that don't use it frequently, top-down testing is another structured programming technique that can have a significant impact on the effectiveness of your development efforts.

Obviously, top-down testing is an idea that is not universally used, just as structured programming has only recently been widely accepted as a style of programming. "Cultural lag" is one factor that accounts for the slow adoption of worthy methods such as these. If you feel pressed, and claim that there is not enough time to practice and learn top-down testing, remember the old admonition, "If we don't have time to do it right, where will we get time to do it over?" That question has relevance to your learning process all the way.

Problem

Rather than have a specific problem for practice here, develop a top-down test plan for your new programming assignment. Compare it with those of your classmates.

Topic 4 **Issue: Acceptable Abbreviations and Verb Conventions**

Orientation

Programmers are instructed to use meaningful names, but often a meaningful name becomes too long and becomes counterproductive in terms of clarity of the source code. The solution to this dilemma is to eliminate unnecessary words, such as INPUT as in INVENTORY–INPUT–FILE, which then becomes INVENTORY–FILE, a name that is just as meaningful. If one worries about loss of clarity when leaving out INPUT, consider that the function of input will probably be clear from its use in the program. Thus, one basic guideline to shortening names is "leave out unnecessary words." The corollary to this rule is "choose words carefully and thoughtfully."

Abbreviations	Full Word	Alternates	Comment
			* = > not normally advisable
ACCUM	ACCUMULATE		
ADDR	ADDRESS		
AMT	AMOUNT		
BR	BRANCH		
CALC	CALCULATE	CALCULATION	
CUST	CUSTOMER		
DA	DAY		*
DEPT	DEPARTMENT		
DESC	DESCRIPTION	DESCR	
DIV	DIVISION	DIVIDE	
DT	DATE		*
EMPL	EMPLOYEE	EMP	
EOF	END OF FILE		
ERR	ERROR		
HI	HIGH		
HR	HOUR		
INS	INSURANCE		
INV	INVENTORY		
INX	INDEX		
LIST	LISTING		
LO	LOW		*
MAST	MASTER		
MO	MONTH		
MULT	MULTIPLY		
NO	NUMBER	NUM, NBR	
PROB	PROBLEM		
PROC	PROCESS		
QTY	QUANTITY		
QUAL	QUALITY		
REP	REPORT		
SLMN	SALESMAN		
ST	STATE		
STR	STREET		
SUB	SUBSCRIPT		
TAB	TABLE		
TERR	TERRITORY		
TRANS	TRANSACTION		
VAL	VALUE		
WORK	WORKED		leave off past tense (-ED's)
YR	YEAR		*

Figure 7–21
List of recommended abbreviations

Using Abbreviations

Of course, the elimination of words reduces the length of data names effectively. To further shorten data names without losing clarity, the programmer may choose acceptable, meaningful, and clear abbreviations. All of the adjectives preceding "abbreviations" in the previous sentence are there to emphasize that careful thought must go into abbreviating. In fact, abbreviations must be chosen more carefully than words, as poor abbreviations will be more confusing and obscure than poorly chosen words.

Here are a few guidelines for abbreviating:

1. Choose abbreviations that have commonly understood meanings. For example, ADDR for ADDRESS versus. AD or ADD (which could be misinterpreted to be an arithmetic function).

2. Do not attempt to abbreviate 3- or 4-letter words. Even abbreviating a 5-letter word is marginally productive. Cases where this rule may be ignored are those where abbreviating will achieve visual balance and the meaning will be clear from the context. For example, one might abbreviate BIRTH–MONTH, BIRTH–DAY, and BIRTH–YEAR as BIRTH–MO, BIRTH–DA, and BIRTH–YR. There are cases in which the abbreviation is nearly as acceptable and understood as the full word, as in using HI instead of HIGH.

3. Indications of tense (especially past tense) are good candidates for abbreviating. For example, HOURS–WORKED may be cut to HOURS–WORK.

4. Often plural indications may be cut to singular names. Thus, HOURS–WORK might be reduced to HR–WORK with no loss of meaning. Note that this example used three of the guidelines presented here.

Probably of more use to the student programmer will be Figure 7–21, which is a list of acceptable abbreviations. The instructor and students are encouraged to add to this list as they work with the concept.

Conventional Verb Meaning

Another factor that will help program clarity is to have a set of verbs with definitions which all programmers accept. That acceptance does not have to be worldwide, although that would be nice. The programmers who work for one company should at least be able to agree to definitions for verbs. Of course, this will normally take management coordination for a set of definitions to be decided on, accepted, and used.

Figure 7–22 is a list of verbs and their definitions which have a reasonable degree of acceptance in industry. The verbs in Figure 7–22 will be used as the official list for this text.

Input verbs	**Suggested meaning**
Accept	In interactive programs, physically accept the data from one field in a screen or from one full screen.
Get	Obtain an acceptable record or set of records. This can be used in a batch or an interactive program. In a batch program, subordinate modules might read a record, edit a record, and dispose of an invalid record. In an interactive program, subordinate modules might accept the data from a screen, edit it, and accept the operator's indication that the data is okay for processing.
Read	Physically read records from a file or database; count records if required.
Return	Sort language that means to make a record available in an output procedure; count records if required.
Output verbs	
Delete	Two related meanings: (1) Physically remove a record from a file or database; (2) Mark a record to indicate that it is deleted.
Display	In interactive programs, physically display the data in one field of a screen or in one full screen.
Print	Do everything associated with preparing a line to be printed on paper. This may include: (1) calling a module to read one or more related records that contain needed data for the print function, (2) formatting the output line or lines, (3) moving a proper spacing value into a space-control field before a line is printed, (4) calling a module to physically write a line, (5) resetting total fields to zero in preparation for the next group of records, and (6) setting up control or data fields in preparation for the next group of records.
Punch	Punch output cards; count records if required. This verb is becoming obsolete.
Put	Two meanings: (1) Format output record and call a module to physically write it on the output file or display it on an interactive screen; (2) Store an entry in a table; count entries if required.
Release	Sort language that means to make a record available in an input procedure; count records if required.

Figure 7-22
A verb list (part 1 of 2)

Output verbs (continued)	Suggested meaning
Rewrite	Physically write an output record in a file or database in the same location on a direct-access device from which the last record was read; count records if required.
Write	Physically write an output record on the output device; count records if required.
Processing verbs	
Accumulate	Develop totals by successive addition of intermediate totals.
Add	Add a record to a file. Subordinate modules might format the output record and physically write the record.
Apply	Apply a transaction to a record that is being updated or maintained without actually writing, rewriting, or deleting the record on the file. This verb is used in update and maintenance programs.
Calculate	Develop results by using any combination of arithmetic operations.
Change	Modify a record in a file. Subordinate modules might format the changed record and physically write the record.
Clear	In an interactive program, return data fields on a screen to blanks or zeros so the operator can enter the data for the next transaction.
Compare	Compare two fields or records.
Convert	Change something from one form to another.
Create	Develop a record, table, or file.
Determine	Find out; may include arithmetic computation.
Edit	Check one or more fields or records for validity.
Format	Prepare output records to be written, but this shouldn't include a call to a module that actually writes them.
Load	Read and store entries in a table; sort them if necessary.
Maintain	Add records to, change records in, or delete records from a master file based on maintenance transactions as opposed to operational transactions. (See **update**.)
Prepare	This is a general verb that should only be used in control modules. It means to prepare output by doing whatever needs to be done. Subordinate modules might read records, accumulate or calculate new data fields, and prepare the output.
Process	This is a general verb that should only be used in control modules. It means operate on the input fields to do whatever needs to be done. Subordinate modules might read records, accumulate or calculate new data fields, and prepare output. Avoid using this verb whenever you can use a more specific verb.
Produce	This is a general verb that should only be used in control modules. It means produce some output by doing whatever needs to be done. Subordinate modules might read records, accumulate or calculate new data fields, and produce output.
Search	Look for in a table or a file.
Sort	Arrange records in a specified order.
Store	Place entries in a table or fields in storage.
Update	The primary meaning is to change records in a master file based on data in an operational transaction as opposed to a maintenance transaction. Sometimes, however, an update function will require adding records to a file or deleting records from a file based on operational data. (See **maintain**.)
Validate	In an interactive program, check the user's sign-on codes to make sure he or she is a valid user of the system.
Verify	In an interactive program, ask the user to give a response that indicates whether or not he or she has sight-verified the data on the screen and is ready to release it for processing.

Figure 7-22
A verb list (part 2 of 2)

Discussion

All of the program examples used in this book have been designed to serve as examples of the principles of structured programming and style being taught. Also notice that the programs consistently have used the verbs and abbreviations discussed here. Use these lists as references when you write programs, and you will find that your time spent on frustrating questions and decisions will lessen. As you practice the concepts presented, you will develop programs in which you take more and more pride.

Part Four

Special Applications of COBOL

The previous pages have covered three major areas of COBOL programming: the basic COBOL command subset, the concepts and style of structured programming, and the logic required for multilevel control breaks. The last part of the text will be devoted to extending your knowledge in four major areas.

First, chapter 8 will present additional commands the professional programmer would use, including how to use subprograms. Second, chapter 9 presents table handling concepts and techniques. Third, chapter 10 introduces file concepts and covers COBOL for sequential files. Finally, the sort/merge feature of COBOL is presented in chapter 11.

It is not expected that you will cover all of these topics in one course. When the course is covered in one academic quarter, you will probably not get to this section. If the duration is one semester, you could get through most of the material on tables in chapter 9. The additional material has been presented so as to allow the student and instructor some flexibility in what is covered. After the first three parts have been learned, the four chapters of part IV could be studied in any sequence, as they are independent subjects.

Chapter 8 A Professional Subset of COBOL

This chapter expands the basic COBOL subset presented in previous chapters by introducing material that should prove helpful to the professional COBOL programmer. Some elements and techniques commonly used by professional programmers are discussed in topic 1. Although these elements do not involve any additional computing functions, they do make it possible for you to code more efficiently. Topic 2 introduces the subject of subprograms, technique for handling commonly used routines. Topic 3 provides some conceptual background to the execution of I/O operations. Finally, topic 4 discusses walkthrough, a cooperative design-evaluating technique which is gaining popularity.

Topic 1 COBOL Elements by Division

Orientation

Once you have an overall understanding of the COBOL language, it is relatively easy to learn additional COBOL elements. Remember, however, that these advanced elements will not allow you to do much more than you can do with the basic elements already presented. In most cases, they will simply allow you to code in a more efficient and less time-consuming manner.

Terminology

collating sequence	figurative constant	relation test
compound condition	flag	relational operator
condition name	linear nesting	

Objective

Apply the COBOL elements described in this topic to appropriate aspects of programming problems.

Identification Division Elements

```
IDENTIFICATION DIVISION.
PROGRAM-ID.  program-name.
[AUTHOR.  [comment-entry]  ...]
[INSTALLATION.  [comment-entry]  ...]
[DATE-WRITTEN.  [comment-entry]  ...]
[DATE-COMPILED.  [comment-entry]  ...]
[SECURITY.  [comment-entry]  ...]
```

Sample Identification Division (1974 standards)

```
 IDENTIFICATION DIVISION.
 PROGRAM-ID.     REVSSPL.
 AUTHOR.         PAUL NOLL  BILL GRAHAM.
 INSTALLATION.   PTT.
 DATE-WRITTEN.   JULY 10, 1986.
 DATE-COMPILED.
 SECURITY.       THIS PROGRAM MAY NOT BE SHOWN TO ANYONE OUTSIDE
                 THE BELL SYSTEM.
*REMARKS.        THIS PROGRAM PRODUCES THE DIVISION OF REVENUE
*                REPORTS FOR SPECIAL SERVICE PRIVATE LINES.
```

Figure 8–1
The Identification Division

Identification Division Elements

Although the division name and PROGRAM–ID are the only lines required in the Identification Division, other identifying information can be given using the formats shown in the first part of Figure 8–1. When these optional paragraphs are used, they must be written in the sequence shown. Then, when the program is compiled, the statements are listed on the program listing; however, no object code is created for them.

The second part of Figure 8–1 illustrates a listing of an Identification Division that uses the optional paragraphs. Most of the statements are self-explanatory; however, you may be wondering why the DATE–COMPILED statement isn't followed by a comment. When this paragraph is used, the compiler substitutes the current date for whatever comment the programmer has written, Thus, it is usually coded with no comment following. Since most compilers print the date-compiled on the top of the first page of each source listing, this paragraph isn't really necessary. However, most programmers include it in the Identification Division.

In the 1968 ANS standards, a REMARKS paragraph was another option in the Identification Division. However, this paragraph has been dropped in the 1974 standards. Under the 74 standards, you are supposed to use comment lines for any additional remarks needed in the Identification Division. That's why the REMARKS paragraph was coded as a comment in the second part of Figure 8–1.

A minor, but pleasant change to the Identification Division has been that many compilers now allow the word IDENTIFICATION to be abbreviated as ID. Since ID has achieved common acceptance as a substitute for the word "identification," there is no loss of meaning, especially in a place that is as standard as a division name.

Environment Division Elements

On many computers the CONFIGURATION SECTION is optional. This means that the Source and Object Computer information given in that section may be left out by those computer installations which have only one type of computer and feel that repeating that information in each program is not useful. The INPUT–OUTPUT SECTION is also optional. It would typically be left out when there are no SELECT statements to specify, as in a subprogram, for example. You will need to check what is allowed by your individual compiler.

The 198X ANSI COBOL standards have made the entire Environment Division optional. This means that in those cases where no files are specified the division may be omitted.

Data Division Elements

There are several Data Division language elements that will make your coding job easier. These elements will be explained, and then you will be shown how to sequence that Data Division code and how to use indentation effectively.

The REDEFINES clause

In some cases, one type of record may differ from another in only a minor way. For instance, two transaction records may differ depending on whether the transaction is an issue from or a receipt to inventory. In the first case, the reference number may be a six-column numeric field representing the invoice number; in the second case, it may be a six-column alphanumeric field representing the order number. To describe the same six columns in both ways, REDEFINES may be used as follows:

```
01  TRAN-RECORD.
    05  TR-TRAN-CODE      PIC X.
    05  TR-DATE           PIC 9(6).
    05  TR-ITEM-NO        PIC 9(6).
    05  TR-QUANTITY       PIC 9(5).
    05  TR-INVOICE-NO     PIC 9(6).
    05  TR-ORDER-NO       REDEFINES TR-INVOICE-NO
                          PIC X(6).
    05  FILLER            PIC X(56).
```

Thereafter in the program, the field that is recorded in columns 19–24 of the transaction records may be called TR–INVOICE–NO, in which case the data is treated as numeric, or TR–ORDER–NO, in which case the data is treated as alphanumeric.

If order number was a five-column numeric field in columns 19–23 and invoice number was a six-column numeric field in columns 19–24, REDEFINES could be used in this way:

```
05  TR-INVOICE-NO      PIC 9(6).
05  TR-ORDER-NO-X      REDEFINES TR-INVOICE-NO.
    10  TR-ORDER-NO    PIC 9(5).
    10  FILLER         PIC X.
```

Thus, REDEFINES can be used in a group item.

You may also redefine a data area more than once. For instance, suppose that in the second example above, there can be a third type of transaction: a return from a customer. In this case, columns 19–24 of the transaction record will contain alphanumeric data. Then, the field could be described like this:

```
05  TR-INVOICE-NO        PIC 9(6).
05  TR-ORDER-NO-X        REDEFINES TR-INVOICE-NO.
    10  TR-ORDER-NO      PIC 9(5).
    10  FILLER           PIC X.
05  TR-RETURN-NO         REDEFINES TR-INVOICE-NO
                         PIC X(6).
```

The format of the REDEFINE clause is this:

```
level-number data-name-1 REDEFINES data-name-2
```

When it is used, it must be the first clause following data-name-1 and must have the same level number as the data name it is redefining (date-name-2). Also, because two or more data names are assigned to the same storage area when REDEFINES is used, VALUE clauses cannot be used *after* the REDEFINES clause. As a result, the following code is illegal:

```
WORKING-STORAGE SECTION.
01  EXAMPLES.
    05  EXAMPLE-1      PIC X(4)     VALUE "ABCD".
    05  EXAMPLE-2      REDEFINES EXAMPLE-1
                       PIC 9(4)     VALUE 100.
```

(It is also illogical and impossible, since two different values cannot be stored in the same storage positions.) A VALUE clause can be used on the field that is being redefined, however. So the following code is legal:

```
WORKING-STORAGE SECTION.
01  EXAMPLES.
    05  EXAMPLE-1      PIC X(4)     VALUE "ABCD".
    05  EXAMPLE-2      REDEFINES EXAMPLE-1
                       PIC 9(4).
```

The preceding discussion shows how to use what is called "explicit redefinition." This means that the REDEFINES clause is actually used. Another type can be called "implicit redefinition," which means that the redefinition is implied, but the REDEFINES clause is not actually used. The following discussion of multiple record types is an example of implicit redefinition.

Multiple record types for one file

In some programs, a single file is made up of two or more different kinds of records. For example, an input file of inventory transactions may start with a record that contains the date on which the batch of records was entered into the computer system for processing and the number of records in the batch. This is normally called a batch control record. That lead record will be followed by the actual inventory transaction records.

Figure 8–2 illustrates coding that describes these two types of records. The FD statement is the same as it would be for any file. But it is followed by two record descriptions instead of one—one for the batch record and one for the transaction record. Notice that each type of record is described in the usual way, starting with an 01 level number. If a file consists of more than two record types, additional record descriptions follow the FD statement.

```
 DATA DIVISION.
*
 FILE SECTION.
*
 FD  INVENTORY-FILE
     LABEL RECORDS ARE STANDARD
     RECORD CONTAINS 80 CHARACTERS.
*
 01  BATCH-RECORD.
*
     05  RECORD-TYPE-CODE      PIC X.
     05  BC-DATE               PIC 9(6).
     05  BC-TOTAL              PIC 9(4).
     05  FILLER                PIC X(69).
*
 01  TRANSACTION-RECORD.
*
     05  RECORD-TYPE-CODE      PIC X.
     05  TR-DATE               PIC 9(6).
     05  TR-ITEM-NO            PIC 9(6).
     05  TR-QUANTITY           PIC 9(5).
     05  TR-REFERENCE-NO       PIC 9(6).
     05  FILLER                PIC X(56).
```

Figure 8–2
Multiple record types

The effect of describing multiple record types in this way is similar to that of the REDEFINES clause. In this case, one input area is used for all record types, but different data names are used to refer to various storage positions within that area. In other words, the input area is redefined by each set of record descriptions. Since the REDEFINES clause was not actually used, the redefinition is considered to be an implied one. After a program checks the record code (RECORD-TYPE-CODE in Figure 8–2) to determine what type of record has been read into the area, the statements of the Procedure Division can refer to the appropriate fields within the record.

Figurative constants

The COBOL words ZERO and SPACE are called *figurative constants*. The complete list of figurative constants for ANS COBOL is given in Figure 8–3. Except for the words ZERO, ZEROS, and ZEROES, these figurative constants act as if they were non-numeric literals. If, for example, a field is described as

```
05  FILLER    PIC X(5)     VALUE ALL "-".
```

the effect is the same as if it were described as

```
05  FILLER    PIC X(5)     VALUE "-----".
```

Similarly,

```
05  QUOTE-EXAMPLE     PIC X     VALUE QUOTE.
```

describes a field of one byte that contains one quotation mark. Because quotation marks are used to enclose non-numeric literals in COBOL, using the word QUOTE is the only way you can store a quotation mark.

The figurative constants HIGH–VALUE and LOW–VALUE represent the highest and lowest values in a computer's collating sequence. This means that a field that is given a value of HIGH–VALUE contains the highest possible value that can be stored in a field of that size. Similarly, a field with a value of LOW–VALUE is given the lowest possible value that can be stored in a field

Constant	Represents
ZERO ZEROS ZEROES	One or more zeros
SPACE SPACES	One or more blanks (spaces)
ALL "character"	One or more occurrences of the character within quotation marks
QUOTE QUOTES	One or more occurrences of the quotation mark
HIGH-VALUE HIGH-VALUES	One or more occurrences of the highest value that can be placed in a storage position of a specific computer
LOW-VALUE LOW-VALUES	One or more occurrences of the lowest value that can be placed in a storage position of a specific computer

Figure 8–3
Figurative constants

of that size. In general, these figurative constants are used when you want to force an unequal comparison (HIGH–VALUE will never be less than another value, and LOW–VALUE will never be more). You saw this used in the module documentation for the report program in Figure 7–7.

Although you can use either the singular or plural forms of figurative constants, it is suggested that you stick to the singular forms (SPACE, ZERO, etc.). Because both the singular and plural forms mean the same thing, the plurals are unnecessary. And the plural forms allow a greater chance of misspelling, with resulting diagnostics.

Indentation

Indentation should be used in the Data Division to show the structure of related data items and to make the code easier to read, as shown in Figure 8–2. As you can see, there should always be two spaces between the level number and the data name, and each successive level should be indented four spaces from the preceding level. As mentioned previously, readability of the program is aided by aligning the various Data Division clauses, such as PICTURE and VALUE. This means beginning all PICTURE clauses in the same position, say 32 or 36, and all VALUE clauses in 48 or 52.

The sequence of elements

To make it easy to locate file or data descriptions in the Data Division, standard coding sequences should be used. For example, the FD statements in the File Section should be coded in the same sequence as the SELECT statements in the Environment Division. Then, the SELECT statements are a directory for finding the FD statements.

Furthermore, the record descriptions in the Working–Storage Section should be coded in the same sequence each time. For instance, you might use a standard sequence like this: (1) switches, (2) flags, (3) work fields, (4) control fields, (5) print fields like LINE–COUNT and SPACE–CONTROL, (6) counters, (7) total fields, (8) subscripts, (9) indexes, (10) tables, (11) input or output record descriptions in the same order as the related files are listed in the SELECT statements. (Numbers 8, 9, and 10 all have to do with repetitive processing, so don't worry about them for now.) When you code the working-storage areas for lines that are associated with print files, you can code them in the same sequence that they are shown on the print chart: (1) heading lines, (2) body lines, and (3) total lines. If you use standard coding sequences like these, it is easier for you to locate code as you go from one of your programs to another.

Procedure Division Elements

This section presents some new Procedure Division elements as well as refinements of some of the statements with which you are already familiar. Also discussed is how to use indentations effectively in the Procedure Division.

Figurative constants

Figurative constants may be used in the Procedure Division as well as in the Data Division. These COBOL words have the same meaning in either division. The following are some examples of their use in the Procedure Division:

```
1.  MOVE ZERO TO CUSTOMER-TOTAL.
2.  MOVE ALL "*" TO PRINT-AREA.
3.  MOVE HIGH-VALUE TO TR-CUSTOMER-NO.
```

In example 1, the value of CUSTOMER–TOTAL is set to zero. In example 2, one asterisk is moved to each storage position in PRINT–AREA. And in example 3, the highest value possible in the computer's collating sequence is moved to TR–CUSTOMER–NO.

The READ INTO option

The READ INTO option of the READ statement reads a record and moves it into an area of working storage. It is thus the equivalent of a READ statement followed by a MOVE. Its format is this:

```
READ file-name RECORD INTO data-name
    AT END imperative-statement.
```

When it is used, the individual fields of the input record are normally defined in the Working–Storage Section rather than in the File Section of the Data Division. This is illustrated in Figure 8–4.

The INTO clause of the READ statement can also specify an output area of another file. Then, input data can be moved directly into an output area by the READ statement. This is often done when processing tape or disk files.

The main reason for using the INTO option is that the data from the last record in a file is available after the AT END clause for that file has been executed. This is often valuable when preparing summary reports or when processing tape or disk files. In contrast, when the data for the last input record hasn't been moved to working storage, it is not available to the program after the end-of-file has been reached. In general, then, you should use the INTO option and process input records in the Working–Storage Section.

The WRITE FROM option

The WRITE FROM option of the WRITE statement is comparable to the READ INTO option of the READ statement. Its format is this:

```
WRITE record-name FROM data-name

[ { BEFORE }  ADVANCING  { integer LINES   } ]
[ { AFTER  }             { data-name LINES } ]
[                        { mnemonic-name   } ]
```

```
 DATA DIVISION
*
 FILE SECTION.
*
 FD  SALES-TRANSACTION-FILE
     LABEL RECORDS ARE STANDARD
     RECORD CONTAINS 100 CHARACTERS
*
 01  SALES-TRANS-AREA          PIC X(100).
          .
          .
*
 WORKING-STORAGE SECTION.
          .
          .
*
 01  SALES-TRANS-REC.
     05  ST-ITEM-CODE          PIC X(05).
     05  ST-REFERENCE-NO       PIC X(06).
          .
          .
*
PROCEDURE DIVISION.
*
          .
          .
     READ SALES-TRANSACTION-FILE INTO SALES-TRANS-REC
         AT END
             MOVE 'Y'          TO SALES-FILE-EOF-SW.
          .
          .
```

Figure 8–4
The READ INTO statement

If the FROM option is used, an output record is moved from an area in working storage to an output area described in the File Section, and then it is printed.

The FROM option is useful when a file has only one record format and the record is described and developed in working storage. Then, the WRITE FROM statement can be used to move the record into the output area and to write it. When a file consists of records with more than one record format, however, using the FROM option results in more than one WRITE statement for the file (one for each record format). And this conflicts with our structured programming goal of one WRITE statement per file. So if you have a file consisting of more than one record format (most print files are that way), don't use the FROM option of the WRITE statement.

Getting the current date

In general, whenever an operating system is used, the current date is stored somewhere in the supervisor area of storage at the start of the day's processing. This date is commonly printing in report headings and on other documents such as invoices or payroll checks.

The ACCEPT statement provides for getting the date, day, or time from the supervisor area. It has this format:

```
                          { DATE }
ACCEPT data-name FROM     { DAY  }
                          { TIME }
```

When executed, date, day, or time is moved to a field described in the user's program. The receiving field can be numeric or numeric edited.

```
The ACCEPT statement:

    WORKING-STORAGE SECTION.
        .
        .
   *
    01  DATE-FIELDS.
   *
        05  PRESENT-DATE.
            10  PD-YEAR         PIC 99.
            10  PD-MONTH        PIC 99.
            10  PD-DAY          PIC 99.
        05  PRESENT-DAY.
            10  FILLER          PIC XX.
            10  PD-DAY-NO       PIC 999.
        05  EDITED-DATE.
            10  ED-MONTH        PIC 99.
            10  FILLER          PIC X        VALUE "/".
            10  ED-DAY          PIC 99.
            10  FILLER          PIC X        VALUE "/".
            10  ED-YEAR         PIC 99.
        .
        .
    PROCEDURE DIVISION.
        .
        .
   *
    100-GET-CURRENT-DATE.
   *
        ACCEPT PRESENT-DATE FROM DATE.
        MOVE PD-MONTH TO ED-MONTH.
        MOVE PD-DAY   TO ED-DAY.
        MOVE PD-YEAR  TO ED-YEAR.
        ACCEPT PRESENT-DAY FROM DAY.
        .
        .
```

Figure 8–5
Getting the current date using the ACCEPT statement

The form of the standard DATE field is an unedited YYMMDD (two-digit year, month, and day), so July 1, 1986 is stored as 860701. Similarly, the form of the standard DAY field is YYDDD, where DDD represents three digits that indicate what number day in the year it is. Thus, July 1, 1986 is stored as 86182 (the 182nd day of 1986). Figure 8–5 illustrates how these fields can be moved into the Working–Storage Section of a user's program. In the example, the date is edited after it is moved, so EDITED–DATE will print July 1, 1986 as 7/01/86.

Although TIME isn't used very often, its standard form is HHMMSSHH (two-digit hours, minutes, seconds, and hundredths of seconds). This assumes a 24-hour clock, so 2:00 P.M. is hour 14. As a result, 2:41 P.M. is stored as 14410000. The minimum value of TIME is 00000000; the maximum is 23595999.

The COMPUTE statement

The format of the COMPUTE statement is this:

```
COMPUTE data-name [ROUNDED] = arithmetic-expression
    [ON SIZE ERROR statement-1 ...]
```

It can be used to express arithmetic calculations in a form that is reasonably close to normal arithmetic notation. For example,

```
COMPUTE NET-PAY ROUNDED =
    EM-HOURS * EM-RATE - TOTAL-DEDUCTIONS
```

can be used to indicate that the contents of the field named EM–HOURS should be multiplied (*) by the contents of the field named EM–RATE and the contents of the field named TOTAL–DEDUCTIONS should be subtracted (–) from the product. The result should be rounded and placed in the field named NET–PAY.

To form an arithmetic expression in COBOL, the following symbols can be used:

Symbol	Meaning
+	Addition
–	Subtraction
*	Multiplication
/	Division
**	Exponentiation

Since exponentiation means "raising to the power of," the COBOL expression X**2 is equivalent to the arithmetic expression X^2. And the COBOL expression X**.5 is equivalent to the arithmetic expression $X^{1/2}$, or $\sqrt{X}$ (the square root of X). Exponentiation is a slow process in COBOL, though, so whenever practical, you should use multiplication instead. For example, X**2 would execute more quickly if you coded it as X*X. When the arithmetic symbols are used to indicate an operation, they must be preceded and followed by one or more spaces.

Sequence of operations

When a series of arithmetic operations is expressed in a single COMPUTE statement, it is important to know the order in which the operations will be executed.

(Before continuing, a caution must be given regarding the data names used in the discussion of the COMPUTE statement. The data names used are single-character names. These short, meaningless names are used to facilitate the discussion of the COMPUTE statement. However, such choices are obvious violations of the structured style guidelines for data names and should never be used in an actual COBOL program.)

To continue, the expression H * R – D, for example, can have different values depending on whether the multiplication or the subtraction is done first. If H = 40, R = 2, and D = 5.00, the value of the expression is 75.00 if the multiplication is done first or – 120.00 if the subtraction is done first (2 – 5.00 = – 3.00; – 3.00 * 40 = – 120).

In COBOL, the order in which arithmetic operations are executed is this: (1) exponentiation, (2) multiplication and division, (3) addition and subtraction. If the same type of operation is used more than once in an expression, the sequence is from left to right for each type. For example, in the statement

```
COMPUTE N = H * R - D
```

multiplication takes place first. In the expression A * B + C * D, first A and B are multiplied, then C and D are multiplied, and then the two products are added together to give the final result.

Sometimes an expression is so complex that it's hard to keep track of which part is evaluated first by the compiler. In such a case, you should use parentheses to indicate the sequence in which the operations will be done. Operations within parentheses are performed before operations outside parentheses. When there are parentheses within parentheses, the operations in the innermost set of parentheses are performed first. Thus, in the expression

```
A + B ** 3 / C - D * E * F
```

parentheses would be used as follows:

```
A + ((B * * 3 ) / C) - (D * E * F)
```

As you can see, this reflects the compiler's sequence of evaluation: exponentiation will be done first, followed by multiplication and division from left to right, and finally addition and subtraction from left to right.

Now suppose that you want to add two values and then cube the sum. How do you make the compiler change its normal sequence of evaluation? Again, you use parentheses. And again, whatever is in the innermost set of parentheses will be evaluated first, followed by the next set of parentheses, and so on. To illustrate, suppose the expression above were written like this:

```
((A + B) * * 3) / ((C - D) * E) * F
```

In this case, the expressions (A + B) and (C − D) would be evaluated first; then the cube of (A + B) would be taken and (C − D) would be multiplied by E; next the result of (A + B) * * 3) would be divided by the result of ((C − D) * E); and finally, the quotient would be multiplied by F. In short, parentheses can dictate as well as clarify the order in which an expression will be evaluated. So use them frequently to improve the clarity of your COMPUTE statements.

Result fields

Since intermediate fields in a COMPUTE statement are the same size as the final result field and since the ON SIZE ERROR clause applies only to final results, errors will occur if intermediate results are larger than the final result field. In the statement

```
COMPUTE RESULT = A * B / C
    ON SIZE ERROR
        PERFORM 170-PRINT-ERROR-MESSAGE.
```

an error will result if A * B is greater than can be stored in the final result field—even if A * B / C is not larger than the result field. As a result, it is the programmer's responsibility to make the result field large enough for any intermediate results. The result field may be described as a numeric item of any USAGE or as a numeric edited item. If it is a numeric edited item, the result is edited as it is moved to this field.

In the 1974 ANS specifications, a minor change was made to the format of the COMPUTE statement. Where formerly only one result field was allowable, a series of result fields is now acceptable. For instance,

```
COMPUTE FIELD-A FIELD-B ROUNDED =
    1.23 * FIELD-X + (FIELD-Y - FIELD-Z)
```

is acceptable under the revised specifications. Here, the result of the arithmetic expression is moved to FIELD–A and FIELD–B, but only FIELD–B is rounded. A statement such as this would be useful for calculating something like interest where you need a rounded result for the current amount as well as an unrounded result for ongoing calculations.

Advanced IF statements

You are already familiar with simple IF statements and with IF statements that have ELSE clauses. You are also familiar with nested IF statements. Now, you will get additional information about the operation and coding of the IF statement.

Evaluating relation tests

Perhaps the most important yet most difficult aspect of the IF statement is determining when a condition is true or false. In a simple *relation test* between two numeric fields—such as IF HOURS—WORKED IS LESS THAN FORTY—the fields are evaluated based on their numeric value; the size or USAGE of the fields does not affect the results. Thus, 30.5 is less than 40 and 58 is greater than 40.00.

When a relation test compares alphanumeric data, the evaluation is made in a different way. The fields are evaluated character by character, from left to right. Since the computer considers A to have the least value and Z to have the greatest, it's fairly easy to compare purely alphabetic fields—for example, JONES comes before (IS LESS THAN) THOMAS. However, it is hard to say whether X–12–13 is less than or greater than X1213. In fact, it depends on the *collating sequence* of a computer and varies by computer model. So you will have to find out what collating sequence is used on your system. In the EBCDIC code, the hypen (–) comes before the digits in the collating sequence, so X–12–13 is less than X1213.

One thing to remember when coding relation tests is to compare numeric items with numeric items and non-numeric with non-numeric items. It is illegal to compare an alphabetic item with a numeric item, and although an alphanumeric item can be compared with a numeric item of DISPLAY usage, the comparison takes place based on collating sequence instead of on the numeric value of the fields. For object program efficiency, numeric items that are compared should have the same number of decimal places. And alphanumeric items should be the same size.

A second point to remember has to do with using the word NOT in a less-than or greater-than condition. For example, this condition

```
FIELD-A NOT GREATER THAN FIELD-B
```

will be true if FIELD–A is less than or *equal to* FIELD–B. It is *not* the same as coding.

```
FIELD-A LESS THAN FIELD-B
```

or

```
FIELD-B GREATER THAN FIELD-A
```

Using relational symbols

Whenever you use the *relational operators* LESS THAN, EQUAL TO, and GREATER THAN in relation tests, you can code them in a couple of different ways. You can use the shorter forms LESS, EQUAL, and GREATER. Or you can use the symbols <, =, and >. The following are examples of the second usage:

```
1.  IF  CR-CUST-ORDER > 200
         PERFORM 430-LIST-SIZE-ERROR.
2.  IF  TR-CODE-2 = "C"
         PERFORM 180-CALCULATE-CALIF-TAX.
```

Before you start using the "less than" and "greater than" symbols, though, check and make sure they're available on your printer. Since some print chains don't have these symbols. A < B can come out looking like A (B on your source listing. Naturally, this can be confusing. So check the printer before you use the symbols.

Using arithmetic expressions

Arithmetic expressions such as those in COMPUTE statements may also be used in relation tests. Some examples follow:

```
1.  IF X + Y EQUAL TO 200
        PERFORM 430-LIST-SIZE-ERROR.
2.  IF .5 * G / T ** 2 NOT LESS THAN 4
        MOVE "Y" TO INVALID-RESULT-SW
        PERFORM 140-PROCESS-INVALID-RESULT
    ELSE
        PERFORM 130-CALCULATE-INT-PAYMENT.
```

If necessary, parentheses can be used within the expression to dictate the order of operations. And they should always be used if they make the expression easier to understand.

In general, though, you should avoid using arithmetic expressions in relation tests. Instead, you should do the calculation in one statement and the relation test in a second statement. For instance, example 2 above can be coded like this:

```
COMPUTE RESULT = .5 * G / T ** 2.
IF RESULT NOT LESS THAN 4
    MOVE "Y" TO INVALID-RESULT-SW
    PERFORM 140-PROCESS-INVALID-RESULT
ELSE
    PERFORM 130-CALCULATE-INT-PAYMENT.
```

Then, if the result of the calculation is needed in another part of the program, you don't have to repeat the calculation. You can simply reference the field named RESULT because it already contains the answer.

Again, remember that field names such as G, T, FIELD–A, FIELD–B, etc., are used only for generality and to shorten the examples, but should never be used in an actual COBOL program.

Sign tests

Although relation tests are the most common, sign tests can also be used in COBOL. The format for a sign test is this:

```
{data-name            }  IS [NOT]  { POSITIVE }
{arithmetic-expression}            { ZERO     }
                                   { NEGATIVE }
```

It simply tests whether a numeric item is greater than, equal to, or less than zero. Zero is considered neither positive nor negative. Here are some examples:

```
1. IF FIELD-1 IS POSITIVE
        PERFORM 210-CALCULATE-PAY-RATE.
2. IF FIELD-2 IS NEGATIVE
        PERFORM 350-PRINT-TOTAL-LINE-INVEST.
```

Thus, whenever FIELD–1 and FIELD–2 contain the value zero, the 210 and 350 modules will not be executed since the sign test will be considered to be false. The sign test can only be used on numeric data items.

Class tests

Besides sign and relation tests, you can also code class tests. The class test format is this:

```
data-name IS [NOT] { NUMERIC    }
                   { ALPHABETIC }
```

The alphabetic form of this test can be performed on an alphabetic or alphanumeric field. If the field consists entirely of the letters A through Z and blanks (SPACE), the field is considered to be alphabetic.

The numeric test can be performed on an elementary item that is an alphanumeric or numeric field with DISPLAY usage. An alphanumeric field is considered numeric if all bytes consist of the digits 0 through 9. Likewise, an *unsigned* numeric field is considered numeric if it contains only digits and does not contain a sign. In a *signed* numeric field, however, the rightmost byte carries the sign of the field. As a result, a field like this is considered numeric if it contains all digits with a valid sign in the rightmost byte.

Compound conditions

A *compound condition* is created by using the words AND and OR, as in these examples:

```
1. IF ER-HOURS IS NUMERIC AND ER-RATE IS NUMERIC
        PERFORM 120-CALCULATE-EMPLOYEE-PAY.
2. IF AP-AGE LESS THAN 18 OR AP-CODE-A EQUAL TO 1
        PERFORM 180-PRINT-ERROR-MESSAGE
   ELSE
        PERFORM 130-LOOKUP-INSURANCE-RATE.
```

In these statements, AND means "both" and OR means "either or both." In other words, when using AND, both conditions must be true before the compound condition is true; when using OR, the compound condition is true if either condition or both conditions are true. In example 1, both ER–HOURS and ER–RATE must be numeric for the program to perform 120– CALCULATE–EMPLOYEE–PAY. In example 2, the program will perform 180–PRINT–ERROR–MESSAGE if AP–AGE is less than 18, if AP–CODE–A is equal to 1, or if AP–AGE is less than 18 and AP–CODE–A is equal to 1.

When more than two conditions are linked in a compound condition, the NOT conditions are evaluated first, followed by the AND conditions and then the OR conditions. Because compound conditions can be very confusing,

```
General form:

    IF       condition-1
          OR condition-2
         AND condition-3
         statement-group-1
     ELSE
         statement-group-2.

Example:

     IF     (CM-TIMES-DUNNED LESS THAN 4
         AND CM-CUST-YEARS GREATER THAN 2)
         AND CM-OVER-60-BAL-OWED EQUAL TO ZERO
         PERFORM 550-PREPARE-SHIPPING-ORDER
     ELSE
         IF      (CM-TIMES-DUNNED GREATER THAN 3
              OR CM-CUST-YEARS NOT GREATER THAN 2)
             AND CM-OVER-60-BAL-OWED GREATER THAN ZERO
                 PERFORM 560-PRINT-REFUSE-CREDIT
         ELSE
             PERFORM 570-PRINT-MANAGER-DECISION.
```

Figure 8–6
Indentation in compound conditions

however, parentheses should be used to make these statements more understandable. For example,

```
A GREATER THAN B OR A EQUAL TO C AND D NOT POSITIVE
```

is confusing, while

```
   (A GREATER THAN B)
OR (A EQUAL TO C AND D NOT POSITIVE)
```

is less confusing. As in arithmetic expressions, conditions within parentheses are evaluated first. And parentheses can be used to override the compiler's normal sequence of evaluation.

Although COBOL allows compound conditions of great complexity, it is best to keep them relatively simple. Then programming errors are less likely to occur and program changes can be made more easily. Remember that the goal of structured COBOL is program clarity.

As an aid to clarity, indentation should be used for each of the conditions within a compound condition. For instance, Figure 8–6 illustrates a two-level nested IF statement with compound conditions at both levels. Because of the use of indentation and parentheses, however, the statement can be understood with relative ease.

Linear nesting

In chapter 3, you saw how to use indentation to make nested IF statements easy to read and understand. However, if a string of nested IF statements merely checks a single field for a succession of independent values, the IF statements can be written without indentation as shown in Figure 8–7. As you can see, this code performs one module if the activity code is equal to 1, performs another module if it is equal to 2, and so on for seven more values. If the activity code isn't equal to a value from 1 to 9, some default code is executed. You will probably agree that this code is at least as clear as it would be with indentation.

```
PROCEDURE DIVISION
       .
       .
   IF TR-ACTIVITY-CODE EQUAL TO 1
       PERFORM 510-DO-CODE-1-FUNCTION
   ELSE IF TR-ACTIVITY-CODE EQUAL TO 2
       PERFORM 510-DO-CODE-2-FUNCTION
   ELSE IF TR-ACTIVITY-CODE EQUAL TO 3
       PERFORM 510-DO-CODE-3-FUNCTION
   ELSE IF TR-ACTIVITY-CODE EQUAL TO 4
       PERFORM 510-DO-CODE-4-FUNCTION
   ELSE IF TR-ACTIVITY-CODE EQUAL TO 5
       PERFORM 510-DO-CODE-5-FUNCTION
   ELSE IF TR-ACTIVITY-CODE EQUAL TO 6
       PERFORM 510-DO-CODE-6-FUNCTION
   ELSE IF TR-ACTIVITY-CODE EQUAL TO 7
       PERFORM 510-DO-CODE-7-FUNCTION
   ELSE IF TR-ACTIVITY-CODE EQUAL TO 8
       PERFORM 510-DO-CODE-8-FUNCTION
   ELSE IF TR-ACTIVITY-CODE EQUAL TO 9
       PERFORM 510-DO-CODE-9-FUNCTION
   ELSE
       MOVE 'Y'            TO INVALID-ACTIVITY-CODE-SW.
```

Figure 8–7
Nested IF statements in linear form

Figure 8–7 is an example of the "case structure" of the IF test where a single data element is being tested for a series of codes or values. The method shown in Figure 8–7, where the ELSE is immediately followed by the IF on the same line, should only be used for the case structure. This method of coding IF statements is sometimes also referred to as *linear nesting* since the IF conditions are tested one right after the other. But note that you should only use linear nesting when a single item is being tested and when each IF statement is contained in the ELSE clause of the IF statement that precedes it. Furthermore, you shouldn't use linear nesting within another IF nest. In other words, the use of linear nesting must be limited as illustrated in this book or it doesn't work toward the goal of clarity.

Whenever several fields are being tested in a nested situation, each ELSE should be on a line by itself, and following IF should be indented below the ELSE on the following line.

Indentation

You have already seen how indentation should be used to clarify the intent of nested IF statements, statements with conditional clauses, and statements with compound conditions. Figure 8–8 shows in more detail how indentation should be used throughout the Procedure Division to show the relationships between the phrases and clauses within a statement.

In general, start the first word of each Procedure Division statement in column 12 of the coding form. If a statement is too long for one coding line, break it up at the start of a clause or phrase and indent the succeeding lines four spaces. In statements like the OPEN, CLOSE, and MOVE (examples 1, 2, and 3), align similar elements like file and data names. Indent conditional clauses, such as AT END and ON SIZE ERROR, by four spaces. If one or more statements are part of the conditional clause of another statement, indent the conditional statements four spaces from their conditional clause. For instance, the two statements following the AT END condition in example 4 of Figure 8–8 are indented four more spaces to show they're part of the AT END condition.

Example 1: **OPEN** statement

```
OPEN INPUT  TRANSACTION-FILE
            OLD-MASTER-FILE
     OUTPUT NEW-MASTER-FILE
            REPORT-FILE
            ERROR-FILE.
```

Example 2: **CLOSE** statement

```
CLOSE   TRANSACTION-FILE
        OLD-MASTER-FILE
        NEW-MASTER-FILE
        REPORT-FILE
        ERROR-FILE.
```

Example 3: **MOVE** statement

```
MOVE SPACE                 TO PR-RECORD.
MOVE TP-ITEM-NO            TO PR-ITEM-NO.
MOVE TP-ITEM-DESC          TO PR-ITEM-DESC.
```

Example 4: **READ** statement

```
READ TRANSACTION-FILE INTO TR-TRANSACTION-REC
    AT END
        MOVE 'Y'           TO TRANS-FILE-EOF-SW
        MOVE HIGH-VALUE    TO TR-ITEM-NO.
```

Example 5: **WRITE** statement

```
WRITE PR-OUTPUT-AREA
    AFTER ADVANCING SPACE-CONTROL LINES.
```

Example 6: **PERFORM - UNTIL** statement

```
PERFORM 100-BUILD-ITEM-CODE-TABLE
    UNTIL TABLE-BUILD-COMPLETE.
```

Example 7: **Arithmetic with GIVING clause**

```
MULTIPLY TR-QUANTITY-SOLD BY TR-RETAIL-PRICE
    GIVING IL-SALES-AMOUNT
    ON SIZE ERROR
        PERFORM 360-PRINT-INVALID-TRANS.
```

Example 8: IF statement (short nested list - OR relation)

```
IF VOLUME-CUSTOMER
    MOVE VOLUME-CUST-RATE             TO DISCOUNT-PERCENT
ELSE
    IF PREFERRED-CUSTOMER
        MOVE PREF-CUST-RATE           TO DISCOUNT-PERCENT
    ELSE
        MOVE ZERO                     TO DISCOUNT-PERCENT.
```

Example 9: IF statement (long nested list - case structure)

```
IF CR-CUST-CODE EQUAL 1
    MOVE .050                         TO DISCOUNT-PERCENT
ELSE IF CR-CUST-CODE EQUAL 2
    MOVE .040                         TO DISCOUNT-PERCENT
        .
        .
```

Figure 8–8
Proper use of indentation and alignment in the Procedure Division (part 1 of 2)

```
ELSE IF CR-CUST-CODE EQUAL 5
    MOVE .010                           TO DISCOUNT-PERCENT
ELSE
    MOVE .000                           TO DISCOUNT-PERCENT.
```

Example 10: IF statement (AND relation)

```
IF FEMALE-EMPLOYEE
    IF EF-EXPERIENCE-YEARS GREATER THAN 5
        IF     (EF-JOB-CATEGORY EQUAL 5
            OR  EF-JOB-CATEGORY EQUAL 10)
            PERFORM 360-PRINT-SELECTED-EMPL.
```

Figure 8–8
Proper use of indentation and alignment in the Procedure Division (part 2 of 2)

In general, nested IF statements are indented by four spaces for each level as shown in example 8 in Figure 8–8. However, if several levels of nesting are used, you may run out of coding space. In this case, you can indent by only two spaces for each level. Furthermore, related IF and ELSE clauses should be aligned, unless you're using a linear nest as in example 9. In either case, the imperative statements that are to be executed if the condition is met are indented.

Since you will undoubtedly encounter statements that are not covered by this simple set of rules, always remember that the goal of indentation is clarity. If you encounter a special situation, code it in the way that is most understandable and most consistent with the rest of your code.

Problems

1. An investment-listing program is shown in Figure 4–11. Modify this program using the ACCEPT statement so that a new first heading line including the current date will print as follows:

   ```
   INVESTMENT LISTING OF XX/XX/XX
   ```

   Add whatever descriptions are needed to the Working-Storage Section, and rewrite the paragraph named 140–PRINT–REPORT–HEADING entirely. Add the ACCEPT statement to paragraph 000–PRODUCE–INVESTMENT–LISTING, not to module 140. (It's more efficient to execute the statement only once rather than each time headings are printed.) The second heading line should print two lines after the first one.

2. Code one COMPUTE statement for each of the following calculations. Use the ROUNDED option as you think necessary.

   a. Gross profit (GROSS–PROFIT) should be calculated by multiplying sales (IR–QTY) by unit cost (IR–UNIT–COST) and subtracting it from sales multiplied by unit price (IR–UNIT–PRICE).

   b. Calculate the new principal on an investment after one compounding period using this formula:

$$\text{New-Principal} = \text{Old-Principal}\left(1 + \frac{\text{Interest-Rate}}{\text{Times-Compounded}}\right)$$

3. Figure 8–9 shows a portion of the File Section of the Data Division for a program that edits input records to make sure they contain valid data. If the transaction code (IT–TRAN–CODE) is a 1, the input record represents an

```
 DATA DIVISION.
*
 FILE SECTION.
*
 FD  INVENTORY-TRANSACTION-FILE
     LABEL RECORDS ARE STANDARD
     RECORD CONTAINS 80 CHARACTERS.
*
 01  INV-TRANS-RECORD.
     05  IT-RECORD-CODE             PIC X(01).
     05  IT-TRAN-CODE               PIC X(01).
         88  IT-ITEM-ISSUED                         VALUE '1'.
         88  IT-ITEM-RECEIVED                       VALUE '2'.
         88  VALID-TRAN-CODE                        VALUE '1' '2'.
     05  IT-CUST-NO                 PIC 9(06).
     05  FILLER                     REDEFINES IT-CUST-NO.
         10  IT-VENDOR-NO           PIC 9(05).
         10  IT-BLANK               PIC X(01).
     05  IT-ITEM-NO                 PIC X(05).
     05  IT-QUANTITY                PIC 9(05).
     05  IT-UNIT-PRICE              PIC 9(03)V99.
     05  FILLER                     PIC X(57).
*
```

Figure 8–9
Use of REDEFINES in a record description

issue transaction, and columns 3–8 of the record should contain a six-digit positive numeric customer number. If IT–TRAN–CODE is a 2, the input record represents a receipt transaction, and columns 3–7 should contain a five-digit positive numeric vendor number followed in column 8 by a blank.

In the Procedure Division, write a procedure that checks the transaction code of each input record and then performs procedures that check columns 3–8 for valid data. If the data is not valid, you should move an N into VALID–TRANSACTION–SW and your program should not check the remaining fields in the record. If the transaction code is neither a 1 or 2, the program should move N into VALID–TRANSACTION–SW and end the editing function. Assume that the portion of the VTOC that represents the editing procedure looks like this:

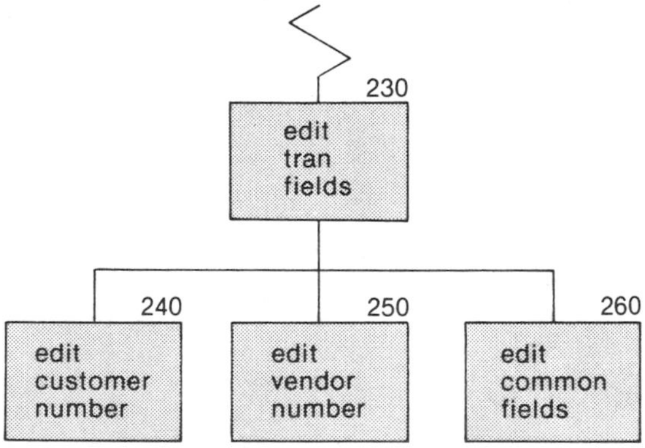
230
edit tran fields
240
edit customer number
250
edit vendor number
260
edit common fields

Now code modules 230, 240, and 250.

Notice two special facets of the record description in Figure 8–9. The first is the condition name VALID–TRAN–CODE. It has two values which will enable the name to be used to make a single test when you want to ensure that the code is valid, but are not concerned with identifying which type of transaction is represented. The second facet is the 05 level

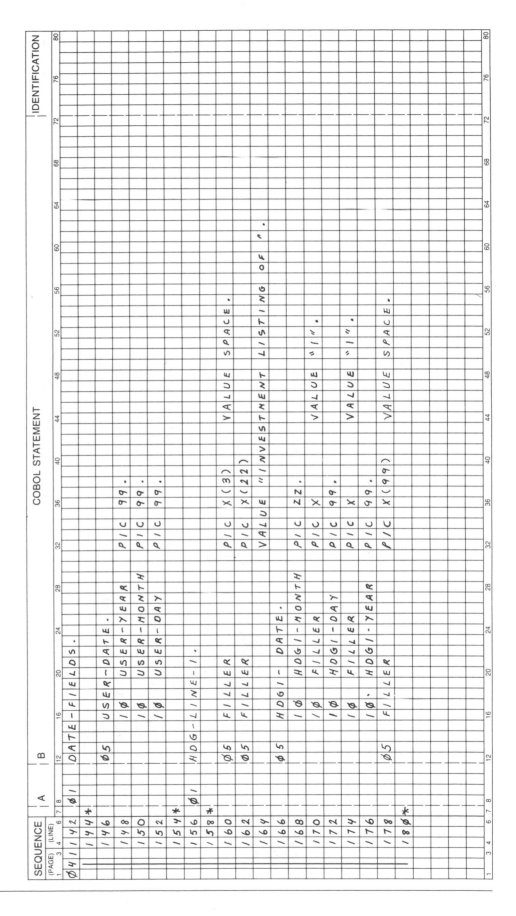

Figure 8–10
Modifications to the investment-listing program using the ACCEPT statement
(part 1 of 2)

```
Ø41142 Ø1  DATE-FIELDS.
   144*
   146     Ø5  USER-DATE.
   148         1Ø  USER-YEAR     PIC 99.
   150         1Ø  USER-MONTH    PIC 99.
   152         1Ø  USER-DAY      PIC 99.
   154*
   156 Ø1  HDG-LINE-1.
   158*
   160     Ø5  FILLER            PIC X(3)   VALUE SPACE.
   162     Ø5  FILLER            PIC X(22)
   164                           VALUE "INVESTMENT LISTING OF ".
   166     Ø5  HDG1- DATE.
   168         1Ø  HDG1-MONTH    PIC ZZ.
   170         1Ø  FILLER        PIC X      VALUE "/".
   172         1Ø  HDG1-DAY      PIC 99.
   174         1Ø  FILLER        PIC X      VALUE "/".
   176         1Ø. HDG1-YEAR     PIC 99.
   178     Ø5  FILLER            PIC X(99)  VALUE SPACE.
   18Ø*
```

```
ØØ6Ø92               ACCEPT USER-DATE FROM DATE.
   Ø94               MOVE USER-MONTH TO HDGI-MONTH.
   Ø96               MOVE USER-DAY   TO HDGI-DAY.
   Ø98               MOVE USER-YEAR  TO HDGI-YEAR.

ØØ814Ø           14Ø-PRINT-REPORT-HEADING.
   16Ø               MOVE HDG-LINE-1 TO PRINT-AREA.
   165               PERFORM 16Ø-WRITE-PAGE-TOP-LINE.
   17Ø               MOVE HDG-LINE TO PRINT-AREA.
   175               MOVE 2 TO SPACE-CONTROL.
   180               PERFORM 15Ø-WRITE-REPORT-LINE.
```

Figure 8–10
Modifications to the investment-listing program using the ACCEPT statement
(part 2 of 2)

REDEFINES. Note that the data name for the 05 level is FILLER. This demonstrates that the reserved word FILLER may be used with REDEFINES. This is often a handy attribute as you can avoid having to think up data names which will not be referred to once the redefinition has been made.

Solutions

1. Figure 8–10 shows acceptable modifications using the ACCEPT statement.
2. a. Here's an acceptable COMPUTE statement:

```
COMPUTE GROSS-PROFIT =
    (IR-QTY * IR-UNIT-PRICE) -
        (IR-QTY * IR-UNIT-COST).
```

   b. Here's an acceptable COMPUTE statement:

```
COMPUTE NEW-PRINCIPAL ROUNDED =
    OLD-PRINCIPAL *
        (1 + (INTEREST-RATE / TIMES-COMPOUNDED)).
```

3. Figure 8–11 is an acceptable solution. Note that the tests for valid data only check that the data in the field is numeric and not equal to zero. Since the input fields aren't signed, their values will be considered positive.

```
 230-EDIT-TRAN-FIELDS.
     MOVE 'Y'                          TO VALID-TRANSACTION-SW.
     IF IT-ITEM-ISSUED
         PERFORM 240-EDIT-CUSTOMER-NUMBER
     ELSE
         IF IT-ITEM-RECEIVED
             PERFORM 250-EDIT-VENDOR-NUMBER
         ELSE
             MOVE 'N'                  TO VALID-TRANSACTION-SW.
     IF      VALID-TRANSACTION
         AND VALID-TRAN-CODE
         PERFORM 260-EDIT-COMMON-FIELDS.
*
 240-EDIT-CUSTOMER-NUMBER.
     IF      IT-CUST-NO NOT NUMERIC
         OR  IT-CUST-NO EQUAL ZERO
         MOVE 'N'                      TO VALID-TRANSACTION-SW.
*
 250-EDIT-VENDOR-NUMBER.
     IF      IT-VENDOR-NO NOT NUMERIC
         OR  IT-VENDOR-NO EQUAL ZERO
         OR  IT-BLANK NOT EQUAL SPACE
         MOVE 'N'                      TO VALID TRANSACTION-SW.
*
```

Figure 8–11
An editing routine

Topic 2 **Using Subprograms**

Orientation

As you gain more experience in programming, you will find that a single processing routine or module is often common to a large number of programs. For example, many programs in an installation may require a routine that converts a two-character state code into the expanded state name. Another popular subroutine is one which will print the name of the company producing the report along with the date, time, and page number. It would be a useless waste of programming effort for each programmer to develop either routine from scratch each time it was needed. Instead, a common routine like this should be coded as a *subprogram*. Once written, the subprogram is converted into an *object module* and is stored in one of the libraries of the operating system, ready to be loaded and executed. Then, any programmer who needs the routine can retrieve it from the library and combine it with the main program at execution time.

There are other benefits to using subprograms besides saving programming time and effort. For one thing, because it's combined with the main program at the object-language level, a subprogram can be written in a different language than the main program is. As a result, functions that are difficult or impossible to code in COBOL can be written as subprograms in assembler or some other language, and then combined with a main COBOL program. Subprograms can also help make the best use of available programming personnel: the most difficult segment of a program can be assigned to the most experienced programmer, the least difficult segment to the least experienced programmer, and so on.

The *linkage-editor program*—one of the programs provided by an operating system—combines the object code of the subprogram with the object code of the main program. In other words, after the main program and subprogram have been written, they are compiled or assembled into object modules, *link-edited* into a single module, and executed as a single program. Linkage editing is not something you have to worry about in COBOL, though. You execute the linkage-editor program through your job-control language for running a program.

Terminology

called program	link editor
calling a subprogram	linkage-editor program
calling program	nested subprograms
entry point	object module
exit point	subprogram

Objectives

1. ***Given the description of a subprogram and a programming problem, write a COBOL calling program that uses the subprogram.***

2. ***Given the description of a subprogram and its calling program, write the subprogram in COBOL.***

3. ***Given the format for an organization's heading, write a subprogram to set up the output lines for the company name and the current date and time, and to number the pages of the report.***

Calling a Subprogram

To illustrate the use of subprograms, suppose that an object module named GRSCALC is combined with a main payroll program. This subprogram calculates the gross pay for an employee from hours-worked and pay-rate fields. In this case, the payroll program is referred to as the *calling program* and the GRSCALC subprogram is the *called program*. When the main program passes control to the subprogram, it is *calling the subprogram*.

Figure 8–12 is a skeleton outline of the coding required to call the subprogram. As you can see, the program is written as usual until it is time to use the subprogram. Then, a CALL statement is used as follows:

```
CALL GRSCALC
    USING EMPLOYEE-FIELDS.
```

```
 IDENTIFICATION DIVISION.
*
 PROGRAM-ID.     PAYROLL.
        .
        .
 DATA DIVISION.
*
 FILE SECTION.
*
 FD  TIME-WORKED-FILE
     LABEL RECORDS ARE STANDARD
     RECORD CONTAINS 56 CHARACTERS.
 01  TIME-WORKED-AREA                  PIC X(56).
*
 FD  PAYROLL-LIST
     LABEL RECORDS ARE STANDARD
     RECORD CONTAINS 133 CHARACTERS.
 01  PRINT-AREA                        PIC X(133).
        .
        .
*
 WORKING-STORAGE SECTION.
        .
        .
 01  EMPLOYEE-FIELDS          COMP-3.
     05  EM-HOURS-WORKED               PIC S99V9.
     05  EM-PAY-RATE                   PIC S999V99.
     05  EM-GROSS-PAY                  PIC S9(05)V99.
        .
        .
01   TIME-WORKED-REC.
     05  TW-EMPLOYEE-ID                PIC 9(03).
     05  TW-HOURS-WORKED               PIC 9(02)V9.
     05  TW-PAY-RATE                   PIC 9(03)V99.
        .
        .
```

Figure 8–12
Calling a subprogram that calculates gross pay (part 1 of 2)

```
 PROCEDURE DIVISION.
*
 000-PRODUCE-PAYROLL-LISTING.
     OPEN INPUT  TIME-WORKED-FILE
          OUTPUT PAYROLL-LIST.
     PERFORM 100-PRODUCE-PAYROLL-LINE
          UNTIL END-TIME-WORKED-FILE.
     CLOSE TIME-WORKED-FILE
           PAYROLL-LIST.
     DISPLAY "PAYROLL  I  1  NORMAL EOJ".
     STOP RUN.
*
 100-PRODUCE-PAYROLL-LINE.
          .
          .
     PERFORM 200-CALC-EMPLOYEE-GROSS.
     PERFORM 300-DEDUCT-EMPLOYEE-TAXES.
     PERFORM 400-PRINT-PAYROLL-LINE.
          .
          .
 200-CALC-EMPLOYEE-GROSS.
     PERFORM 210-READ-TIME-WORKED-FILE.
     IF  MORE-TIME-WORKED-RECS
         MOVE TW-HOURS-WORKED           TO EM-HOURS-WORKED
         MOVE TW-PAY-RATE               TO EM-PAY-RATE
         CALL GRSCALC
             USING EMPLOYEE-FIELDS.
         .
         .
```

Figure 8–12
Calling a subprogram that calculates gross pay (part 2 of 2)

The format of the CALL statement is this:

```
CALL literal [USING data-name ... ]
```

The literal is the name of the subprogram to be called. In general, the rules for forming the subprogram name are the same as those for forming a program name.

The USING clause lists the data names that are going to be used by the subprogram. If more than one data item is used, the order in which they are listed must correspond to the order in which the subprogram is prepared to receive them. Also, the PICTUREs and usages of the fields must correspond to the fields in the subprogram. (You'll learn more about coordinating the fields in the calling program with those in the subprogram in the section on writing subprograms.)

In Figure 8–12, EMPLOYEE–FIELDS contains the three employee fields to be used by the subprogram: the hours-worked and pay-rate fields used in the wage calculation and the gross-pay field used to store the result. Although it's more efficient to group fields as in this example, it isn't necessary. In other words, the three fields in Figure 8–12 could be listed individually, like this:

```
CALL GRSCALC
    USING EM-HOURS-WORKED
          EM-PAY-RATE
          EM-GROSS-PAY.
```

In fact, the fields should be grouped *only* when they are logically related.

When the CALL statement is executed in the main program, control passes to the subprogram named in the statement. When the subprogram ends,

```
 ID DIVISION.
*
 PROGRAM-ID.        GRSCALC.
*
 ENVIRONMENT DIVISION.
*
 DATA DIVISION.
*
 WORKING-STORAGE SECTION.
*
 01  OVERTIME-FIELDS        COMP-3.
     05  REG-HOURS-LIMIT            PIC S9(02)V9      VALUE 40.0.
     05  OVERTIME-HOURS             PIC S9(02)V9.
     05  OVERTIME-RATE              PIC SV99.         VALUE .50.
     05  OVERTIME-PAY               PIC S9(03)V99.
*
 LINKAGE SECTION.
*
 01  EMPLOYEE-PAY-FIELDS    COMP-3.
     05  EP-HOURS-WORKED            PIC X9(02)V9.
     05  EP-REG-PAY-RATE            PIC S9(03)V99.
     05  EP-GROSS-PAY               PIC S9(05)V99.
*
 PROCEDURE DIVISION
     USING EMPLOYEE-PAY-FIELDS.
*
 000-CALCULATE-GROSS-PAY.
     MULTIPLY EP-HOURS-WORKED BY EP-REG-PAY-RATE
         GIVING EP-GROSS-PAY.
     IF EP-HOURS-WORKED GREATER THAN REG-HOURS-LIMIT
         SUBTRACT REG-HOURS-LIMIT FROM EP-HOURS-WORKED
             GIVING OVERTIME-HOURS
         MULTIPLY OVERTIME-RATE BY OVERTIME-HOURS
         MULTIPLY OVERTIME-HOURS BY EP-REG-PAY-RATE
             GIVING OVERTIME-PAY
         ADD OVERTIME-PAY TO EP-GROSS-PAY.
*
 000-CALC-GROSS-PAY-EXIT.
     EXIT PROGRAM.
```

Figure 8–13
The gross-pay calculation subprogram

control is returned to the statement following the CALL statement. In other words, the CALL statement, like the PERFORM statement, is an implementation of the DO structure. As a result, a module in a structured program can either be performed or called.

Notice that nothing has been said about the language in which the subprogram is written. As I explained earlier, since the calling program and the subprogram are linked at the object-program level, the language used doesn't really matter. Whether the subprogram is written in COBOL, assembler language, or some other language, the calling program is the same.

Writing a Subprogram

To write a subprogram in COBOL, some additional language elements are required. Some of these elements are illustrated in Figure 8–13. This is the subprogram that is called by the main program in Figure 8–12 to calculate and employee's gross pay.

The first requirement of the subprogram is the Linkage Section in the Data Division. It follows the Working-Storage Section and describes the fields that correspond to the fields listed in the main program's CALL statement. In Figure 8–13, the Linkage Section is as follows:

```
 LINKAGE SECTION.
*
 01  EMPLOYEE-PAY-FIELDS            COMP-3.
*
     05  EP-HOURS-WORKED            PIC S9(02)V9.
     05  EP-PAY-RATE                PIC X9(03)V99.
     05  EP-GROSS-PAY               PIC S9(05)V99.
```

Notice that the PICTURE and usage of each field correspond exactly to the fields passed from the calling program in Figure 8–12. In addition, the data names in the calling program are different from those in the subprogram. This was done intentionally to emphasize the fact the the two sets of names do not have to be the same. In fact, it is a good idea if they are the same, as consistency is always a good idea. An advantage of the subprogram is that one programmer can do the subprogram, even in a different language, and another programmer can do the calling program. The only communication these two programmers really need is to know the size, type, order, and usage of the fields that the calling and subprograms are both using.

The subprogram, like any other program structure, should have one *entry point* and one *exit point*. The entry point is the start of the Procedure Division. To indicate which data names are passed to the subprogram, the Procedure Division header is written as follows:

```
PROCEDURE DIVISION
    USING EMPLOYEE-PAY-FIELDS.
```

The names listed in the USING clause must be defined as 01-level data items in the Linkage Section. And they must be in the same order as the names passed to the subprogram in the CALL statement. Again, as in the CALL statement, elementary items may be used as well as group items.

To indicate the exit point of a subprogram, the EXIT PROGRAM statement is used. It must be the only statement of a single-statement paragraph. When it is encountered, the computer returns to the first statement following the CALL statement of the calling program.

The use of the EXIT PROGRAM statement illustrates something not generally allowed in structured programming. The exit module (000–CALC–GROSS–PAY–EXIT) is not performed. Instead, control simply "falls through" from the last statement of module 000–CALCULATE–GROSS–PAY. This is one of only a few cases where control is allowed to fall through like this.

Note that not all compilers require a paragraph name prior to use of the EXIT command. In that case you may treat the EXIT the same as the STOP RUN. The EXIT PROGRAM can be the last statement in the 000-module that controls the subroutine. This subroutine could have been written without the 000–CALC–GROSS–PAY–EXIT paragraph name. You will see that approach used in module 000 of Figure 8–16.

Nested Subprograms

In some cases, a main program calls a subprogram that calls another subprogram. This is often referred to as *nested subprograms*. Because the relationship between a called program and a calling program is the same no matter how many levels of nesting are used, no additional coding techniques are involved.

Structured Program Development

As you might guess, subprograms are used fairly frequently in structured programming. Here are some points to remember as you design, document, code, test, and debug structured programs that use the subprograms.

Design

You should consider the use of subprograms early in the development of a structured program. In other words, right after you get the complete program specifications, you should also get listings of any subprograms that might be applicable to the program. Then, when you design the VTOC for the program, you can decide whether or not you actually want to use any of the subprograms. It's important to get copies before you start your VTOC, however, because in some cases the subprograms will affect your design.

On the VTOC, a subprogram module is usually set off from the other modules by "striping." In Figure 8–14, for example, the module called "calculate gross pay" is the CRSCALC subprogram. To show this, the VTOC square is striped and GRSCALC is marked on it. This program also uses three other subprograms (FITCALC, FICACALC, and CITCALC) to determine the amount of taxes to be withheld from the employee's pay.

Documentation

When the program you are writing calls a subprogram that has already been written and is available in object-code form in a system library, you must get all of the documentation available for the subprogram. Then you can be sure that the data you pass to the subprogram in the CALL statement is in the format expected. When your program calls a subprogram that hasn't been written yet, be aware that you may encounter problems later on if the subprogram is coded for one form of data and your program sends it in another form. In any event, the linkage between calling program and called program should be carefully documented.

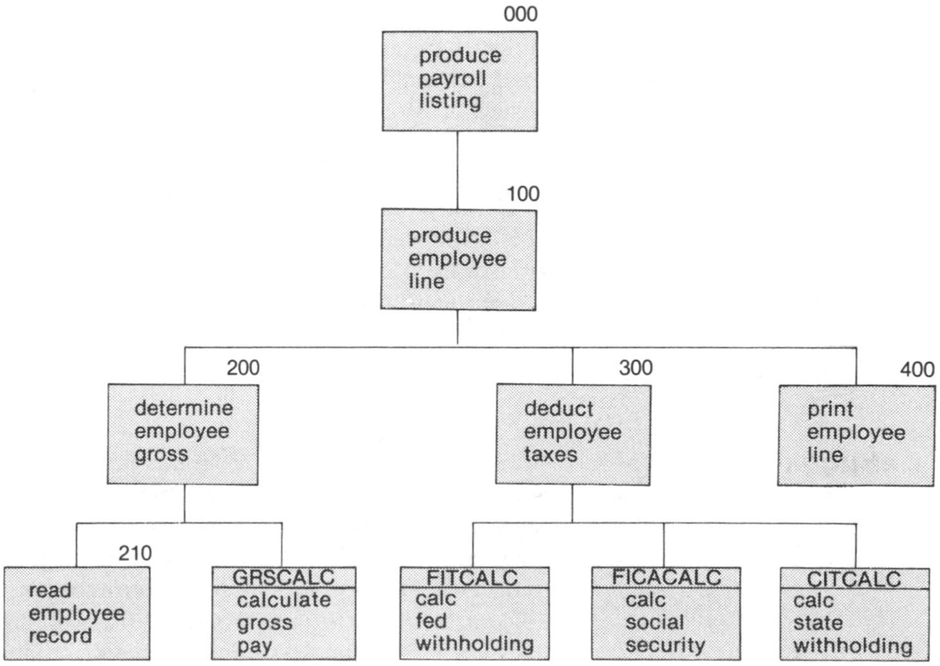
000
produce payroll listing
100
produce employee line
200
determine employee gross
300
deduct employee taxes
400
print employee line
210
read employee record
GRSCALC
calculate gross pay
FITCALC
calc fed withholding
FICACALC
calc social security
CITCALC
calc state withholding

Figure 8–14
VTOC for a payroll program using four subprograms

Coding

To keep your subprograms themselves structured, you should remember a couple of points when you're coding. One is to show program structure by grouping data items that are passed between the called and calling programs whenever the items are logically related. A second consideration deals with multiple entry points. Some compilers allow a subprogram to be entered by a calling program at more than one point through the use of the ENTRY statement. However, in keeping with the guidelines of structured programming, you should always limit your subprograms to one entry point—the beginning of the Procedure Division.

One reason a programmer may want to use more than one entry point is to provide some procedural flexibility in the program. For example, the heading subprogram mentioned previously has an initialization and a continuation function. That is, the initialization function gets the current date and time and sets the page number to one. The continuation function merely adds one to the page number whenever a new page is called for (typically on page overflow). There is no need to repeat the getting of the date and time unless a new time is required for a special operation. Many programs, though, will require that the page numbering be restarted at the beginning for certain reports (for example, one that is printing by geographical region may restart numbering at the beginning of each new region). Thus the program will require two points: an initialization point and a continuation point. To handle this problem without resorting to two entry points in the subprogram, the programmer merely encodes a switch which directs the subprogram to the initial or to the continue point, and then sets the switch as needed in the calling program. The switch then becomes just another data element which is passed between the two programs.

Testing

There are several different sequences in which you can test called and calling programs. To test a subprogram when the main program is complete, it is common to compile, link-edit, and test both modules in the same job. In this case, the first two job steps compile the object modules, the third job step links them, and the fourth step executes the combined modules.

If the main program isn't complete when the subprogram is ready to be tested, it is sometimes necessary to write a simple main program that can be used to test the subprogram. Later, when the main program is finished, a more complete test run can be made.

When you have completed the calling program but the subprogram isn't ready for testing, you can write the subprogram as a dummy module or program stub. Here, your dummy subprogram module simply (1) accepts the data passed to it, (2) displays the data so you can be sure it received it correctly, and (3) passes valid data back to the calling program (not necessarily correct data, just valid data, usually stored in the dummy program as literal values).

Debugging

When you're debugging programs that involve subprograms, you may run into some difficult problems. For example, if an abnormal termination occurs when you're testing your main COBOL program in combination with another programmer's assembler-language subprogram, it may be hard to determine whose object module caused the termination. Even if the last instruction being executed was in the subprogram, the problem may be in the calling program. In such a case, the first thing to check is that the fields passed to the subprogram are in the same sequence and have the same size and form (usage) as that required by the subprogram. If this has been done by the calling program and the program check occurred during the execution of the subprogram, the debugging problem can be turned over to the person who wrote the subprogram. In many cases, however, you will find that the problem stems from the fact that the calling program passed data in a form other than that expected by the subprogram.

Discussion

As you can see from the examples in this topic, a subprogram simply takes the place of a paragraph in the Procedure Division of a COBOL program. There are only two differences: (1) a subprogram is called rather than performed, and (2) a subprogram may consist of more than one Procedure Division paragraph.

There is another difference that is not functional. The subprogram coding will not appear in the source listing of the calling program. This can be advantageous for frequently used functions (such as the company heading routine) that really do not need to be seen in the main program as it would just make the main program longer and clutter it. Of course, if the subprogram were written in another language, the appearance of its code in the calling program would only be confusing.

In terms of structured programming, then, the use of subprograms doesn't create any complications. In fact, in some ways it makes the goals of structured programming easier to achieve. For one thing, program execution is more controlled using subprograms because a subprogram can operate on only a limited amount of data—whatever the calling program passes to it. This restriction, in turn, leads to greater module independence because the programmer coding the subprogram must write it without any consideration for what the calling program will be like. As a result, the subprogram will not be able to operate on data with which it should have no concern, and which should be protected from access by the subprogram. This supports the structured concept of local variables—those variables which should be available only to the module that is working on them. The fact that the subprogram and main program are often written by different programmers and in different languages also contributes to module independence. So subprograms actually make it easier to achieve two key goals of structured programming—controlled program execution and module independence.

You may have been using the COPY facility discussed in chapter 4. If you have understood its use and recognize that you can Copy procedural statements as well as Data Division parts, you may ask "why not use the COPY rather than a subprogram?" The question is very legitimate and the answer has several considerations:

1. Is the function already coded as a subprogram? If so, there is little sense in redoing it.

2. Should the function be coded in a different language? (That is, if it is easier to do or only feasible in a language other than COBOL, then the subprogram is the way to go.)

3. Is the function an aspect of the main program that does not need to be documented? The company heading routine is a good example of a function which would lengthen the source list of a program without adding anything useful to the documentation.

4. Is the function so common that it is likely to be used by many programs? Most all programming languages have a subprogram facility and if a function could be widely used, it has the potential to be included in a program written in a language other than COBOL. Having that function in a subprogram thus lends flexibility to its use which is not otherwise achievable.

Problems

1. (Objective 1) Suppose you are writing a billing program in which some of the customers will get a discount on the merchandise they purchased. To calculate the amount of the discount, you are going to use a subprogram called DISCALC. This program calculates the customer's discount (CUSTOMER–DISCOUNT) based on the customer code (CR–CUST–CODE) and the total amount of the sales (SALES–AMOUNT–TOTAL). The subprogram expects to receive the fields individually in this order: customer code, sales amount, and discount. Write the statement required for calling this subprogram.
2. (Objective 2) Suppose you are assigned to write the subprogram used in problem 1. The three fields that are going to be passed to the subprogram have the following characteristics:

Field	**PICTURE**	**USAGE**
Customer code	X	
Sales total	S9(5)V99	COMP-3.
Discount amount	S9(5)V99	COMP-3.

Your subprogram is to calculate the discount amount as follows:

> The discount is 3 percent if the customer pays cash and is a low-volume buyer, which is indicated by a code of 1.
>
> The discount is 5 percent if the customer pays cash and is a high-volume buyer, which is indicated by a code of 2.
>
> No discount is given if the code is not 1 or 2.

The subprogram will be executed by the CALL statement that's the solution for problem 1. Write the subprogram in COBOL.

3. (Objective 3) Write a subprogram to print a report heading block which will contain the company name on the top line, followed by the current date and time, and the page number on the second line. The following specification shows the suggested format for the output of the heading block.

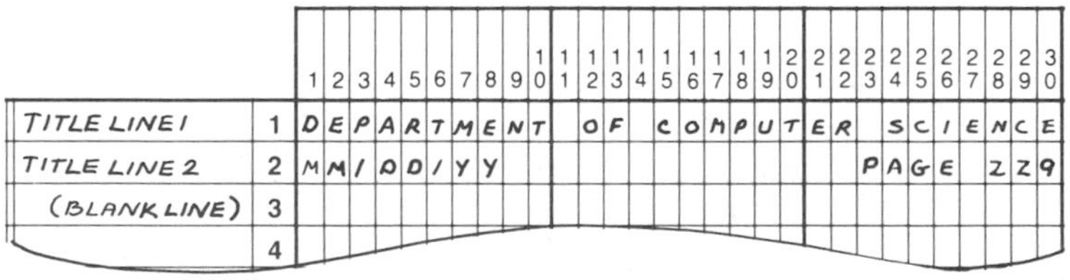
TITLE LINE 1
TITLE LINE 2
(BLANK LINE)
DEPARTMENT OF COMPUTER SCIENCE
MM/DD/YY
PAGE ZZ9

You may wish to actually implement this subprogram for headings in your program assignments, in which case the organization name surely must be changed. You may want to change the format, such as centering it or putting all of the data on one line.

```
ID DIVISION.
*
PROGRAM-ID.        DISCALC.
*
DATA DIVISION.
*
WORKING-STORAGE SECTION.
*
01  WORK-FIELDS             COMP-3.
    05  DISCOUNT-PERCENT.           PIC SV99.
*
LINKAGE SECTION.
*
01  CR-CUST-CODE                    PIC X.
    88  CASH-DISCOUNT                                VALUE '1'.
    88  CASH-VOLUME-DISC                             VALUE '2'.
*
01  SALES-AMOUNT-TOTAL              PIC S9(05)V99            COMP-3.
*
01  CUSTOMER-DISCOUNT               PIC S9(05)V99            COMP-3.
*
PROCEDURE DIVISION
    USING   CR-CUST-CODE
            SALES-AMOUNT-TOTAL
            CUSTOMER-DISCOUNT.
*
000-CALCULATE-CUST-DISCOUNT.
    IF  CASH-DISCOUNT
        MOVE .03                    TO DISCOUNT-PERCENT
    ELSE
        IF  CASH-VOLUME-DISC
            MOVE .05                TO DISCOUNT-PERCENT
        ELSE
            MOVE .0                 TO DISCOUNT-PERCENT.
    MULTIPLY DISCOUNT-PERCENT BY SALES-AMOUNT-TOTAL
        GIVING CUSTOMER-DISCOUNT.
*
000-CALC-CUST-DISC-EXIT.
    EXIT PROGRAM.
```

Figure 8–15
Subprogram for discount calculation

Solutions

1. Here's the statement you would use:

```
CALL DISCALC
    USING CR-CUST-CODE
          SALES-AMOUNT-TOTAL
          CUSTOMER-DISCOUNT
```

2. Figure 8–15 is an acceptable solution. Note that when the USING fields are listed individually, they must be 01 levels in the Linkage Section. In the Procedure Division, linear IFs are used to determine what the discount percentage should be.
3. Figure 8–16 is an acceptable solution. Notice that it allows the calling program to do the physical output. This is necessary in some on-line environments.

```
 IDENTIFICATION DIVISION.
 PROGRAM-ID.    DEPTHEAD.
*
 DATA DIVISION.
*
 WORKING-STORAGE SECTION.
*
 01  DATE-FIELDS.
     05  CURRENT-DATE.
         10  CD-CURRENT-YEAR       PIC 9(02).
         10  CD-CURRENT-MONTH      PIC 9(02).
         10  CD-CURRENT-DAY        PIC 9(02).
     05  FORMATTED-DATE.
         10  FD-CURRENT-MONTH      PIC Z9.
         10  FILLER                PIC X(01)  VALUE '/'.
         10  FD-CURRENT-DAY        PIC 9(02).
         10  FILLER                PIC X(01)  VALUE '/'.
         10  FD-CURRENT-YEAR       PIC 9(02).
*
 01  PAGE-FIELDS.
     05  PF-PAGE-NUMBER            PIC 9(03)  COMP-3.
*
 01  LITERAL-HEAD-FIELDS.
     05  ORGANIZATION-NAME.
         10  FILLER                PIC X(14)  VALUE 'DEPARTMENT OF'.
         10  FILLER                PIC X(09)  VALUE 'COMPUTER'.
         10  FILLER                PIC X(07)  VALUE 'SCIENCE'.
     05  PAGE-LITERAL              PIC X(04)  VALUE 'PAGE'.
*
 01  ERROR-LINE-1.
     05  FILLER                    PIC X(17)  VALUE ' INVALID PROCESS'.
     05  FILLER                    PIC X(14)  VALUE 'CODE PASSED ='.
     05  EL-PROCESS-SW             PIC X(01).
*
 01  ERROR-LINE-2.
     05  FILLER                    PIC X(13)  VALUE ' VALID CODES'.
     05  FILLER                    PIC X(17)  VALUE 'ARE ALPHANUMERIC'.
     05  FILLER                    PIC X(06)  VALUE '1 OR 2'.
*
 LINKAGE SECTION.
*
 01  LINK-SPACE-FIELDS.
     05  LS-PROCESS-SW             PIC X(01).
         88  INIT-DATE-PAGE                   VALUE '1'.
         88  INCREMENT-PAGE-NO                VALUE '2'
*
     05  LS-TITLE-LINE-1.
         10  FILLER                PIC X(01).
         10  LS-ORGANIZTN-NAME     PIC X(30).
         10  FILLER                PIC X(100).
*
     05  LS-TITLE-LINE-2.
         10  FILLER                PIC X(01).
         10  LS-CURRENT-DATE       PIC X(08).
         10  FILLER                PIC X(14).
         10  LS-PAGE-LITERAL       PIC X(05).
         10  LS-PAGE-NUMBER        PIC ZZ9.
         10  FILLER                PIC X(100).
```

Figure 8–16
Solution to heading subroutine (part 1 of 2)

```
*
 PROCEDURE DIVISION
        USING LINK-SPACE-FIELDS.
*
 000-PRODUCE-PAGE-TOP-HEADINGS.
     IF  INIT-DATE-PAGE
         PERFORM 100-INIT-DATE-PAGE
     ELSE
         IF  INCREMENT-PAGE-NO
             PERFORM 200-INCREMENT-PAGE-NO
         ELSE
             PERFORM 300-TRAMSMIT-ERROR-MSG.
     EXIT PROGRAM.
*
 100-INIT-DATE-PAGE.
     ACCEPT CURRENT-DATE FROM DATE.
     MOVE SPACES                         TO LS-TITLE-LINE-1
                                            LS-TITLE-LINE-2.
     MOVE CD-CURRENT-MONTH               TO FD-CURRENT-MONTH.
     MOVE CD-CURRENT-DAY                 TO FD-CURRENT-DAY.
     MOVE CD-CURRENT-YEAR                TO FD-CURRENT-YEAR.
     MOVE FORMATTED-DATE                 TO LS-CURRENT-DATE.
     MOVE ORGANIZTN-NAME                 TO LS-ORGANIZTN-NAME.
     MOVE PAGE-LITERAL                   TO LS-PAGE-LITERAL.
     MOVE 1                              TO PF-PAGE-NUMBER
                                            LS-PAGE-NUMBER.
     MOVE '2'.                           TO LS-PROCESS-SW.
*
 200-INCREMENT-PAGE-NO.
     ADD 1                               TO PF-PAGE-NUMBER.
     MOVE PF-PAGE-NUMBER                 TO LS-PAGE-NUMBER.
*
 300-TRANSMIT-ERROR-MSG.
     MOVE ERROR-LINE-1                   TO LS-TITLE-LINE-1.
     MOVE LS-PROCESS-SW                  TO EL-PROCESS-CODE.
     MOVE ERROR-LINE-2                   TO LS-TITLE-LINE-2.
```

Figure 8–16
Solution to heading subroutine
(part 2 of 2)

Topic 3 **Issue: Overlap and I/O Operations**

Orientation

Until the mid-1960s, most computer systems could perform only one operation at a time. For instance, a typical small system read a card, processed it, and printed an output line on the printer. This sequence was then repeated for the next card record. Similarly, a typical tape system read input, processed it, and gave output—but only one operation at a time. The problem with this method of processing was that most of the components of the computer system were idle, even though the system was running.

To illustrate, suppose a tape system executes a program that reads a tape record, processes it, and writes a tape record. Figure 8–17 might then represent the relative amounts of time that the CPU and the tape drives would be busy during execution of the program. (These percentages, of course, would vary depending on the speed of the components.) In this example, the CPU is busy 44 percent of the time that the system is running, while each tape drive is busy only 28 percent of the time.

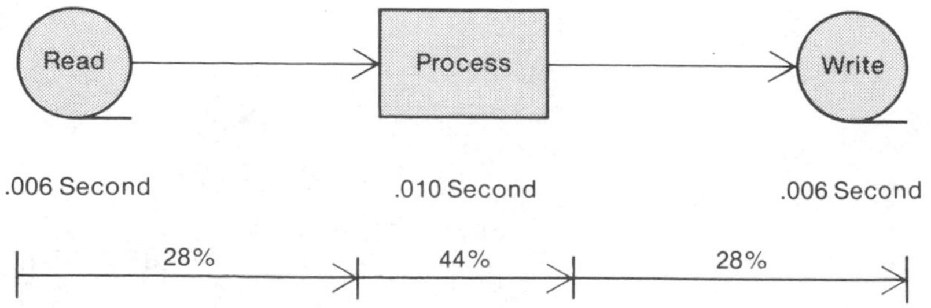
Read
Process
Write
.006 Second
.010 Second
.006 Second
28%
44%
28%

Figure 8–17
The problem of idle computer components

To overcome this problem of idle components, systems were developed to *overlap* I/O operations with CPU processing. The difference between nonoverlapped and overlapped processing is illustrated in Figure 8–18. On system A, the nonoverlapped system, nine time intervals are required to read, process, and write three records. On system B, the overlapped system, nine records have been read, eight have been processed, and seven have been written at the end of nine time intervals. Although this example is based on the unlikely assumption that reading, processing, and writing take equal amounts of time, the message is clear: overlap can significantly increase the amount of work that a computer system can do.

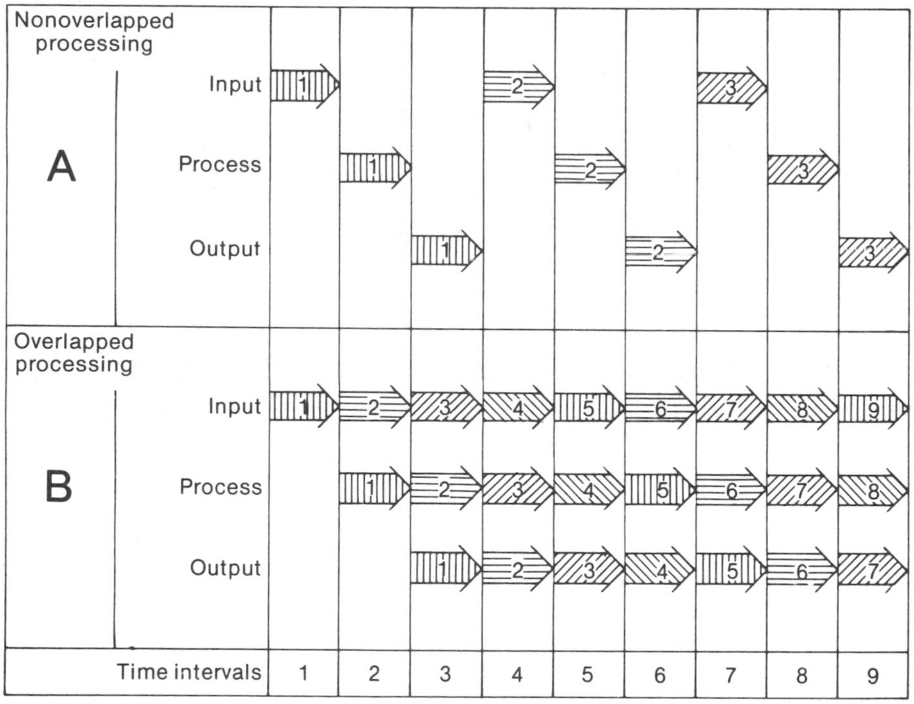
Nonoverlapped processing
A
Input
Process
Output
Overlapped processing
B
Input
Process
Output
Time intervals
1
2
3
4
5
6
7
8
9

Figure 8–18
Overlapped and nonoverlapped processing

Terminology

access cycle	multiplexor channel	selector channel
channel	overlap	storage access cycle
channel command		

Objectives

1. ***Explain how overlap increases the productivity of a computer system.***
2. ***Explain why two I/O areas are required for each input and output device if overlap is to take place.***

Channels

One reason earlier computers weren't able to overlap operations is that the CPU executed all of the instructions of a program, one after the other. In contrast, the CPU of an overlapped system doesn't execute I/O instructions. Instead, *channels* are used to execute the I/O instructions, while the CPU executes the arithmetic, logical, and data-movement instructions. The I/O instructions executed by the channels are called *channel commands*. Figure 8–19 illustrates the components of an overlapped system: one channel executes an input command, a second channel executes an output command, and the CPU executes others instructions of the program—all at the same time. (Although the CPU is generally considered to consist of storage and control circuitry, the CPU and storage are shown separately in the illustration to indicate that both CPU and channels can access data from storage.)

Whenever data is transferred from a channel to storage or from storage to a channel, CPU processing is interrupted for one *storage access cycle* (or just *access cycle*). Because of the tremendous difference between access-cycle speeds and I/O speeds, however, this is a minor interruption. To illustrate, suppose cards read by a 600-card-per-minute card reader are being processed by a computer that transfers two storage positions (or bytes) of data during each access cycle. If each access cycle takes one microsecond (millionth of a second), CPU processing will be interrupted for a total of 40 microseconds to read all 80 card columns into storage. In contrast, the card reader takes 1/10 of a second, of 100,000 microseconds to read all 80 card columns. This means that while each card is read, the CPU can spend over 99 percent of its time—99,960 seconds out of 100,000 to be exact—executing other instructions of the program.

Although tape and disk devices are many times faster than card readers and printers, this same type of inequality is likely to exist between the speeds of these I/O devices and the access-cycle speeds. For example, a tape drive with a 50,000 byte-per-second transfer rate reads or writes one byte of data every 20 microseconds. If the CPU requires one-half microsecond to transfer the byte to or from storage, 19.5 microseconds per byte are available for other processing. In other words, because of the overlap capability, the CPU can spend 97.5 percent of its time executing other instructions.

Since a channel, like a CPU, can execute only one operation at a time, the number of overlapping operations that a system can have is limited by the number of channels on the system. For instance, a one-channel system can overlap one I/O operation with CPU processing, and a three-channel system

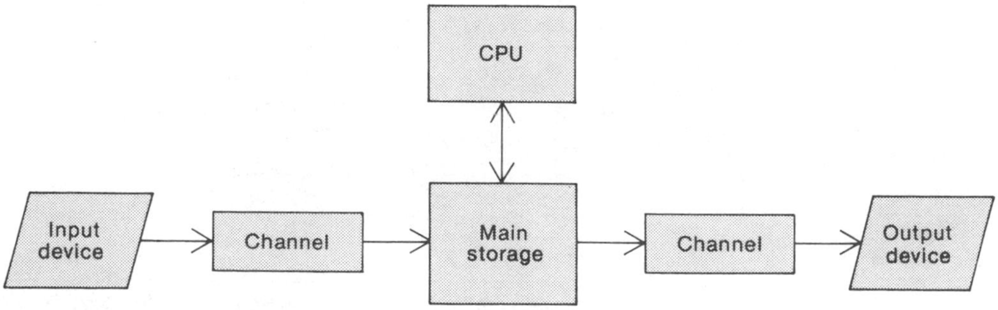
CPU
Input device
Channel
Main storage
Channel
Output device

Figure 8–19
A computer system with overlap capability

can overlap three I/O operations with CPU processing. The one exception to this is the *multiplexor channel*, which can read or write on two or more slow-speed I/O devices at one time.

The multiplexor channel has the ability to alternate between several I/O devices. For example, if a card reader, card punch, and printer are attached to a multiplexor channel, the channel can accept one byte of data from the card reader, send one byte to the card punch, send one byte to the printer, and then accept another byte from the card reader. By switching from one device to another, this single channel can overlap several different devices. Here again, the extreme difference in speeds between I/O devices and access cycles makes this possible.

Figure 8–20 shows a typical configuration of an overlapped system with three disk drives. All of its slow-speed devices—the card reader, card punch, printer, and console typewriter—are attached to a multiplexor channel, while the disk drives are attached to the other type of channel—a *selector channel*. This system, then, can overlap card reading, printing, punching, console-typewriter operations, and reading or writing on one of the disk drives. Because a selector channel can perform only one operation at a time, however, reading from disk drive 1 and writing on disk drive 2 cannot be overlapped. Since disk drives are considerably faster than the slow-speed devices, it is more important that slow-speed operations be overlapped than disk operations.

Dual I/O Areas

One programming complexity resulting from overlap is that two I/O areas in storage must be used for each I/O operation. If only one input area of storage was used for a reading operation, for example, the second record would be read into the input area while the first record was being processed—thus destroying the data from the first record. Instead, the second record must be read into a second input area of storage while the first record is being processed in the first input area. Then, the third record is read into the first input area, while the second record is processed in the second input area. This switching from one input area to the other, which is shown schematically in Figure 8–21, must be continued throughout the program. Similarly, dual I/O areas must be used for all other I/O operations that are overlapped.

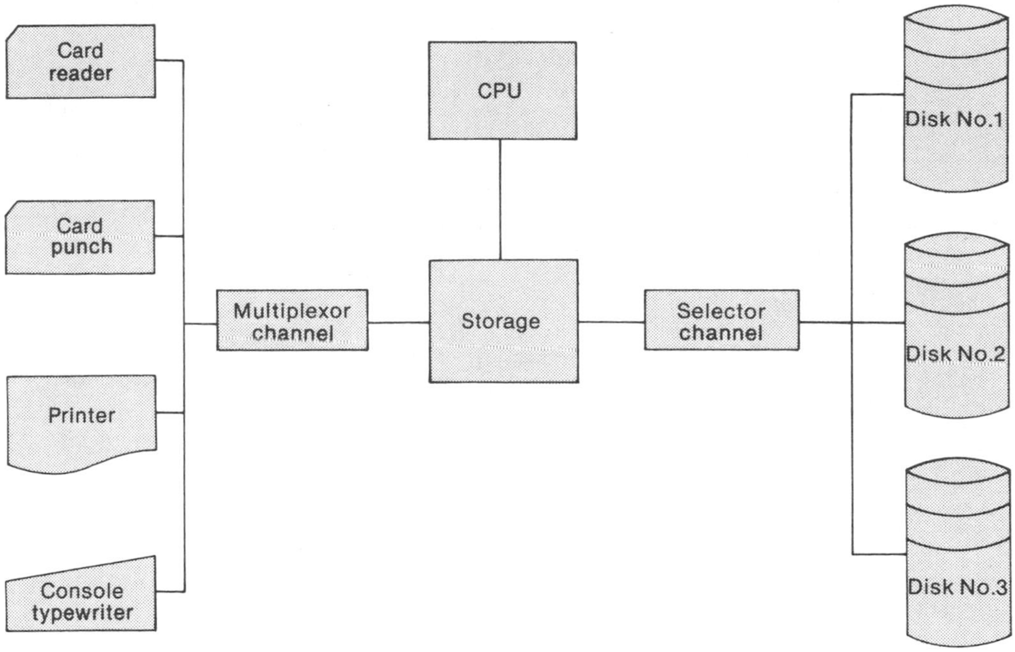
Card reader
Card punch
Printer
Console typewriter
Multiplexor channel
CPU
Storage
Selector channel
Disk No.1
Disk No.2
Disk No.3

Figure 8–20
A typical overlapped system

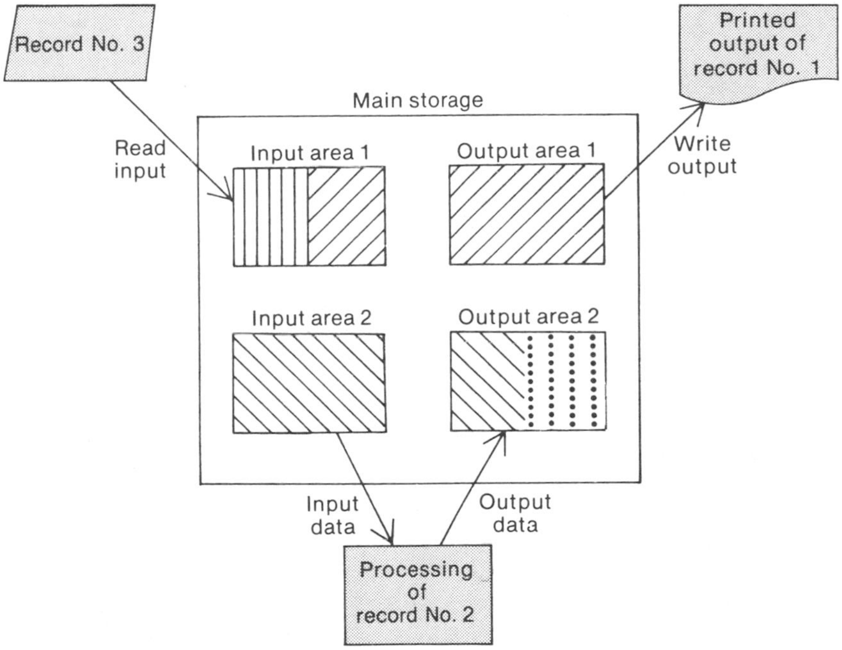
Record No. 3
Read input
Main storage
Input area 1
Output area 1
Input area 2
Output area 2
Printed output of record No. 1
Write output
Input data
Output data
Processing of record No. 2

Figure 8–21
Use of dual I/O areas for overlapped processing

Note: Data is being moved into input area 1 and output area 2

```
Example 1:
         .
         .
     SELECT PRINT-FILE
         ASSIGN TO PFMS.
         .
         .
 DATA DIVISION.
         .
         .
 FD  PRINT-FILE
     LABEL RECORDS ARE STANDARD
     RECORD CONTAINS 133 CHARACTERS.
*
 01  PRINT-RECORD
     05  FILLER                          PIC X(01).
     05  PR-FIELD-1                      PIC Z(05).
     05  FILLER                          PIC X(04).
     05  PR-FIELD-2                      PIC ZZZ.99.
     05  FILLER                          PIC X(04).
     05  PR-FIELD-3                      PIC Z(03).
     05  FILLER                          PIC X(110).
         .
         .
 PROCEDURE DIVISION.
*
 000-PRODUCE-PRINTED-OUTPUT.
     OPEN INPUT ...
          OUTPUT PRINT-FILE.
         .
         .
 130-PRINT-OUTPUT-LINE.
     MOVE SPACE                TO PRINT-RECORD.
     MOVE WS-FIELD-1           TO PR-FIELD-1.
         .
         .
     PERFORM 140-WRITE-OUTPUT-LINE.
*
 140-WRITE-OUTPUT-LINE.
     WRITE PRINT-RECORD
         AFTER ADVANCING SPACE-CONTROL LINES.
```

Figure 8–22
Two ways to clear output areas (part 1 of 2)

COBOL Implications

Fortunately, the COBOL programmer doesn't have to be concerned much with overlap. In fact, all of the COBOL programs illustrated so far have used overlap although the programmer has done nothing to provide for dual I/O areas or switching from one I/O area to another. In general, the COBOL compiler in conjunction with the operating system automatically provides for overlap.

Perhaps the main reason for presenting the concept of overlap is that it explains why the I/O area of an output file (as described by the COBOL program) must be cleared more than once to blanks. In many COBOL programs, for example, you will find a statement such as

```
MOVE SPACE TO OUTPUT-AREA
```

at the start of a routine that constructs an output record for a file. You should now understand that the first time the statement is executed, it clears the first output area for the file; the second time it is executed, it clears the second

```
Example 2:

     SELECT PRINT-FILE
         ASSIGN TO PFMS.
           .
           .
 DATA DIVISION.
           .
           .
 FD  PRINT-FILE
     LABEL RECORDS ARE STANDARD
     RECORD CONTAINS 133 CHARACTERS.
*
 01  PRINT-AREA                          PIC X(133).
           .
           .
 WORKING-STORAGE SECTION.
           .
           .
 01  PRINT-RECORD.
     05  FILLER                          PIC X(01).
     05  PR-FIELD-1                      PIC Z(05).
     05  FILLER                          PIC X(04)       VALUE SPACE.
     05  PR-FIELD-2                      PIC ZZZ.99.
     05  FILLER                          PIC X(04)       VALUE SPACE.
     05  PR-FIELD-3                      PIC Z(03).
     05  FILLER                          PIC X(110)      VALUE SPACE.
           .
           .
 PROCEDURE DIVISION.
*
 000-PRODUCE-PRINTED-OUTPUT.
     OPEN INPUT ...
          OUTPUT PRINT-FILE.
           .
           .
 130-PRINT-OUTPUT-LINE.
     MOVE WS-FIELD-1          TO PR-FIELD-1.
           .
           .
     MOVE PRINT-RECORD        TO PRINT-AREA.
     PERFORM 140-WRITE-OUTPUT-LINE.
*
 140-WRITE-OUTPUT-LINE.
     WRITE PRINT-AREA
         ADVANCING SPACE-CONTROL LINES.
```

Figure 8–22
Two ways to clear output areas (part 2 of 2)

output area. If both areas aren't cleared, data from a previous program or record might be written in an output record.

Figure 8–22 presents two different ways of removing foreign data from all output records when using a compiler that automatically provides two output areas for each output file. Example 1 illustrates the method just described in which SPACE is moved to the output area before each output record is constructed. Thus, both output areas are cleared before an output record is written. This method is used in the reorder-listing program in Figure 3–4.

In example 2, all output data, with all required areas set to blanks, is moved from working storage to the output area and then the line is printed. This is accomplished by a MOVE statement coupled with a statement that performs a write procedure. This is the method most commonly used in structured programs. And it is the one used in the refined reorder-listing program in Figure 4–8.

Discussion

The material on overlap processing is particularly related to the older batch-oriented computer systems. Newer operating systems are often handling overlap problems automatically, thus eliminating it as a question with which the programmer must be concerned.

As a programmer, you should understand the overlap situation and its effects on program speed and on output errors so that you can write more efficient and accurate programs. You must determine how the individual operating system deals with overlap processing so that you will be able to handle the local situation appropriately.

Finally, you should remember the method described in Figure 8–22, which defined the output records in Working–Storage and moved them to the output area before writing. That technique helps avoid the overlap problem of invalid data getting into the output record.

Topic 4 **Issue: Structured Walkthrough**

Orientation

A structured walkthrough is a peer-oriented, cooperative technique to identify design errors in programs. The word *walkthrough* derives from the image that a programmer "walks" his or her fellow programmers "through" the proposed logic of a program or other significant parts of the development process. The word *structure* signifies that the process is very strict in its objectives and in the manner in which it is conducted. The use of the word *structure* has also evolved from its recent popularity as a word used to designate a special way of doing things, particularly those which are computer-related.

The role of the programmer's peers is to help detect errors in the design, weaknesses in the structure, or lack of clarity in the style of the part under examination. The walkthrough is intended to be helpful and, hence, must be devoid of any feeling of put-downs or other demeaning criticism.

A strong feature of the walkthrough is that it enables errors, weaknesses, and other wrong directions to be detected at an early stage of the development process. Studies have shown that the earlier a problem is detected and fixed, the cheaper it is to make the correction. On the other hand, problems discovered later in the development process become more expensive to correct. The later they are discovered the more expensive they are to correct. Thus, it is much less expensive, in terms of dollars, time, and staff frustration, to detect and solve design problems at the earliest possible moment.

As you will see from the following discussion, there are several different types of walkthroughs. A common feature of each type is that the walkthrough takes place before the proposed action. Hence, it always represents an early attempt to answer the question "will this work?" When used properly, it is also a recognition and use of the fact that "two (or more) heads are better than one."

Walkthroughs

General information

Formal walkthroughs can be conducted at several different times during the development of a program. Some typical times for walkthroughs follow:

1. After the program specifications have been developed (a *program specification walkthrough*)
2. After the program is designed (a *design walkthrough* covering structure chart only or structure chart and HIPO diagrams)
3. After the test plan and test data have been developed (a *test plan walkthrough*)
4. After the program or selected modules of a program have been coded, but before they have been tested (a *coding walkthrough*)
5. After the program or selected modules of a program have been coded and tested (a *coding walkthrough*)
6. After the user guide has been prepared (a *user guide walkthrough*)

Find out what kinds of walkthroughs, if any, are required in your shop.

In addition, informal walkthroughs can be held at any time during the development of a program. This can simply mean, for example, that one programmer reviews your coding and user guides, and you do the same for him or her. If you are concerned about any phase of development, you should at least initiate an informal walkthrough.

Walkthrough format

1. A walkthrough is initiated by a programmer when ready for a public review of some phase of the programmer's work.
2. The programmer invites from two to six colleagues to participate in the walkthrough (two or three is usually better than five or six).
3. No managers are allowed at a walkthrough—this is a time for finding errors, not for evaluating programmers.
4. At least 48 hours before the meeting, the programmer gives an agenda like the one in Figure 8–23 to the participants. Besides giving general information about when and where the meeting will be held, the agenda specifies the program name, the type of walkthrough that will be held, the material that will be reviewed, and the walkthrough objectives (that is, what the materials are to be reviewed for).
5. Along with the agenda, the programmer hands out copies of the materials listed on the agenda to each participant. The participants then have at least 48 hours to review the materials so they will be prepared for the actual walkthrough.
6. At the walkthrough, an action list is made of all the questions, errors, and possible trouble spots raised during the meeting. However, no attempt is made at this time to correct anything. The purpose of the walkthrough meeting is error detection, not correction.
7. The programmer follows up the meeting in two ways. First, within an hour of the meeting, the programmer makes and distributes copies of the action list to each of the walkthrough participants. Second, within two days of the meeting, the programmer lets each of the participants know in writing what was done to resolve each of the items on the action list.

Walkthrough Agenda

Notice date: August 25, 1986

Originator: Paul Noll

Meeting date and time: Friday August 27 1:30 P.M.

Location: Room 578

Program: Produce sales report

Type of Walkthrough: Design

Materials:

1 Specifications

2 Structure chart

3 HIPO diagrams for all control modules

4

5

Objectives:
Please review for

1 Completeness and logic

2 Meaningful names

3 Naming consistency

4

5

Team:

	Name	Present	Resolution Initials	Resolution Date
Moderator	Mike Murach	Yes		
Recorder	Doug Lowe	Yes		
Member 1	Judy Taylor	Yes		
Member 2				
Member 3				
Member 4				

Date of resolution August 30, 1986 **Originator's signature** ____________

Figure 8–23
A walkthrough form that serves as an agenda and as a record of follow-up

The meeting

1. Select one participant to be moderator and one to be recorder. In general, the programmer should be neither moderator nor recorder. The moderator's job is to keep the meeting on track; it's up to him or her to make sure the comments don't become too trivial or too personal. The recorder is in charge of writing down items on the action list.

2. The main part of the walkthrough consists of detecting errors. Sometimes, however, the meeting begins with the programmer giving an overview of the program. Since the materials given to the partici pants are usually self-explanatory, a walkthrough should *not* begin with an overview unless there is a solid reason for having one.

3. When a question is raised, the programmer should be given a chance to explain his or her work. If it's agreed that the point is or could be a problem, it goes on the action list.

4. Avoid pointing up trivial errors (such as syntax errors, missing punctuation, or inconsistent names) at the walkthrough. Instead, participants should mark these errors in red on their own materials and hand them to the programmer at the end of the meeting.

5. All of the walkthrough members should participate actively in the meeting. To do this, they have to prepare ahead of time by going through the walkthrough materials the programmer gave them and listing any problems areas and errors they find. Then at the meeting, they'll be able to raise their own questions, as well as intelligently discuss the points raised by the other participants.

Follow-up

1. The easiest way for a programmer to tell the other walkthrough members what he or she did about the items on an action list is to simply write the resolutions on the action list itself. (This is shown in Figure 8–24.) Then the programmer can make copies and distribute them. Notice that the explanations aren't long, but they say enough so the other participants know what action was taken on each point.

2. If a major error is found in a walkthrough, the best resolution may be for the programmer to redo the material and hold another walkthrough.

3. Anytime a formal walkthrough is held, a report should be made to management. The easiest way to do this is to use an agenda form like the one in Figure 8–23. After the participants are satisfied with the programmer's resolution of the points on the action list, they initial the form; then the originator signs it and turns it in. Notice that the form simply gives the agenda and states that all the problems were solved. It doesn't give any indication of who found how many errors, how many errors there were in all, how crucial or trivial the errors were, etc.

Action List

Originator: Paul Noll
Program: Produce sales report
Type of walkthrough: Design

Questions:	Resolution:
1. Is there any unnecessary level in the structure chart? Can modules 130, 140, and 150 be moved from level 3 to level 2?	Changed. The modules have been moved to level 2. See attached structure chart.
2. Will module 120 process the first record in the file?	Changed. It didn't work. See attached HIPO diagram.
3. Should control field changes be made in module 120 (the major control module) rather than in the print modules?	Changed. I moved the control field changes from the print modules to module 120. See attached HIPO diagram.
4. Is the module name for module 120 meaningful?	Changed. From "process sales record" to "produce sales line."
5. Inconsistency in use of TR and TRAN in several HIPO diagrams (marked in red and returned).	Changed. All references are now TRAN.

Figure 8–24
An action list for a design walkthrough including resolution of the questions raised

Checklist for effective walkthroughs

1. No manager present
2. Error detection only
3. Two-hour time limit
4. The right participants
5. Vested interests
6. Show results
7. No counting
8. Professional behavior only

Use of Walkthroughs

Several interesting aspects of walkthroughs appear to be coming to light as more and more computing groups experiment with the technique.

1. Walkthroughs are especially effective whenever a new process is being installed or a new concept is being adopted. One immediate example is the adoption of a common structured style by a programming group. At that time the walkthrough method is an excellent aid in developing the common understandings required among the computer staff to accomplish the project objectives.

2. Walkthroughs are effective in training programmers who are new to the group. This is particularly true for trainee programmers. They need the direction which naturally occurs during walkthroughs, and it is an effective method for helping them to become acquainted with their fellow workers.

3. Walkthroughs are always effective whenever a new project is being undertaken as initial misunderstandings can be caught and clarified at the earliest moment.

4. Walkthroughs become less effective when the group is well-trained. The smarter, quicker programmers and staff often become bored with the process. Whenever boredom sets in, the effort becomes counterproductive on several counts.

5. Walkthroughs can become time-wasters. In any large group there are people who are motivated to make the most of their time and those who want to spend a significant part of their day socializing. When you examine group dynamics, you find that meetings are a form of socializing. Any meeting must be tightly structured in terms of its objectives, processes, and time limits. That is why the guidelines for walkthroughs specify a time limit, have a moderator to keep the discussion on the task, recommend a limited number of participants, and require that the participants be given prior information and come prepared.

6. Walkthroughs, then, should be used as long as they are effective. Whenever they start to become less effective, their frequency should be reduced. Their use should become more specialized, as when working with a trainee programmer. One of managements tasks is to monitor the effectiveness of walkthroughs.

7. How can students use the walkthrough technique? There are probably as many answers as there are programming classes, but three approaches will be suggested.

Classroom: A student is chosen or volunteers to present his or her design solution to the class as a whole. Two walkthrough types that would be effective in this situation are the VTOC and the pseudocode walkthrough. A moderator and a recorder are chosen from the class and perform those functions as described, but the whole class has the opportunity and responsibility to contribute. The project being discussed should probably be one of the class assignments since all of the class would then have the same information.

A variation on this mode would be to allow only the moderator, the recorder, and one or two other students to actively participate during the actual walkthrough.

In either case the presenting student could be given the responsibility of selecting the walkthrough group, or the instructor might want to choose the group to ensure the widest participation.

Classroom: The instructor selects or allows students to select walkthrough groups. The groups have a maximum of four students. Time is planned on a regular schedule for the groups to meet in the classroom and each student to make a presentation of a phase of the current project. The instructor's responsibility at those times is to monitor how each group is conducting the walkthrough and to help them to be more effective by reminding them of the various facets of the process or by modeling some aspect of the walkthrough.

Outside the classroom: After training the students by going through the above approaches, the instructor merely tells the students that they are on their own. They have been organized into walkthrough groups, they have been trained in the method, and now they are to practice the method as often as the individual members of the group feel is needed. The instructor may want to monitor each group's progress occasionally. Techniques to do so may be having each group give a walkthrough for the instructor (although this somewhat violates the dictum that no management be present) or may merely require that a walkthrough form and action list be turned in periodically.

In summary, walkthroughs appear to be very effective in certain situations, but can become counterproductive in others. Since walkthroughs are most effective when the process being discussed is new or when the participants are novices, it would appear that using walkthroughs for students who are learning structured programming would be most timely.

Chapter 9 Table Handling in COBOL

Tables are used in many computer applications. For example, a tax table may be used to look up the amount of income tax to be withheld from paychecks. To find the premium to be charged for an insurance policy, rating tables are often used. In many statistical analyses, tables are printed to show how data breaks down by categories.

Topic 1 discusses the techniques in COBOL that help you handle several fields which have the same characteristics. This is called repetitive processing and is applied to the simple single-level table. Topic 2 shows how that concept applies to single-level tables. Topic 3 introduces indexes as a preferred method for table work, and topic 4 extends your knowledge by showing how multilevel tables are set up and accessed. Since the use of tables is a method to increase the efficiency of programs in appropriate situations, topic 5 discusses two more debugging aids.

The topics that covered control breaks were the first logical hurdle for the novice programmer to get over; the study of tables is the second. The need to set up or accumulate table data and to access tables is a requirement of many solutions to real-world problems. If you can understand and use tables, you are well on your way to developing the skills of a professional programmer.

Topic 1 Repetitive Processing

Orientation

In some programs, several fields of a record must be processed in the same way. Rather than repeat similar code for each field, most programmers use looping techniques for repetitive processing.

To illustrate the use of repetitive processing, consider this problem. A payroll program reads an input record that has the format given in Figure 9–1. To calculate the number of hours an employee worked during the week, one of the procedures of the program must add the seven daily-hours-worked fields. Although this could be done using the subset presented thus far, Figure 9–2 shows how to do it more efficiently using the OCCURS clause, subscripts, and the PERFORM VARYING statement.

Field Name	Employee Data	Daily Hours Worked 1	2	3	4	5	6	7
Characteristics	X(38)	99V9	99V9	99V9	99V9	99V9	99V9	99V9
Usage								
Position	1-38	39-41	42-44	45-47	48-50	51-53	54-56	57-59

Figure 9–1
Employee payroll record format

Terminology

subscript

Objective

Given a problem involving repetitive operations, solve it using the elements or techniques presented in this topic.

The OCCURS Clause

The basic format of the OCCURS clause is this:

```
OCCURS integer TIMES
```

This clause may be used to describe any data name that is not on an 01 level. The integer in the clause refers to the number of times a field or group of fields is repeated. In Figure 9–2, the OCCURS clause indicates that the WP-HOURS-WORKED field is repeated seven times in the WEEKLY-PAY-RECORD area.

Subscripts

To process the fields defined with an OCCURS clause, *subscripts* are used. For example, the first daily-hours-worked field in the employee record may be referred to as WP-HOURS-WORKED (1), the second field as WP-HOURS-WORKED (2), and so on. In each case, the number in parentheses is called the subscript.

A data name can be used as a subscript in the same way that an integer is. Then, the field that is referred to depends on the value of the subscript field at the time an instruction is executed. For example, HOURS-SUB is a subscript in the following statement taken from the program in Figure 9–2:

```
ADD WP-HOURS-WORKED (HOURS-SUB) TO WEEKLY-HOURS.
```

If HOURS-SUB contains a 1 at the time of execution, the first daily-hours-worked field is referred to; if it contains a 2, the second daily-hours-worked field is referred to; and so on. Although a data name used as a subscript can be any USAGE, COMP usage leads to the most efficient object program.

```
WORKING-STORAGE SECTION.
*
     .
     .
*
01  WORK-FIELDS            COMP-3.
*
    05  WEEKLY-HOURS       PIC S99V9.
     .
     .
*
01  SUBSCRIPTS             COMP.
*
    05  HOURS-SUB          PIC 9.
     .
     .
*
01  WEEKLY-PAY-RECORD.
*
    05  WP-EMP-DATA        PIC X(38).
    05  WP-HOURS-WORKED    PIC 99V9 OCCURS 7 TIMES.
     .
     .
*
PROCEDURE DIVISION.
*
     .
     .
    PERFORM 230-ACCUMULATE-WEEKLY-HOURS
        VARYING HOURS SUB FROM 1 BY 1
        UNTIL HOURS SUB GREATER THAN 7.
     .
     .
*
230-ACCUMULATE-WEEKLY-HOURS.
*
    ADD WP-HOURS-WORKED (HOURS-SUB) TO WEEKLY-HOURS.
     .
     .
```

Figure 9–2
Repetitive processing using subscripts and the PERFORM VARYING statement

The PERFORM VARYING statement

To control the repeated processing when subscripts are used, this more advanced form of the PERFORM statement can be used:

```
PERFORM procedure-name-1

    VARYING data-name-1

        FROM  integer-1     BY  integer-2
              data-name-2       data-name-3

    UNTIL condition
```

Data-name-1 is the subscript field, and its initial value is given after the word FROM. Then, each time the procedure named is performed, the value of the subscript field is increased by the amount specified after BY.

When the PERFORM statement in Figure 9–2 is executed, it causes the procedure named 230–ACCUMULATE–WEEKLY–HOURS to be executed seven times—once for each of the values of the subscript named HOURS–SUB. In other words, by varying the subscript value from one to seven and branching to the procedure named 230–ACCUMULATE–WEEKLY–HOURS, the PERFORM statement causes the seven daily-hours-worked fields to be added together. After the seven WP–HOURS–WORKED values are added to WEEKLY–HOURS, the processing continues with the statement following the PERFORM.

It is important to note that the condition in the PERFORM is stated as UNTIL HOURS–SUB GREATER THAN 7, not UNTIL HOURS–SUB EQUAL TO 7, as you might think. This is necessary because the test to see whether the condition has been met is made *before* the procedure named 230–ACCUMULATE–WEEKLY–HOURS is executed. If the condition were stated UNTIL HOURS–SUB EQUAL TO 7, 230–ACCUMULATE–WEEKLY–HOURS would only be executed six times, and the seventh daily-hours-worked field wouldn't be added to WEEKLY–HOURS.

Using Literals as Subscripts

In Figure 9–2, you see how the PERFORM VARYING statement can be used in repetitive processing. However, if you have a fixed number of repetitions, it is often just as quick and easy to repeat certain segments of code using literals as subscripts. For example, the PERFORM statement in Figure 9–2 could be a simply PERFORM that would execute module 230. Then, module 230 could consist of the following code:

```
ADD WP-HOURS-WORKED  (1)
    WP-HOURS-WORKED  (2)
    WP-HOURS-WORKED  (3)
    WP-HOURS-WORKED  (4)
    WP-HOURS-WORKED  (5)
    WP-HOURS-WORKED  (6)
    WP-HOURS-WORKED  (7)
       GIVING WEEKLY-HOURS.
```

The point is, when you have a small, fixed number of repetitions, it's up to you to decide how to control processing—either by using the PERFORM VARYING statement or by coding the repetitive code using literals as subscripts.

Varied Number of Repetitions

Sometimes, the number of fields to be operated on in a repetitive processing loop may vary. For instance, the sixth and seventh daily-hours-worked fields in Figure 9–1 may be blank if an employee works only five days. Then, if the coding shown in Figure 9–2 is used, program cancellation will occur due to data exception (invalid numeric field).

As an alternative, suppose column 38 is used to indicate the number of days an employee has worked. Then, the coding in Figure 9–3 will perform the repetitive processing only as many times as column 38 indicates is necessary. The key change here is that the condition in the PERFORM statement is UNTIL HOURS–SUB GREATER THAN WP–DAYS–WORKED. In a case like this, the PERFORM VARYING statement must be used to control processing. You can't use literals as subscripts because the number of required subscripts varies with each input record.

As you become more sophisticated in the use of computers, in general, and with table handling, specifically, it will occur to you that more and more tasks should be removed from human handling and turned over to the computer program. Requiring a clerk to count and record the days worked in the previous example is one of those situations the computer program can handle quicker with 100 percent accuracy. How do you do that? There are several

```
 WORKING-STORAGE SECTION.
*
     .
     .
*
 01  WORK-FIELDS              COMP-3.
*
     05  WEEKLY-HOURS         PIC S99V9.
     .
     .
*
 01  SUBSCRIPTS               COMP.
*
     05  HOURS-SUB            PIC 9.
     .
     .
*
 01  WEEKLY-PAY-RECORD.
*
     05  WP-EMP-DATA          PIC X(37).
     05  WP-DAYS-WORKED       PIC 9.
     05  WP-HOURS-WORKED      PIC 99V9 OCCURS 7 TIMES.
     .
     .
*
 PROCEDURE DIVISION.
*
     .
     .
     PERFORM 230-TOTAL-WEEKLY-HOURS
         VARYING HOURS-SUB FROM 1 BY 1
         UNTIL HOURS-SUB GREATER THAN WP-DAYS-WORKED.
     .
     .
*
 230-TOTAL-WEEKLY-HOURS.
*
     ADD WP-HOURS-WORKED (HOURS-SUB) TO WEEKLY-HOURS.
     .
     .
```

Figure 9–3
Repetitive processing with a varied number of repetitions

methods, but two that work well are:

1. If the hours worked are listed one after the other for as many days as were worked, test the field for not numeric before adding. Note that the field may have to be redefined as alphanumeric fields to allow the following numeric test to work.

```
PERFORM ACCUMULATE-WEEKLY-HOURS
     VARYING HOURS-SUB FROM 1 BY 1
     UNTIL WP-HRS-WORK-ALPHA (HOURS-SUB) NOT NUMERIC.
```

2. If the position is related to the day of the week, then there will be gaps in the list of hours worked. In that situation the program can check for zero (no hours worked that day) or for blank fields again. The checking for blank fields is preferred as it does not require keying of data into those fields. In this case the testing takes place in the accumulate module.

```
IF WP-HRS-WORK-ALPHA (HOURS-SUB) IS NUMERIC
    ADD WP-HOURS-WORKED (HOURS-SUB) TO WEEKLY-HOURS.
```

```
 WORKING-STORAGE SECTION.
*
        .
        .
*
 01  WORK-FIELDS                  COMP-3.
     05  TEMPERATURE-TOTAL        PIC S9(4).
        .
        .
*
 01  SUBSCRIPTS                   COMP.
     05  TEMP-SUB                 PIC 99.
        .
        .
*
 01  TEMPERATURE-RECORD.
     05  TR-TEMP-DATA             OCCURS 13 TIMES.
         10  TR-TEMP-DATE         PIC X(4).
         10  TR-TEMPERATURE       PIC 99.
     05  FILLER                   PIC XX.
        .
        .
*
 PROCEDURE DIVISION.
*
        .
        .
     PERFORM 120-ADD-RECORD-TEMPS
         VARYING TEMP-SUB FROM 1 BY 1
         UNTIL TEMP-SUB GREATER THAN 13.
        .
        .
*
 120-ADD-RECORD-TEMPS.
     IF TR-TEMP-DATE (TEMP-SUB) EQUAL TO SPACE
         MOVE 99 TO TEMP-SUB
     ELSE
         ADD TR-TEMPERATURE (TEMP-SUB) TO TEMPERATURE-TOTAL.
        .
        .
```

Figure 9–4
Routine for adding temperatures

Problem

A file contains dates and temperatures. Each record can have a maximum of thirteen pairs of four-column dates and two-column temperatures. However, if a four-column date is blank, the rest of the record will be blank also.

The input area for the record is described as follows:

```
 01   TEMPERATURE-RECORD.
*
      05  TR-TEMP-DATA            OCCURS 13 TIMES.
          10  TR-TEMP-DATE        PIC X(4).
          10  TR-TEMPERATURE      PIC 99.
      05  FILLER                  PIC XX.
```

Write a routine that adds the temperatures in each record to a field named TEMPERATURE–TOTAL. Use subscripts and the PERFORM statement to control the repetitive processing. The module that does the addition should be called 120–ADD–RECORD–TEMPS.

Solution

Figure 9–4 illustrates an acceptable solution.

Pay class	Pay rate
1	4.25
2	4.50
3	4.75
4	5.00
5	5.25
6	5.50
7	5.75
8	6.00
9	6.25
10	6.50

Figure 9–5
A single-level pay-rate table

Topic 2 **Handling Single-Level Tables Using Subscripts**

Orientation

A *single-level table* is a table that tabulates data for one variable factor. For instance, the rate table in Figure 9–5 is a single-level table in which the pay class is the variable. As the pay class increases, so does the rate of pay.

The program in Figure 9–6 uses the repetitive processing elements to set up and process the pay-rate table. This program reads payroll records containing employee number, pay class, and hours worked. It then looks up each employee's pay rate in the rate table and calculates the employee's gross pay. The output of the program is one line per employee showing employee number, hours worked, pay rate, and gross pay. Since the point of this program is to show how to use a table, we'll assume there is no need for page overflow or headings on the report.

Terminology

computed access	look-up	single-level table
direct access	look-up access	table access
frequency access	search access	table organization
imbedded table	sequential organization	table use
loaded table	serial organization	variable-length table

Objective

Given a problem involving a single-level table, code a COBOL solution using subscripts.

```
       IDENTIFICATION DIVISION.
      *
       PROGRAM-ID.    RATLKUP.
      *
       ENVIRONMENT DIVISION.
       INPUT-OUTPUT SECTION.
      *
       FILE-CONTROL.
           SELECT EMPLOYEE-FILE
               ASSIGN TO PFMS.
           SELECT PAYROLL-LISTING
               ASSIGN TO PFMS.
      *
       DATA DIVISION.
      *
       FILE SECTION.
      *
       FD  EMPLOYEE-FILE
           LABEL RECORDS ARE STANDARD
           RECORD CONTAINS 80 CHARACTERS.
      *
       01  EMPLOYEE-AREA.
           05  FILLER              PIC X(80).
      *
       FD  PAYROLL-LISTING
           LABEL RECORDS ARE STANDARD
           RECORD CONTAINS 133 CHARACTERS.
      *
       01  PRINT-AREA.
           05  FILLER              PIC X(133).
      *
       WORKING-STORAGE SECTION.
      *
       01  SWITCHES.
           05  EMPLOYEE-EOF-SW     PIC X         VALUE 'N'.
               88  LAST-EMPLOYEE-RECORD          VALUE 'Y'.
               88  MORE-EMPLOYEE-RECORDS         VALUE 'N'.
      *
       01  WORK-FIELDS.
           05  GROSS-PAY           PIC S999V99                COMP-3.
      *
       01  SUBSCRIPTS                                         COMP.
           05  RATE-SUB            PIC 99.
      *
       COPY PAYRTVAL.
       01  RATE-TABLE-VALUES                                  COMP-3.
           05  FILLER              PIC S9V99     VALUE +4.25.
```

Figure 9–6
The produce-payroll-listing program using subscripts (part 1 of 3)

Table Concepts

The topic on repetitive processing presented the essential tools that the COBOL programmer requires to use tables. As you probably know from experience, tables have many uses. However, the general concepts concerning the ways in which tables are set up and used are only a few. As you study the remaining topics, keep in mind the following definitions. They will help you in deciding how to set up, organize, and use tables.

Use

Tables have two possible purposes or ways in which they are used:

1. Reference—Data is found in the table and extracted from it for informational use or as part of a calculation. In Figures 9–5 and 9–6 you will see the pay-rate being used as part of a payroll calculation.

```
       05  FILLER                PIC S9V99        VALUE +4.50.
       05  FILLER                PIC S9V99        VALUE +4.75.
       05  FILLER                PIC S9V99        VALUE +5.00.
       05  FILLER                PIC S9V99        VALUE +5.25.
       05  FILLER                PIC S9V99        VALUE +5.50.
       05  FILLER                PIC S9V99        VALUE +5.75
       05  FILLER                PIC S9V99        VALUE +6.00.
       05  FILLER                PIC S9V99        VALUE +6.25.
       05  FILLER                PIC S9V99        VALUE +6.50.
   COPY PAYRTVAL.
  *
   01  RATE-TABLE                REDEFINES RATE-TABLE-VALUES.
       05  PAY-RATE                  OCCURS 10 TIMES
                                 PIC S9V99                      COMP-3.
  *
   COPY EMPLRECD.
   01  EMPLOYEE-RECORD.
       05  ER-EMP-NO             PIC X(4).
       05  ER-EMP-AGE            PIC 99.
           88  EMPLOYABLE-AGE                     VALUE 16 THRU 65.
       05  FILLER                PIC X(21).
       05  ER-PAY-CLASS          PIC 99.
           88  VALID-PAY-CLASS                    VALUE 0 THRU 10.
       05  ER-HOURS-WORKED       PIC 99V9.
       05  FILLER                PIC X(48).
   COPY EMPLRECD.
  *
   01  EMPLOYEE-LINE.
       05  FILLER                PIC X            VALUE SPACE.
       05  EL-EMP-NO             PIC X(4).
       05  FILLER                PIC X(3)         VALUE SPACE.
       05  EL-PAY-RATE           PIC Z.99.
       05  FILLER                PIC X(3)         VALUE SPACE.
       05  EL-HOURS-WORKED       PIC ZZ.9.
       05  FILLER                PIC X(3)         VALUE SPACE.
       05  EL-GROSS-PAY          PIC ZZZ.99.
  *
   01  ERROR-MESSAGE-LINE.
       05  FILLER                PIC X(16)        VALUE ' RATLKUP  A  2'.
       05  FILLER                PIC X(8)         VALUE 'INVALID'.
       05  FILLER                PIC X(14)        VALUE 'PAY-CLASS FOR'.
       05  FILLER                PIC X(14)        VALUE 'EMPLOYEE NO.'.
       05  EML-EMP-NO            PIC X(4).
       05  FILLER                PIC X(77)        VALUE SPACE.
  *
```

Figure 9–6
The produce-payroll-listing program using subscripts (part 2 of 3)

2. Accumulation—This is often a simple counting function. The program reads the records of a file and counts the number of records in each category. The categories are the elements of the table. For example, the census bureau might create income categories in units of $5000 and determine how many families had annual incomes of $0–5000, how many had incomes of $5001–10,000, how many in $10,001–15,000, etc. Sometimes data that is accumulated may be used later in the program for reference.

Data source

This concerns the manner in which data for reference typically gets into the table. This is an important question as it impacts overall programming efficiency, both in current running times and in continued program maintenance time.

```
       PROCEDURE DIVISION.
      *
       000-PRODUCE-PAYROLL-LISTING.
           OPEN INPUT  EMPLOYEE-FILE
                OUTPUT PAYROLL-LISTING.
           PERFORM 100-PRODUCE-EMPLOYEE-LINE
               UNTIL LAST-EMPLOYEE-RECORD
           CLOSE EMPLOYEE-FILE
                 PAYROLL-LISTING.
           DISPLAY 'RATLKUP  I  1  NORMAL EOJ'.
           STOP RUN.
      *
       100-PRODUCE-EMPLOYEE-LINE.
           PERFORM 110-READ-EMPLOYEE-RECORD.
           IF MORE-EMPLOYEE-RECORDS
               IF  VALID-PAY-CLASS
                   PERFORM 120-CALC-GROSS-PAY
                   PERFORM 130-PRINT-EMPLOYEE-LINE
               ELSE
                   PERFORM 140-PRINT-ERROR-MESSAGE.
      *
       110-READ-EMPLOYEE-RECORD.
           READ EMPLOYEE-FILE INTO EMPLOYEE-RECORD
               AT END
                   MOVE 'Y'                TO EMPLOYEE-EOF-SW.
      *
       120-CALC-GROSS-PAY.
           MOVE ER-PAY-CLASS               TO RATE-SUB.
           MULTIPLY ER-HOURS-WORKED BY PAY-RATE (RATE-SUB)
               GIVING GROSS-PAY ROUNDED.
      *
       130-PRINT-EMPLOYEE-LINE.
           MOVE ER-EMP-NO                  TO EL-EMP-NO.
           MOVE PAY-RATE (RATE-SUB)        TO EL-PAY-RATE.
           MOVE ER-HOURS-WORKED            TO EL-HOURS-WORKED.
           MOVE GROSS-PAY                  TO EL-GROSS-PAY.
           MOVE EMPLOYEE-LINE              TO PRINT-AREA.
           PERFORM 150-WRITE-REPORT-LINE.
      *
       140-PRINT-ERROR-MESSAGE.
           MOVE ER-EMP-NO                  TO EML-EMP-NO.
           MOVE ERROR-MESSAGE-LINE         TO PRINT-AREA.
           PERFORM 150-WRITE-REPORT-LINE.
      *
       150-WRITE-REPORT-LINE.
           WRITE PRINT-AREA
               AFTER ADVANCING 1 LINES.
```

Figure 9–6
The produce-payroll-listing using subscripts (part 3 of 3)

1. Imbedded—The data is built (coded) into the program directly. The RATE-TABLE-VALUES of Figure 9–6 are an example of this.

2. Loaded—The program has a "get ready" function that loads the data from an outside source into the table. Figure 9–9 introduces this technique.

Access

How to access or find the position in the table where the data is to be accumulated, stored, or found makes a significant difference in the way the coding for the table is accomplished. In the case where data is being referenced, this process is also called table look-up.

1. Direct—A code associated with the data is in a one-to-one correspondence with the position of the data in the table. (That is, the data for a code of 1 is in the first table position, the data for code 2 is in the second position, and the data for code 11 is in the eleventh position.) In this case only the data itself needs to be stored in the table. Figure 9–6 shows a direct look-up table.

2. Computed—This is a subcategory of the direct access for tables. In this case the data elements are still the only entries in the table. However, the codes that will lead to finding the data's table position do not point there directly. The codes must first be manipulated via a predefined process to generate the position. A simple example of this would be to subtract 1110 from codes 1111–1220 to generate the numbers 1–120, which would be the 120 table positions required.

3. Search—Due to large and irregular gaps in the code sequence or to the use of non-numeric codes, there can be no possibility of direct or computed conversion of the code to the table position. In this case the code must be stored along with the data. The typical implementation of this situation is to create the table so that each element is actually a code-data pair. To access the needed data element, the codes must be searched one by one for a match or an appropriate range.

The programmer should study the situation carefully since it is generally more efficient if the searching approach can be avoided, even at the expense of a relatively complex position computation.

Organization

The order in which the data and the related codes are stored in the table will have a significant impact on the efficiency of the look-up process. This question is only significant for a search-type access.

1. Serial—The data is simply stored in the table in the order in which it arrives. This essentially means that the data may not be in any predetermined order.

2. Sequential—This is really a subcategory of serial. It means that the data has been sorted in either ascending or descending order of the code before loading into the table. Ascending order is the most common order used.

3. Frequency access—The data is preorganized with those elements having the highest probability of being required placed in the lowest or first position. This is only useful if there is a known, predictable, and significant difference in the potential accesses between the elements. If the probability of access is relatively evenly distributed or not dependable, then the serial or sequential method is better since both demand less work.

The Data Division

Two of the COBOL elements you're already familiar with, the REDEFINES and OCCURS clauses, are used in the Working–Storage Section in Figure 9–6 to store the table. First, the pay rates are given in a group item named RATE–TABLE–VALUES. Then, RATE–TABLE redefines the table-value area using the OCCURS clause. The values in the table can then be referenced using subscripts, as you'll see in a moment. Because VALUE clauses are illegal in statements that redefine a storage area, you must first code the values of a table and then redefine the storage area using the OCCURS clause.

To reduce the coding involved in storing the rate table, the following could be used:

```
 01    RATE-TABLE-VALUES.
*
       05  FILLER  PIC X(15)  VALUE "425450475500525".
       05  FILLER  PIC X(15)  VALUE "550575600625650".
```

However, when this form is used, the rates are more difficult to read, so we don't recommend it. Also, this method of storing table values can't be used if COMP–3 usage is required.

The Procedure Division

In the Procedure Division, paragraph 100 causes an employee record to be read and then checks to be sure that the pay-class field contains a value from one through ten. Otherwise, the pay class won't refer to a value within the rate table. If the value is invalid, an error message is printed and no further processing is done in paragraph 100.

If the value is valid, the program moves EM–PAY–CLASS to RATE–SUB, a COMPUTATIONAL field that will be used as a subscript. A subscript, as you'll recall, specifies which of the fields defined by an OCCURS clause is being referred to. For instance, in PAY–RATE (3), 3 is the subscript that specifies the third value in the rate table, 4.75. In PAY–RATE (RATE–SUB), the value depends on the value of RATE–SUB. For example, if RATE–SUB equals nine, the expression refers to the ninth value in the table, 6.25. Although EM–PAY–CLASS itself could have been used as the subscript for the rate table, COMPUTATIONAL subscripts generally lead to a more efficient object program.

To determine the employee's gross pay, RATE–SUB is used as the subscript in this statement:

```
MULTIPLY EM-HOURS-WORKED BY PAY-RATE (RATE-SUB)
    GIVING GROSS-PAY ROUNDED
```

Here, the table rate referred to by the subscript is the one that is used as the multiplier. If, for example, RATE–SUB has a value of six, the hours-worked field is multiplied by 5.50. Then the rounded result is stored in GROSS–PAY.

Searching a Table

In the program in Figure 9–6, it was not necessary to search the rate table since the pay-class value identified the position of the proper pay rate. The purpose of the table was to look up data and the access method was direct. To illustrate the need for table searching, suppose a program is to look up unit prices using a price table like the one in Figure 9–7. When a transaction record is read, the program must compare the transaction item number with each of the item numbers in the table until a matching number is found. Then, the corresponding unit price in the table is the one used in processing the transaction.

As you study this case, note that the code cannot be manipulated to give the data's table position. Also pay special attention to how the code-data pair is arranged in the table.

Item no.	Unit price
101	12.50
107	50.00
111	7.70
158	5.55
161	62.50
192	25.00
201	.40
213	6.66
277	1.11
297	7.77
305	.10
341	15.00
342	57.50
343	65.00
347	22.50
351	.35
356	8.88
359	2.22

Figure 9–7
A price table

```
 WORKING-STORAGE SECTION.
*
 01  SWITCHES.
*
         .
         .
     05  VALID-ITEM-NO-SW       PIC X.
         88  VALID-ITEM-NO      VALUE "Y".
*
 01  WORK-FIELDS                COMP-3.
*
     05  UNIT-PRICE             PIC S999V99.
*
 01  SUBSCRIPTS                 COMP.
*
     05  ITEM-SUB               PIC 99.
*
 01  ITEM-TABLE-VALUES.
*
     05  FILLER                 PIC X(7)     VALUE "1011250".
     05  FILLER                 PIC X(7)     VALUE "1075000".
     05  FILLER                 PIC X(7)     VALUE "1110770".
     05  FILLER                 PIC X(7)     VALUE "1580555".
     05  FILLER                 PIC X(7)     VALUE "1616250".
     05  FILLER                 PIC X(7)     VALUE "1922500".
     05  FILLER                 PIC X(7)     VALUE "2010040".
     05  FILLER                 PIC X(7)     VALUE "2130666".
     05  FILLER                 PIC X(7)     VALUE "2770111".
     05  FILLER                 PIC X(7)     VALUE "2970777".
     05  FILLER                 PIC X(7)     VALUE "3050010".
     05  FILLER                 PIC X(7)     VALUE "3411500".
     05  FILLER                 PIC X(7)     VALUE "3425750".
     05  FILLER                 PIC X(7)     VALUE "3436500".
     05  FILLER                 PIC X(7)     VALUE "3472250".
     05  FILLER                 PIC X(7)     VALUE "3510035".
     05  FILLER                 PIC X(7)     VALUE "3560888".
     05  FILLER                 PIC X(7)     VALUE "3590222".
*
```

Figure 9–8
Searching the item table using subscripts (part 1 of 2)

```
 01  ITEM-TABLE                  REDEFINES ITEM-TABLE-VALUES.
*
     05  ITEM-TABLE-ENTRY        OCCURS 18 TIMES.
         10  IT-ITEM-NO          PIC 999.
         10  IT-UNIT-PRICE       PIC 99V99.
*
     .
     .
*
 PROCEDURE DIVISION.
*
     .
     .
*
 100-PREPARE-CUSTOMER-INVOICE.
*
     .
     .
     MOVE "N" TO VALID-ITEM-NO-SW.
     PERFORM 120-SEARCH-ITEM-TABLE
         VARYING ITEM-SUB FROM 1 BY 1
         UNTIL VALID-ITEM-NO
            OR ITEM-SUB GREATER 18.
     IF VALID-ITEM-NO
         SUBTRACT 1 FROM ITEM-SUB
         MOVE IT-UNIT-PRICE (ITEM-SUB) TO UNIT-PRICE
         .
         .
     ELSE
         .
         .
*
 120-SEARCH-ITEM-TABLE.
*
     IF TR-ITEM-NO = IT-ITEM-NO (ITEM-SUB)
         MOVE "Y" TO VALID-ITEM-NO-SW.
     .
     .
```

Figure 9–8
Searching the item table using subscripts (part 2 of 2)

Figure 9–8 presents a routine for performing this table search. In the Working-Storage Section, the 18 pairs of item numbers and unit prices are stored in this sequence: the first item number and the first unit price, the second item number and the second unit price, and so on. Then, ITEM–TABLE redefines the table-value area. The OCCURS clause says the ITEM–TABLE–ENTRY occurs 18 times, so subscripts 1 through 18 can be used to refer to the entries in the table.

In the Procedure Division, a PERFORM statement with the VARYING option controls the table search. It does this by manipulating the value of the subscript (ITEM–SUB) from 1 to 18 and executing 120–SEARCH–ITEM–TABLE once for each value. Paragraph 120, in turn, uses the subscript to compare the item number from the transaction record to the item number in the table. If the numbers are equal, Y is moved to VALID–ITEM–NO–SW, indicating that the item number has been found. Once the VALID–ITEM–NO–SW has been turned on or the subscript has been varied through all 18 values, the program continues with the statement after the PERFORM VARYING statement.

There are two other important points to note in paragraph 100. One is the SUBTRACT statement in the IF statement that follows the PERFORM

VARYING statement. As you can see, it subtracts one from the value of ITEM–SUB. Why is this necessary? Because of the way the PERFORM VARYING statement works. Each time it finishes performing module 120, it increases ITEM–SUB by one *before* it checks to see if the condition is true. So to use the subscript later in the program, you have to decrease it by one to get the proper value.

For example, suppose TR–ITEM–NO equals IT–ITEM–NO when ITEM–SUB is three. On its third execution, module 120 will move Y to VALID–ITEM–NO–SW before returning to the PERFORM VARYING statement. The PERFORM VARYING statement will then increase ITEM–SUB to four before it checks for the condition in the UNTIL clause. Since VALID–ITEM–NO–SW is on, the program will continue by executing the IF statement and subtract one from ITEM–SUB. That means ITEM–SUB will be reduced back to three and can be used correctly as a subscript to move the unit price in the table to the working-storage field named UNIT–PRICE.

The second point to note is that VALID–ITEM–NO–SW must be turned off in paragraph 100 before the start of each search. Otherwise, once the switch is turned on, it will indicate that every subsequent item number was found in the table on the first try.

Choosing Table Organization

One other thing you should remember about table searching is that the sequence of entries can affect the efficiency of the search in terms of processing time. Since the table in Figure 9–8 is always searched starting with the first entry and proceeding toward the last, the most used entry should be the first one in the table and the least used entry should be the last. For example, if 60 percent of the transactions involve item number 277, 347, and 356, these table entries should be first in the table. Similarly, the rest of thc table should be sequenced by frequency of use. You can imagine what a difference this type of sequencing can make if item number 359 accounts for 25 percent of the transactions.

Again, remember to give careful consideration to selection of the table organization. The above discussion, of course, presents an obvious application of frequency access loading. If the frequency is not predictable or easily discovered, then a sequential loading may be preferred. Strictly scrial loading is not usually acceptable except for very short tables or ones that are being continually added to and accessed during the program's execution. Direct methods are always prefered since that is the fastest way to access any one element.

Loading a Table

In many cases, particularly if a table requires frequent changes, the values used in the table aren't defined in the program. Instead, the table values are read into storage from a file (cards, tape, or disk) at the beginning of the program. Then the table can be changed without changing the program.

Using the price table again, you might find the table values in a small disk file. To illustrate the code necessary to load the table, assume one pair of entries is stored in each record. Also assume the format of the table is the same as that defined in Figure 9–8. The price-table input records have the item number in columns 1–3 and the unit price in columns 4–7 with an assumed decimal point between columns 5 and 6. Figure 9–9, then, illustrates a routine for loading this table into storage.

```
 FILE SECTION.
*
 FD  TABLE-DATA-FILE
     LABEL RECORDS ARE STANDARD
     RECORD CONTAINS 80 CHARACTERS.
*
 01  TABLE-DATA-AREA              PIC X(80).
*
     .
     .
*
 WORKING-STORAGE SECTION.
*
 01  SWITCHES.
*
     05  TABLE-DATA-EOF-SW        PIC X       VALUE "N".
         88  TABLE-DATA-EOF                   VALUE "Y".
     .
     .
*
 01  SUBSCRIPTS                   COMP.
*
     05  ITEM-SUB                 PIC 99.
     .
     .
*
 01  ITEM-TABLE.
*
     05  ITEM-TABLE-ENTRY         OCCURS 18 TIMES.
         10  IT-ITEM-NUMBER       PIC 999.
         10  IT-UNIT-PRICE        PIC 99V99.
*
 01  TD-RECORD.
*
     05  TD-ITEM-NUMBER           PIC 999.
     05  TD-UNIT-PRICE            PIC 99V99.
     05  FILLER                   PIC X(73).
*
     .
     .
*
```

Figure 9-9
Loading the item table using subscripts (part 1 of 2)

The price table is loaded in a module named 100-LOAD-ITEM-TABLE. This module is performed while the subscript (ITEM-SUB) is varied from 1 until it is greater than 18. Each time it's executed, the load module begins by performing the read module for the file containing the item numbers and prices. Then, it moves the input data into the table area. When the subscript is greater than 18, it means the table is loaded, so the program continues with the next statement following the PERFORM VARYING statement. Any other program that uses the price table will have to have a similar routine to read the table file and construct the table in storage.

```
 PROCEDURE DIVISION.
*
 000-PRODUCE-PRICE-LISTING.
*
     OPEN INPUT  TABLE-DATA-FILE
                 TRANSACTION-FILE
          OUTPUT PRICE-LISTING.
     PERFORM 100-LOAD-ITEM-TABLE
         VARYING ITEM-SUB FROM 1 BY 1
         UNTIL ITEM-SUB GREATER 18.
     .
     .
     CLOSE TABLE-DATA-FILE
           TRANSACTION-FILE
           PRICE-LISTING.
     DISPLAY "LSTPRCE  I  1  NORMAL EOJ".
     STOP RUN.
*
 100-LOAD-ITEM-TABLE.
*
     PERFORM 110-READ-TABLE-DATA-RECORD.
     MOVE TD-ITEM-NUMBER TO IT-ITEM-NUMBER (ITEM-SUB).
     MOVE TD-UNIT-PRICE  TO IT-UNIT PRICE (ITEM-SUB).
*
 110-READ-TABLE-DATA-RECORD.
*
     READ TABLE-DATA-FILE INTO TD-RECORD
         AT END
             MOVE "Y" TO TABLE-DATA-EOF-SW.
*
     .
     .
```

Figure 9–9
Loading the item table using subscripts (part 2 of 2)

Sequential Processing of a Table

Sometimes it is necessary to manipulate the entries of a table in a uniform way. For instance, suppose a table contains the salaries of all employees in a firm. If everybody is to get a ten-percent pay increase, then each entry in the table must be modified. As you might guess, this type of problem can also be done with a PERFORM VARYING statement.

Figure 9–10 illustrates code that prints the contents of the price table. As you can see, the logic is the same as in the load example in Figure 9–9. The PERFORM statement simply executes the print module as it varies the subscript value from 1 to 18. The print module takes care of formatting and writing the output line for each individual table record.

This same logic can be used regardless of the complexity of the problem. If, for example, all of the prices in the table were to be increased by five percent, the statements that print the table could be replaced by statements that do the required calculations.

Variable-Length Tables

In actual practice, the number of entries in a table is likely to change. For instance, a new rate may be added to the pay-rate table or additional items may be added to the price table. For this reason, COBOL provides for processing *variable-length tables*. To illustrate, assume the price table is only 18 items long at the time it is created, but programs that use it should provide for

```
 DATA DIVISION.
*
 FILE SECTION.
*
 FD  PRINT-FILE
     LABEL RECORDS ARE STANDARD
     RECORD CONTAINS 132 CHARACTERS.
*
 01  PRINT-AREA                  PIC X(132).
*
     .
     .
*
 WORKING-STORAGE SECTION.
*
     .
     .
*
 01  SUBSCRIPTS                  COMP.
*
     05  ITEM-SUB                PIC 99.
     .
     .
*
 01  ITEM-TABLE.
*
     05  ITEM-TABLE-ENTRY        OCCURS 18 TIMES.
         10  IT-ITEM-NO          PIC S999.
         10  IT-UNIT-PRICE       PIC S99V99.
*
 01  TABLE-LINE-RECORD.
*
     05  TL-ITEM-NO              PIC ZZZ.
     05  FILLER                  PIC XXX       VALUE SPACE.
     05  TL-UNIT-PRICE           PIC ZZ.99.
     05  FILLER                  PIC X(121)    VALUE SPACE.
*
     .
     .
*
 PROCEDURE DIVISION.
*
     .
     .
     PERFORM 200-PRINT-ITEM-TABLE
         VARYING ITEM-SUB FROM 1 BY 1
         UNTIL ITEM-SUB GREATER 18.
     .
     .
*
 200-PRINT-ITEM-TABLE.
*
     MOVE IT-ITEM-NO (ITEM-SUB)    TO TL-ITEM-NO.
     MOVE IT-UNIT-PRICE (ITEM-SUB) TO TL-UNIT-PRICE.
     MOVE TABLE-LINE-RECORD TO PRINT-AREA.
     PERFORM 210-WRITE-ITEM-LINE.
*
 210-WRITE-ITEM-LINE.
*
     WRITE PRINT-AREA
         AFTER ADVANCING 1 LINES.
*
 .
 .
```

Figure 9–10
Sequentially processing the item table using subscripts

```
 DATA DIVISION.
*
 FILE SECTION.
*
 FD  TABLE-DATA-FILE
     LABEL RECORDS ARE STANDARD
     RECORD CONTAINS 80 CHARACTERS.
*
 01  TABLE-DATA-AREA        PIC X(80).
*
 FD  TRANSACTION-FILE
     LABEL RECORDS ARE STANDARD
     RECORD CONTAINS 80 CHARACTERS.
*
 01  TRAN-AREA              PIC X(80).
*
     .
     .
*
 WORKING-STORAGE SECTION.
*
 01  SWITCHES.
*
     05  TABLE-EOF-SW       PIC X      VALUE "N".
         88  TABLE-EOF                 VALUE "Y".
     05  TRAN-EOF-SW        PIC X      VALUE "N".
         88  TRAN-EOF                  VALUE "Y".
     05  VALID-ITEM-NO-SW   PIC X.
         88  VALID-ITEM-NO             VALUE "Y".
     .
     .
*
 01  TABLE-CONTROL-FIELDS COMP-3.
*
     05  IT-ENTRY-COUNT     PIC 9(03)  COMP-3.
     05  IT-ENTRY-LIMIT     PIC 9(03)  VALUE 100.
     .
*
 01  SUBSCRIPTS             COMP.
*
     05  ITEM-SUB           PIC 9(03)
*
 01  ITEM-TABLE.
*
     05  ITEM-TABLE-ENTRY   OCCURS 100 TIMES.
         10  IT-ITEM-NO     PIC 999.
         10  IT-UNIT-PRICE  PIC 99V99.
*
 01  TD-RECORD.
*
     05  TD-ITEM-NO         PIC 999.
     05  TD-UNIT-PRICE      PIC 99V99.
     05  FILLER             PIC X(73).
*
 01  TR-RECORD.
*
     05  TR-ITEM-NO         PIC 999.
     .
     .
```

Figure 9–11
Loading and searching a variable-length table using subscripts (part 1 of 2)

```
 PROCEDURE DIVISION.
*
 000-PRODUCE-CUST-INVOICES.
*
     OPEN INPUT  TABLE-DATA-FILE
                 TRANSACTION-FILE
          OUTPUT ...
     PERFORM 100-LOAD-ITEM-TABLE
         VARYING ITEM-SUB FROM 1 BY 1
         UNTIL TABLE-EOF.
     IF IT-ENTRY-COUNT NOT GREATER IT-ENTRY-LIMIT
         PERFORM 200-PRODUCE-CUST-INVOICE
             UNTIL TRAN-EOF
     ELSE
         DISPLAY "VLITMTB  A  2  TABLE HAS "
                 IT-ENTRY-COUNT " ENTRIES".
     CLOSE TABLE-DATA-FILE
           TRANSACTION-FILE ...
     DISPLAY "VLITMTB  I  1  NORMAL EOJ".
     STOP RUN.
*
 100-LOAD-ITEM-TABLE.
*
     PERFORM 110-READ-TABLE-RECORD.
     IF NOT TABLE-EOF AND ITEM-SUB NOT GREATER IT-ENTRY-LIMIT
         MOVE TD-ITEM-NO    TO IT-ITEM-NO (ITEM-SUB)
         MOVE TD-UNIT-PRICE TO IT-UNIT-PRICE (ITEM-SUB).
     IF TABLE-EOF
         SUBTRACT 1 FROM ITEM-SUB
         MOVE ITEM-SUB TO IT-ENTRY-COUNT.
*
 110-READ-TABLE-RECORD.
*
     READ TABLE-DATA-FILE INTO TD-RECORD
         AT END
             MOVE "Y" TO TABLE-EOF-SW.
*
 200-PRODUCE-CUST-INVOICE.
*
     PERFORM 210-READ-TRAN-RECORD.
     IF NOT TRAN-EOF
         MOVE "N" TO VALID-ITEM-NO-SW
         PERFORM 220-SEARCH-ITEM-TABLE
             VARYING ITEM-SUB FROM 1 BY 1
             UNTIL VALID-ITEM-NO
                OR ITEM-SUB GREATER IT-ENTRY-COUNT
         .
         .
*
 210-READ-TRAN-RECORD.
*
     READ TRANSACTION-FILE INTO TR-RECORD
         AT END
             MOVE "Y" TO TRAN-EOF-SW.
*
 220-SEARCH-ITEM-TABLE.
*
     IF IT-ITEM-NO (ITEM-SUB) = TR-ITEM-NO
         MOVE "Y" TO VALID-ITEM-NO-SW.
```

Figure 9–11
Loading and searching a variable-length table using subscripts (part 2 of 2)

price table of up to 100 items. Figure 9–11 illustrates the coding for loading and searching this table.

Perhaps the key coding in this example is the UNTIL clause in the first PERFORM VARYING statement:

```
PERFORM 100-LOAD-ITEM-TABLE
    VARYING ITEM-SUB FROM 1 BY 1
    UNTIL TABLE-EOF.
```

Here, instead of performing the load module a fixed number of times, the module is executed until the end of the table file has been reached. Then, module 100 subtracts one from the subscript value to give the actual number of entries in the table and stores it for later use in IT–ENTRY–COUNT.

In the Working–Storage Section, the OCCURS clause for ITEM–TABLE–ENTRY says that the table cannot have more than 100 entries. As a result, the program will abend if it tries to load more than 100 entries. That's why the code in module 100 says to move the information from a table record to the table only if the end of the table file hasn't been reached *and* if ITEM–SUB is less than or equal to IT–ENTRY–LIMIT which has a value of 100. Otherwise, the program bypasses the loading code. Then back in module 000, IT–ENTRY–COUNT is compared with IT–ENTRY–LIMIT. If not greater, processing continues with 200–PRODUCE–CUST–INVOICE. Otherwise, an error message is displayed and the program continues by executing the CLOSE statement.

To process the table, the program simply performs a module IT–ENTRY–COUNT times, or until a subscript or counter is greater than IT–ENTRY–COUNT. For instance, module 200 in Figure 9–11 looks up the price for each transaction item by using a PERFORM VARYING statement just as in Figures 9–8, 9–9, and 9–10. But this time, instead of using a literal value in the PERFORM statement, ITEM–SUB is compared to IT–ENTRY–COUNT, and the program leaves the PERFORM statement if a greater-than condition results. This code insures that no matter how many entries are in the table, the program will check all the table entries before it decides it can't find the correct one.

Discussion

From this introduction to table handling, you should realize that you can process all single-level tables using the elements you are already familiar with: the OCCURS clause, the REDEFINES clause, the PERFORM VARYING statement, and subscripts. Most business applications do not require processing much more sophisticated than this.

The one problem in using these elements is that they tend to be very inefficient in terms of execution speed. For instance, on one IBM system, it takes as many as 16 machine instructions to convert a subscript value to a value representing the number of storage positions that a table entry is from the start of the table. For example, the second value in the price table starts in the eighth position from the beginning of the table (three positions for the first time number and four positions for the first item price). So the subscript 2 must be converted to a value representing the eighth storage position. Since this conversion must be done each time an entry in a table is referenced using a subscript, a table-handling routine can be quite time-consuming.

Topic 3 presents another method of handling tables—one that uses indexes. Here, you will see that indexes are not only more efficient in terms of execution speed, but they are also easier to use when coding a search routine.

The following summary describes the advantages and disadvantages of the various attributes of tables.

Data sources

Advantages
Imbedded data can be seen in the source program and takes no execution time once a correct compile is obtained. Loaded data is more easily changed when the data changes, and the program does not have to be updated and recompiled.

Disadvantages
If imbedded data changes, the program must be updated and recompiled, which is a potential source of error. Loaded data requires handling outside of the program, possibly by another program.

Criteria
The choice should be based on the likelihood of data change. Data sets such as names of states of the union, days of the week, and months of the year should be imbedded since they seldom change. Items subject to change should be loaded. Price lists and transportation schedules are examples of data sets that would normally be loaded since they are subject to frequent change. Data sets that change, but do so infrequently, are borderline cases. Income tax tables probably should be loaded, but since they change usually only once a year it could be more efficient to have them imbedded.

Access

Advantages
Direct and computed are always faster, whereas the search enables accessing of data with scattered code distribution or alphanumeric coding such as state codes.

Disadvantages
If the code is in a one-to-one correspondence with the table position, there is no disadvantage. If a computation is required to generate the position, there are the possibilities of poor documentation, overly cumbersome computations, or even inaccurate computations. Search access requires more items (the codes) to be in the table along with the data. Searching through a table to find a needed position always consumes more times than direct access.

Organization

Advantages
Serial is easy and requires no prior preparation. Sequential is also easy, but requires a prior ordering. However, the ordering is always in ascending or descending order so a sort process is all that is required. Sequential order can also shorten the search. The instant that the search locates an ascending ordered table code which is greater than the search code the search can stop. Since the table codes will only get larger, you know that either the code will not be matched or the desired range has been found. Frequency access can drastically reduce search time if there are a few items which can be predicted to have most of the activity.

Disadvantages

Serial is not necessarily in order and may require searching the entire table to determine whether an item is present. Sequential organization by code requires a prior sorting which may take processing time. If the data comes from an already ordered file, then there is no disadvantage, other than excess execution time if the table could have been loaded in frequency order. Frequency access requires prior study to ensure that the access pattern is significant, predictable, and dependable. A pattern that changes frequently may be worse than treating the data sequentially. Frequency is not as easy to arrange in the desired order as is sequential by the code and may take more time than the sort process.

Table use

There is really no legitimate question of advantage here. The program problem dictates the choice between a look-up or reference use and accumulation.

Problem

Rewrite the program in Figure 9–6 so that you're loading the rate table into storage in the Procedure Division rather than storing it as part of the program. For this, assume the pay rates are entered in successive positions of one input record, starting with position 3. This means as many as 26 pay rates may be entered in positions 3–80 of the table record. Assume the pay-rate table is variable-length with a maximum of 26 entries and that positions 1–2 of the table record contain the actual number of rates to be stored in the table. Figure 9–12 shows a VTOC for this program.

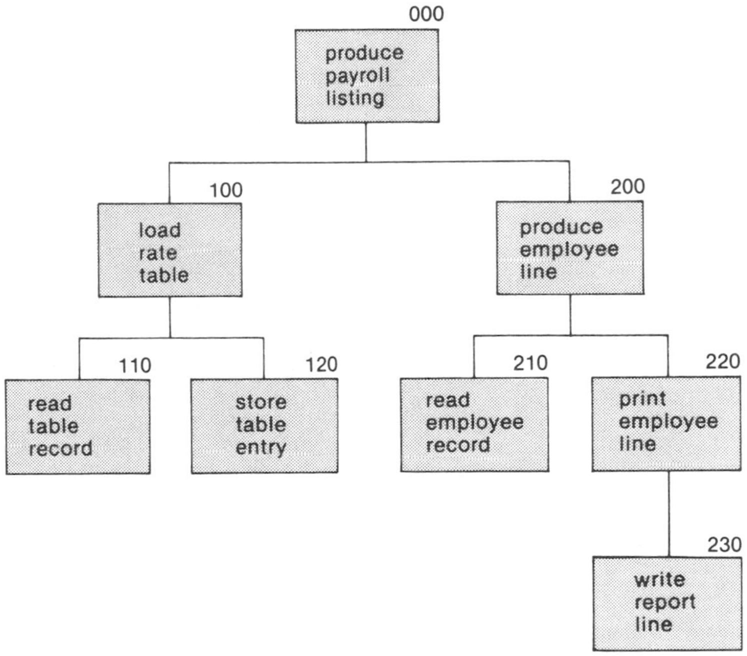
000
produce payroll listing
100
load rate table
200
produce employee line
110
read table record
120
store table entry
210
read employee record
220
print employee line
230
write report line

Figure 9–12
A VTOC for the produce-payroll-listing program

```
 IDENTIFICATION DIVISION.
*
 PROGRAM-ID.  RATLKUP.
*
 ENVIRONMENT DIVISION.
*
 CONFIGURATION SECTION.
*
 SOURCE-COMPUTER.  PRIME 850.
 OBJECT-COMPUTER.  PRIME 850.
*
 INPUT-OUTPUT SECTION.
*
 FILE-CONTROL.
     SELECT PAY-RATE-FILE
         ASSIGN TO PFMS.
     SELECT EMPLOYEE-FILE
         ASSIGN TO PFMS.
     SELECT PAYROLL-LISTING
         ASSIGN TO PFMS.
*
 DATA DIVISION.
*
 FILE SECTION.
*
 FD  PAY-RATE-FILE
     LABEL RECORDS ARE STANDARD
     RECORD CONTAINS 80 CHARACTERS.
*
 01  PAY-RATE-AREA            PIC X(80).
*
 FD  EMPLOYEE-FILE
     LABEL RECORDS ARE STANDARD
     RECORD CONTAINS 80 CHARACTERS.
*
 01  EMPL-AREA                PIC X(80).
*
 FD  PAYROLL-LISTING
     LABEL RECORDS ARE STANDARD
     RECORD CONTAINS 132 CHARACTERS.
*
 01  PRINT-AREA               PIC X(132).
*
 WORKING-STORAGE SECTION.
*
 01  SWITCHES.
*
     05  PAY-RATE-FILE-END-SW  PIC X      VALUE "N".
         88  LAST-PAY-RATE-REC            VALUE "Y".
     05  EMPL-FILE-END-SW      PIC X      VALUE "N".
         88  LAST-EMPL-REC                VALUE 'Y'.
         88  MORE-EMPL-RECS               VALUE 'N'.
*
 01  WORK-FIELDS              COMP-3.
*
     05  GROSS-PAY            PIC S999V99.
*
```

Figure 9–13
Loading and processing the pay-rate table (part 1 of 3)

```
 01  COUNT-FIELDS              COMP-3.
*
     05  TABLE-ENTRY-COUNT     PIC S999.
*
 01  SUBSCRIPTS                COMP.
*
     05  RATE-SUB              PIC 99.
*
 01  RATE-TABLE.               COMP-3.
*
     05  PAY-RATE              OCCURS 26 TIMES
                               PIC 9V99.
*
 01  TD-RECORD.
*
     05  TD-NO-OF-ENTRIES      PIC 99.
     05  TD-ENTRY              OCCURS 26 TIMES
                               PIC 9V99.
*
 01  EM-RECORD.
*
     05  EM-EMP-NO             PIC X(4).
     05  FILLER                PIC X(23).
     05  EM-PAY-CLASS          PIC 99.
     05  EM-HOURS-WORKED       PIC 99V9.
     05  FILLER                PIC X(48).
*
 01  EMPLOYEE-LINE.
*
     05  EL-EMP-NO             PIC X(4).
     05  FILLER                PIC X(3)      VALUE SPACE.
     05  EL-PAY-RATE           PIC Z.99.
     05  FILLER                PIC X(3)      VALUE SPACE.
     05  EL-HOURS-WORKED       PIC ZZ.9.
     05  FILLER                PIC X(3)      VALUE SPACE.
     05  EL-GROSS-PAY          PIC ZZZ.99.
     05  FILLER                PIC X(105)    VALUE SPACE.
*
 PROCEDURE DIVISION.
*
 000-PRODUCE-PAYROLL-LISTING.
*
     OPEN INPUT  TABLE-DATA-FILE
                 EMPLOYEE-FILE
          OUTPUT PAYROLL-LISTING.
     PERFORM 100-LOAD-RATE-TABLE.
     PERFORM 200-PRODUCE-EMPLOYEE-LINE
         UNTIL LAST-EMPL-REC
     CLOSE TABLE-DATA-FILE
           EMPLOYEE-FILE
           PAYROLL-LISTING.
```

Figure 9–13
Loading and processing the pay-rate table (part 2 of 3)

Solution

Figure 9–13 is an acceptable solution. Notice how it differs from Figure 9–6. A third file containing the table data takes the place of supplying the table values in the Working-Storage Section. Module 100 controls the loading of the table using a PERFORM VARYING statement, while module 120 actually stores the input values in the rate table. And TABLE-ENTRY-COUNT is used in the UNTIL clause of the PERFORM VARYING statement in module 100 and again in the validity test for EM-PAY-CLASS in module 200. Otherwise, the program is the same as the one in Figure 9–6.

```
           DISPLAY "RATLKUP  I  1  NORMAL EOJ".
           STOP RUN.
      *
       100-LOAD-RATE-TABLE.
      *
           PERFORM 110-READ-TABLE-RECORD.
           IF NOT-LAST-PAY-RATE-REC
               MOVE TD-NO-OF-ENTRIES TO TABLE-ENTRY-COUNT
               PERFORM 120-STORE-TABLE-ENTRY
                   VARYING RATE-SUB FROM 1 BY 1
                   UNTIL RATE-SUB GREATER THAN TABLE-ENTRY-COUNT.
      *
       110-READ-TABLE-RECORD.
      *
           READ TABLE-DATA-FILE INTO TD-RECORD
               AT END
                   MOVE "Y" TO TABLE-EOF-SW.
      *
       120-STORE-TABLE-ENTRY.
      *
           MOVE TD-ENTRY (RATE-SUB) TO PAY-RATE (RATE-SUB).
      *
       200-PRODUCE-EMPLOYEE-LINE.
      *
           PERFORM 210-READ-EMPLOYEE-RECORD.
           IF MORE-EMPL-FILE-RECS
               IF         EM-PAY-CLASS LESS 1
                       OR EM-PAY-CLASS GREATER TABLE-ENTRY-COUNT
                   DISPLAY "RATLKUP  A  2  INVALID PAY CLASS FOR "
                           "EMPLOYEE NO. " EM-EMP-NO
               ELSE
                   MOVE EM-PAY-CLASS TO RATE-SUB
                   MULTIPLY EM-HOURS-WORKED BY PAY-RATE (RATE-SUB)
                       GIVING GROSS-PAY ROUNDED
                   PERFORM 220-PRINT-EMPLOYEE-LINE.
      *
       210-READ-EMPLOYEE-RECORD.
      *
           READ EMPLOYEE-FILE INTO EM-RECORD
               AT END
                   MOVE "Y" TO EMP-EOF-SW.
      *
       220-PRINT-EMPLOYEE-LINE.
      *
           MOVE EM-EMP-NO            TO EL-EMP-NO.
           MOVE PAY-RATE (RATE-SUB) TO EL-PAY-RATE.
           MOVE EM-HOURS-WORKED      TO EL-HOURS-WORKED.
           MOVE GROSS-PAY            TO EL-GROSS-PAY.
           MOVE EMPLOYEE-LINE        TO PRINT-AREA.
           PERFORM 230-WRITE-REPORT-LINE.
      *
       230-WRITE-REPORT-LINE.
      *
           WRITE PRINT-AREA
               AFTER ADVANCING 1 LINES.
```

Figure 9–13
Loading and processing the pay-rate table (part 3 of 3)

Topic 3 Handling Single-Level Tables Using Indexes

Orientation

This topic presents the table-handling elements that are part of the ANS standard COBOL language. As stated at the end of topic 2, there are some problems with using subscripts for table handling, most notably the inefficiency in terms of program execution. The table-handling elements not only improve execution speed, they also make table-handling routines easier to code. The basic idea is to use *indexes* rather than subscripts to refer to table entries, so all of the statements presented here are related to indexing in some way.

Terminology

binary search	index data item	key field
index	index name	relative indexing

Objective

Given a problem involving single-level tables, code a COBOL solution using the ANS table-handling elements.

Searching a Table Using Indexes

To illustrate the use of indexes, consider the program in Figure 9–14. This is a routine that searches the price table in Figure 9–7 just like the routine in Figure 9–8. The main difference is that this routine most likely will require less core storage and will execute faster.

The INDEXED BY clause

The INDEXED BY clause is the first ANS table handling element you encounter in Figure 9–14. It follows the OCCURS clause and assigns an *index name* of ITEM–INDEX to the table entries named ITEM–TABLE–ENTRY. In the Procedure Division, this index name is used to refer to the entries within the table:

```
MOVE IT-UNIT-PRICE (ITEM-INDEX) TO UNIT-PRICE
```

The unit price that is moved will depend on the value of ITEM–INDEX at the time the statement is executed. As you can see, this coding and execution is similar to the use of subscripts.

An index differs from a subscript, however. A subscript represents an occurrence number while an index represents a displacement value from the start of the table. As a result, valid subscript values in the item table are 1 through 18, while valid index values are 0, 7, 14, 21, 28, 35, 42, 49, 56, 63, 70, 77, 84, 91, 98, 105, 112, and 119. (The values are increased by seven because there are seven positions in each ITEM–TABLE–ENTRY.) Thus, an index value of 0 represents the first item number in the table and corresponds to a subscript of 1; an index value of 35 represents the sixth item number in the table (35 positions from the start of the table) and corresponds to a subscript value of 6. Because index values represent displacements, they don't have to be converted when they are used to refer to table entries, and thus object program efficiency is improved.

```
 WORKING-STORAGE SECTION.
*
 01  SWITCHES.
*
     .
     .
     05  VALID-ITEM-NO-SW        PIC X            VALUE "N".
         88  VALID-ITEM-NO                        VALUE "Y".
*
 01  WORK-FIELDS                 COMP-3.
*
     05  UNIT-PRICE              PIC S999V99.
*
 01  ITEM-TABLE-VALUES.
*
     05  FILLER                  PIC X(7)         VALUE "1011250".
     05  FILLER                  PIC X(7)         VALUE "1075000".
     05  FILLER                  PIC X(7)         VALUE "1110770".
     05  FILLER                  PIC X(7)         VALUE "1580555".
     05  FILLER                  PIC X(7)         VALUE "1616250".
     05  FILLER                  PIC X(7)         VALUE "1922500".
     05  FILLER                  PIC X(7)         VALUE "2010040".
     05  FILLER                  PIC X(7)         VALUE "2130666".
     05  FILLER                  PIC X(7)         VALUE "2770111".
     05  FILLER                  PIC X(7)         VALUE "2970777".
     05  FILLER                  PIC X(7)         VALUE "3050010".
     05  FILLER                  PIC X(7)         VALUE "3411500".
     05  FILLER                  PIC X(7)         VALUE "3425750".
     05  FILLER                  PIC X(7)         VALUE "3436500".
     05  FILLER                  PIC X(7)         VALUE "3472250".
     05  FILLER                  PIC X(7)         VALUE "3510035".
     05  FILLER                  PIC X(7)         VALUE "3560888".
     05  FILLER                  PIC X(7)         VALUE "3590222".
*
 01  ITEM-TABLE                  REDEFINES ITEM-TABLE-VALUES.
*
     05  ITEM-TABLE-ENTRY        OCCURS 18 TIMES
                                 INDEXED BY ITEM-INDEX.
         10  IT-ITEM-NO          PIC 999.
         10  IT-UNIT-PRICE       PIC 99V99.
*
     .
     .
*
 PROCEDURE DIVISION.
*
     .
     .
     PERFORM 120-SEARCH-ITEM-TABLE.
     IF VALID-ITEM-NO
         MOVE IT-UNIT-PRICE (ITEM-INDEX) TO UNIT-PRICE
         .
         .
*
 120-SEARCH-ITEM-TABLE.
*
     SET ITEM-INDEX TO 1.
     SEARCH ITEM-TABLE-ENTRY
         AT END
             MOVE "N" TO VALID-ITEM-NO-SW
         WHEN IT-ITEM-NO (ITEM-INDEX) = TR-ITEM-NO
             MOVE "Y" TO VALID-ITEM-NO-SW.
*
     .
     .
```

Figure 9–14
Searching the item table using indexes

Except when debugging, the COBOL programmer doesn't have to worry about the actual value of an index because the table-handling statements set these values based on occurrence numbers. Knowing the difference between an index value and a subscript value, however, is essential to logical programming. You should note in Figure 9–14 that the INDEXED BY clause automatically defines an index for use with a specific table; that is, the index cannot be defined anywhere else in the Data Division.

Table-handling statements

Because an index value is different than an occurence value, it can be set or modified only by the SET, SEARCH, and PERFORM statements. In Figure 9–14, for example, the SET statement in paragraph 120 causes a value to be moved to ITEM–INDEX that corresponds to an occurrence value of one. The index must always be set to an appropriate value before the first execution of a SEARCH statement.

When the SEARCH statement in Figure 9–14 is executed, it compares in sequence the item numbers in the table with TR–ITEM–NO (the item-number field in the transaction record). If the table item number is never equal to TR–ITEM–NO, the AT END clause is executed after the last entry in the table is compared. This means that N is moved to VALID–ITEM–NO–SW. If the SEARCH statement does reach an equal comparison, Y is moved to VALID–ITEM–NO–SW. Then, the program returns to the module that called the search module.

Because the SEARCH statement causes the index value to be increased so that all item numbers are compared with TR–ITEM–NO, it doesn't matter if the item-number values are in sequence. The item numbers in the table could be reversed in sequence or in no sequence at all; the look-up routine in Figure 9–14 would still work.

The sequence of entries can, however, affect the efficiency of table searching in terms of processing time, just as it does when using subscripts. Since the table in Figure 9–14 is always searched starting with the first entry and proceeding toward the last, the most used entry should be the first one in the table and the least used entry should be the last. For example, if 60 percent of the transactions involve item numbers 277, 347, and 356, these table entries should be first in the table. Similarly, the rest of the table should be sequenced by frequency of use. You can imagine what a difference this type of sequencing can make if item number 359 accounts for 25 percent of the transactions.

Separate search modules

Whenever you use a SEARCH statement, you should set it aside in its own module, as shown in Figure 9–14. There are a couple of reasons for doing this. For one thing, table searching is complex and should be considered a separate program function, even though the SEARCH statement allows you to code it with a single statement. Secondly, many programs require that a single table be searched several times. It's much more efficient to perform the same search module for each search than it would be to code multiple SEARCH statements throughout the program. So treat a SEARCH statement just like an I/O statement—limit yourself to one per table whenever possible and isolate the statement in a separate paragraph. (As with read and write modules, a search module may also include some pertinent subfunction, like setting the index with the SET statement as in Figure 9–14.

```
 WORKING-STORAGE SECTION.
*
 01  SWITCHES.
*
     .
     .
     05  VALID-ITEM-NO-SW       PIC X            VALUE "N".
         88  VALID-ITEM-NO                       VALUE "Y".
*
 01  WORK-FIELDS                COMP-3.
*
     05  UNIT-PRICE             PIC S999V99.
*
 01  ITEM-TABLE-VALUES.
*
     05  FILLER                 PIC X(7)         VALUE "1011250".
     05  FILLER                 PIC X(7)         VALUE "1075000".
     05  FILLER                 PIC X(7)         VALUE "1110770".
     05  FILLER                 PIC X(7)         VALUE "1580555".
     05  FILLER                 PIC X(7)         VALUE "1616250".
     05  FILLER                 PIC X(7)         VALUE "1922500".
     05  FILLER                 PIC X(7)         VALUE "2010040".
     05  FILLER                 PIC X(7)         VALUE "2130666".
     05  FILLER                 PIC X(7)         VALUE "2770111".
     05  FILLER                 PIC X(7)         VALUE "2970777".
     05  FILLER                 PIC X(7)         VALUE "3050010".
     05  FILLER                 PIC X(7)         VALUE "3411500".
     05  FILLER                 PIC X(7)         VALUE "3425750".
     05  FILLER                 PIC X(7)         VALUE "3436500".
     05  FILLER                 PIC X(7)         VALUE "3472250".
     05  FILLER                 PIC X(7)         VALUE "3510035".
     05  FILLER                 PIC X(7)         VALUE "3560888".
     05  FILLER                 PIC X(7)         VALUE "3590222".
*
 01  ITEM-TABLE                 REDEFINES ITEM-TABLE-VALUES.
*
     05  ITEM-TABLE-ENTRY       OCCURS 18 TIMES
                                ASCENDING KEY IS IT-ITEM-NO
                                INDEXED BY ITEM-INDEX.
         10  IT-ITEM-NO         PIC 999.
         10  IT-UNIT-PRICE      PIC 99V99.
*
     .
     .
*
 PROCEDURE DIVISION.
*
     .
     .
     PERFORM 120-SEARCH-ITEM-TABLE.
     IF VALID-ITEM-NO
         MOVE IT-UNIT-PRICE (ITEM-INDEX) TO UNIT-PRICE
         .
         .
*
 120-SEARCH-ITEM-TABLE.
*
     SEARCH ALL ITEM-TABLE-ENTRY
         AT END
             MOVE "N" TO VALID-ITEM-NO-SW
         WHEN IT-ITEM-NO (ITEM-INDEX) = TR-ITEM-NO
             MOVE "Y" TO VALID-ITEM-NO-SW.
*
 .
 .
```

Figure 9–15
Using a binary search

Using a Binary Search

If the frequency of use is evenly distributed over the items in a table or if you are working with a large table, you should consider using the SEARCH ALL statement. Its use is illustrated in the lookup routine in Figure 9–15. When used, the *key field* in the table must be in either ascending or descending sequence. The key field is the field that will be searched during the execution of the SEARCH ALL statement.

On most compilers, the SEARCH ALL statement performs a *binary search* when it is executed. In a binary search, the search begins with an entry near the middle of the table. Based on this comparison, the search continues in either the first half or the second half of the table. The next comparison is near the middle of the half just selected, and the program continues by successively halving the portion of the table remaining. Eventually, an equal key is found, or the statement determines that no equal key is in the table.

Figure 9–15 shows how to use a binary search for the item-number table. Notice there are three changes from the coding in Figure 9–14. First, the ASCENDING KEY clause is used following the OCCURS clause for the table entries. Second, the index doesn't have to be given a starting value since the binary search routine will figure out where to start. So there's no SET statement. And third, the word ALL follows the word SEARCH in the SEARCH statement. Since the compiler doesn't check to make sure that all table entries are in key-field sequence, an out-of-sequence table entry will cause errors during the execution of the search routine. As a result, the table is normally edited and sorted before it's used.

To appreciate the value of a binary search, suppose a price table of 1000 items is being processed. If the frequency of use is evenly distributed over the table, the average sequential search will involve 500 comparisons. In contrast, a binary search will reach any entry in the table in a maximum of 10 comparisons, which is visually demonstrated in Figure 9–16. This reduction of from 500 to 10 searches is proved by the following demonstration:

Search number	Numbers in the possible set after the search
0	1,000
1	500
2	250
3	125
4	68
5	34
6	17
7	8
8	4
9	2
10	1

For this reason the SEARCH ALL statement is recommended for large tables. On the other hand, if only small tables are to be processed and if their entries can be arranged in order of use, a sequential search is adequate.

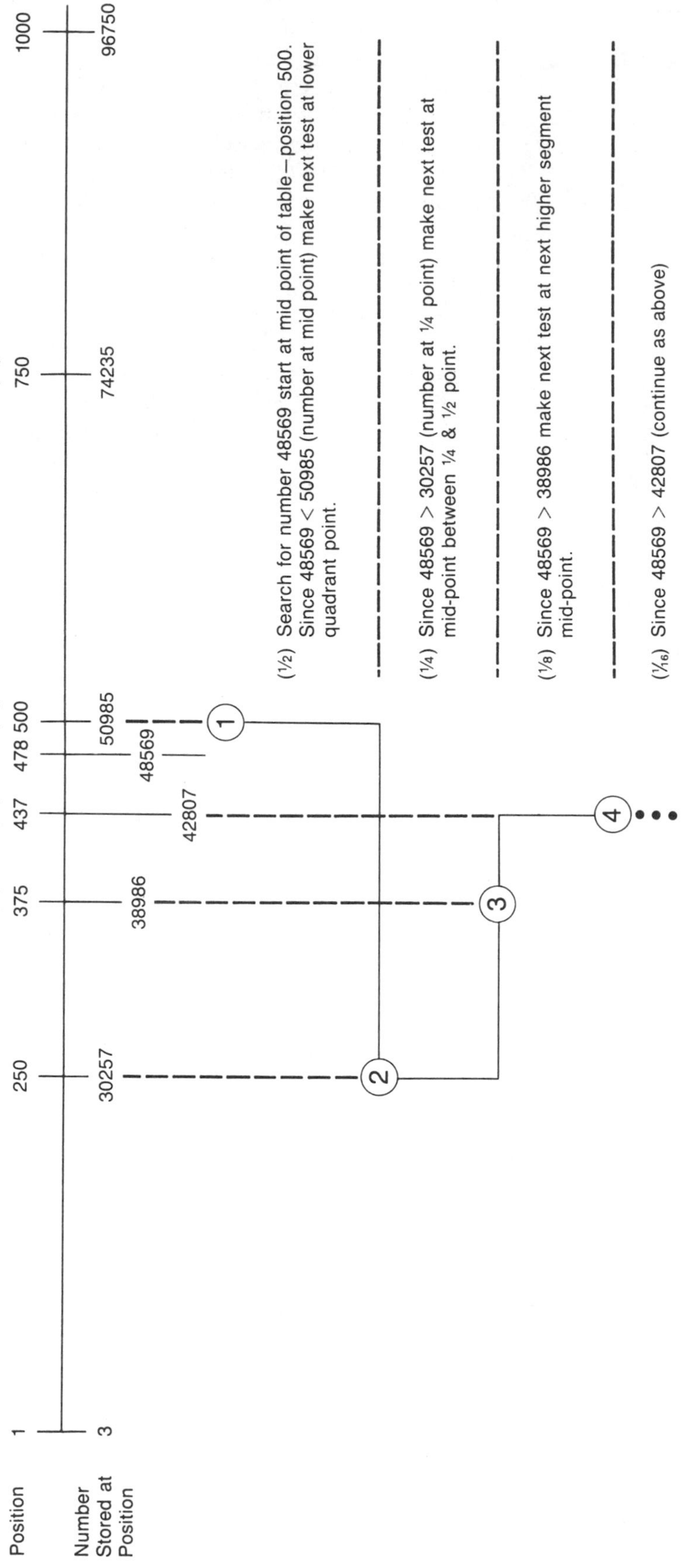
Position
Number Stored at Position
1
3
(1/4)
250
30257
(1/8)
375
38986
(1/16)
437
42807
478
48569
(1/2)
500
50985
(3/4)
750
74235
1000
96750
1
2
3
4
(1/2) Search for number 48569 start at mid point of table—position 500. Since 48569 < 50985 (number at mid point) make next test at lower quadrant point.
(1/4) Since 48569 > 30257 (number at 1/4 point) make next test at mid-point between 1/4 & 1/2 point.
(1/8) Since 48569 > 38986 make next test at next higher segment mid-point.
(1/16) Since 48569 > 42807 (continue as above)

Figure 9–16
Example of binary search

```
 WORKING-STORAGE SECTION.
*
     .
     .
*
 01  ITEM-TABLE.
*
     05  ITEM-TABLE-ENTRY         OCCURS 18 TIMES
                                  INDEXED BY ITEM-INDEX.
         10  IT-ITEM-NUMBER       PIC 999.
         10  IT-UNIT-PRICE        PIC 99V99.
*
     .
     .
*
 PROCEDURE DIVISION.
*
 000-PRODUCE-PRICE-LISTING.
*
     OPEN INPUT  TABLE-DATA-FILE
                 TRANSACTION-FILE
          OUTPUT PRICE-LISTING.
     PERFORM 100-LOAD-ITEM-TABLE
         VARYING ITEM-INDEX FROM 1 BY 1
         UNTIL ITEM-INDEX GREATER 18.
     .
     .
     CLOSE TABLE-DATA-FILE
           TRANSACTION-FILE
           PRICE-LISTING.
     DISPLAY "LSTPRCE  I  1  NORMAL EOJ".
     STOP RUN.
*
 100-LOAD-ITEM-TABLE.
*
     PERFORM 110-READ-TABLE-DATA-RECORD.
     MOVE TD-ITEM-NUMBER TO IT-ITEM-NUMBER (ITEM-INDEX).
     MOVE TD-UNIT-PRICE  TO IT-UNIT-PRICE (ITEM-INDEX).
*
 110-READ-TABLE-DATA-RECORD.
*
     READ TABLE-DATA-FILE INTO TD-RECORD
         AT END
             MOVE "Y" TO TABLE-DATA-EOF-SW.
*
     .
     .
```

Figure 9–17
Loading a table using indexes

Loading a Table Using Indexes

Figure 9–17 illustrates a routine that uses indexes to load the price table in Figure 9–7 into storage. Since this program is so similar to the one in Figure 9–9, you should have no difficulty understanding how it works.

The key here, as in Figure 9–9, is the PERFORM VARYING statement that controls the actual loading of the table. In this case, when the statement says to vary ITEM–INDEX FROM 1 BY 1, the index values are changed in a way that corresponds to changing occurrence numbers. And when the UNTIL clause is executed, the occurrence number corresponding to the value of ITEM–INDEX is compared with the literal 18. As a result, the PERFORM statement varies the index values in a way that causes 100–LOAD–ITEM–TABLE to be executed 18 times. The point here is that you code the PERFORM statement the same way for both indexes and subscripts. Although there are differences in internal execution, they are unimportant to you at this level.

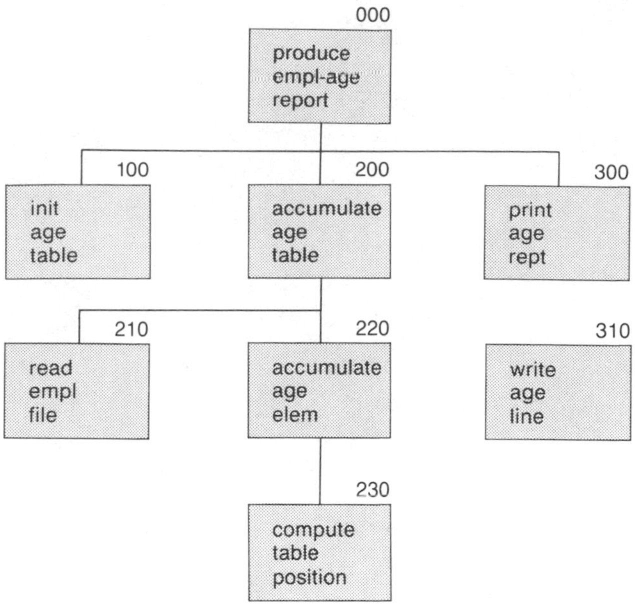
000
produce empl-age report
100
init age table
200
accumulate age table
300
print age rept
210
read empl file
220
accumulate age elem
310
write age line
230
compute table position

Figure 9–18
VTOC for produce-employee-age report

An Accumulated Table with Computed Access

Figure 9–18 is the VTOC for a program to count the number of employees in ten age categories. The program example demonstrates the concept of accumulating the data that is desired in the table. So far all of the examples have been used for reference purposes, but accumulating data in a table is a common and useful application. At the same time the program presents one example of computing table positions, rather than doing a search of identifiers to locate the desired position.

The program shown in Figure 9–19 is to read an employee file and determine the table element to count in by applying a set of calculations to the employee ages that are stored on the file. The output format will look like the following, which will ignore headings, but will print the age ranges of the different categories:

```
Age group    Number of employees

16-20          ZZZ
21-25          ZZZ
26-30          ZZZ
31-35          ZZZ
36-40          ZZZ
41-45          ZZZ
46-50          ZZZ
51-55          ZZZ
56-60          ZZZ
61-65          ZZZ
INVALID        ZZZ
```

```
ID DIVISION.
*
PROGRAM-ID.    AGETABL.
*
ENVIRONMENT DIVISION.
INPUT-OUTPUT SECTION.
*
FILE-CONTROL.
    SELECT EMPLOYEE-FILE
        ASSIGN TO PFMS.
    SELECT AGE-TABLE-LISTING
        ASSIGN TO PFMS.
*
DATA DIVISION.
*
FILE SECTION.
*
FD  EMPLOYEE-FILE
    LABEL RECORDS ARE STANDARD
    RECORD CONTAINS 56 CHARACTERS.
*
01  EMPLOYEE-AREA.
    05  FILLER              PIC X(56).
*
FD  AGE-TABLE-LISTING
    LABEL RECORDS ARE STANDARD
    RECORD CONTAINS 133 CHARACTERS.
*
01  AGE-PRINT-AREA.
    05  FILLER              PIC X(133).
*
WORKING-STORAGE SECTION.
*
01  SWITCHES.
    05  EMPLOYEE-EOF-SW     PIC X          VALUE 'N'.
        88  LAST-EMPLOYEE-RECORD           VALUE 'Y'.
        88  MORE-EMPLOYEE-RECORDS          VALUE 'N'.
*
01  WORK-FIELDS                                       COMP-3.
    05  AGE-FIELD           PIC S9(03).
        88  VALID-AGE-RANGE                VALUE 16 THRU 65.
    05  AGE-TABL-POSITION   PIC S9(02).
*
01  LIMIT-FIELDS                                      COMP-3.
    05  AGE-TABLE-LIMIT     PIC S9(03)     VALUE 11.
    05  LOW-AGE-LIMIT       PIC S9(03)     VALUE 16.
    05  TABLE-AGE-INCR      PIC S9(03)     VALUE 5.
    05  HI-LOW-DIFFERENCE   PIC S9(01)     VALUE 4.
*
01  AGE-TABLE                                         COMP-3.
    05  AT-EMPL-COUNT       PIC 9(03)      OCCURS 11
                                       INDEXED BY AGE-INDEX.
*
01  EMPLOYEE-RECORD.
    05  FILLER              PIC X(04).
    05  ER-EMPL-AGE         PIC 9(02).
    05  FILLER              PIC X(50).
*
01  AGE-TABLE-LINE.
    05  FILLER              PIC X(01)      VALUE SPACE.
    05  TL-AGE-RANGE.
        10  TL-LOW-AGE      PIC 9(02).
        10  FILLER          PIC X(01)      VALUE '-'.
        10  TL-HIGH-AGE     PIC 9(02).
        10  FILLER          PIC X(04)      VALUE SPACE.
    05  TL-EMPL-COUNT       PIC ZZ9.
*
```

Figure 9–19
Creating and printing an age table (part 1 of 2)

```
 PROCEDURE DIVISION.
*
 000-PRODUCE-EMPL-AGE-REPT.
     OPEN INPUT  EMPLOYEE-FILE
          OUTPUT AGE-TABLE-LISTING.
     PERFORM 100-INIT-AGE-TABLE
         VARYING AGE-INDEX FROM 1 BY 1
         UNTIL AGE-INDEX GREATER THAN AGE-TABLE-LIMIT.
*
     PERFORM 200-ACCUMULATE-AGE-TABLE
         UNTIL LAST-EMPLOYEE-RECORD.
     PERFORM 300-PRINT-AGE-REPT
         VARYING AGE-INDEX FROM 1 BY 1
         UNTIL AGE-INDEX GREATER THAN AGE-TABLE-LIMIT.
     CLOSE EMPLOYEE-FILE
           AGE-TABLE-LISTING.
     DISPLAY 'AGETABL  I  1  NORMAL EOJ'.
     STOP RUN.
*
 100-INIT-AGE-TABLE.
     MOVE ZERO                    TO AT-EMPL-COUNT (AGE-INDEX).
*
*
 200-ACCUMULATE-AGE-TABLE.
     PERFORM 210-READ-EMPLOYEE-RECORD.
     IF MORE-EMPLOYEE-RECORDS
         PERFORM 220-ACCUMULATE-AGE-ELEM.
*
 210-READ-EMPLOYEE-RECORD.
     READ EMPLOYEE-FILE INTO EMPLOYEE-RECORD
         AT END
             MOVE 'Y'             TO EMPLOYEE-EOF-SW.
*
 220-ACCUMULATE-AGE-ELEM.
     MOVE ER-EMPL-AGE             TO AGE-FIELD.
     IF VALID-AGE-RANGE
         PERFORM 230-COMPUTE-TABLE-POSITION
     ELSE
         SET AGE-INDEX            TO AGE-TABLE-LIMIT.
     ADD 1                        TO AT-EMPL-COUNT (AGE-INDEX).
*
 230-COMPUTE-TABLE-POSITION.
     COMPUTE AGE-TABL-POSITION =
         ((AGE-FIELD - LOW-AGE-LIMIT) / TABLE-AGE-INCR) + 1.
     SET AGE-INDEX                TO AGE-TABL-POSITION.
*
 300-PRINT-AGE-REPT.
     SET AGE-TABL-POSITION        TO AGE-INDEX.
     COMPUTE AGE-FIELD =
         LOW-AGE-LIMIT + TABLE-AGE-INCR * (AGE-TABL-POSITION - 1).
     MOVE AGE-FIELD               TO TL-LOW-AGE.
     ADD AGE-FIELD HI-LOW-DIFFERENCE
         GIVING TL-HIGH-AGE.
     IF AGE-INDEX EQUAL AGE-TABLE-LIMIT
         MOVE 'INVALID'           TO TL-AGE-RANGE.
     MOVE AT-EMPL-COUNT (AGE-INDEX)
                                  TO TL-EMPL-COUNT.
     MOVE AGE-TABLE-LINE          TO AGE-PRINT-AREA.
     PERFORM 310-WRITE-AGE-LINE.
*
 310-WRITE-AGE-LINE.
     WRITE AGE-PRINT-AREA
         AFTER ADVANCING 1 LINES.
```

Figure 9–19
Creating and printing an age table (part 2 of 2)

The program also demonstrates the use of condition names to check for valid data. Actually, the INVALID category should not be necessary if the data is coming from a permanent disk or tape file since it should have been edited before ever getting on the file. However, that part of the program is useful for demonstration purposes.

Module 000–PRODUCE–EMPL–AGE–REPT performs three modules in the get-ready, principal-process, and follow-up mode. Note that module 100–INIT–AGE–TABLE is simply a move of zero to each one of the table elements. Why was this done rather than simply creating a table with table values equal to zero? One main reason is that the elements must be set to zero before attempting to add to them, otherwise the program may have an abnormal termination or, worse, accumulate inaccurate counts. Another is that the elements in an accumulation table should be defined with COMP–3 usage since each one will be continually involved in computations. Recall that to be defined in DISPLAY usage (the default) would require the field to be packed, computed, and unpacked each time it was involved in a computation. Since each is defined as a COMP–3 field, initializing the table with a DISPLAY value such as the following one would be inconsistent usage.

```
05  AGE-TABLE-VALUES              PIC X(33)         VALUE ZERO.
```

The 200–ACCUMULATE–AGE–TABLE shows just two modules that it controls directly, 210–READ–EMPL–FILE, the typical input module, and 220–ACCUMULATE–AGE–ELEM, which controls computing of and adding to the proper table position. Notice that there is no output module as is typical with most principal-function modules. The reason is that in table accumulation functions output does not normally take place until the table is totally accumulated. In this instance the accumulation process is complete when the end of the employee file is reached, as that was the source of the data for the table.

Module 220–ACCUMULATE–AGE–ELEM controls the location of the proper table element for each employee read, adding to the element when it is found. Note the use of the condition name VALID–AGE–RANGE to test for employee ages in the valid range of the table. The eleventh table element is being reserved to count any employees whose records may have an age that is not valid. The assumption is that no employees should be younger than 16 nor older than 65.

The focal point of this example is in module 230–COMPUTE–TABLE–POSITION, which determines the proper table element to add to by doing a computation involving the employee's age. To understand the computation you must take into consideration the lower age limit (16), the increment or range for one age group (5), and the fact that fractional parts of calculations are ignored unless the result field is defined with a fractional part. Of course, the position for a table element must be expressed as an integer so the result field is an integer. You should take a little time to study and prove that the algorithm for determining table position works accurately.

Module 300–PRINT–AGE–REPT is executed after the table has been completely accumulated. It is especially interesting since it also involves a computation, but this time the computation is used to generate part of the output. The output generated is the numbers which indicate the age ranges for which the counts are being reported. Again, the proof of the accuracy of the computations will require a little study, but you should do it because it will enhance your programming sophistication.

A question of style as related to clarity arises from this example. The question is, "Has the programmer become too cute with the position computation and lost program clarity as a result?" Quite honestly, that may be a legitimate charge. The program could have been programmed with the age ranges imbedded in the table so that they would not have to be computed for the output. A search access could have also been used, although the direct access could have also been employed. The example is a borderline case. Since the table is short, perhaps the imbedding of the age ranges would have been more efficient. If possible, a similar table with many elements (30, 50, or more) probably should be coded as this example was. One aspect of programming you should consider is, what is feasible and easy to do in a short table may be much too much effort in a long table. Of course, you should remember that text examples are just that, examples presented to demonstrate a concept or technique. In a professional situation the programmer of this example might have done it differently.

Finally, module 310–WRITE–AGE–LINE is the basic physical output module. The only thing worth noting is the use of the integer for space control. If headings were involved, the variable option would be used instead.

Handling Variable-Length Tables Using Indexes

Handling a variable-length table is much the same using indexes as it is using subscripts. Figure 9–20 shows a program that loads and searches the item table if the table can contain up to 100 entries. It functions in the same way as the program in Figure 9–11.

In the Working–Storage Section of Figure 9–20, IT–ENTRY–COUNT is given INDEX usage. This means that the field can store an index value, although it can't be used to index a table. This is done to reduce the conversion involved in storing an index in a normal data item. More about this later.

In the Procedure Division, the table is loaded in 100–LOAD–ITEM–TABLE. Because the index value is increased *before* each table record is read, module 100 must set the value of the index down by one when it reaches the end of the table file to get the correct index value. Then, IT–ENTRY–COUNT is set to the value of the index, so the number of entries is saved. (Like an index, an item with INDEX usage requires the use of the SET statement.) This part of the coding is nearly the same as it is using subscripts in Figure 9–11. The main difference is replacing the SUBTRACT and MOVE statements by SET statements.

In paragraph 220, the SEARCH statement searches the table until the proper item number is found or the index is equal to IT–ENTRY–COUNT. Both of these conditions are tested in the WHEN clauses of the SEARCH statement, and the validity switch (VALID–ITEM–NO–SW) is set accordingly. This switch can be tested later to determine if the search was successful.

```
 DATA DIVISION.
*
 FILE SECTION.
*
 FD  TABLE-DATA-FILE
     LABEL RECORDS ARE STANDARD
     RECORD CONTAINS 80 CHARACTERS.
*
 01  TABLE-DATA-AREA                        PIC X(80).
*
 FD  TRANSACTION-FILE
     LABEL RECORDS ARE STANDARD
     RECORD CONTAINS 80 CHARACTERS.
*
 01  TRAN-AREA                              PIC X(80).
*
     .
     .
*
 WORKING-STORAGE SECTION.
*
 01  SWITCHES.
*
     05  TABLE-EOF-SW                       PIC X          VALUE "N".
         88  TABLE-EOF                                     VALUE "Y".
     05  TRAN-EOF-SW                        PIC X          VALUE "N".
         88  TRAN-EOF                                      VALUE "Y".
     05  VALID-ITEM-NO-SW                   PIC X          VALUE "N".
         88  VALID-ITEM-NO                                 VALUE "Y".
     .
     .
*
 01  COUNT-FIELDS.
*
     05  IT-ENTRY-COUNT                     INDEX.
     .
     .
*
 01  ITEM-TABLE.
*
     05  ITEM-TABLE-ENTRY                   OCCURS 100 TIMES
                                            INDEXED BY ITEM-INDEX.
         10  IT-ITEM-NO                     PIC 999.
         10  IT-UNIT-PRICE                  PIC 99V99.
*
 01  TD-RECORD.
*
     05  TD-ITEM-NO                         PIC 999.
     05  TD-UNIT-PRICE                      PIC 99V99.
     05  FILLER                             PIC X(73).
*
 01  TR-RECORD.
*
     05  TR-ITEM-NO                         PIC 999.
     .
     .
*
```

Figure 9–20
Loading and searching a variable-length table using indexes (part 1 of 2)

```
 PROCEDURE DIVISION.
*
 000-PRODUCE-CUST-INVOICES.
*
     OPEN INPUT  TABLE-DATA-FILE
                 TRANSACTION-FILE
          OUTPUT ...
     PERFORM 100-LOAD-ITEM-TABLE
         VARYING ITEM-INDEX FROM 1 BY 1
         UNTIL TABLE-EOF.
     IF ITEM-INDEX NOT GREATER 100
         PERFORM 200-PRODUCE CUST-INVOICE
             UNTIL TRAN-EOF
     ELSE
         DISPLAY "VLITMTB  A  2  TABLE HAS TOO MANY ENTRIES".
     CLOSE TABLE-DATA-FILE
           TRANSACTION-FILE...
     DISPLAY "VLITMTB  I  1  NORMAL EOJ".
     STOP RUN.
*
 100-LOAD-ITEM-TABLE.
*
     PERFORM 110-READ-TABLE-RECORD.
     IF NOT TABLE-EOF AND ITEM-INDEX NOT GREATER 100
         MOVE TD-ITEM-NO    TO IT-ITEM-NO (ITEM-INDEX)
         MOVE TD-UNIT-PRICE TO IT-UNIT-PRICE (ITEM-INDEX).
     IF TABLE-EOF
         SET ITEM-INDEX DOWN BY 1
         SET IT-ENTRY-COUNT TO ITEM-INDEX.
*
 110-READ-TABLE-RECORD.
*
     READ TABLE-DATA-FILE INTO TD-RECORD
         AT END
             MOVE "Y" TO TABLE-EOF-SW.
*
 200-PRODUCE-CUST-INVOICE.
*
     PERFORM 210-READ-TRAN-RECORD.
     IF NOT TRAN-EOF
         PERFORM 220-SEARCH-ITEM-TABLE
         .
         .
*
 210-READ-TRAN-RECORD.
*
     READ TRANSACTION-FILE INTO TR-RECORD
         AT END
             MOVE "Y" TO TRAN-EOF-SW.
*
 220-SEARCH-ITEM-TABLE.
*
     SET ITEM-INDEX TO 1.
     SEARCH ITEM-TABLE-ENTRY
         WHEN IT-ITEM-NO (ITEM-INDEX) = TR-ITEM-NO
             MOVE "Y" TO VALID-ITEM-NO-SW
         WHEN ITEM-INDEX = IT-ENTRY-COUNT
             MOVE "N" TO VALID-ITEM-NO-SW.
```

Figure 9–20
Loading and searching a variable-length table using indexes (part 2 of 2)

```
Relative indexing

    data-name (index-name [± literal])

Table definition

    OCCURS integer TIMES

    [{ASCENDING }  KEY IS data-name-1  [data-name-2]...] ...
    [{DESCENDING}                                      ]

    [INDEXED BY index-name-1  [index-name-2]...]

Index data item definition

    [USAGE IS] INDEX

The SET statement

    Format 1:
                                                      {data-name-3 }
    SET {data-name-1   [data-name-2]... }  TO  {index-name-3}
        {index-name-1  [index-name-2]...}      {literal-1   }

    Format 2:

    SET index-name-1 [index-name-2]... {UP BY  } {data-name-1}
                                       {DOWN BY} {literal-1  }
```

Figure 9–21
ANS 1974 table-handling elements including the PERFORM statement (part 1 of 2)

The Formats of the ANS Table-Handling Elements

With the background provided so far, you should be able to code most types of table-handling routines involving single-level tables. In special cases, however, you may need some additional coding flexibility. For this reason, a summary of the ANS table-handling elements is given in Figure 9–21.

Relative indexing

Relative indexing is another method of referring to an element in a table. To use it, you start with an index value and increase or decrease it by some literal value. For example, if you coded

```
TR-ITEM-NO = IT-ITEM-NO (ITEM-INDEX + 3)
```

three would be converted to its corresponding index value and added to the index value of ITEM-INDEX. Or, to put it another way, the occurrence number of IT-ITEM-NO (ITEM-INDEX) would be increased by three. To illustrate, look back at the table in Figure 9–7 and assume it is defined as in Figure 9–14.

```
The SEARCH statement

Format 1:

SEARCH data-name
    [AT END imperative-statement-1]

    WHEN condition-1 {imperative-statement-2}
                     {NEXT SENTENCE         }

    WHEN condition-2 {imperative-statement-3}
                     {NEXT SENTENCE         }

Format 2:

SEARCH ALL data-name-1 [AT END imperative-statement-1]

    WHEN indexed-key-field-1 {IS EQUAL TO} {data-name-2             }
                             {IS =       } {literal-1               }
                                           {arithmetic-expression-1 }

      [AND indexed-key-field-2 {IS EQUAL TO} {data-name-3             }] . . .
      [                        {IS =       } {literal-2               }]
      [                                      {arithmetic-expression-2 }]

      {imperative-statement-2}
      {NEXT SENTENCE         }

The PERFORM statement

PERFORM procedure-name

    VARYING {data-name-1 } FROM {data-name-2 }
            {index-name-1}      {index-name-2}
                                {literal-1   }

     BY {data-name-3} UNTIL condition-1
        {literal-2  }
```

Figure 9–21
ANS 1974 table-handling elements including the PERFORM statement (part 2 of 2)

If the occurrence value of ITEM–INDEX is two, IT–ITEM–NO (ITEM–INDEX + 3) will be the fifth entry in the table, item number 161. Likewise, IT–ITEM–NO (ITEM–INDEX – 1) will be the first entry, item number 101. When you use relative indexing, you must leave a space on either side of the plus or minus sign.

You should generally avoid relative indexing. Such programming schemes are often based on specific patterns. If the pattern were to change, the whole scheme could become invalid and necessitate program changes, or worse, remain operable while providing incorrect output. There are undoubtedly situations where such processing is appropriate, but you should try to find other, more flexible methods before resorting to relative indexing.

The OCCURS clause

As shown in the format for the OCCURS clause, you may use more than one key field with the SEARCH ALL statement and more than one index for a single table. However, you'll rarely need to use these options. The complete statement format has been presented so you'll be familiar with it if you run into multiple keys and multiple indexes.

INDEX usage

As shown in Figure 9–20, you can use *index data items* to store index values without converting them to occurrence numbers:

```
05  IT-ENTRY-COUNT     USAGE IS INDEX.
```

In this case, the compiler will set up a field large enough to store any index value. When INDEX usage is specified, PICTURE and VALUE clauses aren't allowed since the field size is always the same and the purpose of an index data item is to store an index value for later use.

One important point about items with INDEX usage is that they can only be specified in a SET statement or in a relation test with an index or another index data item. That's why ITEM–INDEX was used in the IF statement in module 000 of Figure 9–20 instead of using IT–ENTRY–COUNT as in Figure 9–11.

The SET statement

The SET statement is used to create index values that correspond to occurrence numbers, and vice versa. If you look at the table in Figure 9–22, you can see that different conversions are performed depending on the nature of the sending and receiving fields. If a literal or numeric item is the sending field and an index item is the receiving field, an occurrence number is converted to an appropriate index value. If an index value is the sending field and a numeric item is the receiving field, an index value is converted to an occurrence number. When an index value is sent to an index data item, no conversion takes place.

Note in Figure 9–21 that a series of receiving fields can be modified by one SET statement, regardless of the format you're using. When format 2 of the SET statement is used, the index or indexes are increased or decreased by a value that corresponds to the number of occurrences indicated by the data name or literal. You saw both formats illustrated in the program in Figure 9–20:

```
Format 1:  SET IT-ENTRY-COUNT TO ITEM-INDEX.
Format 2:  SET ITEM-INDEX DOWN BY 1.
```

The SEARCH statement

As shown in Figure 9–20, you can code a series of WHEN clauses in the SEARCH statement during a sequential search (format 1 in Figure 9–21). If this is done, the SEARCH statement ends when any of the conditions in a WHEN clause is satisfied. For example, consider this statement:

```
SEARCH ITEM-TABLE-ENTRY
    AT END
        MOVE "N" TO VALID-ITEM-NO-SW
    WHEN IT-ITEM-NO (ITEM-INDEX) = TR-ITEM-NO
        MOVE "Y" TO VALID-ITEM-NO-SW
    WHEN IT-ITEM-NO (ITEM-INDEX) GREATER TR-ITEM-NO
        MOVE "N" TO VALID-ITEM-NO-SW.
```

Here, the search will end whenever TR–ITEM–NO becomes equal to or smaller than the current item number in the table. For a small table in ascending sequence by item number, this coding will end the search before all entries are tested.

One thing to remember when coding multiple WHEN clauses is that the first WHEN condition will be checked first, the second condition next, and so on. However, once a condition is true, the program leaves the SEARCH statement without testing the remaining WHEN clauses. So in some cases, it will make a difference which WHEN clause you code first, second, and so on.

Receiving Field	Sending Item		
	Index	Literal or numeric item	Index data item
Index	Set to value corresponding to occurrence number unless indexes refer to same table. If for same table, move value without converting.	Set to value corresponding to occurrence number.	Move without conversion.
Numeric item	Set to occurrence number represented by index value.	Illegal	Illegal
Index data item	Move without conversion.	Illegal	Move without conversion.

Figure 9–22
Operation of the SET statement

In format 2, the SEARCH ALL statement, the conditions that can be used in the WHEN clause are more restricted than in format 1. Here, a properly indexed key field must be tested for an equal comparison with an arithmetic expression, a literal, or a data name. Also in format 2, compound conditions testing multiple key fields can be specified in the WHEN clause by using AND connectors. In such a case, all of the conditions must be satisified before the WHEN clause is executed. However, as was said in the discussion of the OCCURS clause, there's seldom any reason to use multiple keys. So you'll rarely code compound conditions in the WHEN clause.

The PERFORM statement

As illustrated in Figures 9–17 and 9–20, the PERFORM statement can be used to modify an index value. When it is used in this way, however, both the FROM and the BY values must be integer data items. The index is then modified in the same way that it is using the SET statement. The integer FROM value is converted to an index value and is used as the starting index value; the integer BY value is used to increase the index value by a number corresponding to the number of occurrences indicated.

Discussion

Because coding with indexes generally leads to a more efficient object program and is not really much more complex than coding with subscripts, you should use indexes for most table-handling applications. Also, you should use the binary search facility of the SEARCH ALL statement for all large tables.

Whether you use indexes or subscripts, you should be aware of the likelihood of debugging problems in table-handling routines. Two conditions to guard against are (1) failing to initialize an index before issuing the SEARCH statement or before referencing an indexed field and (2) using a subscript or index that is not within the acceptable range for a table. Both error conditions can lead to program cancellation, and the cause of cancellation can be very difficult to isolate.

Whenever you must design a table and its associated search routine, your goals should be (1) to cover all possible conditions and (2) to maximize processing efficiency. To this end, subscript or index values should be checked for validity before the program enters a search routine. Also, for a sequential search, table entries should be arranged by frequency of use if the frequencies are known; otherwise, a binary search should be considered.

```
 IDENTIFICATION DIVISION.
*
 PROGRAM-ID. RATLKUP.
*
 ENVIRONMENT DIVISION.
*
 CONFIGURATION SECTION.
*
 SOURCE-COMPUTER.  PRIME 850.
 OBJECT-COMPUTER.  PRIME 850.
*
 INPUT-OUTPUT SECTION.
*
 FILE-CONTROL.
     SELECT TABLE-DATA-FILE
         ASSIGN TO PFMS.
     SELECT EMPLOYEE-FILE
         ASSIGN TO PFMS.
     SELECT PAYROLL-LISTING
         ASSIGN TO PFMS.
*
 DATA DIVISION.
*
 FILE SECTION.
*
 FD  TABLE-DATA-FILE
     LABEL RECORDS ARE STANDARD
     RECORD CONTAINS 80 CHARACTERS.
*
 01  TABLE-DATA-AREA          PIC X(80).
*
 FD  EMPLOYEE-FILE
     LABEL RECORDS ARE STANDARD
     RECORD CONTAINS 80 CHARACTERS.
*
 01  EM-AREA                  PIC X(80).
*
 FD  PAYROLL-LISTING
     LABEL RECORDS ARE STANDARD
     RECORD CONTAINS 132 CHARACTERS.
*
 01  PRINT-AREA               PIC X(132).
*
 WORKING-STORAGE SECTION.
*
 01  SWITCHES.
*
     05  TABLE-EOF-SW         PIC X        VALUE "N".
         88  TABLE-EOF                     VALUE "Y".
     05  EMP-EOF-SW           PIC X        VALUE "N".
         88  EMP-EOF                       VALUE "Y".
*
 01  WORK-FIELDS              COMP-3.
*
     05  GROSS-PAY            PIC S999V99.
*
```

Figure 9–23
Loading and processing the pay-rate table (part 1 of 3)

One final thing to keep in mind when coding table-handling routines is the advisability of sorting a table when you load it. For example, suppose you want to do a binary search of a 5000-entry part-number table, but you know the entries aren't in order by the key field you want to use. Then, as part of your loading routine, you could use the SORT statement to arrange the part-number field in sequential order.

```
 01  COUNT-FIELDS                COMP-3.
*
     05  TABLE-ENTRY-COUNT       PIC S999.
*
 01  RATE-TABLE                  COMP-3.
*
     05  PAY-RATE                OCCURS 26 TIMES
                                 INDEXED BY RATE-INDEX
                                 PIC 9V99.
*
 01  TD-RECORD.
*
     05  TD-NO-OF-ENTRIES        PIC 99.
     05  TD-ENTRY                OCCURS 26 TIMES
                                 INDEXED BY TABLE-INDEX
                                 PIC 9V99.
*
 01  EM-RECORD.
*
     05  EM-EMP-NO               PIC X(4).
     05  FILLER                  PIC X(23).
     05  EM-PAY-CLASS            PIC 99.
     05  EM-HOURS-WORKED         PIC 99V9.
     05  FILLER                  PIC X(48).
*
 01  EMPLOYEE-LINE.
*
     05  EL-EMP-NO               PIC X(4).
     05  FILLER                  PIC X(3)    VALUE SPACE.
     05  EL-PAY-RATE             PIC Z.99.
     05  FILLER                  PIC X(3)    VALUE SPACE.
     05  EL-HOURS-WORKED         PIC ZZ.9.
     05  FILLER                  PIC X(3)    VALUE SPACE.
     05  EL-GROSS-PAY            PIC ZZZ.99.
     05  FILLER                  PIC X(105)  VALUE SPACE.
*
 PROCEDURE DIVISION.
*
 000-PRODUCE-PAYROLL-LISTING.
*
     OPEN INPUT  TABLE-DATA-FILE
                 EMPLOYEE-FILE
          OUTPUT PAYROLL-LISTING.
     PERFORM 100-LOAD-RATE-TABLE.
     PERFORM 200-PRODUCE-EMPLOYEE-LINE
         UNTIL EMP-EOF.
     CLOSE TABLE-DATA-FILE
           EMPLOYEE-FILE
           PAYROLL-LISTING.
     DISPLAY "RATLKUP  I  1  NORMAL EOJ".
     STOP RUN.
*
```

Figure 9–23
Loading and processing the pay-rate table (part 2 of 3)

Problem

Rewrite the program in Figure 9–6 so that it uses indexes instead of subscripts. Also, load the rate table into storage in the Procedure Division rather than storing it as part of the program. For this, assume the pay rates are entered in successive positions of one input record, starting with position 3. This means as many as 26 pay rates may be entered in positions 3–80 of the table record. Assume the pay-rate table is variable-length with a maximum of 26 entries and that positions 1–2 of the table record contain the actual number of rates to be stored in the table. Figure 9–12 shows a VTOC for this program.

```
 100-LOAD-RATE-TABLE.
*
     PERFORM 110-READ-TABLE-RECORD.
     IF NOT TABLE-EOF
         MOVE TD-NO-OF-ENTRIES TO TABLE-ENTRY-COUNT
         PERFORM 120-STORE-TABLE-ENTRY
             VARYING RATE-INDEX FROM 1 BY 1
             UNTIL RATE-INDEX GREATER THAN TABLE-ENTRY-COUNT.
*
 110-READ-TABLE-RECORD.
*
     READ TABLE-DATA-FILE INTO TD-RECORD
         AT END
             MOVE "Y" TO TABLE-EOF-SW.
*
 120-STORE-TABLE-ENTRY.
*
     SET TABLE-INDEX TO RATE-INDEX.
     MOVE TD-ENTRY (TABLE-INDEX) TO PAY-RATE (RATE-INDEX).
*
 200-PRODUCE-EMPLOYEE-LINE.
*
     PERFORM 210-READ-EMPLOYEE-RECORD.
     IF NOT EMP-EOF
         IF        EM-PAY-CLASS LESS 1
                OR EM-PAY-CLASS GREATER TABLE-ENTRY-COUNT
             DISPLAY "RATLKUP  A  2  INVALID PAY CLASS FOR "
                     "EMPLOYEE NO. " EM-EMP-NO
         ELSE
             SET RATE-INDEX TO EM-PAY-CLASS
             MULTIPLY EM-HOURS-WORKED BY PAY-RATE (RATE-INDEX)
                 GIVING GROSS-PAY ROUNDED
             PERFORM 220-PRINT-EMPLOYEE-LINE.
*
 210-READ-EMPLOYEE-RECORD.
*
     READ EMPLOYEE-FILE INTO EM-RECORD
         AT END
             MOVE "Y" TO EMP-EOF-SW.
*
 220-PRINT-EMPLOYEE-LINE.
*
     MOVE EM-EMP-NO              TO EL-EMP-NO.
     MOVE PAY-RATE (RATE-INDEX)  TO EL-PAY-RATE.
     MOVE EM-HOURS-WORKED        TO EL-HOURS-WORKED.
     MOVE GROSS-PAY              TO EL-GROSS-PAY.
     MOVE EMPLOYEE-LINE          TO PRINT-AREA.
     PERFORM 230-WRITE-REPORT-LINE.
*
 230-WRITE-REPORT-LINE.
*
     WRITE PRINT-AREA
         AFTER ADVANCING 1 LINES.
```

Figure 9–23
Loading and processing the pay-rate table (part 3 of 3)

Solution

Figure 9–23 is an acceptable solution. The rates in the input record are indexed by TABLE–INDEX, while RATE–INDEX is used for the table in working storage. The SET statement is used twice: in module 120, to set TABLE–INDEX so it is varied with RATE–INDEX; and in module 200, to store the value of EM–PAY–CLASS in RATE–INDEX so RATE–INDEX will specify the proper rate for the calculation that follows.

Topic 4 **Multilevel Tables**

Orientation

For many table-handling problems, single-level tables are either inadequate or inconvenient. For instance, income tax withholdings vary based on two factors: amount of pay and number of dependents. To handle a problem like this using single-level tables, you would have to define a separate table for each possible number of dependents. If, for example, there could be from zero to ten dependents, you would have eleven single-level tables. Then, you would look up the amount to be withheld in the appropriate table.

Terminology

multilevel table | three-level table | two-level table

Objective

Given a problem involving multilevel tables, code a COBOL solution.

Table

Age	Class 1	Class 2	Class 3	Class 4
18-34	$23.50	$27.05	$35.25	$52.90
35-39	24.00	27.55	35.75	53.40
40-44	24.60	28.15	36.35	54.00
45-49	25.30	28.85	37.05	54.70
50-54	26.30	29.85	38.05	55.70
55-59	28.00	31.55	39.75	57.40

Subscript notation

Age	Class 1	Class 2	Class 3	Class 4
18-34	(1,1)	(1,2)	(1,3)	(1,4)
35-39	(2,1)	(2,2)	(2,3)	(2,4)
40-44	(3,1)	(3,2)	(3,3)	(3,4)
45-49	(4,1)	(4,2)	(4,3)	(4,4)
50-54	(5,1)	(5,2)	(5,3)	(5,4)
55-59	(6,1)	(6,2)	(6,3)	(6,4)

Table description

```
 01  RATE-TABLE.
*
     05  AGE-GROUP              OCCURS 6 TIMES
                                INDEXED BY AGE-INDEX.
         10  INS-RATE           OCCURS 4 TIMES
                                INDEXED BY CLASS-INDEX
                                PIC S99V99.
```

Table entry reference

```
INS-RATE (AGE-INDEX, CLASS-INDEX)
```

Figure 9–24
Two-level table description

Table

Age	Men		Women	
	Class 1	Class 2	Class 1	Class 2
18-34	$23.50	$27.05	$24.75	$28.45
35-39	24.00	27.55	25.80	29.50
40-44	24.60	28.15	27.10	30.80
45-49	25.30	28.85	29.10	32.80
50-54	26.30	29.85	31.55	35.25
55-59	28.00	31.55	35.00	38.70

Subscript notation

Age	Men		Women	
	Class 1	Class 2	Class 1	Class 2
18-34	(1,1,1)	(1,1,2)	(1,2,1)	(1,2,2)
35-39	(2,1,1)	(2,1,2)	(2,2,1)	(2,2,2)
40-44	(3,1,1)	(3,1,2)	(3,2,1)	(3,2,2)
45-49	(4,1,1)	(4,1,2)	(4,2,1)	(4,2,2)
50-54	(5,1,1)	(5,1,2)	(5,2,1)	(5,2,2)
55-59	(6,1,1)	(6,1,2)	(6,2,1)	(6,2,2)

Table description

```
 01  RATE-TABLE.
*
         05  AGE-GROUP                 OCCURS 6 TIMES
                                       INDEXED BY AGE-INDEX.
             10  SEX-GROUP             OCCURS 2 TIMES
                                       INDEXED BY SEX-INDEX.
                 15  INS-RATE          OCCURS 2 TIMES
                                       INDEXED BY CLASS-INDEX
                                       PIC S99V99.
```

Table entry reference

```
INS-RATE (AGE-INDEX, SEX-INDEX, CLASS-INDEX)
```

Figure 9–25
Three-level table description

A Multilevel Table Example

An easier way to do the kind of problem outlined above would be to use a *two-level table*. With a table like this, two indexes or subscripts are used to refer to the correct table entry. For example, Figure 9–24 illustrates a two-level insurance rating table. Two variable factors—age and job class—determine the premium to be charged.

Three-level tables are also relatively common. Figure 9–25, for example, is a three-level insurance rating table similar to the two-level table in Figure 9–24. Here, one more variable factor, the applicant's sex, has been added. Thus, age, sex, and job class are used to determine the premium.

To describe a *multilevel table* in COBOL, OCCURS clauses within OCCURS clauses are used. If you look at the table description in Figure 9–24, you can see that a field named AGE–GROUP is said to occur six times. Then, the field named INS–RATE with a PICTURE of S99V99 occurs four times within each field named AGE–GROUP. As a result, the area named RATE–TABLE consists of 24 rate fields.

To refer to the fields within a two-level table, subscripts or indexes are used. In Figure 9–24, indexes are used, so

```
INS-RATE (AGE-INDEX, CLASS-INDEX)
```

can refer to any of the 24 rates in the table, depending on the values of AGE–INDEX and CLASS–INDEX. Using occurrence number, or subscript, notation as shown in the second part of Figure 9–24, INS–RATE (1, 1) refers to the rate corresponding to age group 1 and class 1. Similarly, INS–RATE (3, 4) refers to age group 3 and class 4; and INS–RATE (6, 2) refers to age group 6 and class 2. When writing a two-level subscript or index, one or more spaces must separate the subscripts or indexes.

For three-level table descriptions and references, the notation used for two-level tables is simply extended. In Figure 9–25, for example, the table is described by an OCCURS clause within an OCCURS clause within an OCCURS clause. Then, three index names are used to refer to the entries within the table, as in this example:

```
INS-RATE (AGE-INDEX, SEX-INDEX, CLASS-INDEX)
```

Thus, INS–RATE (4, 1, 2) refers to the rate corresponding to age group 4, sex group 1, and class 2. When using subscripts or indexes, their order corresponds to the order in which the table is described.

Searching a Multilevel Table

There are many alternative ways to code routines for multilevel tables. In general, though, you can think of multilevel tables as tables within tables, and then treat each level as a single-level table. In fact, the SEARCH statement can search only one level of a table at a time, so multiple SEARCH statements are often used for multilevel tables.

Searching a two-level table

Figure 9–26 illustrates a routine for finding the appropriate rate in the two-level insurance table shown in Figure 9–24. The table values are coded as part of the program. If you check the table description, you will see that each AGE–GROUP field is made up of two parts—a two-digit field named HIGH–AGE (which occurs once within each of the six AGE–GROUP areas) and a four-digit field named INS–RATE (which occurs four times within each of the six AGE–GROUP areas). Then, if you check RATE–TABLE–VALUES, you will see that the highest age in each age group is stored as the first two positions of the 18-digit field representing one line of the table. These age values are 34, 39, 44, 49, 54, and 59. They are then followed by the four class rates for their age group.

In the Procedure Division, the applicant's age (AP–AGE) and class (AP–CLASS) are checked to make sure they are within valid limits before starting the search. If they are invalid, N is moved to VALID–APPLICANT–SW. Otherwise, AGE–GROUP is searched in module 120. When the applicant's age is less than or equal to (NOT GREATER) the table age, AGE–INDEX represents the proper age index value, and Y is moved to AGE–GROUP–FOUND–SW. Notice that this part of the routine is a single-level search.

```
 DATA DIVISION.
*
 FILE SECTION.
*
 FD  APPLICANT-FILE
     LABEL RECORDS ARE STANDARD
     RECORD CONTAINS 80 CHARACTERS.
*
 01  APPLICANT-AREA          PIC X(80).
*
     .
     .
*
 WORKING-STORAGE SECTION.
*
 01  SWITCHES.
     .
     .
     05  VALID-APPLICANT-SW   PIC X        VALUE "N".
         88  VALID-APPLICANT               VALUE "Y".
     05  AGE-GROUP-FOUND-SW   PIC X        VALUE "N".
         88  AGE-GROUP-FOUND               VALUE "Y".
     .
     .
*
 01  WORK-FIELDS              COMP-3.
*
     05  POLICY-RATE          PIC S999V99.
     .
     .
*
 01  RATE-TABLE-VALUES.
*
     05  FILLER               PIC X(18)    VALUE "342350270535255290".
     05  FILLER               PIC X(18)    VALUE "392400275535755340".
     05  FILLER               PIC X(18)    VALUE "442460281536355400".
     05  FILLER               PIC X(18)    VALUE "492530288537055470".
     05  FILLER               PIC X(18)    VALUE "542630298538055570".
     05  FILLER               PIC X(18)    VALUE "592800315539755740".
*
 01  RATE-TABLE               REDEFINES RATE-TABLE-VALUES.
*
     05  AGE-GROUP            OCCURS 6 TIMES
                              INDEXED BY AGE-INDEX.
         10  HIGH-AGE         PIC 99.
         10  INS-RATE         OCCURS 4 TIMES
                              INDEXED BY CLASS-INDEX
                              PIC 99V99.
*
 01  AP-RECORD.
*
     05  AP-AGE               PIC 99.
     05  AP-CLASS             PIC 9.
     .
     .
```

Figure 9–26
Searching a two-level table
(part 1 of 2)

To address the appropriate class, the class index is set to the applicant's class given in the input record. Since the applicant's class and the class index are the same, no search is involved, and

```
INS-RATE (AGE-INDEX, CLASS-INDEX)
```

addresses the appropriate premium. Thus, the two-level search routine is completed.

```
*
 PROCEDURE DIVISION.
*
     .
     .
     IF       AP-AGE LESS 18
           OR AP-AGE GREATER 59
         MOVE "N" TO VALID-APPLICANT-SW.
     IF       AP-CLASS LESS 1
           OR AP-CLASS GREATER 4
         MOVE "N" TO VALID-APPLICANT-SW.
     IF VALID-APPLICANT
         PERFORM 120-SEARCH-INS-RATE-TABLE
         IF AGE-GROUP-FOUND
             SET CLASS-INDEX TO AP-CLASS
             MOVE INS-RATE (AGE-INDEX, CLASS-INDEX) TO POLICY-RATE
         ELSE ...
     ELSE ...
     .
     .
*
 120-SEARCH-INS-RATE-TABLE.
*
     SET AGE-INDEX TO 1.
     SEARCH AGE-GROUP
         WHEN AP-AGE NOT GREATER HIGH-AGE (AGE-INDEX)
             MOVE "Y" TO AGE-GROUP-FOUND-SW.
*
 .
 .
```

Figure 9–26
Searching a two-level table (part 2 of 2)

Searching a three-level table

Figure 9–27 illustrates a more complex search routine involving the three-level table given in Figure 9–25. Again, the table values are coded as part of the program. In this example, both the low-age limit and the high-age limit are stored. Before entering the search routine, the applicant's age is checked to make sure that it isn't less than the low age of the first age group or greater than the high age of the last age group. Then, the applicant's sex code and class code are checked to make sure they are 1 or 2. If all three fields are valid, the program executes the search module.

At the beginning of the search module, three SET statements are issued. These set the AGE–INDEX to an occurrence value of one and set the class and sex indexes to the values indicated by the input fields. When the SEARCH statement is executed, it does a single-level search of the high-age field. This search, like the one in Figure 9–26, ends when an applicant's age is not greater than the high age in the table. Then,

```
INS-RATE (AGE-INDEX, SEX-INDEX, CLASS-INDEX)
```

refers to the desired entry. Thus, while processing a three-level table is complex in terms of checking for valid input data and setting up index fields, the search itself is quite simple.

```
 DATA DIVISION.
*
 FILE SECTION.
*
 FD  APPLICANT-FILE
     LABEL RECORDS ARE STANDARD
     RECORD CONTAINS 80 CHARACTERS.
*
 01  APPLICANT-AREA           PIC X(80).
*
     .
     .
*
 WORKING-STORAGE SECTION.
*
 01  SWITCHES.
*
     .
     .
     05  VALID-APPLICANT-SW   PIC X        VALUE "N".
         88  VALID-APPLICANT               VALUE "Y".
     05  AGE-GROUP-FOUND-SW   PIC X        VALUE "N".
         88  AGE-GROUP-FOUND               VALUE "Y".
     .
     .
*
 01  WORK-FIELDS              COMP-3.
*
     05  POLICY-RATE          PIC S999V99.
     .
     .
*
 01  RATE-TABLE-VALUES.
*
     05  FILLER               PIC X(20)    VALUE "18342350270524752845".
     05  FILLER               PIC X(20)    VALUE "35392400275525802950".
     05  FILLER               PIC X(20)    VALUE "40442460281527103080".
     05  FILLER               PIC X(20)    VALUE "45492530288529103280".
     05  FILLER               PIC X(20)    VALUE "50542630298531553525".
     05  FILLER               PIC X(20)    VALUE "55592800315535003870".
*
 01  RATE-TABLE               REDEFINES RATE-TABLE-VALUES.
*
     05  AGE-GROUP            OCCURS 6 TIMES
                              INDEXED BY AGE-INDEX.
         10  LOW-AGE          PIC 99.
         10  HIGH-AGE         PIC 99.
         10  SEX-GROUP        OCCURS 2 TIMES
                              INDEXED BY SEX-INDEX.
             15  INS-RATE     OCCURS 2 TIMES
                              INDEXED BY CLASS-INDEX
                              PIC 99V99.
*
 01  AP-RECORD.
*
     05  AP-AGE               PIC 99.
     05  AP-CLASS             PIC 9.
     .
     .
```

Figure 9–27
Searching a three-level table
(part 1 of 2)

```
*
 PROCEDURE DIVISION.
*
     .
     .
     IF        AP-AGE LESS LOW-AGE (1)
            OR AP-AGE GREATER HIGH-AGE (6)
         MOVE "N" TO VALID-APPLICANT-SW.
     IF        AP-SEX LESS 1
            OR AP-SEX GREATER 2
         MOVE "N" TO VALID-APPLICANT-SW.
     IF        AP-CLASS LESS 1
            OR AP-CLASS GREATER 2
         MOVE "N" TO VALID-APPLICANT-SW.
     IF VALID-APPLICANT
         PERFORM 120-SEARCH-INS-RATE-TABLE
         IF AGE-GROUP-FOUND
             MOVE INS-RATE (AGE-INDEX, SEX-INDEX, CLASS-INDEX)
                 TO POLICY-RATE
         ELSE ...
     ELSE ...
     .
     .
*
 120-SEARCH-INS-RATE-TABLE.
*
     SET AGE-INDEX TO 1.
     SET SEX-INDEX TO AP-SEX.
     SET CLASS-INDEX TO AP-CLASS.
     SEARCH AGE-GROUP
         WHEN AP-AGE NOT GREATER HIGH-AGE (AGE-INDEX)
             MOVE "Y" TO AGE-GROUP-FOUND-SW.
*
```

Figure 9–27
Searching a three-level table (part 2 of 2)

Loading a Table

In many cases, of course, a table will be loaded into storage at the start of a program from a card, tape, or disk file, instead of being coded as part of the Data Division. To illustrate, suppose the two-level insurance table is to be loaded from a rate file and is followed by the applicant file. The table records have the high limit of each age group in columns 1–2 followed by four rates, one for each class. As a result, there are six table records. Then, the routine in Figure 9–28 will load the insurance table.

Two PERFORM VARYING statements control the table loading. The first PERFORM statement in module 000 executes module 100 while it varies the value of AGE–INDEX from one to six. As a result, module 100, which actually causes the table to be loaded, is executed six times. Each time, it reads a new table record, moves the high age in the record to the proper position in RATE–TABLE according to the value of AGE–INDEX, and executes the second PERFORM VARYING statement. This statement varies the TABLE–INDEX from one to four while it executes module 120. Thus, the four class rates within each age group are stored in the table area. Note that CLASS–INDEX is set to TABLE–INDEX in module 120 so it will be varied along with TABLE–INDEX as the rates are stored. Once the table is loaded, the program continues with the next statement following the PERFORM VARYING statement in module 000.

```
 DATA DIVISION.
*
 FILE SECTION.
*
 FD  TABLE-DATA-FILE
     LABEL RECORDS ARE STANDARD
     RECORD CONTAINS 80 CHARACTERS.
*
 01  TABLE-DAIA-AREA           PIC X(80).
*
  .
  .
*
 WORKING-STORAGE SECTION.
*
     .
     .
*
 01  RATE-TABLE.
*
     05  AGE-GROUP             OCCURS 6 TIMES
                               INDEXED BY AGE-INDEX.
         10  HIGH-AGE          PIC 99.
         10  INS-RATE          OCCURS 4 TIMES
                               INDEXED BY CLASS-INDEX
                               PIC 99V99.
*
 01  TD-RECORD.
*
     05  TD-HIGH-AGE           PIC 99.
     05  TD-INS-RATE           OCCURS 4 TIMES
                               INDEXED BY TABLE-INDEX
                               PIC 99V99.
     05  FILLER                PIC X(62).
*
  .
  .
*
 PROCEDURE DIVISION.
*
 000-DETERMINE-INS-PREMIUMS.
*
     OPEN INPUT  TABLE-DATA-FILE
                 APPLICANT-FILE
          OUTPUT PREMIUM-LISTING.
     PERFORM 100-LOAD-RATE-TABLE
         VARYING AGE-INDEX FROM 1 BY 1
         UNTIL AGE-INDEX GREATER 6.
     .
     .
     CLOSE TABLE-DATA-FILE
           APPLICANT-FILE
           PREMIUM-LISTING.
     DISPLAY "INSPREM  I  1  NORMAL EOJ".
     STOP RUN.
*
 100-LOAD-RATE-TABLE.
*
     PERFORM 110-READ-TABLE-DATA-RECORD.
     IF NOT TABLE-DATA-EOF
         MOVE TD-HIGH-AGE TO HIGH-AGE (AGE-INDEX)
         PERFORM 120-STORE-INS-RATE
             VARYING TABLE-INDEX FROM 1 BY 1
             UNTIL TABLE-INDEX GREATER 4.
*
```

Figure 9–28
Loading the two-level insurance table (part 1 of 2)

```
 110-READ-TABLE-DATA-RECORD.
*
     READ TABLE-DATA-FILE INTO TD-RECORD
         AT END
             MOVE "Y" TO TABLE-DATA-EOF-SW.
*
 120-STORE-INS-RATE.
*
     SET CLASS-INDEX TO TABLE-INDEX.
     MOVE TD-INS-RATE (TABLE-INDEX)
         TO INS-RATE (AGE-INDEX, CLASS-INDEX).
*
```

Figure 9–28
Loading the two-level insurance table (part 2 of 2)

```
 WORKING-STORAGE SECTION.
*
     .
     .
*
 01  WORK-FIELDS             COMP-3.
*
     05  RATE-TOTAL          PIC S9(3)V99            VALUE ZERO.
     05  AVERAGE-RATE        PIC S9(3)V99.
     .
     .
*
 01  RATE-TABLE.
*
     05  AGE-GROUP           OCCURS 6 TIMES
                             INDEXED BY AGE-INDEX.
         10  LOW-AGE         PIC 99.
         10  HIGH-AGE        PIC 99.
         10  SEX-GROUP       OCCURS 2 TIMES
                             INDEXED BY SEX-INDEX.
             15  INS-RATE    OCCURS 2 TIMES
                             INDEXED BY CLASS-INDEX
                             PIC 999V99.
*
     .
     .
*
 PROCEDURE DIVISION.
*
     .
     .
     PERFORM 210-ACCUMULATE-RATE-TOTAL
         VARYING AGE-INDEX FROM 1 BY 1
         UNTIL AGE-INDEX GREATER 6
             AFTER SEX-INDEX FROM 1 BY 1
             UNTIL SEX-INDEX GREATER 2
                 AFTER CLASS-INDEX FROM 1 BY 1
                 UNTIL CLASS-INDEX GREATER 2.
     DIVIDE RATE-TOTAL BY 24
         GIVING AVERAGE-RATE.
     .
     .
*
 210-ACCUMULATE-RATE-TOTAL.
*
     ADD INS-RATE (AGE-INDEX, SEX-INDEX, CLASS-INDEX)
         TO RATE-TOTAL.
     .
     .
```

Figure 9–29
Using the three-level PERFORM statement

```
PERFORM procedure-name

    VARYING {data-name-1 }  FROM {data-name-2 }
            {index-name-1}       {index-name-2}
                                 {literal-1   }

        BY {data-name-3}  UNTIL condition-1
           {literal-2  }

   [AFTER {data-name-4 }  FROM {data-name-5 }
          {index-name-3}       {index-name-4}
                               {literal-3   }

        BY {data-name-6}  UNTIL condition-2
           {literal-4  }

   [AFTER {data-name-7 }  FROM {data-name-8 }
          {index-name-5}       {index-name-6}
                               {literal-5   }

        BY {data-name-9}  UNTIL condition-3]]
           {literal-6  }
```

Figure 9–30
The format of the PERFORM statement

The PERFORM Statement with Multiple VARYING Clauses

When a series of values in a two- or three-level table is to be manipulated, an expanded form of the PERFORM statement can be used. To illustrate, suppose all the rates in the three-level insurance table are to be added together. Figure 9–29 shows how the PERFORM statement can be used for this purpose.

Since the PERFORM statement has the expanded format given in Figure 9–30, up to three different subscripts or indexes can be varied by one statement. In Figure 9–29, the PERFORM statement varies AGE–INDEX from an occurrence value of one through six, SEX–INDEX from one through two, and CLASS–INDEX from one through two. As a result, 210–ACCUMULATE–RATE–TOTAL is executed 24 times. The first time it is executed, INS–RATE (1, 1, 1) is added to RATE–TOTAL; the second time, INS–RATE (1, 1, 2) is added; then INS–RATE (1, 2, 1); then INS–RATE (1, 2, 2); then INS–RATE (2, 1, 1); and so on. After the PERFORM statement is executed, the next statement in sequence is executed.

In Figure 9–31, a PERFORM statement with three levels of VARYING clauses has been broken down into three PERFORM statements, each with only one VARYING clause. In both cases, the indexes are varied in the same way: first, INDEX–3 is varied from one to five, then INDEX–2 is varied from one to five, and finally INDEX–1 is varied from one to five. In other words, both segments of code achieve the same result—125 values are loaded into the rate table by module 110. From this illustration, the function of the PERFORM with multiple VARYING clauses should be clear.

```
Three-level PERFORM statement:

   PERFORM 110-LOAD-RATE-TABLE
       VARYING INDEX-1 FROM 1 BY 1
       UNTIL INDEX-1 GREATER 5
           AFTER INDEX-2 FROM 1 BY 1
           UNTIL INDEX-2 GREATER 5
               AFTER INDEX-3 FROM 1 BY 1
               UNTIL INDEX-3 GREATER 5.

Nested PERFORM statements:

       PERFORM VARY-INDEX-2
           VARYING INDEX-1 FROM 1 BY 1
           UNTIL INDEX-1 GREATER 5.

   VARY-INDEX-2.
*
       PERFORM VARY-INDEX-3
           VARYING INDEX-2 FROM 1 BY 1
           UNTIL INDEX-2 GREATER 5.

   VARY-INDEX-3.
*
       PERFORM 110-LOAD-RATE-TABLE
           VARYING INDEX-3 FROM 1 BY 1
           UNTIL INDEX-3 GREATER 5.

Load module:
   110-LOAD-RATE-TABLE.
  *
       MOVE TD-RATE TO RATE (INDEX-1, INDEX-2, INDEX-3).
```

Figure 9–31
Using PERFORM to vary three levels of indexes or subscripts

How often should you use multiple VARYING clauses? That depends on the situation. It's all right to use them as long as the meaning of the code is clear and easy to follow. Once the statement gets confusing, however, you should break it down into separate modules and use nested PERFORM statements like those in Figure 9–31. In other words, always remember that one of the goals of structured programming is program readability and clarity. So if several levels of PERFORM statements with only one VARYING clause are easier for you to understand than a single, multilevel PERFORM statement, by all means use them.

Discussion

From these illustrations, you should be able to see that handling multilevel tables is simply an extension of the principles for handling single-level tables. Table descriptions, subscript and index notation, the SEARCH statement, and even the PERFORM statement can all be seen as defining or operating on single-level tables within single-level tables.

One thing you should realize is that the programs in this topic are designed to show the basic table-handling elements. In actual practice, though, you won't always use subscripts or indexes for a table with only two or three elements. For example, in the three-level insurance table, you probably wouldn't subscript or index the sex code. Instead, you would use condition names in the input record. Then, you would set up two two-level tables, one for men and one for women, and process them according to the value of AP–SEX. This is shown in a search routine in Figure 9–32.

```
 DATA DIVISION.
*
 FILE SECTION.
*
 FD  APPLICANT-FILE
     LABEL RECORDS ARE STANDARD
     RECORD CONTAINS 80 CHARACTERS.
*
 01  APPLICANT-AREA            PIC X(80).
*
     .
     .
*
 WORKING-STORAGE SECTION.
*
 01  SWITCHES.
*
     .
     .
     05  VALID-APPLICANT-SW    PIC X           VALUE "N".
         88  VALID-APPLICANT                   VALUE "Y".
     05  AGE-GROUP-FOUND-SW    PIC X           VALUE "N".
         88  AGE-GROUP-FOUND                   VALUE "Y".
     .
     .
*
 01  WORK-FIELDS               COMP-3.
*
     05  POLICY-RATE           PIC S999V99.
     .
     .
*
 01  MENS-RATE-TABLE-VALUES.
*
     05  FILLER                PIC X(12)       VALUE "183423502705".
     05  FILLER                PIC X(12)       VALUE "353924002755".
     05  FILLER                PIC X(12)       VALUE "404424602815".
     05  FILLER                PIC X(12)       VALUE "454925302885".
     05  FILLER                PIC X(12)       VALUE "505426302985".
     05  FILLER                PIC X(12)       VALUE "555928003155".
*
 01  MENS-RATE-TABLE           REDEFINES MENS-RATE-TABLE-VALUES.
*
     05  MRT-AGE-GROUP         OCCURS 6 TIMES
                               INDEXED BY AGE-INDEX.
         10  MRT-LOW-AGE       PIC 99.
         10  MRT-HIGH-AGE      PIC 99.
         10  MRT-INS-RATE      OCCURS 2 TIMES
                               INDEXED BY CLASS-INDEX
                               PIC 99V99.
*
 01  WOMENS-RATE-TABLE-VALUES.
*
     05  FILLER                PIC X(12)    VALUE "183424752845".
     05  FILLER                PIC X(12)    VALUE "353925802950".
     05  FILLER                PIC X(12)    VALUE "404427103080".
     05  FILLER                PIC X(12)    VALUE "454929103280".
     05  FILLER                PIC X(12)    VALUE "505431553525".
     05  FILLER                PIC X(12)    VALUE "555935003870".
*
 01  WOMENS-RATE-TABLE         REDEFINES WOMENS-RATE-TABLE-VALUES.
*
```

Figure 9–32
An alternative to using a three-level table: two two-level tables and condition names (part 1 of 2)

```
        05  WRT-AGE-GROUP          OCCURS 6 TIMES
                                   INDEXED BY AGE-INDEX.
            10  WRT-LOW-AGE        PIC 99.
            10  WRT-HIGH-AGE       PIC 99.
            10  WRT-INS-RATE       OCCURS 2 TIMES
                                   INDEXED BY CLASS-INDEX
                                   PIC 99V99.
*
 01  AP-RECORD.
*
        05  AP-AGE                 PIC 99.
        05  AP-CLASS               PIC 9.
        05  AP-SEX                 PIC 9.
            88  MAN                             VALUE 1.
            88  WOMAN                           VALUE 2.
        .
        .
*
 PROCEDURE DIVISION.
*
        .
        .
        IF VALID-APPLICANT
            IF MAN
                PERFORM 120-SEARCH-MENS-RATE-TABLE
            ELSE
                PERFORM 130-SEARCH-WOMENS-RATE-TABLE.
        .
        .
*
 120-SEARCH-MENS-RATE-TABLE.
*
        SET AGE-INDEX TO 1.
        SET CLASS-INDEX TO AP-CLASS.
        SEARCH MRT-AGE-GROUP
            WHEN AP-AGE NOT GREATER MRT-HIGH-AGE (AGE-INDEX)
                MOVE "Y" TO AGE-GROUP-FOUND-SW.
*
 130-SEARCH-WOMENS-RATE-TABLE.
*
        SET AGE-INDEX TO 1.
        SET CLASS-INDEX TO AP-CLASS.
        SEARCH WRT-AGE-GROUP
            WHEN AP-AGE NOT GREATER WRT-HIGH-AGE (AGE-INDEX)
                MOVE "Y" TO AGE-GROUP-FOUND-SW.
*
 .
 .
```

Figure 9–32
An alternative to using a three-level table: two two-level tables and condition names (part 2 of 2)

In short, if the number of elements in some level of a table is small, always consider alternative ways of coding. You'll probably find that two levels of OCCURS clauses are all you need in most cases. And when you're deciding how to code a problem that could use a multilevel table, keep in mind the structured programming goal of clarity. For example, in the three-level insurance table, it doesn't make much sense to reduce the applicant's sex to a number. It's easier to follow what's going on if you use condition names as in Figure 9–32. On the other hand, the applicant's class number directly relates to the class that determines his or her insurance rate. So it makes sense to use the class to index the table. In any event, you can see that you have a lot of

```
 DATA DIVISION.
*
 FILE SECTION.
*
 FD  TABLE-DATA-FILE
     LABEL RECORDS ARE STANDARD
     RECORD CONTAINS 80 CHARACTERS.
*
 01  TABLE-DATA-AREA            PIC X(80).
*
     .
     .
*
 WORKING-STORAGE SECTION.
*
 01  SWITCHES.
*
     05  TABLE-DATA-EOF-SW      PIC X            VALUE "N".
         88  TABLE-DATA-EOF                      VALUE "Y".
     .
     .
*
 01  RATE-TABLE.
*
     05  AGE-GROUP              OCCURS 6 TIMES
                                INDEXED BY AGE-INDEX.
         10  LOW-AGE            PIC 99.
         10  HIGH-AGE           PIC 99.
         10  SEX-GROUP          OCCURS 2 TIMES
                                INDEXED BY SEX-INDEX.
             15  INS-RATE       OCCURS 2 TIMES
                                INDEXED BY CLASS-INDEX
                                PIC 99V99.
*
 01  TD-RECORD.
*
     05  TD-LOW-AGE             PIC 99.
     05  TD-HIGH-AGE            PIC 99.
     05  TD-SEX-GROUP           OCCURS 2 TIMES
                                INDEXED BY TD-SEX-INDEX.
         10  TD-INS-RATE        OCCURS 2 TIMES
                                INDEXED BY TD-CLASS-INDEX
                                PIC 99V99.
     05  FILLER                 PIC X(60).
*
 .
 .
```

Figure 9–33
Partial Data Division for the program that loads the three-level insurance table

Dept. No.	Men			Women		
	Bachelor's	Master's	Doctor's	Bachelor's	Master's	Doctor's
1						
2						
3						
4						
5						
6						
7						
8						
9						
10						
11						
12						

Figure 9–34
Teachers' table

leeway when deciding how to code a program that involves a multilevel table. So you'll have to make some value judgments to determine which is the best way.

Problems

1. Assume that the data for the three-level table searched by the routine in Figure 9–27 is stored in a file that is to be loaded into the program at execution time. The file consists of six records with this format:

Positions	Data
1–2	Lower age limit
3–4	Upper age limit
5–8	Rate for men class 1
9–12	Rate for men class 2
13–16	Rate for women class 1
17–20	Rate for women class 2

   Using the partial Data Division in Figure 9–33, write a routine for loading this table at the start of the program.

2. Suppose there is a file of input records with one record for each teacher in a college. The records include a field for sex (1 = male, 2 = female), a field for the highest degree earned by the teacher (1 = bachelor's, 2 = master's, 3 = doctor's), and a field for the teacher's department (1 through 12). From this file, a table in the form shown in Figure 9–34 could be created showing the number of teachers in each classification.

   Figure 9–35 presents the code to be used in the exercises that follow. The Data Division gives the input record description, the table description, the indexes that can be used (SEX–INDEX, DEGREE–INDEX, and DEPT–INDEX), and some other required fields. (As mentioned in the discussion for this topic, you might not code a table with only two or three elements in this way. But the purpose of this problem is to familiarize you with the coding for three-level tables.) The partial coding for paragraph 000 shows when and how often modules 100 and 200 will be executed.

   a. Code a routine that creates the table by reading and processing the input file. For each input record, you must add one to the appropriate table entry.

   b. Once the table is created, you have to find the total number of male teachers in the school. The answer should be accumulated in the field named TOTAL–MEN. Write the PERFORM statement that will be used in module 200 to execute the totaling routine. Then code the routine in a paragraph named 210–ACCUMULATE–TOTAL–MEN.

   c. Now find the total number of female teachers with doctor's degrees. The answer should be accumulated in the field named TOTAL–WOMAN–PHDS. Write the PERFORM statement that will be used in module 200 to execute the totaling routine. Then code the routine in a paragraph named 220–ACCUMULATE–WOMEN–PHDS.

   d. Now find the total number of teachers in the college. The answer should be accumulated in the field named TOTAL–TEACHERS. Write the PERFORM statement that will be used in module 200 to execute the totaling routine. Then code the routine in a paragraph named 230–TOTAL–COLLEGE–TEACHERS.

```
DATA DIVISION.
*
FILE SECTION.
*
FD  TEACHER-FILE
    LABEL RECORDS ARE STANDARD
    RECORD CONTAINS 80 CHARACTERS.
*
01  TEACHER-AREA             PIC X(80).
*
    .
    .
*
WORKING-STORAGE SECTION.
*
01  SWITCHES.
*
    05  TEACHER-EOF-SW       PIC X          VALUE "N".
        88  TEACHER-EOF                     VALUE "Y".
    .
    .
*
01  TOTAL-FIELDS             COMP-3.
*
    05  TOTAL-TEACHERS       PIC S9(3)      VALUE 0.
    05  TOTAL-MEN            PIC S9(3)      VALUE 0.
    05  TOTAL-WOMAN-PHDS     PIC S9(3)      VALUE 0.
*
01  TEACHER-TABLE            COMP-3.
*
    05  TT-SEX               OCCURS 2 TIMES
                             INDEXED BY SEX-INDEX.
        10  TT-DEGREE        OCCURS 3 TIMES
                             INDEXED BY DEGREE-INDEX.
            15  TT-DEPT      OCCURS 12 TIMES
                             INDEXED BY DEPT-INDEX
                             PIC 99.
*
01  TEACHER-RECORD.
*
    05  TR-SEX               PIC X.
    05  TR-DEGREE            PIC X.
    05  TR-DEPT-NO           PIC XX.
    05  FILLER               PIC X(76).
*
    .
    .
*
PROCEDURE DIVISION.
*
000-DETERMINE-TEACHER-TOTALS.
*
    .
    .
    MOVE ZERO TO TEACHER-TABLE.
    PERFORM 100-CREATE-TEACHER-TABLE
        UNTIL TEACHER-EOF.
    PERFORM 200-ACCUMULATE-TEACHER-TOTALS.
    .
    .
```

Figure 9–35
Partial coding of Data Division and module 000 for the teachers' table program

```
 PROCEDURE DIVISION.
*
      .
      .
      PERFORM 100-LOAD-RATE-TABLE
          VARYING AGE-INDEX FROM 1 BY 1
          UNTIL AGE-INDEX GREATER 6.
      .
      .
*
 100-LOAD-RATE-TABLE.
*
      PERFORM 110-READ-TABLE-DATA-RECORD.
      IF NOT TABLE-DATA-EOF
          MOVE TD-LOW-AGE  TO LOW-AGE (AGE-INDEX)
          MOVE TD-HIGH-AGE TO HIGH-AGE (AGE-INDEX)
          PERFORM 120-STORE-INS-RATE
              VARYING TD-SEX-INDEX FROM 1 BY 1
              UNTIL TD-SEX-INDEX GREATER 2
                  AFTER TD-CLASS-INDEX FROM 1 BY 1
                  UNTIL TD-CLASS-INDEX GREATER 2.
*
 110-READ-TABLE-DATA-RECORD.
*
      READ TABLE-DATA-FILE INTO TD-RECORD
          AT END
              MOVE "Y" TO TABLE-DATA-EOF-SW.
*
 120-STORE-INS-RATE.
*
      SET SEX-INDEX   TO TD-SEX-INDEX.
      SET CLASS-INDEX TO TD-CLASS-INDEX.
      MOVE TD-INS-RATE (TD-SEX-INDEX, TD-CLASS-INDEX)
          TO INS-RATE (AGE-INDEX, SEX-INDEX, CLASS-INDEX).
*
      .
      .
```

Figure 9–36
Loading the three-level table

Solutions

1. Figure 9–36 is an acceptable solution. Note how the SET statements are used in 120–STORE–INS–RATE. Here, an index for one table is set to a value that corresponds to the occurrence number of the index value of another table. This program also uses the PERFORM statement with two levels of VARYING to control the loading of the table.

2. Figure 9–37 shows acceptable solutions.
   a. Module 120 does most of the work in this routine. It sets the three indexes to the values in the input record so they'll refer to the right field in the table. Then, it adds one to the field indicated by the indexes.
   b. Here, a two-level PERFORM statement is used in module 200 to control the execution of module 210. It varies the degree and department indexes through all their possible values. The sex index, however, is simply coded as 1 in module 210. Because only the men are being counted, this index doesn't have to be varied.
   c. Only a single-level PERFORM statement is needed here to vary the department index from 1 to 12 as module 220 is executed. The sex and degree indexes can be coded as 2 and 3 respectively in the ADD statement because only the women teachers with doctorates are being counted.

d. To find the total number of teachers in the college, all three indexes must be varied through all their possible values so that all the entries in the table are added together. That's why module 200 uses a three-level PERFORM statement to execute module 230.

Acceptable code for problem 2a

```
 100-CREATE-TEACHER-TABLE.
*
     PERFORM 110-READ-TEACHER-RECORD.
     IF NOT TEACHER-EOF
         PERFORM 120-ACCUMULATE-TABLE-VALUES.
     .
     .
*
 110-READ-TEACHER-RECORD.
*
     READ TEACHER-FILE INTO TEACHER-RECORD
         AT END
             MOVE "Y" TO TEACHER-EOF-SW.
*
 120-ACCUMULATE-TABLE-VALUES.
*
     SET SEX-INDEX TO TR-SEX.
     SET DEGREE-INDEX TO TR-DEGREE.
     SET DEPT-INDEX TO TR-DEPT-NO.
     ADD 1 TO TT-DEPT (SEX-INDEX, DEGREE-INDEX, DEPT-INDEX).
*
```

Acceptable code for problem 2b

The PERFORM statement:

```
     PERFORM 210-ACCUMULATE-TOTAL-MEN
         VARYING DEGREE-INDEX FROM 1 BY 1
         UNTIL DEGREE-INDEX GREATER 3
             AFTER DEPT-INDEX FROM 1 BY 1
             UNTIL DEPT-INDEX GREATER 12.
```

Module 210:

```
 210-ACCUMULATE-TOTAL-MEN.
*
     ADD TT-DEPT (1, DEGREE-INDEX, DEPT-INDEX) TO TOTAL-MEN.
*
```

Acceptable code for problem 2c

The PERFORM statement:

```
     PERFORM 220-ACCUMULATE-WOMAN-PHDS
         VARYING DEPT-INDEX FROM 1 BY 1
         UNTIL DEPT-INDEX GREATER 12.
```

Module 220:

```
 220-ACCUMULATE-WOMAN-PHDS
*
     ADD TT-DEPT (2, 3, DEPT-INDEX) TO TOTAL-WOMAN-PHDS.
*
```

Figure 9–37
Coding solution for the teacher's table program (part 1 of 2)

```
Acceptable code for problem 2d

   The PERFORM statement:

         PERFORM 230-TOTAL-COLLEGE-TEACHERS
             VARYING SEX-INDEX FROM 1 BY 1
             UNTIL SEX-INDEX GREATER 2
                 AFTER DEGREE-INDEX FROM 1 BY 1
                 UNTIL DEGREE-INDEX GREATER 3
                     AFTER DEPT-INDEX FROM 1 BY 1
                     UNTIL DEPT-INDEX GREATER 12.

    Module 230:

     230-TOTAL-COLLEGE-TEACHERS.
    *
         ADD TT-DEPT (SEX-INDEX, DEGREE-INDEX, DEPT-INDEX)
             TO TOTAL-TEACHERS.
    *
```

Figure 9–37
Coding solution for the teacher's table program (part 2 of 2)

Topic 5 **Issue: Two More Debugging Aids**

The DISPLAY statement was discussed previously. You were shown how to use it to help debug programs that seemed to be extra troublesome and where you were not able to locate the logical errors by careful inspection of the source list. As the programs and their attendant logic statements become more complex, your debugging problems will probably also become more complex and you will need more tools than just the DISPLAY statement to help you. Some COBOL compilers have two additional tools, the EXHIBIT statement and the TRACE statement, which are extensions to the ANSI COBOL standards. You should check the COBOL reference guide for your computer to see if these are available.

The EXHIBIT Statement

The EXHIBIT statement functions about the same as the DISPLAY. Like the DISPLAY, it will display data on the user terminal (or whichever device is defined as the system output device), but it will also print out the name of the field being shown if you request it. The format of the EXHIBIT is:

```
             ⎧literal          ⎫
EXHIBIT      ⎨                 ⎬...
             ⎩NAMED data-name  ⎭
```

If you use the literal option it will act just like the literal option of the DISPLAY. For example the statement EXHIBIT 'module 100' will show that literal data (module 100) on the terminal.

If you use the named option, the name of the field, an equal sign, and the contents of the field will be displayed. For example, the statement EXHIBIT NAMED PF–EMPL–NUMBER will display PF–EMPL–NUMBER = 950 on the terminal if the contents of PF–EMPL–NUMBER is the number 950.

If you want to display the name of the field along with the field contents, you can see that the EXHIBIT statement has some advantages over the DISPLAY. To do the same thing with the DISPLAY you would have to name a literal in addition to the field, such as the statement

```
DISPLAY 'PF-EMPL-NUMBER = ' PF-EMPL-NUMBER.
```

The TRACE Statement

If you want to track the execution of the modules of your program to see whether they are (1) all being executed and (2) being executed in the order you assumed, you can cause the module names to be displayed as they are executed by using the TRACE command. This function can be turned on and turned off. The reason for turning the function on and off is that in a complex program you may want to track module execution in only one part of the program, but not in all parts of the program.

The command to turn the trace function on is READY TRACE and the command to turn it off is RESET TRACE. For instance, look at the VTOC in Figure 9–12. If you wanted to track the execution of the program from beginning to end, you would put the READY TRACE command in as the first line in module 000. That is that type of action, however, that only novices take. A more efficient approach is to use the trace only in the part of the program where you are having trouble. Suppose that the load-rate-table module did not appear to be doing its job. To track what is happening, you might turn on the trace just before performing the 100 module and turn it off after it is done. The following statements show how to do that:

```
READY TRACE.
PERFORM 100-LOAD-RATE-TABLE.
RESET TRACE.
```

The results of that particular set of commands would be a display of each module name each time it was executed. For example:

```
trace: 100-LOAD-RATE-TABLE
trace: 110-READ-TABLE-RECORD
trace: 120-STORE-TABLE-ENTRY
trace: 110-READ-TABLE-RECORD
trace: 120-STORE-TABLE-ENTRY
  .       .
  .       .
trace: 110-READ-TABLE-RECORD
trace: 120-STORE-TABLE-ENTRY
trace: 110-READ-TABLE-RECORD
```

This example assumes that the modules worked somewhat as they were intended to work. If something was wrong, however, such as the end-of-file switch not being initialized properly—you might get only one line of output from the trace. On the other hand, if the end-of-file switch was not set properly when the end of file was reached you could get an infinite trace list, or perhaps the program would just blow up. A test would be to the feed load-table module only a limited number of records that were easy to count (three or four). If it went through the cycle fewer times than it should or more time than it should you could then begin to isolate the problem from the way that the execution of the modules worked.

A final word of advice is that you should resort to these debugging techniques only when careful desk checking has not enabled you to find the problem. Careful design and a thoughtful test plan should save you in most instances from having to use these tools.

Chapter 10 Introduction to File Handling

If you have written programs with secondary storage input or output in another language or have taken a course that emphasized secondary storage concepts, these topics may be largely review for you. Topic 1 presents the basic tape concepts and topic 2 introduces disk concepts. Topic 3 discusses sequential file organization and programming considerations. Topic 4 presents COBOL language elements for fixed-length sequential files. More advanced topics, such as Indexed Sequential Access Method files, direct files, and variable-length records, are left for the advanced course.

Topic 1 Tape Concepts

Orientation

Since the memory of the computer is an expensive and limited resource, the massive quantities of data that must be available in machine-readable form are stored on what are called secondary memory devices. The data must not only be in machine-readable form, but also must be able to be read over and over and to give consistent results each time it is read. Obviously, having a human input the data each time it is needed is horribly slow, but more importantly, that method will not give consistent results. The use of punched cards was one of the first satisfactory answers to those problems, but was not completely satisfactory due to the speed at which cards could be read and punched. Also, cards could easily get out of place in a deck or even lost, thus causing consistency problems. Tape was the first medium that was truly satisfactory in regard to ease and speed of handling and providing consistent data. Tape is still widely used today since it remains the least expensive secondary storage medium.

Terminology

BCD
Binary Coded Decimal
bit
block
blocking
blocking factor
bpi
check bit
density
horizontal check character
horizontal parity checking
IBG
interblock gap
interrecord gap
IRG
KB
load-point marker
logical record
longitudinal check character
magnetic tape
nine-track tape
parity bit
physical record
record
seven-track tape
start/stop time
tape drive
transfer rate
transfer speed
vertical parity checking

Objectives

1. ***Explain how vertical and horizontal parity checking assure the accuracy of tape I/O operations.***

2. ***Name two benefits derived from blocking records on tape.***

3. ***Describe how the block factor for a tape file is determined; specifically, name the factors that must be considered.***

Magnetic Tape

Figure 10–1 illustrates a reel of the *magnetic tape* used in computer operations. Similar to the tape used for tape records, it is a continuous strip of plastic coated on one side with a metal oxide. In general, it is half an inch wide and comes in lengths of 250, 600, 1200, and 2400 feet, wound on plastic reels of varying sizes.

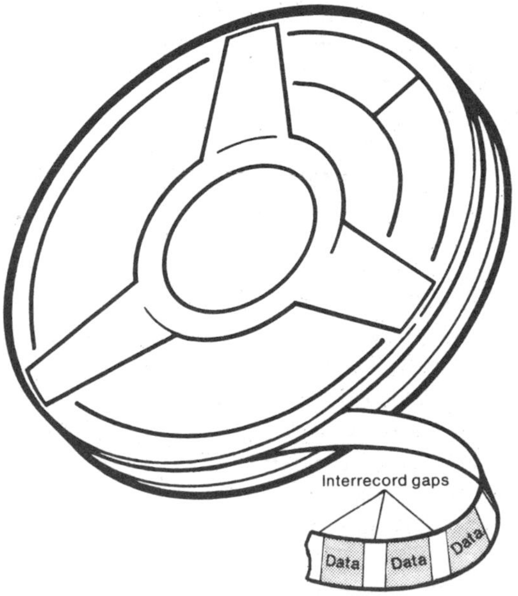

Interrecord gaps
Data
Data
Data

Figure 10–1
A magnetic tape

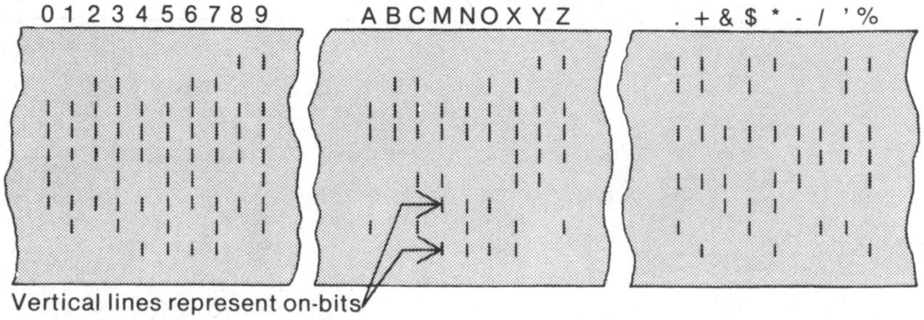
0 1 2 3 4 5 6 7 8 9
A B C M N O X Y Z
. + & $ * - / ' %
Vertical lines represent on-bits

Figure 10–2
Coding on tape

Data is recorded on the coated surface of the tape in patterns of magnetized spots called *bits*. A succession of these patterns strung together forms a *record*—that is, a collection of related data fields. Between individual data records on the tape are spaces where no data is recorded. These spaces, shown in Figure 10–1, are called *interrecord gaps*, or *IRGs*. Although there are some limitations, for most uses a data record can be as short or as long as necessary.

To get a clearer idea of how bits are used to record data on tape, look at Figure 10–2. For each letter, number, and special character, there are nine vertical positions on the tape in which a bit may or may not be recorded. In other words, each character is represented by its own code made up of a unique combination of "on" and "off" bits. (In Figure 10–2, the on-bits are indicated by a line in a bit position, the off-bits by a space.) The nine vertical bit positions in each code correspond to a byte of computer storage.

Actually, though, the code for each character uses only eight of the nine bit positions. The ninth bit, called a *check bit* or *parity bit*, is used as a check on the accuracy of tape operations. This bit is set either off or on to make the number of on-bits in the individual codes either all odd or all even, depending on the computer. For example, if the total number of on-bits in each code is supposed to be odd and a tape character with an even number of on-bits is read, the computer system has detected an input error. This type of checking is called *vertical parity checking*.

A second type of check is performed in the horizontal direction. At the end of each tape record—the last byte before the interrecord gap—is a *horizontal*, or *longitudinal*, *check character*. The bits of this byte are set on or off to form a parity check for each of the horizontal tracks. Then, if a computer that uses even parity finds an odd number of bits in a track, it has detected an input error. With the combination of vertical and *horizontal parity checking*, most tape input errors can be caught. While it isn't necessary for you as a programmer to understand parity checking completely, you should realize that all input and output operations on tape are checked.

The tape in Figure 10–2 is called a *nine-track tape* because each vertical position consists of nine bit positions. Although these tapes are the most common right now, *seven-track tapes* were formerly used by many companies. Seven-track tapes are recorded in a code called *Binary Coded Decimal*, or *BCD*. In this code, seven bits are used to represent one character of data—six data bits plus one parity bit. Parity checking takes place on seven-track tapes just as it does on nine-track tapes. The ASCII code discussed in chapter 1 is also a seven-bit code. It is probably the most-used code structure and is coded onto nine-track tapes. Often the developer of the tape system will devise a special method to use the two extra tracks of a nine-track system to store more than one byte of data across one tape position. The EBCDIC code, also discussed in chapter 1, is the second most-used code. EBCDIC is an extension

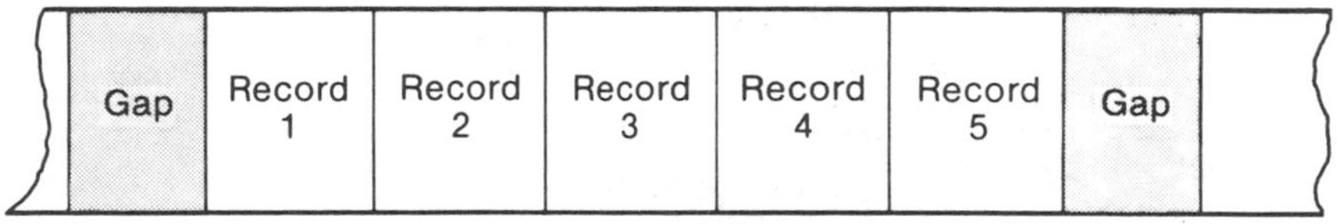
Gap
Record 1
Record 2
Record 3
Record 4
Record 5
Gap

Figure 10–3
Blocked records

of the BCD code. The EBCDIC code can encode more characters than the BCD, and nine-track tape is designed especially for it.

Often in tape operations, more than one tape record is recorded between IRGs. This is called *blocking* records. Figure 10–3, for instance, shows how a *block* of five records would look on tape. Here, the *blocking factor* of the file is five, since five records (often called *logical records*) are stored in each tape block (often called a *physical record*). Because blocking is such a common practice, the IRG is often referred to as an *interblock gap*, or *IBG*. Blocking is commonly used because it increases the storage capacity of a reel of tape as well as the speed at which the records on the tape can be read or written.

The Tape Drive

The *tape drive* is the hardware unit that reads and writes the data on tape. To mount a tape on one of the older tape drives, the computer operator threads the tape through a read/write mechanism in the center of the unit and then onto an empty takeup reel, as shown in Figure 10–4. This process is similar to mounting a tape on a tape recorder. On the newer tape drives, threading of the tape is done by the drive itself so the operator can change tapes more rapidly.

Once the tape is mounted, the operator pushes the start button, and the tape drive locates the first record on the file by searching for a *load-point marker*, which is a reflective spot on the surface of the tape. Tape records can then be read or written under control of a stored program. When data is read from a tape, the data on the tape remains unaltered, so it can be read many times. When data is written on a tape, it replaces (and thus destroys) the data that was on the tape. Before a tape is removed from the tape drive, it is rewound onto the original reel, ready to be read or written again.

During reading operations, input records are checked for vertical and horizontal parity as discussed earlier. In writing operations, output records can be checked for vertical and horizontal parity as soon as a character, record, or block of records is written, because the reading mechanism is located just after the writing mechanism.

Although the basic programmable functions of a tape drive are reading and writing records, there are a number of others. For example, tape drives can be programmed to rewind a tape, to backspace a tape one block of records, and to skip over faulty sections of tape. In addition, some tape drives can be programmed to read tapes backwards, which can increase the speed of tape operations in some applications.

Many computer systems used tape drives extensively, even though their primary I/O form was the disk. For instance, a medium-sized system frequently included from two to six tape drives, while larger systems may have had several dozen or more.

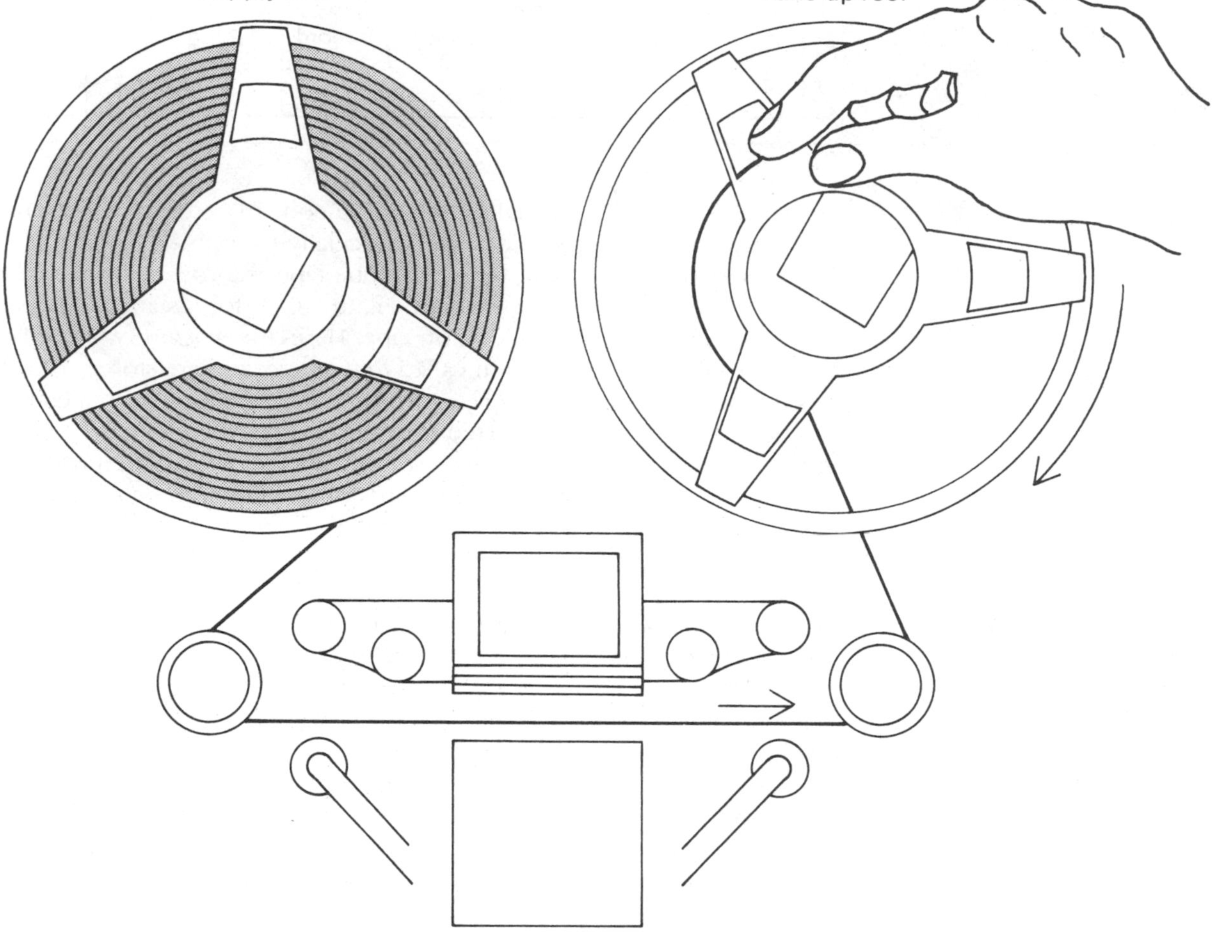
Supply reel
Take-up reel
Read/write assembly

Figure 10–4
Mounting a tape

Tape Speed and Capacity

One measure of the speed of tape operations is the *transfer rate*, or *transfer speed*, of a tape drive. It measures how long it takes in bytes per second to transfer data from the tape drive to storage, or vice versa. For example, one common tape drive has a transfer rate of 60,000 bytes per second. (This speed is often referred to as 60 *KB*, where KB means thousands of bytes per second.) Other tape drives have speeds that range from 5 KB all the way up to 1250 KB. To appreciate tape speeds, consider that a transfer rate of 80,000 bytes per second (80 KB) is the equivalent of reading 1000 80-column cards per second, or 60,000 cards—a stack 35 feet high—in one minute.

Transfer rate is somewhat misleading, however, because a tape drive actually stops and starts every time that it comes to an IBG. Yet transfer rate does not reflect this *start/stop time*. To appreciate the effect of starting and stopping between each physical record, suppose that a file of 6000 records, each 100 bytes long, is stored on a tape with a blocking factor of 1. At 60 KB, it takes 10 seconds to read the data in the file (600,000 bytes at 60,000 bytes per second). However, the tape also has to stop and start 6000 times. Since the start/stop time of a typical tape drive is 8/1000 of a second (8 milliseconds), the time required for starting and stopping is an additional 48 seconds. In other words, the tape drive spends 10 seconds reading data and 48 seconds starting and stopping. The effective processing rate is therefore much less than 60 KB.

Now suppose the records are blocked with a blocking factor of 10. Ten seconds are still required for reading the 600,000 bytes of data, but only 4.8 seconds are required for starting and stopping. Since the total time for reading the file is reduced from 58 seconds to 14.8 seconds, you can see the effect of blocking on the speed of tape operations.

The capacity of a reel of tape depends on the length of the tape and the *density* of the tape. Density is a measure of the number of bytes of data that can be recorded on one inch of tape. For example, one older model type drive has a density of 800 *bpi* (bytes per inch) and has an IBG of 0.6 inch. Common densities are 800, 1600, and 6250 bpi; common lengths are 0.6 and 0.75 inch.

Blocking also affects the capacity of a tape. To illustrate, suppose there is a sample file of 8000 records, 100 bytes each. At 1600 bpi, the 800,000 bytes require 500 inches of tape. With a blocking factor of 1, the 8000 IBGs (at 6/10 inch) use 4800 inches of tape. The total file then requires 5300 inches of tape. If the blocking factor is increased to 10, however, only 800 IBGs are required. Then, only 480 inches of tape is used for IBGs, and the file is reduced from 5300 inches to 980 inches.

How large can a blocking factor be? On smaller systems, it depends to some extent on the computer's available CPU storage. If, for example, a program is to be run in 16K of storage and the instructions by themselves take 14K, the blocking factors must be kept relatively small. Assuming four files were processed by a program, each requiring two I/O areas, the average block size would have to be 250 bytes (2K divided by eight I/O areas).

On medium-size to large systems, storage restrictions are generally *not* a factor in determining block size. In such cases you should choose a blocking factor that will make optimum use of the resources of the computer system. Based on past experience, a block size of around 4000 bytes has proven to be efficient. Any increase in block size contributes little to I/O speed, even though it increases the requirements for internal storage. Most manufacturers provide tables that can be used to determine the most efficient block size for any record size. However, due to the nature of tape and of disk, the block size is more critical for disk.

Discussion

Because of decreased cost per byte of computer hardware in general and secondary storage equipment in particular, the use of tape is decreasing. In actuality, there are more tape drives being used than before since the computer is being used more. However, as a percent of the total secondary storage being used today, tape usage has declined and disk usage has increased tremendously.

Another factor in the percent reduction of tape use is the trend toward on-line access as opposed to batch. With hardware costs down and operating sophistication and reliability up, on-line access is becoming more common. Multiuser on-line systems are also becoming more popular. All of these advances call for increased disk capacity and less reliance on tape files for working master files.

Tapes still represent the least expensive method of data storage, and as such will be used for several years. They are used extensively in on-line environments as an inexpensive medium for back-up and for archive files which must be retained for a long time.

Technological advances are on the horizon which may replace tape and disk. You are seeing the first commercial applications of some of these advances in the compact disk for playing music. Laser technology and other discoveries will probably make a significant impact on the secondary storage market in the coming years.

Topic 2 **Direct-Access Concepts**

Orientation

A substantial majority of today's data-processing systems are direct-access systems. Direct-access storage devices (DASD) provide large amounts of storage with fast access to any of the stored records. Unlike sequential devices such as a card reader or a tape drive, a record on a direct-access file can be read or written without reading or writing the records that precede it. To process the 500th record in a direct-access file, it is possible to bypass the previous 499 records and go directly to the 500th, hence the word *direct* when speaking of access.

Direct-access devices also differ from tape devices in that they vary considerably in physical characteristics. For example, *disks* record data on platters that are somewhat analogous to phonograph records in a stack. There are significant differences in the disks of the various manufacturers, and that fact precludes a detailed discussion of those differences. However, since COBOL is a standardized language, this means that your knowledge should be almost totally applicable on all computer systems that run COBOL. Once you understand how to write a COBOL program that accesses files on one computer system, the new information needed to work on another system will be relatively minor and easy to learn.

This part of the text is intended to provide an introduction to disk processes. As such it will not become very involved in the complexities and methods of the random-access methods, such as direct and indexed. Those discussions are left to an advanced COBOL book, and this one only introduces those concepts so that you will know that they exist and are used.

Terminology

access mechanism
access-mechanism movement
alternate track
blocking
blocking routine
coarse index
count area
count-data format
count-key-data format
cyclic check characters
cylinder
cylinder index
DASD
data area
data transfer
deblocking routine
detail index
direct file organization
disk
disk address
disk drive
disk label-checking routine
disk pack
end-of-file label
end-of-reel marker
end-of-volume label
error-recovery routine
file label
file-label checking
fine index
general index
head switching

Terminology (continued)

header label
home address
I/O commands
index
indexed file organization
internal label
key area
latency
master index
module
multifile reel
multifile volume
multivolume file
random processing
randomizing routine
read
rotational delay
search
seek
seek time
sequential file organization
spindle
standard labels
synonym
tape label-checking routine
tape switching
track
track index
trailer label
volume label
Volume Table of Contents
volume-label checking
VTOC
write
write-verify

Objectives

1. *List and describe the physical operations required by the disk in order to access and read or write a record from a file in (1) count-data format and (2) count-key-data format.*

2. *List the I/O commands that must be executed to access and read or write a record on the disk.*

3. *Explain how blocking can (1) increase the number of records that can be stored on a disk and (2) decrease the time required to read or write a sequential file on disk.*

4. *Describe the function of a randomizing routine as applied to direct files.*

5. *Explain how general and detail indexes are used to access a record (1) sequentially and (2) directly.*

6. *Describe the purpose of error-recovery, blocking, deblocking, and label-checking routines.*

7. *Distinguish between a multifile volume and a multivolume file.*

The Direct-Access Storage Device

The two basic elements of a disk system are the disk pack and the disk drive. The *disk pack* is the device on which data is recorded; the *disk drive* is the I/O unit that writes data on and reads data from a disk pack. The disk pack and disk drive will be discussed; following those discussions the types of I/O commands that can be executed by the disk systems will be explained. Rather than attempting to discuss several disk systems, or to even discuss the low and the high end of disk systems that are available, this discussion will point out the capabilities and features of a middle of the road system. The data given will be for a typical disk system that is currently available, the kind that is present in 60 to 75 percent of the computer centers you might visit.

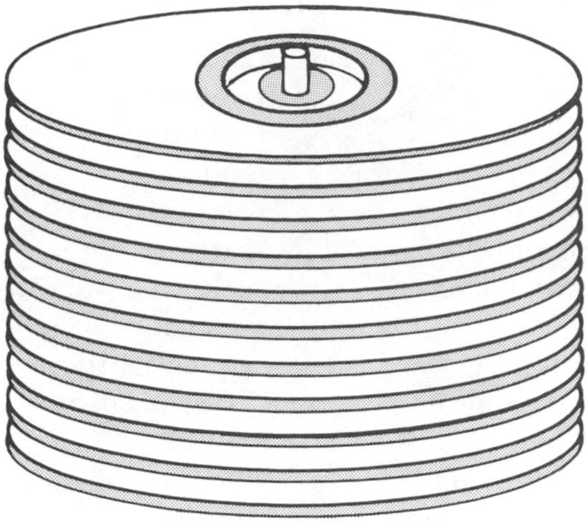

Figure 10–5
The disk pack

The disk pack

The physical structure of a commonly used disk pack is illustrated in Figure 10–5. It consists of 11 metal disks, each 14 inches in diameter, which are permanently stacked on a central *spindle*. When the disk pack is mounted on the drive, a common rotational speed is 3600 revolutions per minute. When the disk pack is removed from the disk drive, a protective plastic cover is placed over it for storage.

Except for the top surface of the top disk and the bottom surface of the bottom disk, data can be recorded on both sides of the 11 disks that make up the pack; this is similar to sound being recorded on both sides of a phonograph record. As a result, this disk pack has a total of 20 recording surfaces, each of

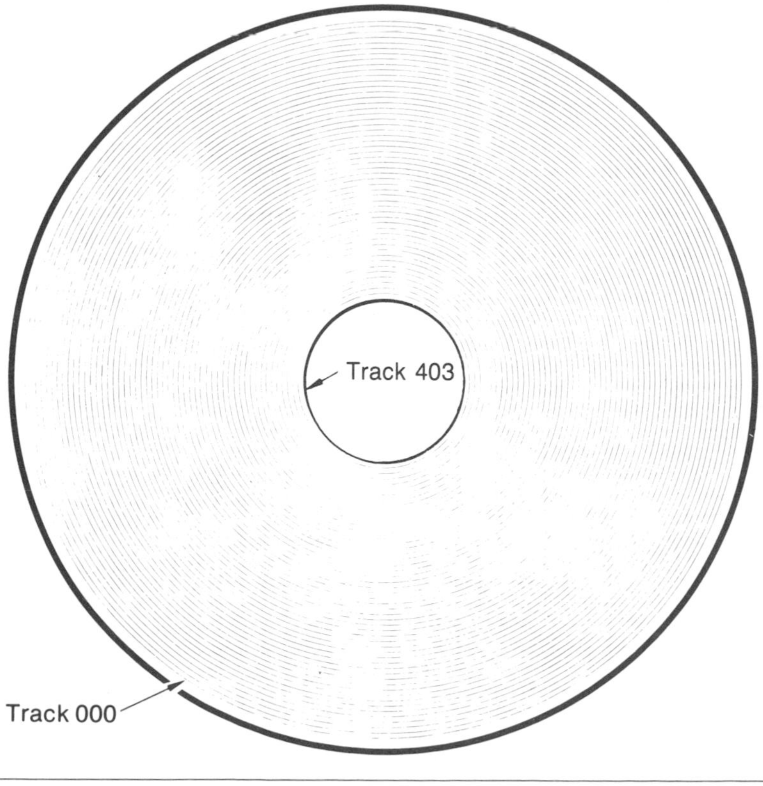
Track 403
Track 000

Figure 10–6
Tracks on a disk surface

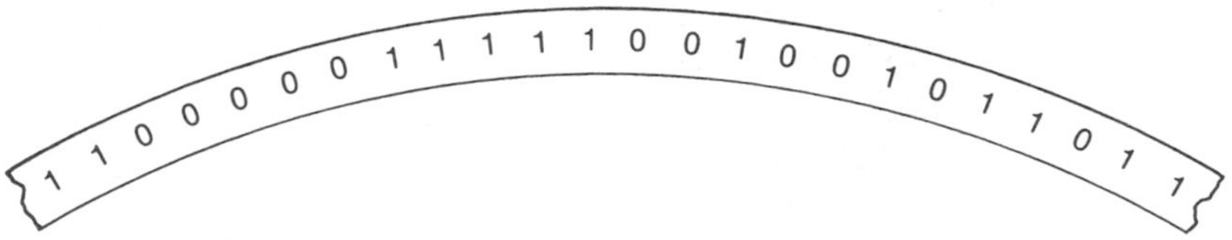
1 1 0 0 0 0 0 1 1 1 1 1 0 0 1 0 0 1 0 1 1 0 1 1

Figure 10–7
Coding on one section of a track

which has a magnetic coating on which data can be recorded. Each disk is coated top and bottom with a metal oxide, which is the medium used to record data. Spots on the oxide are magnetized or demagnetized to represent bits turned on or off. Ordered combinations of these bits become the various characters of fields and records.

On each of the 20 recording surfaces are concentric circles called *tracks*, as illustrated in Figure 10–6. The tracks are numbered beginning with 000 through 403 for a system with 404 tracks, or 000 through 807 for a system with 808 tracks. A disk system which is less expensive, but with less capacity, would access the 404 tracks per surface, while a system with greater capacity, but which would also be more expensive, would access 808 tracks. The capacity of the pack would depend more on the technology of the disk drive than on the disk pack itself. With either system there would still be 20 surfaces, which on the large capacity disk would mean that there were 16,160 addressable tracks. Although the tracks get smaller toward the center of the disk, each of the tracks can hold the same amount of data, a maximum of 13,030 bytes.

Bits are used to record data on a track of a disk pack, just as they are on tape. On disk, the bits are strung together, one following the other around the track, so that eight bits make up one byte of data. To illustrate, suppose that Figure 10–7 represents a portion of one track on one recording surface. If 0 represents an off-bit and 1 an on-bit, this portion of track contains three bytes of data. In EBCDIC code, which corresponds to DISPLAY usage, the first byte, 11000001, represents the letter A; the second byte, 11110010, represents the digit 2; and the third byte, 01011011, represents the special character $.

The actual number of records on any track of a disk pack varies depending on the size of the records being stored. For example, one track can hold one record of 13,030 bytes, two records of 6447 bytes each, three records of 4,253 bytes each, etc. You can see that the capacity of a track decreases as the number of records on the track increases. If the records are stored one per track, the capacity is 13,030 bytes; if two per track, the capacity is 12,894 bytes (two records of 6447 bytes each), and so on. By the time you get to records that are 100 bytes long, the track capacity is only 56 records or 5,600 bytes. This loss of capacity is due to interrecord gaps, just as on tape.

Storage Formats

Count-data storage format

When records are stored on a disk pack, they can be stored in either of two track formats. The first, called the *count-data format*, is illustrated in Figure 10–8. In this format, each record (*data area*) on a track is preceded by a *count area*. (The disk is revolving in a counterclockwise direction, so the read/write device would read or write the count area before the data area.) Since the illustration, which represents only one track, has four data areas, there are four count areas on the track. These count areas contain the *disk addresses* and lengths of the records following them. Just as a storage address identifies one and only one storage position, a disk address identifies one

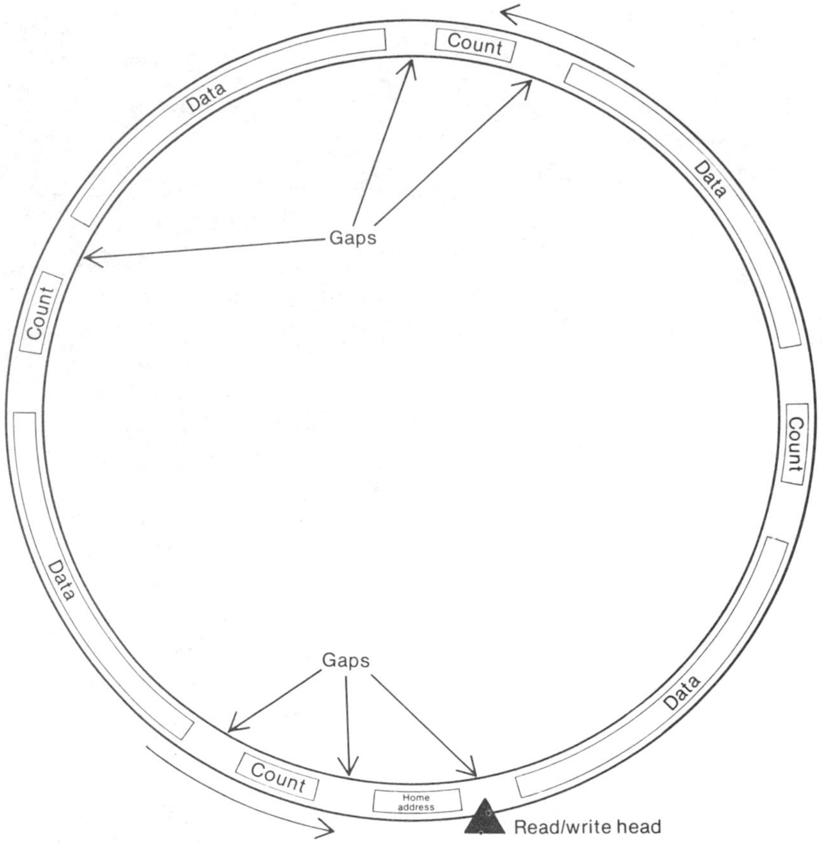
Count
Data
Data
Gaps
Count
Count
Data
Data
Gaps
Count
Home address
Read/write head

Figure 10–8
Count-data format

and only one data area on a disk pack. By using the count area, each of the records on a disk pack can be directly accessed and read or written.

In addition to count areas and data areas, each track in the count-data format has a *home address*. The home address, which comes immediately before the first count area on a track, uniquely identifies each of the tracks on a disk pack.

Count-key-data storage format

The second track format that can be used is called the *count-key-data format*. Like the count-data format, there is a home address at the start of each track. However, unlike the count-data format, there is a *key area* between each count and data area as shown in Figure 10–9. This key area contains the control data that uniquely identifies a record in a file. For example, in a file of inventory master records, the part number would logically be recorded in the key area. In a file of master payroll records, the employee number would be recorded in the key area. The difference, then, between count and key areas is that the count area contains a disk address that uniquely identifies a record location on the disk pack, and the key area contains a control field that uniquely identifies a record in a file. As you will see later, both count and key areas can be used to locate records when directly accessing them.

Because the count-key-data format has gaps separating the key from the count and data areas, the track capacity of this format is less than that of the count-data format. For example, with one record per track (one home address, one count, one key, and one data area), the track capacity is 12,974 bytes

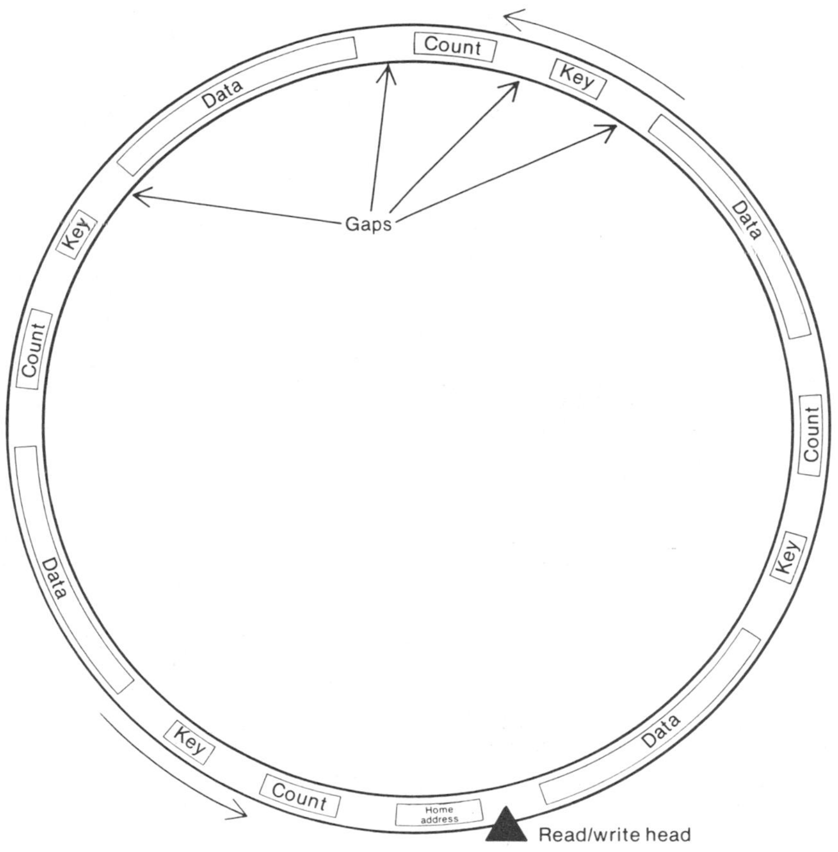
Count
Key
Data
Gaps
Key
Count
Data
Count
Key
Data
Key
Count
Home address
Data
Read/write head

Figure 10–9
Count-key-data format

This includes both key and data areas. Recall that the capacity of the track in count-data format was 13,030 bytes, or 56 bytes difference just for the extra gap. If the record size is only 100 bytes, a maximum of 45 records in the count-key-data format can be stored on the track, which is 11 records fewer than the count-data format. That is a loss of 1,100 bytes to gaps.

The disk drive

The disk drive is the I/O unit which writes data on and reads data from the disk pack. The typical drive contains only one pack, but some disk facilities may contain several packs. These are essentially independent drives housed in a large unit, and the individual drives are called *modules*.

To mount a disk pack, the operator opens the lid on the drive (or possibly pulls out a drawer containing the drive unit), places the disk pack on the drive's spindle, unscrews the pack's plastic protective cover, and closes the drive unit. When the operator pushes the start button of the unit, the disk pack begins rotating until it reaches the prescribed rotational speed for that particular device. A common speed for the type of drive described is 3600 rpm. When the pack reaches the correct speed, it is then ready for I/O activity. The drive may then read data from or write data on the pack's several recording surfaces. When it reads data, the data on the disk pack remains unchanged (called a nondestructive read); when it writes data, the data that is written replaces the data previously stored at that particular position on the pack.

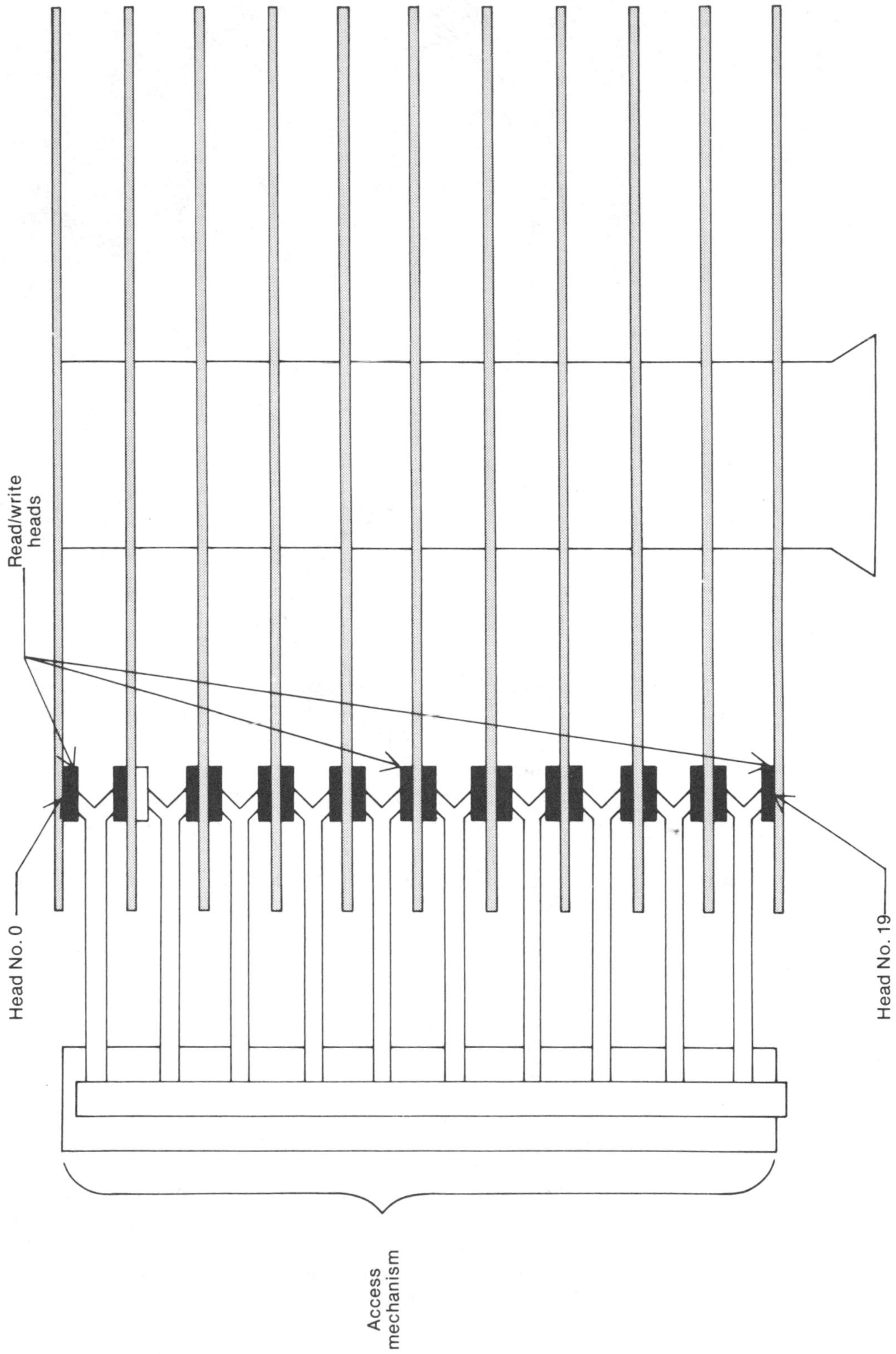
Read/write heads
Head No. 0
Head No. 19
Access mechanism

Figure 10–10
Side view of the access mechanism

The access mechanism

The machanism used to read and write data on the disk is called the *access mechanism* and is illustrated in side view in Figure 10–10. It consists of 20 read/write heads, one for each of the 20 recording surfaces. These heads are numbered from 0 through 19. Only one of the 20 heads can be turned on at any one time; thus, only one track can be operated on at one time. Each of the heads can both read and write data but can do only one operation at a time.

To operate on a recording surface, the access mechanism moves to the track that is to be operated on. When the access mechanism moves, all 20 heads move in unison so that they are positioned at the same track on each of the 20 recording surfaces. Then, these 20 tracks, which are said to make up one *cylinder* of data, can be operated on, one right after another, without the access mechanism having to move to another setting. In other words, if the access mechanism is positioned at the 75th cylinder, the 75th track on each recording surface can be read or written, one track right after another. If the particular drive can access 404 tracks on each surface, then there are 404 different settings of the access mechanism and 404 cylinders. A drive with 808 tracks has 808 different access mechanism settings and 808 cylinders.

An interesting aspect of disk technology is that quite often the drive's capacity is not the total number of tracks that can be accessed. For example, when it was said that the drive could access 404 tracks, the actual capacity may only be 400 tracks. The reason is that in manufacturing a pack, or after use, one or more tracks may have or develop a flaw which renders that track unusable. Rather than allowing that to cause the whole pack to be unusable, most disk systems can have the bad track taken out of service, so to speak, and a previously unused track brought into service to replace the bad one. For instance, suppose that only tracks 000 through 399 were available for normal use. If it were discovered that track 187 was bad, a standard list of usable tracks would be updated to indicate that track 187 is not to be used and that track 400 is now to be used to replace it.

Accessing a disk record

Any programming references to data records on disk are eventually reduced to cylinder number, head (track) number, and either record number or key. The cylinders are numbered 0 through say 399, the heads 0 through 19, and the record number starts at 0 and continues through the maximum number of records that can be stored on the track. Because record number 0 is used by the operating system, data records always begin with record number 1.

When directly accessing and reading a record on a disk, there are four phases that the disk drive goes through. During the first phase, called *access-mechanism movement*, the access mechanism moves to the cylinder that is going to be operated on. The time required for this movement depends on the number of cylinders moved. If it is just one cylinder—for instance, a move from the 25th to the 26th cylinder—may take just 6 milliseconds (6/1000 second). On the other hand, if the move is from the first to the last cylinder, the move may take 55ms (55 milliseconds). Another meaningful time is the average time, which will be about 30ms if the file uses all of the cylinders on a pack. This time to move the access mechanism and find a desired cylinder is also commonly called *seek time*, or the time to seek another cylinder.

Once the heads are moved to the correct cylinder, the appropriate read/write head must be turned on. This is called *head switching*. If a track on the third recording surface is supposed to be read, head number 2 is turned on. In Figure 10–10, head number 2, which is on, is colored white while the others are black. Since head switching takes place at electronic speeds, it has a negligible effect on the total amount of time required to read or write a record.

After the head is turned on, there is a delay while the appropriate record rotates around under the head. This phase is called *rotational delay* (or *latency*). One complete rotation on a disk pack that is being rotated at 3600 rpm is 16.67ms. This means that the maximum time of rotational delay could only be 16.7ms. On the other hand, the desired record may just be reaching the head when the head is switched on. In this case, rotational delay could be as little as 0ms. Since rotational delay can then vary between 0 and 16.67ms, the average delay is about 8.33ms.

The last phase in the process of accessing and reading a record is called *data transfer*. Here, data is transferred from the disk to storage in the CPU. Data transfer can take place at rates as high as 1,209,600 bytes per second, or 1.2 MB (megabytes). At that speed a 1,200 byte record theoretically requires less than 1 millisecond for data transfer.

When accessing and writing a record, the same four phases are completed. First, the access mechanism is moved; second, the appropriate head is turned on; third, rotational delay takes place; and fourth, the data is transferred from storage to disk. In either a reading or writing operation, access-mechanism movement and rotational delay are by far the most time-consuming phases.

Verifying I/O operations

Like other I/O devices on a computer system, the disk drive checks to make sure that reading and writing take place without error. Although not mentioned before, there are actually two *cyclic check characters* at the end of each count, key, and data area that are used as a check on accuracy. During a writing operation, these characters are calculated based on the combinations of bits used in the count, key, or data area. Then, when a record is read, the cyclic check characters are recalculated and compared with those that are read. If they don't agree, an input error is indicated.

A writing operation may be checked by using the write-verify instruction. When it is executed following a write instruction, the data that has just been written is read and the cyclic check characters are checked as in a read operation. If there is a discrepancy, it indicates that the writing operation did not take place correctly. Unfortunately, the write-verify is time-consuming since the disk must make one complete rotation before the record that has been written can be read. Nevertheless, write-verification is often used when recording permanent files.

I/O commands

The actual *I/O commands* that a disk can be programmed to execute are many. These commands can be broken down into five types: seek, search, read, write, and write-verify.

The *seek* command causes the access mechanism to be moved to the specified cylinder and the specified head to be turned on. A typical *search* command tries to locate a record by searching a track until it finds a count or key equal to the one specified in the command. If the specified key or count isn't found, the search may be continued on successive tracks in the cylinder.

Once the seek and search have been executed, a *read* or *write* may take place. This is the data-transfer phase of the operation. In a typical business program, data alone or data plus key is transferred during a read or write command. Following the write command, a *write-verify* may be executed as described above.

To illustrate the use of the commands, suppose the 5th record on the 7th track of the 120th cylinder must accessed and read. The seek command would specify that the access mechanism be moved to the 120th cylinder and the 7th head (head number 6) be turned on. Next, a search command would compare the counts on the track with the count specified in the command. Since the count for a record indicates the cylinder number, head number, and record number on the track, the count for this record would indicate that it is the 5th record on the track. When the count in the command and the count on the track were equal, the read command would be issued, thus causing the data area following the count to be read.

When using the count-key-data format, a slightly different set of instructions may be used. First, the seek finds the selected cylinder and turns on the selected head. Second, the search looks for a key on the track that is equal to the one specified in the command. When they match, a read command is issued, thus transferring the data area following the selected key into storage.

Other direct-access devices

The disk system just described is one of many that are available on the market today. As cost of secondary storage has been reduced, the variety of storage devices has correspondingly increased. Probably the greatest boom has been in the direct-access area.

In recent years the microcomputer has become commercially feasible and has created a large market for the so-called floppy disk. A sealed-environment system, usually known as the Winchester disk, is available for micros as well as large systems.

The largest capacity secondary storage device currently available is the mass-storage device. Mass-storage systems combine the technologies of tape and disk into a large unit that has many cartridges. Each cartridge is a wide, but relatively short roll of tape. The direct-access aspect comes from the system's ability to pick out any one of the cartridges for processing. The cartridge is automatically mounted on a read station in the unit, the tape extracted from the cartridge and read sequentially.

File Organization

For a device such as a tape drive or a card reader, the records in a file may be organized in only one way: sequentially. On a direct-access device, however, there are a number of different ways in which a file may be organized. This section presents three of the most common methods of file organization: (1) sequential, (2) direct, and (3) indexed.

Sequential file organization

Due to its physical characteristics, a card file is always a sequential file. A card reader can only read a deck of cards from the first card to the last card in its physical sequence. Similarly, a tape file is always a sequential file. The tape drive reads the file from beginning to end starting with the first record on the tape. Because blocking increases the speed at which a tape file can be read, tape records are usually blocked.

Although direct-access devices were designed for directly accessing records, they too may store and process records sequentially. In fact, *sequential organization* is the most efficient method for some files. When writing records sequentially on a disk device, the first record of the file is stored in the first record position on the first track of the first cylinder of the file, the second record is stored in the second record position on the first track of the first cylinder of the file, and so on.

When reading the records in a sequential file, they are read beginning with the first physical location of the file and continuing consecutively until an end-of-file record is reached. Because the records in a sequential file are almost always processed sequentially, keys aren't needed and the count-data format is used.

Blocking

To make efficient use of direct-access storage, the records in a sequentially organized file are usually *blocked*. This means that more than one record is read or written in a single read or write command. To illustrate, suppose a block consists of five 100-byte records. On disk, there will be 500 bytes in the data area following each count and five records will be read by one read command.

Blocking is important because it reduces the time required to read or write a sequential file. With unblocked records, one search and, therefore, one rotational delay is required for each record that is accessed. If the records are blocked, however, only one search (rotational delay) is required for each block of records. When one read command is executed, an entire block of records is read into storage. By eliminating rotational delay, blocking can significantly reduce the time required to read the records in a sequential file.

Blocking also affects the storage capacity of a direct-access device. On the typical disk, for example, 7100 100-byte records will take about 129 tracks to hold all of the records in unblocked form. On a disk with 19 or 20 tracks per cylinder, this file would consume between six and seven cylinders. However, if the file were blocked 9 records per block, then 12 such blocks, or 108 records, could be stored on each track. The file would then only use 67 tracks, or three-plus cylinders.

Direct file organization

When *direct file organization* is used, the records on the direct-access device are in no particular sequence. When a program is ready to read or write a record using this organization, it must supply the information required to locate the record on the device. The program must supply the cylinder and head number of the desired record before the seek command can be executed. And before the search can be executed, either the record location on the track or the key of the desired record must be supplied. The trick in processing records in direct file organization, then, is determining the direct-access address for each record that is to be processed. This information is normally developed in a programming routine called a *randomizing routine*.

A randomizing routine is a set of program instructions which manipulate the record key in various ways to generate a disk address that is in the predefined range of the file. The best of randomizing routines will sometimes generate addresses that are the same for more than one record. Those duplicate addresses are called *synonyms* and must be dealt with via special programming, because two records obviously may not occupy the same area on the disk. To minimize the number of synonyms, the disk space allocated to the file typically is increased 15–20 percent more than the space required by the anticipated number of records. When there is little extra space for the file, more synonyms will be generated, but when there is more extra space, the number of synonyms will be reduced since there are then more addresses for the same number of records. The creation of a randomizing routine that will generate the fewest number of synonyms and the extra programming required to handle the synonyms that do occur are the main drawbacks to the use of direct organization files.

Blocking

When records in a direct file are blocked, additional programming routines are required. When loading a file, the records have to be randomized to a block of records rather than to an individual storage location. Blocking is likely to improve the use of the available disk storage, but it will probably decrease the speed at which records are accessed and read. Thus, the use of blocking depends on considerations such as the addressing characteristics of the device used, and access speeds required, and the available storage capacity.

Frequency of use

In actual practice, direct files aren't commonly used for two reasons. First, it is usually difficult to develop an efficient randomizing routine. Second, the programmer must code file-maintenance routines that keep track of available record spaces as records are added to and deleted from a file. These routines can be very complex. Together these two problems make direct files very difficult to use.

Indexed file organization

Although sequential and direct file organizations have their advantages, they also have their limitations. For example, while a blocked sequential file may make maximum use of the storage capacity of a direct-access device, it has many of the limitations of a tape file. To update a sequential file, all of the records in the file are read instead of just those affected by transactions, and the entire file has to be rewritten to add a record to the file. On the other hand, while direct file organization allows a record to be accessed rapidly, it wastes storage capacity. In addition, a direct file must usually be sorted into sequential order before a sequential report can be prepared from it.

Indexed file organization is designed to allow both sequential and direct, or random, processing. (*Random* means that the records aren't processed in any particular sequence.) There are many ways in which this can be accomplished, but the common procedure is for the file to be loaded in key sequence (sequential order) and the keys to be stored in an index which contains the key and the disk address of the record. Then, when any random processing is required, the index is searched for the key and the address part of the index is used to read the record from that address on the disk. If a record is added to the file later, it is placed at the end of the file in a special overflow area, and its key is entered into the index in sequence with the record's address. When sequential processing is called for, the records are read in sequence by key and are located by using the addresses in the index.

In actual practice no processing is as simple as explained above. Any method of indexed file organization has to provide for hundreds or even thousands of records. In processing a record randomly, it still could be time-consuming to search an index with thousands of keys to locate one. Thus, most indexed methods employ several levels of indexes in a process that is reminiscent of the binary search. Typically, there would be two levels of index, the first being a *general index* (also called *cylinder* or *coarse index*). This discussion will be for those systems that use the cylinder index concept. The cylinder (general) index normally only keeps the highest key that is on a cylinder of the disk along with the cylinder number. The access method moves to the cylinder specified in the index where a lower level of index is stored. This second index is called the *track index* (also the *detail* or *fine index*) and contains, in sequential order, the highest key on each track along with the track number. The access method moves to the appropriate track and reads the record from the track.

If the required record was added later, the record will be in an overflow area, but the access method will handle that situation by having the track index point to the overflow area rather than the disk area where the records were stored when the file was built. Any record in overflow will still be able to be accessed sequentially since the indexes will provide addresses of any record that is physically out of sequence so that it can be accessed in logical sequence.

Some index methods will provide a higher level of indexing if the general or cylinder index itself requires too long a search. The general rule for cylinder/track-oriented methods is that a *master index* should be specified if the cylinder index is more than four tracks in length. This is not difficult to do since it only requires an additional specification in the SELECT statement in COBOL programs.

Although the basic concepts are much the same for all indexed files, the programming details may vary extensively as you move from one system to another or from one type of direct-access device to another. Rather than loading a file sequentially, the file may be loaded in some other order. Chaining fields may be used so the records in a file can be accessed sequentially; or the indexes may be sorted to allow sequential access. When records are added to a file, they may be added at the end of the file or in a separate overflow area. And so on.

Regardless of these variations, any indexed file can be processed in sequential or random order with relative ease. That is the major feature of this method of file organization. When processing sequentially, though, an indexed file is likely to be slower than a sequential file. (Consider the extra access-mechanism movement if customer 201 is on cylinder 21, customer 202 on cylinder 40, and customer 203 back on cylinder 21.) Similarly, when processed randomly, an indexed file is likely to be slower than a direct file. (Consider the time required to find the appropriate detail or track index before the record can actually be read.) Because each type of file organization has its advantages and limitations, you can decide which type of organization to use only after considering a file's characteristics, as well as all of the uses to which the file will be put.

Programming Considerations

You're now familiar with the physical aspects of tape and direct-access files and know something about how they're accessed. You should also be aware that there are some complications with tape and direct-access files that must be handled by programming. Some of the most important of these are error recovery, record blocking and deblocking, and label checking. For the most part, these complications are handled by routines that are part of the operating system, so no special coding is required of the applications programmer. Nevertheless, the programmer should be familiar with what these routines do.

Error-recovery routines

When an error is detected during a reading operation, the error may often be recovered by an *error-recovery routine*. If, for example, a piece of dust or dirt on the surface of the tape or disk causes an error, it may be brushed off as the reading mechanism passes over that part of the recording surface. Then if that area is reread, the data can be transferred to storage without error. (A tape must be backspaced to be reread; a disk record is reread by waiting one complete revolution until the record rotates under the read/write head again.) In a typical error-recovery routine, the record is reread a number of times. If the error persists, an error message is printed so the operator can decide what action to take.

The same type of routine is used in a writing operation. For example, if a writing error is detected on tape, the tape is backspaced and the write instruction is tried again. After a number of attempts, the program may skip a certain amount of tape—the equivalent of a long IRG—and try again. On disk, the error-recovery routine may try to write the record on an *alternate track*. A direct-access device commonly has several cylinders or tracks that can be used for alternate tracks in the event of writing errors. In any event, if the attempt to write the record takes place without error, the program continues. Otherwise, an error message is printed for operator action.

Blocking and deblocking routines

When a tape or disk drive executes a read command, it reads an entire block of records into storage. The program, however, is usually written to process only one record at a time. *Deblocking routines* are used to keep track of which record in a block is being processed and to issue read commands to the drive only when a new block of records is required.

A similar situation exists when creating blocked output files. Each time the processing portion of the main program writes an individual record, a *blocking routine* moves the record to the output area. Only when the entire block is filled does the blocking routine actually issue a write command to the tape or disk drive.

Label-checking routines

Tape files

The instructions given to a computer operator for running a job tell which reel of tape to mount on which tape drive. The reels of tape are identified by external labels on the outside of the reels. Suppose, however, that the operator makes a mistake. The operator mounts a tape containing current accounts-receivable records on a tape drive that is going to write a file of updated inventory records. If this mistake isn't caught, the accounts-receivable records will be destroyed.

To prevent this type of error, *internal labels*—labels that are actually records on the tape itself—are used. For example, a typical tape file with *standard labels* contains the three label records shown in Figure 10–11. (IBGs aren't shown in this illustration.) The *volume label*, which comes immediately after the load-point marker, identifies the reel of tape. The *header label*, which contains information such as the file name, the date the file was created, and the date after which it can be destroyed, identifies the file. The *trailer label*, found after the data records of the file, contains the same data as the header label plus a block count indicating the number of blocks of data that the file contains.

On a typical system, these labels are processed by comparing the data that the labels contain with data supplied by job-control data at the time the object program is run. The job-control data indicate which program should

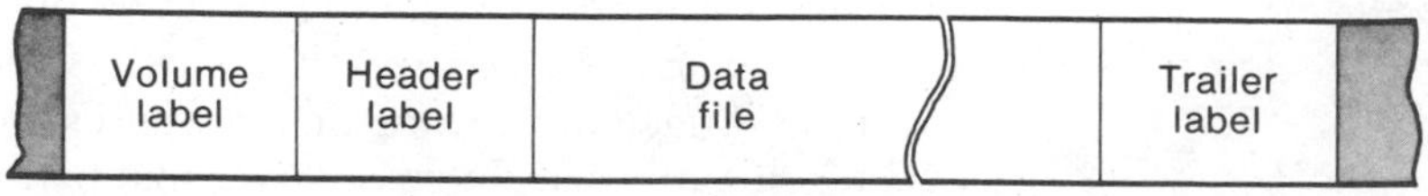
Volume
label
Header
label
Data
file
Trailer
label

Figure 10–11
Labels for a tape file

be loaded and executed, as well as which file should be mounted on which tape drive and what the volume and header labels should contain.

To appreciate the value of label checking, consider the label processing that is done on a typical system before writing a tape output file. First, the volume and header labels are read and analyzed. If the volume number agrees with the volume number given in the job-control data and the expiration date has passed (that is, the file can be destroyed), the routine backspaces the tape, writes a new header label for the output file, and begins processing. Otherwise, a message is printed to the operator indicating that the wrong file has been mounted, and thus, what might have been a costly error is avoided.

For input files, the header label is checked to make sure that the identifying information agrees with the information given in the job-control data. At the end of the file, the block count in the trailer label is compared with a block count accumulated during processing. If the counts are the same, all the input blocks have been processed. If they are different, the routine prints a message to the operator telling that an error has occurred.

In some cases, a file of records will require more than one reel (volume) of tape. This is referred to as a *multivolume file* and requires additional label-checking routines. When writing a multivolume file, the tape drive must check for a reflective spot near the end of each tape—this is the *end-of-reel marker*. When it is encountered, the label-checking routines write a trailer label, called an *end-of-volume label*, that includes the block count for that reel of tape. The routines then check the labels on the next reel of tape. If the next reel is accepted for processing, a header label is written that contains a volume sequence number indicating the order in which the reels of tape should be read. This switching from one reel of tape to another is called *tape switching*. On the last reel of the multivolume file, the program writes a file trailer label, called an *end-of-file label*, containing the block count for the reel. A four-volume multivolume file and its associated labels are illustrated in Figure 10-12.

VL = Volume label
HL = Header label
VOL = Volume
EOV = End of volume
TL = Trailer label
EOF = End of file

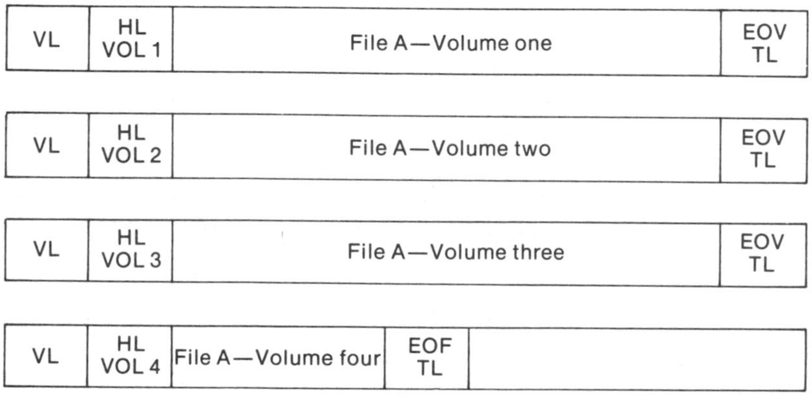
VL
HL
VOL 1
File A—Volume one
EOV
TL
VL
HL
VOL 2
File A—Volume two
EOV
TL
VL
HL
VOL 3
File A—Volume three
EOV
TL
VL
HL
VOL 4
File A—Volume four
EOF
TL

Figure 10–12
A multivolume file

VL = Volume label
HL = Header label
TL = Trailer label

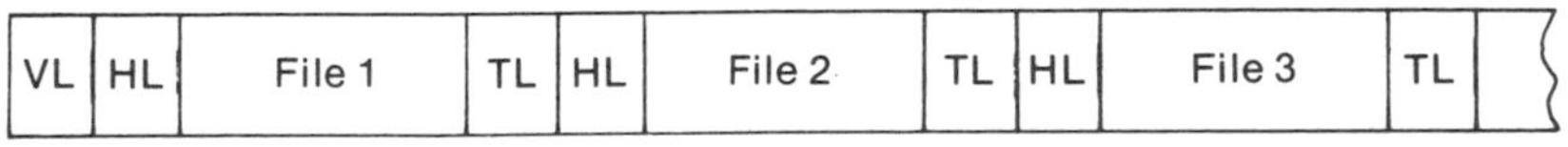
VL
HL
File 1
TL
HL
File 2
TL
HL
File 3
TL

Figure 10–13
A multifile volume

For multivolume input files, the label-checking routines check the header label of each reel to be sure that the correct file is being processed and that the reels are being processed in sequence. Thus, the first reel in the file must have volume sequence number 1, the second must have sequence number 2, and so on. If the wrong file has been mounted, a message is printed and the program is halted. At the end of each reel, prior to tape switching, the program checks the block count in the trailer label against a block count accumulated by the program to determine if all blocks have been read.

One final aspect of tape label-checking routines concerns *multifile volumes* or *multifile reels*). These are reels that have more than one file stored on them—for example, an inventory file, a billing file, and a sales-reporting file. In this case, each file is preceded by a header label and followed by a trailer label, as illustrated in Figure 10–13. When reading a file from a multifile volume, the label-checking routines must scan the tape until the correct label is located. When writing a file in any but the first position of a multifile volume, the label-checking routines must locate the correct position for the output file.

Disk files

A single disk pack normally contains many files, with each file assigned to a particular area on the pack. For example, a pack might have an accounts-receivable file in cylinders 1–30, a payroll master file in cylinders 36–55, and other files on the rest of the pack. A second pack could have cylinders 1–10 allocated as a temporary work area for record sorting and cylinders 11–20 assigned to a customer master file. These file allocations are illustrated in Figure 10–14.

Again, as on tape, internal labels are used for each file on the disk to protect it from being destroyed by mistake. On disk, the entire label area is often found in cylinder 0 and is called the *Volume Table of Contents*, or *VTOC*. (Yes the abbreviation is the same as that given for the visual table of contents, or structure chart, in chapter 6.)

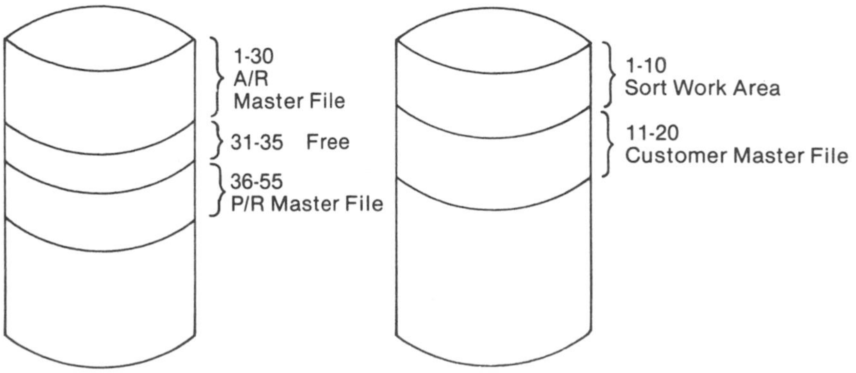
1-30
A/R
Master File
31-35 Free
36-55
P/R Master File
1-10
Sort Work Area
11-20
Customer Master File

Figure 10–14
Disk pack allocation

The first record in the VTOC is a *volume label* containing a serial number assigned to the pack. Then, for each file on the disk, there are one or more records called *file labels*. These labels give the name of the file, its organization, its location on the disk, and its expiration date. The expiration date indicates when a file is no longer needed so that its area can be assigned to another file. If a file is to be found in more than one area of the disk—cylinder 11–20 and 41–49, for example—this information is also given in the file label. Each area of a file is referred to as an *extent* of the file.

Label-checking routines similar to those for tape records compare the data in the labels with data supplied in job-control data at the time the program is executed. These job-control data indicate which disk pack should be mounted on which disk drive and what information the volume and file labels should contain. They also indicate the extents of each file that is going to be processed.

When a disk file is opened for processing, the volume label is compared to the one supplied in the job-control data. This is called *volume-label checking*. If the volume codes don't match, the operator is notified by a message and is thus given the opportunity to mount the proper pack.

Once the volume label is checked, *file-label checking* takes place. This level of label processing actually performs two types of checking. First, the file name is checked. For an input file, the name of the file as supplied in the job-control data is compared to the list of file names on the pack. If an equal name is found, the file is opened for processing. Otherwise, a message is issued to the operator for appropriate action. For output files, the list of file names is checked to see if a file with the same name already exists on the pack. If a duplicate is found, a message is displayed on the console.

If a duplicate name for an output file does not exist, the second type of file-label checking is performed. The disk extents in the job-control data are compared with the extents given in the file labels of all the other files on the disk pack. As long as the new file does not overlap any active file, the program continues. If, however, the new file will overlap an area already assigned to some other file, processing stops and a message is issued to the operator.

Referring to Figure 10–14, suppose that a programmer wanted to use the free area in cylinders 31–35 on disk 1. By mistake, however, he assigns cylinders 30–35 for his new file. Extent checking will prevent the last cylinder of the accounts-receivable file from being destroyed. When this new program tries to open the output file, the overlap with cylinder 30 will be found and the operator will be alerted to the problem.

When a direct-access file is stored on more than one disk pack, the labels for all the packs are checked and processed. For a sequentially organized file, this processing takes place when the end of the first disk pack is reached. Thus, the label-checking routines provide for switching from one disk pack to the next.

What the programmer must know

As you can see, tape and disk programs can be considerably more complicated than card and printer programs. Fortunately for the COBOL programmer, various modules of the operating system contain the code to perform all these tape and disk functions. So programmers don't have to worry about error-recovery, blocking, deblocking, or label-checking routines.

What, then, must programmers know? They must know the blocking characteristics of the file—what the length of each record is and how many records are in each block. When using direct-access files, they must know which track format is being used, and, if keys are used, what the key length is. They must be able to specify the exact file organization being used, including such details as how overflow records or synonyms are to be handled; and they must know whether the records are to be processed in sequential or random order. Once these specifications are given, the programmer uses simple statements that automatically generate the required I/O routines. When writing programs for direct files, however, the programmer is completely responsible for the logic of the randomizing routine.

Discussion

As stated at the beginning of this topic, the subject of direct-access devices has received only a cursory treatment here. The sequential aspects received more in-depth discussion than the random, but that was appropriate as sequential processing is all that will be covered in this text. However, you have been introduced to the random aspects and can look forward to a different kind of challenge in the second course, namely that of working with files as they are commonly used in the commercial environment today. The following topic will provide you with the COBOL tools to process sequential files.

Topic 3 **COBOL for Sequential Files**

Orientation

Most sequential files on tape or disk consist of blocks of fixed-length records—for example, ten records to a block, each record 120 bytes long. When coding COBOL programs, these files are handled much like card or printer files. Only minor adjustments are required in the Environment, Data, and Procedure Divisions.

From a conceptual point of view, a tape file and a sequentially organized file on a direct-access device are the same. When you read a tape file, you start with the first record and continue sequentially until you reach the end of the file. When you read a sequential file on disk, you read the record in the first physical record location assigned to the file and continue in sequence with the records in the next physical record locations until you reach the end of the file. The idea is the same when writing a sequential file on tape or disk; you move in sequence from the first physical record to the last.

In terms of COBOL, however, there are some minor variations depending on whether you are coding for a tape file or a direct-access file.

To show you how to use the sequential file handling elements, a simple file-to-printer program is illustrated in Figure 10–15 and 10–16. Figure 10–15 is a VTOC for this program and, as you can see, the printed output requires no headings, page overflow, or final totals. This will let you concentrate on the coding for the input file. The complete program listing is given in COBOL in Figure 10–16.

Terminology

control field	unmatched transaction
file maintenance	update program

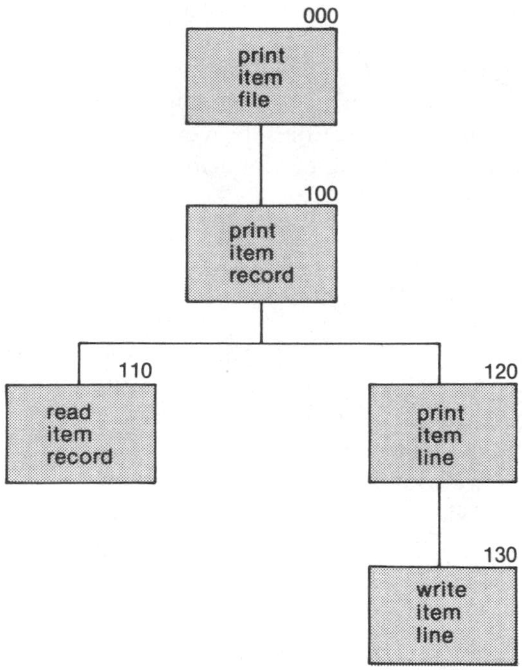
000
print
item
file
100
print
item
record
110
read
item
record
120
print
item
line
130
write
item
line

Figure 10–15
VTOC for the sequential file-to-printer program

Objective

Given a problem involving sequential files with fixed-length records, code a COBOL solution. The problem may require more than one input or output file, such as an update program with an output error file.

The Environment Division

The ASSIGN clause

The only entry in the Environment Division that needs to be discussed for sequential files is the ASSIGN clause of the SELECT statement. The SELECT statement for the item file of Figure 10–16 is:

```
SELECT ITEM-FILE
    ASSIGN TO MT9.
```

On the Prime computer MT9 is the system-name for a nine-track magnetic tape. If the file was accessed on disk, the designation would be PFMS for Prime File Management System. Recall that the PFMS designation has been used for the printer also. All that means is that, since the Prime computer is on-line–oriented rather than batch-oriented, the programs will output print files to disk libraries which are later spooled to the printer as requested and as the operating system gets time to do that task.

```
IDENTIFICATION DIVISION.
*
PROGRAM-ID. ITEMLST.
*
ENVIRONMENT DIVISION.
*
CONFIGURATION SECTION.
*
SOURCE-COMPUTER. PRIME 850.
OBJECT-COMPUTER. PRIME 850.
*
INPUT-OUTPUT SECTION.
*
FILE-CONTROL.
*
    SELECT ITEM-FILE
        ASSIGN TO MT9.
    SELECT ITEM-LISTING
        ASSIGN TO PFMS.
*
DATA DIVISION.
*
FILE SECTION.
*
FD  ITEM-FILE
    LABEL RECORDS ARE STANDARD
    RECORD CONTAINS 100 CHARACTERS
    BLOCK CONTAINS 40 RECORDS.
*
01  IT-RECORD.
*
    05  IT-ITEM-NUMBER       PIC X(5).
    05  IT-ITEM-DESC         PIC X(20).
    05  IT-ON-HAND           PIC S9(5)   COMP-3.
    05  FILLER               PIC X(72).
*
FD  ITEM-LISTING
    LABEL RECORDS ARE STANDARD
    RECORD CONTAINS 132 CHARACTERS.
*
01  PR-RECORD.
*
    05  PR-ITEM-NUMBER       PIC X(5).
    05  FILLER               PIC X(3).
    05  PR-ITEM-DESC         PIC X(20).
    05  FILLER               PIC X(3).
    05  PR-ON-HAND           PIC Z(5).
    05  FILLER               PIC X(96).
*
WORKING-STORAGE SECTION.
*
01  SWITCHES.
*
    05  ITEM-EOF-SW          PIC X    VALUE "N".
        88  ITEM-EOF                  VALUE "Y".
*
```

Figure 10–16
A sequential file-to-printer program (part 1 of 2)

```
 PROCEDURE DIVISION.
*
 000-PRINT-ITEM-FILE.
*    OPEN INPUT  ITEM-FILE
          OUTPUT ITEM-LISTING.
     PERFORM 100-PRINT-ITEM-RECORD
         UNTIL ITEM-EOF.
     CLOSE ITEM-FILE
           ITEM-LISTING.
     DISPLAY "ITEMLST  I  1  NORMAL EOJ".
     STOP RUN.
*
 100-PRINT-ITEM-RECORD.
*
     PERFORM 110-READ-ITEM-RECORD.
     IF NOT ITEM-EOF
         PERFORM 120-PRINT-ITEM-LINE.
*
 110-READ-ITEM-RECORD.
*
     READ ITEM-FILE
         AT END
             MOVE "Y" TO ITEM-EOF-SW.
*
 120-PRINT-ITEM-LINE.
*
     MOVE SPACE          TO PR-RECORD.
     MOVE IT-ITEM-NUMBER TO PR-ITEM-NUMBER.
     MOVE IT-ITEM-DESC   TO PR-ITEM-DESC.
     MOVE IT-ON-HAND     TO PR-ON-HAND.
     PERFORM 130-WRITE-ITEM-LINE.
*
 130-WRITE-ITEM-LINE.
*
     WRITE PR-RECORD
         AFTER ADVANCING 1 LINES.
```

Figure 10–16
A sequential file-to-printer program (part 2 of 2)

Some other manufacturer's system-name designations for tape and disk are listed below:

System-name	Manufacturer device
ASSIGN TO TAPE-E	Datapoint—Tape EBDIC Code
DISK-F-D-ITEMFLE-TEXT	Datapoint—Disk fixed-length with external name
TAPE	Burroughs—Tape
DISK	Burroughs—Disk
SYS010-UT-2400-S-ITEMFLE	IBM-DOS—Tape with external name
SYS020-UT-2314-S-ITEMFLE	IBM-DOS—Disk with external name
UT-S-ITEMFILE	IBM-OS—Any sequential file

As you see, the system-names vary with each manufacturer and even with different operating systems of the same manufacturer. The only means of knowing which designation to use is to consult the COBOL manual for the computer on which you are working.

ANS COBOL for tape files

```
IDENTIFICATION DIVISION.
     .
     .
ENVIRONMENT DIVISION.
     .
     .
INPUT-OUTPUT SECTION.
FILE-CONTROL.
    SELECT file-name ASSIGN TO system-name
     .
     .
DATA DIVISION.
FILE SECTION.
FD  file-name
    LABEL RECORDS ARE STANDARD
    [RECORD CONTAINS integer CHARACTERS]
    [BLOCK CONTAINS integer RECORDS].
     .
     .
PROCEDURE DIVISION.
    OPEN {INPUT  file-name} ...
         {OUTPUT file name}

    READ file-name RECORD
        [INTO data-name]
        AT END imperative-statement.

    WRITE record-name
        [FROM data-name].

    CLOSE file-name...
```

Figure 10–17
Syntax summary for sequential file handling (part 1 of 2)

Other clauses for direct-access files

If you look at the language summary in Figure 10–17, you'll see that other clauses besides the ASSIGN clause can be coded in the SELECT statement for a direct-access file. On a '74 compiler a SELECT statement for a sequential disk file might be coded like this:

```
SELECT ITEM-FILE ASSIGN TO DISK-F-D-ITEMFLE-TXT
                 ORGANIZATION IS SEQUENTIAL
                 ACCESS MODE IS SEQUENTIAL.
```

These '74 clauses are always optional, however. If they're omitted, sequential organization and access are assumed.

The Data Division

The FD statement

In the FD statement in the Data Division, the programmer gives the characteristics of the sequential file. In Figure 10–16, these characteristics are given:

```
FD  ITEM-FILE
    LABEL RECORDS ARE STANDARD
    RECORD CONTAINS 100 CHARACTERS
    BLOCK CONTAINS 40 RECORDS.
```

ANS COBOL for direct-access files

```
IDENTIFICATION DIVISION.
    .
    .
ENVIRONMENT DIVISION.
    .
    .
INPUT-OUTPUT SECTION.
FILE-CONTROL.
    SELECT file-name ASSIGN TO system-name
                     [ORGANIZATION IS SEQUENTIAL]
                     [ACCESS MODE IS SEQUENTIAL].
    .
    .
DATA DIVISION.
FILE SECTION.
FD  file-name
    LABEL RECORDS ARE STANDARD
    [RECORD CONTAINS integer CHARACTERS]
    [BLOCK CONTAINS integer RECORDS].
    .
    .
PROCEDURE DIVISION.

    OPEN {INPUT  file-name } ...
         {OUTPUT file name }

    READ file-name RECORD
        [INTO data-name]
        AT END imperative-statement.

    WRITE record-name
        [FROM data-name].

    CLOSE file-name...
```

Figure 10–17
Syntax summary for sequential file handling (part 2 of 2)

This code is similar to what you've seen for other files. For a tape or direct-access file, the LABEL RECORDS clause indicates that the labels used are in the manufacturer's standard format. Although the labels can be omitted or can conform to a user's format, they are standard in almost all cases. The RECORD CONTAINS clause tells how many characters there are in each record.

The only new code in the FD statement, then, is the BLOCK CONTAINS clause. As you might guess, it gives the blocking factor for the file; that is, the number of records in each block. In this case, ITEM–FILE consists of blocks of 40 each.

Record description

After the FD statement for the sequential file in Figure 10–16, the record and its fields are described just as is done for a card or printer file:

```
01  IT-RECORD.
    05  IT-ITEM-NUMBER      PIC X(5).
    05  IT-ITEM-DESC        PIC X(20).
    05  IT-ON-HAND          PIC S9(5)       COMP-3.
    05  FILLER              PIC X(72).
```

Regardless of the blocking factor, only one record is described, because all of the records in the file are the same.

Unlike card and printer files and data from terminals, the fields in tape and direct-access files can have a computational usage. In Figure 10–16, for example, IT–ON–HAND has COMP–3 usage. One advantage of COMP–3 fields is found in reducing the amount of data conversion required during the execution of the COBOL program (meaning that IT–ON–HAND can be operated on arithmetically without first being converted to COMP–3 usage).

Additionally, COMP–3 usage stores more than one character of data in a single byte of storage, thus affecting some savings of storage space. As a programmer, you must be aware of how computational type fields (COMP and COMP–3) are stored on your system because it affects your code in the Data Division. For example, if the program in Figure 10–16 was run on a system which did not store the five digits of IT–ON–HAND in three storage bytes, the record would be 102 characters long instead of 100.

The Procedure Division

As you can see from the summary in Figure 10–17, OPEN, CLOSE, READ, and WRITE statements are used in the Procedure Division in much the same way that they are used for card and printer files. There is one exception, the use of the INVALID KEY clause with the WRITE statement, and that will be covered in detail in a few moments. In the program in Figure 10–16, the OPEN, READ, and CLOSE statement for the item file are exactly the same as before.

I/O routines

What about blocking and deblocking, error-recovery, and label-checking routines? These are all taken care of by the OPEN, CLOSE, READ, and WRITE statements. For example, when an OPEN statement is executed for a tape input file, the volume and header labels are checked to make sure that the correct tape has been mounted. Similarly, the CLOSE statement takes care of checking and creating trailer labels and rewinding files, while the READ and WRITE statements handle error-recovery, blocking, and deblocking routines. If an input or output file requires more than one volume, the READ and WRITE statements also process the trailer labels at the end of one tape and the volume and header labels at the start of the next. In short, though many more machine-language instructions are executed for a tape I/O routine than for a card or printer routine, the COBOL programmer codes them both in approximately the same way.

The idea is the same for sequential files on direct-access devices. For an input file, for example, the appropriate label routines are executed when the OPEN statement is executed: the volume and file labels are checked to make sure that the right pack containing the right file is mounted on the right disk drive. Similarly, the READ and WRITE statements handle error-recovery, blocking, and deblocking routines. If an input or output file requires more than one disk pack, the READ and WRITE statements also process the labels for additional packs. And, if an input or output file is stored on more than one area of the disk, say cylinders 31–50, 81–100, and 121–140, the READ and WRITE statements handle the switching from one area to the next.

INVALID KEY

In the Procedure Division the only variation in the language for sequential files involves the INVALID KEY clause of the WRITE statement for direct-access files. The statements specified in this clause are executed when the

WRITE statement tries to write a record beyond the disk area assigned to the file. If, for example, 35 cylinders are allocated to a sequential disk file, the INVALID KEY clause is executed when a program tries to write a record in the first record location in the 36th cylinder. In a case like this, the statements in the INVALID KEY clause usually display an error message and set a switch so that the program can return to module 000 and come to a normal program termination. This is illustrated as follows:

```
WRITE MASTER-FILE-AREA FROM WS-MASTER-FILE
    INVALID KEY
        DISPLAY 'MSCREATE  A  2  THE FILE LIMITS '
                'HAVE BEEN EXCEEDED WHILE WRITING '
                'ITEM-NUMBER ' MF-ITEM-NUMBER
                ' --JOB ABORTED.'
        MOVE 'Y'          TO MASTER-FILE-EOF-SW.
```

System flowchart:

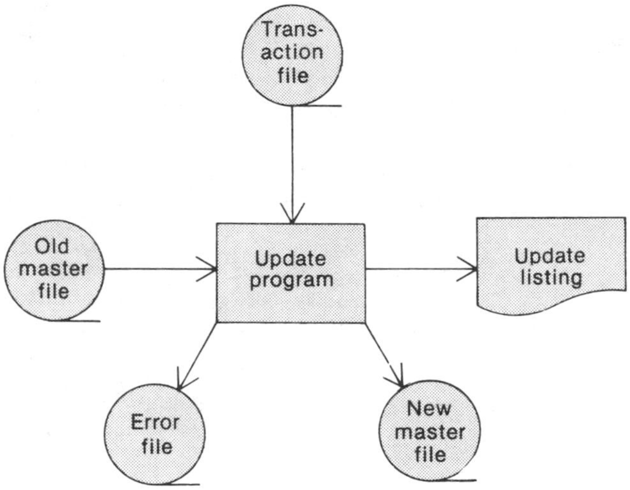
Trans-
action
file
Old
master
file
Update
program
Update
listing
Error
file
New
master
file

Record layouts:

Inventory Master Record

Field Name	Item No.	Item Description	On Hand	Unused
Characteristics	X(5)	X(20)	S9(5)	X(72)
Usage			COMP	
Position	1-5	6-25	26-28	29-100

Transaction and Error Record

Field Name	Item No.	Vendor No.	Receipt Date	Receipt Quantity	Unused
Characteristics	X(5)	X(5)	X(6)	S9(5)	X(5)
Usage				COMP	
Position	1-5	6-10	11-16	17-19	20-24

Figure 10–18
Specifications for a master-file update program (part 1 of 2)

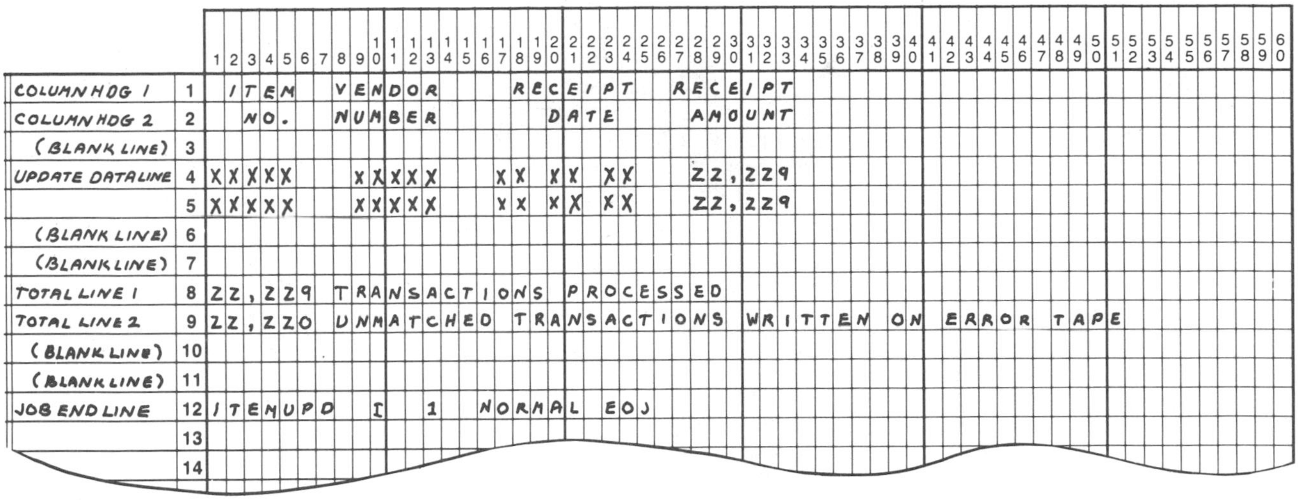
COLUMN HDG 1 — ITEM VENDOR RECEIPT RECEIPT
COLUMN HDG 2 — NO. NUMBER DATE AMOUNT
(BLANK LINE)
UPDATE DATA LINE — XXXXX XXXXX XX XX XX ZZ,ZZ9
XXXXX XXXXX XX XX XX ZZ,ZZ9
(BLANK LINE)
(BLANK LINE)
TOTAL LINE 1 — ZZ,ZZ9 TRANSACTIONS PROCESSED
TOTAL LINE 2 — ZZ,ZZ0 UNMATCHED TRANSACTIONS WRITTEN ON ERROR TAPE
(BLANK LINE)
(BLANK LINE)
JOB END LINE — ITEMUPD I 1 NORMAL EOJ

Narrative:

1. Use transaction records to update master records by adding the receipt amount in the transaction record to the on-hand amount in the master record. There may be none, one, or several transactions for each master, and both files are in item-number sequence.
2. Print an update report with one line for each valid transaction record showing item number, vendor number, receipt date, and receipt quantity.
3. Write a record on the error file if an unmatched transaction is detected.
4. At the end of the report, print total lines showing the number of transactions processed and the number of unmatched transactions.

Figure 10–18
Specifications for a master-file update program (part 2 of 2)

The use of the INVALID KEY depends on your compiler. The variations below point out the difference between the ANSI standards and the individual developer's implementation of a COBOL compiler. For instance, the clause was required in the '68 ANSI standards, but some '68 compilers allowed its omission. In the '74 standards, the INVALID KEY clause has been eliminated, so theoretically you cannot code it—however, you may find that some '74 compilers allow it. So there are some older programs that do not have to be changed by eliminating the clause (and all of the attendant impacts) and then recompiling them. The answer is to be familiar with the latest standards so that your code is as up to date as possible, but to check the compiler being used to see what is allowed and what is required. And remember, the clause is always illegal for tape files.

An Update Program

At this point, you should realize that tape or direct-access input and output presents few coding problems. However, the logic of a tape or direct-access program can become complex because several files can be processed by a single program.

To illustrate, consider a sequential *update program* such as the one described in Figure 10–18. As you can see by the system flowchart, there are two input files—a transaction file and an inventory master file—and two output files—an updated, or new, master file and an error file of unmatched transactions. (An *unmatched transaction* is one that doesn't have a master record with the same *control-field* number—in this case, item number.) The program will

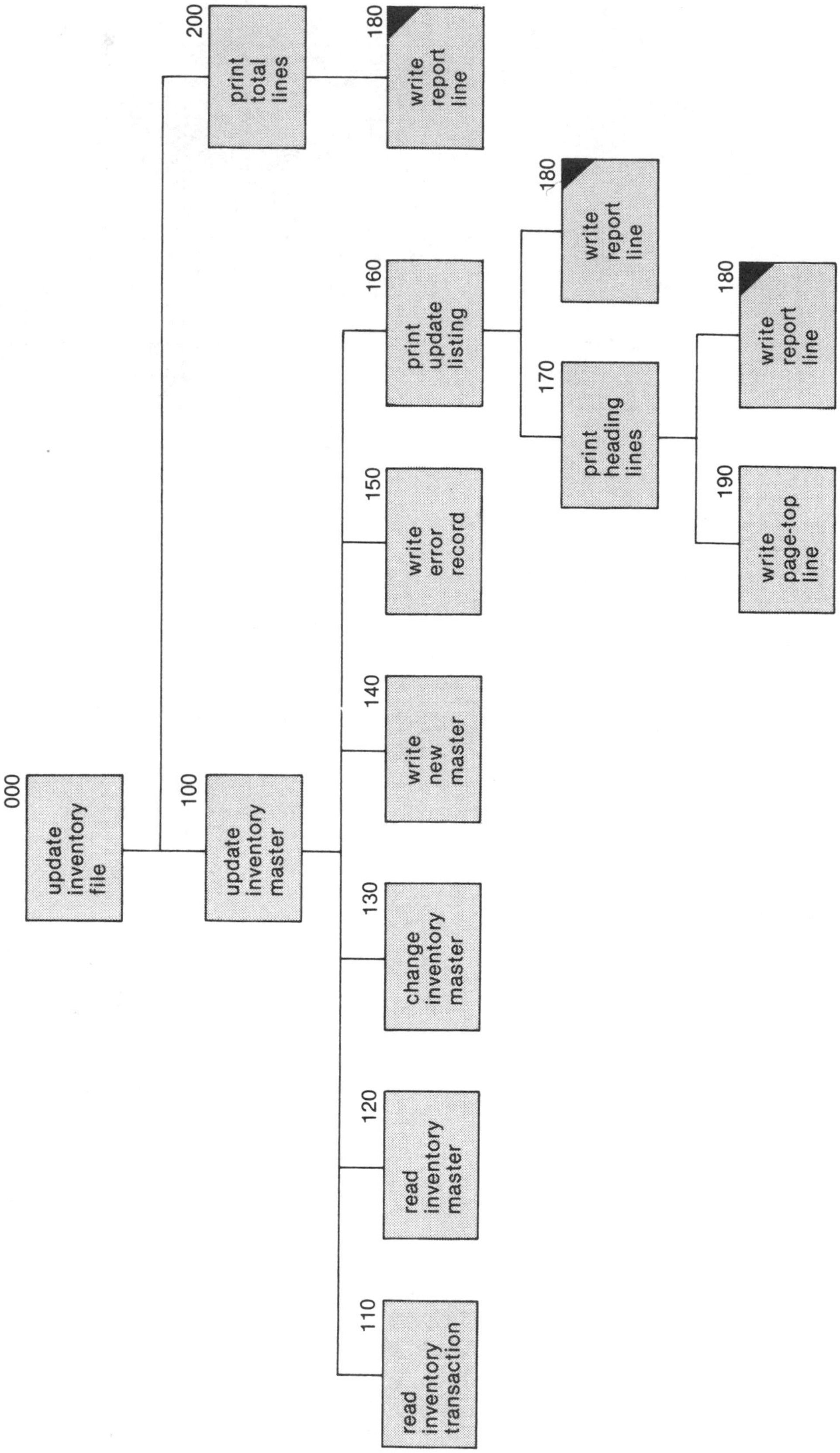
000
update inventory file
100
update inventory master
200
print total lines
180
write report line
110
read inventory transaction
120
read inventory master
130
change inventory master
140
write new master
150
write error record
160
print update listing
170
print heading lines
180
write report line
180
write report line
190
write page-top line

Figure 10–19
VTOC for the sequential update program

also produce a printed summary of the update run. In the system flowchart, the tape symbol is used for sequential files, but these files could be stored on tape or a direct-access device.

Figure 10–19 shows a VTOC for this update program. The main control module, 100–UPDATE–INVENTORY–MASTER, causes one transaction and one master record to be read. It then compares the control fields of the two records and performs one or more of four modules depending on the result of this comparison. To control processing in this way, the module relies on the fact that the records in both the transaction and master files are arranged in ascending sequence by item number.

Figure 10–20 is the COBOL listing for this program. Perhaps the key here is the action that results when the control field of the transaction record is compared with the control field of the master record in module 100. If the control fields are equal and the transaction item number is not HIGH–VALUE, the transaction is used to update the old master (module 130) and a report line is printed (module 160). In addition, Y is moved to NEED–TRANSACTION–SW to show that another transaction should be read. If the transaction is greater than the master, module 140 is performed. This module uses a WRITE FROM statement to write the master record, which may have been updated if it matched a previous transaction, on the new master file. Then Y is moved to NEED–MASTER–SW so another master will be read. Finally, if the transaction is less than the master, an unmatched transaction is indicated, and the record is written on the error file (module 150). Again, Y is moved to NEED–TRANSACTION–SW so another transaction will be read.

When a program reads two input files, as this one does, eventually all the records in one file will have been read while the other still contains some records to be processed. Note how the update program handles this problem. The AT END clauses in both the READ statements move HIGH–VALUE to the item-number fields. If the transaction file ends first, the rest of the master records will all have control fields lower than HIGH–VALUE since HIGH–VALUE is the highest value possible in the computer's collating sequence. So when the control fields are compared in module 100, the program will perform the code for a greater-than comparison and write the remaining master records on the new master file. If the master file ends first, the comparison will indicate that the transaction is less than the master for the rest of the records in the transaction file. So these unmatched transactions will be written on the error file. After all the records in both files have been read, the comparison will show that the item-number fields are equal. So when the program checks and finds TR–ITEM–NUMBER equal to HIGH–VALUE, Y will be moved to the ALL–RECORDS–PROCESSED switch, and the program will continue with the statements after the PERFORM UNTIL in 000–UPDATE–INVENTORY–FILE.

To control processing in this way, you must use the INTO option of the READ statement. Without it, it would be impossible to move HIGH–VALUE into the item-number fields, since fields in an input area aren't available to a program after the AT END clause has been executed. And be sure to move HIGH–VALUE, not all 9s, into the control fields when the ends of the files are reached. If you move all 9s to a field in a situation like this, there's always the chance of running into a valid control field of all 9s. Then the comparison would be equal, and the program logic wouldn't work properly.

```
 IDENTIFICATION DIVISION.
*
 PROGRAM-ID. ITEMUPD.
*
 ENVIRONMENT DIVISION.
*
 CONFIGURATION SECTION.
*
 SOURCE-COMPUTER.  PRIME 850.
 OBJECT-COMPUTER.  PRIME 850.
 SPECIAL-NAMES.
     C01 IS PAGE-TOP.
*
 INPUT-OUTPUT SECTION.
*
 FILE-CONTROL.
     SELECT TRANSACTION-FILE
         ASSIGN TO MT9.
     SELECT OLD-MASTER-FILE
         ASSIGN TO MT9.
     SELECT NEW-MASTER-FILE
         ASSIGN TO MT9.
     SELECT ERROR-FILE
         ASSIGN TO MT9.
     SELECT UPDATE-LISTING
         ASSIGN TO PFMS.
*
 DATA DIVISION.
*
 FILE SECTION.
*
 FD  TRANSACTION-FILE
     LABEL RECORDS ARE STANDARD
     RECORD CONTAINS 24 CHARACTERS
     BLOCK CONTAINS 166 RECORDS.
*
 01  TR-AREA               PIC X(24).
*
 FD  OLD-MASTER-FILE
     LABEL RECORDS ARE STANDARD
     RECORD CONTAINS 100 CHARACTERS
     BLOCK CONTAINS 40 RECORDS.
*
 01  OM-AREA              PIC X(100).
*
 FD  NEW-MASTER-FILE
     LABEL RECORDS ARE STANDARD
     RECORD CONTAINS 100 CHARACTERS
     BLOCK CONTAINS 40 RECORDS.
*
 01  NM-AREA              PIC X(100).
*
 FD  ERROR-FILE
     LABEL RECORDS ARE STANDARD
     RECORD CONTAINS 24 CHARACTERS
     BLOCK CONTAINS 166 RECORDS.
*
 01  ER-RECORD                         PIC X(24).
*
 FD  UPDATE-LISTING
     LABEL RECORDS ARE STANDARD
     RECORD CONTAINS 132 CHARACTERS.
*
 01  PRINT-AREA                        PIC X(132).
*
```

Figure 10–20
The sequential update program (part 1 of 5)

```
 WORKING-STORAGE SECTION.
*
 01  SWITCHES.
*
     05  ALL-RECORDS-PROCESSED-SW      PIC X          VALUE "N".
         88  ALL-RECORDS-PROCESSED                    VALUE "Y".
     05  NEED-TRANSACTION-SW           PIC X          VALUE "Y".
         88  NEED-TRANSACTION                         VALUE "Y".
     05  NEED-MASTER-SW                PIC X          VALUE "Y".
         88  NEED-MASTER                              VALUE "Y".
*
 01  COUNT-FIELDS                      COMP-3.
*
     05  TRANS-PROCESSED-COUNT         PIC S9(5)      VALUE ZERO.
     05  UNMATCHED-TRANS-COUNT         PIC S9(5)      VALUE ZERO.
*
 01  PRINT-FIELDS                      COMP-3.
*
     05  LINE-COUNT                    PIC S99        VALUE +99.
     05  LINES-ON-PAGE                 PIC S99        VALUE +57.
     05  SPACE-CONTROL                 PIC S9.
*
 01  TR-RECORD.
*
     05  TR-ITEM-NUMBER                PIC X(5).
     05  TR-VENDOR-NUMBER              PIC X(5).
     05  TR-RECEIPT-DATE               PIC X(6).
     05  TR-RECEIPT-QUANTITY           PIC S9(5)      COMP-3.
     05  FILLER                        PIC X(5).
*
 01  MA-RECORD.
*
     05  MA-ITEM-NUMBER                PIC X(5).
     05  MA-ITEM-DESCR                 PIC X(20).
     05  MA-ON-HAND                    PIC S9(5)      COMP-3.
     05  MA-FILLER                     PIC X(72).

*
 01  HDG-LINE-1.
*
     05  FILLER                        PIC X(1)    VALUE SPACE.
     05  FILLER                        PIC X(4)    VALUE "ITEM".
     05  FILLER                        PIC X(2)    VALUE SPACE.
     05  FILLER                        PIC X(6)    VALUE "VENDOR".
     05  FILLER                        PIC X(4)    VALUE SPACE.
     05  FILLER                        PIC X(7)    VALUE "RECEIPT".
     05  FILLER                        PIC X(2)    VALUE SPACE.
     05  FILLER                        PIC X(7)    VALUE "RECEIPT".
     05  FILLER                        PIC X(99)   VALUE SPACE.
*
 01  HDG-LINE-2.
*
     05  FILLER                        PIC X(2)    VALUE SPACE.
     05  FILLER                        PIC X(3)    VALUE "NO".
     05  FILLER                        PIC X(4)    VALUE SPACE.
     05  FILLER                        PIC X(3)    VALUE "NO".
     05  FILLER                        PIC X(6)    VALUE SPACE.
     05  FILLER                        PIC X(4)    VALUE "DATE".
     05  FILLER                        PIC X(4)    VALUE SPACE.
     05  FILLER                        PIC X(6)    VALUE "AMOUNT".
     05  FILLER                        PIC X(100)  VALUE SPACE.
*
```

Figure 10–20
The sequential update program
(part 2 of 5)

```
 01  NEXT-REPORT-LINE.
*
     05  NRL-ITEM-NUMBER     PIC X(5).
     05  FILLER              PIC X(3)    VALUE SPACE.
     05  NRL-VENDOR-NUMBER   PIC Z(5).
     05  FILLER              PIC X(3)    VALUE SPACE.
     05  NRL-RECEIPT-DATE    PIC 99B99B99.
     05  FILLER              PIC X(3)    VALUE SPACE.
     05  NRL-RECEIPT-AMOUNT  PIC ZZZZ9.
     05  FILLER              PIC X(100)  VALUE SPACE.
*
 01  TOTAL-LINE-1.
*
     05  TL1-TRANS-PROCESSED PIC ZZ,ZZ9.
     05  FILLER              PIC X(23)
                             VALUE " TRANSACTIONS PROCESSED".
     05  FILLER              PIC X(103)  VALUE SPACE.
*
 01  TOTAL-LINE-2.
*
     05  TL2-UNMATCHED-TRANS PIC ZZ,ZZ9.
     05  FILLER              PIC X(23)
                             VALUE " UNMATCHED TRANSACTIONS".
     05  FILLER              PIC X(22)
                             VALUE " WRITTEN ON ERROR TAPE".
     05  FILLER              PIC X(81)   VALUE SPACE.
*
 PROCEDURE DIVISION.
*
 000-UPDATE-INVENTORY-FILE.
*
     OPEN INPUT  TRANSACTION-FILE
                 OLD-MASTER-FILE
          OUTPUT NEW-MASTER-FILE
                 ERROR-FILE
                 UPDATE-LISTING.
     PERFORM 100-UPDATE-INVENTORY-MASTER
         UNTIL ALL-RECORDS-PROCESSED.
     PERFORM 200-PRINT-TOTAL-LINES.
     CLOSE TRANSACTION-FILE
           OLD-MASTER-FILE
           NEW-MASTER-FILE
           ERROR-FILE
           UPDATE-LISTING.
     DISPLAY "ITEMUPD  I  1  NORMAL EOJ".
     STOP RUN.
*
 100-UPDATE-INVENTORY-MASTER.
*
     IF NEED-TRANSACTION
         PERFORM 110-READ-INVENTORY-TRANSACTION
         MOVE "N" TO NEED-TRANSACTION-SW.
     IF NEED-MASTER
         PERFORM 120-READ-INVENTORY-MASTER
         MOVE "N" TO NEED-MASTER-SW.
     IF TR-ITEM-NUMBER EQUAL TO MA-ITEM-NUMBER
         IF TR-ITEM-NUMBER EQUAL TO HIGH-VALUE
             MOVE "Y" TO ALL-RECORDS-PROCESSED-SW
         ELSE
             PERFORM 130-CHANGE-INVENTORY-MASTER
             PERFORM 160-PRINT-UPDATE-LISTING
             MOVE "Y" TO NEED-TRANSACTION-SW
     ELSE
         IF TR-ITEM-NUMBER GREATER THAN MA-ITEM-NUMBER
             PERFORM 140-WRITE-NEW-MASTER
             MOVE "Y" TO NEED-MASTER-SW
```

Figure 10–20
The sequential update program
(part 3 of 5)

```
           ELSE
               PERFORM 150-WRITE-ERROR-RECORD
               MOVE "Y" TO NEED-TRANSACTION-SW.
*
 110-READ-INVENTORY-TRANSACTION.
*
     READ TRANSACTION-FILE INTO TR-RECORD
         AT END
             MOVE HIGH-VALUE TO TR-ITEM-NUMBER.
     IF TR-ITEM-NUMBER NOT EQUAL TO HIGH-VALUE
         ADD 1 TO TRANS-PROCESSED-COUNT.
*
 120-READ-INVENTORY-MASTER.
*
     READ OLD-MASTER-FILE INTO MA-RECORD
         AT END
             MOVE HIGH-VALUE TO MA-ITEM-NUMBER.
*
 130-CHANGE-INVENTORY-MASTER.
*
     ADD TR-RECEIPT-QUANTITY TO MA-ON-HAND.
*
 140-WRITE-NEW-MASTER.
*
     WRITE NM-AREA FROM MA-RECORD.
*
 150-WRITE-ERROR-RECORD.
*
     WRITE ER-RECORD FROM TR-RECORD.
     ADD +1 TO UNMATCHED-TRANS-COUNT.
*
 160-PRINT-UPDATE-LISTING.
*
     IF LINE-COUNT GREATER THAN LINES-ON-PAGE
         PERFORM 170-PRINT-HEADING-LINES.
     MOVE TR-ITEM-NUMBER       TO NRL-ITEM-NUMBER.
     MOVE TR-VENDOR-NUMBER     TO NRL-VENDOR-NUMBER.
     MOVE TR-RECEIPT-DATE      TO NRL-RECEIPT-DATE.
     MOVE TR-RECEIPT-QUANTITY  TO NRL-RECEIPT-AMOUNT.
     MOVE NEXT-REPORT-LINE     TO PRINT-AREA.
     PERFORM 180-WRITE-REPORT-LINE.
     MOVE 1 TO SPACE-CONTROL.
*
 170-PRINT-HEADING-LINES.
*
     MOVE HDG-LINE-1 TO PRINT-AREA.
     PERFORM 190-WRITE-PAGE-TOP-LINE.
     MOVE HDG-LINE-2 TO PRINT-AREA.
     MOVE 1 TO SPACE-CONTROL.
     PERFORM 180-WRITE-REPORT-LINE.
     MOVE 2 TO SPACE-CONTROL.
*
 180-WRITE-REPORT-LINE.
*
     WRITE PRINT-AREA
         AFTER ADVANCING SPACE-CONTROL LINES.
     ADD SPACE-CONTROL TO LINE-COUNT.
*
 190-WRITE-PAGE-TOP-LINE.
*
     WRITE PRINT-AREA
         AFTER ADVANCING PAGE-TOP.
     MOVE ZERO TO LINE-COUNT.
*
```

Figure 10–20
The sequential update program (part 4 of 5)

```
 200-PRINT-TOTAL-LINES.
*
     MOVE TRANS-PROCESSED-COUNT TO TL1-TRANS-PROCESSED.
     MOVE TOTAL-LINE-1 TO PRINT-AREA.
     MOVE 3 TO SPACE-CONTROL.
     PERFORM 180-WRITE-REPORT-LINE.
     MOVE UNMATCHED-TRANS-COUNT TO TL2-UNMATCHED-TRANS.
     MOVE TOTAL-LINE-2 TO PRINT-AREA.
     MOVE 1 TO SPACE-CONTROL.
     PERFORM 180-WRITE-REPORT-LINE.
```

Figure 10–20
The sequential update program (part 5 of 5)

File Maintenance

File maintenance refers to the process of changing the fields within the records in a file, adding records to a file, and deleting records from a file. To perform any of these jobs on a sequential file, the file should be rewritten with necessary changes being made as it is written. You have already seen how changes are made to fields in the update program in Figure 10–20. To add records, the additional records are inserted in sequence as the file is rewritten. To delete records, all the records in a file except those that must be deleted are rewritten on the new file.

In actual practice, it is seldom efficient to perform only one maintenance operation at a time. If, for example, you had only 10 records to add to a 1000-record file, you'd be wasting computer time to rewrite the entire file. So a single-file maintenance program usually provides for adding, deleting, and changing records in a file.

Although a program like this might appear to be rather complex, the coding involves nothing more than has been illustrated in this topic. Even the design of the program is no more than a variation of the VTOC in Figure 10–19. For example, Figure 10–21 is a structure chart for a program that does all the file-maintenance chores. Here, module 130 has become the control module that determines which of four modules should be performed based on the control-field comparison. Three of these modules—160, 170, and 180—actually do the work of maintaining the file. The fourth, module 190, controls the creation of the error file. Thus, even the most complicated file-maintenance program will follow the basic pattern of the update program in Figure 10–19 and 10–21. (Incidentally, the verb "put" for a tape or disk file is equivalent to the verb "print" for a printer file.)

Discussion

In keeping with the philosophy of this book, the material presented in this chapter is a subset of the COBOL language for sequential file handling. By using this subset, you'll give your programs maximum flexibility. Only the SELECT statements and the INVALID KEY clauses in the WRITE statements will vary between tape and disk files or between compilers. As for the language omitted, it isn't anything you'll need to use at this point.

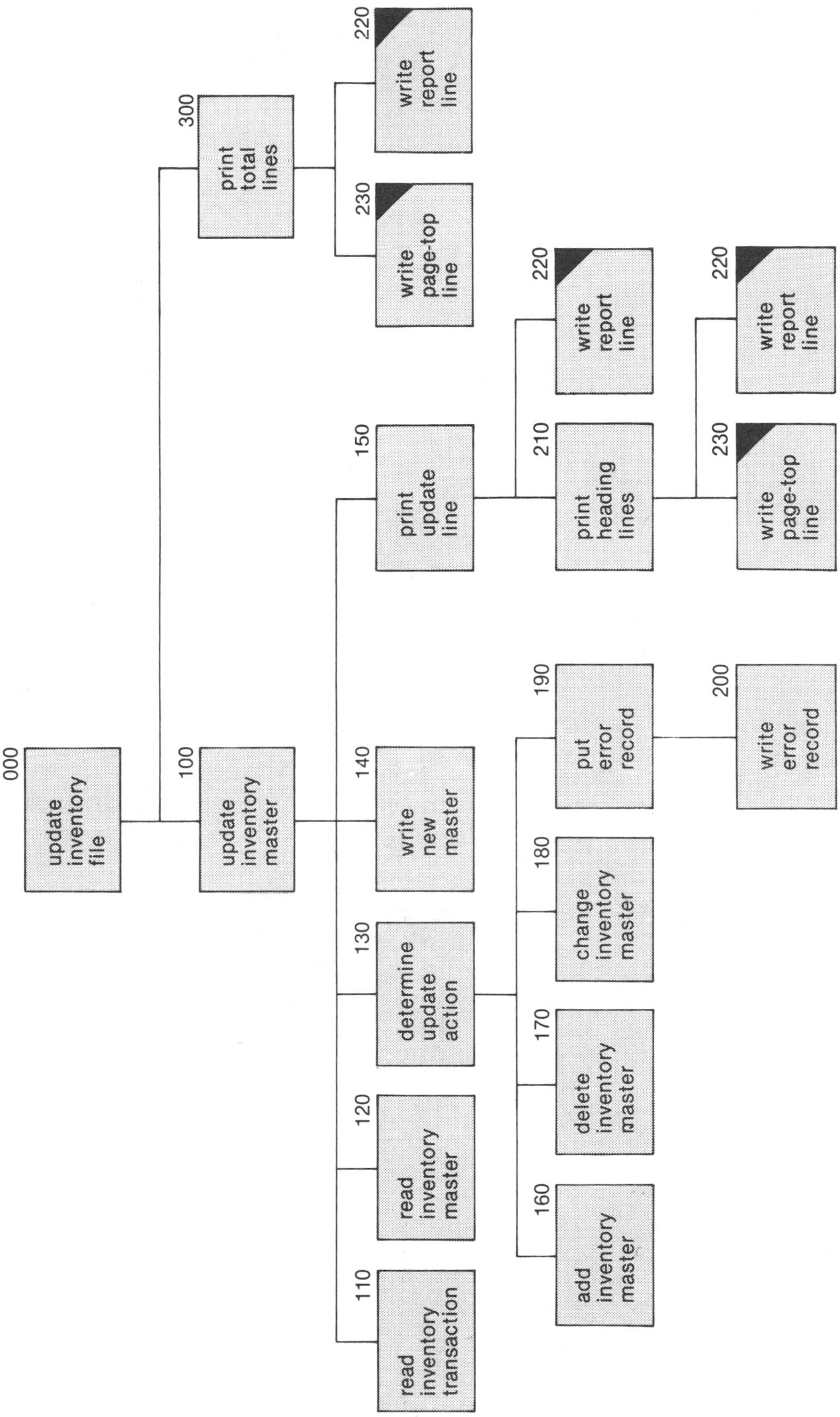
000
update inventory file
100
update inventory master
300
print total lines
110
read inventory transaction
120
read inventory master
130
determine update action
140
write new master
150
print update line
230
write page-top line
220
write report line
160
add inventory master
170
delete inventory master
180
change inventory master
190
put error record
210
print heading lines
220
write report line
200
write error record
230
write page-top line
220
write report line

Figure 10–21
VTOC for a file-maintenance program that adds, deletes, and changes records

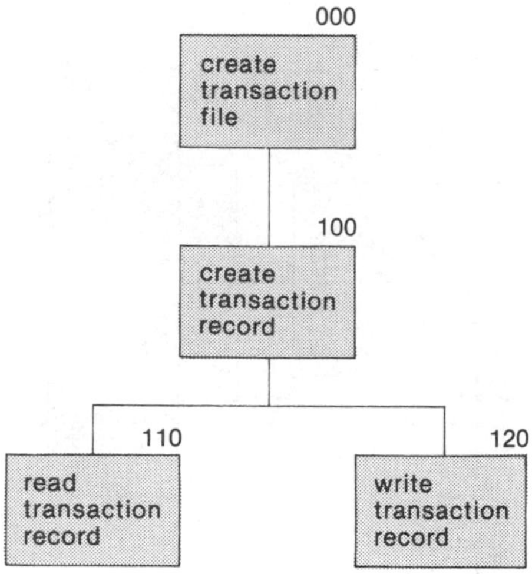
000
create transaction file
100
create transaction record
110
read transaction record
120
write transaction record

Figure 10–22
VTOC for a sequential file-creation program

Problems

1. A third type of sequential file program is referred to as a file-creation program. For instance, suppose the transaction tape in Figure 10–21 was created with a format like this:

Field Name	Card Code	Item No.	Vendor No.	Receipt Date	Receipt Quantity	Unused
Characteristics	=3	X(5)	X(5)	X(6)	S9(5)	X(60)
Usage					COMP-3	
Position	1	2-6	7-11	12-17	18-20	21-80

   Although this type of program would normally check the input records to make sure all fields contain valid or reasonable data, we'll assume this program merely reads the cards and creates the tape file.

   a. Create a VTOC for this program.

   b. Write the program using the VTOC you created in part a.

2. What changes would you have to make to the program you wrote in problem 1 above if the transaction file were to be recorded on disk instead of tape?

Solutions

1. **a.** Figure 10–22 is an acceptable solution.

   b. Figure 10–23 is an acceptable solution on a Datapoint system. The system names must conform to the requirements of your system.

2. The system name for TRANSACTION–FILE would have to be changed to show it was a disk file.

```
 IDENTIFICATION DIVISION.
*
 PROGRAM-ID.  TRCREAT.
*
 ENVIRONMENT DIVISION.
*
 CONFIGURATION SECTION.
*
 SOURCE-COMPUTER.  PRIME 850.
 OBJECT-COMPUTER.  PRIME 850.
*
 INPUT-OUTPUT SECTION.
*
 FILE-CONTROL.
     SELECT TRANSACTION-CARDS
         ASSIGN TO READER.
     SELECT TRANSACTION-FILE
         ASSIGN TO MT9.
*
 DATA DIVISION.
*
 FILE SECTION.
*
 FD  TRANSACTION-CARDS
     LABEL RECORDS ARE STANDARD
     RECORD CONTAINS 80 CHARACTERS.
*
 01  TC-AREA                PIC X(80).
*
 FD  TRANSACTION-FILE
     LABEL RECORDS ARE STANDARD
     RECORD CONTAINS 24 CHARACTERS
     BLOCK CONTAINS 166 RECORDS.
*
 01  TR-AREA                PIC X(24).
*
 WORKING-STORAGE SECTION.
*
 01  SWITCHES.
*
     05  TRAN-EOF-SW        PIC X         VALUE "N".
         88  TRAN-EOF                     VALUE "Y".
*
 01  TC-RECORD.
*
     05  FILLER             PIC X.
     05  TC-ITEM-NUMBER     PIC X(5).
     05  TC-VENDOR-NUMBER   PIC X(5).
     05  TC-RECEIPT-DATE    PIC X(6).
     05  TC-RECEIPT-QUANTITY PIC 9(5).
     05  FILLER             PIC X(58).
*
 01  TR-RECORD.
*
     05  TR-ITEM-NUMBER     PIC X(5).
     05  TR-VENDOR-NUMBER   PIC X(5).
     05  TR-RECEIPT-DATE    PIC X(6).
     05  TR-RECEIPT-QUANTITY PIC S9(5)    COMP-3.
     05  FILLER             PIC X(3).
*
 PROCEDURE DIVISION.
*
```

Figure 10–23
The sequential file-creation program (part 1 of 2)

```
 000-CREATE-TRANSACTION-FILE.
*
     OPEN INPUT  TRANSACTION-CARDS
          OUTPUT TRANSACTION-FILE.
     PERFORM 100-CREATE-TRANSACTION-RECORD
         UNTIL TRAN-EOF.
     CLOSE TRANSACTION-CARDS
           TRANSACTION-FILE.
     DISPLAY "TRCREAT  I  1  NORMAL EOJ".
     STOP RUN.
*
 100-CREATE-TRANSACTION-RECORD.
*
     PERFORM 110-READ-TRANSACTION-RECORD.
     IF NOT TRAN-EOF
         MOVE TC-ITEM-NUMBER      TO TR-ITEM-NUMBER
         MOVE TC-VENDOR-NUMBER    TO TR-VENDOR-NUMBER
         MOVE TC-RECEIPT-DATE     TO TR-RECEIPT-DATE
         MOVE TC-RECEIPT-QUANTITY TO TR-RECEIPT-QUANTITY
         PERFORM 120-WRITE-TRANSACTION-RECORD.
*
 110-READ-TRANSACTION-RECORD.
*
     READ TRANSACTION-CARDS INTO TC-RECORD
         AT END
             MOVE "Y" TO TRAN-EOF-SW.
*
 120-WRITE-TRANSACTION-RECORD.
*
     WRITE TR-AREA FROM TR-RECORD.
```

Figure 10–23
The sequential file-creation program (part 2 of 2)

Chapter 11 The COBOL Sort/Merge Feature and ANSI 198X Standards

The first topic in this chapter discusses the sort/merge feature of COBOL.

In any computer installation, much of the processing requires that records be arranged in certain sequences. As a result, a file may have to be *sorted*. For example, any time you are comparing item numbers from two or more files during a master-file update program, you must first be sure that the input files are sorted into item-number sequence. Likewise, if you're editing entries in one file by comparing them to table records in another or if you're extracting data from a file for a report, you must sort the input files into the proper sequence.

A related function is *merging* two separate files that are already in sequence into a single sequenced file. Suppose, for example, that two transaction files, both containing the same type of records, are going to be used to update a master file. Once the transaction files are in order, they can be merged together to form one file so the master file can be updated in a single run.

Topic 2 discusses the 198X ANSI standards.

Topic 1 The Sort/Merge Feature

Orientation

Although sorting and merging may take as much as 40 percent of the total running time of a computer system, the programs that perform these functions are much the same. They differ primarily in the length of the records in the files to be sorted or merged, the blocking factors used, the length and location of the fields on which the file is to be sequenced, the number of I/O devices to be used, and the number of files in a merge operation. As a result, an operating system typically provides a *sort/merge program* that can be used for many different jobs. The user supplies coded specifications for the variable factors, and the sort/merge program adjusts accordingly. As a result, the applications programmer doesn't have to write his or her own sort/merge programs.

In the COBOL compiler, special links have been included to allow access to the operating system's sort/merge program so the sort specifications are passed to the sort/merge program by the COBOL program. This allows you, the COBOL programmer, to arrange a file in the order you want and to process the records of that file before sorting, after sorting, or both.

Terminology

dummy module	merge work file	sort
input procedure	output procedure	sort/merge program
key field	section	sort work file
merge	section name	

Objectives

1. ***Given the proper program specifications, write a COBOL sort program. It may contain an input procedure, an output procedure, or both.***
2. ***Given the proper program specifications, write a COBOL merge program with an output procedure.***

Sorting in COBOL

A sort in a COBOL program consists of three main elements: (1) the work file used for the sort; (2) the sort specifications; and (3) the processing of data before or after the sort. Figure 11–1 shows the formats of the additional language you will need to code these three elements.

To illustrate the use of the COBOL sort elements, look at the program described in Figure 11–2. The problem here is to produce bulk-mail labels for random customers in the company's customer master file. Since the master file is arranged in customer-number sequence, the customer records chosen for the mailing must be sorted into zip-code order before the labels are printed (the sender is required to sort bulk-mail pieces into zip-code order).

Although all the input and output records in this program are contained in two files, the program requires a third file—the *scrt work file*. This is the work space the operating system's sort program uses to keep track of the records to be sorted so it can hand them back to the COBOL program in the proper sequence. Actually, "sort work file" is a misleading term because the sort program usually uses three or more files for work space. However, in COBOL you're only required to code a SELECT statement and file description for one file, as you'll see in a moment. The sort work file is always on tape or disk.

Figure 11–3 is a VTOC for the mailing-label program. The level-1 modules reflect the three main jobs of the program: (1) select every tenth record from the customer master file; (2) sort the selected records into zip-code sequence; and (3) print mailing labels for the records in the sorted file. The COBOL coding for the program is given in Figure 11–4. Take a minute to look it over and get acquainted with the new statements whose formats are given in Figure 11–1. Now, it will be explained how and why each statement is coded in the program.

Input-Output Section:

```
SELECT sort-file-name ASSIGN TO system-name.
```

File Section:

```
SD  sort-file-name
    [RECORD CONTAINS integer CHARACTERS].
```

Note: The keys named in the SORT statement must be described in the File Section as fields within the sort record.

Procedure Division:

```
SORT sort-file-name

    ON {ASCENDING }  KEY data-name-1...
       {DESCENDING}

       [ON {ASCENDING }  KEY data-name-2...]...
           {DESCENDING}

   {INPUT PROCEDURE IS section-name-1}
   {USING file-name-1                }

   {OUTPUT PROCEDURE IS section-name-2}.
   {GIVING file-name-2                }
```

```
RELEASE sort-record-name
    [FROM identifier].
```

Note: The RELEASE statement must be used in an input procedure.

```
RETURN sort-file-name RECORD
    [INTO identifier]
    AT END imperative-statement.
```

Note: The RETURN statement must be used in an output procedure.

```
paragraph-name.  EXIT.
```

Figure 11–1
Language formats for the sort feature

The SELECT statement

The sort work file, like any other file, requires a SELECT statement in the Environment Division. In Figure 11–4 the SELECT statement was coded for the work file just as for any other sequential disk file. Some systems, though, have special requirements for the system names used for sort work files. So check your reference manual to find out how the system name should be coded for your compiler.

The SD statement

You must describe the sort file to the compiler just as you describe other files. Instead of using an FD statement, though, you use an SD (Sort-file Description) statement. The two statements are basically the same; however, if you look back at the format in Figure 11–1, you'll see that the RECORD CONTAINS clause is the only optional clause given for the SD statement. The LABEL RECORDS clause is not part of the ANS standards, although some compilers allow you to use it. And you don't specify BLOCK CONTAINS because the sort program will control the blocking factor of the sort file.

System flowchart:

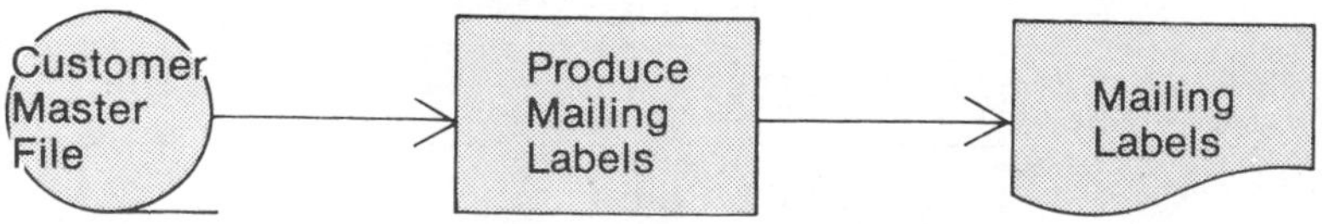
Customer Master File
Produce Mailing Labels
Mailing Labels

Record layouts:

Customer master record

Field Name	Customer No.	Unused	Customer Name	Address	City	State	Zip Code
Characteristics	X(5)	X(12)	X(30)	X(30)	X(21)	XX	X(5)
Usage							
Position	1-5	6-17	18-47	48-77	78-98	99-100	101-105

Mailing Labels

Name
Address
City/State/Zip Code

```
XXXXXXXXXXXXXXXXXXXXXXXXXXXXXX
XXXXXXXXXXXXXXXXXXXXXXXXXXXXXX
XXXXXXXXXXXXXXXXXXXXX XX XXXXX

XXXXXXXXXXXXXXXXXXXXXXXXXXXXXX
XXXXXXXXXXXXXXXXXXXXXXXXXXXXXX
XXXXXXXXXXXXXXXXXXXXX XX XXXXX
```

Narrative:

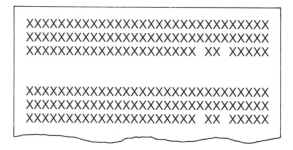

1. The customer master file is in customer-number sequence.
2. Print a mailing label for every 10th record in the master file. The labels should be printed in zip-code order.
3. Skip three lines between labels.
4. At the end of the labels, print a total line showing how many labels were printed.

Figure 11–2
Specifications for the mailing-label program

Record description

Like other files, a sort work file requires a record description (01-level) in the Data Division. Here you must define one or more *key fields*. A key field is the field you want to use to arrange the file in sequence. In Figure 11–4, SR–ZIP–CODE is the field we wish to use to sequence the customer file, so it's an 05-level item within the SORT–RECORD. In addition to key fields, you may also define other fields to be used for processing.

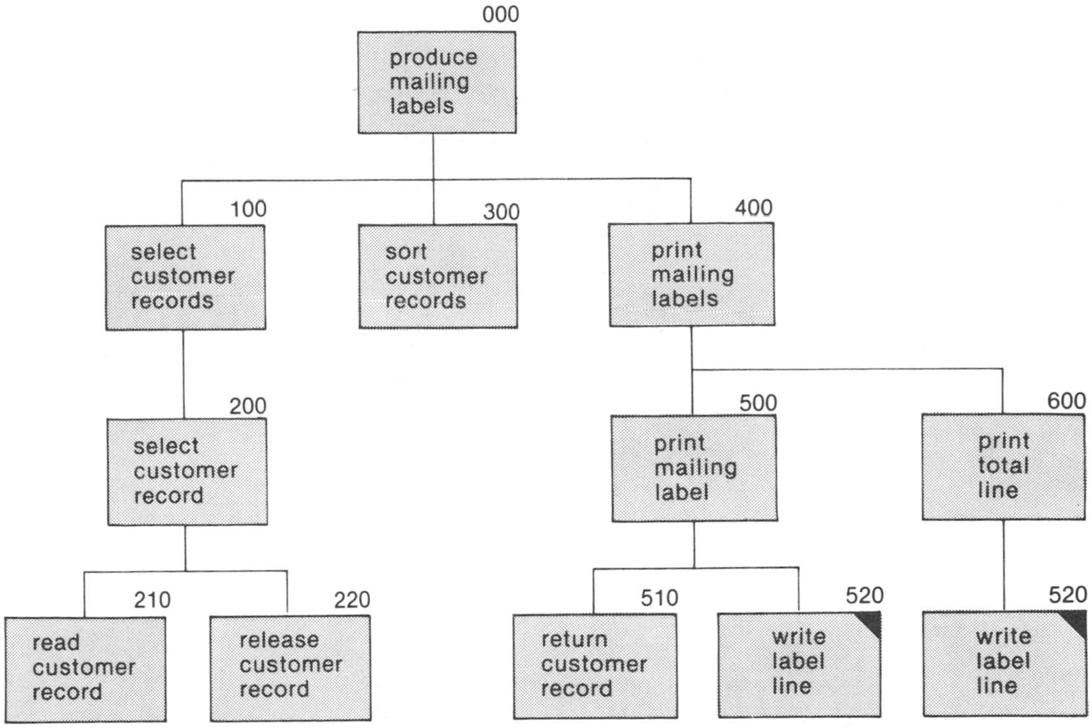
000
produce mailing labels
100
select customer records
300
sort customer records
400
print mailing labels
200
select customer record
500
print mailing label
600
print total line
210
read customer record
220
release customer record
510
return customer record
520
write label line
520
write label line

Figure 11–3
VTOC for the mailing-label program

There are a couple of syntax rules you might want to be aware of when coding key fields. First, a key field cannot contain an OCCURS clause or be subordinate to an item with an OCCURS clause. Second, you can have multiple record descriptions for the sort file; however, the key field must be in the same relative position in every record. For example, if the customer file in Figure 11–2 consisted of records with two different formats, the zip code would have to be in the same five bytes in both sets of records. Because the key field has to be in the same relative position in every record, you only have to describe it in the record description for one set of records. The compiler will figure out its position in the other sets of records. If you do decide to specify the key field in each additional record description, be sure to give it the same name, picture, and position each time.

The SORT statement

The SORT statement is the driving element of the sort feature. It specifies the name of the sort file, the sequence of the sort, the input file or input processing procedure, and the output file or output processing procedure. For instance, here's the SORT statement in Figure 11–4:

```
SORT SORT-FILE
    ON ASCENDING KEY SR-ZIP-CODE
    INPUT  PROCEDURE IS 100-I-SELECT-CUSTOMER-RECORDS
    OUTPUT PROCEDURE IS 400-O-PRINT-MAILING-LABELS.
```

After the word SORT, the sort work file, SORT–FILE, is specified. The next three lines give additional information about how and when the sorting is to be done. The following subtopics will explain these coding lines, discuss other clauses in the SORT statement, and point out some structured programming considerations that relate to the SORT statement.

```
 IDENTIFICATION DIVISION.
*
 PROGRAM-ID.  LBLSORT.
*
 ENVIRONMENT DIVISION.
*
 CONFIGURATION SECTION.
*
 SOURCE-COMPUTER.  PRIME 850.
 OBJECT-COMPUTER.  PRIME 850.
*
 INPUT-OUTPUT SECTION.
*
 FILE-CONTROL.
     SELECT CUSTOMER-MASTER
         ASSIGN TO MT9.
     SELECT LABELS
         ASSIGN TO PFMS.
     SELECT SORT-FILE
         ASSIGN TO PFMS.
*
 DATA DIVISION.
*
 FILE SECTION.
*
 FD  CUSTOMER-MASTER
     LABEL RECORDS ARE STANDARD
     RECORD CONTAINS 105 CHARACTERS
     BLOCK CONTAINS 40 RECORDS.
*
 01  CM-AREA                 PIC X(105).
*
 FD  LABELS
     LABEL RECORDS ARE STANDARD
     RECORD CONTAINS 30 CHARACTERS.
*
 01  PRINT-AREA              PIC X(30).
*
 SD  SORT-FILE
     RECORD CONTAINS 105 CHARACTERS.
*
 01  SORT-RECORD.
*
     05  FILLER              PIC X(100).
     05  SR-ZIP-CODE         PIC X(5).
*
 WORKING-STORAGE SECTION.
*
 01  SWITCHES.
*
     05  CUSTOMER-EOF-SW     PIC X        VALUE "N".
         88  CUSTOMER-EOF                 VALUE "Y".
     05  SORT-EOF-SW         PIC X        VALUE "N".
         88  SORT-EOF                     VALUE "Y".
*
 01  PRINT-FIELDS            COMP-3.
*
     05  SPACE-CONTROL       PIC S9.
*
 01  COUNT-FIELDS            COMP-3.
*
     05  CUSTOMER-COUNT      PIC S999.
     05  LABEL-COUNT         PIC S9(5)    VALUE ZERO.
*
 01  CUSTOMER-RECORD.
```

Figure 11–4
The produce-mailing-labels program (part 1 of 2)

```
*
     05  CR-CUSTOMER-NUMBER   PIC X(5).
     05  FILLER               PIC X(12).
     05  CR-NAME              PIC X(30).
     05  CR-ADDRESS           PIC X(30).
     05  CR-CITY              PIC X(21).
     05  CR-STATE             PIC XX.
     05  CR-ZIP-CODE          PIC X(5).
*
 01  LABEL-LINE-1             PIC X(30).
*
 01  LABEL-LINE-2.
*
     05  LBL2-CITY            PIC X(21).
     05  FILLER               PIC X         VALUE SPACE.
     05  LBL2-STATE           PIC XX.
     05  FILLER               PIC X         VALUE SPACE.
     05  LBL2-ZIP-CODE        PIC X(5).
*
 01  TOTAL-LINE-1.
*
     05  TOT1-LABEL-COUNT     PIC ZZZZ9.
     05  FILLER               PIC X(15)     VALUE " LABELS PRINTED".
     05  FILLER               PIC X(10)     VALUE SPACE.
*
 PROCEDURE DIVISION.
*
 000-C-PRODUCE-MAILING-LABELS SECTION.
*
 000-PRODUCE-MAILING-LABELS.
*
     OPEN INPUT  CUSTOMER-MASTER
          OUTPUT LABELS.
     SORT SORT-FILE
         ON ASCENDING KEY SR-ZIP-CODE
         INPUT  PROCEDURE IS 100-I-SELECT-CUSTOMER-RECORDS
         OUTPUT PROCEDURE IS 400-O-PRINT-MAILING-LABELS.
     CLOSE CUSTOMER-MASTER
           LABELS.
     DISPLAY "LBLSORT  I  1  NORMAL EOJ".
     STOP RUN.
*
 100-I-SELECT-CUSTOMER-RECORDS SECTION.
*
 100-SELECT-CUSTOMER-RECORDS.
*
     PERFORM 200-SELECT-CUSTOMER-RECORD
         UNTIL CUSTOMER-EOF.
     GO TO 100-EXIT.
*
 200-SELECT-CUSTOMER-RECORD.
*
     PERFORM 210-READ-CUSTOMER-RECORD
         VARYING CUSTOMER-COUNT FROM 1 BY 1
         UNTIL CUSTOMER-COUNT GREATER 10
            OR CUSTOMER-EOF.
     IF NOT CUSTOMER-EOF
         PERFORM 220-RELEASE-CUSTOMER-RECORD.
*
 210-READ-CUSTOMER-RECORD.
*
     READ CUSTOMER-MASTER
         AT END
             MOVE "Y" TO CUSTOMER-EOF-SW.
*
```

Figure 11–4
The produce-mailing-labels program (part 2 of 3)

```
 220-RELEASE-CUSTOMER-RECORD.
*
     RELEASE SORT-RECORD FROM CM-AREA.
*
 100-EXIT.
*
     EXIT.
*
 300-SORT-CUSTOMER-RECORDS.
*
*    DUMMY MODULE DONE BY SORT STATEMENT.
*
 400-0-PRINT-MAILING-LABELS SECTION.
*
 400-PRINT-MAILING-LABELS.
*
     PERFORM 500-PRINT-MAILING-LABEL
         UNTIL SORT-EOF.
     PERFORM 600-PRINT-TOTAL-LINE.
     GO TO 400-EXIT.
*
 500-PRINT-MAILING-LABEL.
*
     PERFORM 510-RETURN-CUSTOMER-RECORD.
     IF NOT SORT-EOF
         MOVE CR-NAME TO LABEL-LINE-1
         MOVE LABEL-LINE-1 TO PRINT-AREA
         MOVE 3 TO SPACE-CONTROL
         PERFORM 520-WRITE-LABEL-LINE
         MOVE CR-ADDRESS TO LABEL-LINE-1
         MOVE LABEL-LINE-1 TO PRINT-AREA
         MOVE 1 TO SPACE-CONTROL
         PERFORM 520-WRITE-LABEL-LINE
         MOVE CR-CITY     TO LBL2-CITY
         MOVE CR-STATE    TO LBL2-STATE
         MOVE CR-ZIP-CODE TO LBL2-ZIP-CODE
         MOVE LABEL-LINE-2 TO PRINT-AREA
         PERFORM 520-WRITE-LABEL-LINE.
*
 510-RETURN-CUSTOMER-RECORD.
*
     RETURN SORT-FILE INTO CUSTOMER-RECORD
         AT END
             MOVE "Y" TO SORT-EOF-SW.
     IF NOT SORT-EOF
         ADD 1 TO LABEL-COUNT.
*
 520-WRITE-LABEL-LINE.
*
     WRITE PRINT-AREA
         AFTER ADVANCING SPACE-CONTROL LINES.
*
 600-PRINT-TOTAL-LINE.
*
     MOVE LABEL-COUNT TO TOT1-LABEL-COUNT.
     MOVE TOTAL-LINE-1 TO PRINT-AREA.
     MOVE 3 TO SPACE-CONTROL.
     PERFORM 520-WRITE-LABEL-LINE.
*
 400-EXIT.
*
     EXIT.
```

Figure 11–4
The produce-mailing-labels program (part 3 of 3)

EBCDIC Collating Sequence

No.	Symbol	Character
1.		(space)
2.	.	(period)
3.	<	(less than)
4.	(	(left parenthesis)
5.	+	(plus)
6.	$	(dollar sign)
7.	*	(asterisk)
8.	)	(right parenthesis)
9.	;	(semicolon)
10.	-	(hyphen, minus, dash)
11.	/	(stroke, slash)
12.	,	(comma)
13.	>	(greater than)
14.	'	(apostrophe, single quotation mark)
15.	=	(equal to)
16.	"	(quotation mark)
17-42.	A through Z	
43-52.	0 through 9	

ASCII Collating Sequence

No.	Symbol	Character
1.		(space
2.	"	(quotation mark)
3.	$	(dollar sign)
4.	'	(apostrophe, single quotation mark)
5.	(	(left parenthesis)
6.	)	(right parenthesis)
7.	*	(asterisk)
8.	+	(plus)
9.	,	(comma)
10.	-	(hyphen, minus, dash)
11.	.	(period)
12.	/	(stroke, slash)
13-22.	0 through 9	
23.	;	(semicolon)
24.	<	(less than)
25.	=	(equal to)
26.	>	(greater than)
27-52.	A through Z	

Figure 11–5
Collating sequences in ascending order

The ASCENDING/DESCENDING KEY clause

The KEY clause specifies the order in which the sort file is to be arranged. As a result, it uses one or more of the key fields defined in the sort record description. If you look back at the statement format in Figure 11–1, you'll see that a file can be arranged in key sequence in either ascending or descending order. The SORT statement in Figure 11–4 says to arrange the records in SORT–FILE in ascending sequence according to the values of SR–ZIP–CODE.

If you have more than one key field in the file, you can mix ASCENDING and DESCENDING in the same SORT statement. For example, let's say you want to print an open-accounts report showing balance-due (INV–BAL–DUE) in descending order. However, if there are duplicate amounts for different customers, these are to be shown in ascending customer-number (INV–CUST–NO) sequence. Then, you can code a SORT statement like this:

```
SORT SORT-FILE
    ON DESCENDING KEY INV-BAL-DUE
       ASCENDING KEY  INV-CUST-NO
```

The records will then be arranged in ascending customer-number sequence within descending balance-due sequence.

The actual sequence of the sorted records depends not only on the ASCENDING/DESCENDING clause, but also on the collating sequence of the computer. One common collating sequence is the EBCDIC collating sequence partially shown from lowest value to highest in Figure 11–5, along with the ASCII code. Using this collating sequence, if you specified ASCENDING KEY in the SORT statement, a record with a key of 0123B would be placed *before* a record with a key of 0123C. If you specified DESCENDING sequence, the record with 0123B in its key field would be placed *after* the record with 0123C in its key field. You should find out what collating sequence is used on your computer if you haven't already done so.

Input and output procedures

An *input procedure* is the processing that's to be done before a file is sorted; an *output procedure* is the processing that's to be done using the sorted file. In Figure 11–4, 100–I–SELECT–CUSTOMER–RECORDS is the input procedure given in the SORT statement; 400–O–PRINT–MAILING–LABELS is the output procedure.

An input or output procedure is given control by a SORT statement in much the same way that a COBOL paragraph is given control by a PERFORM statement. The difference is that each input or output procedure must be a *section* in a COBOL program.

What is a section? It's a Procedure Division unit that is made up of one or more paragraphs and has a single *section name*. A section name is any valid procedure name followed by a blank, the word SECTION, and a period. It must appear on a coding line by itself, and, in standard COBOL, it must be followed by a paragraph name. A section continues until the next section name or the end of the program is reached.

Because an input or output procedure must be a section, the other parts of a COBOL sort program should also be contained in sections. As a result, Figure 11–4 consists of three sections: 000–C–PRODUCE–MAILING–LABELS; 100–I–SELECT–CUSTOMER–RECORDS, the input procedure; and 400–O–PRINT–MAILING–LABELS, the output procedure. Notice that the section names are the same as the corresponding module names in the VTOC in Figure 11–3, except that an extra character is inserted between the module number and description: C in section 000 stands for "control" since this is the top-level control section; I in section 100 stands for "input" since this is the input procedure; and O in section 400 stands for "output" since this is the output procedure. (In some cases, the addition of these characters will cause the section name to be over 30 characters long, so you'll have to shorten some of the words used in the name.) The first paragraph name in each section is formed following the same guidelines used for creating any other paragraph name.

One other important point about input and output procedures is that they can only receive control from and return control to a SORT statement. In other words, an input or output procedure cannot be named in a PERFORM statement; it cannot contain PERFORM statements that pass control to paragraphs outside of the section; and it can't contain any SORT statements.

The USING clause

If you do not want to process the input file before it's sorted, you do not need to code an input procedure nor specify one in the SORT statement. Instead, all you need to do is name the input file that is to be sorted in the USING clause. Suppose, for example, that the program is not to select any of the input records in the program Figure 11–4. The program is to sort the whole customer file and to print the labels. Then the SORT statement would be coded like this:

```
SORT SORT-FILE
       ON ASCENDING KEY SR-ZIP-CODE
       USING CUSTOMER-MASTER
       OUTPUT PROCEDURE IS 400-O-PRINT-MAILING LABELS.
```

The USING option would open the customer file, read it into the sort work file, and close it. Later in this topic you will see a program that does not have an input procedure, as a further illustration of the USING clause.

The GIVING clause

Just as a USING clause replaces an input procedure, a GIVING clause replaces an output procedure. For instance, suppose that the program is to select certain customers before sorting, but not to produce the mailing labels. The selected, sorted records are to be written to a file named SELECTED–CUSTOMERS for later processing by another program. In that case, the output procedure would be left out and the SORT statement would be coded like this:

```
SORT SORT-FILE
       ON ASCENDING KEY SR-ZIP-CODE
       INPUT PROCEDURE IS 100-I-SELECT-CUSTOMER-RECORDS
       GIVING SELECTED-CUSTOMERS
```

The GIVING option would open the output file, write the sorted records, and close the file. To further illustrate the use of the GIVING clause, you will see a problem program at the end of this topic that does not have an output procedure.

Structured programming considerations

If you've compared the coding Figure 11–4 to the VTOC in Figure 11–3, you may be wondering why the SORT statement is coded in module 000. Why isn't it in module 300, "sort customer records?"

The SORT statement must be coded in module 000 because it controls the execution of the rest of the program. In other words, the SORT statement controls all three of the functions defined by the level-1 modules in Figure 11–3—it processes the unsorted records in an input procedure (modules 100 through 220), it sorts the records (module 300), and it processes the sorted records in an output procedure (modules 400 through 600). The sort module, then, is empty because the actual sorting is done by the sort program that's provided by the operating system and executed by the SORT statement. It's called a *dummy module* and is coded as a comment in Figure 11–4. If the SORT statement contained a USING clause instead of an input procedure, module 100 would be a dummy module too; if it contained a GIVING clause, module 400 would be a dummy module.

Do you understand the structure in Figure 11–3 a little better now? The programmer drew level-1 modules to show the processing that would be done by the SORT statement in module 000. You should structure your own

COBOL sort programs this way. In other words, use three modules (input, sorting, and output) to represent the processing for each SORT statement, even though one or more of the modules will always be empty. This will make your VTOCs conceptually correct.

A SORT Example

The input procedure: 100–I–SELECT–CUSTOMER–RECORDS section

In an input procedure, you normally loop through instructions that read input records, process those records, and release the records to the sort program. Once all the records have been processed, control should be returned to the SORT statement.

That's just what happens in the input procedure in Figure 11–4. Module 100, the top-level module of the procedure, executes module 200 repeatedly until the end of the customer file is reached. Module 200, in turn, performs a paragraph to read each customer master, selects every tenth customer, and then performs a paragraph to release each selected record to the sort program. At the end of the input, module 100 passes control back to the SORT statement by using a GO TO statement to branch to the section exit point (100–EXIT). This is one of only two situations in which a GO TO statement is acceptable in structured programming.

Notice that the top-level module in an input procedure represents the processing for all the records in a file, so it's roughly equivalent to a 000 module in other programs. That's why its subordinate module has a module number that's a multiple of 100, instead of a multiple of 10.

The RELEASE statement

The RELEASE statement is similar to the WRITE statement in that it is an output verb. It makes the record in the sort work area available to the sort program, ready for sorting. It must be part of an input procedure. Also, since it is an output verb like the WRITE statement, it should be coded in its own separate module.

If you look at the statement format in Figure 11–1, you'll see you can use a FROM option with a RELEASE statement just as you can with a WRITE statement. This causes an input or working-storage record to be moved to the sort work area and be released for sorting. For example, since the input and sort record lengths and formats in Figure 11–4 are the same, the code was:

```
RELEASE SORT-RECORD FROM CM-AREA.
```

This is equivalent to

```
MOVE CM-AREA TO SORT-RECORD.
RELEASE SORT-RECORD.
```

With or without the FROM option, a record must be read and moved to the sort work area before it can be released.

The EXIT statement

The EXIT statement is a one-word statement that does not cause any processing to take place. As shown in the format in Figure 11–1, it must be the only statement in a paragraph when it's used.

The EXIT statement is used in the sort feature to allow the programmer to maintain the structure and modularity of the program. Placed at the end of the input procedure in Figure 11–4, it allows the program to reach the end of the input-procedure section, return to the SORT statement, and continue processing from there. Remember that a GO TO statement is required at the end of module 100 to branch around paragraphs 200 through 220 and get to the exit paragraph.

The output procedure: 400–O–PRINT–MAILING–LABELS section

In an output procedure, you normally loop through instructions that return sorted records from the sort program, process those records, and produce output records. At the end of the sorted file, control should be returned to the SORT statement. And that's just what happens in the output procedure in Figure 11–4. Module 400, the top-level module of the procedure, executes module 500 repeatedly until all the sorted customer masters have been processed. Module 500, in turn, performs a paragraph to return the sorted records from the sort program and controls the printing of the labels. At the end of the sorted records, module 400 causes a total line to print. It then passes control back to the SORT statement by using a GO TO statement to branch to the section exit point (400–EXIT). As mentioned in the discussion of the input procedure, the sort feature is one of two structures in which it is acceptable to use a GO TO statement.

Just as in an input procedure, the top-level module of an output procedure represents the processing for all the records in a file, so it's equivalent to a 000 module in other programs. Again, that's why the two modules on the next level down in the VTOC are numbered by 100s, not 10s.

The RETURN statement

The RETURN statement is similar to the READ statement in that it is an input verb. It makes the next sorted record available to the program in the sort work area. Just as a RELEASE verb can only be coded in an input procedure, the RETURN verb must be part of an output procedure. Also, since RETURN is an input verb like the READ statement, it should be isolated in its own separate module.

If you look at the format in Figure 11–1, you'll see that you can use an INTO option with a RETURN statement just as you can with a READ statement. This causes the sorted record to be made available to the program and automatically moved to an output or working-storage area. In Figure 11–4, the RETURN INTO option was used in module 510. So once this RETURN statement is executed, the sorted record is in the working-storage field named CUSTOMER–RECORD, ready for further processing.

The EXIT statement

As in an input procedure, an EXIT statement is required at the end of an output procedure so the program can reach the end of the section and control can return to the SORT statement. Here again, a GO TO statement like the one at the end of module 400 is required to branch to the EXIT statement, since the EXIT must be coded in its own separate paragraph.

System flowchart:

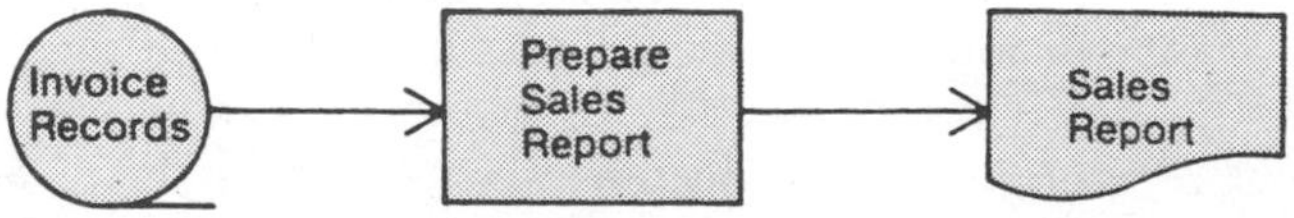
Invoice Records
Prepare Sales Report
Sales Report

Print chart:

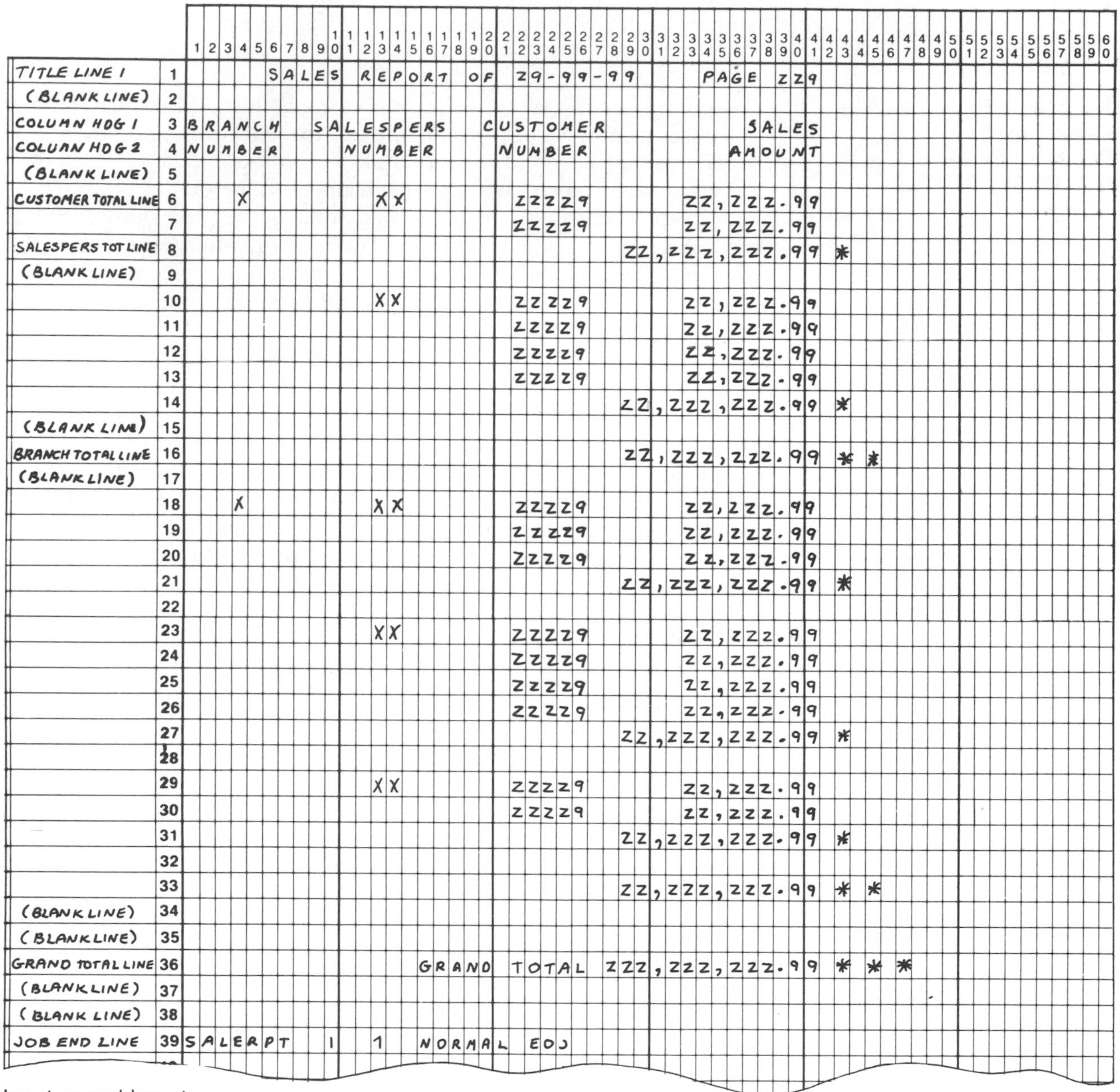
TITLE LINE 1 — 1 — SALES REPORT OF Z9-99-99 PAGE ZZ9
(BLANK LINE) — 2
COLUMN HDG 1 — 3 — BRANCH SALESPERS CUSTOMER SALES
COLUMN HDG 2 — 4 — NUMBER NUMBER NUMBER AMOUNT
(BLANK LINE) — 5
CUSTOMER TOTAL LINE — 6 — X XX ZZZZ9 ZZ,ZZZ.99
7 — ZZZZ9 ZZ,ZZZ.99
SALESPERS TOT LINE — 8 — ZZ,ZZZ,ZZZ.99 *
(BLANK LINE) — 9
10 — XX ZZZZ9 ZZ,ZZZ.99
11 — ZZZZ9 ZZ,ZZZ.99
12 — ZZZZ9 ZZ,ZZZ.99
13 — ZZZZ9 ZZ,ZZZ.99
14 — ZZ,ZZZ,ZZZ.99 *
(BLANK LINE) — 15
BRANCH TOTAL LINE — 16 — ZZ,ZZZ,ZZZ.99 * *
(BLANK LINE) — 17
18 — X XX ZZZZ9 ZZ,ZZZ.99
19 — ZZZZ9 ZZ,ZZZ.99
20 — ZZZZ9 ZZ,ZZZ.99
21 — ZZ,ZZZ,ZZZ.99 *
22
23 — XX ZZZZ9 ZZ,ZZZ.99
24 — ZZZZ9 ZZ,ZZZ.99
25 — ZZZZ9 ZZ,ZZZ.99
26 — ZZZZ9 ZZ,ZZZ.99
27 — ZZ,ZZZ,ZZZ.99 *
28
29 — XX ZZZZ9 ZZ,ZZZ.99
30 — ZZZZ9 ZZ,ZZZ.99
31 — ZZ,ZZZ,ZZZ.99 *
32
33 — ZZ,ZZZ,ZZZ.99 * *
(BLANK LINE) — 34
(BLANK LINE) — 35
GRAND TOTAL LINE — 36 — GRAND TOTAL ZZZ,ZZZ,ZZZ.99 * * *
(BLANK LINE) — 37
(BLANK LINE) — 38
JOB END LINE — 39 — SALERPT 1 1 NORMAL EOJ

Input record layout:

Field Name	Invoice No.	Invoice Date	Branch No.	Salespers No.	Customer No.	Quantity	Item No.	Unit Cost	Unit Price
Characteristics	X(5)	9(6)	X	X(2)	X(5)	9(3)	X(5)	999V99	999V99
Usage						COMP-3		COMP-3	COMP-3
Position	1-5	6-11	12	13-14	15-19	20-21	22-26	27-29	30-32

Figure 11–6
Specifications for the three-level report program (part 1 of 2)

```
        SALES REPORT OF  8-21-86     PAGE   1
BRANCH  SALESPERS  CUSTOMER            SALES
NUMBER    NUMBER    NUMBER             AMOUNT
   1        12          111          3,668.50
                        189          1,002.00
                      23298         37,383.75
                                    42,054.25 *

            17          512            219.95
                       5394             85.50
                                       305.45 *

                                    42,359.70 * *

   2        28          911         37,342.00
                       1023             40.00
                                    37,382.00 *

            36         1199          1,099.75
                                     1,099.75 *

            39        20032          2,591.50
                      29879             29.80
                                     2,621.30 *

            47        14212            194.25
                      28400          2,584.50
                                     2,778.75 *

                                    43,881.80 * *
   3        72          312          2,732.00
                       1148         12,402.75
                                    15,134.75

            94        77650              2.00
                                         2.00 *

                                    15,136.75 * *

                   GRAND TOTAL     101,378.25 * * *
SALERPT  I  1      NORMAL EOJ
```

Narrative:

1. The invoice records are in invoice-number sequence.
2. There may be one or more invoices for each customer. However, only one line should print for each customer showing the total amount invoiced for that customer. The amount invoiced is quantity multiplied by unit price.
3. Totals will be printed for each salesperson and branch. At the end of the report, the grand total of all sales will be printed.

Figure 11–6
Specifications for the three-level report program (part 2 of 2)

Another Example

To give you a little more feel for the COBOL sort structure and language, another example is provided. Look at the program specifications in Figure 11–6. This program uses an invoice file in invoice-number order to print a summary report showing total sales at three levels—by branch, by salesperson, and by customer. As a result, the invoice records will have to be sorted using three keys—branch number, salesperson number, and customer number—instead of only one, as in the mailing-label program.

The VTOC

Figure 11–7 is a VTOC for this program. Here, as in Figure 11–3, the three level-1 modules reflect the processing that is done by the SORT statement in module 000. In this case, however, there is no need to process the records before sorting them. So module 100 will be empty. And, as always, the sort

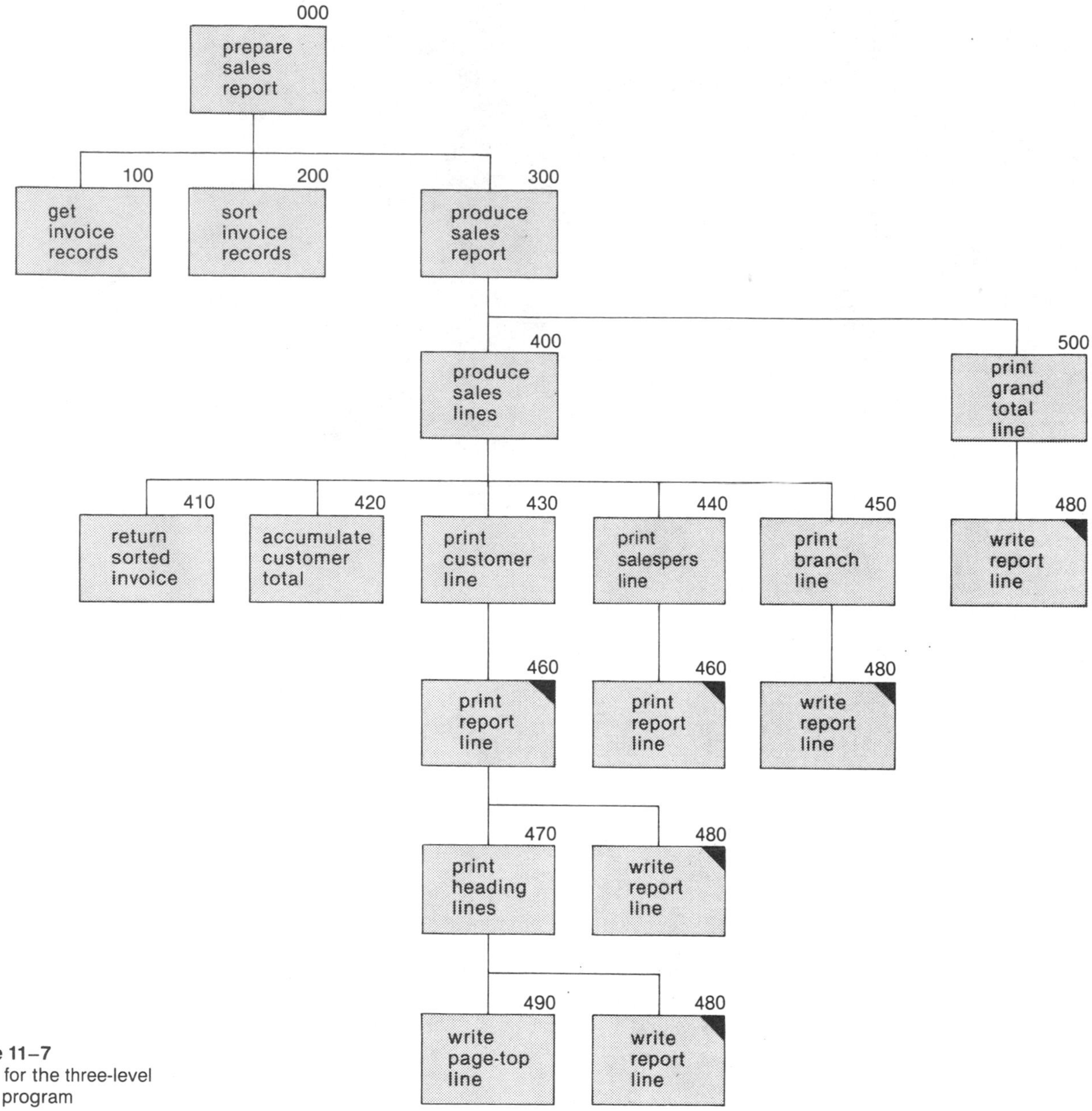
000
prepare sales report
100
get invoice records
200
sort invoice records
300
produce sales report
400
produce sales lines
500
print grand total line
410
return sorted invoice
420
accumulate customer total
430
print customer line
440
print salespers line
450
print branch line
480
write report line
460
print report line
460
print report line
480
write report line
470
print heading lines
480
write report line
490
write page-top line
480
write report line

Figure 11–7
VTOC for the three-level report program

module will be empty because the sorting's done by the system's sort program under the control of the SORT statement.

The output module, module 300, is the top-level module of the output procedure and is equivalent to a 000 module. It executes module 400, the main control module. Module 400, in turn, executes modules that return invoice records from the sort, accumulate customer totals, and print customer, salesperson, and branch total lines whenever there's a control-field change.

Module 460, a subordinate of modules 430 and 440, is the top-level module of a general print routine that checks for when to print heading lines. Since the designer doesn't want to skip to a new page between the printing of a salesperson total line and a branch total line (that is, the designer doesn't want the last salesperson line for a branch on one page and the branch total on the next), only module 480 is subordinate to module 450. At the end of the report, module 500 prints a grand total line.

The coding

Figure 11–8 gives partial coding for the report-printing program. As you can see, this program contains the same basic sort elements as the one in Figure 11–4: the sort work file is selected and defined; the sort specifications are given; and an output procedure is used to process the data after the sort.

After the SD statement, the record description for SORT–RECORD includes the three key fields: SR–BRANCH–NO, SR–SALESPERS–NO, and SR–CUSTOMER–NO. These fields are then specified in the SORT statement in module 000 of the program:

```
SORT SORT-FILE
    ON ASCENDING KEY SR-BRANCH-NO
                     SR-SALESPERS-NO
                     SR-CUSTOMER-NO
    USING INVOICE-FILE
    OUTPUT PROCEDURE IS 300-O-PRODUCE-SALES-REPORT.
```

Once this statement is executed, the invoice records will be arranged in ascending customer-number sequence within salesperson number sequence within branch-number sequence.

Notice that since the invoice records don't require any processing before they're sorted, the SORT statement contains a USING clause, not an input procedure, to open the file and read the records into the sort program. So you can't open INVOICE–FILE in the OPEN statement. Also, since the USING clause does the function of module 100 in the VTOC in Figure 11–7, module 100, like module 200, is coded as a dummy module. Once the records are sorted, however, control passes to the output procedure, just as it did in the program in Figure 11–4.

Can you follow the processing in the output-procedure modules shown in Figure 11–8? Module 300, the top-level module in the output procedure, simply executes module 400 repeatedly until the end of the sorted invoice file is reached. Then it executes module 500 to print the final total line on the report and branches to the exit point of the procedure so the program can return to module 000.

Module 400 is the main control module in the program. After executing module 410 to return a sorted invoice, it checks the FIRST–RECORD–SW and sets up the control fields in working storage if the switch is on. If the switch is off, it compares the values in the invoice record to the control fields in working storage. Whenever a control-field change occurs, it prints the required total lines and resets the control-field values in working storage. Whether there's been a control-field change or not, it then performs module 420 as long as the end of the invoice file hasn't been reached.

As said earlier, an output procedure must contain a RETURN statement, not a READ statement, to make each sorted record available for processing. In Figure 11–8, the RETURN statement in module 410 uses the INTO option to return a sorted invoice into INVOICE–RECORD in working storage. When it reaches the end of the sorted invoices, the statement moves Y to INVOICE–EOF–SW and HIGH–VALUE to the invoice branch number. This means that when the invoice branch is compared to the old branch in module 400, a greater-than relationship will be found. So the last customer, salesperson, and branch total lines will be printed before the program executes module 500. The section ends with an exit paragraph so that control can return to the SORT statement in module 000.

```
 ENVIRONMENT DIVISION.
*
     .
     .
     SELECT SORT-FILE ASSIGN TO DISK-F-D-SORTFLE-TXT.
     .
     .
*
 DATA DIVISION.
*
     .
     .
*
 SD  SORT-FILE
     RECORD CONTAINS 32 CHARACTERS.
*
 01  SORT-RECORD.
*
     05  FILLER              PIC X(11).
     05  SR-BRANCH-NO        PIC X.
     05  SR-SALESPERS-NO     PIC XX.
     05  SR-CUSTOMER-NO      PIC X(5).
     05  FILLER              PIC X(18).
*
     .
     .
*
 WORKING-STORAGE SECTION.
*
 01  SWITCHES.
*
     05  FIRST-RECORD-SW     PIC X          VALUE "Y".
         88  FIRST-RECORD                   VALUE "Y".
     05  INVOICE-EOF-SW      PIC X          VALUE "N".
         88  INVOICE-EOF                    VALUE "Y".
*
 01  CONTROL-FIELDS.
*
     05  OLD-CUSTOMER-NO     PIC X(5).
     05  OLD-SALESPERS-NO    PIC XX.
     05  OLD-BRANCH-NO       PIC X.
*
     .
     .
*
 01  INVOICE-RECORD.
*
     05  FILLER              PIC X(11).
     05  IR-BRANCH-NO        PIC X.
     05  IR-SALESPERS-NO     PIC XX.
     05  IR-CUSTOMER-NO      PIC X(5).
     05  IR-QUANTITY         PIC 9(3)       COMP-3.
     05  FILLER              PIC X(8).
     05  IR-UNIT-PRICE       PIC 9(3)V99    COMP-3.
*
     .
     .
```

Figure 11–8
Partial coding for the three-level report program (part 1 of 3)

One final thing to note in the coding in Figure 11–8 is the language forced upon the program by the SORT statement. First, the output procedure must be a section, so the portion of the program containing module 000 should be a section too. Second, a GO TO statement is required at the end of module 300 to branch to the end of the section. And third, an EXIT statement must be coded in its own paragraph so the paragraph can reach the end of the section and control can return to module 000.

```
*
 PROCEDURE DIVISION.
*
 000-C-PREPARE-SALES-REPORT SECTION.
*
 000-PREPARE-SALES-REPORT.
*
     OPEN OUTPUT SALES-REPORT.
     SORT SORT-FILE
         ON ASCENDING KEY SR-BRANCH-NO
                          SR-SALESPERS-NO
                          SR-CUSTOMER-NO
         USING INVOICE-FILE
         OUTPUT PROCEDURE IS 300-O-PRODUCE-SALES-REPORT.
     CLOSE SALES-REPORT.
     DISPLAY "SLSRPRT  I  1  NORMAL EOJ".
     STOP RUN.
*
*100-GET-INVOICE-RECORDS.
*
*    DUMMY MODULE DONE BY SORT STATEMENT.
*
*200-SORT-INVOICE-RECORDS.
*
*    DUMMY MODULE DONE BY SORT STATEMENT.
*
 300-O-PRODUCE-SALES-REPORT SECTION.
*
 300-PRODUCE-SALES-REPORT.
*
     PERFORM 400-PRODUCE-SALES-LINES
         UNTIL INVOICE-EOF.
     PERFORM 500-PRINT-GRAND-TOTAL-LINE.
     GO TO 300-EXIT.
 400-PRODUCE-SALES-LINES.
*
     PERFORM 410-RETURN-SORTED-INVOICE.
     IF FIRST-RECORD
         MOVE IR-BRANCH-NO    TO OLD-BRANCH-NO
         MOVE IR-SALESPERS NO TO OLD-SALESPERS-NO
         MOVE IR-CUSTOMER-NO  TO OLD-CUSTOMER-NO
         MOVE "N" TO FIRST-RECORD-SW
     ELSE
         IF IR-BRANCH-NO GREATER OLD-BRANCH-NO
             PERFORM 430-PRINT-CUSTOMER-LINE
             PERFORM 440-PRINT-SALESPERS-LINE
             PERFORM 450-PRINT-BRANCH-LINE
             MOVE IR-BRANCH-NO    TO OLD-BRANCH-NO
             MOVE IR-SALESPERS-NO TO OLD-SALESPERS-NO
             MOVE IR-CUSTOMER-NO  TO OLD-CUSTOMER-NO
         ELSE
             IF IR-SALESPERS-NO GREATER OLD-SALESPERS-NO
                 PERFORM 430-PRINT-CUSTOMER-LINE
                 PERFORM 440-PRINT-SALESPERS-LINE
                 MOVE IR-SALESPERS-NO TO OLD-SALESPERS-NO
                 MOVE IR-CUSTOMER-NO TO OLD-CUSTOMER-NO
             ELSE
                 IF IR-CUSTOMER-NO GREATER OLD-CUSTOMER-NO
                     PERFORM 430-PRINT-CUSTOMER-LINE
                     MOVE IR-CUSTOMER-NO TO OLD-CUSTOMER-NO.
     IF NOT INVOICE-EOF
         PERFORM 420-ACCUMULATE-CUSTOMER-TOTAL.
*
```

Figure 11–8
Partial coding for the three-level report program (part 2 of 3)

```
 410-RETURN-SORTED-INVOICE.
*
        RETURN SORT-FILE INTO INVOICE-RECORD
            AT END
                MOVE "Y" TO INVOICE-EOF-SW
                MOVE HIGH-VALUE TO IR-BRANCH-NO.
*
        .
        .
*
 300-EXIT.
*
        EXIT.
```

Figure 11–8
Partial coding for the three-level report program (part 3 of 3)

Merging in COBOL

Under the 1974 ANSI COBOL standard, a COBOL program can contain a merge function, which is logically related to the sort function. Merging, in data processing terms, means placing two or more files that are already in the same sequence into one sequenced file. For example, suppose a report has somehow become separated and now you have two piles of pages which you wish to put back together. The pages in each of the two piles have remained in sequence so that the first pile is numberd 1, 2, 4, 5, 7, and the second contains page numbers 3 and 6. Merging the two piles would result in one pile numbered 1, 2, 3, 4, 5, 6, 7.

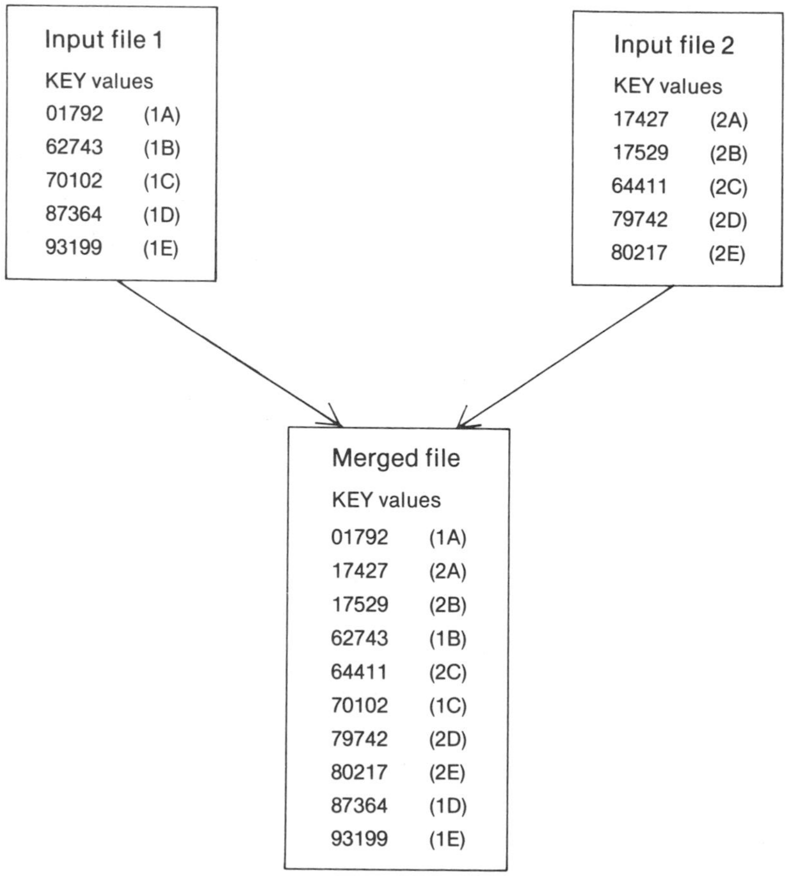
Input file 1
KEY values
01792 (1A)
62743 (1B)
70102 (1C)
87364 (1D)
93199 (1E)
Input file 2
KEY values
17427 (2A)
17529 (2B)
64411 (2C)
79742 (2D)
80217 (2E)
Merged file
KEY values
01792 (1A)
17427 (2A)
17529 (2B)
62743 (1B)
64411 (2C)
70102 (1C)
79742 (2D)
80217 (2E)
87364 (1D)
93199 (1E)

Figure 11–9
Example of the merge function

Figure 11–9 shows another, more realistic example of merging for computer purposes. As you can see, each input file is already in sequence by key. The merged file is simply a combination of the two with all key fields arranged in order.

Figure 11–10 summarizes the COBOL statements for the 1974 merge feature. As you can see, the language for merging is identical to the sort language in most ways. However, although the MERGE statement follows the same basic format as the SORT statement, it cannot contain an input procedure. So there are no RELEASE statements in COBOL merge programs. Instead, every COBOL MERGE statement must contain a USING clause to cause the input files to be opened and closed and input records to be made available to the merge operation.

Aside from these points, the merge feature is the same as the sort feature. A *merge work file* must be selected and then defined by an SD statement and record description. The record description must include one or more key fields that will be used to merge the input files. The rules governing key fields are the same as they are in a sort program.

Input-Output Section:

```
SELECT merge-file-name ASSIGN TO system-name.
```

File Section:

```
SD  merge-file-name
    [RECORD CONTAINS integer CHARACTERS].
```

Note: The keys named in the MERGE statement must be described in the File Section as fields within the merge record.

Procedure Division:

```
MERGE merge-file-name

    ON { ASCENDING  } KEY data-name-1...
       { DESCENDING }

    [ON { ASCENDING  } KEY data-name-2...]...
        { DESCENDING }

    USING file-name-1 file-name-2 [file-name-3]...

   { OUTPUT PROCEDURE IS section-name }.
   { GIVING file-name-4               }
```

```
RETURN merge-file-name RECORD
    [INTO identifier]
    AT END imperative-statement.
```

Note: The RETURN statement must be used in an output procedure.

```
paragraph-name.  EXIT.
```

Figure 11–10
Language formats for the merge feature

If the MERGE statement specifies an output procedure, the program will consist of two sections—one for the output procedure and one for the rest of the program. The output procedure must contain a RETURN statement to return merged records into the program. The top-level module of the procedure will end with a GO TO statement that branches to an exit paragraph at the end of the procedure. This paragraph will contain an EXIT statement that will allow control to return to the MERGE statement.

Thus, a merge program is designed and coded in basically the same way as a sort program. You'll see an example in the problems at the end of this topic.

The Effect of the Sort/Merge Feature on Structured Programming

As you have seen, the COBOL sort/merge feature poses some problems for the structured programmer. First, it prevents the programmer from coding all the modules in the VTOC. At the least, the sort/merge module is always empty, because the SORT/MERGE statement takes care of this function at a higher level. What's more, the input module for the file that's to be sorted or merged is a dummy module when a USING clause is used; and the output module for a sorted or merged file is a dummy module when a GIVING clause is used.

Aside from design implementation, the SORT and MERGE statements cause other coding problems by forcing the COBOL programmer to use sections, GO TO statements, and EXIT statements. In short, then, the COBOL sort/merge feature forces restrictions on the programmer that are not in the best interests of structured programming.

Discussion

In spite of the structured-programming problems, the COBOL sort feature is a valuable tool that can help you solve one of your most frequently occurring problems in one logical, orderly task. The merge feature, though, isn't nearly as useful. There just aren't that many instances in which input files are already sorted into key-sequence order before they have to be merged. And if the files aren't in key-sequence order, it's better to do a sort with multiple reads than to sort the files individually and then merge them. So while the SORT statement will save you lots of coding, time, and headaches, the MERGE statement won't really help you too much. You can always get along without it.

Problems

1. (Objective 1) Figure 11–11 gives the specifications for a program that edits, or checks, sales transactions for validity, prints a report of invalid transactions, sorts the valid transactions, and writes them on an output file.
   - **a.** Design a VTOC for this program. (Use the VTOC for the edit program in Figure 6–17 as a guide for designing the editing portion of the program.)
   - **b.** Code the SELECT statement, SD statement, and record description for the sort work file. Then, using the VTOC in Figure 11–13, code modules 000, 100, 380, 500, 600, and the exit module. Release the sort record from a field called TRAN–RECORD.

Figure 11–11
Specifications for the edit program (part 1 of 2)

System flowchart:

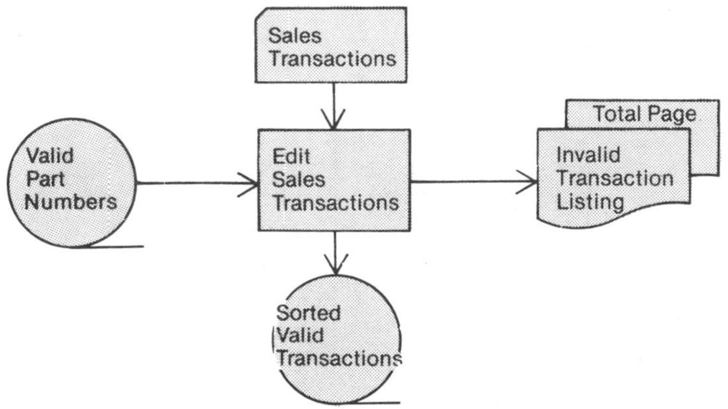
Sales Transactions
Valid Part Numbers
Edit Sales Transactions
Total Page
Invalid Transaction Listing
Sorted Valid Transactions

Record layouts:

Valid part number record

Field Name	Part Number	Date of last price change	Unit Cost	Unit Price
Characteristics	X(5)	9(6)	9(4)V99	9(4)V99
Usage				
Position	1-5	6-11	12-17	18-23

Sales transaction

Field Name	Update Code	Part No.	Tran Type	Customer Order No.	Order Date (mo/day/yr)	Branch No.	Salespers No.	Customer No.	Quantity	Unused
Characteristics	C	X(5)	1	X(10)	X(6)	X(2)	X(3)	X(5)	9(3)	X(6)
Usage										
Position	1	2-6	7	8-17	18-23	24-25	26-28	29-33	34-36	37-42

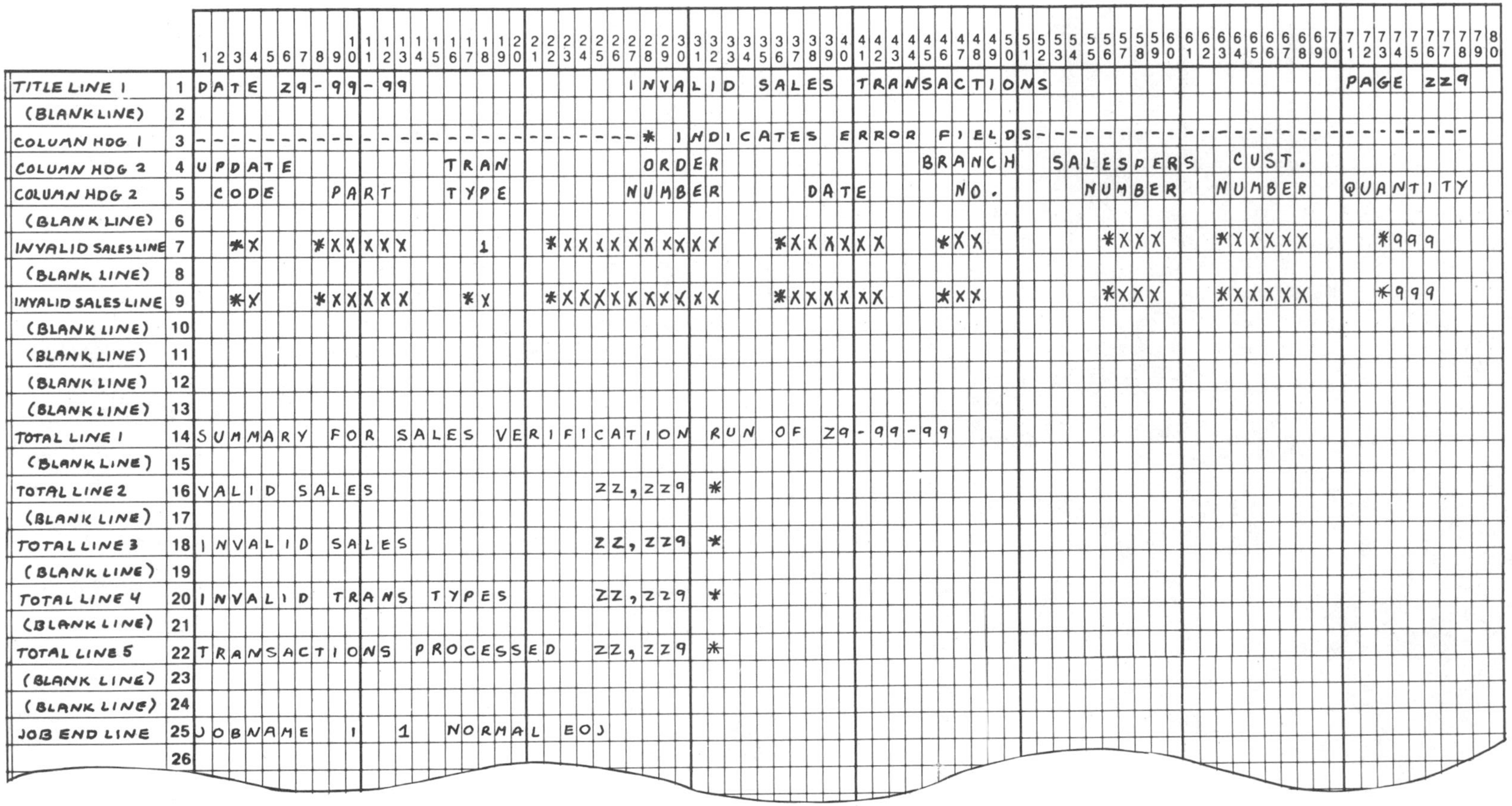
TITLE LINE 1 | 1 | DATE Z9-99-99 INVALID SALES TRANSACTIONS PAGE ZZ9
(BLANK LINE) | 2
COLUMN HDG 1 | 3 | ---------------------------* INDICATES ERROR FIELDS---------------------------
COLUMN HDG 2 | 4 | UPDATE TRAN ORDER BRANCH SALESPERS CUST.
COLUMN HDG 2 | 5 | CODE PART TYPE NUMBER DATE NO. NUMBER NUMBER QUANTITY
(BLANK LINE) | 6
INVALID SALES LINE | 7 | *X *XXXXX 1 *XXXXXXXXXX *XXXXXX *XX *XXX *XXXXX *999
(BLANK LINE) | 8
INVALID SALES LINE | 9 | *X *XXXXX *X *XXXXXXXXXX *XXXXXX *XX *XXX *XXXXX *999
(BLANK LINE) | 10
(BLANK LINE) | 11
(BLANK LINE) | 12
(BLANK LINE) | 13
TOTAL LINE 1 | 14 | SUMMARY FOR SALES VERIFICATION RUN OF Z9-99-99
(BLANK LINE) | 15
TOTAL LINE 2 | 16 | VALID SALES ZZ,ZZ9 *
(BLANK LINE) | 17
TOTAL LINE 3 | 18 | INVALID SALES ZZ,ZZ9 *
(BLANK LINE) | 19
TOTAL LINE 4 | 20 | INVALID TRANS TYPES ZZ,ZZ9 *
(BLANK LINE) | 21
TOTAL LINE 5 | 22 | TRANSACTIONS PROCESSED ZZ,ZZ9 *
(BLANK LINE) | 23
(BLANK LINE) | 24
JOB END LINE | 25 | JOBNAME 1 1 NORMAL EOJ
26

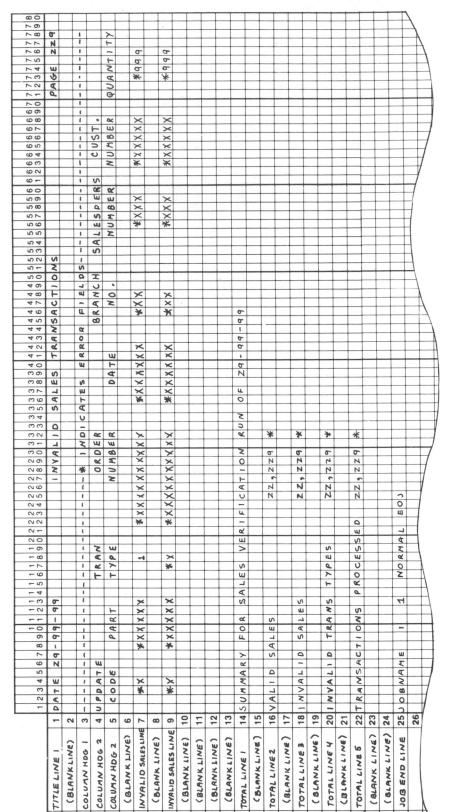

Figure 11–11
Specifications for the edit program (part 2 of 2)

Narrative:

1. Detailed editing specifications for the sales transactions will be developed later on. However, the update code must be C (for change) and the transaction type must be 1 (for sale). Also, the part number in each transaction must be matched against the valid part numbers in the valid part-number file. If no match is found, the part number will be considered invalid.
2. The valid part-number file has a maximum of 100 records in it. These are in order of transaction frequency; the first part number has the most activity and the last number has the least.
3. The output listing must be printed in the same order that the transactions are read.
4. The totals for this program are to be printed on a separate output page.
5. The sorted output file is to be sequenced by (1) part number in ascending order, (2) order date in year-month-day ascending order, (3) customer number in ascending order, and (4) quantity in descending order.

2. (Objective 2) Figure 11–12 gives the specifications for a file-maintenance program. It uses the file of valid sales transactions created in problem 1 and a file of addition and deletion records to update the master file.
   a. Design a VTOC for this program. (Use the VTOC for the update program in Figure 10–22 as a guide for designing the updating portion of this program.)
   b. Code the SELECT statement, SD statement, and record description for the merge work file. Then, using the VTOC in Figure 11–15, code modules 000, 300, 410, and the exit module. Do not use the INTO option of the RETURN statement. (You'd have to check the update code before moving the merge record into the proper working-storage field.) Add one to a field named TOTAL–TRANS–PROCESSED for each transaction that's returned. When you reach the end of the transactions, move Y to MERGE–EOF–SW.

Solutions

1. a. Figure 11–13 is an acceptable solution.
   b. You will have to code a SELECT statement that's acceptable on your system. Otherwise, Figure 11–14 is an acceptable solution. Notice that six fields must be described in the sort record description so they can be used as key fields in the SORT statement in module 000. Also note that the SORT statement uses a GIVING clause; there's no output procedure in this program, so module 600 is a dummy module.
2. a. Figure 11–15 is an acceptable solution.
   b. You will have to code a SELECT statement that's acceptable on your system. Otherwise, Figure 11–16 is an acceptable solution. You can see that the merge feature has the same elements as the sort feature: the merge file requires SELECT and SD statements; the merge record description includes the key field, MR–PART–NO; the MERGE statement merges VALID–SALES–TRANS and ADDITION–DELETION–TRANS in order by MR–PART–NO and then processes the merged file in an output procedure named 300–O–UPDATE–INVENTORY–FILE; the output procedure must be a section, so the rest of the program should be a section, too; module 300 requires a GO TO statement to branch to the end of the output procedure; and an exit paragraph allows the program to return to module 000.

Figure 11–12
Specifications for the update program (part 1 of 2)

System flowchart:

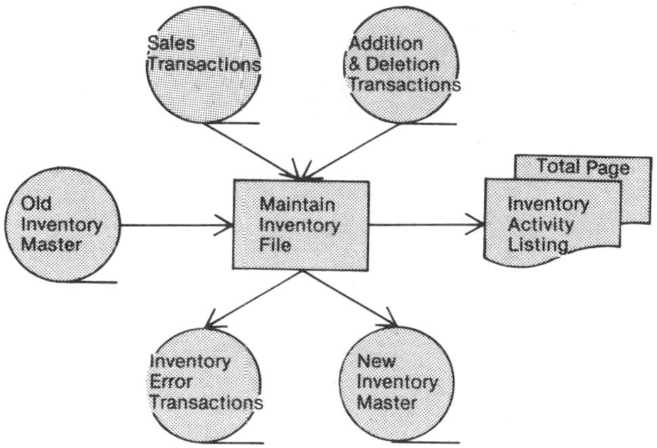

Sales Transactions
Addition & Deletion Transactions
Old Inventory Master
Maintain Inventory File
Total Page
Inventory Activity Listing
Inventory Error Transactions
New Inventory Master

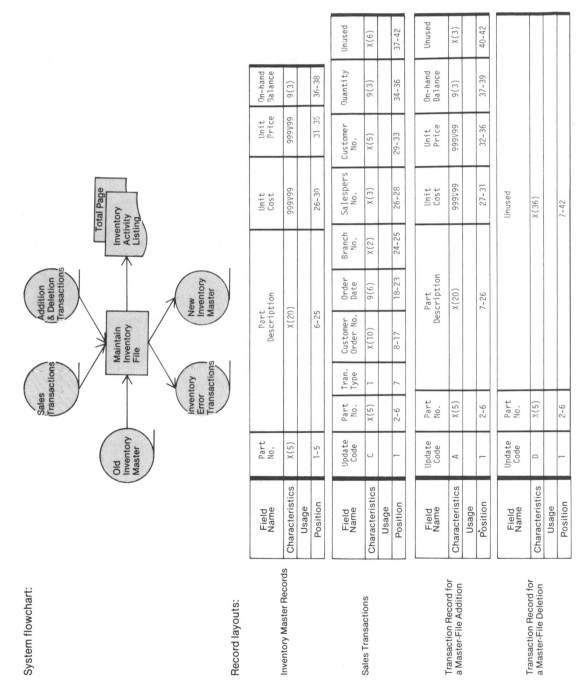

Record layouts:

Inventory Master Records

Field Name	Part No.	Part Description	Unit Cost	Unit Price	On-hand Balance
Characteristics	X(5)	X(20)	999V99	999V99	9(3)
Usage					
Position	1-5	6-25	26-30	31-35	36-38

Sales Transactions

Field Name	Update Code	Part No.	Tran. Type	Customer Order No.	Order Date	Branch No.	Salespers No.	Customer No.	Quantity	Unused
Characteristics	C	X(5)	1	X(10)	9(6)	X(2)	X(3)	X(5)	9(3)	X(6)
Usage										
Position	1	2-6	7	8-17	18-23	24-25	26-28	29-33	34-36	37-42

Transaction Record for a Master-File Addition

Field Name	Update Code	Part No.	Part Description	Unit Cost	Unit Price	On-hand Balance	Unused
Characteristics	A	X(5)	X(20)	999V99	999V99	9(3)	X(3)
Usage							
Position	1	2-6	7-26	27-31	32-36	37-39	40-42

Transaction Record for a Master-File Deletion

Field Name	Update Code	Part No.	Unused
Characteristics	D	X(5)	X(36)
Usage			
Position	1	2-6	7-42

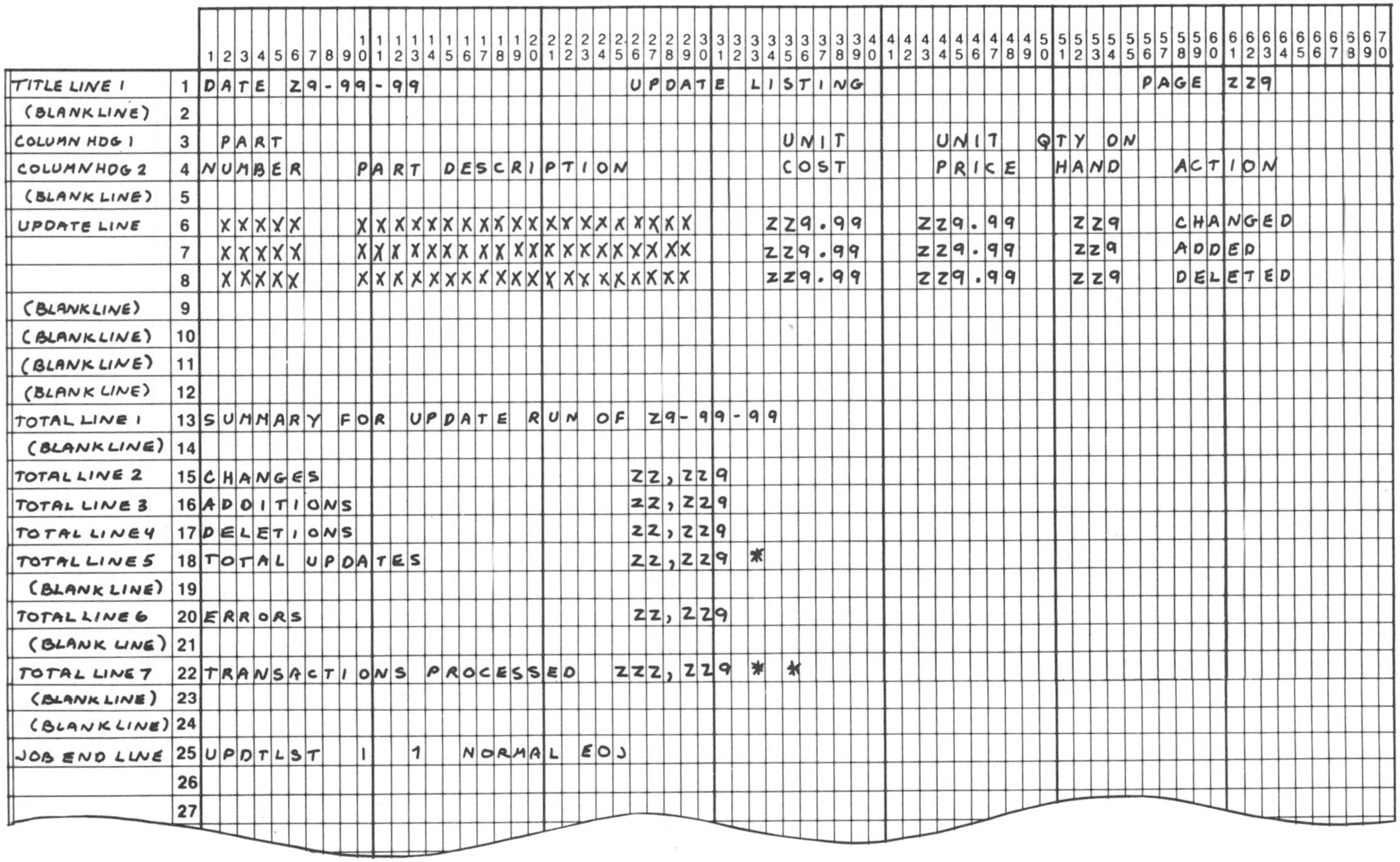
TITLE LINE 1
(BLANK LINE)
COLUMN HDG 1
COLUMN HDG 2
(BLANK LINE)
UPDATE LINE
(BLANKLINE)
(BLANKLINE)
(BLANKLINE)
(BLANK LINE)
TOTAL LINE 1
(BLANKLINE)
TOTAL LINE 2
TOTAL LINE 3
TOTAL LINE 4
TOTAL LINE 5
(BLANK LINE)
TOTAL LINE 6
(BLANK LINE)
TOTAL LINE 7
(BLANK LINE)
(BLANK LINE)
JOB END LINE
DATE Z9-99-99 UPDATE LISTING PAGE ZZ9
PART UNIT UNIT QTY ON
NUMBER PART DESCRIPTION COST PRICE HAND ACTION
XXXXX XXXXXXXXXXXXXXXXXXXX ZZ9.99 ZZ9.99 ZZ9 CHANGED
XXXXX XXXXXXXXXXXXXXXXXXXX ZZ9.99 ZZ9.99 ZZ9 ADDED
XXXXX XXXXXXXXXXXXXXXXXXXX ZZ9.99 ZZ9.99 ZZ9 DELETED
SUMMARY FOR UPDATE RUN OF Z9-99-99
CHANGES ZZ,ZZ9
ADDITIONS ZZ,ZZ9
DELETIONS ZZ,ZZ9
TOTAL UPDATES ZZ,ZZ9 *
ERRORS ZZ,ZZ9
TRANSACTIONS PROCESSED ZZZ,ZZ9 * *
UPDTLST 1 1 NORMAL EOJ

Figure 11–12
Specifications for the update program (part 2 of 2)

Narrative:

1. Use the sales, addition, and deletion transactions to update the master records. There may be none, one, or several transactions for each master. The transaction files and master file are all in ascending part-number sequence.
2. The amount in the quantity field of a sales transaction should be subtracted from the on-hand balance in the corresponding master record.
3. Print an update report with one line for each valid transaction record as shown in the print chart. The totals for the program are to be printed on a separate output page.
4. Write a record on the error if an unmatched transaction is detected. The error record should have the same format as the transaction record.

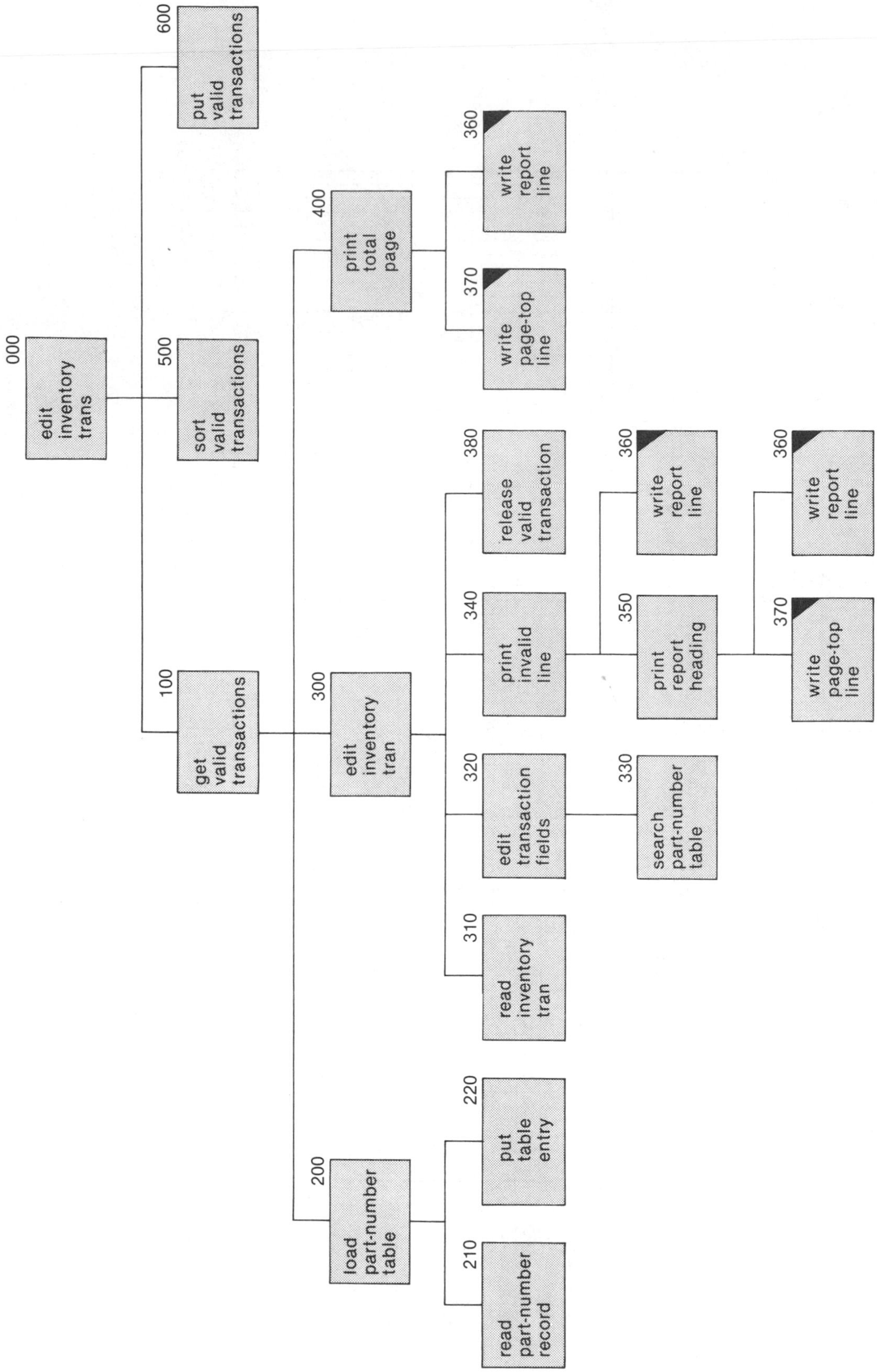
000
edit inventory trans
100
get valid transactions
500
sort valid transactions
600
put valid transactions
200
load part-number table
210
read part-number record
220
put table entry
300
edit inventory tran
310
read inventory tran
320
edit transaction fields
330
search part-number table
340
print invalid line
350
print report heading
370
write page-top line
360
write report line
360
write report line
380
release valid transaction
400
print total page
370
write page-top line
360
write report line

Figure 11–13
VTOC for the edit program

The SD statement and sort record description:

```
 SD  SORT-FILE
     RECORD CONTAINS 42 CHARACTERS.
*
 01  SORT-RECORD.
     05  FILLER         PIC X.
     05  SR-PART-NO     PIC X(5).
     05  FILLER         PIC X(11).
     05  SR-MONTH       PIC X(2).
     05  SR-DAY         PIC X(2).
     05  SR-YEAR        PIC X(2).
     05  FILLER         PIC X(5).
     05  SR-CUST-NO     PIC X(5).
     05  SR-QUANTITY    PIC 9(3).
     05  FILLER         PIC X(6).
*
```

Modules 000, 100, 380, 100-EXIT, 500, and 600:

```
 000-C-EDIT-INVENTORY-TRANS SECTION.
*
 000-EDIT-INVENTORY-TRANS.
     OPEN INPUT  SALES-TRANSACTIONS
                 PART-NUMBER-FILE
          OUTPUT INVALID-TRAN-LISTING.
     SORT SORT-FILE
         ON ASCENDING KEY  SR-PART-NO
                           SR-YEAR
                           SR-MONTH
                           SR-DAY
                           SR-CUST-NO
            DESCENDING KEY SR-QUANTITY
         INPUT PROCEDURE IS 100-I-GET-VALID-TRANSACTIONS
         GIVING VALID-SALES-TRANS.
     CLOSE SALES-TRANSACTIONS
           PART-NUMBER-FILE
           INVALID-TRAN-LISTING.
     DISPLAY "SLSEDIT  I  1  NORMAL EOJ".
     STOP RUN.
*
 100-I-GET-VALID-TRANSACTIONS SECTION.
*
 100-GET-VALID-TRANSACTIONS.
     PERFORM 200-LOAD-PART-NUMBER-TABLE
         VARYING PN-TABLE-INDEX FROM 1 BY 1
         UNTIL PART-NUMBER-EOF.
     PERFORM 300-EDIT-INVENTORY-TRAN
         UNTIL INVENTORY-EOF.
     PERFORM 400-PRINT-TOTAL-PAGE.
     GO TO 100-EXIT.
     .
     .
 380-RELEASE-VALID-TRANSACTION.
     RELEASE SORT-RECORD FROM TRAN-RECORD.
     .
     .
 100-EXIT.
     EXIT.
*
*500-SORT-VALID-TRANSACTIONS.
*    DUMMY MODULE DONE BY SORT STATEMENT.
*
*600-PUT-VALID-TRANSACTIONS.
*    DUMMY MODULE DONE BY SORT STATEMENT.
```

Figure 11–14
Sort code for the edit program

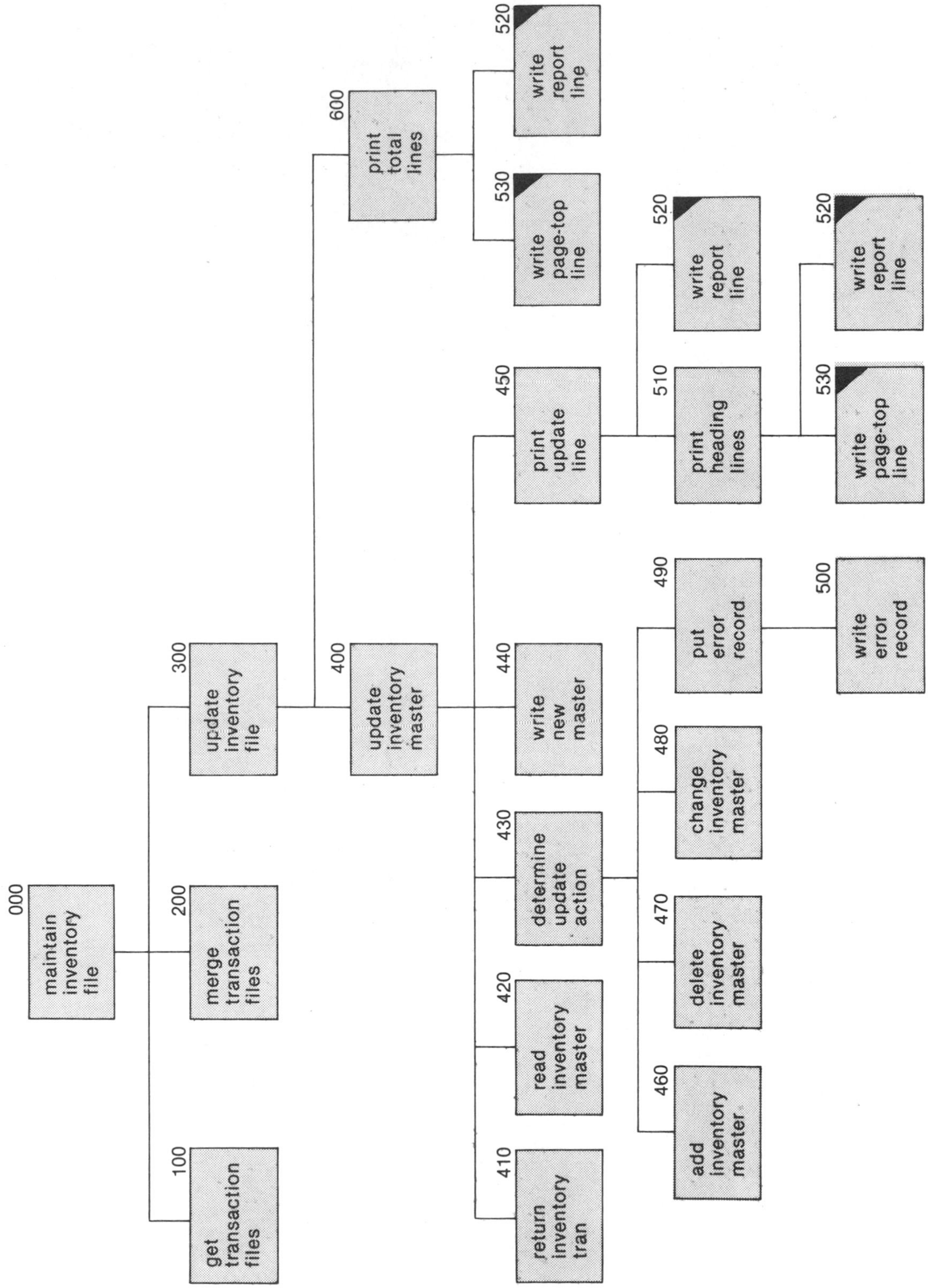
000
maintain inventory file
100
get transaction files
200
merge transaction files
300
update inventory file
400
update inventory master
600
print total lines
410
return inventory tran
420
read inventory master
430
determine update action
440
write new master
450
print update line
530
write page-top line
520
write report line
460
add inventory master
470
delete inventory master
480
change inventory master
490
put error record
510
print heading lines
520
write report line
500
write error record
530
write page-top line
520
write report line

Figure 11–15
VTOC for the update program

The SD statement and merge record description:

```
 SD  MERGE-FILE
     RECORD CONTAINS 42 CHARACTERS.
*
 01  MERGE-RECORD.
*
     05  MR-UPDATE-CODE      PIC X.
         88  SALE                    VALUE "C".
         88  ADDITION                VALUE "A".
         88  DELETION                VALUE "D".
     05  MR-PART-NO          PIC X(5).
     05  FILLER              PIC X(36).
```

The coding for modules 000, 300, 410, and 300-EXIT:

```
 000-C-MAINTAIN-INVENTORY-FILE SECTION.
*
 000-MAINTAIN-INVENTORY-FILE.
*
     OPEN INPUT  OLD-INVENTORY-MASTER
          OUTPUT NEW-INVENTORY-MASTER
                 INVENTORY-ACTIVITY-LISTING
                 INVENTORY-ERROR-TRANS.
     MERGE MERGE-FILE
         ON ASCENDING KEY MR-PART-NO
         USING VALID-SALES-TRANS
               ADDITION-DELETION-TRANS
         OUTPUT PROCEDURE IS 300-O-UPDATE-INVENTORY-FILE.
     CLOSE OLD-INVENTORY-MASTER
           NEW-INVENTORY-MASTER
           INVENTORY-ACTIVITY-LISTING
           INVENTORY-ERROR-TRANS.
     DISPLAY "SEQUPDT  I  1  NORMAL EOJ".
     STOP RUN.
*
     .
     .
*
 300-O-UPDATE-INVENTORY-FILE SECTION.
*
 300-UPDATE-INVENTORY-FILE.
*
     PERFORM 400-UPDATE-INVENTORY-MASTER
         UNTIL ALL-RECORDS-PROCESSED.
     PERFORM 600-PRINT-TOTAL-LINES.
     GO TO 300-EXIT.
*
     .
     .
*
 410-RETURN-INVENTORY-TRAN.
*
     RETURN MERGE-FILE
         AT END
             MOVE "Y" TO MERGE-EOF-SW.
     IF NOT MERGE-EOF
         ADD 1 TO TOTAL-TRANS-PROCESSED.
*
     .
     .
*
 300-EXIT.
*
     EXIT.
```

Figure 11–16
Merge code for the update program

Topic 2 Issue: The 198X ANSI Standards

Orientation

As discussed in chapter 3, a new ANSI COBOL standard is expected sometime during the 1980s. Since it has not yet appeared, it is being referred to as the 198X standard, or just the 8X standard. Even if the standards are released this year, your programming knowledge will not be immediately outdated. It will take time for new compilers to be developed, accepted, and installed.

Actually, IBM has released a new COBOL compiler that supports the 198X standards. When released, it was controlled to run only on a selected system, but it is expected to be available on all IBM mainframes eventually.

Whenever most textbooks show the programming formats, what is shown is a subset of the total ANSI standards for COBOL. There are several reasons for not showing all of the facilities that have been part of the formal COBOL standards. One, the complete set is rather large and often specialized, and as a result is not useful to the student in the typical one- or two-semester course. Many of the language facilities that are concerned with data base handling will not appear in beginning COBOL books, even in the second-semester texts. Secondly, the majority of compilers developed have not implemented the exact ANSI standard. Most compilers do not include some of the standards which the developers felt were only marginally useful, yet do include special extensions of the language which were felt to be very useful even though not in the standard. Two simple examples of extensions that are useful are the ability to abbreviate IDENTIFICATION as ID and the COMP–3 usage.

This topic is not intended to be an exhaustive discussion of the proposed standard. Rather, the intention is to introduce you to what will very likely become the standard.

A List of the Proposed Facilities

To introduce this discussion on the 198X standard, a list of the more important reserved words which will be new to COBOL is given.

New reserved words

```
ALPHABET                 FALSE
ALPHABETIC-LOWER         GLOBAL
ALPHABETIC-UPPER         INITIALIZE
ALPHANUMERIC             NUMERIC-EDITED
ALPHANUMERIC-EDITED      ORDER
ANY                      OTHER
BINARY                   PACKED-DECIMAL
CLASS                    PADDING
COMMON                   PURGE
CONTENT                  REFERENCE
CONTINUE                 STANDARD-2
CONVERTING               TEST
DAY-OF-WEEK              THEN
EVALUATE                 TRUE
EXTERNAL
```

Structured delimiters

The sentence delimiter, the period, is also the symbol for ending a conditional statement. It is difficult and often impossible to construct sentences from several successive conditional statements. The following new reserved words are intended to address this problem.

```
END-ADD
END-CALL
END-COMPUTE
END-DIVIDE
END-EVALUATE
END-IF
END-MULTIPLY
END-PERFORM
END-READ
END-RETURN
END-SEARCH
END-SUBTRACT
END-WRITE
```

If you have had any experience with non–COBOL pseudocode, with other so-called structured languages such as Pascal, and with structured programming as taught for those languages, you can see that this list of END–... statements coincides with newer approaches to coding. The delimiters listed here are those which are related to previous discussions in this text.

Other new facilities

Action paths

Several of the old standard statements allow action to be taken when a specific situation occurs, but have no action path if it does not occur. The following allow action when a condition has not occured:

```
NOT ON SIZE ERROR
NOT AT END
NOT END-OF-PAGE
NOT ON OVERFLOW
```

Character set

Lowercase letters may be used in alphanumeric constants. This is due to the flexibility of new printers, especially the dot matrix, more than inherent attributes of COBOL. The comma, semicolon, and space may be used interchangeably, but remember that only the space is recommended.

Optional entries

```
ENVIRONMENT DIVISION and all its sections
LABEL RECORDS (STANDARD is assumed)
FILLER
PROCEDURE DIVISION
EXIT PROGRAM(in subprograms)
```

STOP RUN

The STOP RUN statement will cause all open files to be closed automatically.

Discussion

Not all the elements that will be available in the new standard have been presented. For one thing, the standard has not been finalized, and secondly, it is not appropriate to discuss all facets of the language in a book like this. However, the intent was to alert you to some of the more important new parts of the language.

Some people feel that the new standards will have a very positive effect on program quality and programmer productivity. Others feel that the way in which the language is used has more positive effect than the new language elements. COBOL is a language with a very rich command set and has most of the facilities necessary for quality work. The text has made a strong point that well-designed COBOL programs that use carefully structured organization and style will promote program quality and programmer productivity more than any inherent parts of the language.

COBOL programs of poor quality have been written since the language was first used. Unfortunately, COBOL programs of poor quality are still being written. But then, programs of poor quality are being written in FORTRAN, in BASIC, in PL/1, in PASCAL, and in any language that you can name. Programs of poor quality will continue to be written until the language can itself force the programmer to write well-organized, understandable code, using meaningful data and procedure names. The new standards will not make that much of a change unless programmers make a commitment to design and write programs in a style that has clarity of the code as its goal. All that the new standards can do is to provide a few more tools to help the programmer who already knows how or is willing to learn to design and write a high-quality program. That has been one of the main goals of this book and it is felt that students who have learned these lessons will be able to judge which of the new tools will promote program quality, and they will be able to use those tools in the most effective manner.

Appendix A Problem Programs

COBOL Program Problem Assignments by Chapter

Number	Description	Part	Chapter	Topic
1	Name and address listing	II	3	1
2	Receipt register	II	4	1
3	Loan problem	II	4	1
4	Group-printed sales report	III	5	4
5	Coin problem	III	6	3
6	Four-up labels	III	6	3
7	Two-level sales report	III	7	1
8	Three-level sales report	III	7	2
9	Input validation	IV	8	1
10	Inventory location listing	IV	9	1
11	One-level table in grading program	IV	9	2
12	Tax table look-up	IV	9	3
13	Subprogram state look-up	IV	9	3
14	Shipping-rate look-up with a two-level table	IV	9	4
15	Two-level table accumulation program	IV	9	4
16	Three-level classification table	IV	9	4
17	Payroll checks with subprogram	IV	9	4
18	Subprogram for FIT calculation	IV	9	4
19	Subprogram for FICA calculation	IV	9	4
20	Creating a student semester file	IV	10	3
21	Maintaining the student semester file	IV	10	3
22a	Sorting grade records and updating the student semester file	IV	11	1
22b	Printing a grade-point-average listing	IV	11	1

1. Name and address listing

Write a program that lists the contents of a file of name and address records. Count the number of records listed, and print the count at the end of the listing. You do not need to print headings or to worry about page overflow on this program.

Output

The following is the printer format for this problem. The headings in parentheses are just to indicate the contents of the columns and are not intended to be printed.

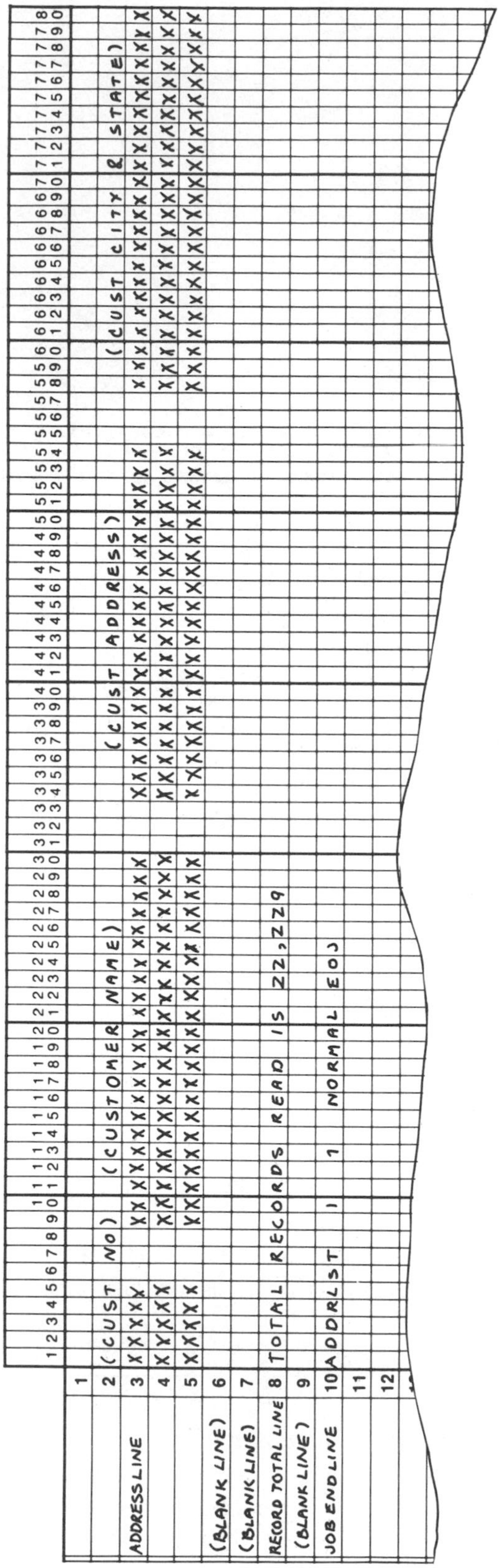
ADDRESS LINE
(BLANK LINE)
(BLANK LINE)
RECORD TOTAL LINE
(BLANK LINE)
JOB END LINE
(CUST NO)
(CUSTOMER NAME)
(CUST ADDRESS)
(CUST CITY & STATE)
TOTAL RECORDS READ IS ZZ,ZZ9
ADDRLST 1 NORMAL EOJ

PROBLEM 1
Name and address listing

Input

The following is the description of the input record for this program. Note that the program does not require you to use all of the fields.

Field Name	Record Code	Branch	Salespers No.	Customer No.	State No.	City No.	Name	Address	City, State
Characteristics	1	X	XX	X(5)	XX	XXX	X(22)	X(21)	X(23)
Usage									
Position	1	2	3-4	5-9	10-11	12-14	15-36	37-57	58-80

VTOC

If you have not yet learned how to design a structured program, your instructor will supply you with a VTOC for this program.

Test Data

POS. 1	2	3-4	5-9	15-36	37-57	58-80
1	1	12	00111	A & A DISTRIBUTING	148 N. MAPLE AVE.	CHICAGO, ILL.
1	1	12	00189	GOLDEN STATE RUGS	1441 W. CLINTIN	DEARBORN, CA.
1	1	12	03217	PACIFIC MFG. CO.	4575 PINE AVE.	DENTON, CA.
1	1	12	23298	B & B FENCE CO.	1553 E. HOME AVE.	FRESNO, CA.
1	1	17	00512	FEDERAL SUPPLY CO.	177 UNIVERSITY	DEARBORN, CA.
1	1	17	05394	WILSON'S HARDWARE	1447 WALNUT ST.	FRESNO, CA.
1	1	19	04215	PICKER PARTS CO.	1530 N. WEST AVE.	MILWAUKEE, WISC.
1	1	19	67843	NESBITT MFG.	2110 VLIET ST.	OMAHA, NEBR.
1	1	19	68111	A-1 SUPPLY	1177 VINE ST.	BAKERSFIELD, CA.
1	1	19	68141	CONSOLIDATED MFG.	WILSON & BROWN ST.	NEW HAVEN, CONN.
1	1	19	68197	A G WATERS CO.	1929 N. 49 ST.	CAMBRIDGE, MASS.
1	1	19	68217	INDEPENDENT PAPER CO.	311 SHERIDAN	MADISON, WISC.
1	2	28	00911	CLACK AND WILSON	1442 RIVER ROAD	MINNEAPOLIS, MINN.
1	2	28	01023	CODY BROS.	833 GLENVIEW ROAD	INDIANAPOLIS, IND.
1	2	36	00912	TOWNSLEY SUPPLY CO.	BOX 294	BALTIMORE, MD.
1	2	36	01199	VALLEY PUMP CO.	7173 BLACKSTONE	PALO ALTO, CA.
1	2	36	21377	JOHNSON AND RILEY	1735 VENTURE RD.	HAYWARD, CA.
1	2	36	21894	WEIL RADIATORS	2432 RAILROAD AVENUE	FONTAIN, CA.
1	2	36	77777	WESTCO MFG.	844 N. FULTON	GENOA, CA.
1	2	39	20032	PEERLESS MFG.	P.O. BOX 947	NUMIS, NEBR.
1	2	39	29879	WORTHINGTON & RYAN	1326 VAN NESS	IOWA CITY, IOWA
1	2	47	14212	ERICKSON MUSIC CO.	422 N. SHIELDS	RENO, NEV.
1	2	47	19876	EASTON LUMBER CO.	605 S. FRUIT	TAHOE CITY, CA.
1	2	47	28400	SUPREME SUPPLY INC.	4771 GRANT AVE.	TWILLEY, COLO.
1	3	72	00312	JONES HARDWARE	1869 HEDGES AVE.	DENTON, CA.
1	3	72	00928	CRAVER RENTALS	1560 MARKS AVE.	BAKERSFIELD, CA.
1	3	72	01148	BUSY BEAVER INC.	2730 BELMONT DRIVE	NEW HAVEN, CONN.
1	3	91	02117	WESTERN MFG.	1221 E. WISCONSIN	FONTAIN, CA.
1	3	91	94300	JOHN WARDS	911 FRUIT STREET	PALO ALTO, CA.
1	3	94	77650	NATIONAL INDUSTRIES	1023 FENCED LANE	NUMIS, NEBR.

2. Receipt register

Write a program to print a receipt register from a file whose records represent receipts to inventory. The records are in sequence by order number within vendor number. On the receipt register, the SHIPMENT BALANCE column is the result of subtracting quantity received from quantity ordered. If the result is negative, the literal OVER SHIPMENT should be printed in the REMARKS column. If the result is positive, print UNDER SHIPMENT in the REMARKS column. When the result is zero, nothing should be printed in the REMARKS column.

Output

The following is the printer format for this problem.

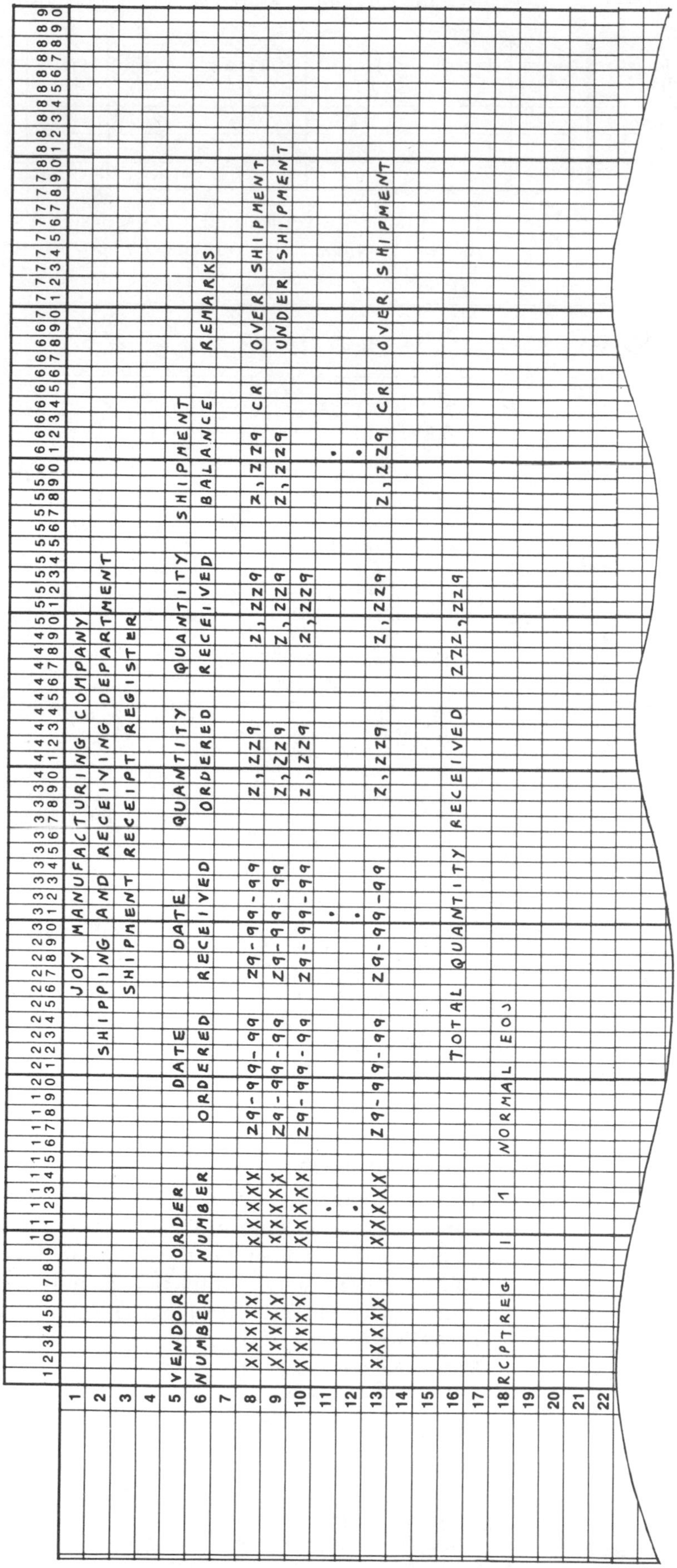
JOY MANUFACTURING COMPANY
SHIPPING AND RECEIVING DEPARTMENT
SHIPMENT RECEIPT REGISTER
VENDOR NUMBER
ORDER NUMBER
DATE ORDERED
DATE RECEIVED
QUANTITY ORDERED
QUANTITY RECEIVED
SHIPMENT BALANCE
REMARKS
XXXXX XXXXX Z9-99-99 Z9-99-99 Z,ZZ9 Z,ZZ9 Z,ZZ9 CR OVER SHIPMENT
XXXXX XXXXX Z9-99-99 Z9-99-99 Z,ZZ9 Z,ZZ9 Z,ZZ9 UNDER SHIPMENT
XXXXX XXXXX Z9-99-99 Z9-99-99 Z,ZZ9 Z,ZZ9
XXXXX XXXXX Z9-99-99 Z9-99-99 Z,ZZ9 Z,ZZ9 Z,ZZ9 CR OVER SHIPMENT
TOTAL QUANTITY RECEIVED ZZZ,ZZ9
RCPTREG I 1 NORMAL EOJ

Input

The following is the description of the input record for this program.

Field Name	Record Code	Unused	Vendor No.	Unused	Order No.	Date Recv'd. Mo/Day/Yr	Quantity Received	Item Description	Item No.	Unit Cost	Unit Price	Date Ordered Mo/Day/Yr	Quantity Ordered	Unused
Characteristics	3	X(3)	X(5)	X(5)	X(5)	9(6)	9(4)	X(20)	X(5)	999V99	999V99	9(6)	9(4)	X(6)
Usage														
Position	1	2-4	5-9	10-14	15-19	20-25	26-29	30-49	50-54	55-59	60-64	65-70	71-74	75-80

VTOC

If you have not yet learned how to design a structured program, your instructor will supply you with a VTOC for this program.

Test Data

POS. 1	5-9	15-19	20-25	26-29	30-49	50-54	55-59	60-64	65-70	71-74
3	01408	22771	041779	0075	ITEM B3	13909	00636	00750	021179	0075
3	01408	36499	041779	0300	PRODUCT D	47821	01000	01295	040779	0750
3	01408	36499	042179	0450	PRODUCT D	47821	01000	01295	040779	0750
3	01408	31004	041879	0075	PRODUCT F	48771	02015	02555	031079	0100
3	60019	21433	041779	0300	PRODUCT I	58911	00750	01000	011979	0300
3	60019	34988	041879	0012	ITEM L1	70019	42550	54995	033179	0010
3	64009	36509	042179	0500	PRODUCT N	92780	00298	00349	040779	0500
3	64009	22870	041979	0100	PRODUCT O	92811	03875	04550	021179	0075
3	78212	33440	041779	1000	PRODUCT P	93404	00031	00049	032479	1000
3	78212	36909	041979	0025	PRODUCT Q	94777	23177	28999	040779	0030
3	78212	21009	042079	0250	PRODUCT R	94779	00636	00750	020979	0250

3. Loan problem

When you make a monthly payment on a loan, a certain amount of the payment is applied toward paying back the principal (the amount you borrowed) and a certain amount is applied toward paying the yearly interest on the unpaid balance (the amount not yet paid back). The portion that goes toward interest is calculated by multiplying the unpaid balance by the interest rate and dividing by 12 (assuming that you are making monthly payments). The remainder of the payment is then applied toward the principal, thus reducing the unpaid balance.

Write a program that calculates how many loan payments must be made before the principal being paid is greater than the interest being paid. The input to the program is a set of records representing a series of loans made by a loan company. The output is a listing, one line per record, that gives the amount of the loan, the interest rate, the monthly payment, and the number of the payment in which the principal paid is greater than the interest paid.

Output

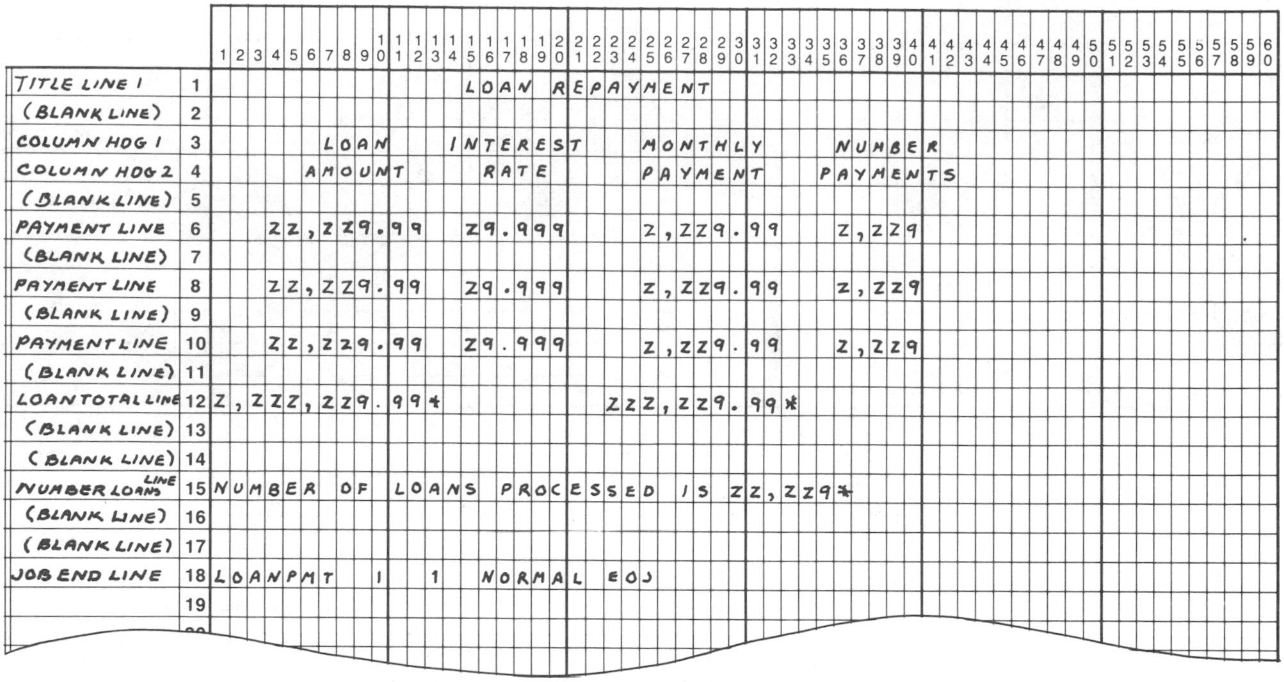
TITLE LINE 1 | 1 | LOAN REPAYMENT
(BLANK LINE) | 2
COLUMN HDG 1 | 3 | LOAN INTEREST MONTHLY NUMBER
COLUMN HDG 2 | 4 | AMOUNT RATE PAYMENT PAYMENTS
(BLANK LINE) | 5
PAYMENT LINE | 6 | ZZ,ZZ9.99 Z9.999 Z,ZZ9.99 Z,ZZ9
(BLANK LINE) | 7
PAYMENT LINE | 8 | ZZ,ZZ9.99 Z9.999 Z,ZZ9.99 Z,ZZ9
(BLANK LINE) | 9
PAYMENT LINE | 10 | ZZ,ZZ9.99 Z9.999 Z,ZZ9.99 Z,ZZ9
(BLANK LINE) | 11
LOAN TOTAL LINE | 12 | Z,ZZZ,ZZ9.99* ZZZ,ZZ9.99*
(BLANK LINE) | 13
(BLANK LINE) | 14
NUMBER LOANS LINE | 15 | NUMBER OF LOANS PROCESSED IS ZZ,ZZ9*
(BLANK LINE) | 16
(BLANK LINE) | 17
JOB END LINE | 18 | LOANPMT 1 1 NORMAL EOJ
19

Input

Field Name	Amount of Loan	Interest Rate	Monthly Payment	Unused
Characteristics	99999V99	99V999	9999V99	X(62)
Usage				
Position	1-7	8-12	13-18	19-80

Test Data

Pos.	1-7	8-12	13-18
	2000000	08000	015000
	2000000	12000	025000
	2000000	14500	025000
	2000000	16250	050000
	2000000	18000	050000
	2000000	21000	050000
	5000000	06250	030000
	5000000	12000	060000
	5000000	18500	110000

4. Group-printed sales report

Write a program to print a summary report from a file of invoice records. The input records are in sequence by customer number, and there will be one or more records for each customer. On the report, however, only one line should print for each customer. That line should show the total amount invoiced for that customer.

Output

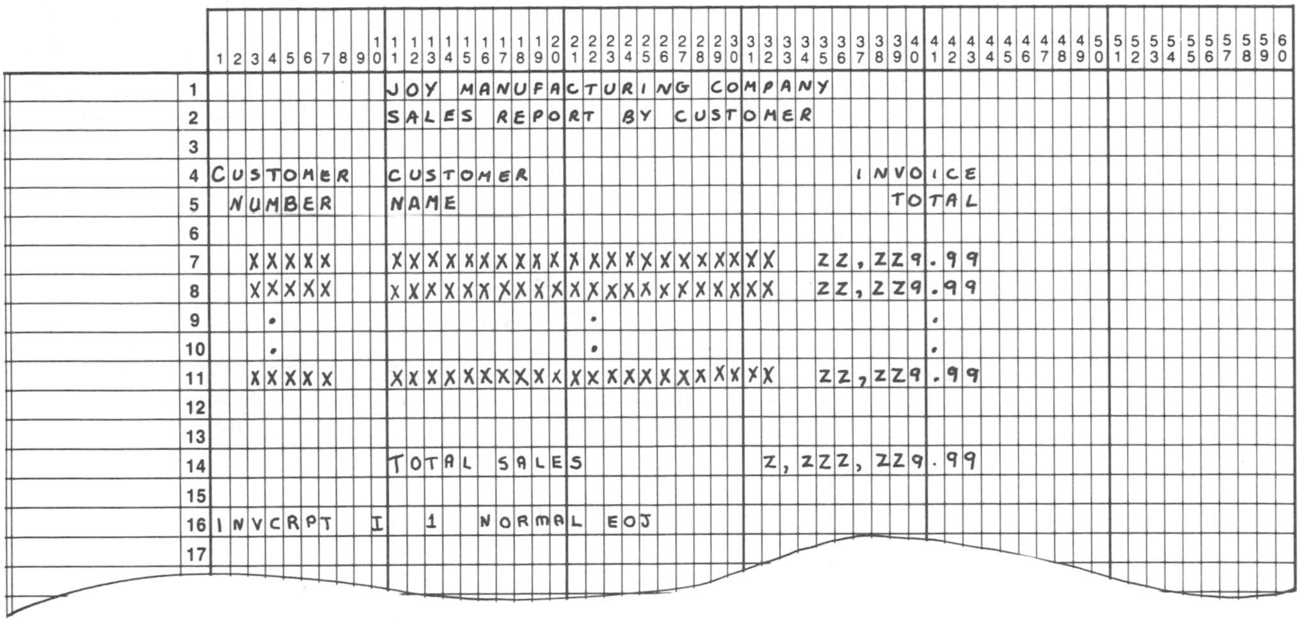
JOY MANUFACTURING COMPANY
SALES REPORT BY CUSTOMER
CUSTOMER
NUMBER
CUSTOMER
NAME
INVOICE
TOTAL
XXXXX
XXXXXXXXXXXXXXXXXXXXXX
ZZ,ZZ9.99
TOTAL SALES
Z,ZZZ,ZZ9.99
INVCRPT I 1 NORMAL EOJ

Input

Field Name	Record Code	Branch	Slspers. No.	Cust. No.	State No.	City No.	Invoice No.	Invoice Date Mo/Day/Yr	Cust. Name	Invoice Amount	Unused
Characteristics	5	X	XX	X(5)	XX	XXX	X(5)	9(6)	X(22)	99999V99	X(26)
Usage											
Position	1	2	3-4	5-9	10-11	12-14	15-19	20-25	26-47	48-54	55-80

Test Data

POS. 1	2	3-4	5-9	10-11	12-14	15-19	20-25	26-47	48-54
5	1	12	00111	31	123	70012	050579	A & A DISTRIBUTING	0031200
5	1	12	00111	31	123	70124	050779	A & A DISTRIBUTING	0432005
5	1	12	00111	31	123	73820	051979	A & A DISTRIBUTING	0001295
5	1	17	00512	48	047	62741	041279	FEDERAL SUPPLY CO.	0048541
5	1	17	00512	48	047	63920	041879	FEDERAL SUPPLY CO.	0066666
5	1	17	00512	48	047	70420	050179	FEDERAL SUPPLY CO.	0077430
5	1	17	00512	48	047	72391	051779	FEDERAL SUPPLY CO.	0920032
5	2	28	00911	29	090	21111	122378	CLACK AND WILSON	0006780
5	2	28	01023	33	039	41782	021279	CODY BROS.	0004215
5	2	28	01023	33	039	50143	030579	CODY BROS.	0023299
5	2	28	01023	33	039	61111	041879	CODY BROS.	0018900
5	3	72	01148	06	038	75420	051279	BUSY BEAVER INC.	0041200
5	3	94	02117	48	068	71112	050579	WESTERN MFG.	0049800
5	1	12	03217	48	022	31420	032179	PACIFIC MFG. CO.	0021170
5	1	12	03217	48	022	47859	040379	PACIFIC MFG. CO.	0009500
5	1	19	04215	30	118	72984	051279	PICKER PARTS CO.	0114800
5	1	19	04215	30	118	73420	051979	PICKER PARTS CO.	0007765
5	1	17	05394	48	038	76841	052979	WILSON'S HARDWARE	0031200
5	2	36	21377	48	097	67840	053179	JOHNSON AND RILEY	0283700
5	1	12	23298	48	038	72480	051579	B & B FENCE CO.	0277430
5	1	19	68141	06	038	71005	050579	CONSOLIDATED MFG.	0028400
5	1	19	68217	30	079	77990	052979	INDEPENDENT PAPER CO.	4028400
5	3	94	77650	35	002	72100	050779	NATIONAL INDUSTRIES	0020000
5	3	94	77650	35	002	72314	050979	NATIONAL INDUSTRIES	0001295

5. Coin problem

Write a program that calculates the number of different coin combinations that make up one dollar. For example, two half-dollars are one combination, one half-dollar and two quarters are another combination, and so forth. The output should be the combination number and the number of each type of coin involved.

6. Four-up labels

Write a program to print three-line mailing labels from a file of name and address records. To increase the speed at which the labels can be printed, blank label sheets are ordered which have four blank labels across the sheet. There are 30 print positions from the left margin of one label to the left margin of the next label. The program should space three lines between the bottom line of one label and the top line of the next.

Output

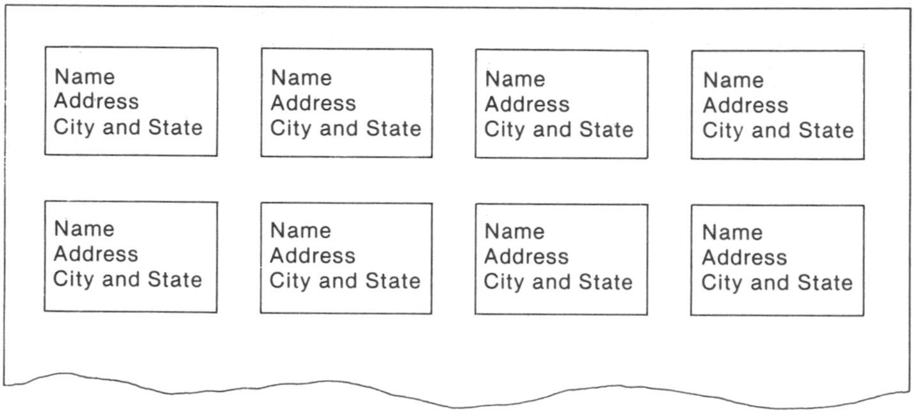
Name
Address
City and State
Name
Address
City and State
Name
Address
City and State
Name
Address
City and State
Name
Address
City and State
Name
Address
City and State
Name
Address
City and State
Name
Address
City and State

Input Use the same format as problem number 1.

Test data Use the same data used for problem 1.

7. Two-level sales report

Write a program that prepares a sales by salesperson report from a file of sales records. The sales file is preceded by a data record that gives the last day of the month for which the report is being prepared. The file is in sequence by customer number within salesperson number, and there may be more than one record for each customer. The sales report should have one summary line for each customer and one total line for each salesperson (indicated by one asterisk). Pay careful attention to the group indication for the salesperson number. When there are no more input records, a total of all sales amounts is to be printed, followed by two asterisks.

Output

```
 1        COLLEGE BOOK COMPANY
 2        MONTHLY SALES REPORT
 3
 4  FOR THE MONTH ENDING 29/99/99
 5
 6 SALESPERS  CUSTOMER        SALES
 7  NUMBER     NUMBER        AMOUNT
 8
 9    XXX       XXXXX    ZZ,ZZ9.99
10              XXXXX    ZZ,ZZ9.99
11     .          .          .
12     .          .          .
13              XXXXX    ZZ,ZZ9.99
14                      ZZZ,ZZ9.99  *  (SALESPERSON TOTAL LINE)
15
16    XXX       XXXXX    ZZ,ZZ9.99
17              XXXXX    ZZ,ZZ9.99
18                      ZZZ,ZZ9.99  *
19
20                    Z,ZZZ,ZZ9.99  ** (GRAND TOTAL LINE)
21
22 SLSRPT   1   1  NORMAL  EOJ
```

Input

Field Name	Record Code	Date Mo/Day/Yr	Unused
Characteristics	-	9(6)	X(73)
Usage			
Position	1	2-7	8-80

Field Name	Record Code	Salespers No.	Customer No.	Sales Amount	Unused
Characteristics	1	XXX	X(5)	99999V99	X(64)
Usage					
Position	1	2-4	5-9	10-16	17-80

Test Data

POS. 1	2-4	5-9	10-16	1	2-4	5-9	10-16
1	012	10155	0507272	1	101	13777	0590000
1	012	10155	0001020	1	101	14900	0711195
1	012	10155	0074321	1	101	23750	0001205
1	012	17722	0701155	1	101	23750	0194200
1	012	18805	0051100	1	101	58740	2750000
1	012	18805	0029995	1	101	58740	0014295
1	012	19722	0070799	1	101	81111	0660050
1	012	19722	0040350	1	295	11477	0942811
1	012	19722	0001945	1	295	12111	0705595
1	015	16555	1500095	1	295	12111	0004095
1	015	16555	0004500	1	312	23333	0311050
1	015	18212	1499011	1	312	23333	0077490
1	015	18212	0000435	1	312	66666	0050050
1	015	19944	0001095	1	312	66666	0143295

8. Three-level sales report

Write a program to prepare a report by customer within salesperson within sales branch. The input is a file of sales records that is in the specified sequence. There will be more than one record for each customer, and each of these records should be printed. Pay careful attention to group indication for each of the three control elements, since this is not a summary report. To obtain the sales amount for each sales record, you must multiply the unit price times the quantity.

Output

```
      MURACH WHOLESALE DISTRIBUTORS
     REPORT OF SALES BY BRANCH NO. X

BRANCH  SALESPERS  CUSTOMER        SALES
NUMBER   NUMBER     NUMBER        AMOUNT

   X       XX        XXXXX     ZZ,ZZ9.99
                               ZZ,ZZ9.99
                              ZZZ,ZZ9.99 *

                     XXXXX     ZZ,ZZ9.99
                               ZZ,ZZ9.99
                               ZZ,ZZ9.99
                              ZZZ,ZZ9.99 *

     ** TOTAL SALESPERS XX  Z,ZZZ,ZZ9.99 **

           XX        XXXXX     ZZ,ZZ9.99
                               ZZ,ZZ9.99
                              ZZZ,ZZ9.99 *

     ** TOTAL SALESPERS XX  Z,ZZZ,ZZ9.99 **


    *** TOTAL BRANCH    X  ZZ,ZZZ,ZZ9.99 ***

       <---(NOTE: ADVANCE TO NEW PAGE WHEN THE BRANCH CHANGES)
      MURACH WHOLESALE DISTRIBUTORS
     REPORT OF SALES BY BRANCH NO. X

BRANCH  SALESPERS  CUSTOMER        SALES
NUMBER   NUMBER     NUMBER        AMOUNT

   X       XX        XXXXX     ZZ,ZZ9.99
                               ZZ,ZZ9.99
                              ZZZ,ZZ9.99 *

     ** TOTAL SALESPERS XX  Z,ZZZ,ZZ9.99 **


    *** TOTAL BRANCH    X  ZZ,ZZZ,ZZ9.99 ***

       <--(NOTE: NEW PAGE)
         MURACH WHOLESALE DISTRIBUTORS
                REPORT OF SALES

   **** FINAL TOTAL       ZZZ,ZZZ,ZZ9.99 ****

BRSLSRP  I  1 NORMAL EOJ
```

Input

Field Name	Unused	Branch	Slspers. No.	Cust. No.	State No.	City No.	Ref. No.	Tran. Date Mo/Day/Yr	Quantity	Item Desc.	Item No.	Unit Price	Unit Cost	Unused
Characteristics	X	X	XX	X(5)	XX	XXX	X(5)	9(6)	9(4)	X(20)	X(5)	999V99	999V99	X(16)
Usage														
Position	1	2	3-4	5-9	10-11	12-14	15-19	20-25	26-29	30-49	50-54	55-59	60-64	65-80

Test Data

POS.	2	3-4	5-9	26-29	30-49	50-54	55-59	60-64
	1	12	00111	0001	PRODUCT A	00311	00200	00160
	1	12	00111	0010	PRODUCT C	41222	21995	19000
	1	12	00111	0100	PRODUCT D	47821	01295	01000
	1	12	00111	0010	PRODUCT E	48541	01720	01200
	1	12	00189	0001	PRODUCT A	00311	00200	00160
	1	12	00189	0002	PRODUCT J	61111	50000	42000
	1	12	23298	0001	PRODUCT B	03987	00425	00395
	1	12	23298	0010	PRODUCT K	61234	01295	01000
	1	12	23298	0100	PRODUCT XXXXXXXXXXXX	77430	03800	03300
	1	12	23298	1000	PRODUCT L	66666	03345	02837
	1	17	00512	0001	PRODUCT C	41222	21995	19000
	1	17	05394	0002	PRODUCT D	47821	01295	01000
	1	17	05394	0003	PRODUCT E	48541	01720	01200
	1	17	05394	0004	PRODUCT A	00311	00200	00160
	1	19	04215	0001	PRODUCT J	61111	50000	42000
	1	19	04215	0010	PRODUCT C	41222	21995	19000
	1	19	04215	0100	PRODUCT B	03987	00425	00395
	1	19	04215	1000	PRODUCT B	03987	00425	00395
	1	19	04215	0001	PRODUCT K	61234	01295	01000
	1	19	67843	0001	PRODUCT C	41222	21995	19000
	1	19	67843	0002	PRODUCT A	00311	00200	00160
	1	19	67843	0003	PRODUCT L	66666	03345	02837
	1	19	68111	0004	PRODUCT D	47821	01295	01000
	1	19	68111	0005	PRODUCT XXXXXXXXXXXX	77430	03800	03300
	1	19	68141	0006	PRODUCT XXXXXXXXXXXX	77430	03800	03300
	1	19	68141	0007	PRODUCT E	48541	01720	01200
	1	19	68141	0008	PRODUCT L	66666	03345	02837
	1	19	68141	0009	PRODUCT A	00311	00200	00160
	1	19	68197	0001	PRODUCT XXXXXXXXXXXX	77430	03800	03300
	1	19	68197	0010	PRODUCT XXXXXXXXXXXX	77430	03800	03300
	1	19	68214	0100	PRODUCT F	48771	02555	02015
	1	19	68214	1000	PRODUCT K	61234	01295	01000
	2	28	00911	5000	PRODUCT A	00311	00200	00160
	2	28	00911	9000	PRODUCT G	48911	00298	00250
	2	28	00911	0001	PRODUCT J	61111	50000	42000
	2	28	00911	0002	PRODUCT B	03987	00425	00395
	2	28	00911	0003	PRODUCT H	57777	00450	00350
	2	28	01023	0004	PRODUCT I	58911	01000	00750
	2	36	01199	0005	PRODUCT C	41222	21995	19000
	2	39	20032	0006	PRODUCT I	58911	01000	00750
	2	39	20032	0007	PRODUCT H	57777	00450	00350
	2	39	20032	0005	PRODUCT J	61111	50000	42000
	2	39	29879	0010	PRODUCT G	48911	00298	00250
	2	47	14212	0015	PRODUCT D	47821	01295	01000
	2	47	28400	0020	PRODUCT K	61234	01295	01000
	2	47	28400	0025	PRODUCT F	48771	02555	02015
	2	47	28400	0030	PRODUCT E	48541	01720	01200
	2	47	28400	0035	PRODUCT L	66666	03345	02837
	3	72	00312	0040	PRODUCT F	48771	02555	02015
	3	72	00312	0045	PRODUCT XXXXXXXXXXXX	77430	03800	03300
	3	72	01148	0050	PRODUCT C	41222	21995	19000
	3	72	01148	0055	PRODUCT F	48771	02555	02015
	3	94	77650	0001	PRODUCT A	00311	00200	00160

9. Input validation

Write a program that checks a file of accounts receivable records for validity. The output should list only those records which have invalid data. The listing should be triple-spaced and the fields that contain invalid data should be indicated by hyphens on the line below them. Thus,

```
5  1  21  54823  52  12K  12345 MURPHY'S         5512400
                 --  ---                         -------
```

would indicate three fields in error. A field is considered invalid if any of the following conditions are *not* met:

1. All fields other than customer name should be numeric.

2. All numeric fields other than the invoice amount should be positive.

3. The record code must be equal to 5.

4. Branch numbers must be less than 6, and the state number must be less than 51.

5. Check the date for a valid range:
   a. month range is from 1 through 12.
   b. day range is from 1 through 31.

6. The invoice amount field should be checked to see if it is reasonable. The first digit in the customer number, position 5, indicates what amount is reasonable. If the digit is from 0 through 3, the amount should not exceed $10,000; otherwise, the amount should not exceed $50,000.

Note the message(s) at the bottom of the report. The first message is to be issued if there are *no* errors. The second message is to be issued if any errors were discovered in the data. You will need to use two sets of test data for this program and run it twice, once for each set of data.

Output

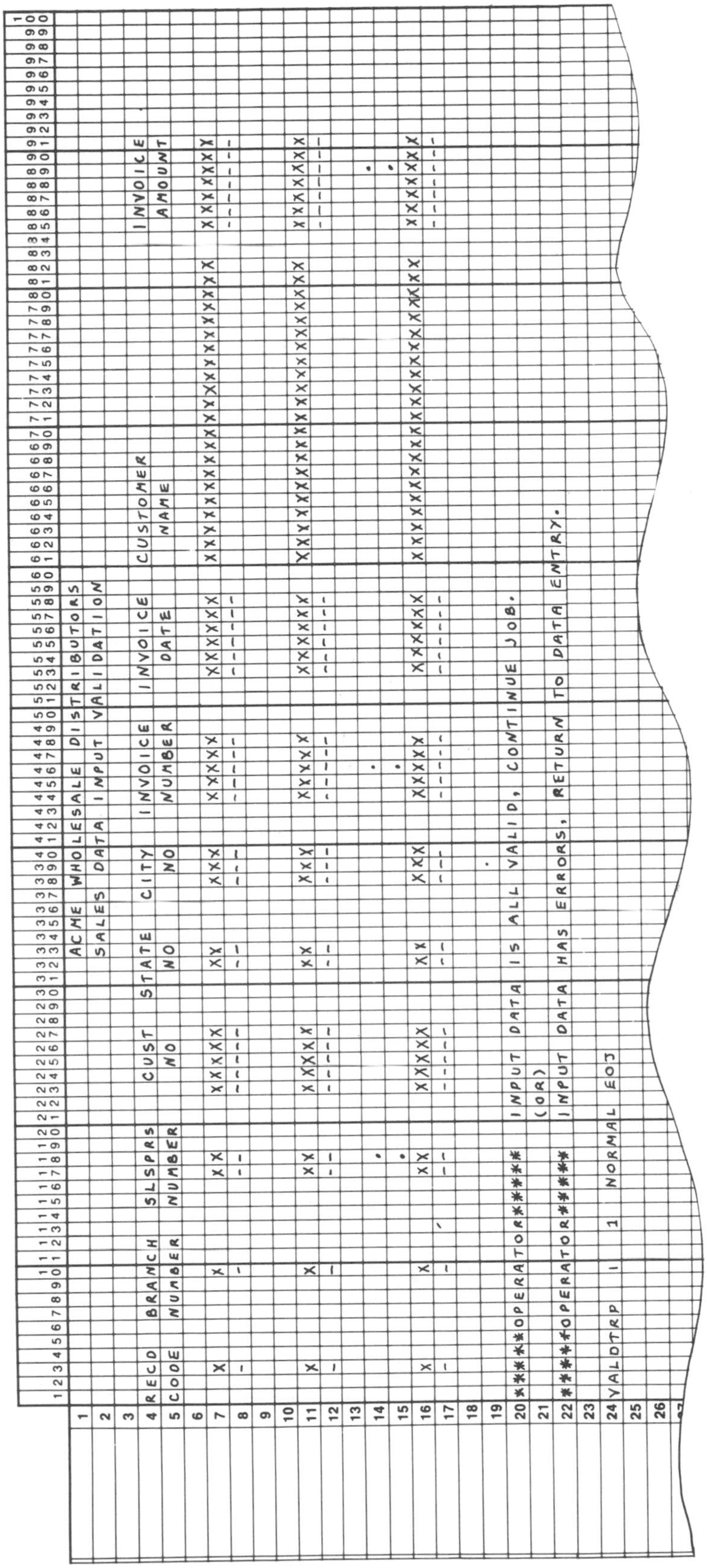
ACME WHOLESALE DISTRIBUTORS
SALES DATA INPUT VALIDATION
RECD BRANCH SLSPRS CUST STATE CITY INVOICE INVOICE CUSTOMER INVOICE
CODE NUMBER NUMBER NO NO NO NUMBER DATE NAME AMOUNT
X X XX XXXXX XX XXX XXXXX XXXXXX XXXXXXXXXXXXXXXXXXXXXXXX XXXXXXX
*****OPERATOR***** INPUT DATA IS ALL VALID, CONTINUE JOB.
(OR)
*****OPERATOR***** INPUT DATA HAS ERRORS, RETURN TO DATA ENTRY.
VALDTRP 1 1 NORMAL EOJ

Input

Use the same format as problem number 4.

Test Data

For the first run use the test data from problem number 4. For the second run use the following test data.

POS.	1	2	3-4	5-9	10-11	12-13	15-19	20-25	26-47	48-54
	5	1	12	1249K	05	012	J-123	040379	MURPHY'S	012345M
	5	1	2J	00095	J4	024	12345	040979	DUN & DUNNING	0222222
	E	1	12	1MN23	10	048	11111	044579	NELSON AND GRIESE	0A33333
	5	2	B1	01234	15	096	22222	122079	BACK MFG.	044444D
	5	9	19	00123	59	112	33333	043079	BOGUS SUPPLY	1500000
	5	2	19	00480	20	132	44444	053179	LUCID SYSTEMS	1234567
	5	2	31	99876	25	1K4	55555	053579	TRAP'S HARDWARE	4900000
	5	3	47	42194	30	148	66666	122079	S & I SUPPLY	0555555
	2	3	50	31234	35	152	77777	142979	JOHNSON'S MOTORS	5954900
	3	K	E5	3123K	B4	B-2	1234K	5K1579	ANALYTIC SYSTEMS	0666666

10. Inventory location listing

Write a program to print an inventory report from a file of inventory records. Each item may be stored in from one to ten different locations as indicated by the record layout. If a location ID field is blank, the item is not stored in that location nor is it stored in any subsequent location.

Output

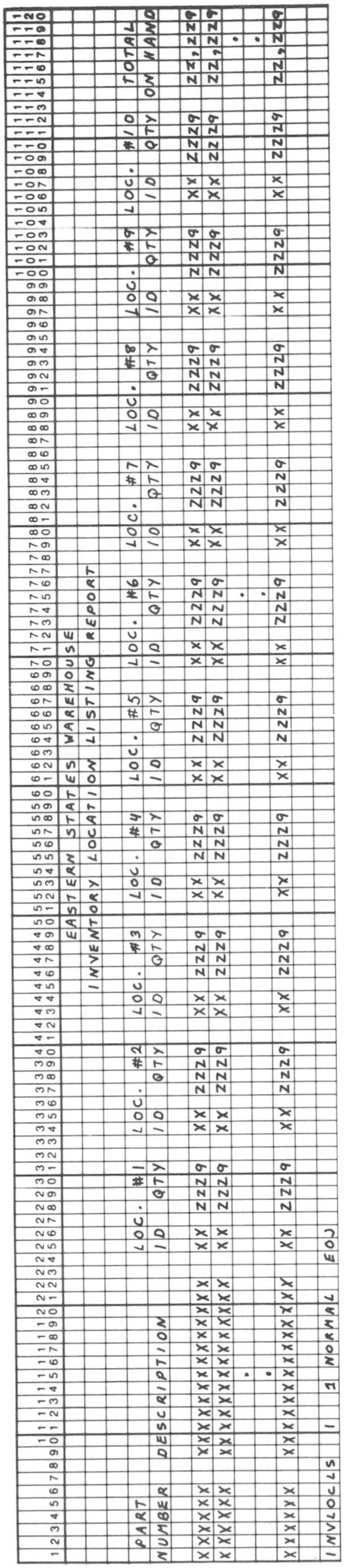
EASTERN STATES WAREHOUSE
INVENTORY LOCATION LISTING REPORT
PART LOC. #1 LOC. #2 LOC. #3 LOC. #4 LOC. #5 LOC. #6 LOC. #7 LOC. #8 LOC. #9 LOC. #10 TOTAL
NUMBER DESCRIPTION ID QTY ID QTY ID QTY ID QTY ID QTY ID QTY ID QTY ID QTY ID QTY ID QTY ON HAND
XXXXXX XXXXXXXXXXXXXX XX ZZZ9 XX ZZZ9 XX ZZZ9 XX ZZZ9 XX ZZZ9 XX ZZZ9 XX ZZZ9 XX ZZZ9 XX ZZZ9 XX ZZZ9 ZZ,ZZ9
INVLOCLS 1 3 NORMAL EOJ

Input

Field Name	Item No.	Item Desc.	Location 1		Location 2		Location 3		Location 4		Location 5	
			ID	Qty.	ID	Qty.	ID	Qty.	ID	Qty.	ID	Qty.
Characteristics	X(6)	X(14)	XX	9999	XX	9999	XX	9999	XX	9999	XX	9999
Usage												
Position	1-6	7-20	21-22	23-26	27-28	29-32	33-34	35-38	39-40	41-44	45-46	47-50

Location 6		Location 7		Location 8		Location 9		Location 10		
ID	Qty.	ID	Qty.	ID	Qty.	ID	Qty.	ID	Qty.	
XX	9999	XX	9999	XX	9999	XX	9999	XX	9999	
51-52	53-56	57-58	59-62	63-64	65-68	69-70	71-74	75-76	77-80	

Test Data

POS.	1-6	7-20	21-26	27-32	33-38	39-44	45-50	51-56	57-62	63-68	69-74	75-80
	003044	HANDLE	B70040	D40028	M60126							
	003810	HANDLE PIN	L91386	F20624								
	004462	BOLT. 1/4	C70320	X40213	L30040	K20418	N80083	E60092	T30026	R70118	H10202	J40070
	005071	AXLE PIN	T60846	A70120	L40083	G10078						
	005302	WHEEL	P31000	S21000	Y61000							
	006657	BLADE	Q80500	V90500	V80500	Z20500						
	008129	REAR BRACE	D30126	D50150	D60150	M10300	M20300	M30300				
	008844	NUT. 1/4	F61200	F71200								
	011263	MOWER BODY	N20060	N30060	U20024	W40036	A20016	C60048	C80060	C90060		
	012768	ROLLER	H70100	H80100	H90100	G20100	G30100					

11. One-level table in a grading program

Write a program that will grade multiple-choice tests of 50 questions. A lead input record gives the correct answers to the test. Student answers are recorded on the following records. The answers for one student are recorded on each record. For each test question there are five choices, A through E, and only one of these choices is correct. The student's choices are entered as the digits 1 through 5 in positions 31 through 80 of the answer records. Thus, a 2 in position 32 indicates that B is the answer given for question 2. In the lead record (the correct answer key), positions 1 through 50 correspond to the 50 correct answers. Print a line showing the correct answers, followed by lines with the student identifying information and answers and a percent correct. Vertically align the correct answer key and the student responses as shown and express the percent correct as a whole number.

Output

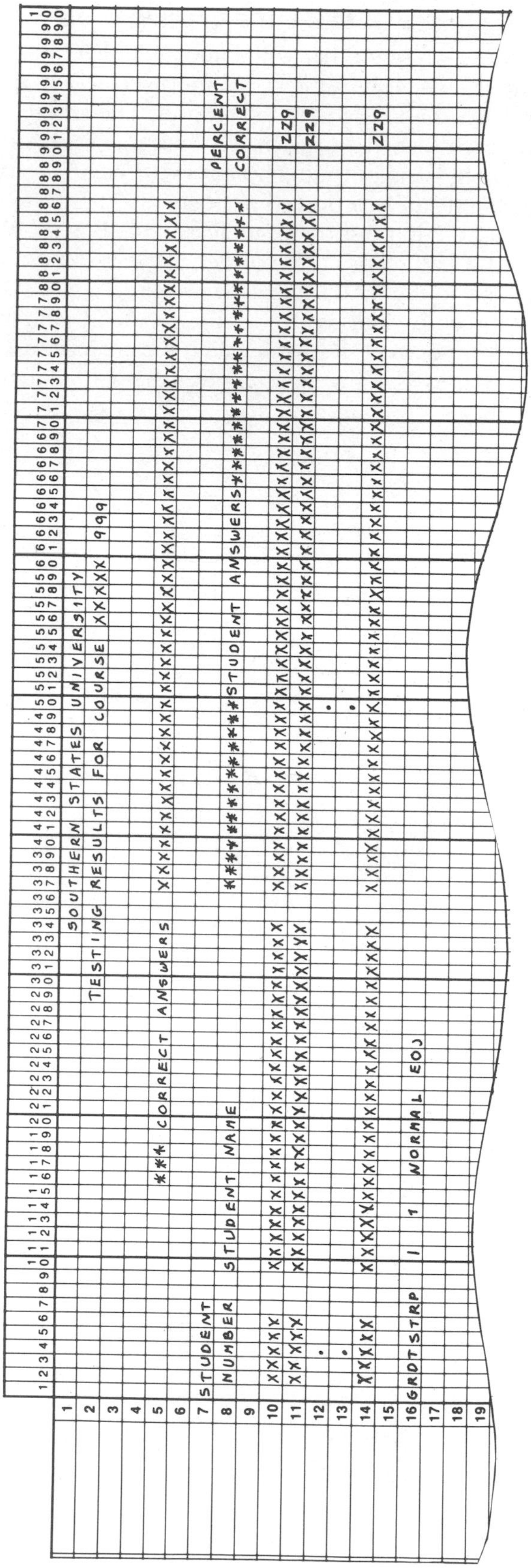
SOUTHERN STATES UNIVERSITY
TESTING RESULTS FOR COURSE XXXXX 999
** CORRECT ANSWERS
STUDENT NUMBER
STUDENT NAME
STUDENT ANSWERS
PERCENT CORRECT
GRDTSTRP 1 NORMAL EOJ

Input

Record layout:

LEAD RECORD

Field Name	Correct Answers	Dept. Name	Course Number	Unused
Characteristics	9(50)	X(5)	9(03)	X(22)
Usage				
Position	1-50	51-55	56-58	59-80

STUDENT ANSWER RECORD

Field Name	Student Number	Student Name	Student Answers	
Characteristics	X(5)	X(20)	9(50)	
Usage				
Position	1-5	6-30	31-80	

Test Data

LEAD RECORD

```
                                                      55    5
POS.   1                                              01   68

       14253311342355543212123345211243211234221122454321COMSC220
```

STUDENT ANSWER RECORDS

```
POS.   1                                                                        80

       00103STUDENTAAAAAAAAAAAAA14252311242355443211121345215253212234211223543222
       01125STUDENTBBBBBBBBBBBBB14243351532151542132242355114212111224322122434253
       11111STUDENTCCCCCCCCCCCCC24344351122152542232244355113211311224322425412133
       12222STUDENTDDDDDDDDDDDDD14252211341355543111113345111153211234221112454321
       13333STUDENTEEEEEEEEEEEEE21344153132254443242255314212252541254122223445213
       14444STUDENTFFFFFFFFFFFFF21344153132254443242255314212252541254122223545213
       15555STUDENTGGGGGGGGGGGGG24354351142251543252252315212251421235522521423143
       16666STUDENTHHHHHHHHHHHHH34455311212352544152214325313213351214222324451123
       17777STUDENTIIIIIIIIIIIII14153341342355513212123344211253111234121122454321
       18888STUDENTJJJJJJJJJJJJJ41541123322454145212225335415213431244522112243425
       19999STUDENTKKKKKKKKKKKKK14213311332355443211124345215213211134222122453321
       21111STUDENTLLLLLLLLLLLLL54152333442551541122232344514252511225322425412233
       22222STUDENTMMMMMMMMMMMMM11253311342355513212123315211254211234221132454321
       23333STUDENTNNNNNNNNNNNNN11243141532152542232241355113211441254422122434153
       24444STUDENTPPPPPPPPPPPPP21344351122254543242252315212213311225322521423143
```

12. Tax table look-up

Write a program that reads a tax table into storage and then uses the table to look up income tax amounts to be paid. The table is read into storage from a separate reference file. The individual tax payroll records are input from a separate file.

Output

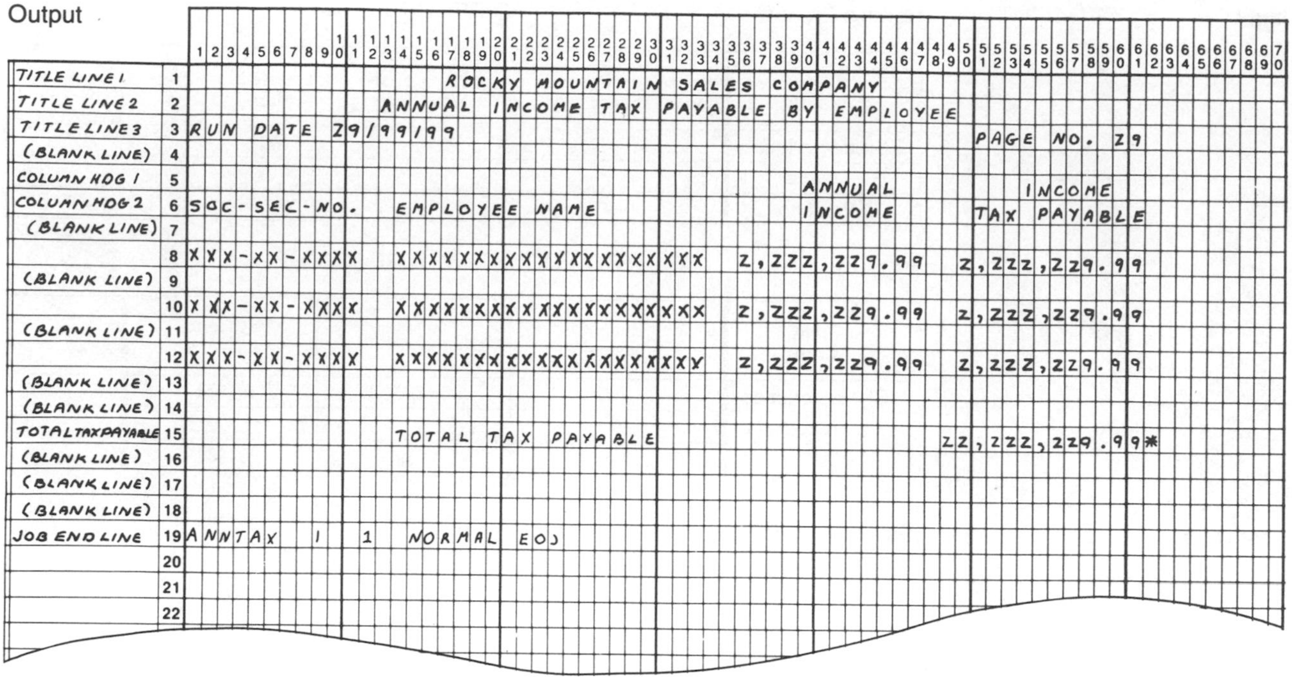
TITLE LINE 1 — ROCKY MOUNTAIN SALES COMPANY
TITLE LINE 2 — ANNUAL INCOME TAX PAYABLE BY EMPLOYEE
TITLE LINE 3 — RUN DATE Z9/99/99 PAGE NO. Z9
(BLANK LINE)
COLUMN HDG 1 — ANNUAL INCOME
COLUMN HDG 2 — SOC-SEC-NO. EMPLOYEE NAME INCOME TAX PAYABLE
(BLANK LINE)
XXX-XX-XXXX XXXXXXXXXXXXXXXXXXXXXXXXXXXXXX Z,ZZZ,ZZ9.99 Z,ZZZ,ZZ9.99
(BLANK LINE)
XXX-XX-XXXX XXXXXXXXXXXXXXXXXXXXXXXXXXXXXX Z,ZZZ,ZZ9.99 Z,ZZZ,ZZ9.99
(BLANK LINE)
XXX-XX-XXXX XXXXXXXXXXXXXXXXXXXXXXXXXXXXXX Z,ZZZ,ZZ9.99 Z,ZZZ,ZZ9.99
(BLANK LINE)
(BLANK LINE)
TOTAL TAX PAYABLE — TOTAL TAX PAYABLE ZZ,ZZZ,ZZ9.99*
(BLANK LINE)
(BLANK LINE)
(BLANK LINE)
JOB END LINE — ANNTAX 1 1 NORMAL EOJ

Table Data

Tax table

If the adjusted gross income is: / The amount of income tax to be withheld is:

Not over $2,300 — $0

Over	But not over		Of excess over
$2,300	$3,400	11%	$2,300
3,400	4,400	$121 plus 12%	3,400
4,400	6,500	241 plus 14%	4,400
6,500	8,500	535 plus 15%	6,500
8,500	10,800	835 plus 16%	8,500
10,800	12,900	1,203 plus 18%	10,800
12,900	15,000	1,581 plus 20%	12,900
15,000	18,200	2,001 plus 23%	15,000
18,200	23,500	2,737 plus 26%	18,200
23,500	28,800	4,115 plus 30%	23,500
28,800	34,100	5,705 plus 34%	28,800
34,100	41,500	7,507 plus 38%	34,100
41,500	55,300	10,319 plus 42%	41,500
55,300	81,800	16,115 plus 48%	55,300
81,800	------	28,835 plus 50%	81,800

Input

Table record

Field Name	Taxable Income	Tax on Amt. in 1st Column of Table	Percent of Excess	Unused
Characteristics	9(6)	9(6)	99	X(66)
Usage				
Position	1-6	7-12	13-14	15-80

Data record

Field Name	Soc. Sec. No.	Name	Yearly Income	Unused
Characteristics	9(9)	X(20)	9(7)V99	X(42)
Usage				
Position	1-9	10-29	30-38	39-80

Test Data

POS.	1-9	10-29	30-38
	120125017	NORMART	027584300
	250023003	MATHIESEN	000011275
	347225035	MC KEIGHAN	000073245
	353560888	O'BRIEN	000127550
	359022238	GALLAGHER	000172000
	380099938	MCNAMARA	000200000
	528175005	BENNINGTON	000410000
	470030590	COLDERIDGE	008500000
	612033374	SMITH J.	009275000
	431400747	MILLER	017500000
	600791009	MUELLER	012500000
	320000779	POHL	214368200

13. Subprogram state look-up

Addresses are part of many of the records maintained in data processing installations. To conserve tape or disk space, the state portion of these addresses is often stored as a two-character code. Then, whenever the full state name is needed, a program can use the two-character code to look up the full name in the table.

Write a program to convert a two-character state code to a 20-character state name. The name of this subprogram should be CONVST, and the subprogram should accept two fields from the calling programs: (1) the two-character state code field and (2) a 20-character field in which the subprogram can place the full state name. If the look-up is unsuccessful, the subprogram should place the word INVALID STATE in the state name field. The calling program should test the state name for INVALID STATE and print a blank name or print just the two-character code, or take other appropriate action. The appropriate action will depend on the function of the calling program and is to be defined in class.

To test the subprogram, modify program 1 (the name and address listing) to read the data below and print a listing of company, name, street, city, state (full name) and zip code. The calling program should print appropriate column headings. The calling program can be linked with the subprogram and the subprogram can then be tested. Be sure to use the top-down testing techniques for this problem.

Output

Modify the output format of problem number 1 to fit this problem.

Input

See the test data for the input record format.

Test Data

POS.	1	21	41	61	63
	HOMEWOOD LUMBER	6238 HIGH PASS RD.	CRESTED BUTTE	MT	59902
	WESTON HARDWARE	46 ASPEN WAY	KETCHUM	ID	83340
	REDWOOD SUPPLIES	847 HIWAY 88	JACKSON	CA	95642
	QUADE LUMBER	2776 PIONEER DR.	EUGENE	OR	97405
	THOMPSON TREE FARM	87 OLYMPIC LANE	ACME	WA	98220
	TETON LUMBER	8724 YELLSTONE WAY	JACKSON	WY	83025
	WESTERN SUPPLY	16404 PIKE AVE.	DURANGO	CO	81301
	MULLEN LUMBER	63 WHEELER AVE.	RATON	NM	87740
	MINING SUPPLIES	44 GOLD RUN	PARK CITY	UT	84064
	SUNRISE LUMBER	1011 EAST RIDGE	KINGMAN	AZ	86401

State table

Code	State name	Code	State name	Code	State name
AL	Alabama	LA	Lousiana	OH	Ohio
AK	Alaska	ME	Maine	OK	Oklahoma
AZ	Arizona	MD	Maryland	OR	Oregon
AR	Arkansas	MA	Massachusetts	PA	Pennsylvania
CA	California	MI	Michigan	RI	Rhode Island
CO	Colorado	MN	Minnesota	SC	South Carolina
CT	Connecticut	MS	Mississippi	SD	South Dakota
DE	Delaware	MO	Missouri	TN	Tennessee
FL	Florida	MT	Montana	TX	Texas
GA	Georgia	NE	Nebraska	UT	Utah
HI	Hawaii	NV	Nevada	VT	Vermont
ID	Idaho	NH	New Hampshire	VA	Virginia
IL	Illinois	NJ	New Jersey	WA	Washington
IN	Indiana	NM	New Mexico	WV	West Virginia
IA	Iowa	NY	New York	WI	Wisconsin
KS	Kansas	NC	North Carolina	WY	Wyoming
KY	Kentucky	ND	North Dakota		

14. Shipping-rate look-up with a two-level table

Write a program to print a report of the estimated costs for orders identified by shipment records. The shipping rate per pound depends on the total weight of the order and on the district to which the order is to be shipped. The table that follows shows these cost-per-pound rates as dollar figures. For instance, .030 equals 3 cents per pound. You should define this table in your program and use it to look up the proper shipping rate to use in calculating the estimated cost of shipping each order.

Output

Shipping rate per pound

Order weight	Shipping district				
	1	2	3	4	5
0-50	.030	.032	.034	.036	.038
51-100	.028	.029	.029	.030	.031
101-499	.024	.025	.026	.027	.028
500-999	.020	.022	.023	.025	.026
1000-1999	.014	.015	.016	.017	.018
2000 & over	.010	.011	.012	.013	.014

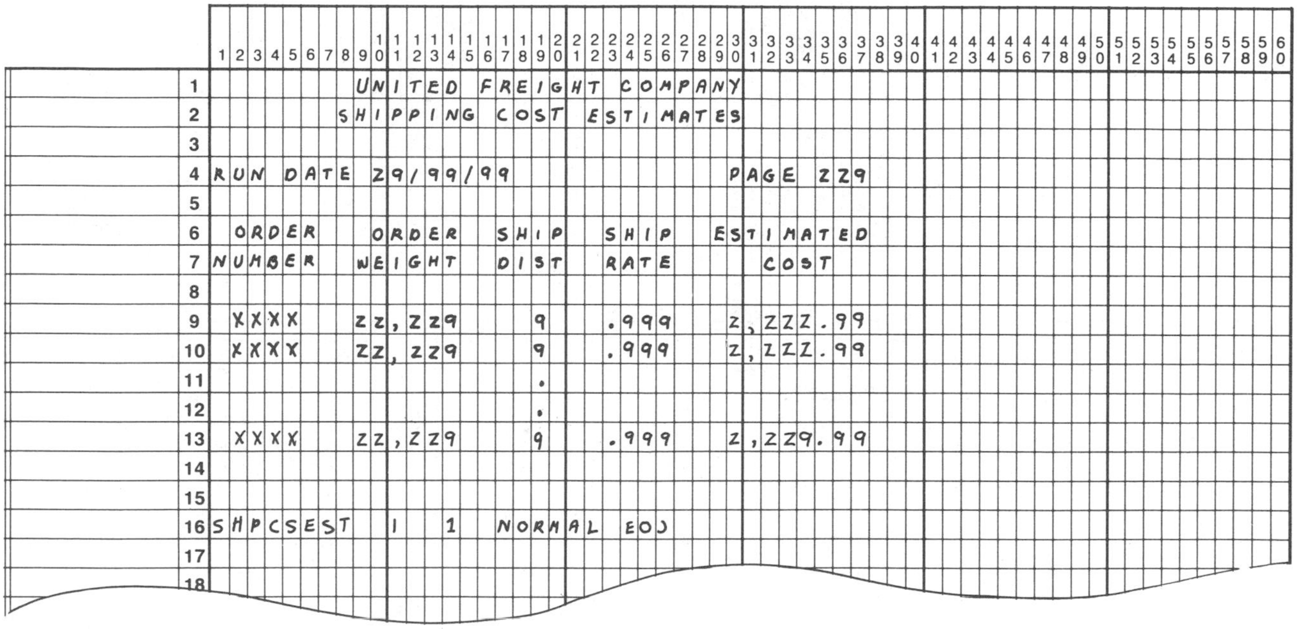
UNITED FREIGHT COMPANY
SHIPPING COST ESTIMATES
RUN DATE Z9/99/99
PAGE ZZ9
ORDER
NUMBER
ORDER
WEIGHT
SHIP
DIST
SHIP
RATE
ESTIMATED
COST
XXXX ZZ,ZZ9 9 .999 Z,ZZZ.99
XXXX ZZ,ZZ9 9 .999 Z,ZZZ.99
XXXX ZZ,ZZ9 9 .999 Z,ZZ9.99
SHPCSEST 1 1 NORMAL EOJ

Input

Field Name	Order No.	Order Weight	Shipping District	Unused
Characteristics	X(4)	9(5)	9	X(70)
Usage				
Position	1-4	5-9	10	11-80

Test Data

```
4728000363
4729012161
4730001005
4731027341
4732004991
4733000514
4734340832
```

15. Two-level table accumulation program

Write a program that prints two summary tables of data taken from a file of personel records for teachers in a college. The input file is to be read only once, and both tables are to be printed after the input has been read.

Output

```
                              Print position
                            1         2         3         4         5
                   12345678901234567890123456789012345678901234567890
TITLE LINE 1         1                IVYWILD COLLEGE OF THE SOUTH
TITLE LINE 2         2                    STAFF ANALYSIS REPORT
(BLANK LINE)         3
COLUMN HDG 1         4     AGE    ---------------DEPARTMENT--------------
COLUMN HDG 2         5    GROUP    1    2    3    4    5    6    7    8
(BLANK LINE)         6
AGE DEPARTMENT LINE  7    21-25   ZZZ  ZZZ  ZZZ  ZZZ  ZZZ  ZZZ  ZZZ  ZZZ
(BLANK LINE)         8
                     9    26-30   ZZZ  ZZZ  ZZZ  ZZZ  ZZZ  ZZZ  ZZZ  ZZZ
(BLANK LINE)        10
                    11    31-35   ZZZ  ZZZ  ZZZ  ZZZ  ZZZ  ZZZ  ZZZ  ZZZ
(BLANK LINE)        12
                    13    36-40   ZZZ  ZZZ  ZZZ  ZZZ  ZZZ  ZZZ  ZZZ  ZZZ
(BLANK LINE)        14
                    15    41-45   ZZZ  ZZZ  ZZZ  ZZZ  ZZZ  ZZZ  ZZZ  ZZZ
(BLANK LINE)        16
                    17    46-50   ZZZ  ZZZ  ZZZ  ZZZ  ZZZ  ZZZ  ZZZ  ZZZ
(BLANK LINE)        18
                    19    51-55   ZZZ  ZZZ  ZZZ  ZZZ  ZZZ  ZZZ  ZZZ  ZZZ
(BLANK LINE)        20
                    21    56-60   ZZZ  ZZZ  ZZZ  ZZZ  ZZZ  ZZZ  ZZZ  ZZZ
(BLANK LINE)        22
                    23    61-65   ZZZ  ZZZ  ZZZ  ZZZ  ZZZ  ZZZ  ZZZ  ZZZ
(BLANK LINE)        24
(BLANK LINE)        25
(BLANK LINE)        26
COLUMN HDG 3        27     AGE    -----------DEGREE---------
COLUMN HDG 4        28    GROUP   BACHELORS  MASTERS    PHD
(BLANK LINE)        29
AGE DEPARTMENT LINE 30    21-25      ZZZ       ZZZ      ZZZ
(BLANK LINE)        31
                    32    26-30      ZZZ       ZZZ      ZZZ
(BLANK LINE)        33
                    34    31-35      ZZZ       ZZZ      ZZZ
(BLANK LINE)        35
                    36    36-40      ZZZ       ZZZ      ZZZ
(BLANK LINE)        37
                    38    41-45      ZZZ       ZZZ      ZZZ
(BLANK LINE)        39
                    40    46-50      ZZZ       ZZZ      ZZZ
(BLANK LINE)        41
                    42    51-55      ZZZ       ZZZ      ZZZ
(BLANK LINE)        43
                    44    56-60      ZZZ       ZZZ      ZZZ
(BLANK LINE)        45
                    46    61-65      ZZZ       ZZZ      ZZZ
(BLANK LINE)        47
(BLANK LINE)        48
JOB END LINE        49    TCHANLS  1  1  NORMAL  EOJ
                    50
```

Input

Field Name	Sex	Dept. No.	Age	Degree	Unused
Characteristics	9	9	99	9	X(75)
Usage					
Position	1	2	3-4	5	6-80

Notes: Sex: 1 = male, 2 = female
Department: Ranges from 1 through 8
Degree: 1 = bachelor's, 2 = master's, 3 = doctorate

Test Data

POS.	1	2	3-4	5	POS.	1	2	3-4	5	POS.	1	2	3-4	5	POS.	1	2	3-4	5
	1	8	24	1		1	1	29	1		1	6	31	2		1	8	22	1
	2	6	35	2		1	2	28	2		2	5	37	2		1	1	66	1
	1	4	43	3		2	3	44	2		1	4	39	2		2	4	22	1
	1	2	54	3		1	2	61	3		2	3	47	3		1	4	19	3
	2	3	33	2		1	8	58	3		1	8	58	3		2	4	33	1
	1	5	26	2		2	7	33	3		1	7	60	3		2	5	44	3
	1	7	28	1		1	3	22	1		1	2	55	2		2	3	51	3

16. Three-level classification table

Write a program to print information in the form of a three-level table. The data for the output is to be accumulated in a three-level table. The data for the table is to be collected from a group of college personnel records. The purpose of the report is to use in the analysis of promotion practices to ensure that no discrimination is taking place.

Special Instructions:

1. Set row designators (Bachelor, etc.) up in a small single-level table and access them from that table.

2. You should be able use the same output line description for the total line that you used for the detail lines (i.e., no need to encode a "total" line description). In fact, the designator TOTAL should be included in the table mentioned in instruction 1 above. See if you can do this.

3. The output line should be subscripted (preferably indexed).

Output

```
 1                                      PSEUDO INTELLECT COLLEGE
 2                                         RANK-DEGREE-SEX TABLE
 3
 4               INSTRUCTOR         ASSISTANT        ASSOCIATE          PROFESSOR            TOTAL
 5          MALE FEM INV TOT    MALE FEM INV TOT   MALE FEM INV TOT   MALE FEM INV TOT    MALE FEM INV TOT
 6
 7 BACHELOR   ZZZ ZZZ ZZZ ZZZ    ZZZ ZZZ ZZZ ZZZ    ZZZ ZZZ ZZZ ZZZ    ZZZ ZZZ ZZZ ZZZ    ZZZ ZZZ ZZZ ZZZ
 8 MASTER     ZZZ ZZZ ZZZ ZZZ    ZZZ ZZZ ZZZ ZZZ    ZZZ ZZZ ZZZ ZZZ    ZZZ ZZZ ZZZ ZZZ    ZZZ ZZZ ZZZ ZZZ
 9 DOCTOR     ZZZ ZZZ ZZZ ZZZ    ZZZ ZZZ ZZZ ZZZ    ZZZ ZZZ ZZZ ZZZ    ZZZ ZZZ ZZZ ZZZ    ZZZ ZZZ ZZZ ZZZ
10
11 TOTAL      ZZZ ZZZ ZZZ ZZZ    ZZZ ZZZ ZZZ ZZZ    ZZZ ZZZ ZZZ ZZZ    ZZZ ZZZ ZZZ ZZZ    ZZZ ZZZ ZZZ ZZZ
12
13 RDSTBREP  I   1 NORMAL EOJ
```

Input

Field Name	Soc Sec Number	Name	Birth Date	High Degree	Rank	Sex	Other data
Characteristics	9(9)	X(25)	9(6)	9	9	9	X(37)
Usage							
Position	1-9	10-34	35-40	41	42	43	44-80

Test Data

Line	Columns 1–34	Columns 35–43	Columns 50–58
1	123456789Aaaaaaaaaaaaaaaaaaaaaaaaa	112233342	123TRA456
2	522389995SMITH, SAMUAL	010136221	223MIB888
3	531840024JONES, JAMES	092255111	554TRB909
4	00134?876RHODES, ROCQUE	122529222	987MKL005
5	111222345READY, HELEN	112456330	765REB007
6	855446754MIX, THOMAS	050555321	223MNB844
7	345231234RANGER, LONE	081144231	987MKI321
8	458765099WONDER, ALICE	060352332	823MCI383
9	283746352PRIME, PRICILLA	081260232	834KEU374
10	293846145SHANK, THAYNE	101048111	294QW0394
11	023974724BRILLIANT, ASHLEY	120329341	455ASD498
12	345875856CARVER, KEITH	031560331	395ASD345
13	945874756MEDLEY, DONALD	060947231	856KGJ845
14	948573457FREE, WORLD B.	071860331	945LOP348
15	000000001LOVELACE, ADA	092501342	098AER123
16	374628374NASTER, MICHAEL	101056331	2341ER384
17	573984724DALE, NELSON	022250332	7451RI485
18	398574756ORSHALLEY, RONALD	110345231	934ORT324
19	345873456WELLHART, TYLER	093056321	478PLO435
20	005060007HANSEN, DAVID	051247341	394EER487
21			
22			
23			

17. Payroll checks with subprograms

Write a program that prints payroll checks from input records that contain current earnings and year-to-date totals. The check to be printed is, of course, a preprinted form, so there are actually only five data lines printed by the program. You will use line counting for forms control. For check protection the amount figure should be printed with a floating dollar sign or with a fixed dollar sign and asterisk check protection.

In preparing this program, there are two subprograms that should be used. The first, described in problem 18, will calculate the federal withholding amount. It is named FITCALC and requires these four fields in order: the current-gross field, the marital-status field, the number-of-exemptions field, and a five-digit field that will receive the amount of federal income tax to be deducted for this pay period.

The second subprogram, described in problem 19, will calculate the social security tax (FICA) to be deducted. It is named FICACALC and requires these three fields in order: the current-gross field, the year-to-date FICA field, and a four-digit field that will receive the amount of FICA to be deducted for this pay period.

Output

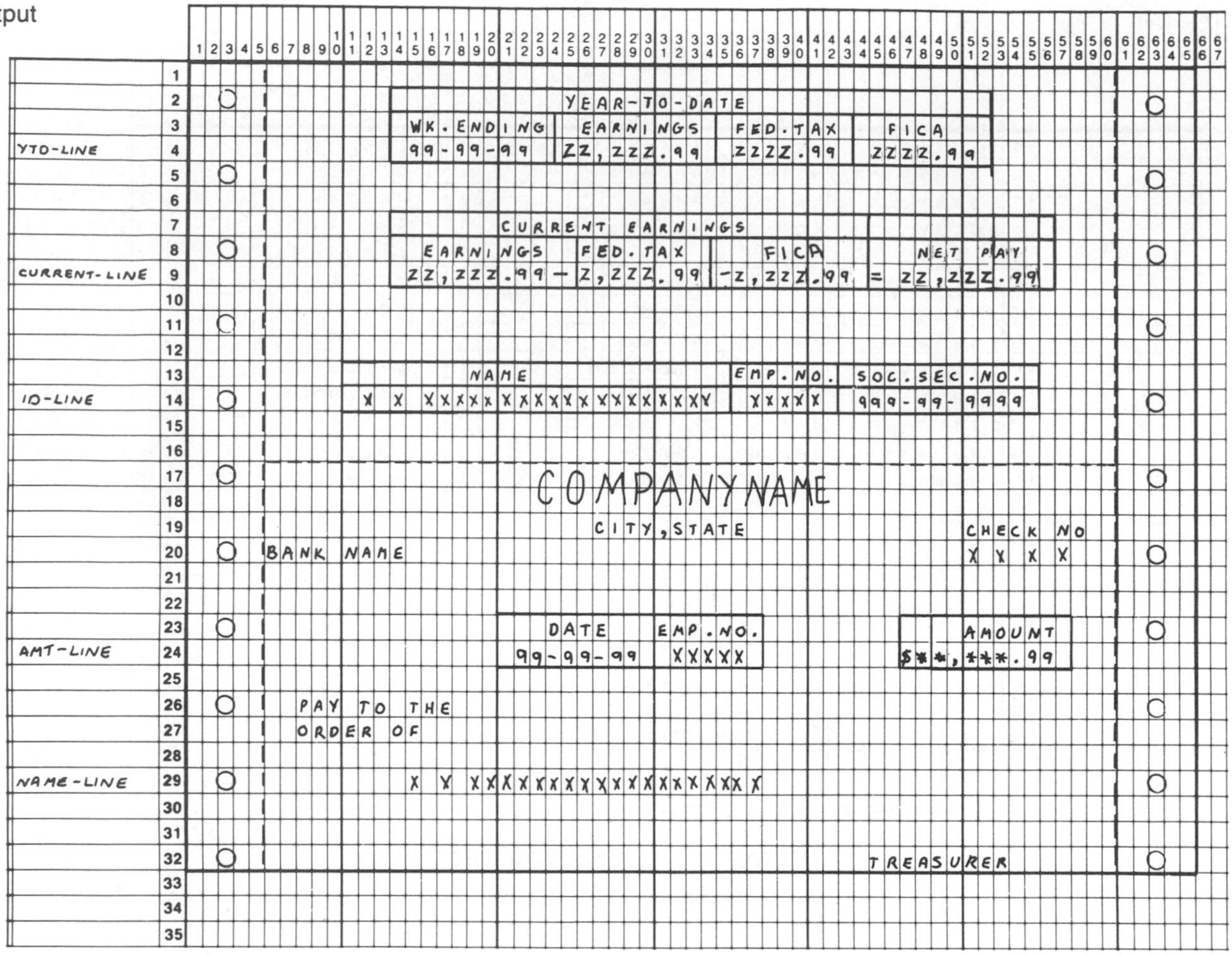

YTD-LINE
CURRENT-LINE
ID-LINE
AMT-LINE
NAME-LINE
YEAR-TO-DATE
WK. ENDING
EARNINGS
FED. TAX
FICA
99-99-99
ZZ,ZZZ.99
ZZZZ.99
ZZZZ.99
CURRENT EARNINGS
EARNINGS
FED. TAX
FICA
NET PAY
ZZ,ZZZ.99 − Z,ZZZ.99 −Z,ZZZ.99 = ZZ,ZZZ.99
NAME
EMP. NO.
SOC. SEC. NO.
X X XXXXXXXXXXXXXXXXXXX
XXXXX
999-99-9999
COMPANY NAME
CITY, STATE
CHECK NO
XXXX
BANK NAME
DATE
EMP. NO.
99-99-99
XXXXX
AMOUNT
$**,***.99
PAY TO THE
ORDER OF
X X XXXXXXXXXXXXXXXXXXX
TREASURER

Input

The employee records are preceded by a date record that contains the date of the pay period and the date to be used on the payroll checks.

Date record

Field Name	Check Date	Pay-period Date	Unused
Characteristics	9(6)	9(6)	X(68)
Usage			
Position	1-6	7-12	13-80

Employee record

Field Name	Emp. No.	Emp. Name	First Initial	Middle Initial	Soc. Sec. No.	Marital Status	Exempt.	YTD Gross	YTD Fed. Tax	YTD FICA
Characteristics	X(5)	X(19)	X	X	9(9)	X	99	9(6)V99	9(5)V99	9(5)V99
Usage										
Position	1-5	6-24	25	26	27-35	36	37-38	39-46	47-53	52-57

Current Gross	Unused
9(4)V99	X(14)
61-66	67-80

Test Data 1. A leading date record such as the following:

Positions	1-6	7-12	80
	100286	101486	-

Test Data 2. Payroll records

Pos.	1-5	6-24	25	26	27-35	36	37-38	39-46	47-53	54-60	61-66
	01206	ASTOR	W	V	131680549	S	01	00302000	0019770	0021291	009900
	01342	DUFFY	A	F	268444678	S	01	01000000	0123200	0070500	025000
	01518	ENGLEHART	B	H	528431646	M	03	01190000	0162660	0083895	029750
	01615	FARLEY	F	L	716411783	M	04	07100000	2226800	0279180	177500
	01703	BARTLETT	J	E	111237642	M	07	01500000	0182160	0105750	037500
	02418	BRIANT	F	A	392280401	S	01	02110000	0407120	0148755	052750
	02479	HARRIS	M	W	398380775	M	02	03700000	0812560	0260850	092500
	02488	HARRISON	B	R	726412888	M	11	01400000	0164160	0098700	035000
	02512	HUNT	S	L	123445555	M	03	00500000	0096920	0035250	025000

18. Subprogram for FIT calculation

Write a subprogram that calculates the amount of federal withholding tax (FIT) to be withheld from a weekly payroll. The calling program will send these four fields in the order listed: a six-digit current-gross field (two decimal positions), a one-character marital-status field (S = single, M = married), a two-digit number-of-exemptions field, and a six-digit field that will receive the amount of federal income tax to be withheld (two decimal positions). The name of this subprogram is to be FITCALC.

To calculate federal withholding tax, multiply the number of exemptions by $13.50, and subtract this amount from current gross; the result is adjusted income. Then, use the following table to look up the factors to be used in the actual calculation. For example, if the adjusted gross income for a single person is $20.00, the withholding tax is $1.26, plus 15% of $7.00, or $2.31. To test this subprogram, write your own calling program or use the main program written for problem 17. In either case, you can use the test data from problem 17.

Tax Table

Single person

If the adjusted gross income is:		The amount of income tax to be withheld is:	
Not over $44		$0	
Over	But not over		Of excess over
$44	$65	11%	$44
65	85	$2.33 plus 12%	65
85	125	4.63 plus 14%	85
125	163	10.29 plus 15%	125
163	208	16.06 plus 16%	163
208	248	23.13 plus 18%	208
248	288	30.40 plus 20%	248
288	350	38.48 plus 23%	288
350	452	52.63 plus 26%	350
452	554	79.13 plus 30%	452
554	656	109.71 plus 34%	554
656	798	144.37 plus 38%	656
798	1,063	198.44 plus 42%	798
1,063	1,573	309.90 plus 48%	1,063
1,573	-----	554.52 plus 50%	1,573

Married person

If the adjusted gross income is:		The amount of income tax to be withheld is:	
Not over $65		$0	
Over	But not over		Of excess over
$65	$106	11%	$65
106	146	$4.44 plus 12%	106
146	229	9.29 plus 14%	146
229	308	20.87 plus 16%	229
308	388	33.48 plus 18%	308
388	473	48.02 plus 22%	388
473	575	66.63 plus 25%	473
575	677	92.12 plus 28%	575
677	881	120.65 plus 33%	677
881	1,154	187.92 plus 38%	881
1,154	1,646	291.69 plus 42%	1,154
1,646	2,104	498.65 plus 45%	1,646
2,104	3,123	704.42 plus 49%	2,104
3,123	-----	1,203.85 plus 50%	3,123

19. Subprogram for FICA calculation

Write a subprogram that calculates the amount of social security tax (FICA) to be withheld from a weekly paycheck. The calling program will send these three fields in the order listed: a six-digit current-gross field (two decimal positions), a seven-digit year-to-date FICA field (two decimal positions), and a six-digit field that will receive the amount of FICA to be deducted for this pay period (two decimal positions). The name of this subprogram is to be FICACALC.

To calculate FICA, multiply current gross by 7.05 percent. However, when a certain maximum year-to-date figure is reached, an employee no longer pays FICA. As a result, the subprogram must test to see whether the maximum has been reached. If the maximum was reached in a previous pay period, the employee pays no FICA for the rest of the year. However, if the maximum is reached in the current pay period, FICA is normally calculated by subtracting the year-to-date FICA from the maximum. In 1985 the maximum was $39,600, but this will be increased in subsequent years.

To test this subprogram, write your own calling program or use the main program written for problem 17. In either case, you can use the test data from problem 17 even though it is based on a maximum FICA of $39,600 which may no longer be in effect. Since this maximum is changed every year, you should write the subprogram so that it can be easily modified.

Sequential File Problems

The following problems require you to create, maintain, and update a file of student semester records. In addition, one of the problem requires printing a report from this master file.

The sequential student semester file can be stored on tape or disk, depending on what you or your instructor decide. At any rate, this decision should be made at the start; you can then be consistent in programming your solutions.

For the master record format, assume that a student can take from one to seven courses. That means positions 1–26 of the record will contain the basic student information and will be followed by the information for one to seven courses. If the first character of the second through seventh course segment is blank, the rest of the record will be blank, too. The record layout for the master records is given below.

To test the creation, maintenance, and update programs, you can use a tape-to-printer or disk-to-printer utility program following the execution of each of these programs. The utility specifications or the proper utilities manual for your system are available from your instructor. Or, you can write a simple program of your own that lists the contents of the master file.

20. Creating a student semester file

Write a program to create a sequential file of student semester records using course records as input. These records will be in sequence by course number within department code within student number. At the end of the program, print the number of records written on the file, the number of records *not* processed, and the total number of input records read.

In all cases, the grade portions of each record (bytes 27–31 in each course segment) along with the usused portion of the record should be blank. If a student has more than seven course cards, print an error message for each record over seven and ignore these records.

Record Layout

ID segment

Field Name	Student No.	Student Name (Last name first)	No. of Courses
Characteristics	X(6)	X(19)	9
Usage			
Position	1-6	7-25	26

Course information segment:

Field Name	Course Title	Dept.	Course No.	Section No.	Semester Hours	Three Grade Periods	Final Exam Grade	Final Course Grade
Characteristics	X(6)	X(4)	999	99	9	XXX	X	X
Usage								
Position	1-16	17-20	21-23	24-25	26	27-29	30	31

Note: A student may take from one to seven courses, so the total record length is 243 bytes.

Input

Field Name	Student No.	Student Name (Last name first)	Course Title	Dept.	Course No.	Section No.	Semester Hours	Unused
Characteristics	9(6)	X(19)	X(16)	X(4)	999	99	9	X(29)
Usage								
Position	1-6	7-25	26-41	42-45	46-48	49-50	51	52-80

Test Data

POS.	1-6	7-25	26-41	42-45	46-48	49-50	51
	101450	MC QUILLEN, KEVIN	BIOCHEM	CHEM	011	02	5
	101450	MC QUILLEN, KEVIN	INTRO ECON	ECON	010	03	3
	101450	MC QUILLEN, KEVIN	INTRO AMER LIT	ENG	101	07	3
	101450	MC QUILLEN, KEVIN	INTRO MECH ENGR	M E	050	01	5
	194007	POHL, GARY	COBOL	DP	015	01	3
	194007	POHL, GARY	INTRO DP	DP	050	09	3
	194007	POHL, GARY	INTRO FORTRAN	DP	065	02	2
	194007	POHL, GARY	CREATIVE WRITING	ENG	003	02	3
	194007	POHL, GARY	INTRO DRAMA	ENG	121	03	3
	194007	POHL, GARY	SHAKESPEARE	ENG	150	02	3
	194007	POHL, GARY	INTRO MUSIC	MUS	011	04	2
	200943	FURY, MICHAEL	INTRO ANTHRO	ANTH	001	07	3
	200943	FURY, MICHAEL	FREEHND DRAWING	ART	010	02	2
	200943	FURY, MICHAEL	INTRO WRITING	ENG	002	14	3
	200943	FURY, MICHAEL	AMER HIST 1929-P	HIST	010	03	2
	200943	FURY, MICHAEL	INTRO SYMPHONY	MUS	010	03	2
	200943	FURY, MICHAEL	INTRO MUSIC	MUS	011	04	2
	200943	FURY, MICHAEL	ESTHETICS	PHIL	121	01	3
	200943	FURY, MICHAEL	INTRO SOC SCI	SOC	001	11	3
	214433	ROGERS, SALLY	INTRO ACCTG	COM	009	03	3
	214433	ROGERS, SALLY	CORP FIN	COM	043	02	3
	214433	ROGERS, SALLY	INTRO ASSEMBLER	DP	100	01	3
	214888	NELSON, GRACE	BOTANY	BIO	010	01	5
	214888	NELSON, GRACE	INTRO DP	DP	050	07	3
	214888	NELSON, GRACE	INTRO WRITING	ENG	002	12	3
	214888	NELSON, GRACE	PHYSICS	PHYS	020	03	5
	214888	NELSON, GRACE	INTRO POL SCI	POL	010	02	3

21. Maintaining the student semester file

Write a program that maintains the student semester file using the change records described below. These records should be in sequence by student number only (not course number within student number). However, all drop records should precede any add records.

If a course has been dropped by a student, that portion of the record should be set to blanks. Then, all course data following the deleted record should be moved up one record segment. If a course is added, it should be placed in its proper sequence in the record. If the code field in the change record contains a 3 (indicating withdrawal from school), the entire student record should be deleted from the file.

If an input sequence error is detected or if a course to be dropped can't be found in the master record (compare on department code and course number), print an error message and ignore the record. If a student has more than seven courses because of additions, print an error message for each course over seven and ignore these records. At the end of the program, print the number of records in the old file, the number of records deleted, the number of records in the new file, the number of courses added, the number of courses dropped, and the number of input change records ignored.

Input

Field Name	Student No.	Student Name (Last name first)	Course Title	Dept.	Course No.	Section No.	Semester Hours	Change Code	Unused
Characteristics	9(6)	X(19)	X(16)	X(4)	999	99	9	9	X(28)
Usage									
Position	1-6	7-25	26-41	42-45	46-48	49-50	51	52	53-80

Note: For the change code, 1 = drop, 2 = add, and 3 = withdrawal from school.

Test Data

POS. 1-6	7-25	26-41	42-45	46-48	49-50	51	52
101450	MC QUILLEN, KEVIN	INTRO ANTHRO	ANTH	001	07	3	2
194007	POHL, GARY	FREEHND DRAWING	ART	010	03	2	2
194007	POHL, GARY	INTRO FORTRAN	DP	065	02	2	2
194007	POHL, GARY	CREATIVE WRITING	ENG	003	02	3	1
194007	POHL, GARY	INTRO SYMPHONY	MUS	010	03	2	2
200943	FURY, MICHAEL	FREEHND DRAWING	ART	010	02	2	1
200943	FURY, MICHAEL	AMER HIST 1929-P	HIST	010	03	2	1
200943	FURY, MICHAEL	INTRO MUSIC	MUS	011	04	2	1
214433	ROGERS, SALLY						

22a. Sorting grade records and updating the student semester file

Write a program that updates the grade portion of the student semester records. The input to this program is a file of grade records that must be sorted into sequence by course number within department code within student number. These records are preceded by a lead record containing an asterisk in position 1 and 1, 2, 3, or F in position 2 to indicate the grading period (first, second, third, or final).

To update a semester record, the grade for a course is placed in the appropriate grading area. If the lead record contains an F, position 16 of the grade records contains the final exam grade and position 17 contains the course grade. Otherwise, position 16 is blank and position 17 contains the period grade. If no grade record is received for a course, student number, student name, and the course description should be printed along with the message NO GRADE RECEIVED.

To make sure that a grade record matches a course stored in the student semester record, department and course number in the transaction should be compared with those in the master record. If they don't match, the contents of the unmatched grade record should be printed along with the message UNMATCHED GRADE RECORD.

Write the following grade report program (22b) to test the update of the student file.

Input

Field Name	Student No.	Dept.	Course No.	Section No.	Final Exam Grade	Period/Course Grade	Unused
Characteristics	9(6)	X(4)	999	99	X	X	X(63)
Usage							
Position	1-6	7-10	11-13	14-15	16	17	18-80

Test Data

POS.	1-6	7-10	11-13	14-15	16	17
	101450	CHEM	011	02	C	C
	101450	ECON	010	03	B	C
	101450	ENG	101	07	B	B
	101450	M E	050	01	A	A
	194007	DP	015	01	D	C
	194007	DP	050	09	B	B
	194007	ENG	003	02	B	B
	194007	ENG	121	03	A	A
	194007	ENG	150	02	B	A
	194007	MUS	011	04	C	B
	200943	ANTH	001	07	B	B
	200943	ART	010	02	A	A
	200943	ENG	002	14	B	B
	200943	MUS	010	03	A	B
	200943	HIST	010	03	B	A
	200943	MUS	011	04	A	A
	200943	PHIL	121	01	A	A
	200943	SOC	001	11	C	C
	214433	COM	009	03	D	D
	214433	COM	043	02	C	C
	214433	DP	100	01	B	B
	214888	BIO	010	01	F	F
	214888	DP	050	07	C	C
	214888	ENG	002	12	B	B
	214888	PHYS	020	03	C	C
	214888	POL	010	02	B	C

22b. Printing a grade-point average listing

Write a program that calculates and prints final grade-point averages (GPAs) for all the students in the student semester file. To calculate this average, let a grade of A equal 4 points per semester hour, B equal 3 points, C equal 2, D equal 1, and F equal 0. Thus, a grade of B in a three-hour course equals 9 points. For each student, then, divide the total semester hours into the total grade points to obtain the GPA.

Output

Create a print chart for a listing with the following general format. If a student is missing a grade for one or more courses, print INCOMPLETE GRADES in the remarks column and leave all columns except student name blank.

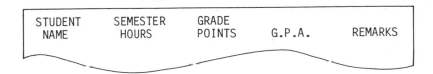

```
STUDENT     SEMESTER     GRADE
 NAME        HOURS       POINTS     G.P.A.      REMARKS
```

Appendix B COBOL Reserved Words and PICTURE Symbols

ACCEPT
ACCESS
ADD
ADVANCING
AFTER
ALL
ALPHABET
ALTER
ALTERNATE
AND
ARE
AREA
AREAS
ASSIGN
AT
AUTHOR
BEFORE
BLANK
BLOCK
BY
CALL
CHARACTER
CHARACTERS
CLOSE
COBOL
CODE
CODE-SET
COMMA
COMP
COMPUTATIONAL
COMPUTE
CONFIGURATION
CONTAINS
COPY
CORR
CORRESPONDING
COUNT
CURRENCY
DATA
DATE
DATE-COMPILED
DATE-WRITTEN
DAY
DECIMAL-POINT
DECLARATIVES
DELETE
DELIMITED
DELIMITER
DEPENDING
DISPLAY
DIVIDE
DIVISION
DOWN
DUPLICATES
DYNAMIC
ELSE
END
ENTER
ENVIRONMENT
EQUAL
ERROR
EVERY
EXCEPTION
EXIT
EXTEND
FD
FILE
FILE-CONTROL
FILLER
FIRST
FOR
FROM
GIVING
GO
GREATER
HIGH-VALUE
HIGH-VALUES
I-O
I-O-CONTROL
IDENTIFICATION
IF
IN
INDEX
INDEXED
INITIAL
INPUT
INPUT-OUTPUT
INSPECT
INSTALLATION
INTO
INVALID
IS
JUST
JUSTIFIED
KEY
LABEL
LEADING
LEFT
LENGTH
LESS
LINE
LINES
LINKAGE
LOW-VALUE
LOW-VALUES
MODE
MOVE
MULTIPLY
NATIVE
NEGATIVE
NEXT
NOT
NUMBER
NUMERIC
OBJECT-COMPUTER
OCCURS
OF
OFF
OMITTED
ON
OPEN
OR
ORGANIZATION
OUTPUT
OVERFLOW
PAGE
PERFORM
PIC
PICTURE
POINTER
POSITION
POSITIVE
PROCEDURE
PROCEDURES
PROCEED
PROGRAM
PROGRAM-ID
QUOTE
QUOTES
RANDOM
READ
RECORD
RECORDS
REDEFINES
RELATIVE
RELEASE
RENAMES
REPLACING
RESERVE
RETURN
REWRITE
RIGHT
ROUNDED
RUN
SAME
SEARCH
SECTION
SECURITY
SELECT
SENTENCE
SEPARATE
SEQUENTIAL
SET
SIGN
SIZE
SORT
SOURCE-COMPUTER
SPACE
SPACES
SPECIAL-NAMES
STANDARD
START
STATUS
STOP
STRING
SUBTRACT
SYNC
SYNCHRONIZED
TABLE
TALLYING
TAPE
TERMINAL
THAN
THROUGH
THRU
TIME
TIMES
TO
TRACE
TRAILING
UNSTRING
UNTIL
UP
UPON
USAGE
USE
USING
VALUE
VALUES
VARYING
WHEN
WITH
WORKING-STORAGE
WRITE
ZERO
ZEROES
ZEROS
+
-
*
/
>
<
=

Common Manufacturer's Extensions to ANSI Reserved Words

ASCII	OWNER
ASSEMBLER	PRINTER
COMP-3	PUNCH
COMPUTATIONAL-3	READER
CONSOLE	READY
EXHIBIT	REMARKS
ID	UNCOMPRESSED
NAMED	WORDS

Permissible PICTURE clause symbols

Symbol	Meaning
A	Any alphabetic character or space
B	Space insertion character
P	Assumed decimal scaling position
S	Operational sign
V	Assumed decimal point
X	Any character
Z	Zero suppression and space replacement character
9	Any numeric character
/	Stroke insertion character
,	Comma insertion character
.	Decimal point
+	Plus sign insertion character
–	Minus sign insertion character
CR	Credit placement characters
DB	Debit placement characters
*	Zero suppression and asterisk replacement character
$	Currency sign insertion character

Appendix C COBOL Reference Summary

The COBOL reference formats listed here cover only those elements discussed in this text. They do not include all of the ANSI formats for the COBOL language, which would be quite extensive. For complete coverage of the available elements for a specific compiler, you must refer to the appropriate reference manual. This is particularly true since many existing compilers receive periodic modification. The formats presented here are based on the ANSI 1974 standards. No attempt has been made to include any of the 1968 standards since it has been assumed that the vast majority of compilers on which students will be working would more nearly conform to the 1974 standards.

The summary that follows is divided into two parts. In the first, general COBOL information is presented. In the second, a summary of the language formats is given. The notation used in the language summary conforms to these rules:

1. Words printed entirely in capital letters are COBOL reserved words.
2. Words printed in lowercase letters are names or words supplied by the programmer.
3. Braces { } enclosing a group of items indicate that the programmer must use one of the items.
4. Square brackets [ ] indicate the enclosed item may be used or omitted, depending on the requirements of the program.
5. The ellipsis ... indicates that an element may appear either once or any number of times in succession.
6. Underlined reserved words are required unless the element itself is optional, but reserved words not underlined are optional.

Unlike the formats given in the chapters themselves, those given in this summary use the word *identifier*. An identifier is simply a data name followed by a correct combination of subscripts or indexes.

General COBOL Information

Character set

Characters used for words and names:
A–Z
0–9
– (hyphen)

Characters used for punctuation:
. ( ) space "
, ;

Characters used in arithmetic expressions:
+ – * / **

Characters used to show relations:
= < >

Characters used in editing:
B 0 = – CR Z * $, .
DB (never discussed but used like CR)
/ (stroke)

Logical operators:
NOT
OR, AND

Name formation

Program name:
1. Maximum of 30 characters.
2. Letters, numbers, and hyphens only.
3. May be all numeric.

Data name:
1. Maximum of 30 characters.
2. Letters, numbers, and hyphens only.
3. Must contain at least one letter.
4. Must start with a letter.

Procedure name:
1. Maximum of 30 characters.
2. Letters, numbers, and hyphens only.
3. May be all numeric.
4. Need not start with a letter.

File name, record name, and mnemonic name:
Same as for data name.

Condition name:
Same as for data name.

Figurative constants

ZERO	LOW–VALUE
ZEROS, ZEROES	LOW–VALUES
SPACE	QUOTE
SPACES	QUOTES
HIGH–VALUE	ALL literal
HIGH–VALUES	

Rules for forming literals

Numeric literals:
1. From 1 through 18 digits.
2. Consisting of 0–9, + or –, and the decimal point.
3. Only one sign character (if unsigned, assumed positive).
4. Only one decimal point.

Non-numeric literals:
1. From 1 through 120 characters.
2. Enclosed in quotation marks.

Use of A and B margins

A margin:

Division headers	01 level numbers
Section names	Any other level numbers
Paragraph names	
FD	

B margin:
All other entries

Use of coding form

1. Use of sequence numbers is optional.
2. Use of program identification (columns 73–80) is optional.
3. If sequence numbers are used, they should be in ascending sequence. If not, an error message (diagnostic) may print, but compilation will still take place.

Comment lines

1. An asterisk (*) must be punched in column 7.
2. Columns 8–72 can contain any characters.

Blank lines

A blank line is any card that is blank in columns 7–72.

MISCELLANEOUS FORMATS

Subscripting

```
{data-name     }  (subscript [,subscript]...)
{condition-name}
```

Indexing

```
{data-name     } ({index-name [{±} literal-2]} [{index-name [{±} literal-4]}]...)
{condition-name} ({literal-1                 } [{literal-3                 }]   )
```

CONDITION FORMATS

Relation conditions

```
   {identifier-1             } {IS [NOT] GREATER THAN} {identifier-2             }
IF {literal-1                } {IS [NOT] LESS THAN   } {literal-2                }
   {arithmetic-expression-1  } {IS [NOT] EQUAL TO    } {arithmetic-expression-2  }

   {identifier-1             } {IS [NOT] >} {identifier-2             }
IF {literal-1                } {IS [NOT] <} {literal-2                }
   {arithmetic-expression-1  } {IS [NOT] =} {arithmetic-expression-2  }
```

Class condition

```
IF identifier IS [NOT] {NUMERIC   }
                       {ALPHABETIC}
```

Sign condition

```
                                     {POSITIVE}
IF arithmetic-expression IS [NOT]    {NEGATIVE}
                                     {ZERO    }
```

Condition-name condition

```
IF condition-name
```

Compound conditions

```
IF condition {AND} condition [{AND} condition] ...
             {OR }           [{OR }          ]
```

NOT condition

```
IF NOT condition
```

GENERAL FORMAT FOR IDENTIFICATION DIVISION

```
IDENTIFICATION DIVISION.
PROGRAM-ID. program-name.
[AUTHOR. [comment-entry]...]
[INSTALLATION. [comment-entry]...]
[DATE-WRITTEN. [comment-entry]...]
[DATE-COMPILED. [comment-entry]...]
[SECURITY. [comment-entry]...]
[REMARKS. [comment-entry]...]
```

GENERAL FORMAT FOR ENVIRONMENT DIVISION

```
ENVIRONMENT DIVISION.
CONFIGURATION SECTION.
SOURCE-COMPUTER. computer-name.
OBJECT-COMPUTER. computer-name.
[SPECIAL-NAMES. implementor-name IS mnemonic-name
                [implementor-name IS mnemonic-name]...]

INPUT-OUTPUT SECTION.
FILE-CONTROL.
    {file-control-entry}...
```

GENERAL FORMAT FOR FILE-CONTROL-ENTRY

Format 1 (sequential file)

```
SELECT file-name
    ASSIGN TO system-name
    [ACCESS MODE IS SEQUENTIAL]
    [ORGANIZATION IS SEQUENTIAL].
```

Format 2 (sort file)

```
SELECT file-name
    ASSIGN TO system-name.
```

GENERAL FORMAT FOR DATA DIVISION

```
DATA DIVISION.
FILE SECTION.
[FD  file-name
     [BLOCK CONTAINS integer-1 {RECORDS   }]
                               {CHARACTERS}
     [RECORD CONTAINS integer-2 CHARACTERS]
     LABEL {RECORD IS  } {STANDARD} .
           {RECORDS ARE} {OMITTED }
[SD  file-name
     [RECORD CONTAINS integer CHARACTERS].
[record-description-entry]...]...
[WORKING-STORAGE SECTION.
[record-description-entry]...]
[LINKAGE SECTION.
[record-description-entry]...]
```

GENERAL FORMAT FOR DATA DESCRIPTION ENTRY

Format 1

```
level-number {data-name-1}
             {FILLER     }
[REDEFINES data-name-2]
[{PICTURE} IS character-string]
[{PIC    }                    ]
[            {COMPUTATIONAL  }]
[            {COMP           }]
[[USAGE IS]  {COMPUTATIONAL-3}]
[            {COMP-3         }]
[            {DISPLAY        }]

[[USAGE IS] INDEX]
[OCCURS integer TIMES
     [{ASCENDING } KEY IS data-name-1 [data-name-2]...] ...
     [{DESCENDING}                                    ]
     [INDEXED BY index-name-1 [index-name-2]...]]
[BLANK WHEN ZERO]
[VALUE IS literal].
```

Format 2

```
88 condition-name {VALUE IS  } literal-1 [{THROUGH} literal-2]
                  {VALUES ARE}           [{THRU   }          ]
     [literal-3 [{THROUGH} literal-4]] ... .
     [          [{THRU   }          ]]
```

GENERAL FORMAT FOR PROCEDURE DIVISION

Format 1

```
PROCEDURE DIVISION.
section-name SECTION.
paragraph-name.
```

Format 2

```
PROCEDURE DIVISION USING identifier-1 [identifier-2]... .
section-name SECTION.
paragraph-name.
```

GENERAL FORMAT FOR VERBS

```
                              {DATE}
ACCEPT identifier FROM        {DAY }
                              {TIME}

ADD {identifier-1} [identifier-2] ... TO identifier-m [ROUNDED]
    {literal-1   } [literal-2   ]

    [identifier-n [ROUNDED]]...
    [ON SIZE ERROR imperative-statement]

ADD {identifier-1} {identifier-2} [identifier-3] ...
    {literal-1   } {literal-2   } [literal-3   ]

    GIVING identifier-m [ROUNDED]
    [identifier-n [ROUNDED]]...
    [ON SIZE ERROR imperative-statement]

CALL {identifier-1} [USING identifier-2 [identifier-3]...]
     {literal-1   }

CLOSE file-name.
CLOSE file-name-1 [file-name-2]...
COMPUTE identifier-1 [ROUNDED]
    [identifier-2 [ROUNDED]]...
    = arithmetic-expression [ON SIZE ERROR imperative-statement]
COPY library-name.
COPY library-name

    [                     {word-2      }   [          {word-4      }]     ]
    [REPLACING word-1 BY  {identifier-1}   [word-3 BY {identifier-2}] ... ]
    [                     {literal-1   }   [          {literal-2   }]     ]
```

Note: A *word* in this format is any one of the following: data-name, procedure-name, condition-name, mnemonic-name, or file-name.

```
DISPLAY {identifier-1} [identifier-2] ...
        {literal-1   } [literal-2   ]

DIVIDE {identifier-1} INTO identifier-2 [ROUNDED]
       {literal-1   }

     [identifier-3 [ROUNDED]]...
     [ON SIZE ERROR imperative-statement]

DIVIDE {identifier-1} INTO {identifier-2} GIVING identifier-3 [ROUNDED]
       {literal-1   }      {literal-2   }

     [identifier-4 [ROUNDED]]...
     [ON SIZE ERROR imperative-statement]

DIVIDE {identifier-1} BY {identifier-2} GIVING identifier-3 [ROUNDED]
       {literal-1   }    {literal-2   }

     [identifier-4 [ROUNDED]]...
     [ON SIZE ERROR imperative-statement]

DIVIDE {identifier-1} INTO {identifier-2} GIVING identifier-3 [ROUNDED]
       {literal-1   }      {literal-2   }

     REMAINDER identifier-4 [ON SIZE ERROR imperative-statement]

DIVIDE {identifier-1} BY {identifier-2} GIVING identifier-3 [ROUNDED]
       {literal-1   }    {literal-2   }

     REMAINDER identifier-4 [ON SIZE ERROR imperative-statement]

EXIT.

EXIT PROGRAM.

GO TO procedure-name

IF condition {statement-1   } {ELSE statement-2   }
             {NEXT SENTENCE } {ELSE NEXT SENTENCE }

MERGE file-name-1 ON {ASCENDING } KEY data-name-1 [data-name-2]...
                     {DESCENDING}

     [ON {ASCENDING } KEY data-name-3 [data-name-4]...]...
         {DESCENDING}

     USING file-name-2 file-name-3 [file-name-4]...

    {OUTPUT PROCEDURE IS section-name}
    {GIVING file-name-5              }

MOVE {identifier-1} TO identifier-2 [identifier-3]...
     {literal     }
```

```
MULTIPLY {identifier-1} BY identifier-2 [ROUNDED]
         {literal-1   }

    [identifier-3 [ROUNDED]]...
    [ON SIZE ERROR imperative-statement]

MULTIPLY {identifier-1} BY {identifier-2} GIVING identifier-3 [ROUNDED]
         {literal-1   }    {literal-2   }

    [identifier-4 [ROUNDED]]...
    [ON SIZE ERROR imperative-statement]

OPEN {INPUT } file-name
     {OUTPUT}

OPEN {INPUT file-name-1 [file-name-2]...  } ...
     {OUTPUT file-name-3 [file-name-4]... }

OPEN {INPUT file-name-1 [file-name-2]...  } ...
     {OUTPUT file-name-3 [file-name-4]... }

PERFORM procedure-name
PERFORM procedure-name UNTIL condition-1
PERFORM procedure-name

    VARYING {identifier-2} FROM {identifier-3}
            {index-name-1}      {index-name-2}
                                {literal-1   }

      BY {identifier-4} UNTIL condition-1
         {literal-3   }

    [AFTER {identifier-5} FROM {identifier-6}
           {index-name-3}      {index-name-4}
                               {literal-3   }

      BY {identifier-7} UNTIL condition-2
         {literal-4   }

    [AFTER {identifier-8} FROM {identifier-9}
           {index-name-5}      {index-name-6}
                               {literal-5   }

      BY {identifier-10} UNTIL condition-3]]
         {literal-6    }
```

```
READ file-name RECORD AT END imperative-statement

READ file-name RECORD [INTO identifier] [AT END imperative-statement]

READ file-name RECORD [INTO identifier] [INVALID KEY imperative-statement]
RELEASE record-name

RELEASE record-name [FROM identifier]

RETURN file-name RECORD AT END imperative-statement

RETURN file-name RECORD [INTO identifier] AT END imperative-statement

SEARCH identifier-1  [VARYING {identifier-2 }]  [AT END imperative-statement-1]
                     [        {index-name-1 }]

     WHEN condition-1 {imperative-statement-2}
                      {NEXT SENTENCE         }

    [WHEN condition-2 {imperative-statement-3}] ...
    [                 {NEXT SENTENCE         }]

SEARCH ALL identifier-1 [AT END imperative-statement-1]

          {data-name-1    {IS EQUAL TO} {identifier-3            }}
     WHEN {               {IS =       } {literal-1               }}
          {                             {arithmetic-expression-1 }}
          {condition-name-1                                       }

         [AND {data-name-2      {IS EQUAL TO}   {identifier-4            }}] ...
         [    {                 {IS =       }   {literal-2               }}]
         [    {condition-name-2                 {arithmetic-expression-2 }}]

         {imperative-statement-2}
         {NEXT SENTENCE         }

SET {identifier-1  [identifier-2]...}  TO {identifier-3}
    {index-name-1  [index-name-2]...}     {index-name-3}
                                          {literal-1   }

SET index-name-4 [index-name-5]... {UP BY  } {identifier-4}
                                   {DOWN BY} {literal-2   }

SORT file-name-1 ON {ASCENDING } KEY data-name-1 [data-name-2]...
                    {DESCENDING}

   [ON {ASCENDING } KEY data-name-3 [data-name-4]...]...
       {DESCENDING}

   {INPUT PROCEDURE IS section-name-1}
   {USING file-name-2                }
   {       [file-name-3]...          }

   {OUTPUT PROCEDURE IS section-name-2}
   {GIVING file-name-4                }

STOP RUN
```

```
SUBTRACT {identifier-1} [identifier-2] ... FROM identifier-m [ROUNDED]
         {literal-1   } [literal-2   ]
    [identifier-n [ROUNDED]] ...
    [ON SIZE ERROR imperative-statement]

SUBTRACT {identifier-1} [identifier-2] ... FROM {identifier-m}
         {literal-1   } [literal-2   ]          {literal-m   }
    GIVING identifier-n [ROUNDED]
    [identifier-o [ROUNDED]] ...
    [ON SIZE ERROR imperative-statement]

WRITE record-name [FROM identifier-1]
    [{BEFORE} ADVANCING {{identifier-2} [LINE ]}]
    [{AFTER } ADVANCING {{integer     } [LINES]}]
    [                   {{mnemonic-name}      }]
    [                   {{PAGE         }      }]

WRITE record-name [FROM identifier] [INVALID KEY imperative-statement]
```

Index